N. M. Beguesse.

Art & Story by N. M. Beguesse

Visit me at:
angelboy.com

Volume 2 version 1.2

Angelboy

Volume 2

CAIN

Story & Art by

N. M. Beguesse

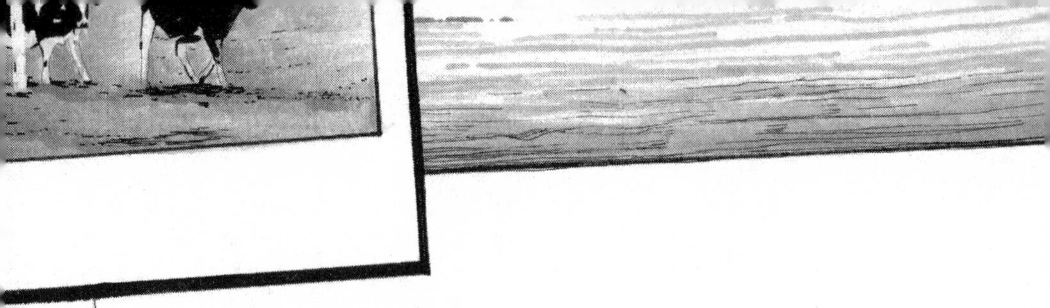

My Story so far...

I'm in South Ohio now... How cool is that? I've come a long way since I was *killed*... it's a weird story... I was murdered, but get this-- I came back to life, and now I have angel wings! And no one can see me or hear me. That really sucks! But its also kind of cool.

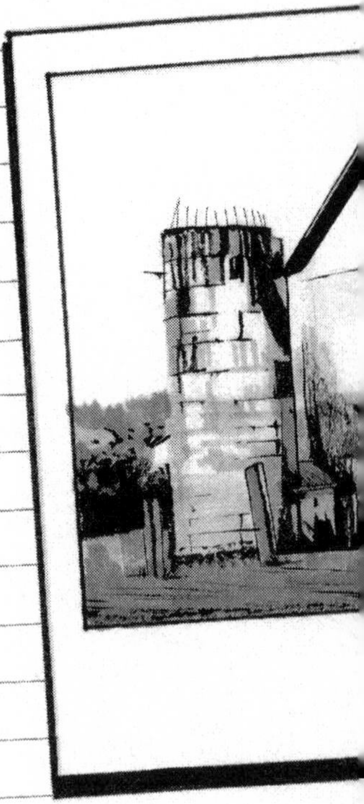

Well... there was that one dude who could see me.
And there was that one time when I pulled a sword out of my spine and had to slay that demon... monster... thing. What was that thing?
...What does it all mean?
Anyway, I'm just glad I'm still here on Earth... Even if I'm invisible. It's all good.

I can't wait to reach back to my hometown...

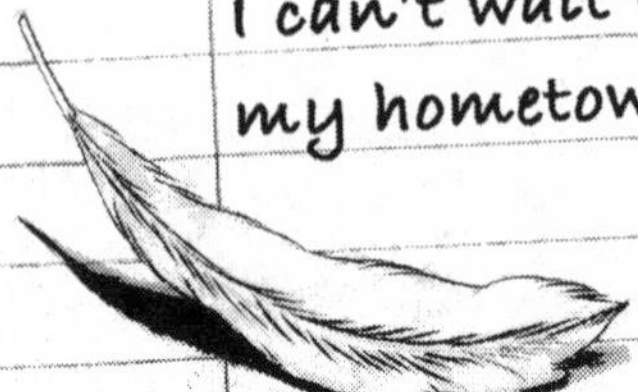

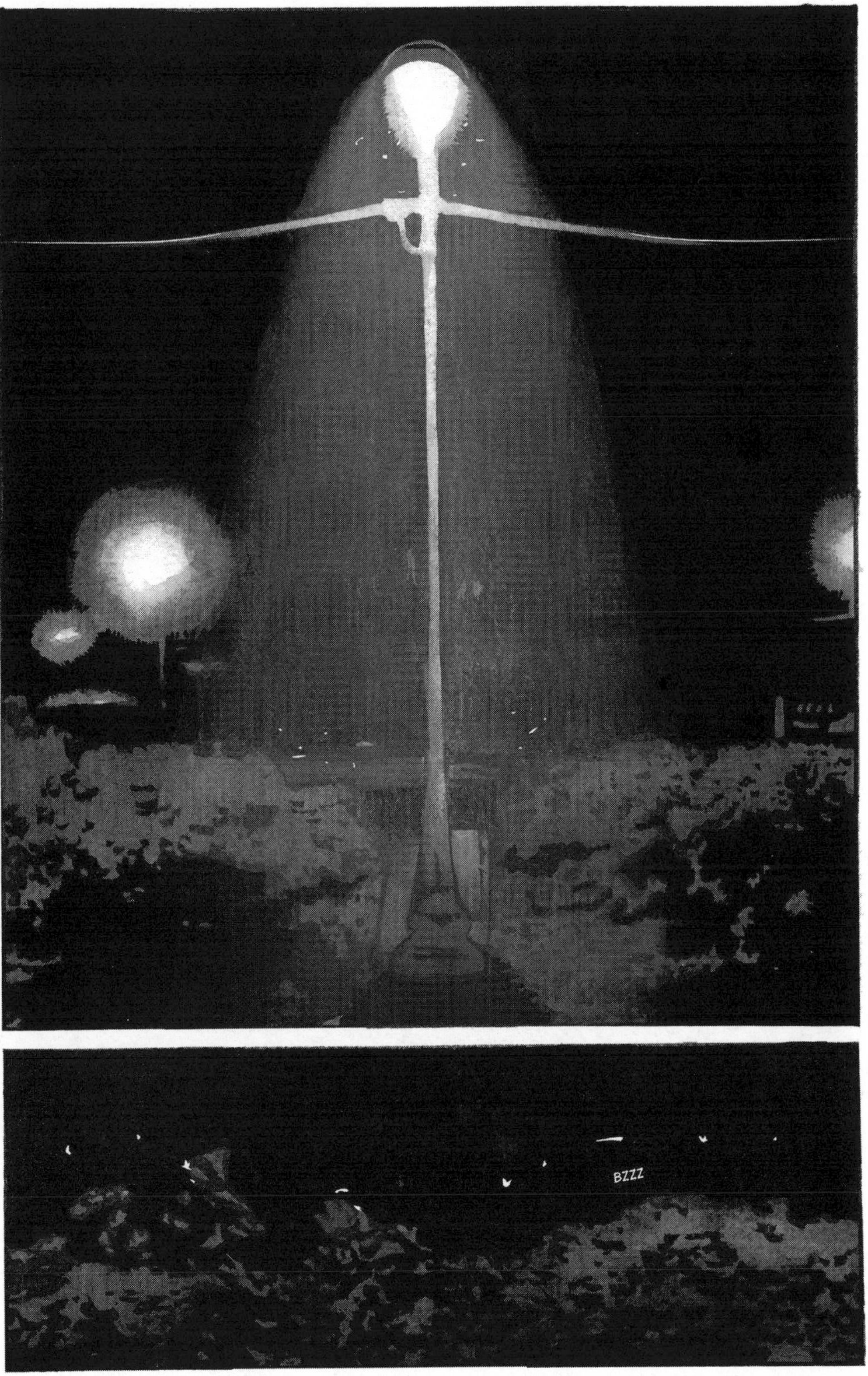
BZZZ

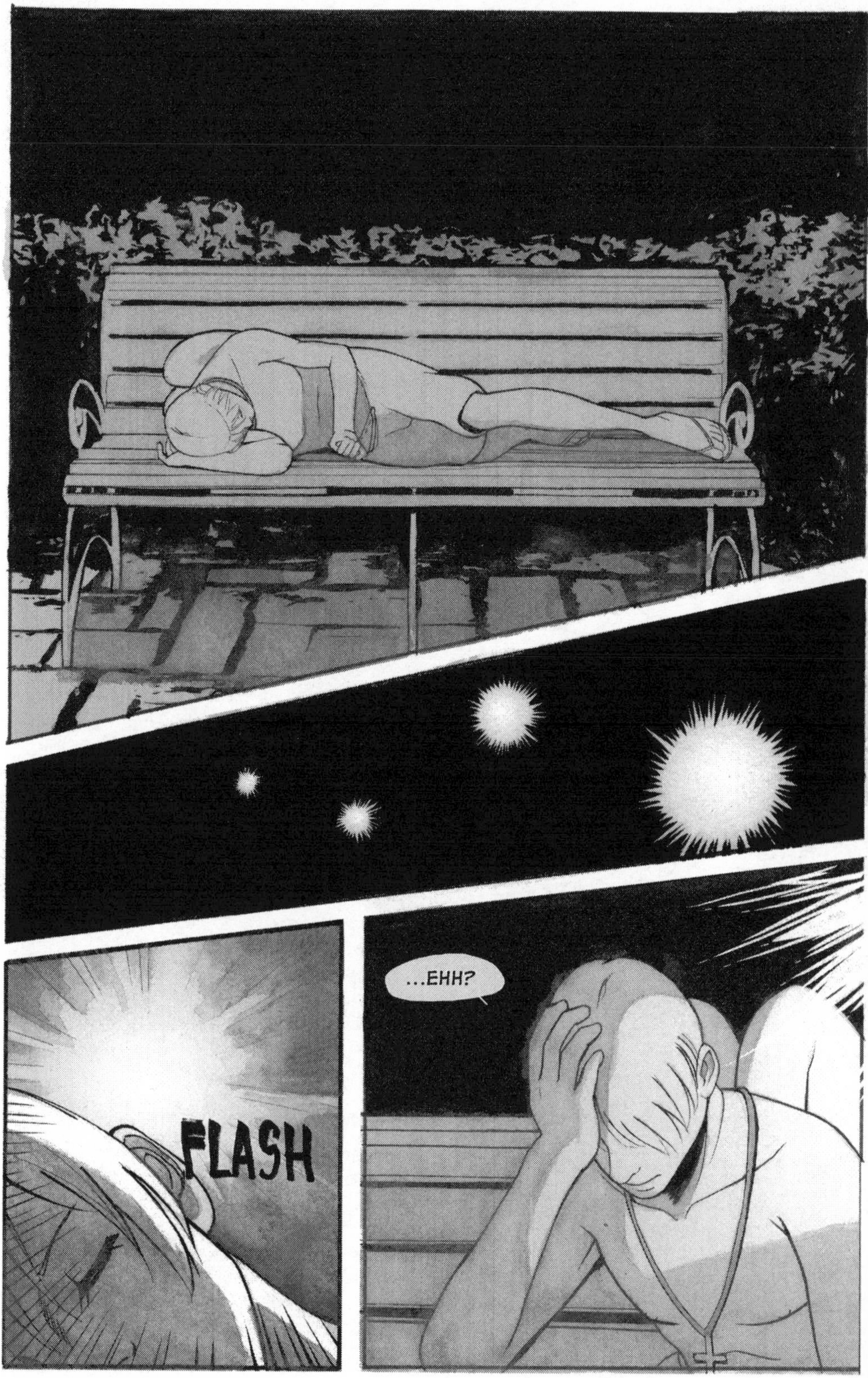
FLASH
...EHH?

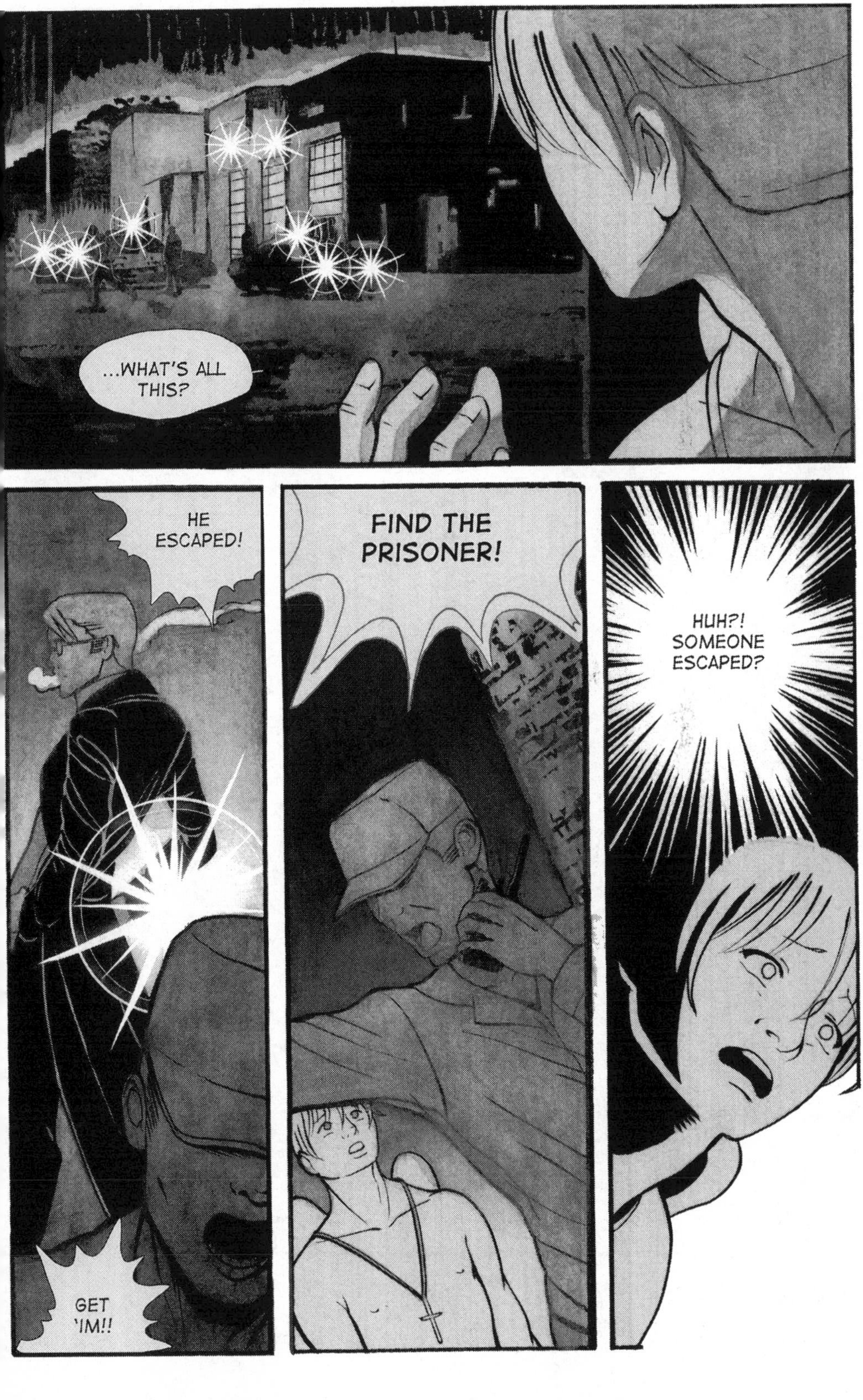
...WHAT'S ALL THIS?
HE ESCAPED!
GET 'IM!!
FIND THE PRISONER!
HUH?! SOMEONE ESCAPED?

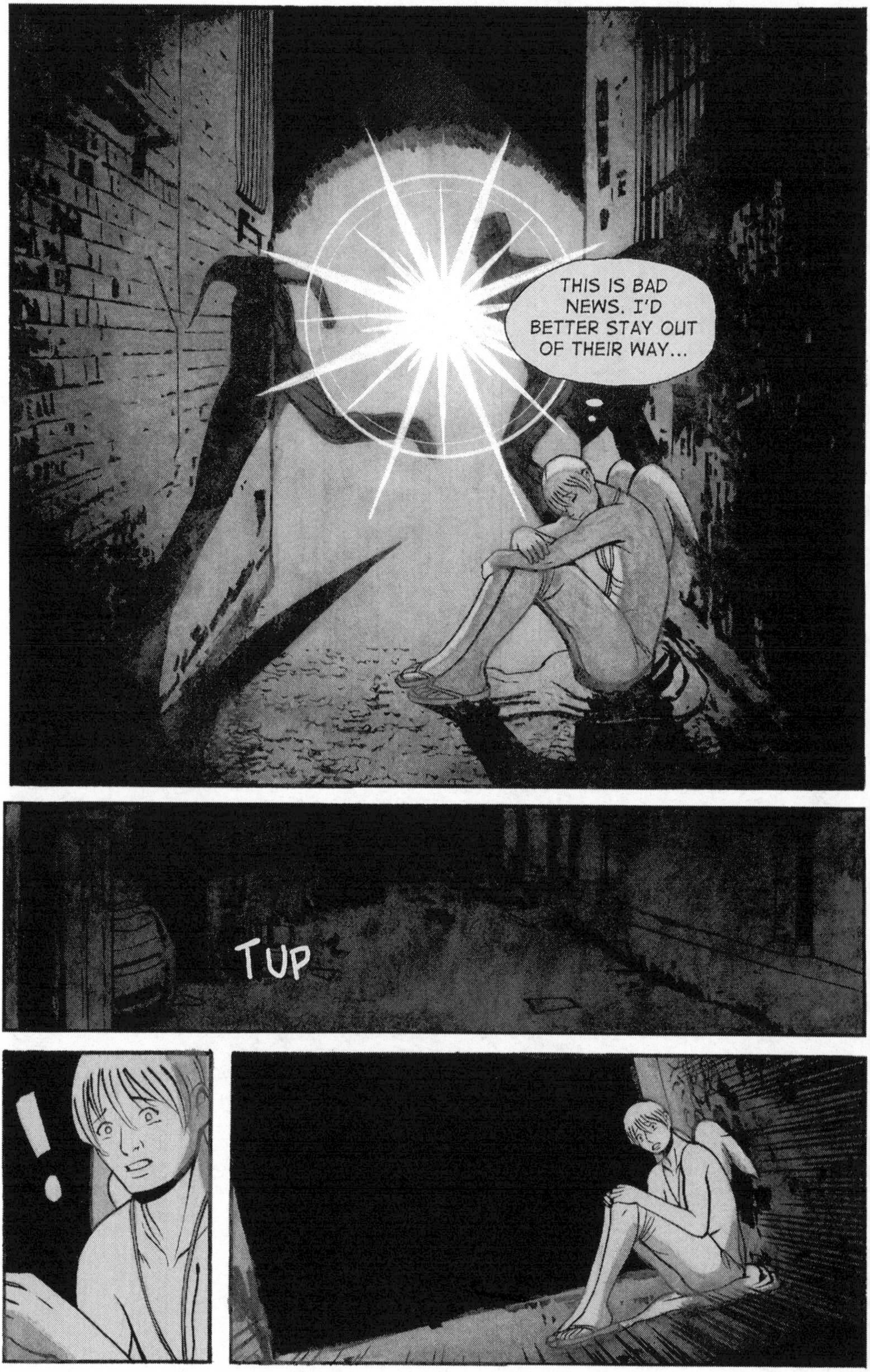
THIS IS BAD NEWS. I'D BETTER STAY OUT OF THEIR WAY...
TUP
!

EXCUSE ME... SIR...
IF YOU COULD, DO YOU THINK YOU COULD HELP ME OUT OF THIS? THE STRAPS ARE ON THE BACK.

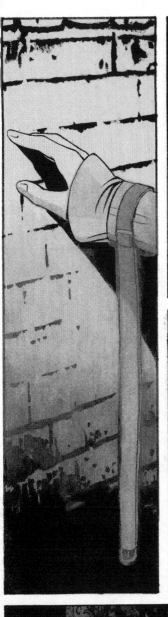

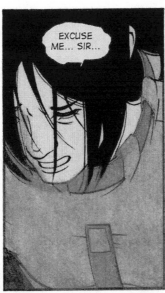

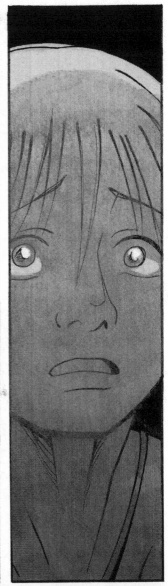

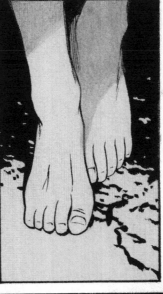

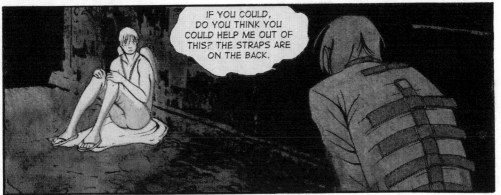

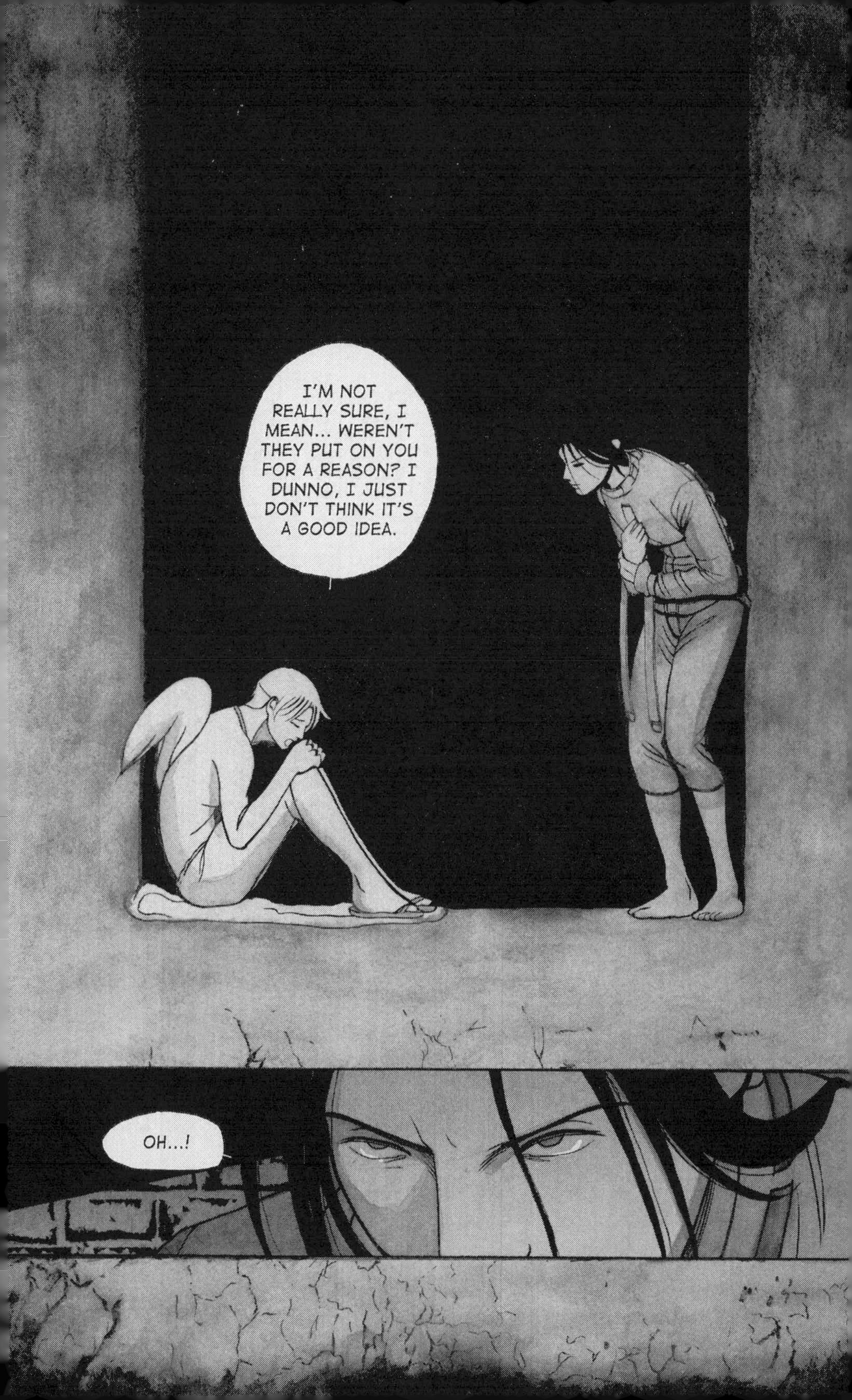
I'M NOT REALLY SURE, I MEAN... WEREN'T THEY PUT ON YOU FOR A REASON? I DUNNO, I JUST DON'T THINK IT'S A GOOD IDEA.
OH...!

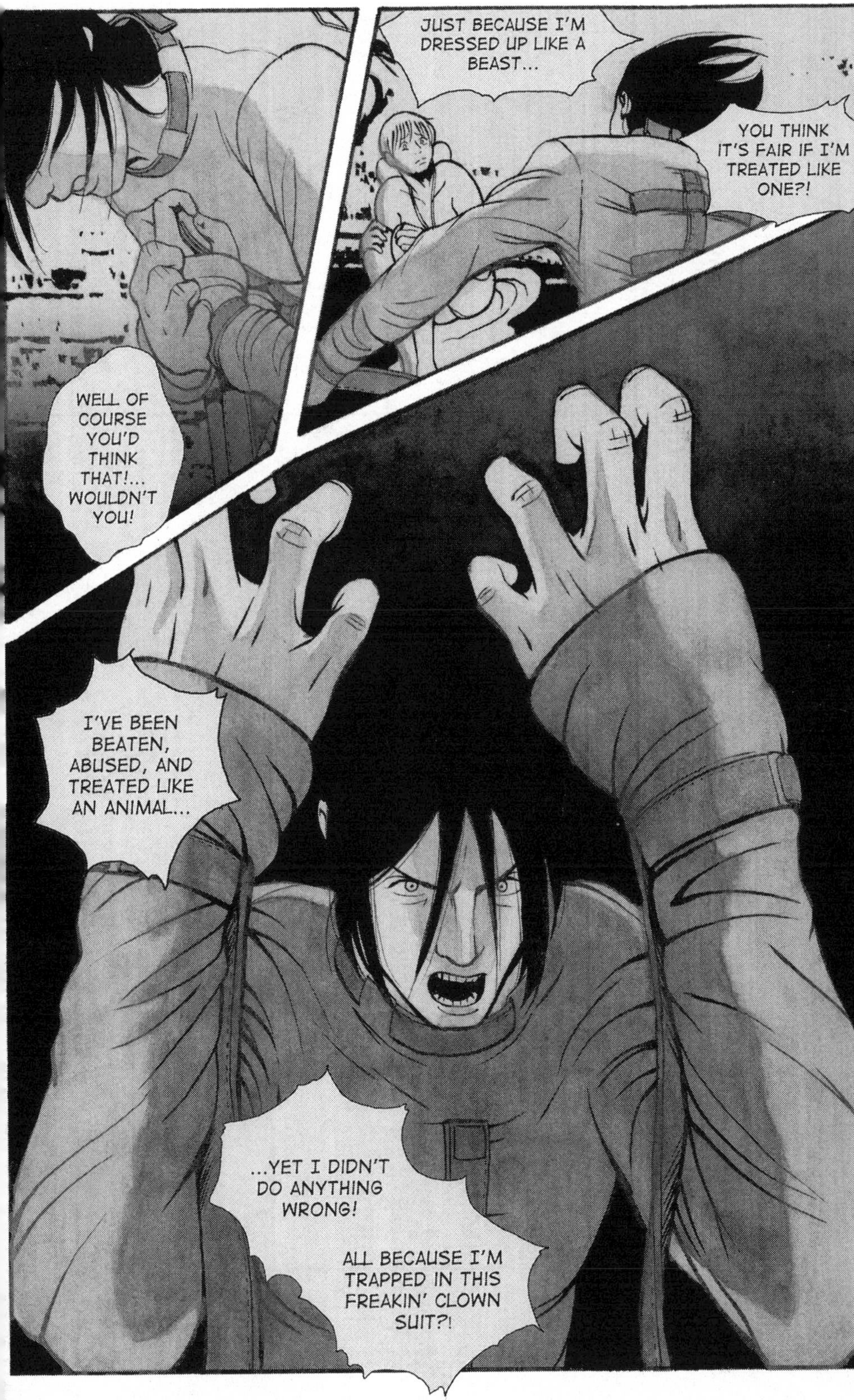
JUST BECAUSE I'M DRESSED UP LIKE A BEAST...
YOU THINK IT'S FAIR IF I'M TREATED LIKE ONE?!
WELL OF COURSE YOU'D THINK THAT!... WOULDN'T YOU!
I'VE BEEN BEATEN, ABUSED, AND TREATED LIKE AN ANIMAL...
...YET I DIDN'T DO ANYTHING WRONG!
ALL BECAUSE I'M TRAPPED IN THIS FREAKIN' CLOWN SUIT?!

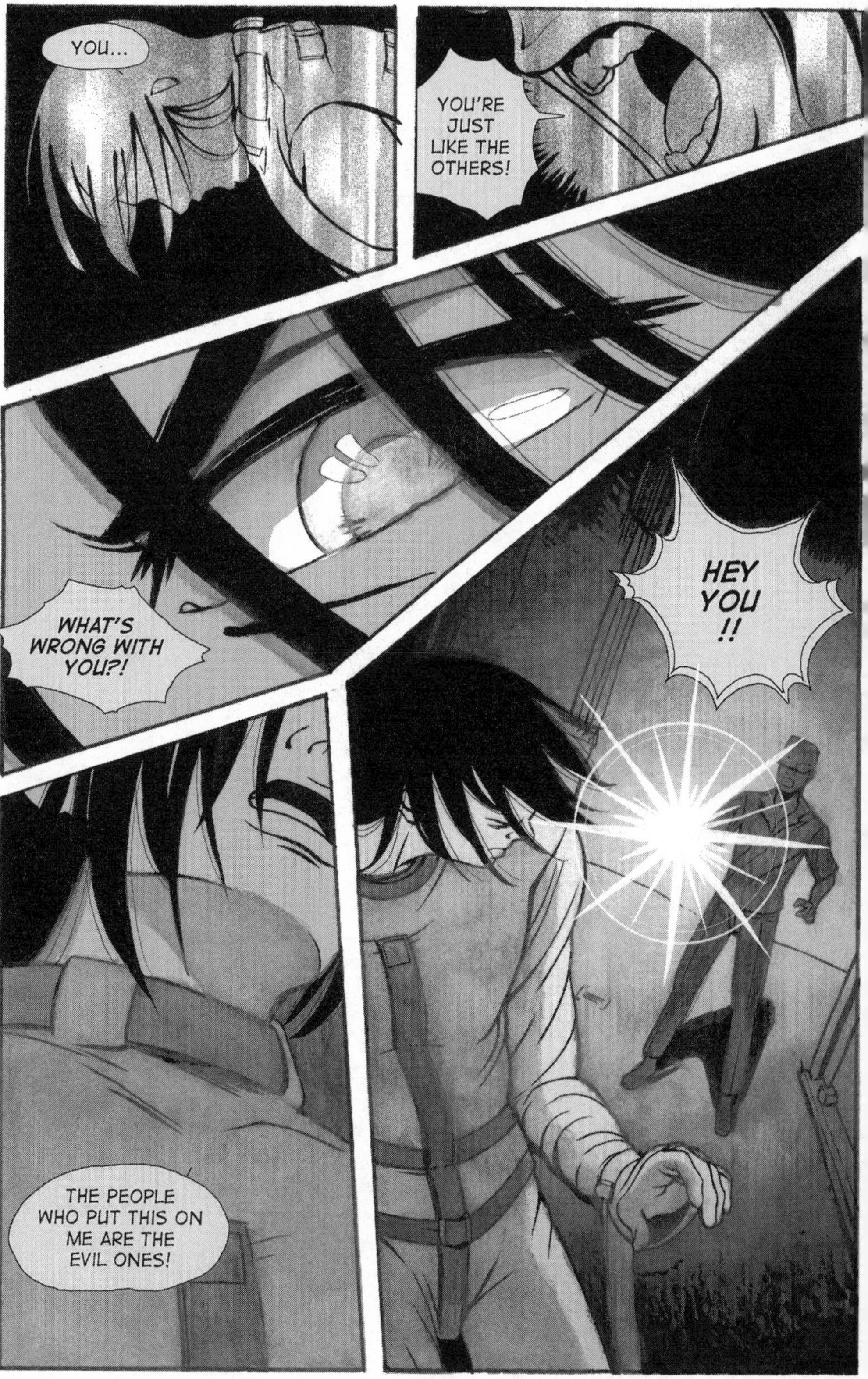
YOU...
YOU'RE JUST LIKE THE OTHERS!
WHAT'S WRONG WITH YOU?!
HEY YOU !!
THE PEOPLE WHO PUT THIS ON ME ARE THE EVIL ONES!

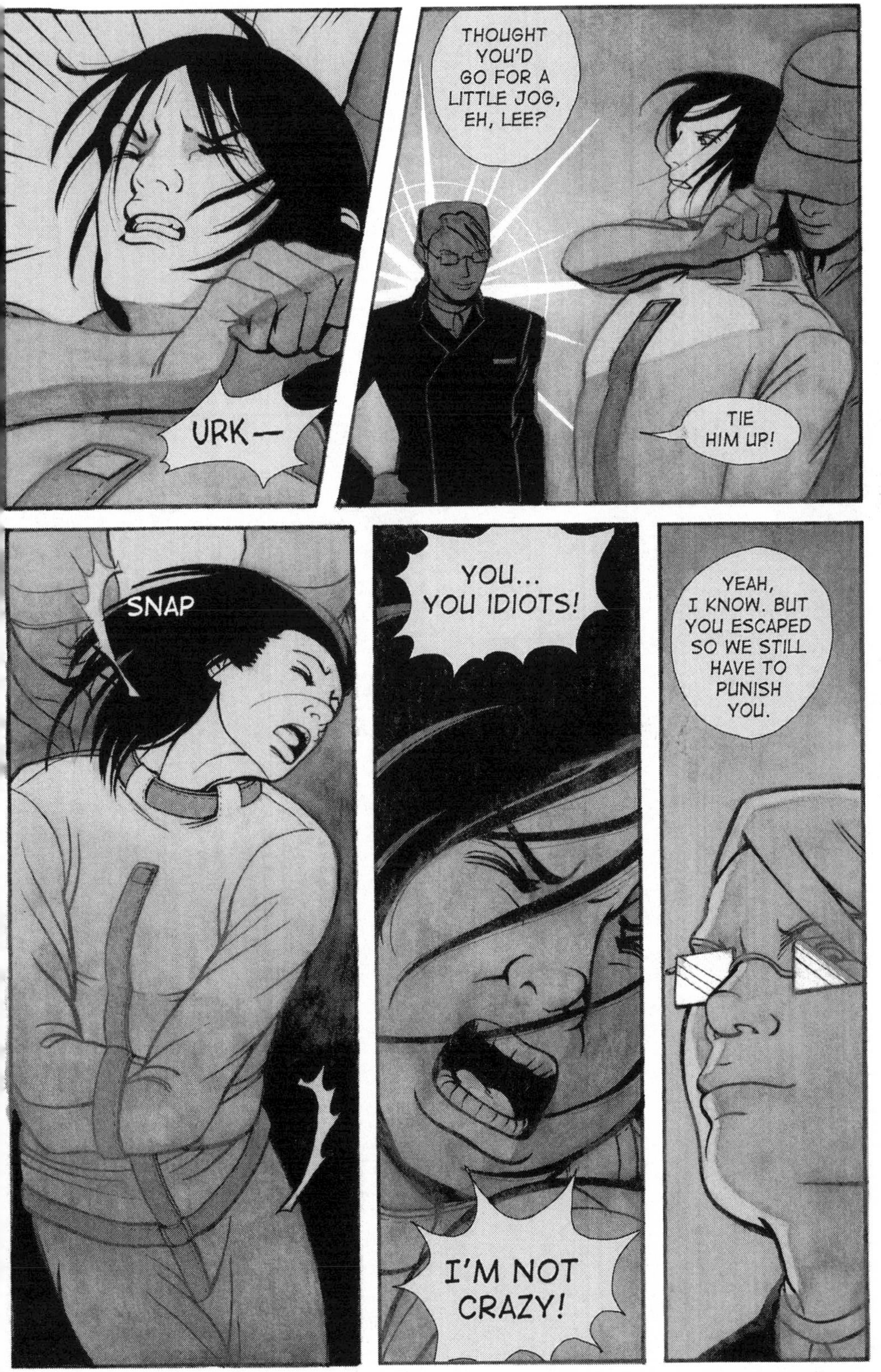
URK—
THOUGHT YOU'D GO FOR A LITTLE JOG, EH, LEE?
TIE HIM UP!
SNAP
YOU... YOU IDIOTS!
I'M NOT CRAZY!
YEAH, I KNOW. BUT YOU ESCAPED SO WE STILL HAVE TO PUNISH YOU.

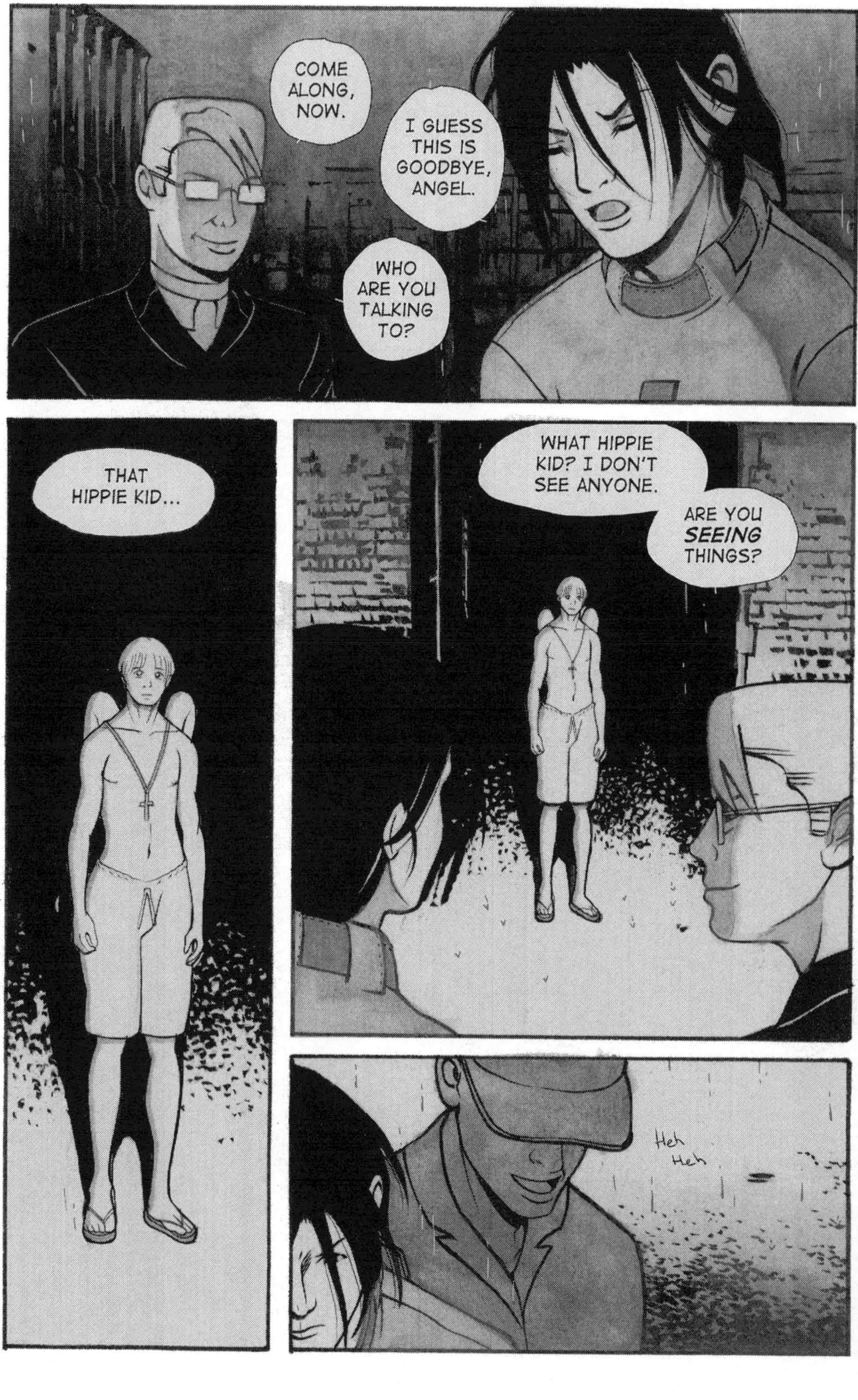
COME ALONG, NOW.
I GUESS THIS IS GOODBYE, ANGEL.
WHO ARE YOU TALKING TO?
THAT HIPPIE KID...
WHAT HIPPIE KID? I DON'T SEE ANYONE.
ARE YOU *SEEING* THINGS?
Heh Heh

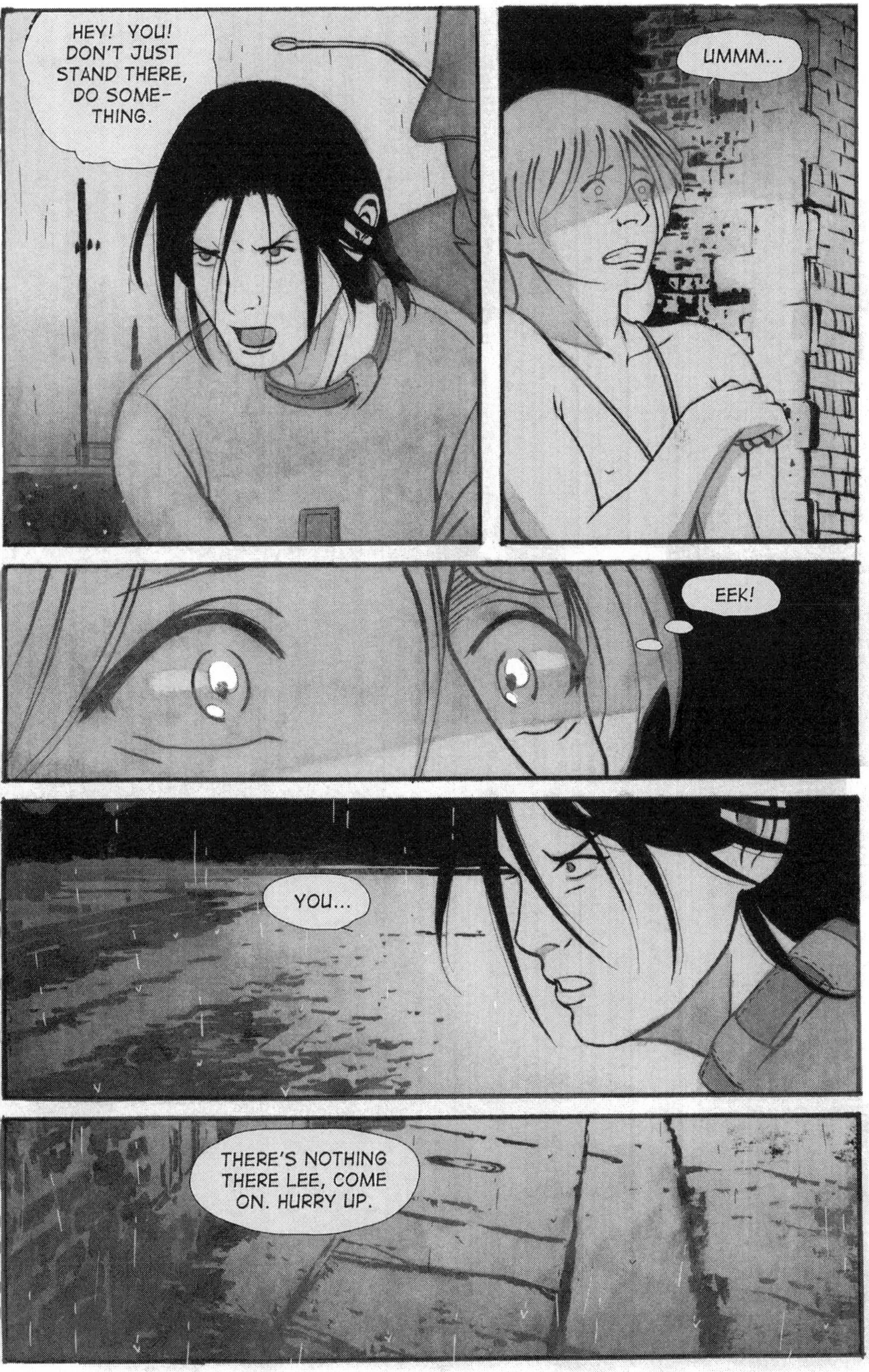
HEY! YOU! DON'T JUST STAND THERE, DO SOME-THING.
UMMM...
EEK!
YOU...
THERE'S NOTHING THERE LEE, COME ON. HURRY UP.

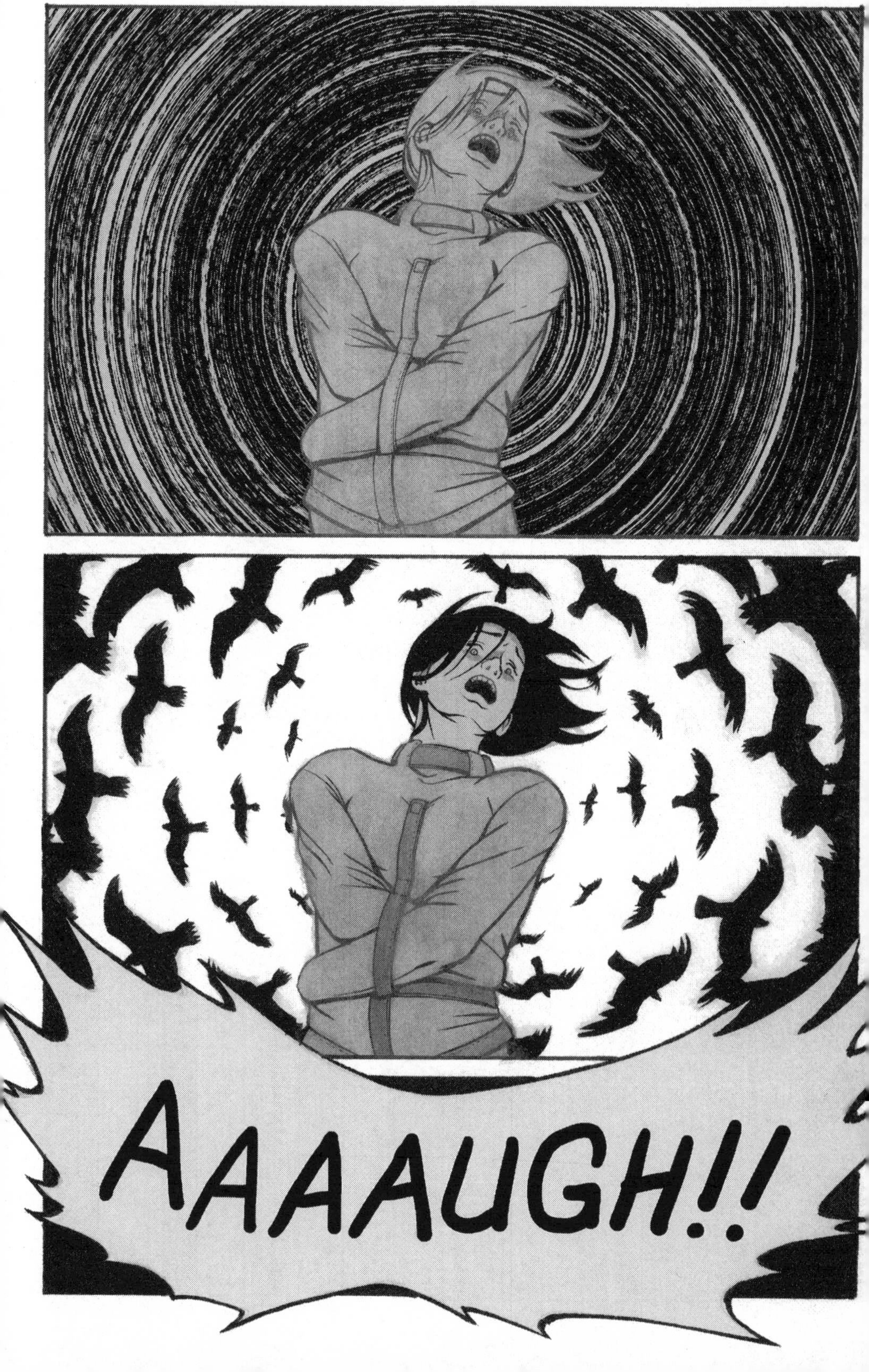
AAAAUGH!!

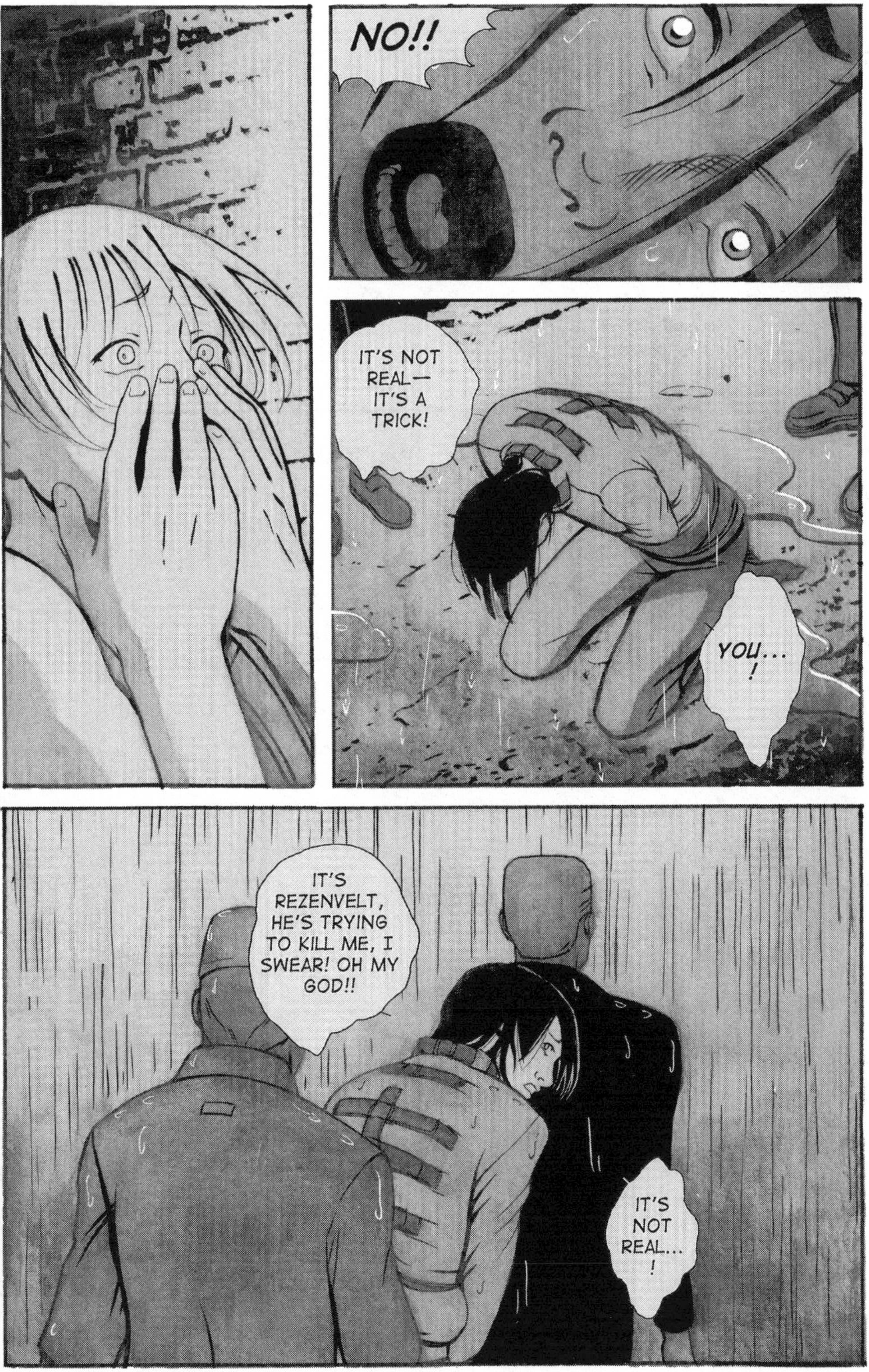
NO!!
IT'S NOT REAL— IT'S A TRICK!
YOU... !
IT'S REZENVELT, HE'S TRYING TO KILL ME, I SWEAR! OH MY GOD!!
IT'S NOT REAL... !

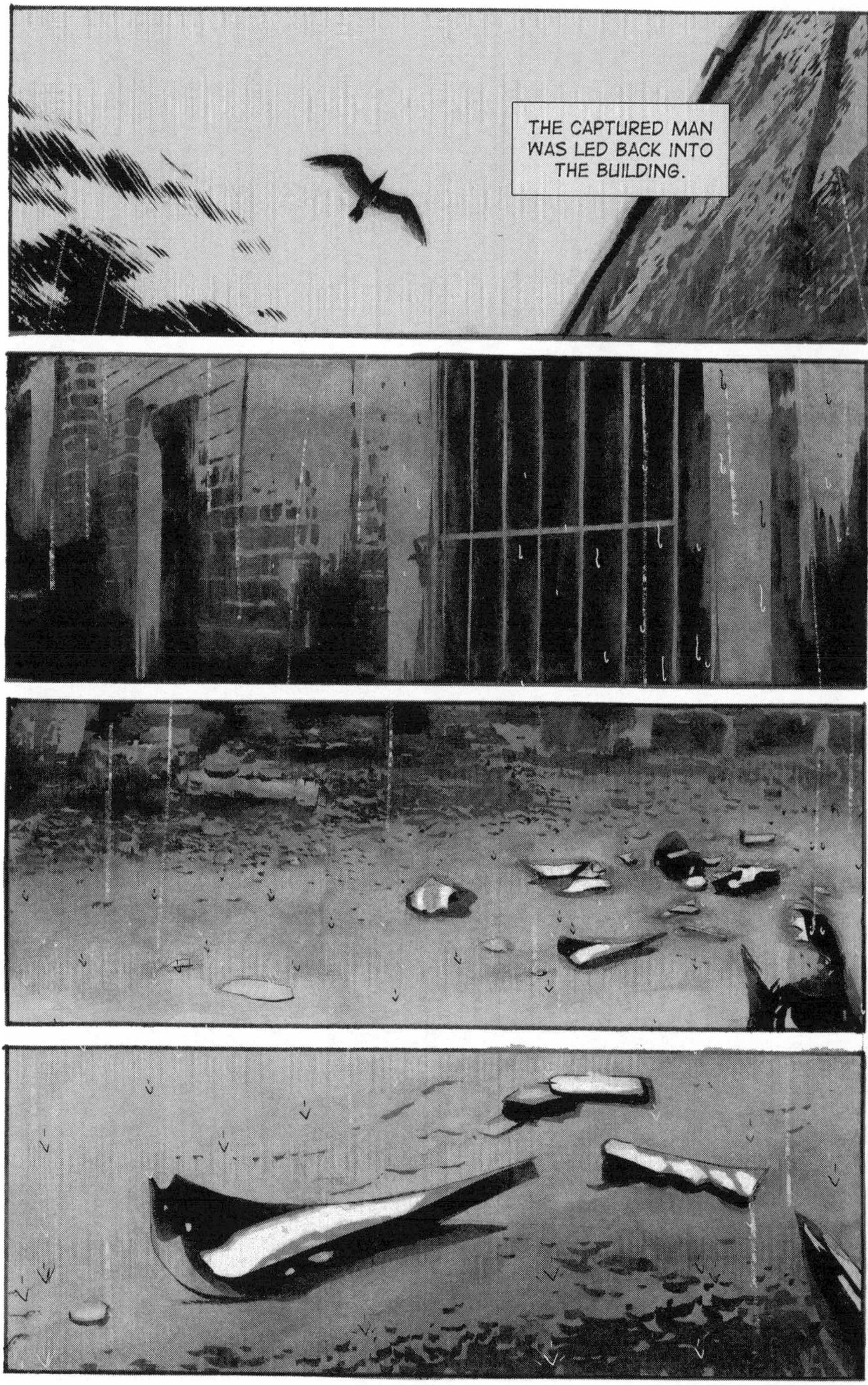
THE CAPTURED MAN WAS LED BACK INTO THE BUILDING.

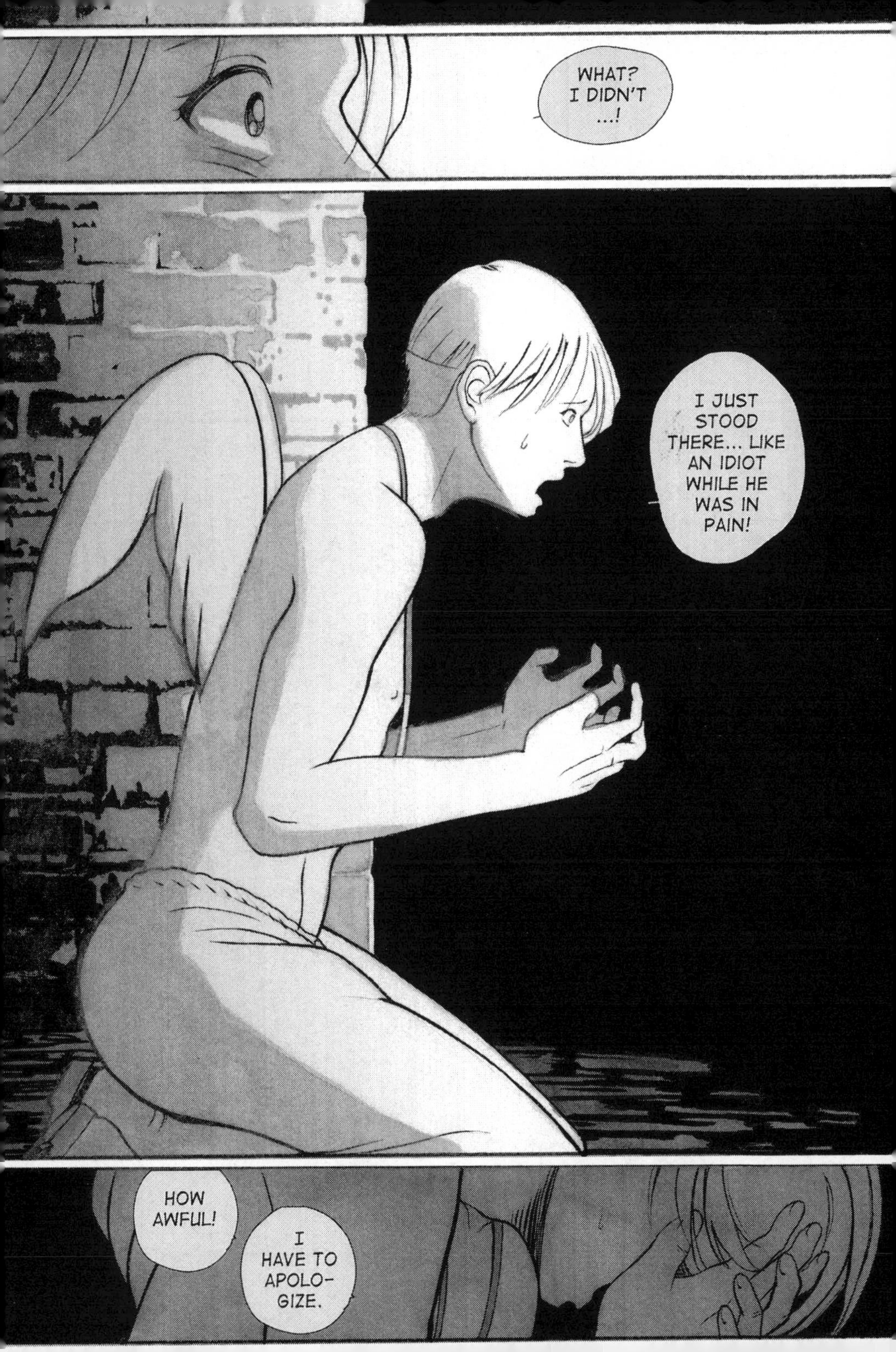
WHAT? I DIDN'T ...!
I JUST STOOD THERE... LIKE AN IDIOT WHILE HE WAS IN PAIN!
HOW AWFUL!
I HAVE TO APOLO-GIZE.

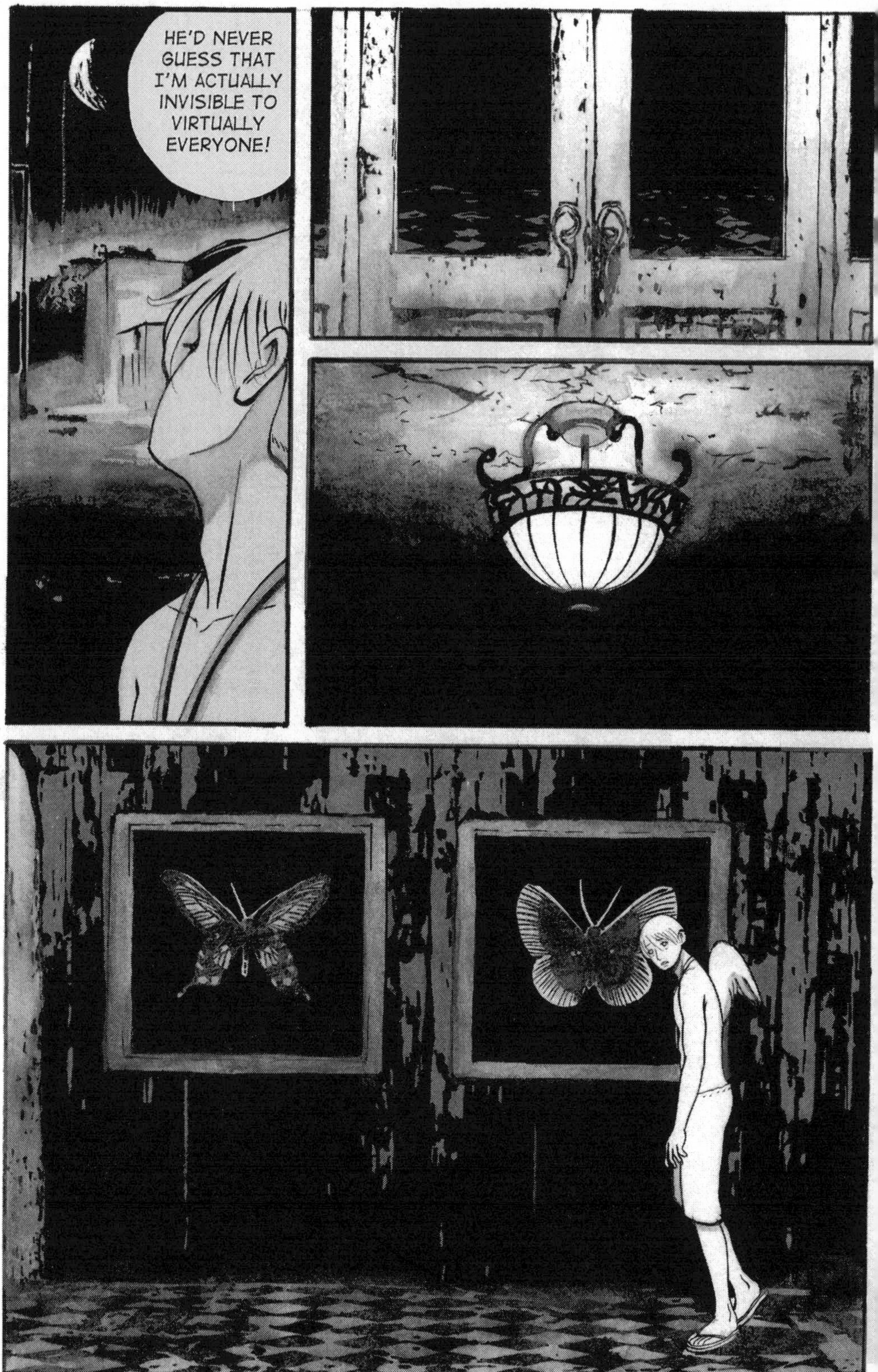
HE'D NEVER GUESS THAT I'M ACTUALLY INVISIBLE TO VIRTUALLY EVERYONE!

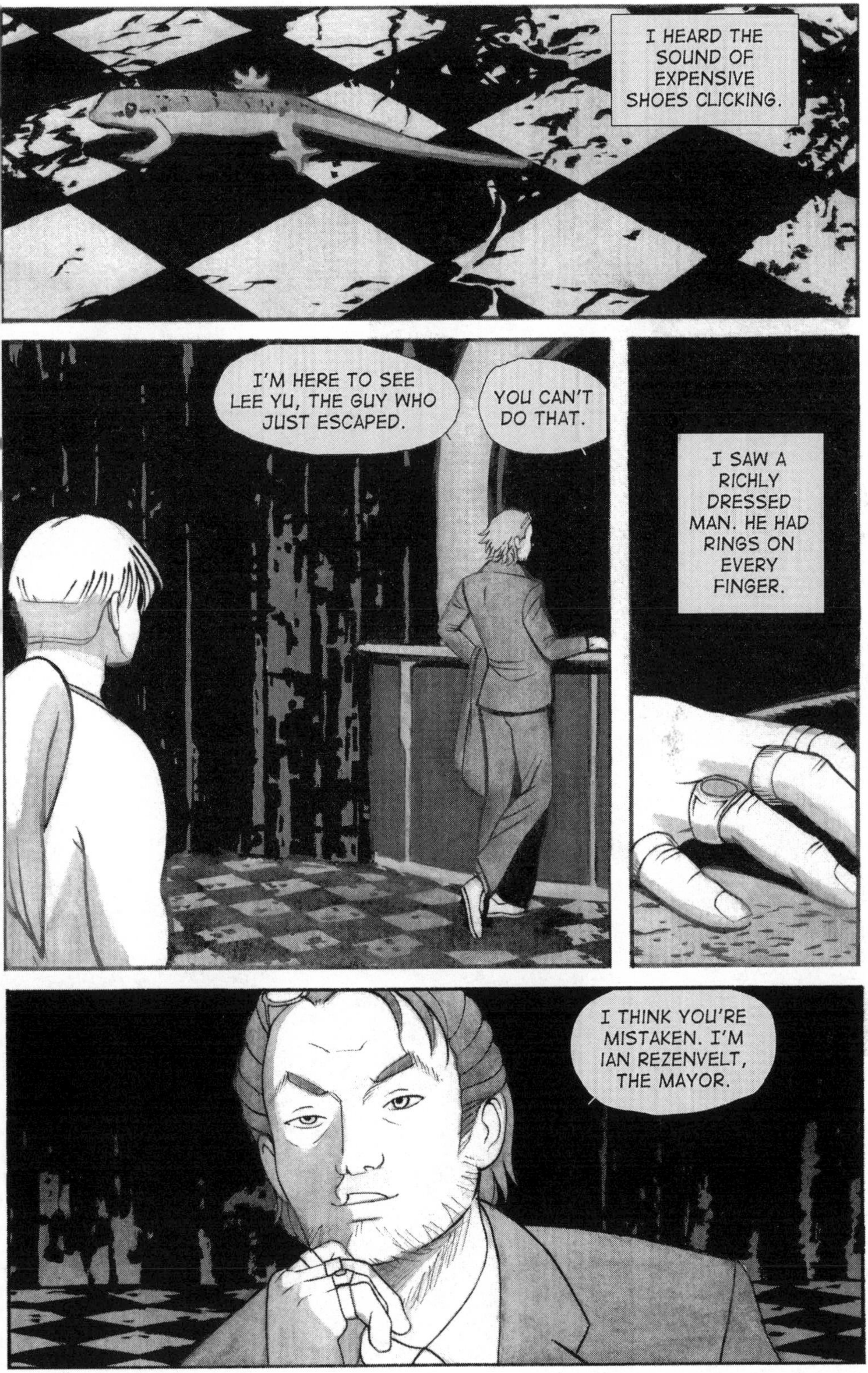
I HEARD THE SOUND OF EXPENSIVE SHOES CLICKING.
I'M HERE TO SEE LEE YU, THE GUY WHO JUST ESCAPED.
YOU CAN'T DO THAT.
I SAW A RICHLY DRESSED MAN. HE HAD RINGS ON EVERY FINGER.
I THINK YOU'RE MISTAKEN. I'M IAN REZENVELT, THE MAYOR.

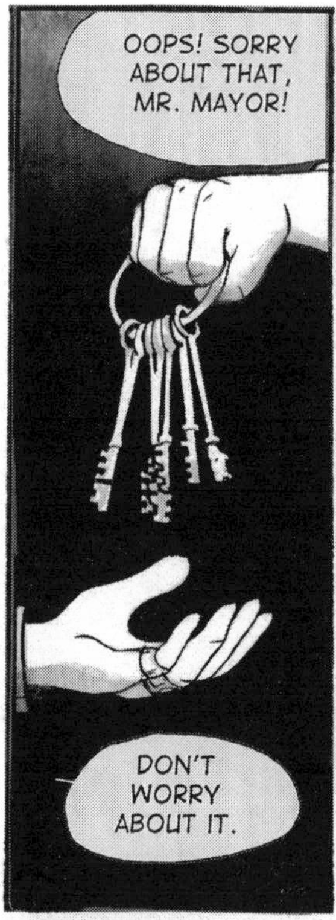
OOPS! SORRY ABOUT THAT, MR. MAYOR!
DON'T WORRY ABOUT IT.

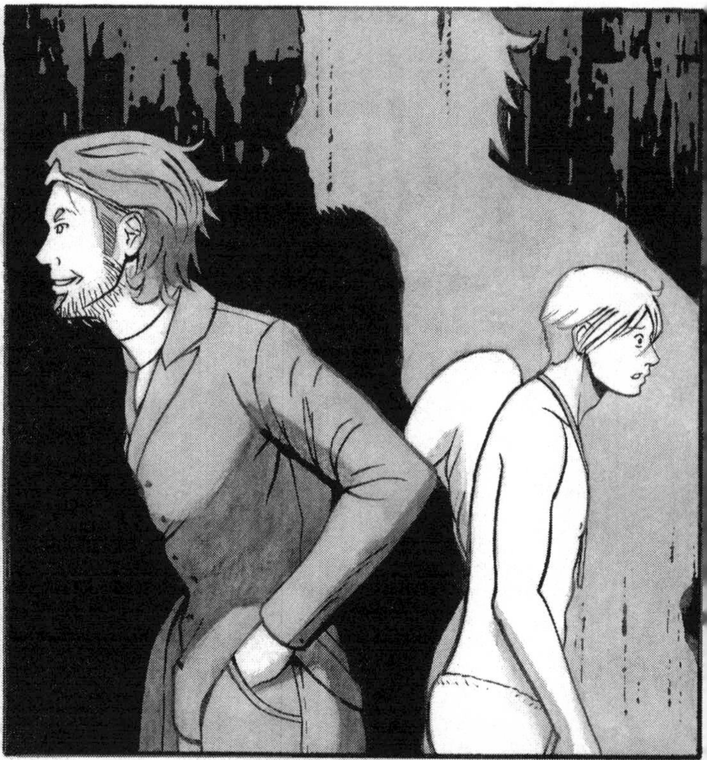

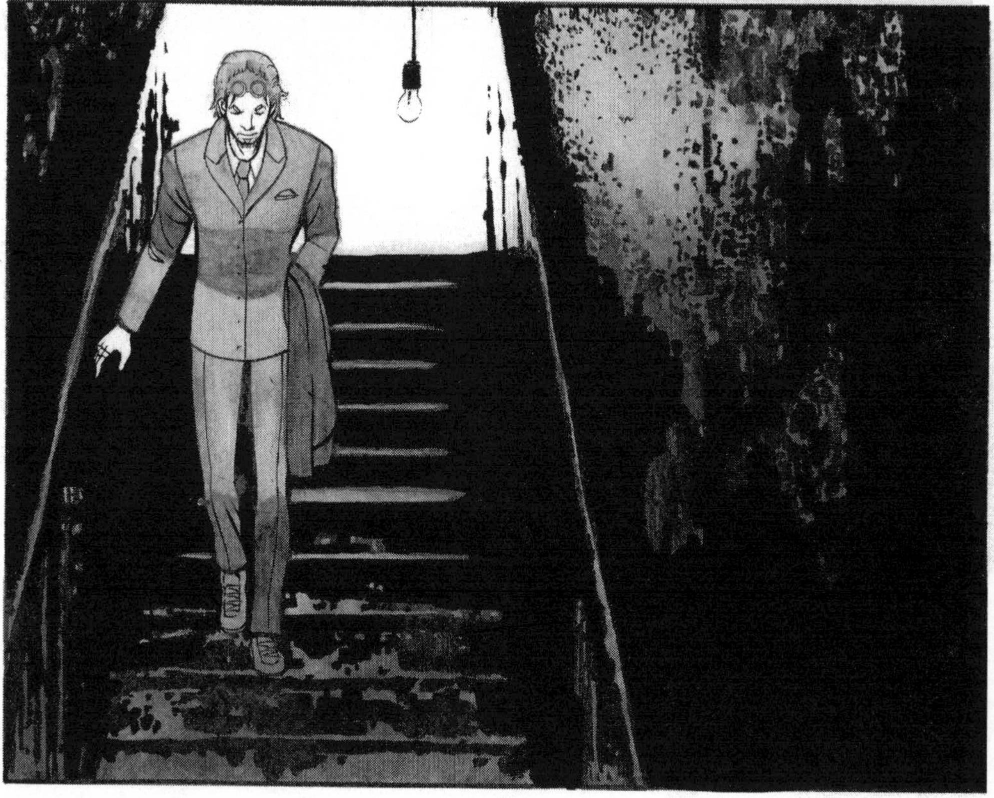

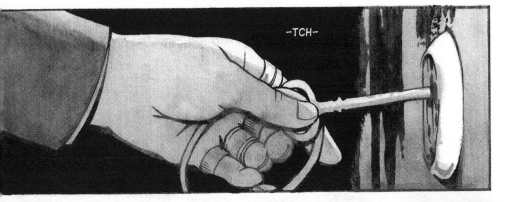

-TCH-

HELLO, LEE!

SO MY FRIENDS CALLED AND TOLD ME YOU TRIED TO ESCAPE.

TRIED TO FLY THE COOP, HUH?

AND THEY ALSO TOLD ME...

...THAT YOU HAD A *VISION*.

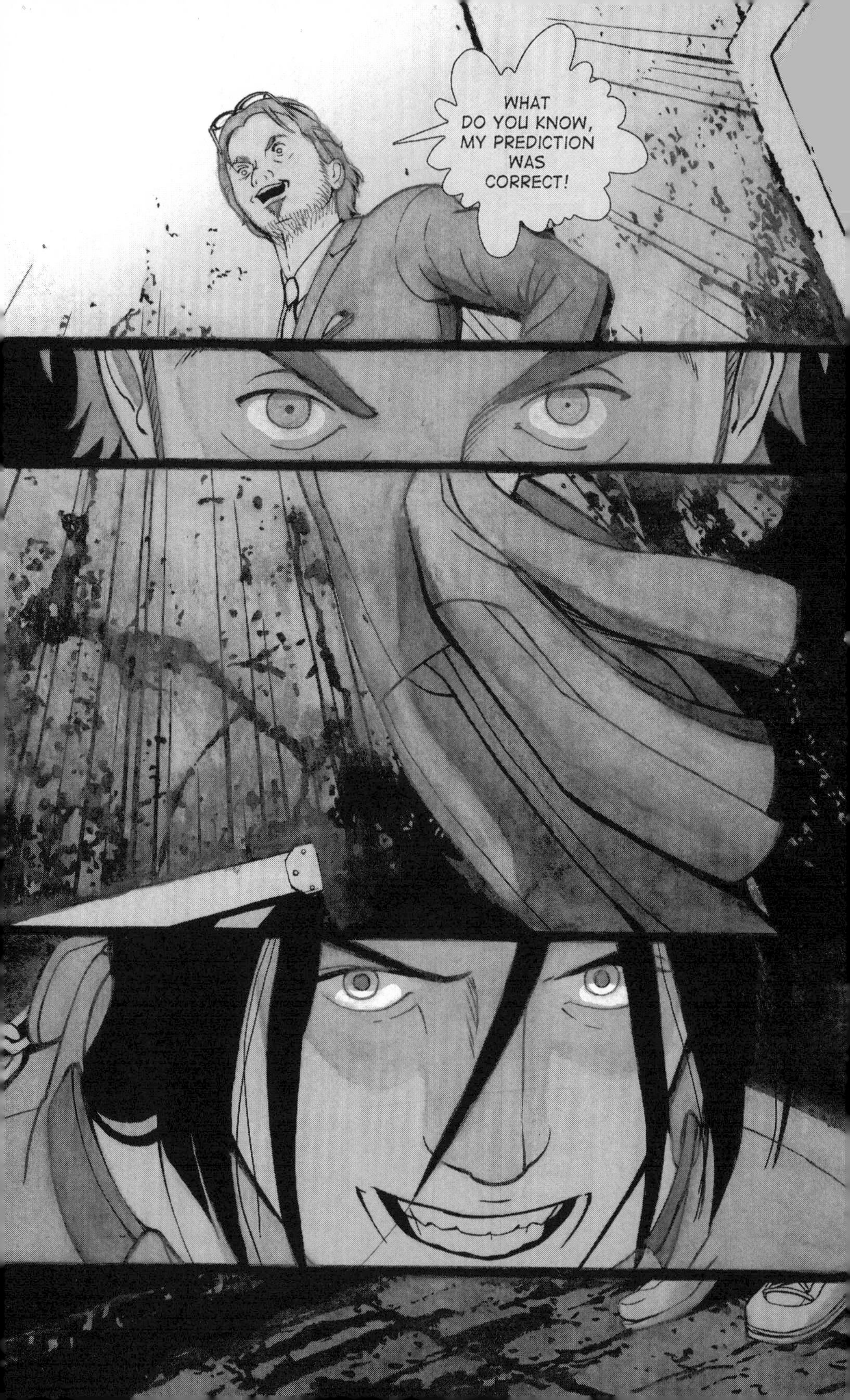
WHAT DO YOU KNOW, MY PREDICTION WAS CORRECT!

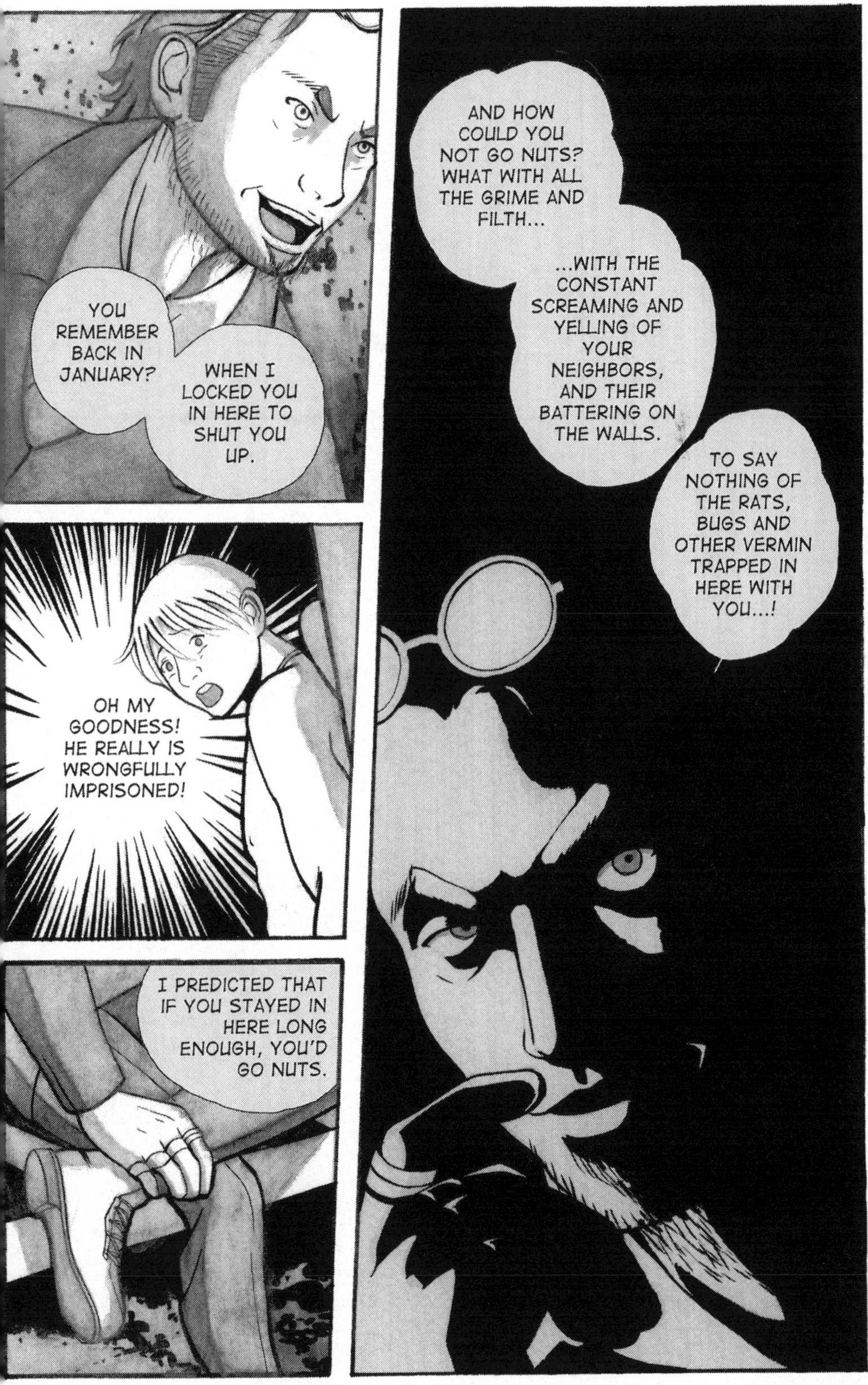
YOU REMEMBER BACK IN JANUARY?
WHEN I LOCKED YOU IN HERE TO SHUT YOU UP.
OH MY GOODNESS! HE REALLY IS WRONGFULLY IMPRISONED!
I PREDICTED THAT IF YOU STAYED IN HERE LONG ENOUGH, YOU'D GO NUTS.
AND HOW COULD YOU NOT GO NUTS? WHAT WITH ALL THE GRIME AND FILTH...
...WITH THE CONSTANT SCREAMING AND YELLING OF YOUR NEIGHBORS, AND THEIR BATTERING ON THE WALLS.
TO SAY NOTHING OF THE RATS, BUGS AND OTHER VERMIN TRAPPED IN HERE WITH YOU...!

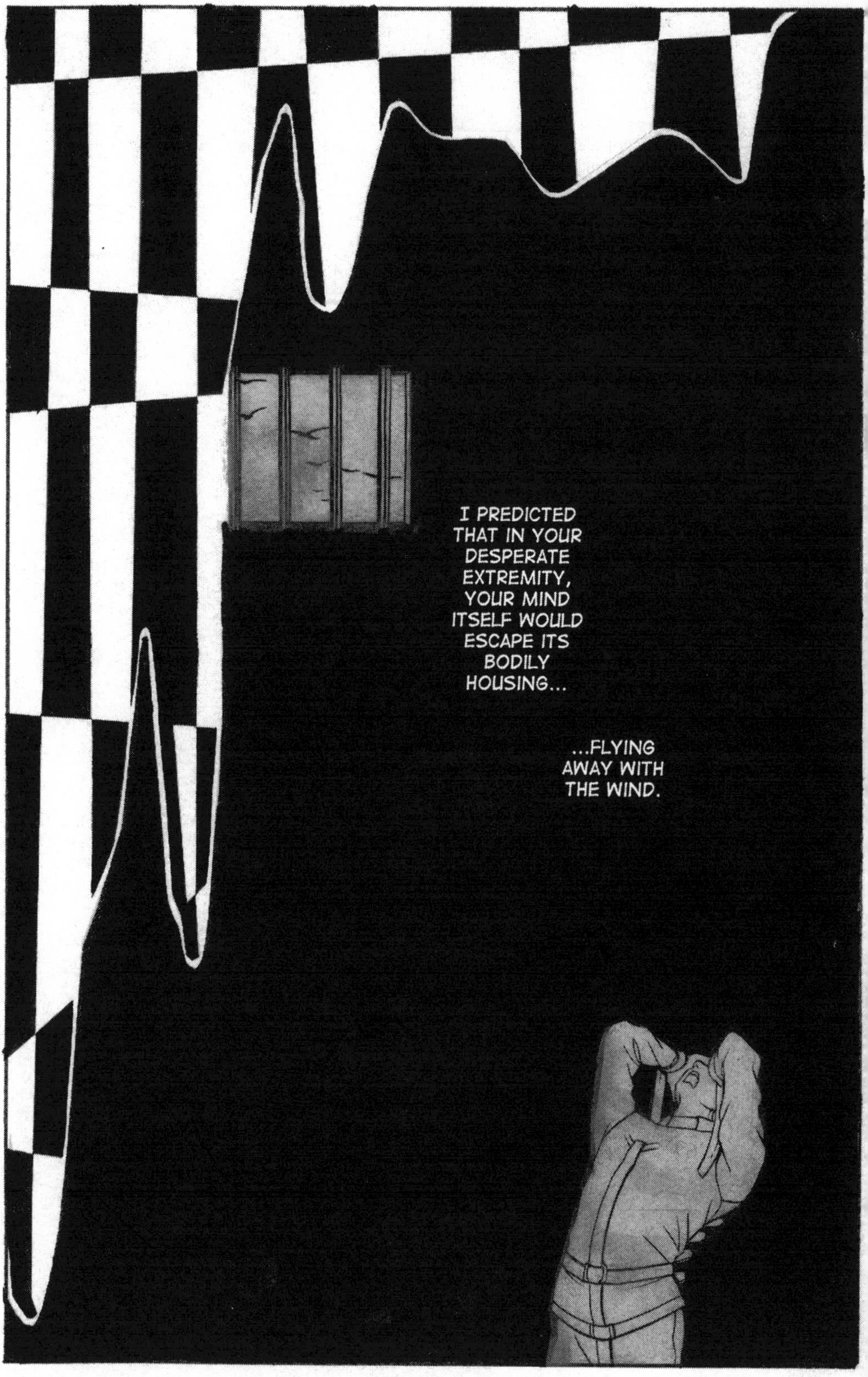
I PREDICTED THAT IN YOUR DESPERATE EXTREMITY, YOUR MIND ITSELF WOULD ESCAPE ITS BODILY HOUSING...
...FLYING AWAY WITH THE WIND.

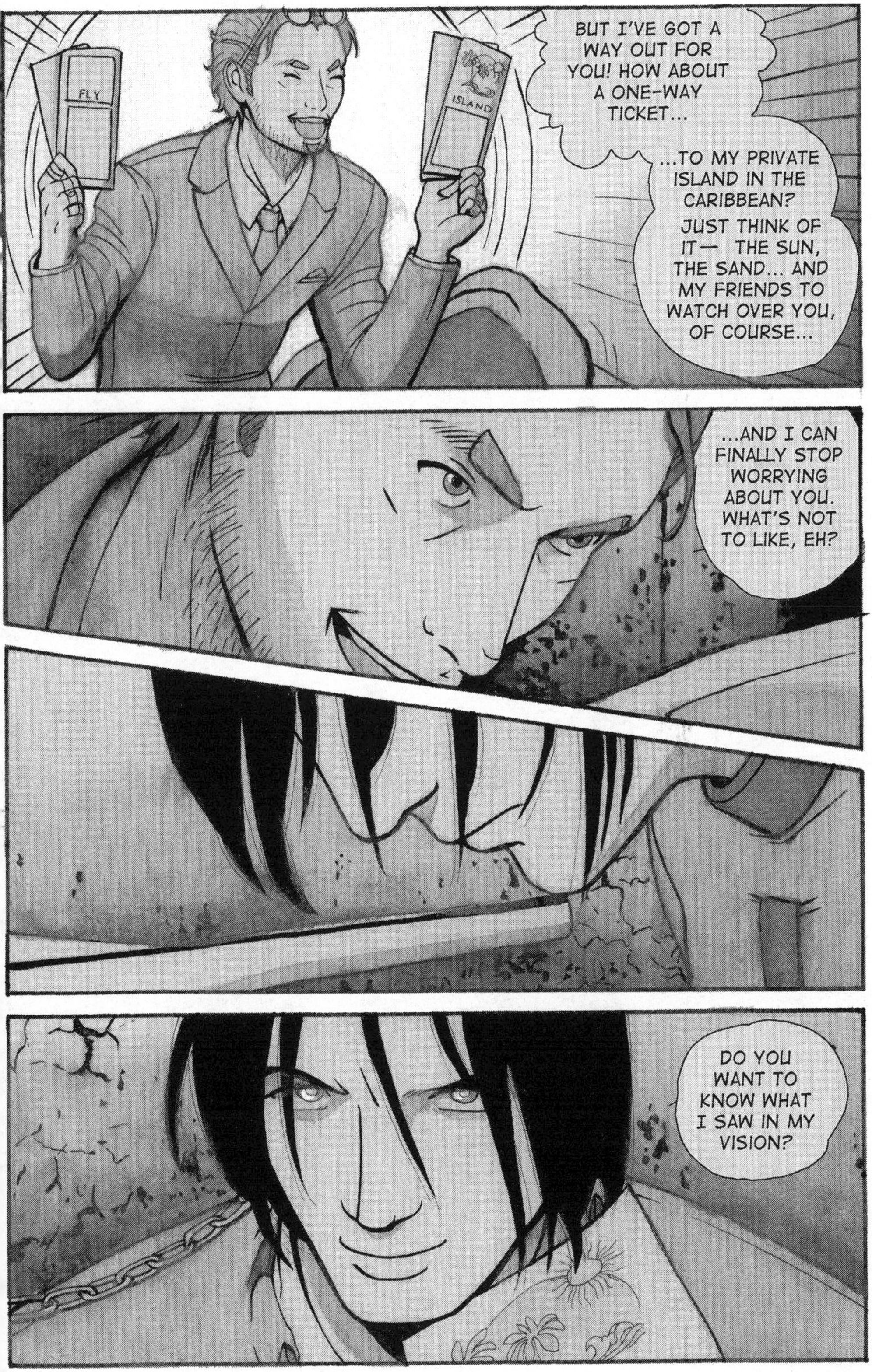
BUT I'VE GOT A WAY OUT FOR YOU! HOW ABOUT A ONE-WAY TICKET...
...TO MY PRIVATE ISLAND IN THE CARIBBEAN?
JUST THINK OF IT— THE SUN, THE SAND... AND MY FRIENDS TO WATCH OVER YOU, OF COURSE...
FLY
ISLAND
...AND I CAN FINALLY STOP WORRYING ABOUT YOU. WHAT'S NOT TO LIKE, EH?
DO YOU WANT TO KNOW WHAT I SAW IN MY VISION?

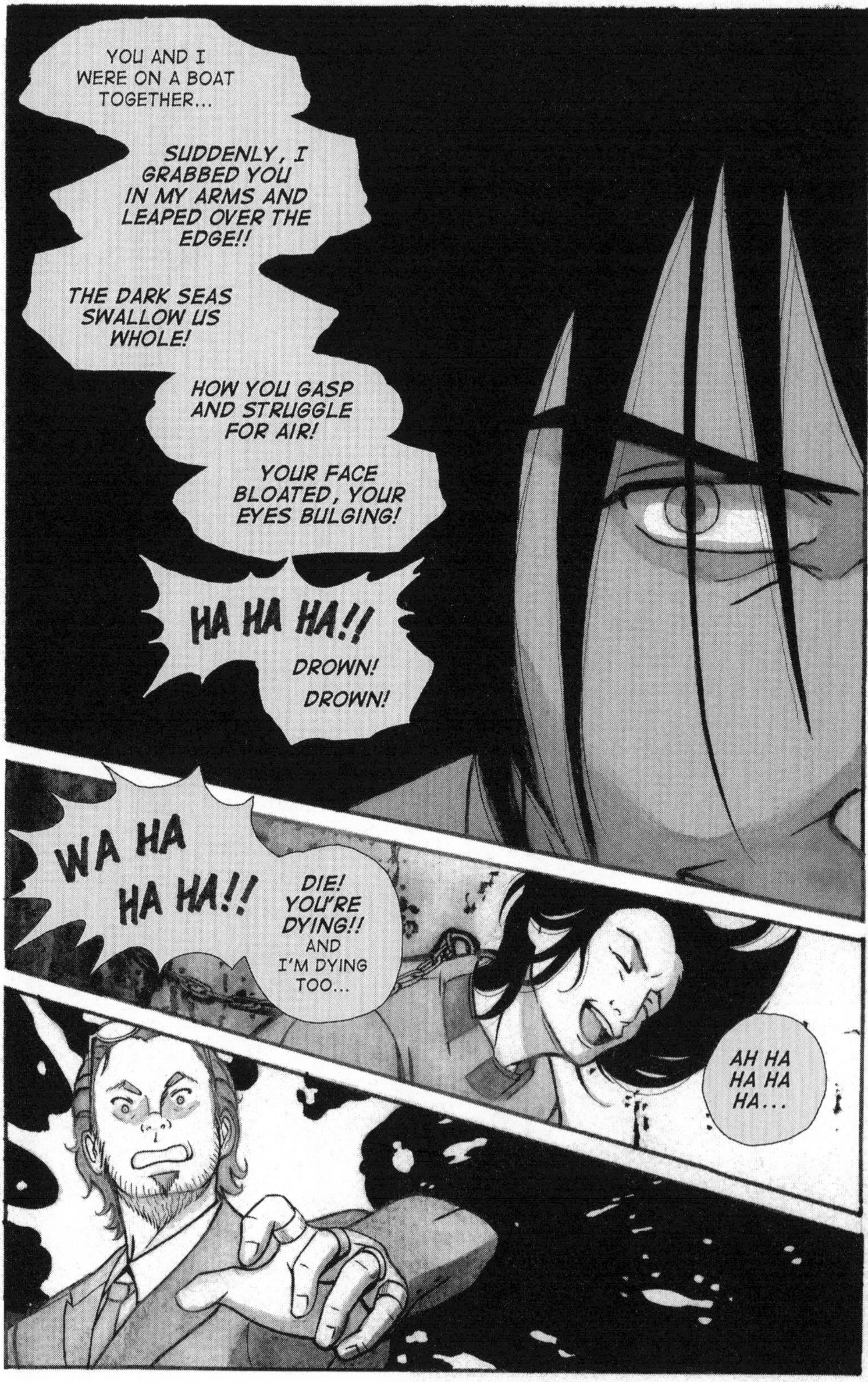
YOU AND I WERE ON A BOAT TOGETHER...
SUDDENLY, I GRABBED YOU IN MY ARMS AND LEAPED OVER THE EDGE!!
THE DARK SEAS SWALLOW US WHOLE!
HOW YOU GASP AND STRUGGLE FOR AIR!
YOUR FACE BLOATED, YOUR EYES BULGING!
HA HA HA!!
DROWN! DROWN!
WA HA HA HA!!
DIE! YOU'RE DYING!! AND I'M DYING TOO...
AH HA HA HA HA...

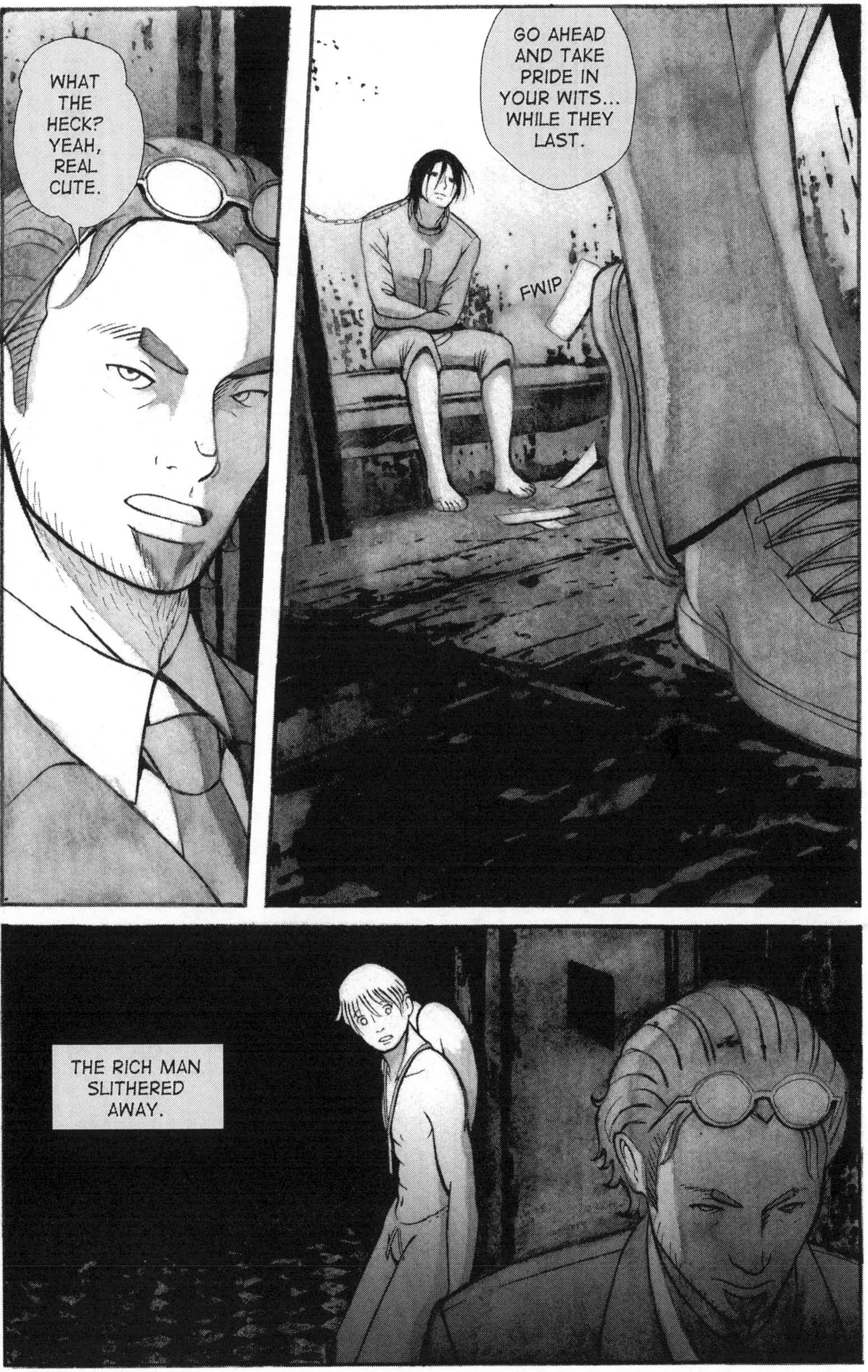
WHAT THE HECK? YEAH, REAL CUTE.
GO AHEAD AND TAKE PRIDE IN YOUR WITS... WHILE THEY LAST.
FWIP
THE RICH MAN SLITHERED AWAY.

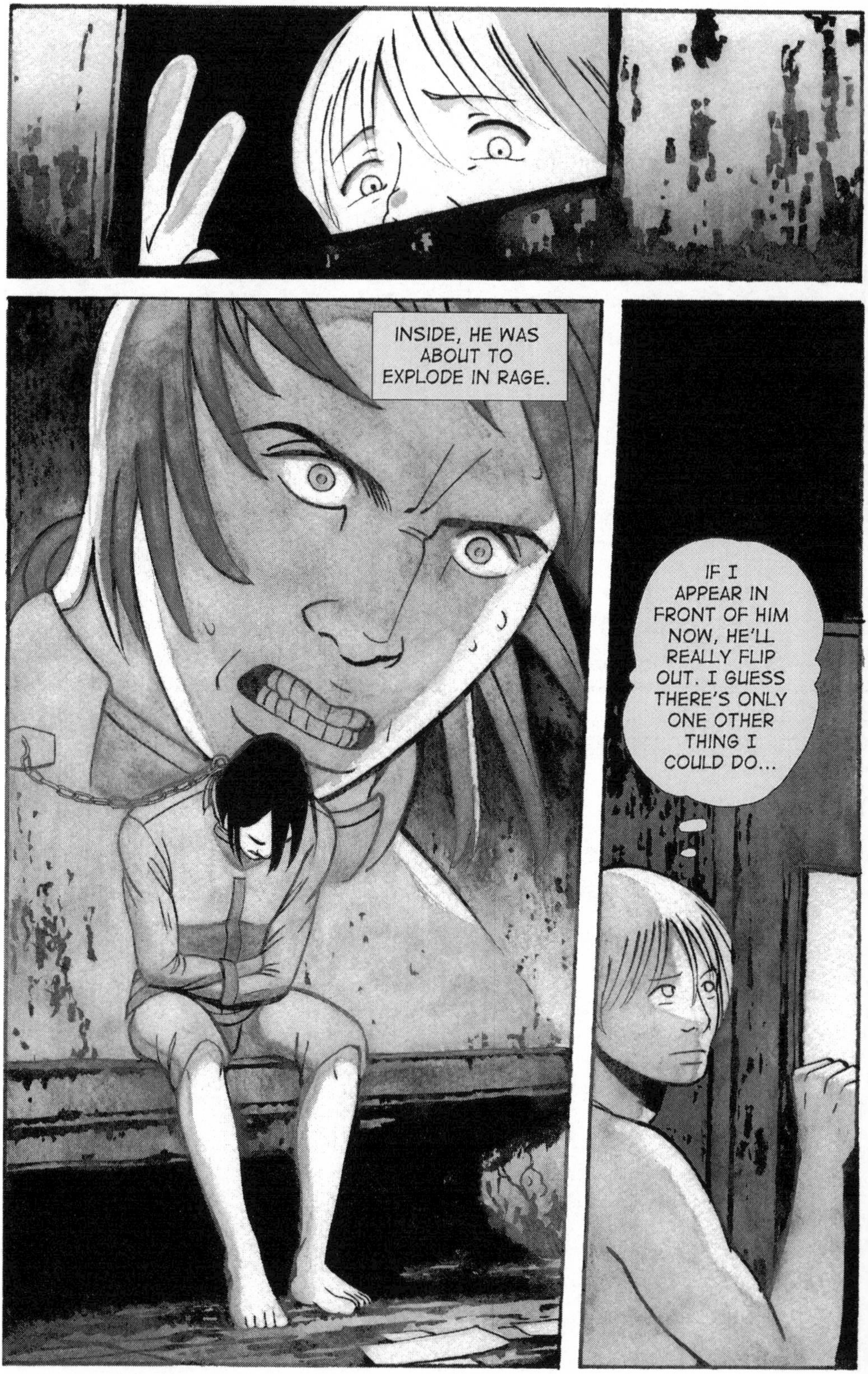
INSIDE, HE WAS ABOUT TO EXPLODE IN RAGE.
IF I APPEAR IN FRONT OF HIM NOW, HE'LL REALLY FLIP OUT. I GUESS THERE'S ONLY ONE OTHER THING I COULD DO...

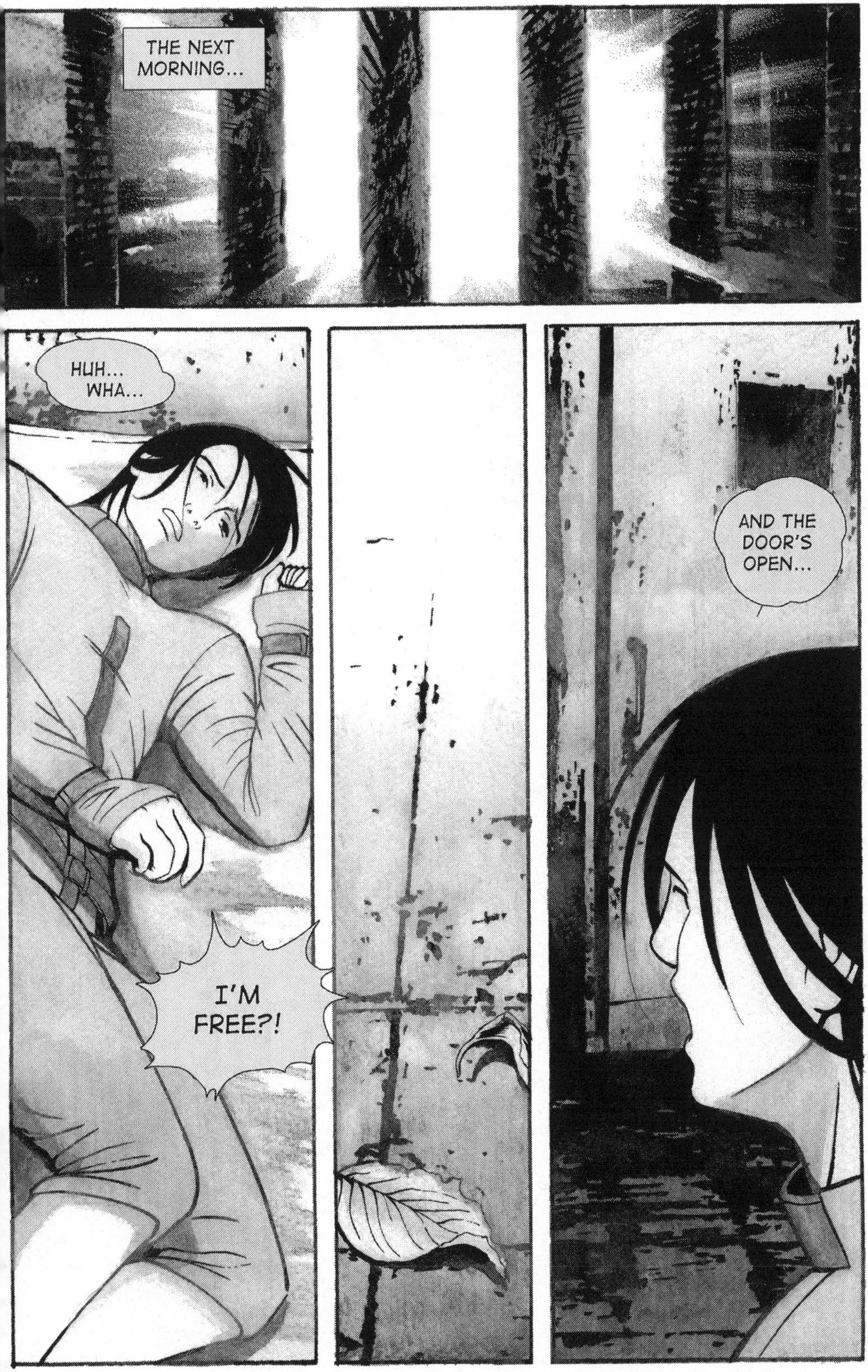
THE NEXT MORNING...
HUH... WHA...
I'M FREE?!
AND THE DOOR'S OPEN...

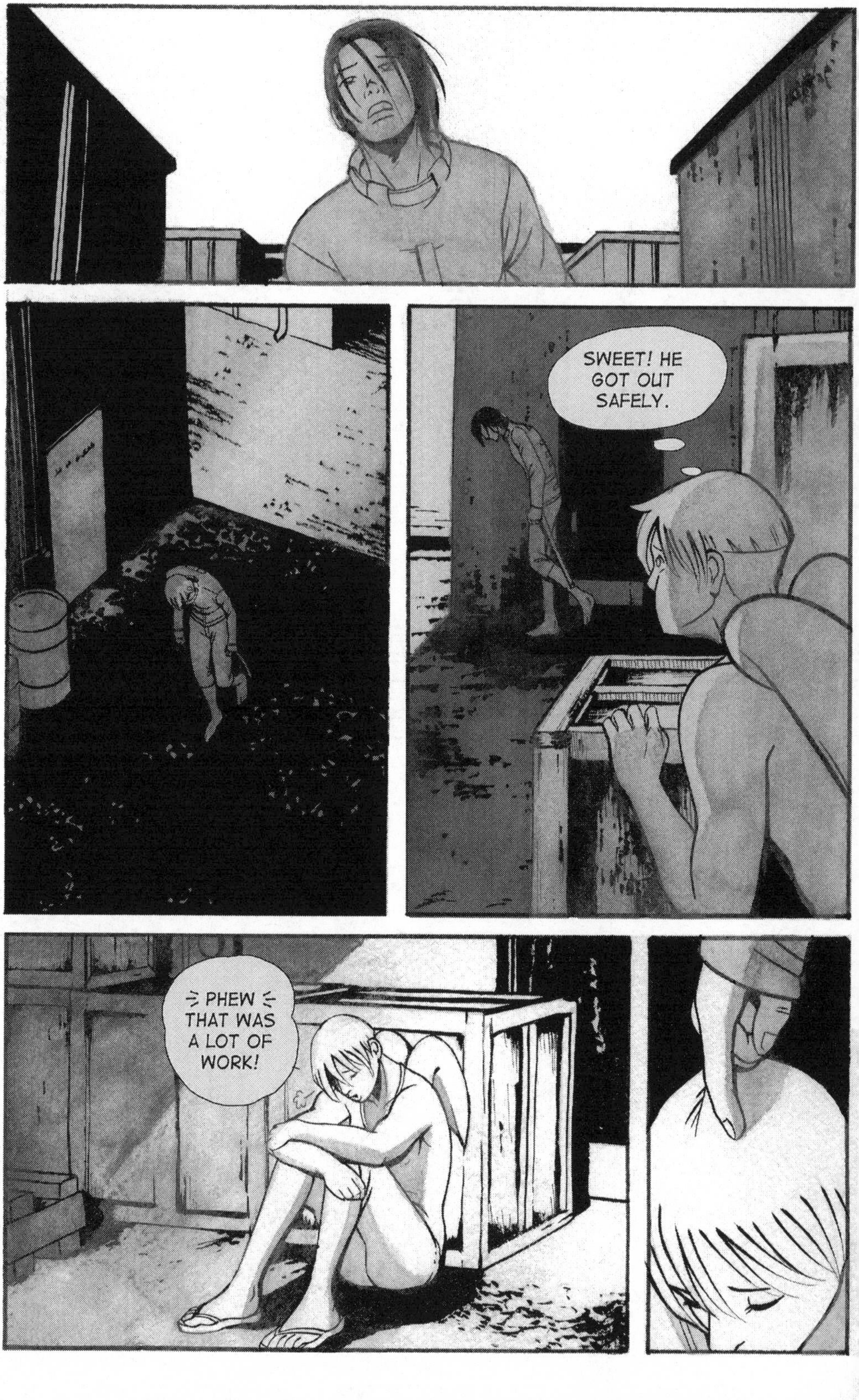
SWEET! HE GOT OUT SAFELY.
PHEW THAT WAS A LOT OF WORK!

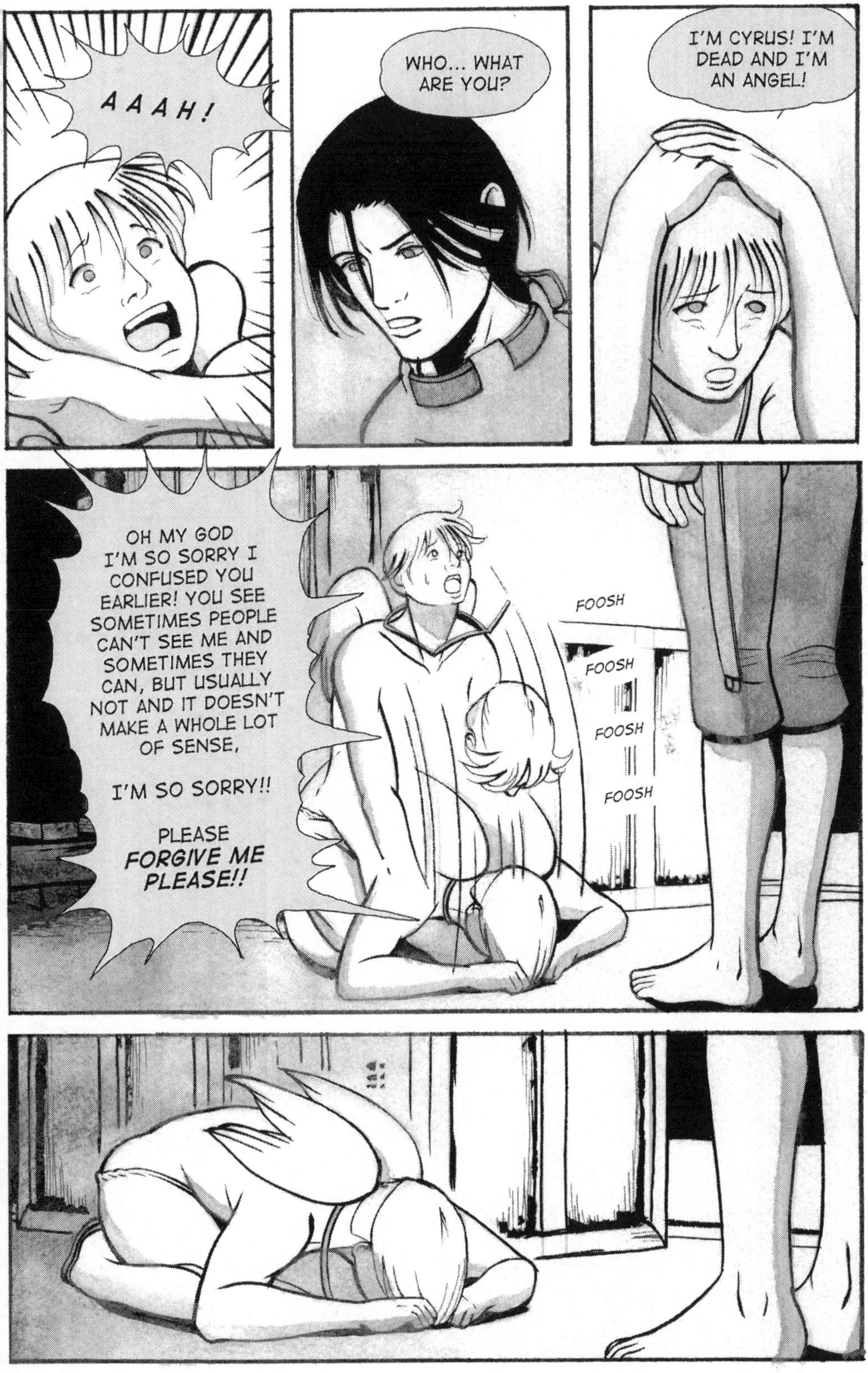
AAAH!
WHO... WHAT ARE YOU?
I'M CYRUS! I'M DEAD AND I'M AN ANGEL!
OH MY GOD I'M SO SORRY I CONFUSED YOU EARLIER! YOU SEE SOMETIMES PEOPLE CAN'T SEE ME AND SOMETIMES THEY CAN, BUT USUALLY NOT AND IT DOESN'T MAKE A WHOLE LOT OF SENSE,
I'M SO SORRY!!
PLEASE *FORGIVE ME PLEASE!!*
FOOSH
FOOSH
FOOSH
FOOSH

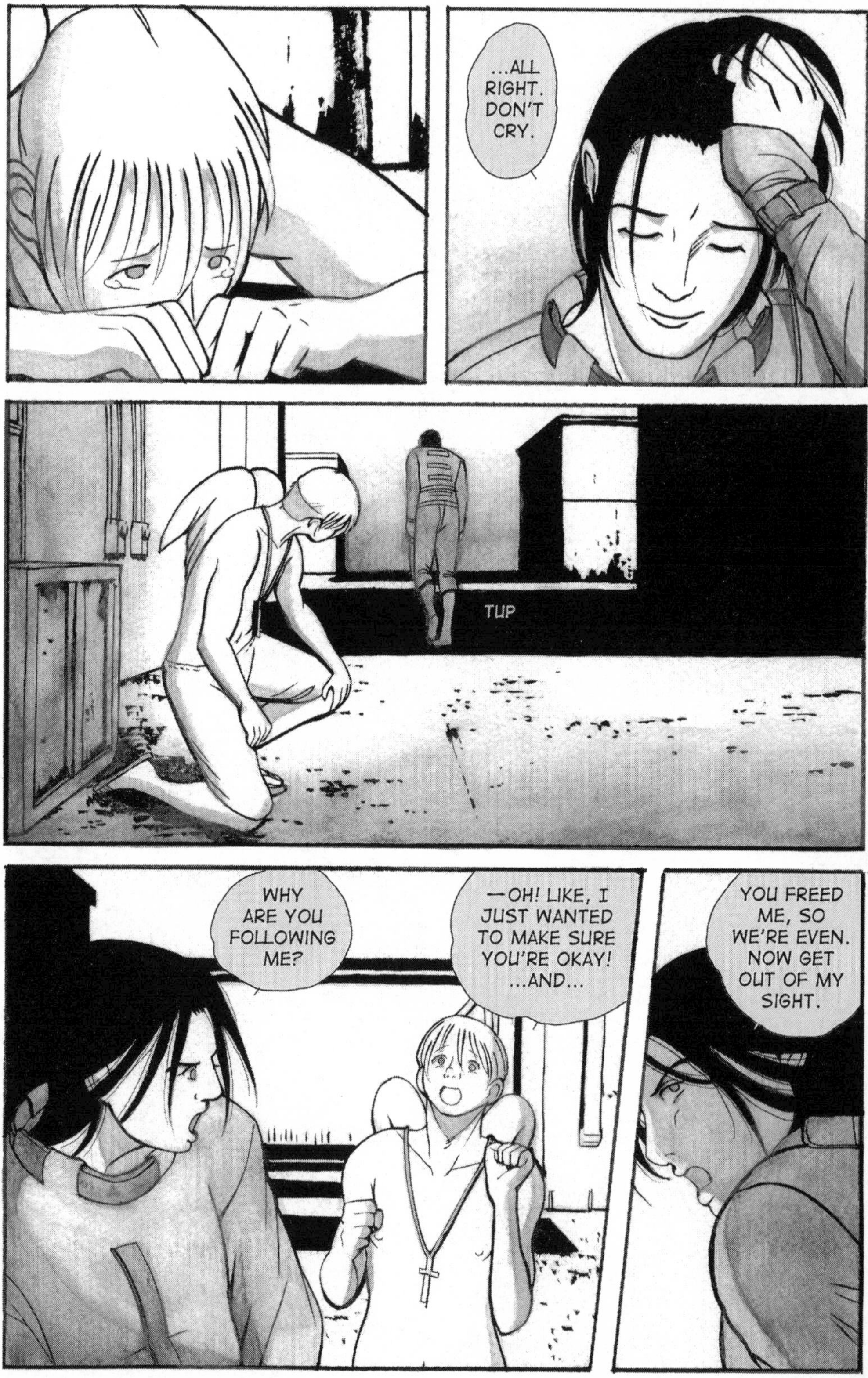
...ALL RIGHT. DON'T CRY.
TUP
WHY ARE YOU FOLLOWING ME?
—OH! LIKE, I JUST WANTED TO MAKE SURE YOU'RE OKAY! ...AND...
YOU FREED ME, SO WE'RE EVEN. NOW GET OUT OF MY SIGHT.

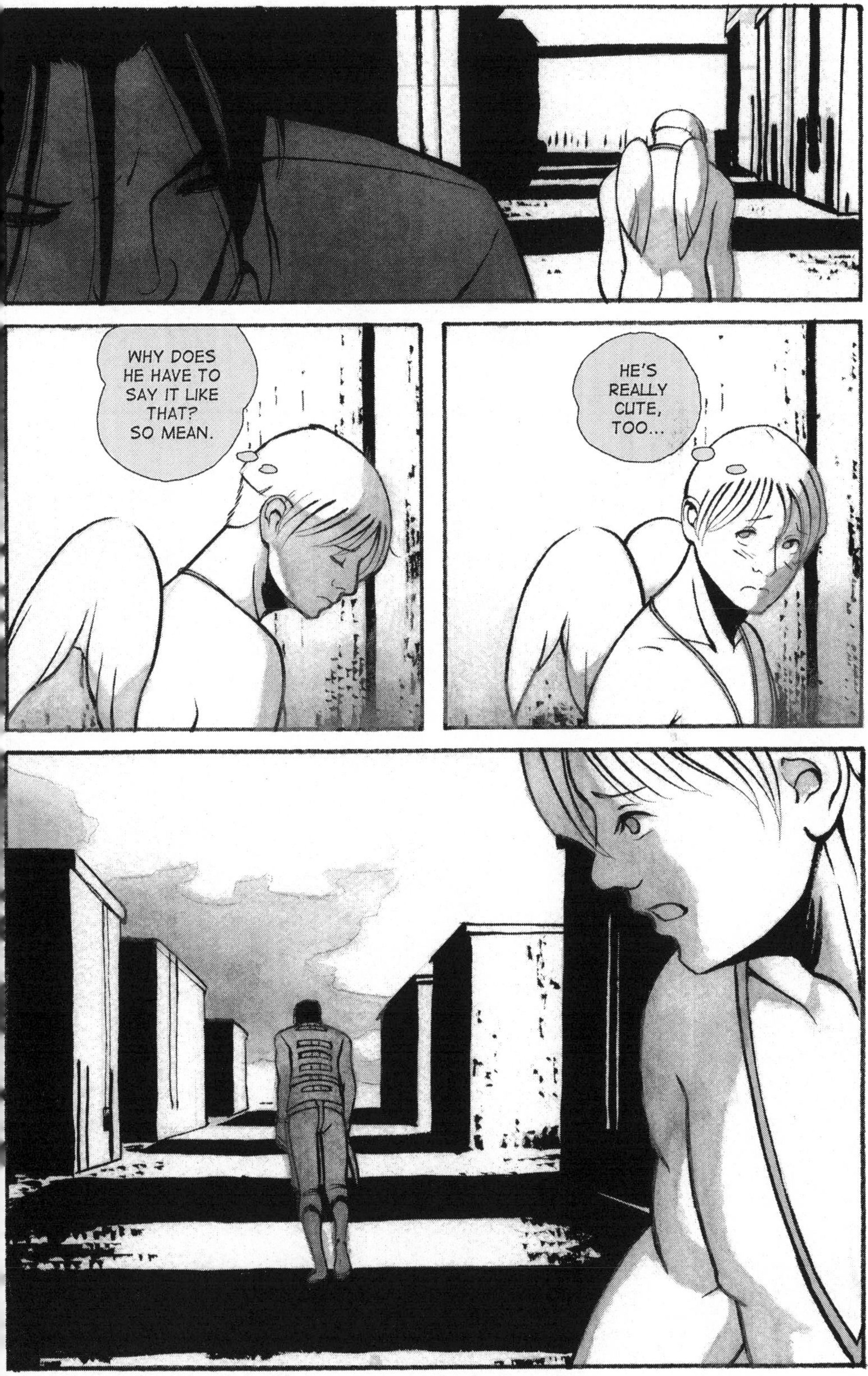
WHY DOES HE HAVE TO SAY IT LIKE THAT? SO MEAN.
HE'S REALLY CUTE, TOO...

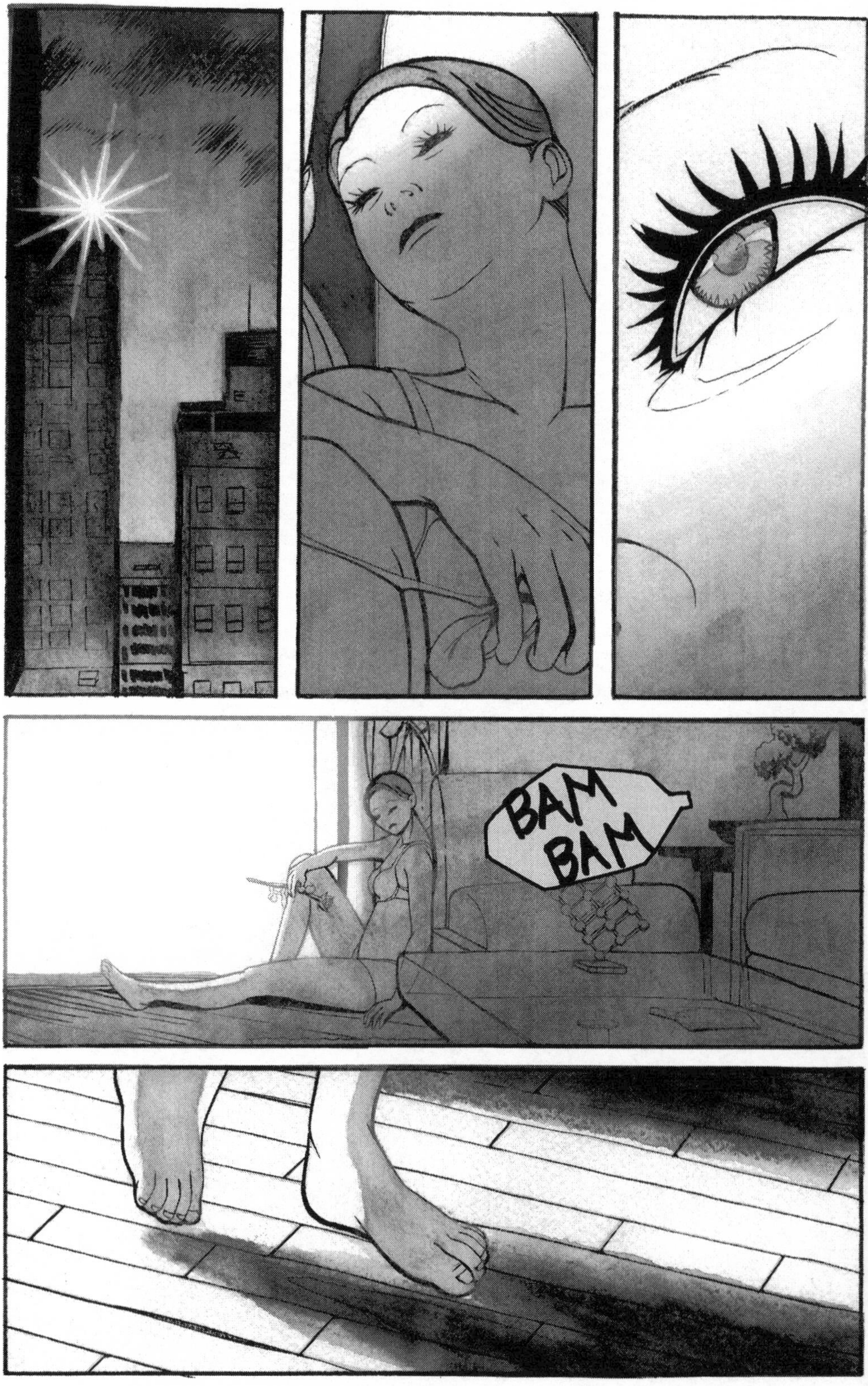
BAM BAM

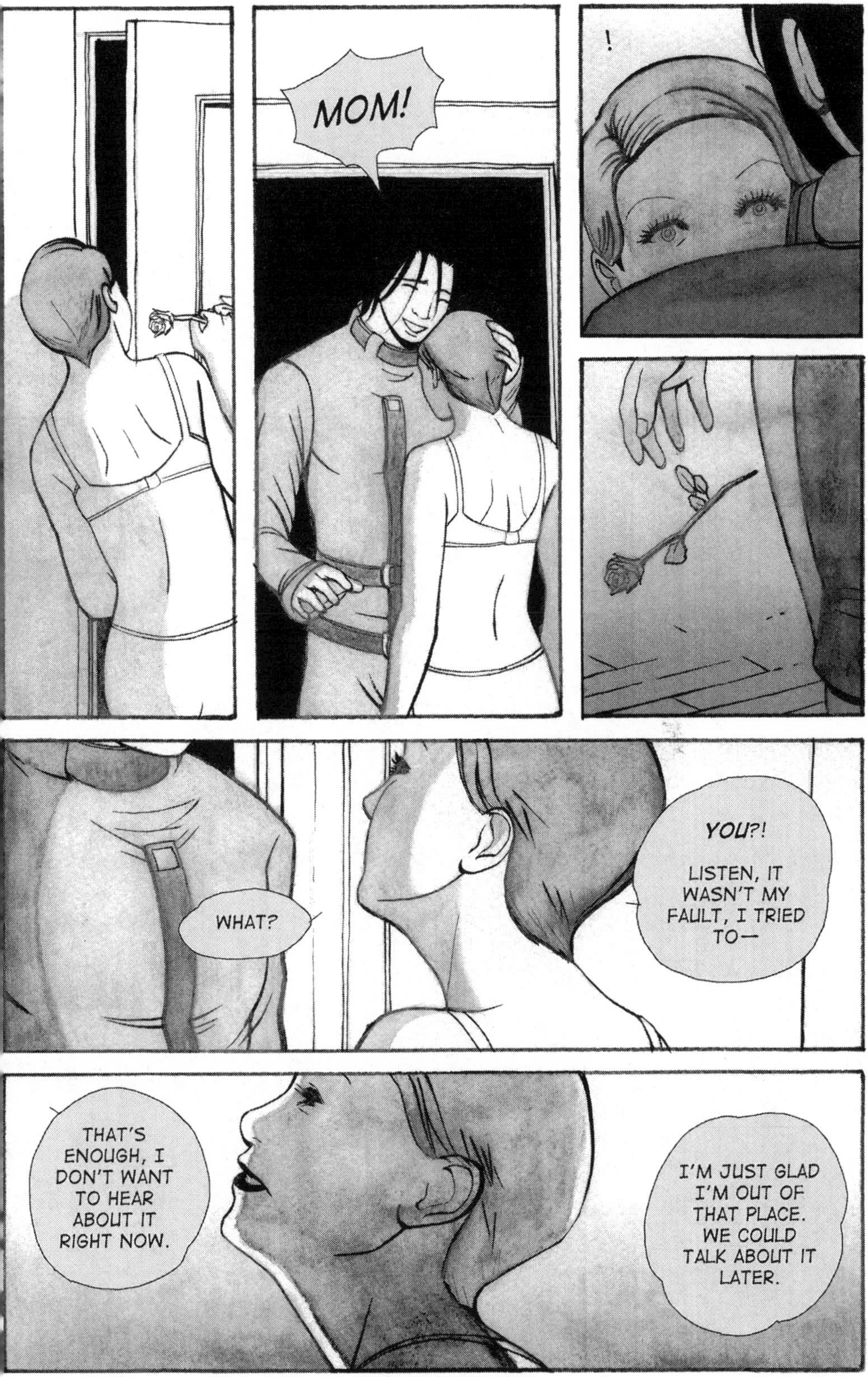
MOM!
!
WHAT?
YOU?!
LISTEN, IT WASN'T MY FAULT, I TRIED TO—
THAT'S ENOUGH, I DON'T WANT TO HEAR ABOUT IT RIGHT NOW.
I'M JUST GLAD I'M OUT OF THAT PLACE. WE COULD TALK ABOUT IT LATER.

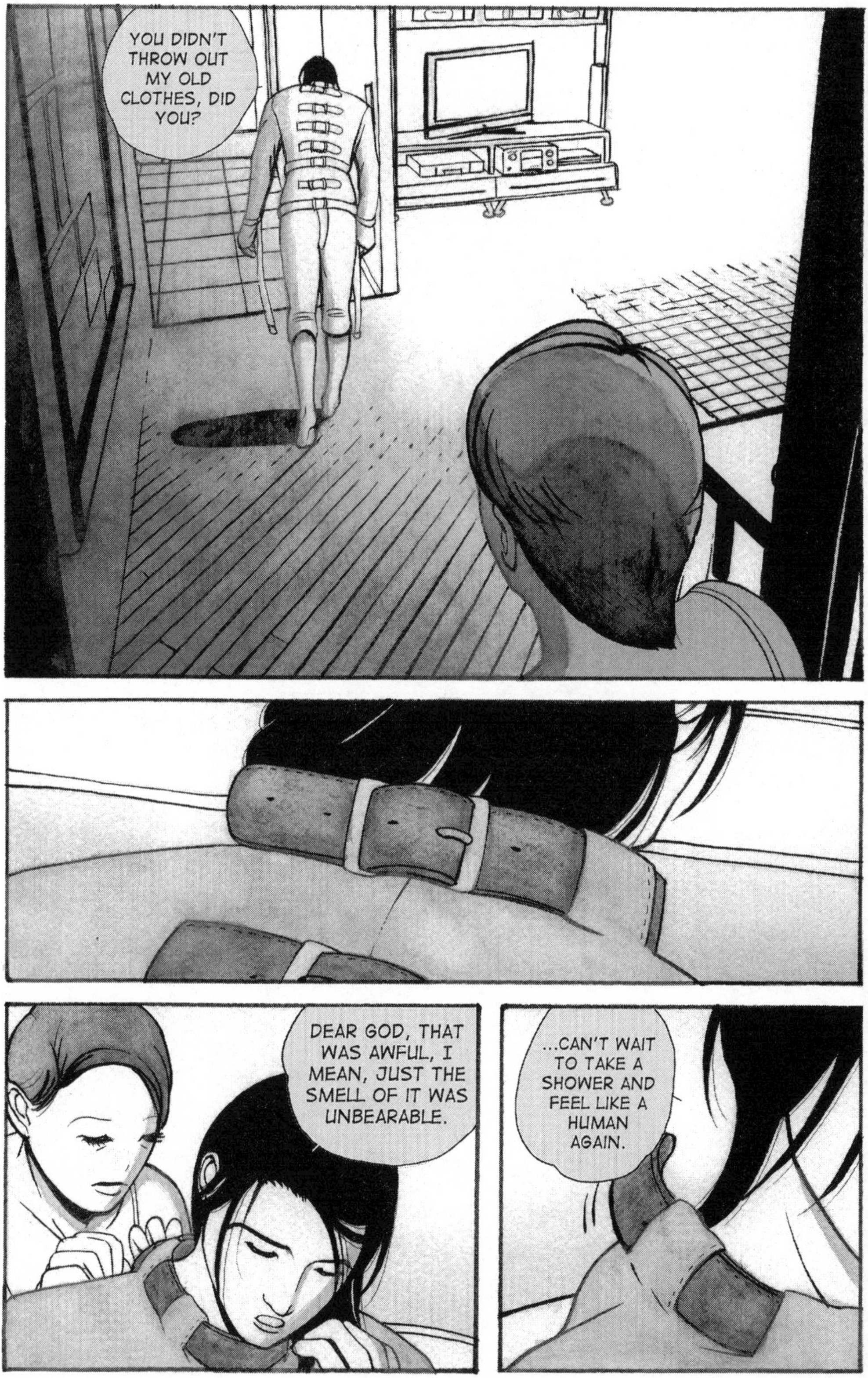
YOU DIDN'T THROW OUT MY OLD CLOTHES, DID YOU?
DEAR GOD, THAT WAS AWFUL, I MEAN, JUST THE SMELL OF IT WAS UNBEARABLE.
...CAN'T WAIT TO TAKE A SHOWER AND FEEL LIKE A HUMAN AGAIN.

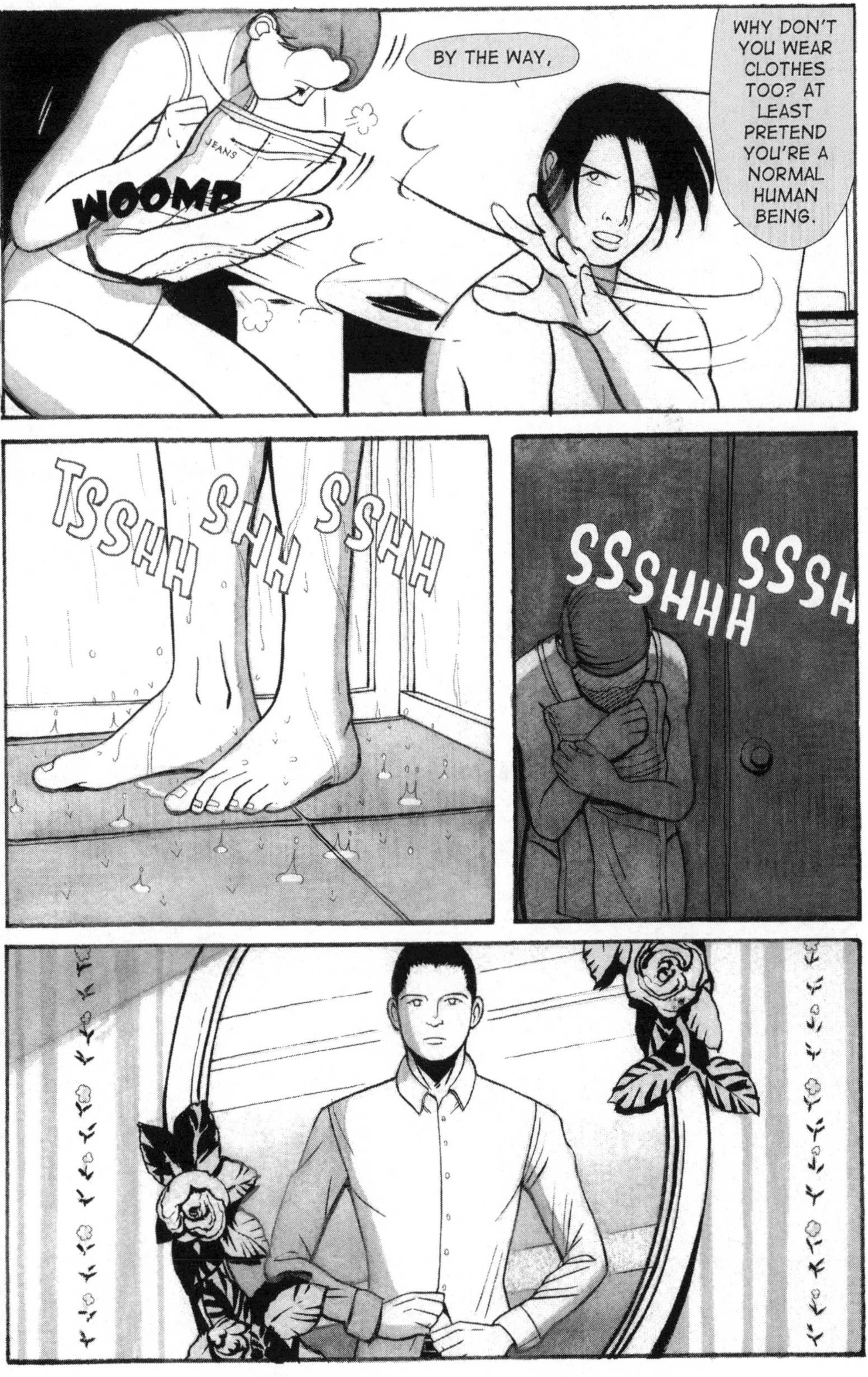
BY THE WAY,
WHY DON'T YOU WEAR CLOTHES TOO? AT LEAST PRETEND YOU'RE A NORMAL HUMAN BEING.
JEANS
WOOMP
TSSHH SHH SSHH
SSSHHH SSSH

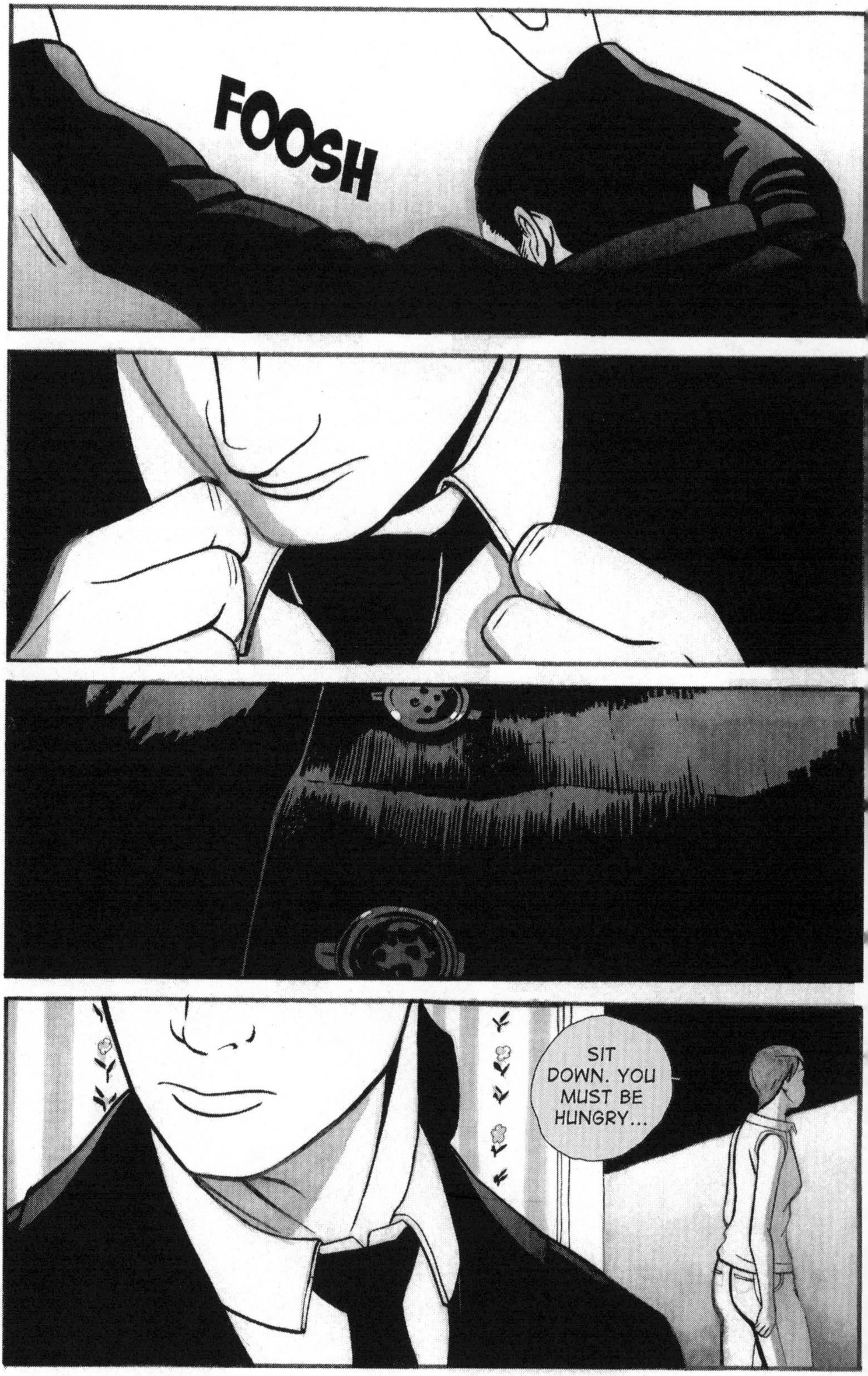
FOOSH
SIT DOWN. YOU MUST BE HUNGRY...

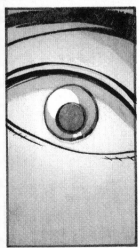

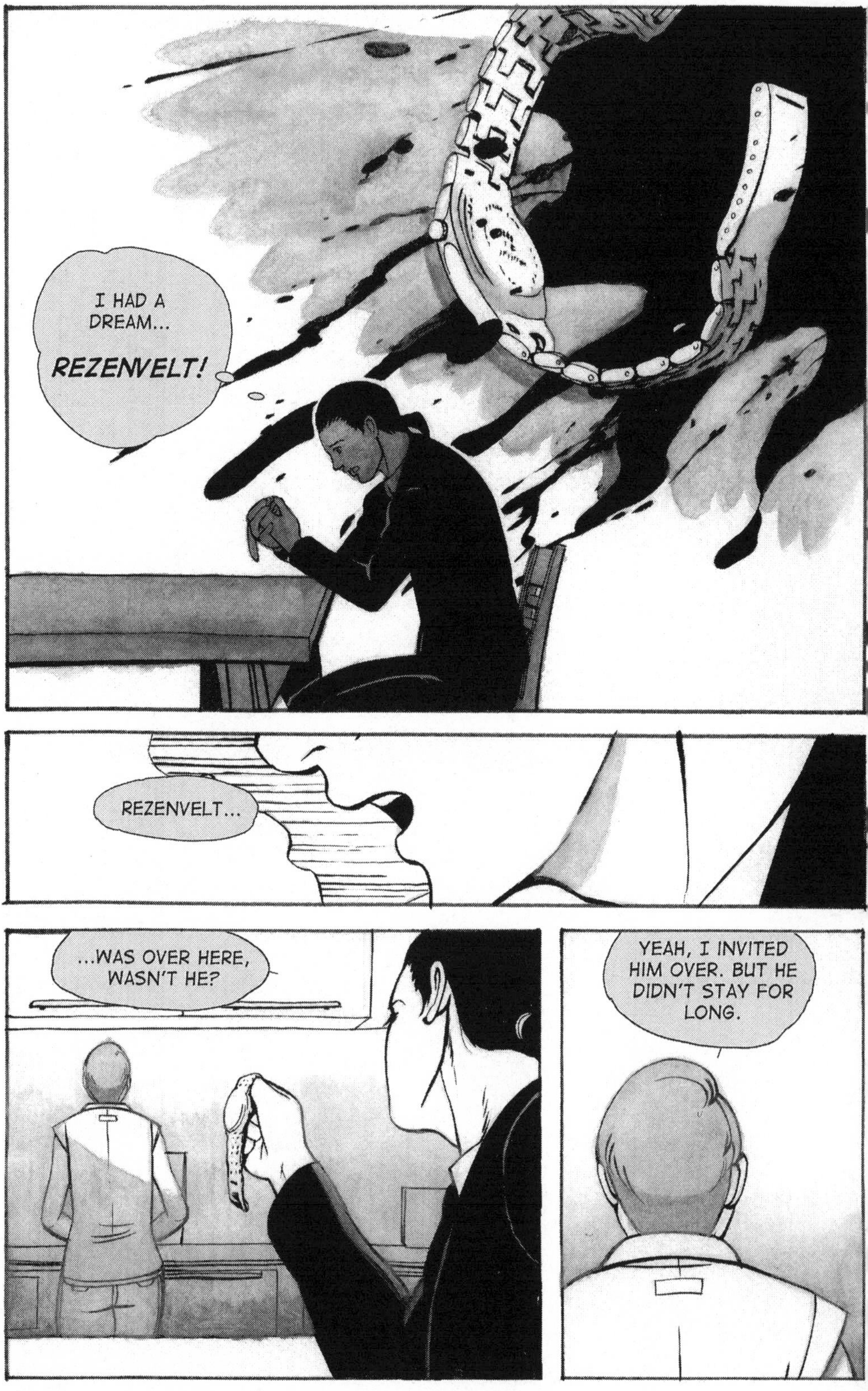
I HAD A DREAM...
REZENVELT!
REZENVELT...
...WAS OVER HERE, WASN'T HE?
YEAH, I INVITED HIM OVER. BUT HE DIDN'T STAY FOR LONG.

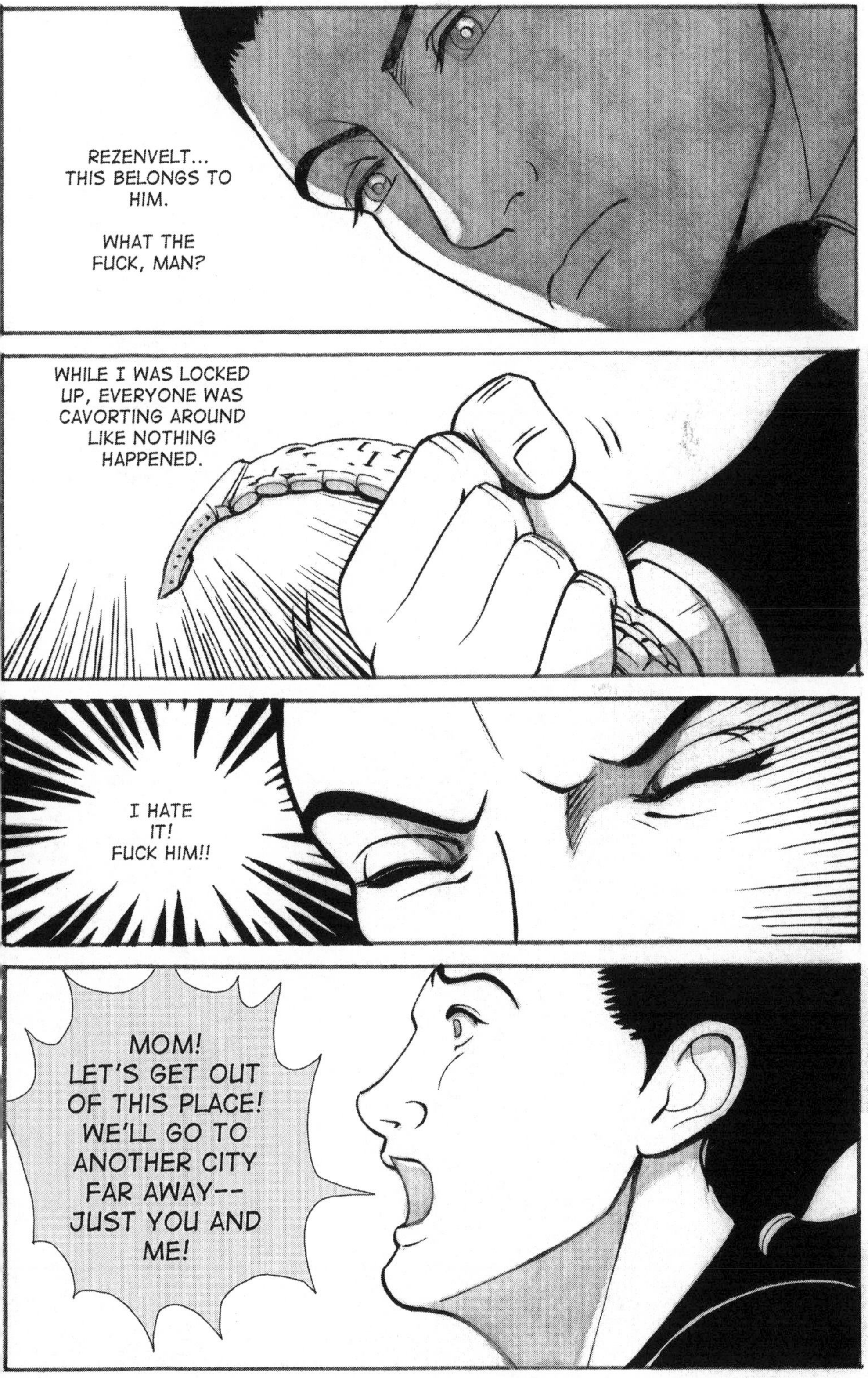
REZENVELT... THIS BELONGS TO HIM.
WHAT THE FUCK, MAN?
WHILE I WAS LOCKED UP, EVERYONE WAS CAVORTING AROUND LIKE NOTHING HAPPENED.
I HATE IT! FUCK HIM!!
MOM! LET'S GET OUT OF THIS PLACE! WE'LL GO TO ANOTHER CITY FAR AWAY-- JUST YOU AND ME!

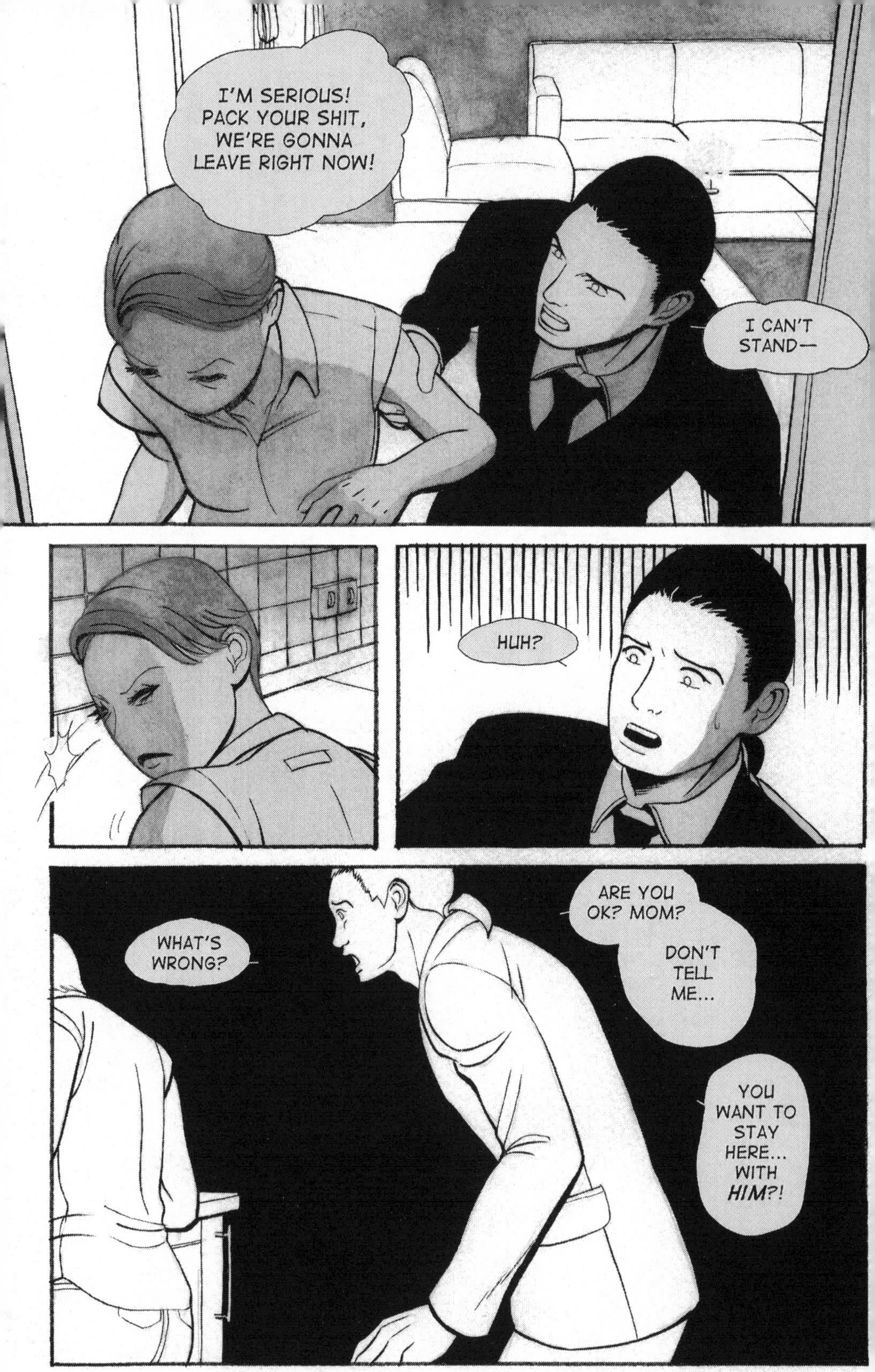
I'M SERIOUS! PACK YOUR SHIT, WE'RE GONNA LEAVE RIGHT NOW!
I CAN'T STAND—
HUH?
WHAT'S WRONG?
ARE YOU OK? MOM?
DON'T TELL ME...
YOU WANT TO STAY HERE... WITH *HIM*?!

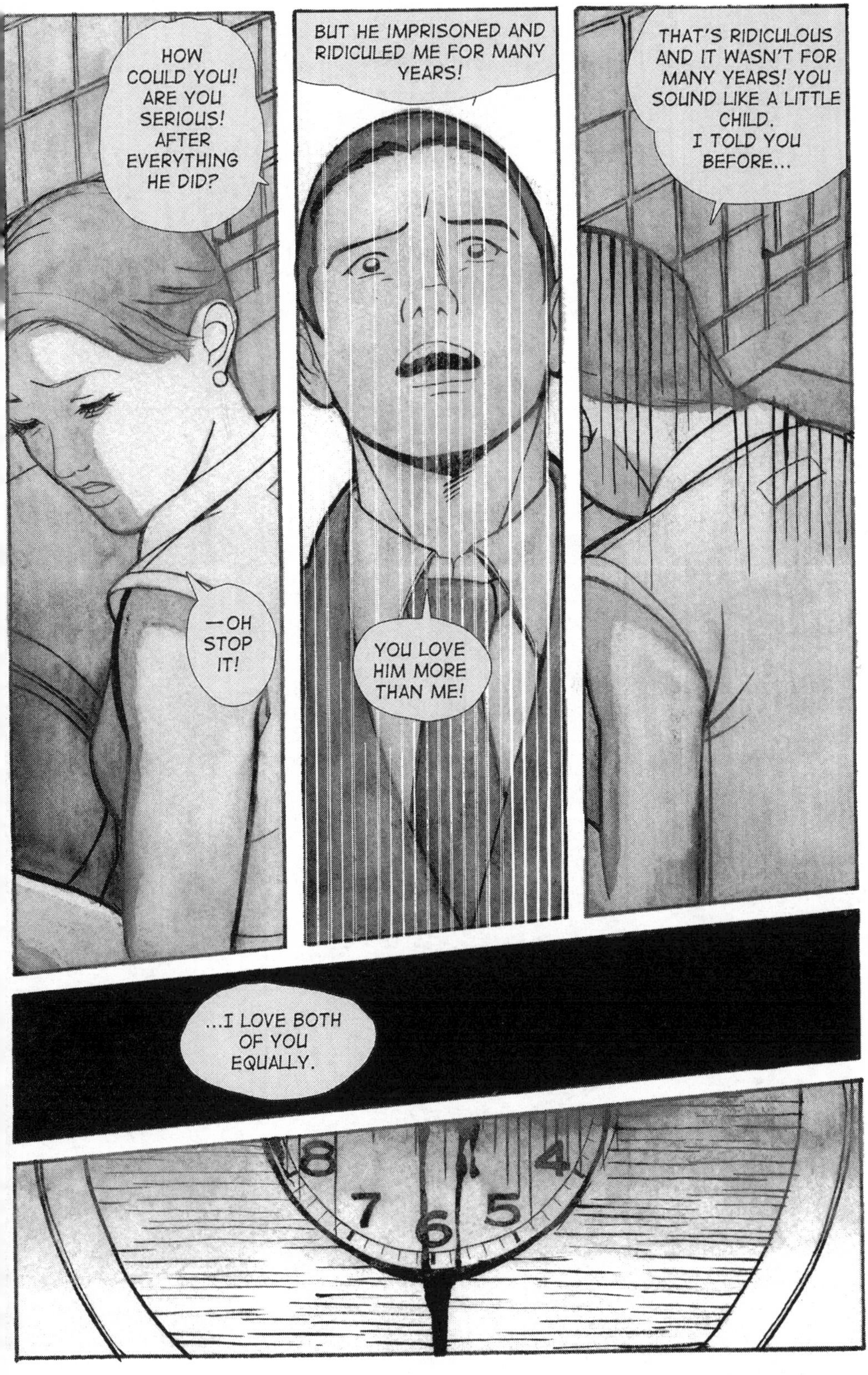
HOW COULD YOU! ARE YOU SERIOUS! AFTER EVERYTHING HE DID?
—OH STOP IT!
BUT HE IMPRISONED AND RIDICULED ME FOR MANY YEARS!
YOU LOVE HIM MORE THAN ME!
THAT'S RIDICULOUS AND IT WASN'T FOR MANY YEARS! YOU SOUND LIKE A LITTLE CHILD. I TOLD YOU BEFORE...
...I LOVE BOTH OF YOU EQUALLY.
8 4 7 6 5

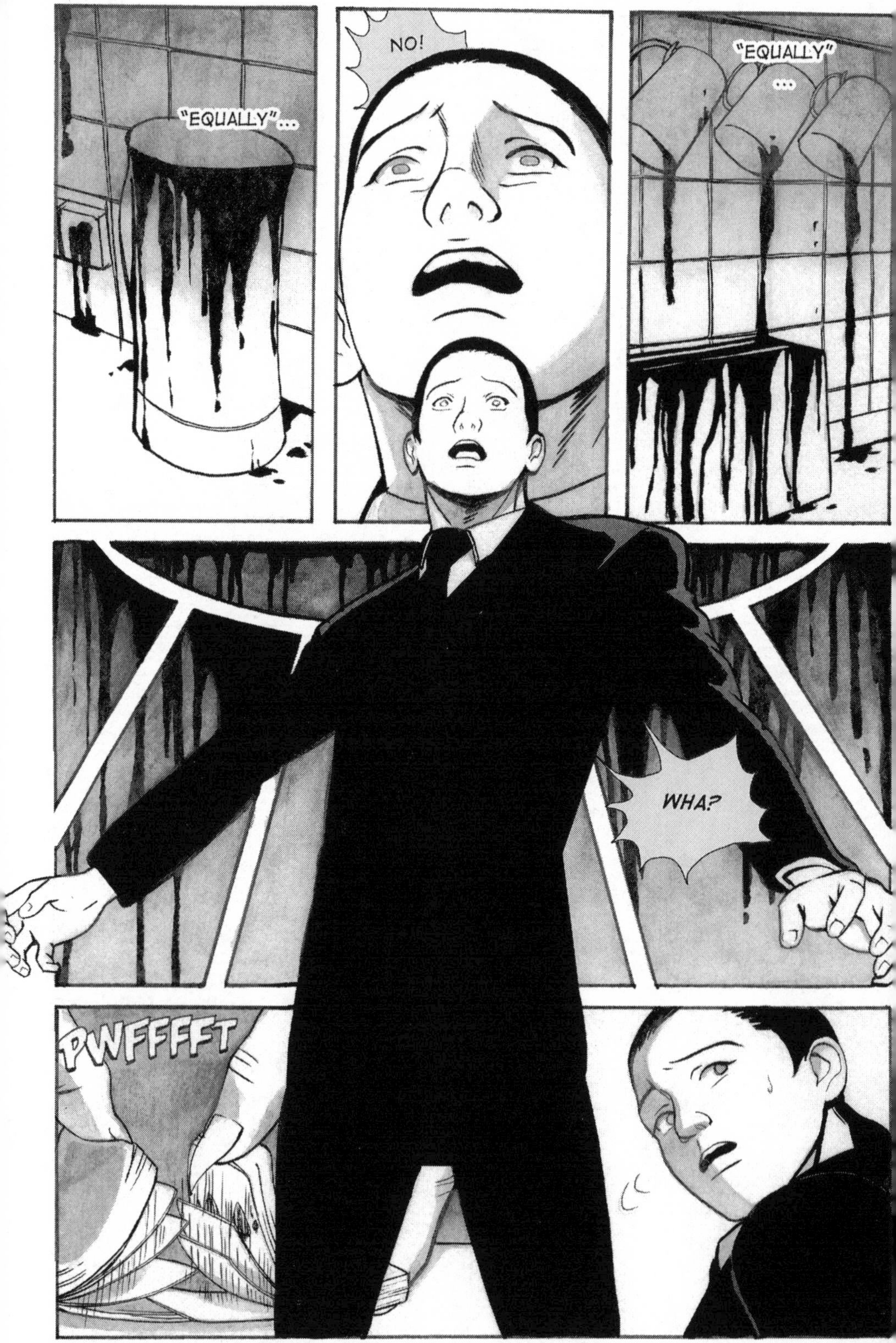
"EQUALLY"...
NO!
"EQUALLY"
...
WHA?
PWFFFFT

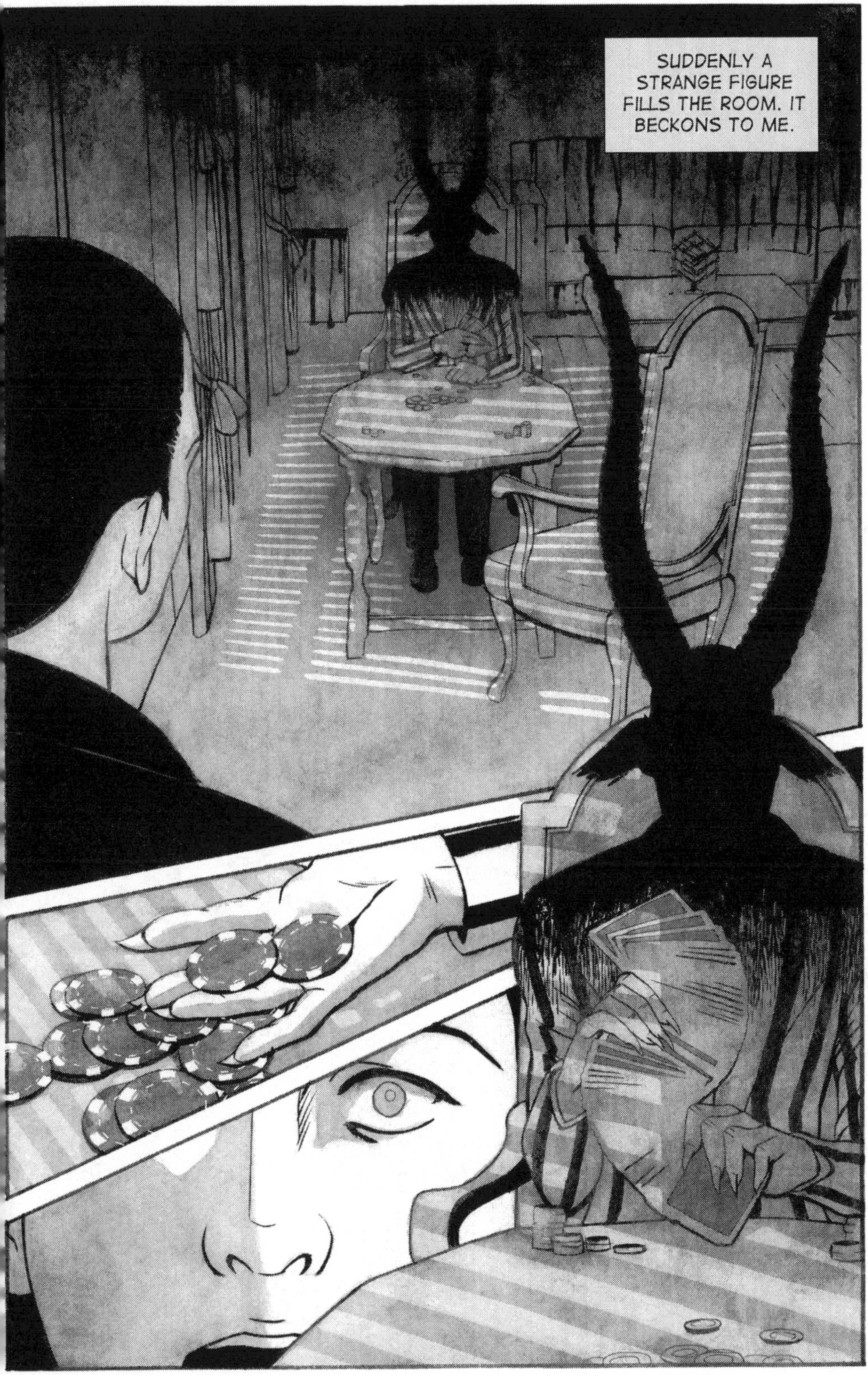
SUDDENLY A STRANGE FIGURE FILLS THE ROOM. IT BECKONS TO ME.

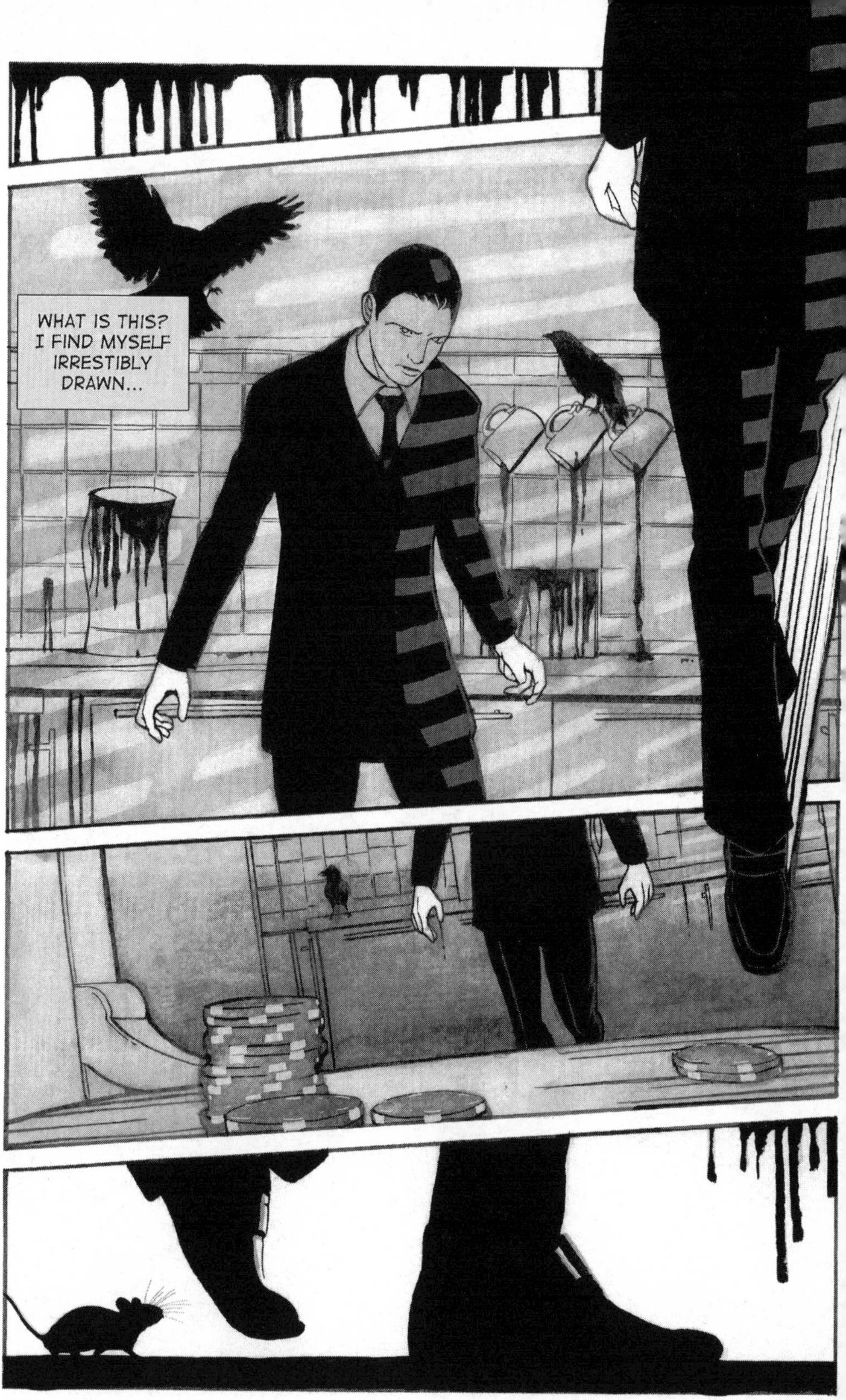
WHAT IS THIS? I FIND MYSELF IRRESTIBLY DRAWN...

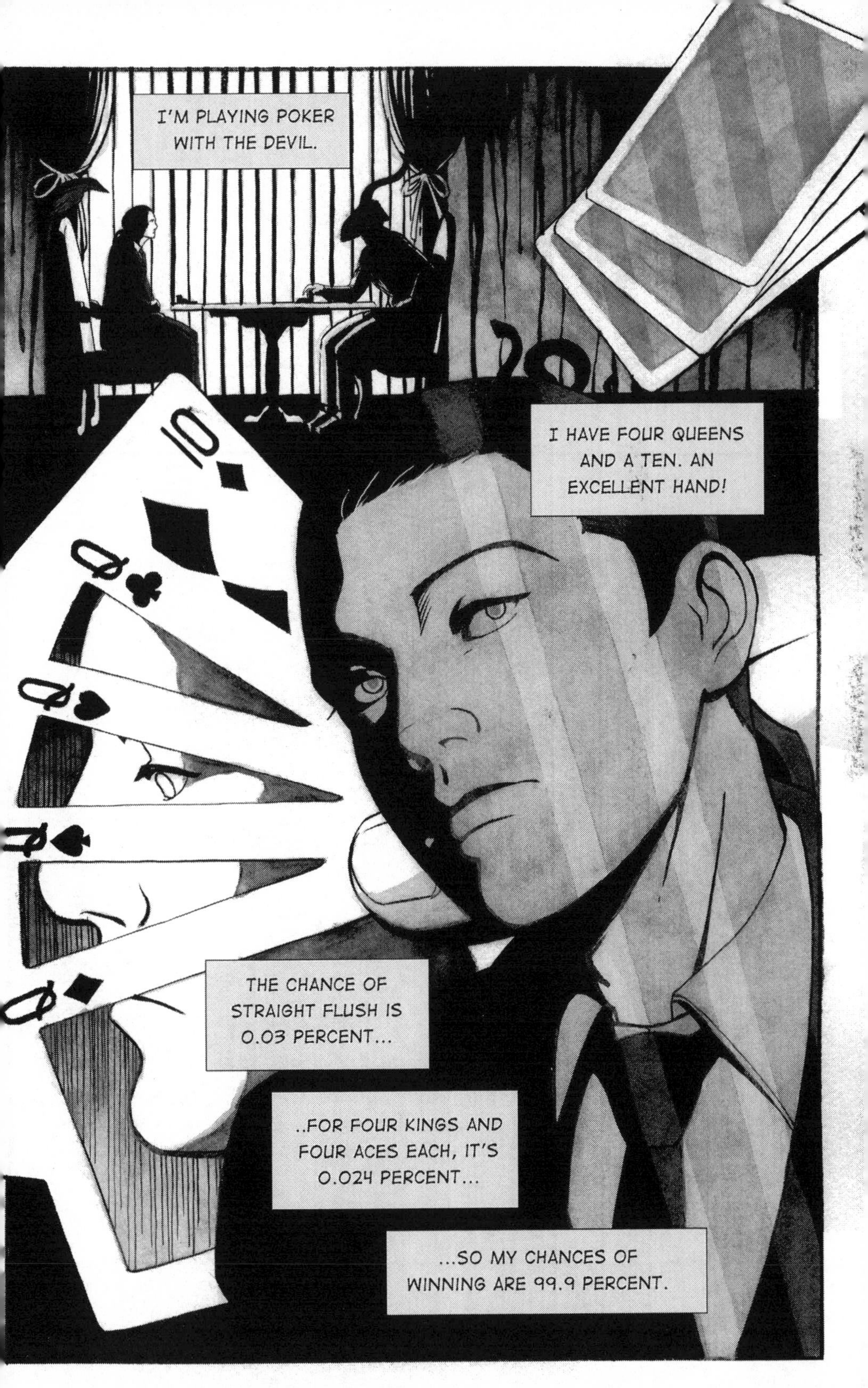
I'M PLAYING POKER WITH THE DEVIL.
I HAVE FOUR QUEENS AND A TEN. AN EXCELLENT HAND!
THE CHANCE OF STRAIGHT FLUSH IS 0.03 PERCENT...
..FOR FOUR KINGS AND FOUR ACES EACH, IT'S 0.024 PERCENT...
...SO MY CHANCES OF WINNING ARE 99.9 PERCENT.

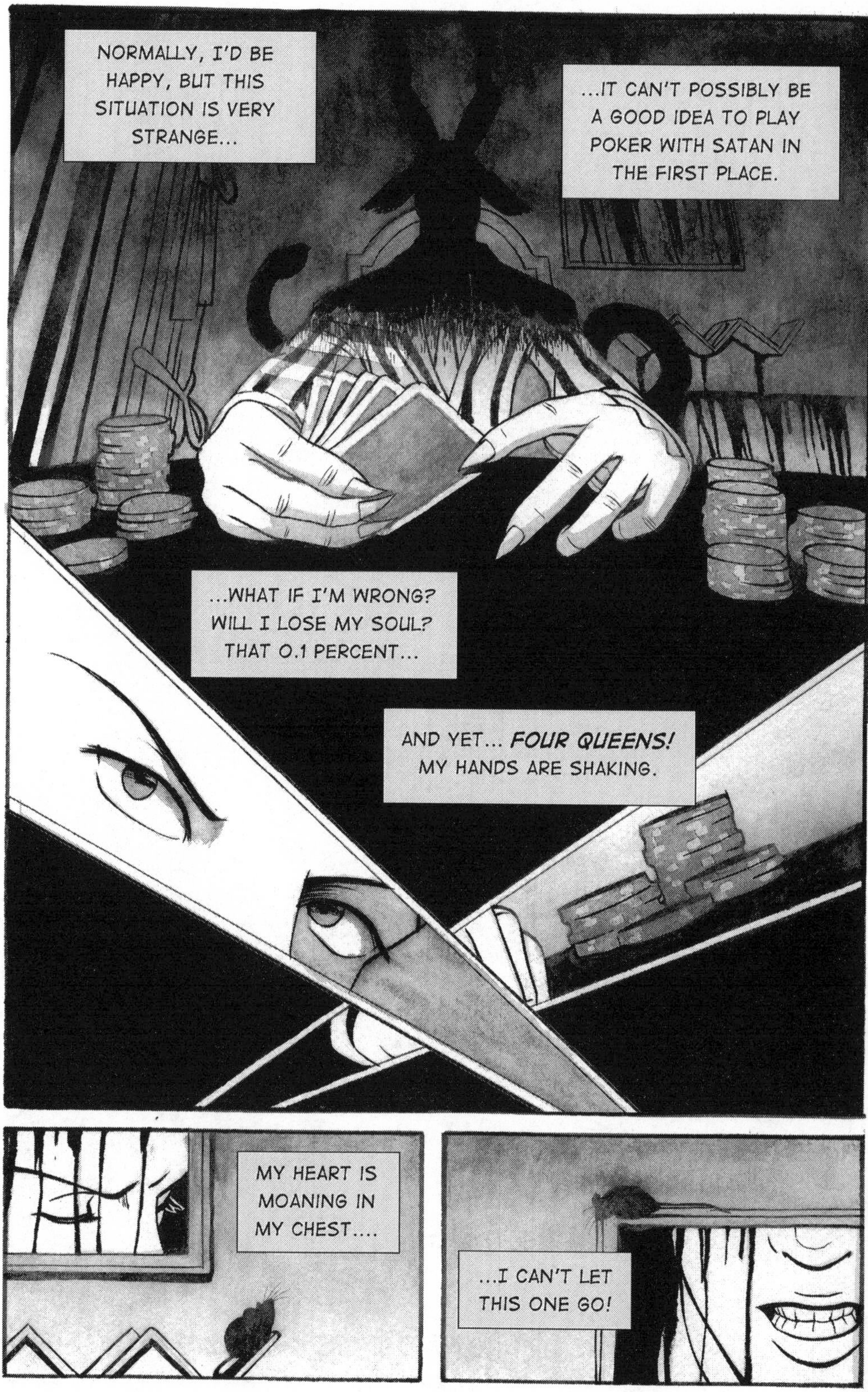
NORMALLY, I'D BE HAPPY, BUT THIS SITUATION IS VERY STRANGE...
...IT CAN'T POSSIBLY BE A GOOD IDEA TO PLAY POKER WITH SATAN IN THE FIRST PLACE.
...WHAT IF I'M WRONG? WILL I LOSE MY SOUL? THAT 0.1 PERCENT...
AND YET... *FOUR QUEENS!* MY HANDS ARE SHAKING.
MY HEART IS MOANING IN MY CHEST....
...I CAN'T LET THIS ONE GO!

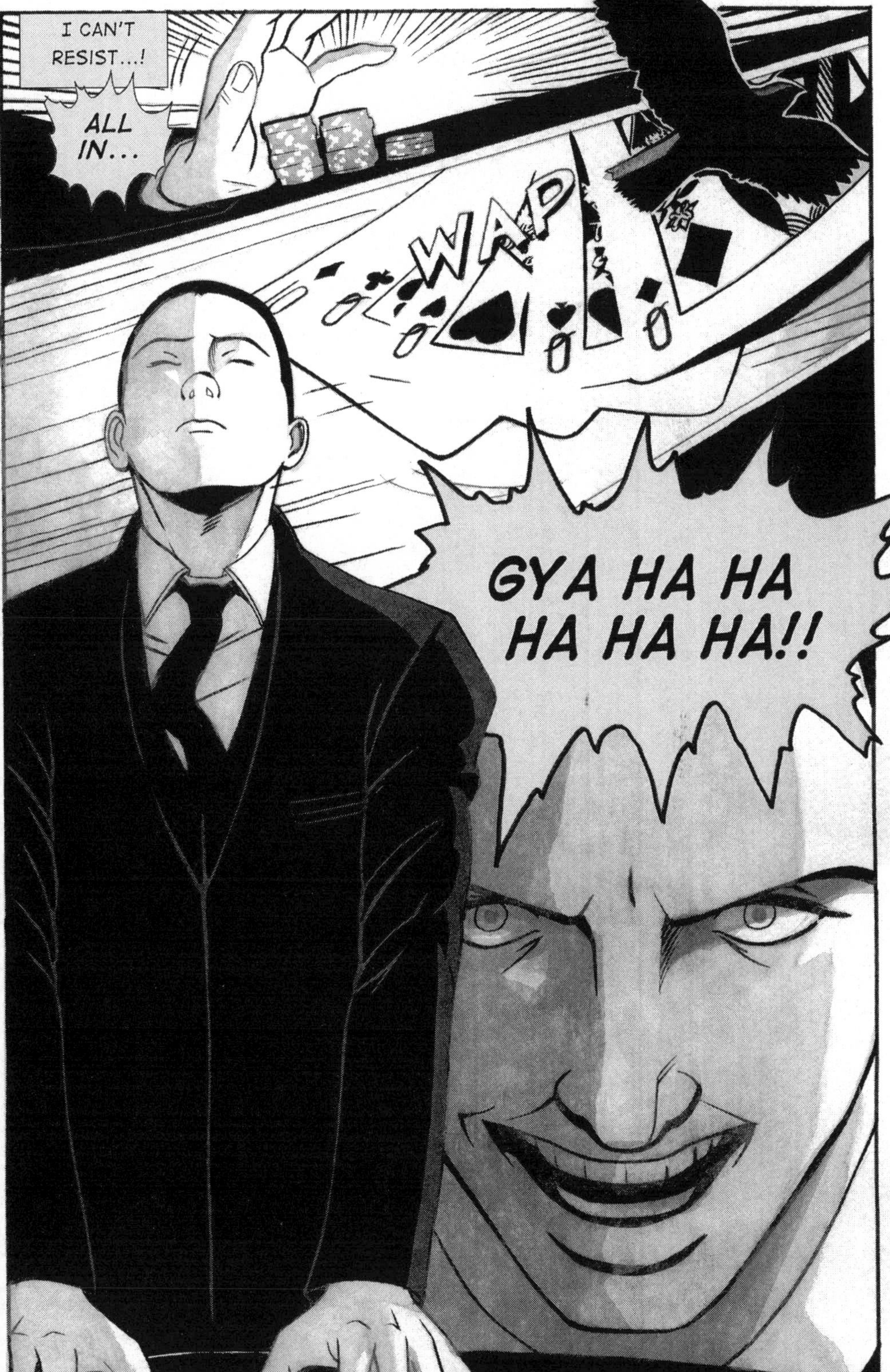

I CAN'T RESIST...!
ALL IN...
WAP
GYA HA HA HA HA HA!!

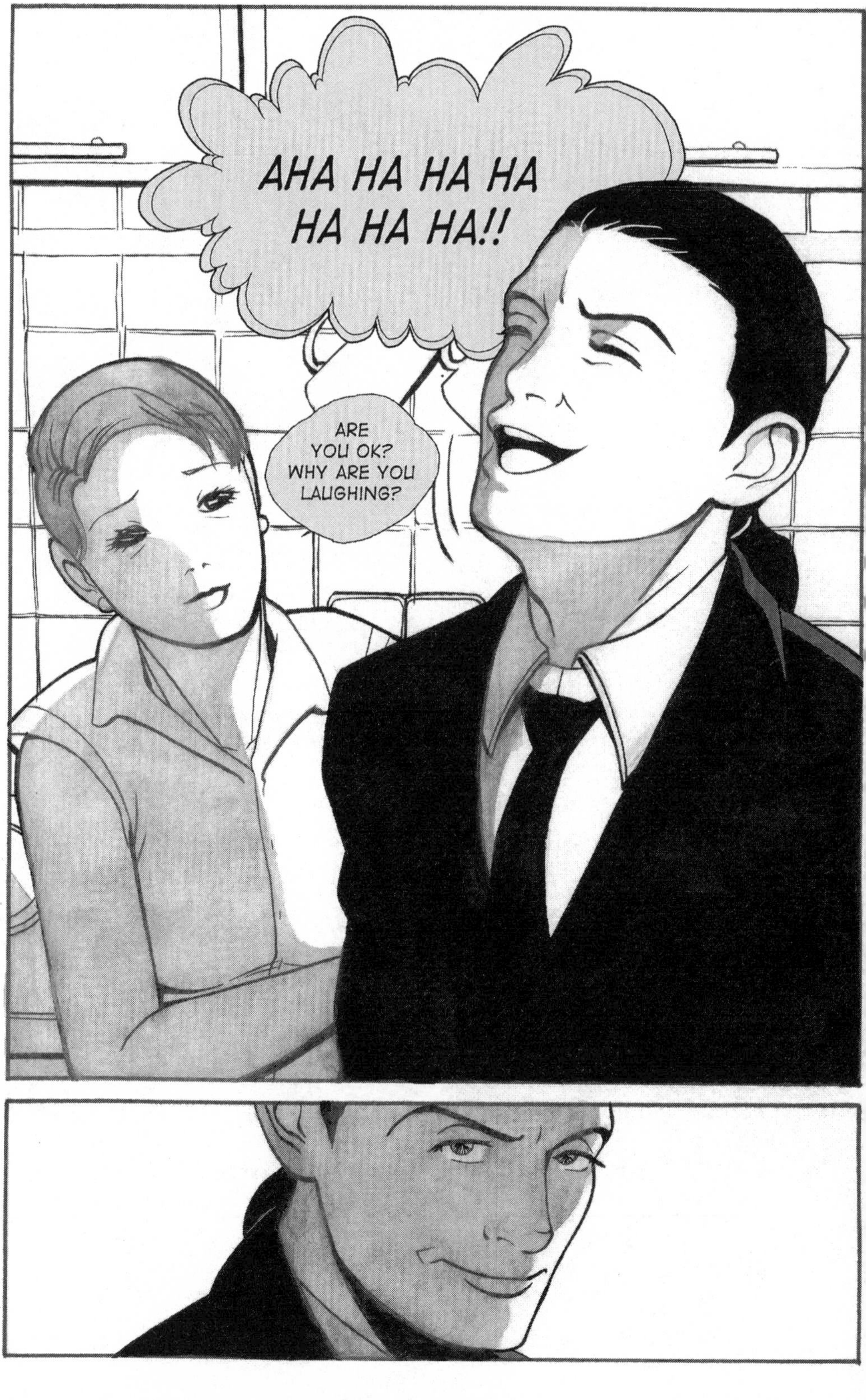
AHA HA HA HA
HA HA HA!!
ARE YOU OK? WHY ARE YOU LAUGHING?

I CAN'T TELL YOU, MOM.

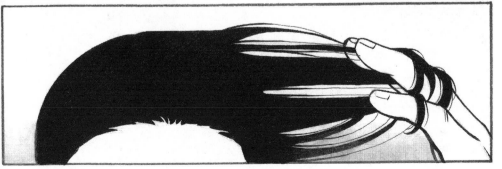

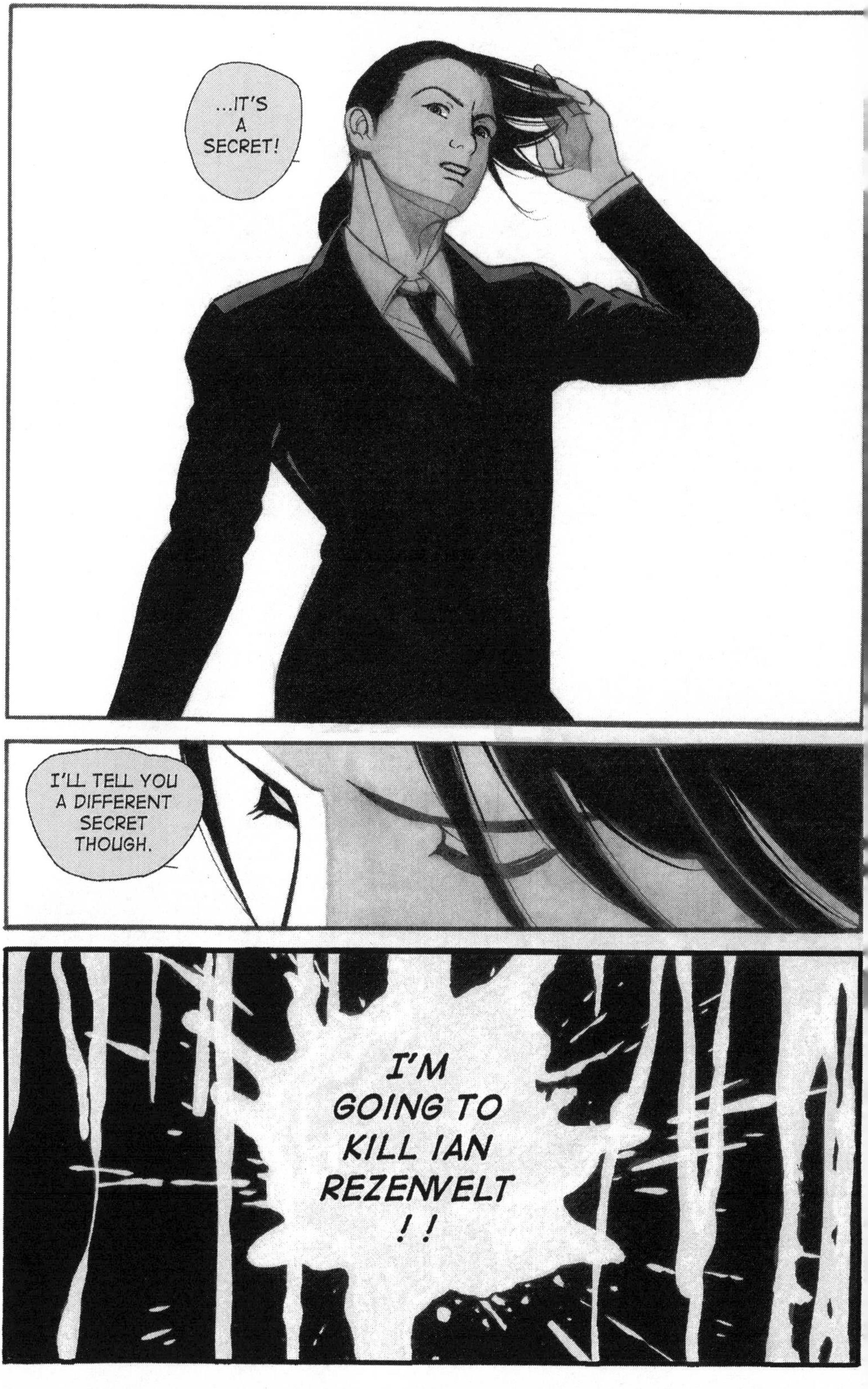
...IT'S A SECRET!
I'LL TELL YOU A DIFFERENT SECRET THOUGH.
I'M GOING TO KILL IAN REZENVELT !!

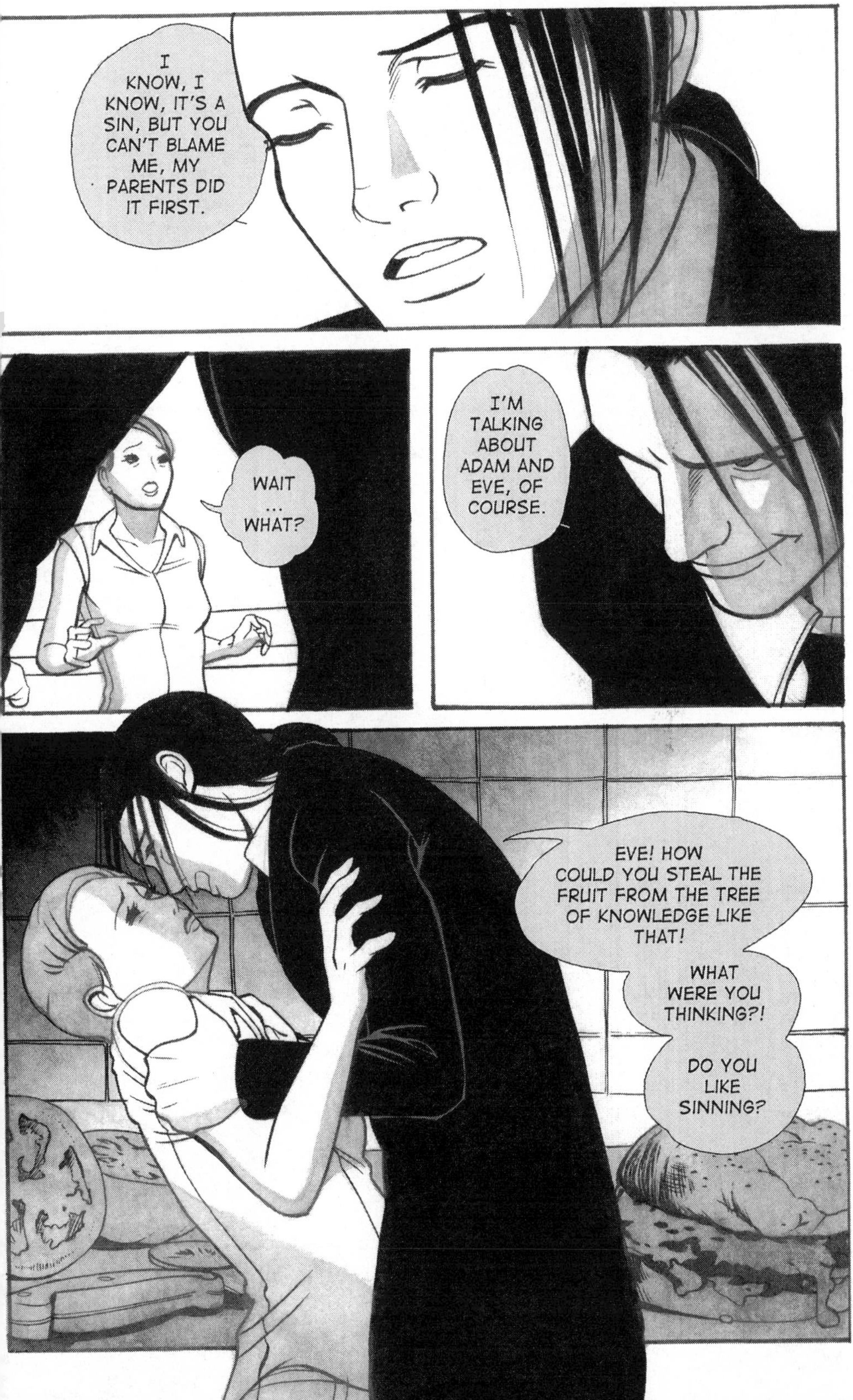
I KNOW, I KNOW, IT'S A SIN, BUT YOU CAN'T BLAME ME, MY PARENTS DID IT FIRST.
WAIT ... WHAT?
I'M TALKING ABOUT ADAM AND EVE, OF COURSE.
EVE! HOW COULD YOU STEAL THE FRUIT FROM THE TREE OF KNOWLEDGE LIKE THAT!
WHAT WERE YOU THINKING?!
DO YOU LIKE SINNING?

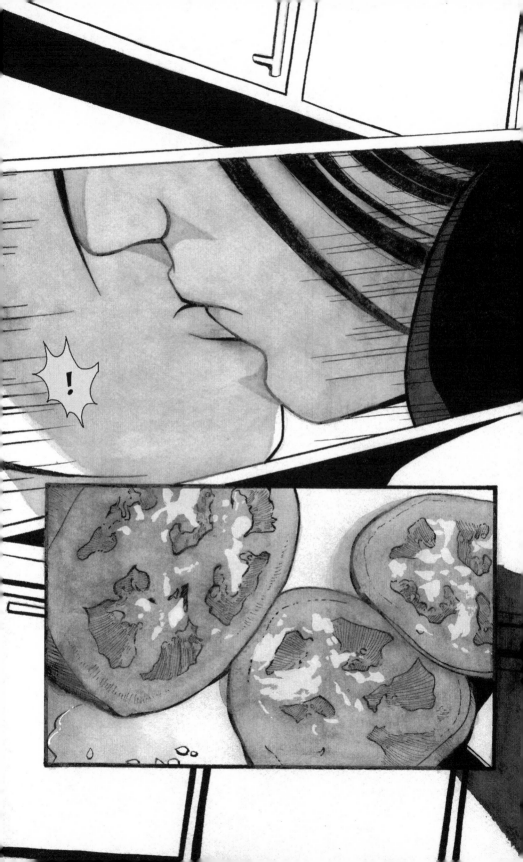

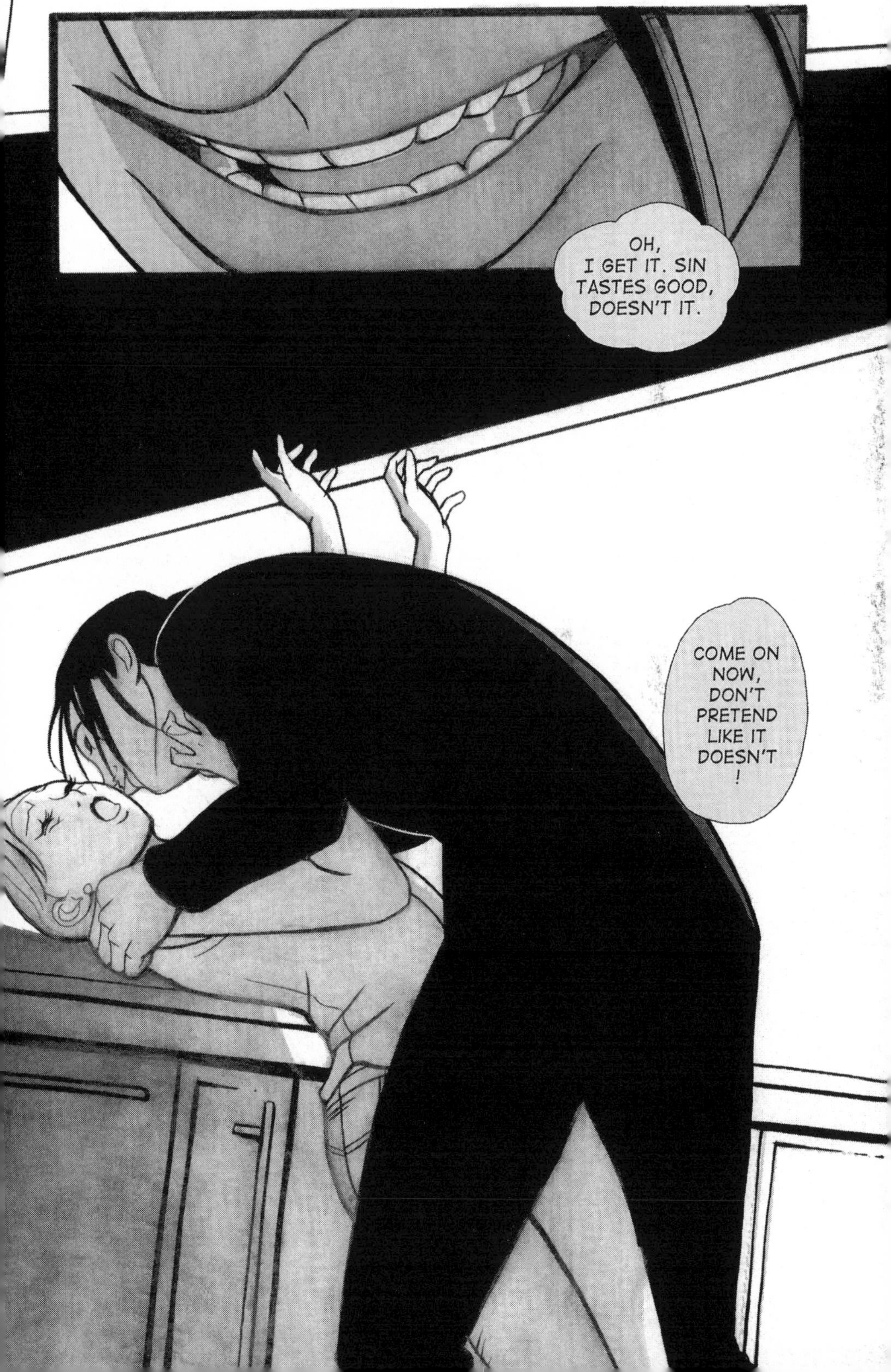
OH, I GET IT. SIN TASTES GOOD, DOESN'T IT.
COME ON NOW, DON'T PRETEND LIKE IT DOESN'T!

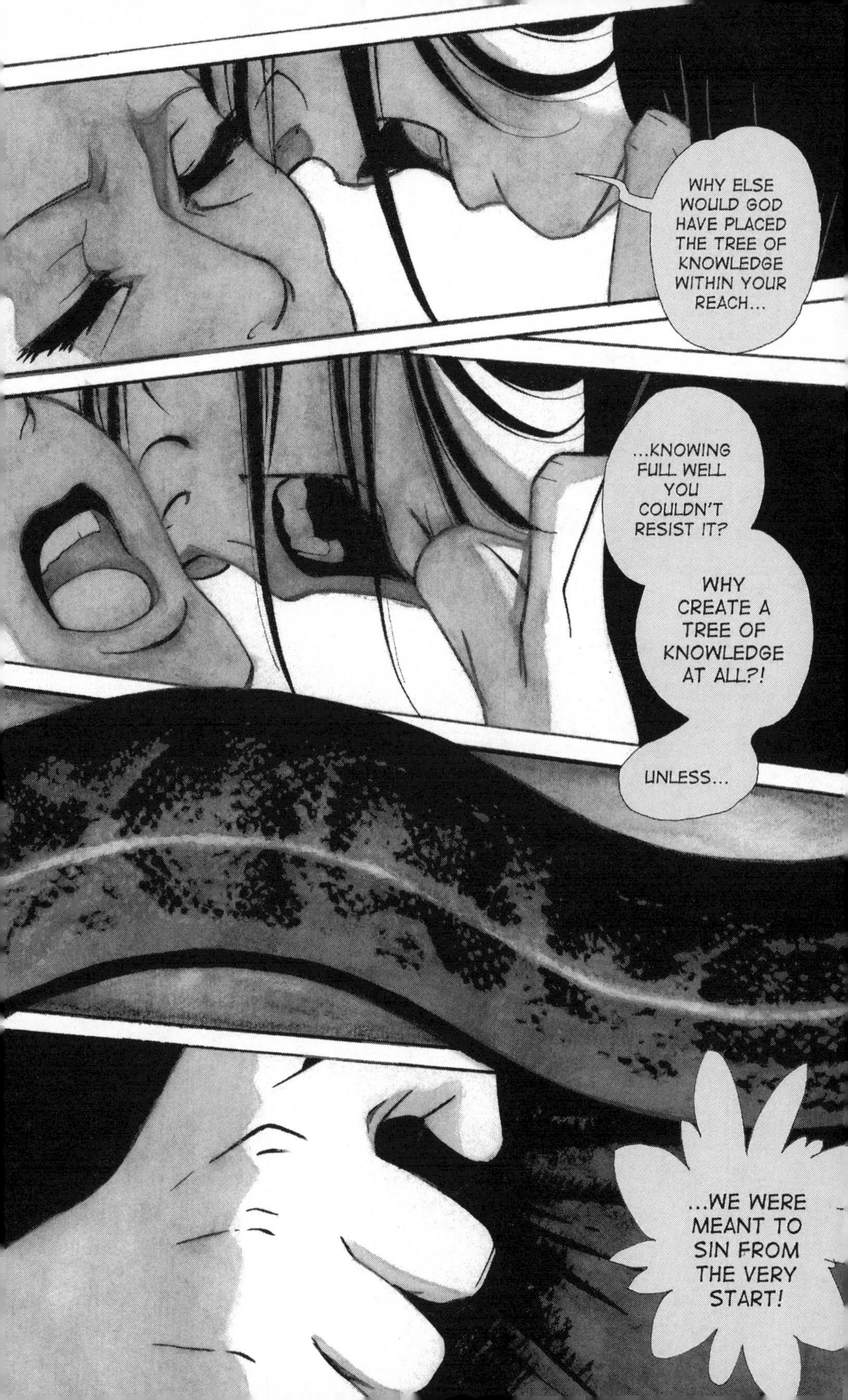
WHY ELSE WOULD GOD HAVE PLACED THE TREE OF KNOWLEDGE WITHIN YOUR REACH...
...KNOWING FULL WELL YOU COULDN'T RESIST IT?
WHY CREATE A TREE OF KNOWLEDGE AT ALL?!
UNLESS...
...WE WERE MEANT TO SIN FROM THE VERY START!

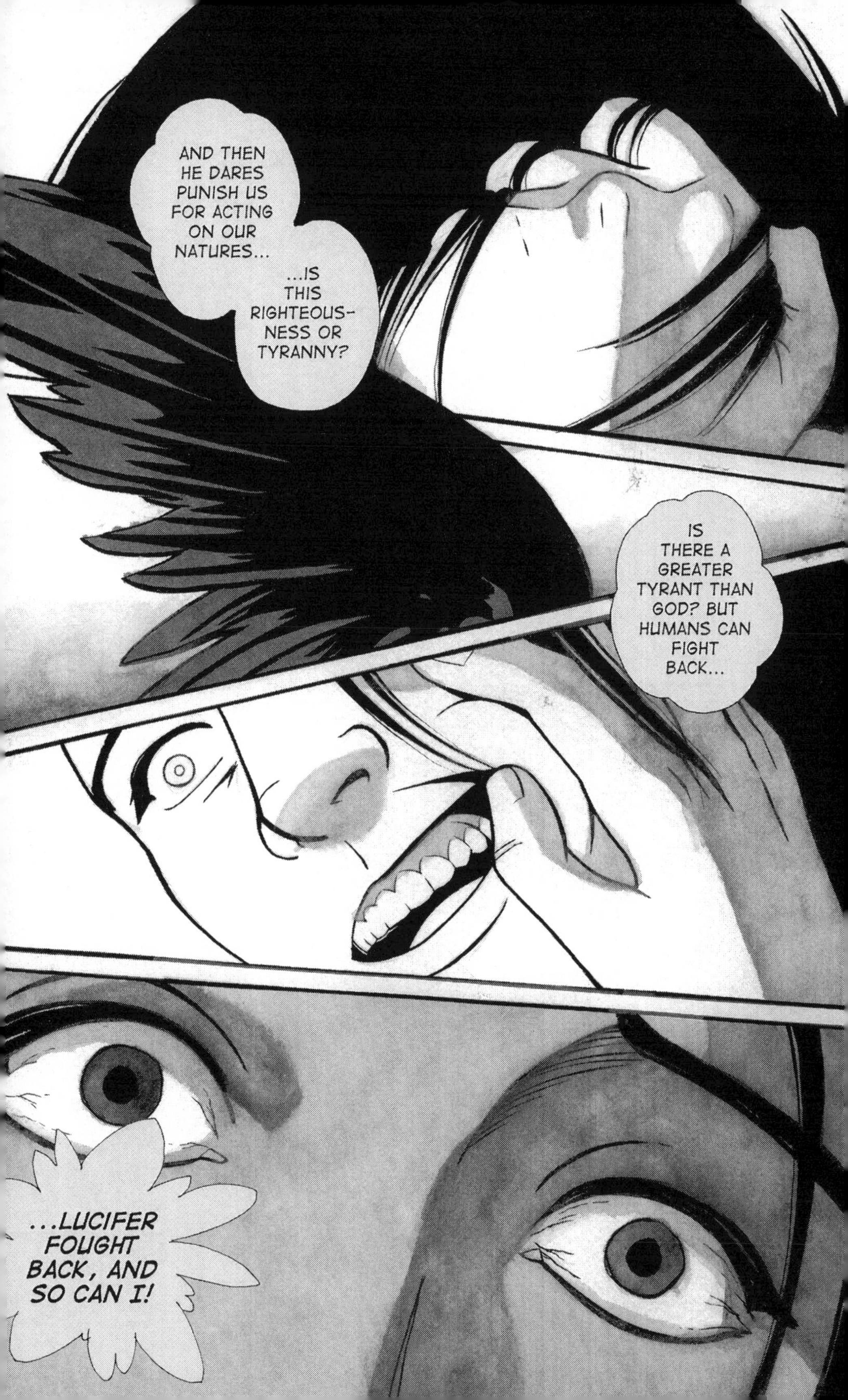
AND THEN HE DARES PUNISH US FOR ACTING ON OUR NATURES...
...IS THIS RIGHTEOUS-NESS OR TYRANNY?
IS THERE A GREATER TYRANT THAN GOD? BUT HUMANS CAN FIGHT BACK...
...LUCIFER FOUGHT BACK, AND SO CAN I!

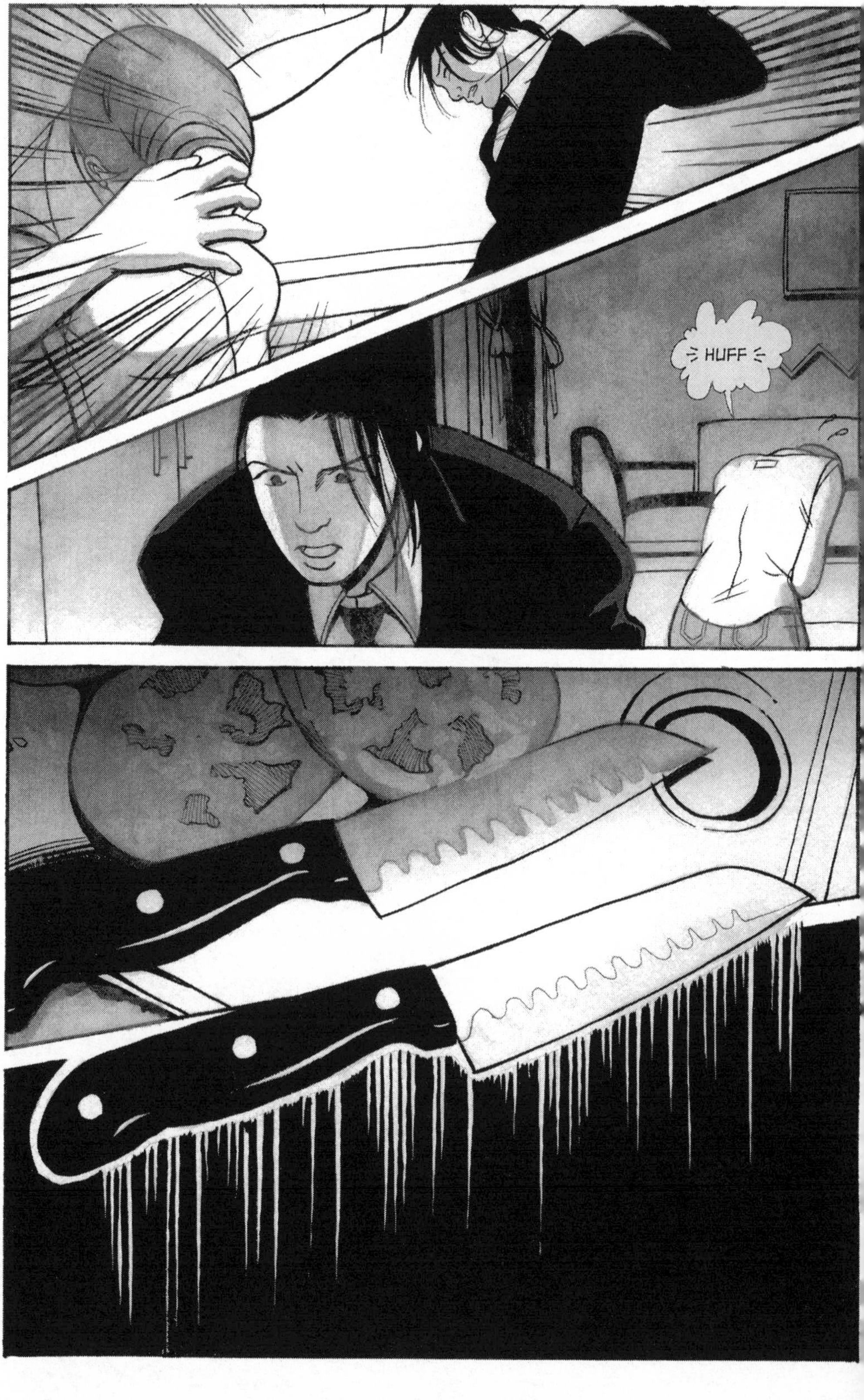
HUFF

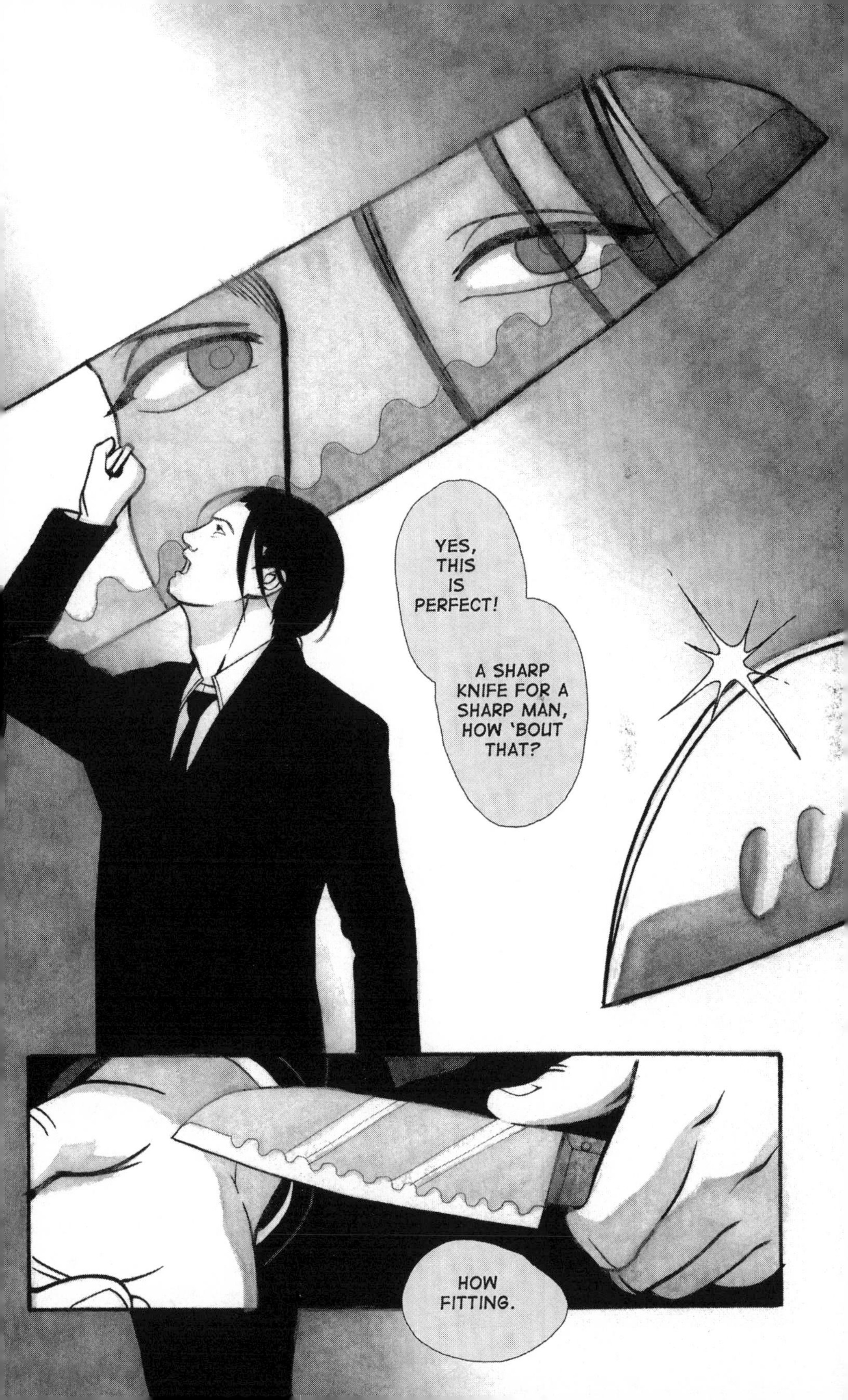
YES, THIS IS PERFECT!
A SHARP KNIFE FOR A SHARP MAN, HOW 'BOUT THAT?
HOW FITTING.

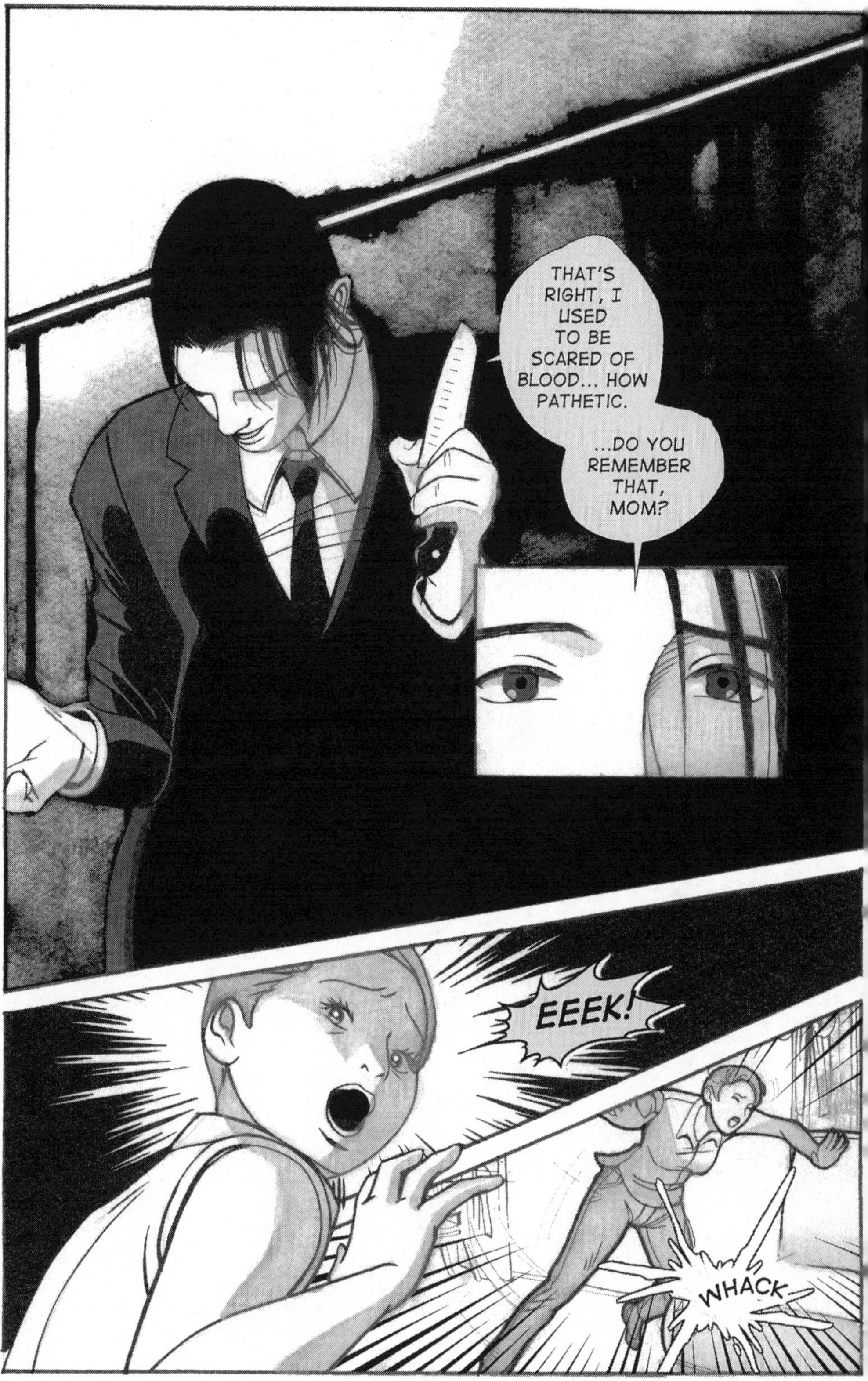
THAT'S RIGHT, I USED TO BE SCARED OF BLOOD... HOW PATHETIC.
...DO YOU REMEMBER THAT, MOM?
EEEK!
WHACK

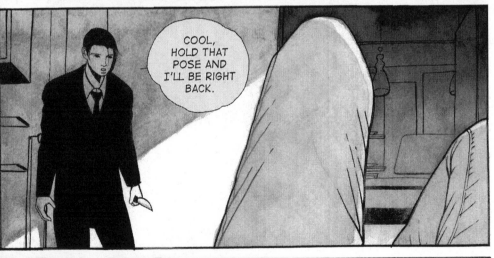

COOL,
HOLD THAT
POSE AND
I'LL BE RIGHT
BACK.

SEE YOU SOON.

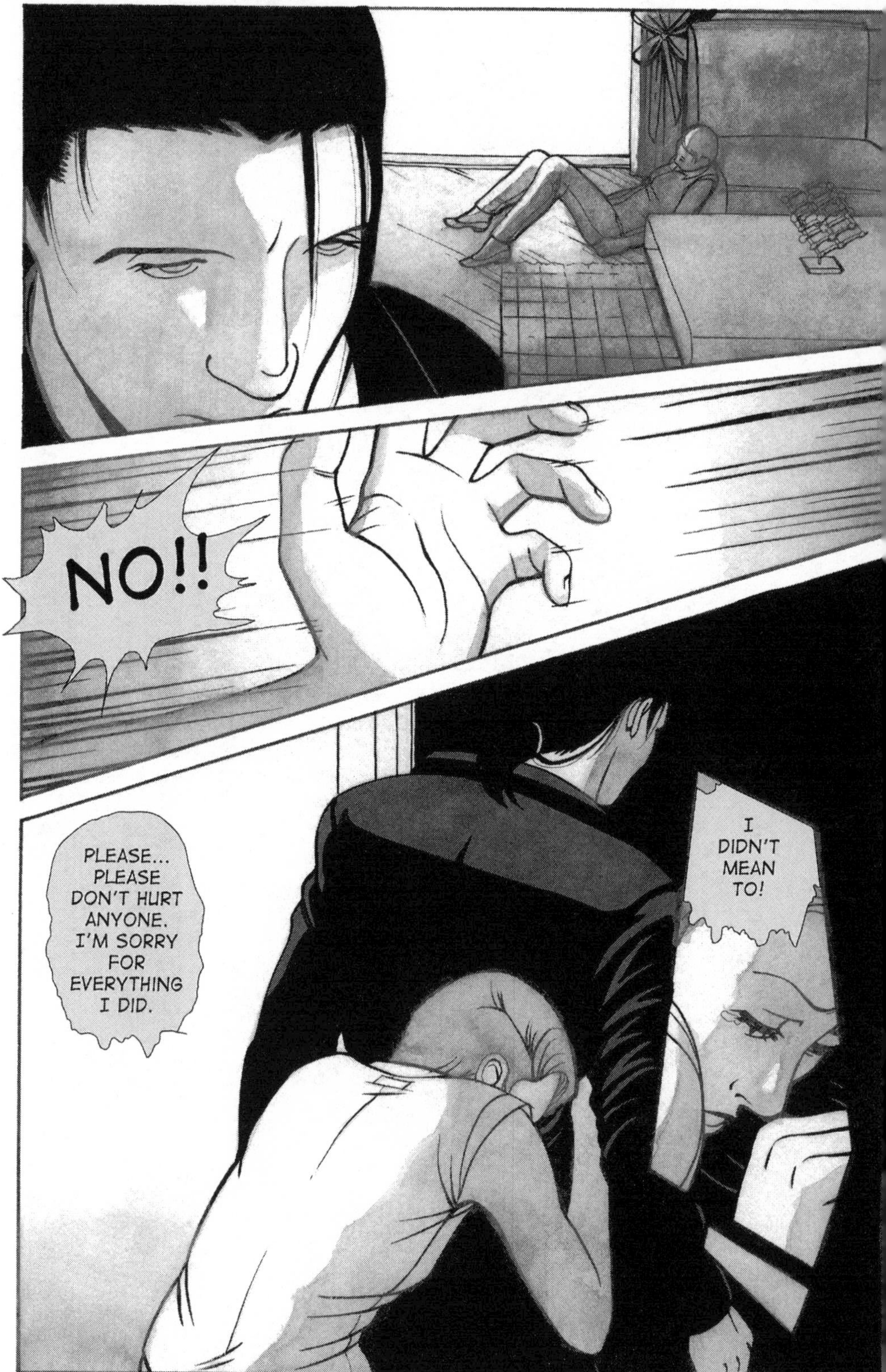
NO!!
PLEASE... PLEASE DON'T HURT ANYONE. I'M SORRY FOR EVERYTHING I DID.
I DIDN'T MEAN TO!

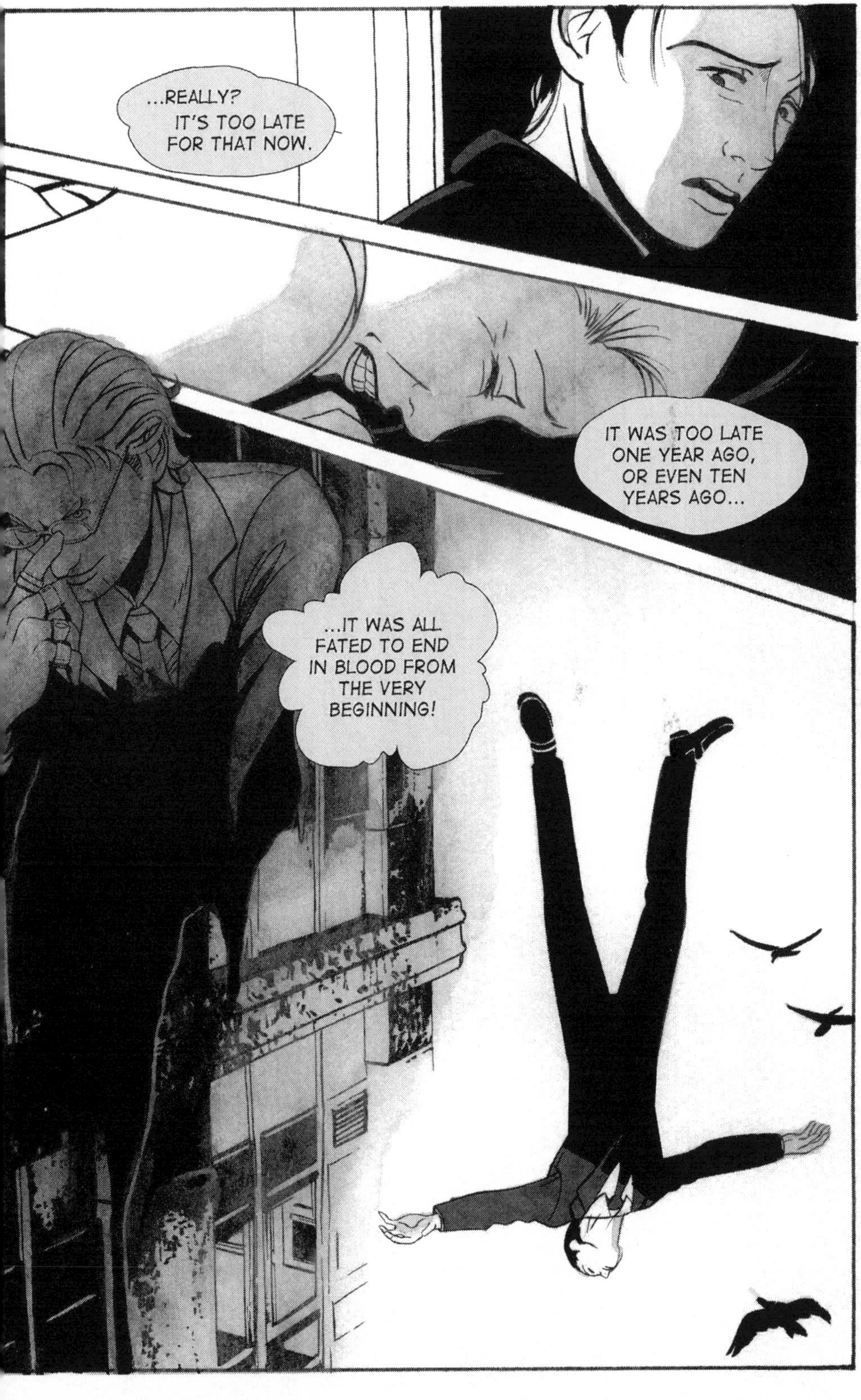
...REALLY? IT'S TOO LATE FOR THAT NOW.
IT WAS TOO LATE ONE YEAR AGO, OR EVEN TEN YEARS AGO...
...IT WAS ALL FATED TO END IN BLOOD FROM THE VERY BEGINNING!

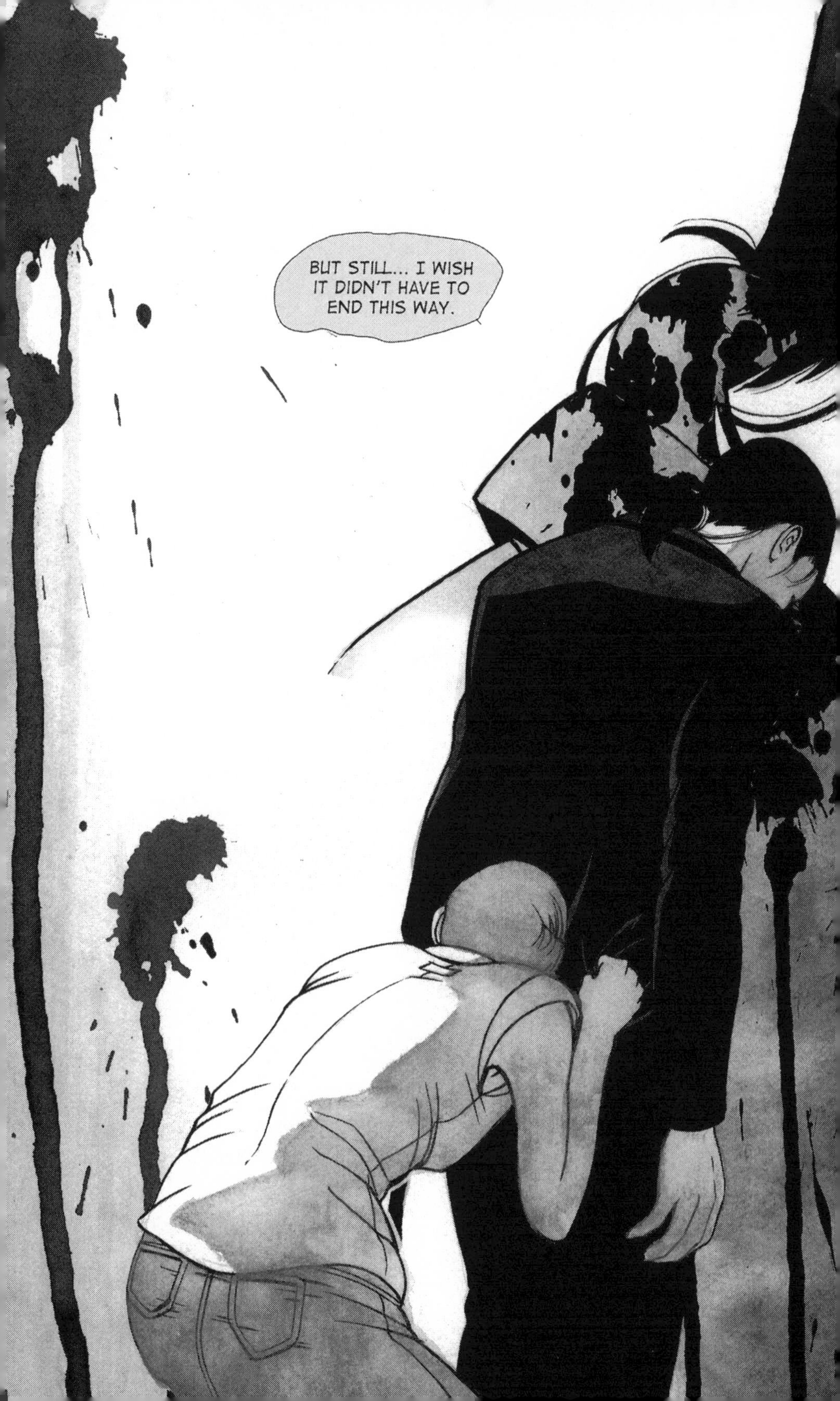
BUT STILL... I WISH IT DIDN'T HAVE TO END THIS WAY.

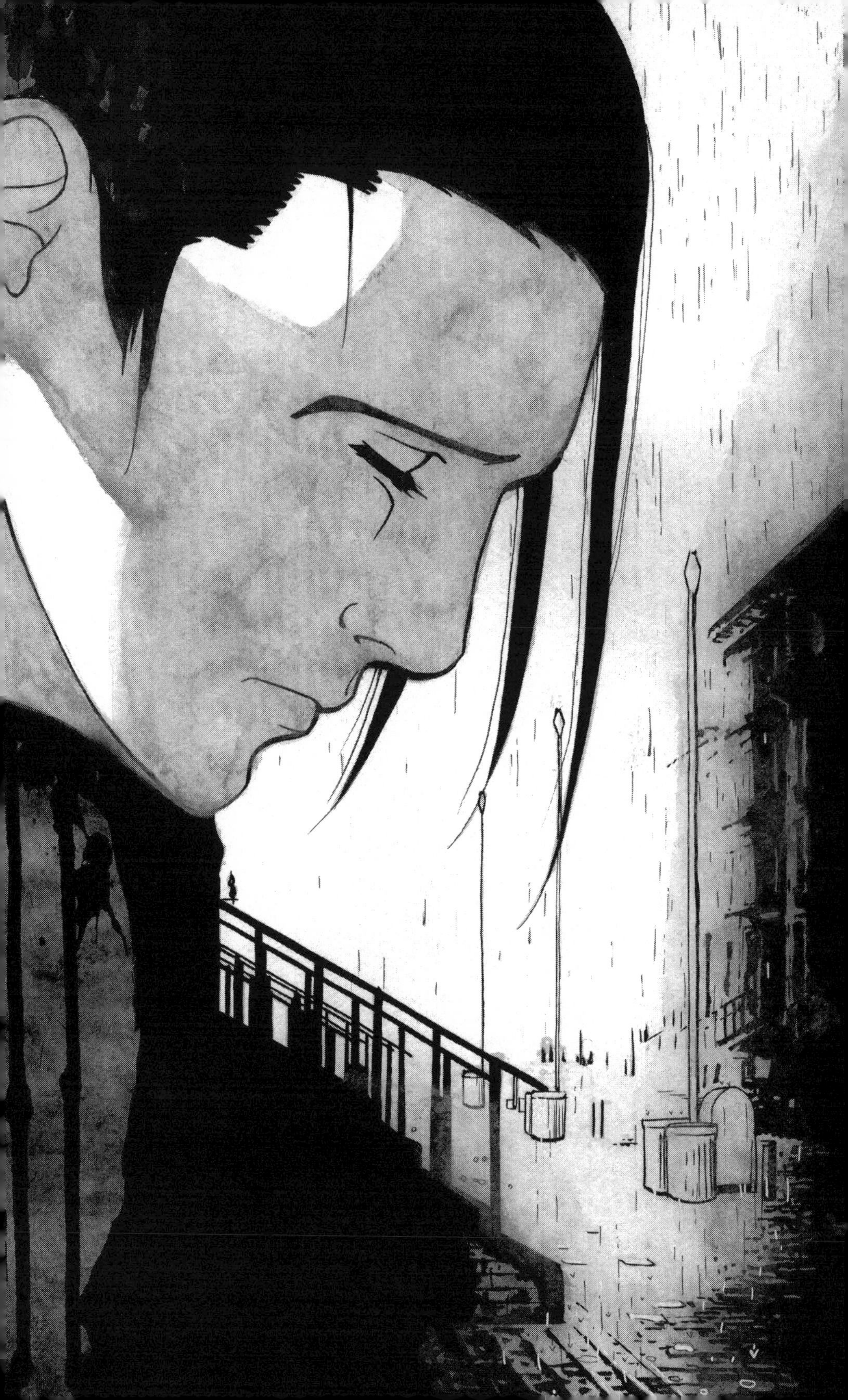

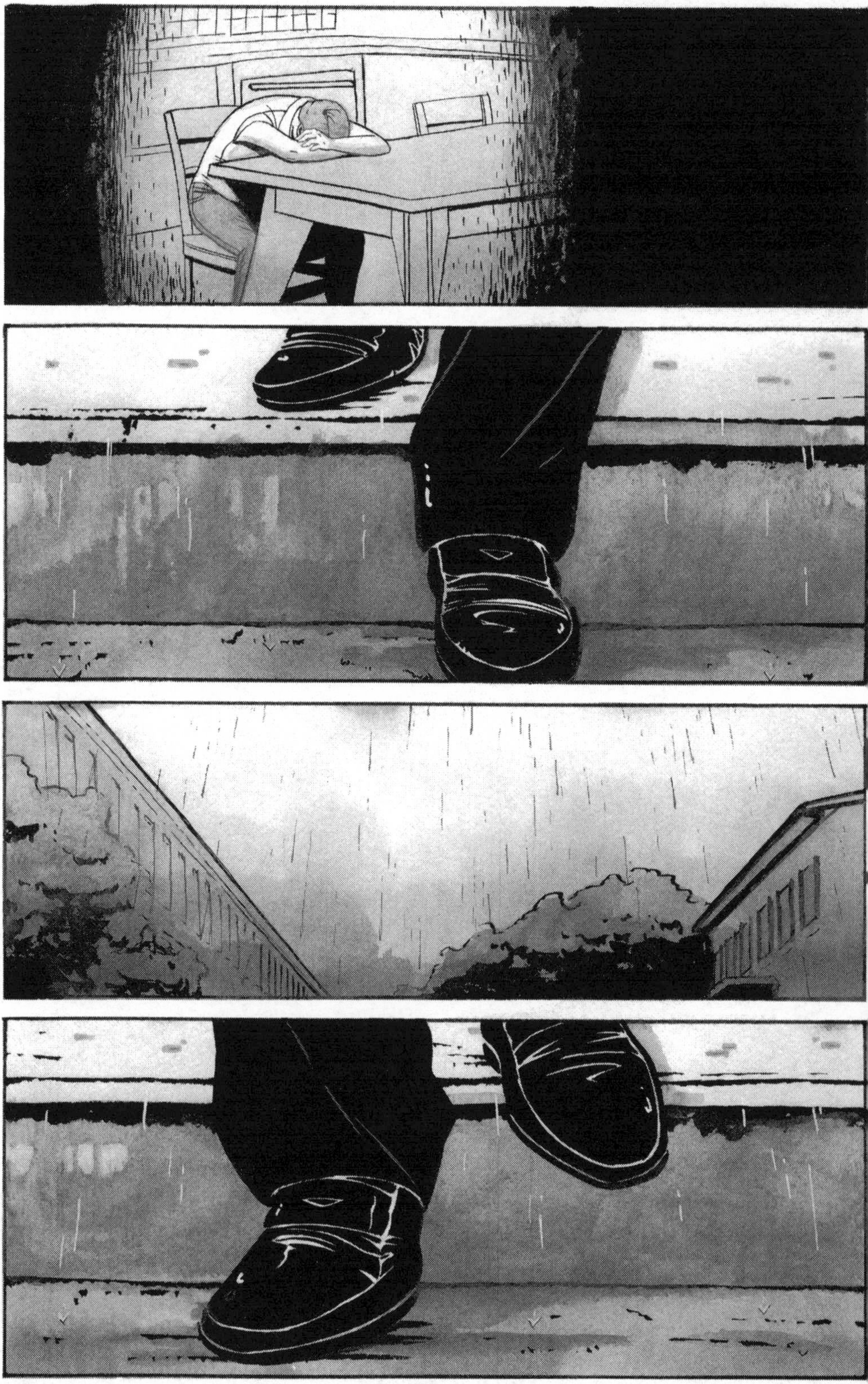

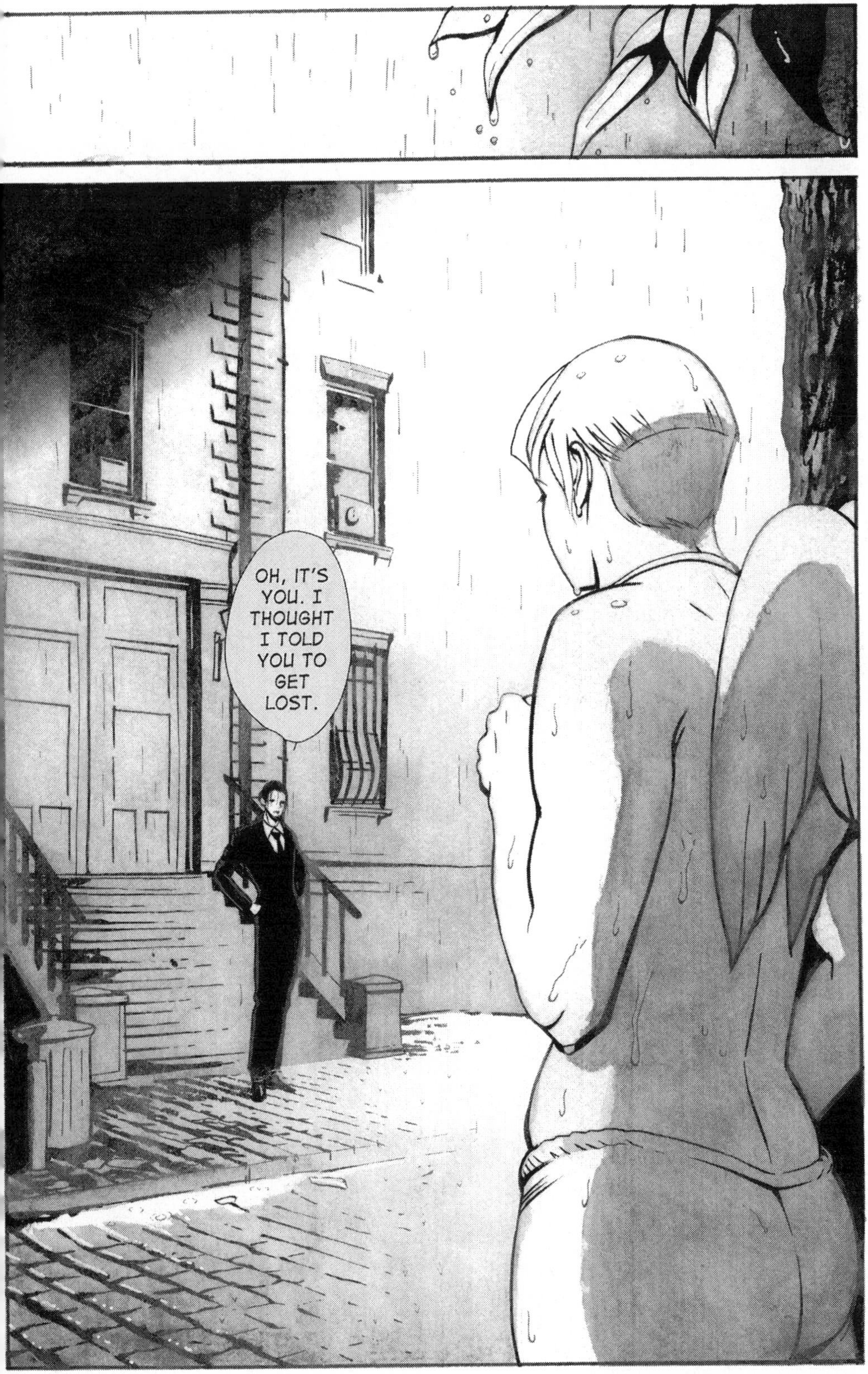
OH, IT'S YOU. I THOUGHT I TOLD YOU TO GET LOST.

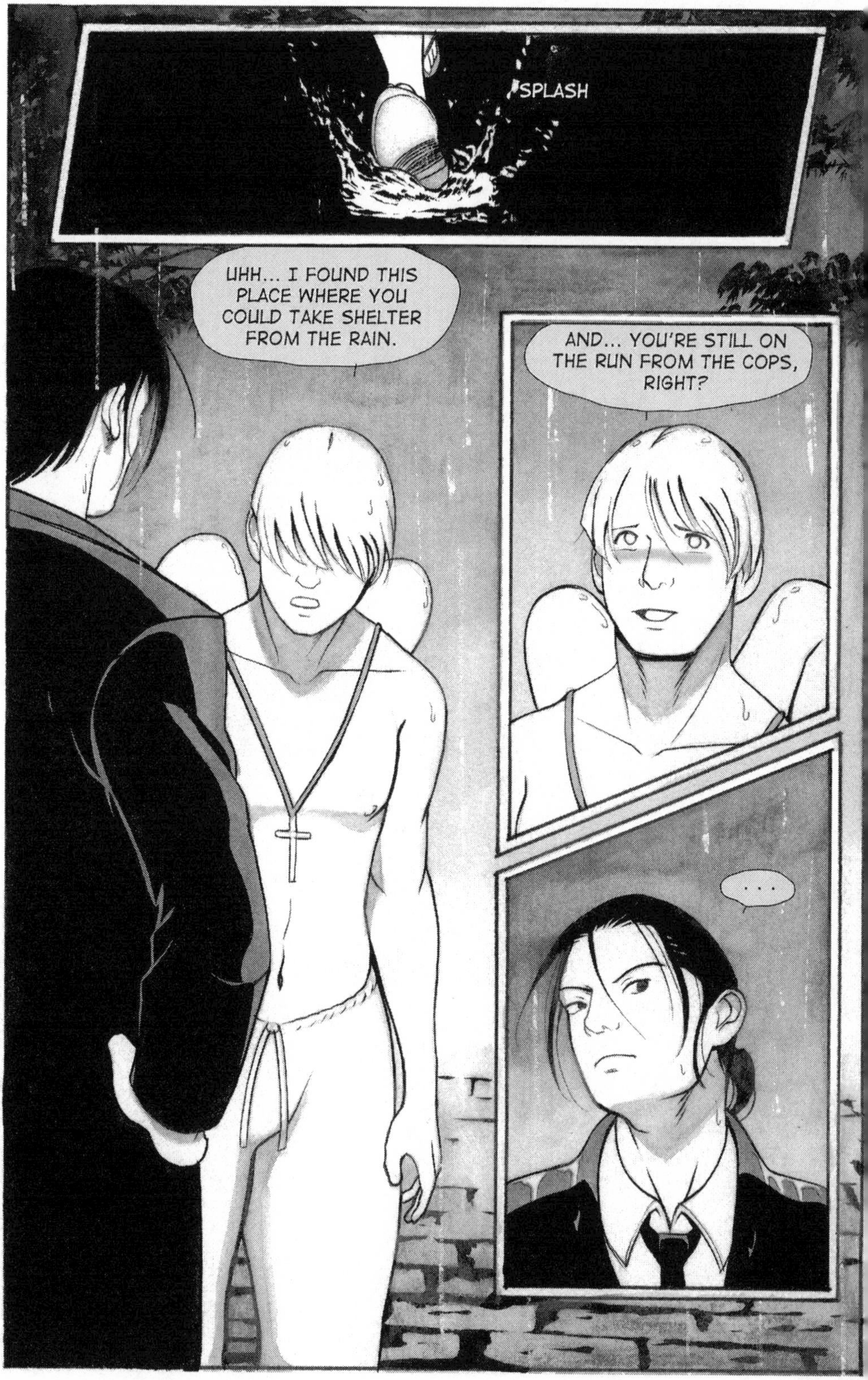
SPLASH
UHH... I FOUND THIS PLACE WHERE YOU COULD TAKE SHELTER FROM THE RAIN.
AND... YOU'RE STILL ON THE RUN FROM THE COPS, RIGHT?
...

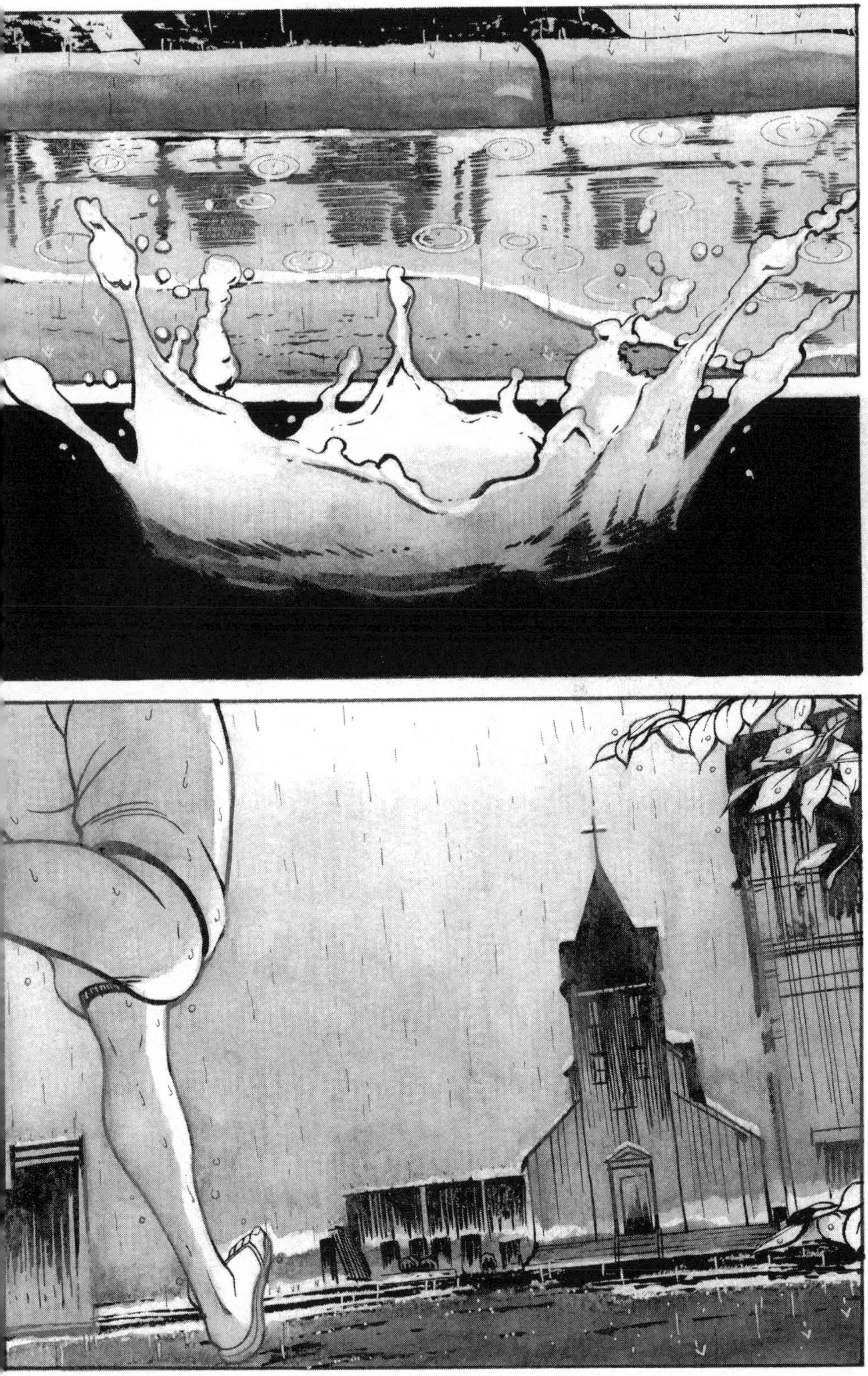

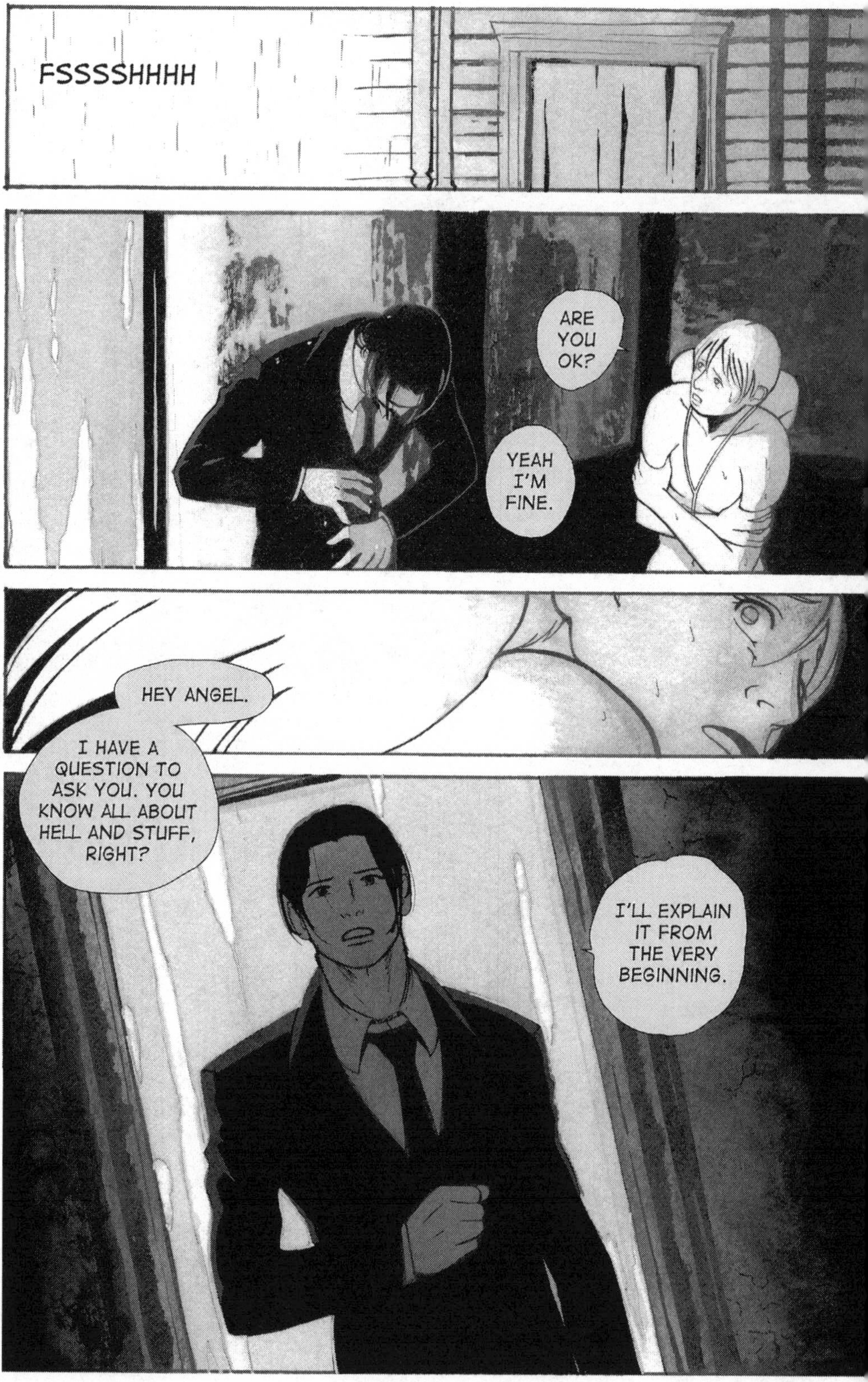
FSSSSHHHH
ARE YOU OK?
YEAH I'M FINE.
HEY ANGEL.
I HAVE A QUESTION TO ASK YOU. YOU KNOW ALL ABOUT HELL AND STUFF, RIGHT?
I'LL EXPLAIN IT FROM THE VERY BEGINNING.

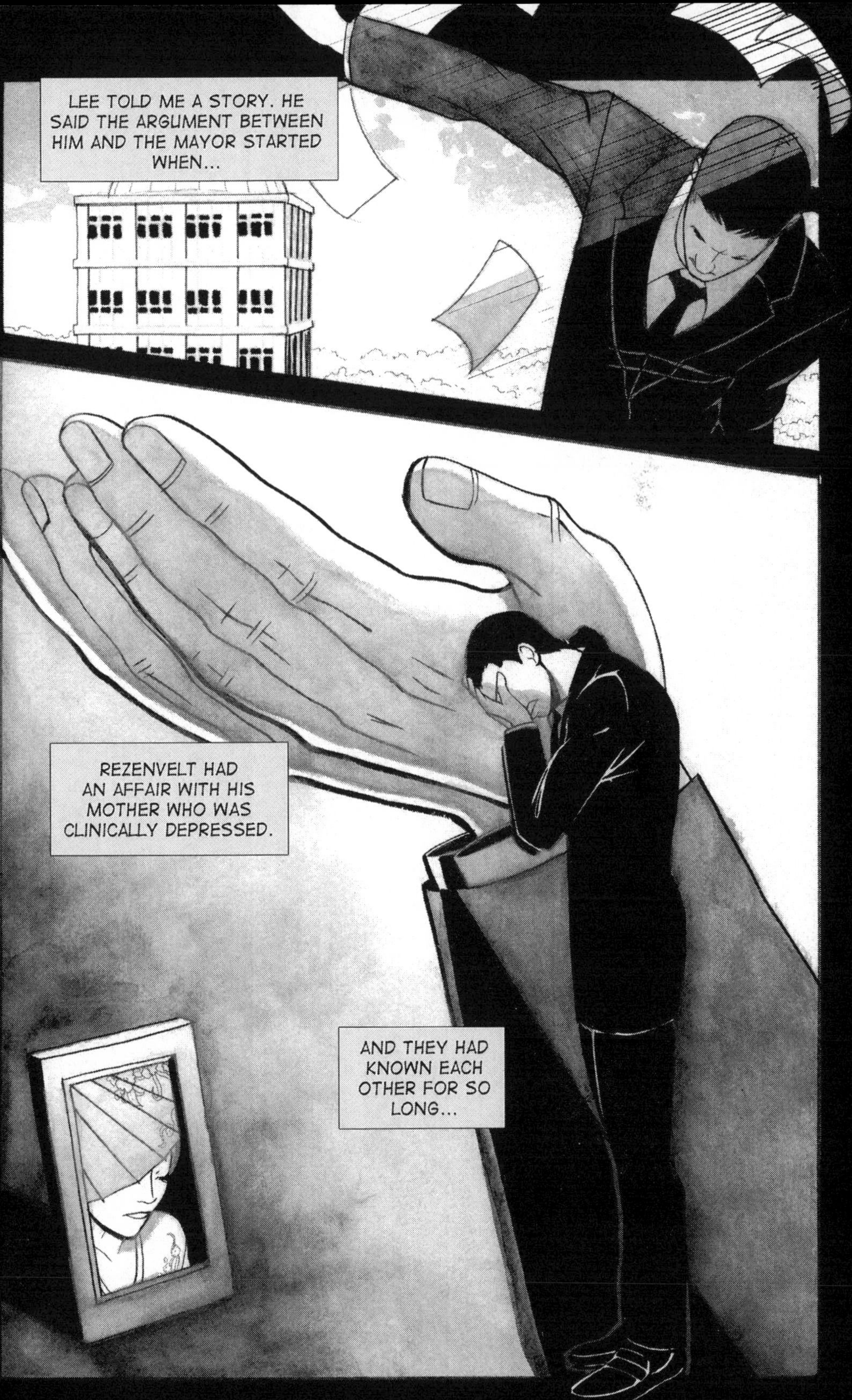
LEE TOLD ME A STORY. HE SAID THE ARGUMENT BETWEEN HIM AND THE MAYOR STARTED WHEN...
REZENVELT HAD AN AFFAIR WITH HIS MOTHER WHO WAS CLINICALLY DEPRESSED.
AND THEY HAD KNOWN EACH OTHER FOR SO LONG...

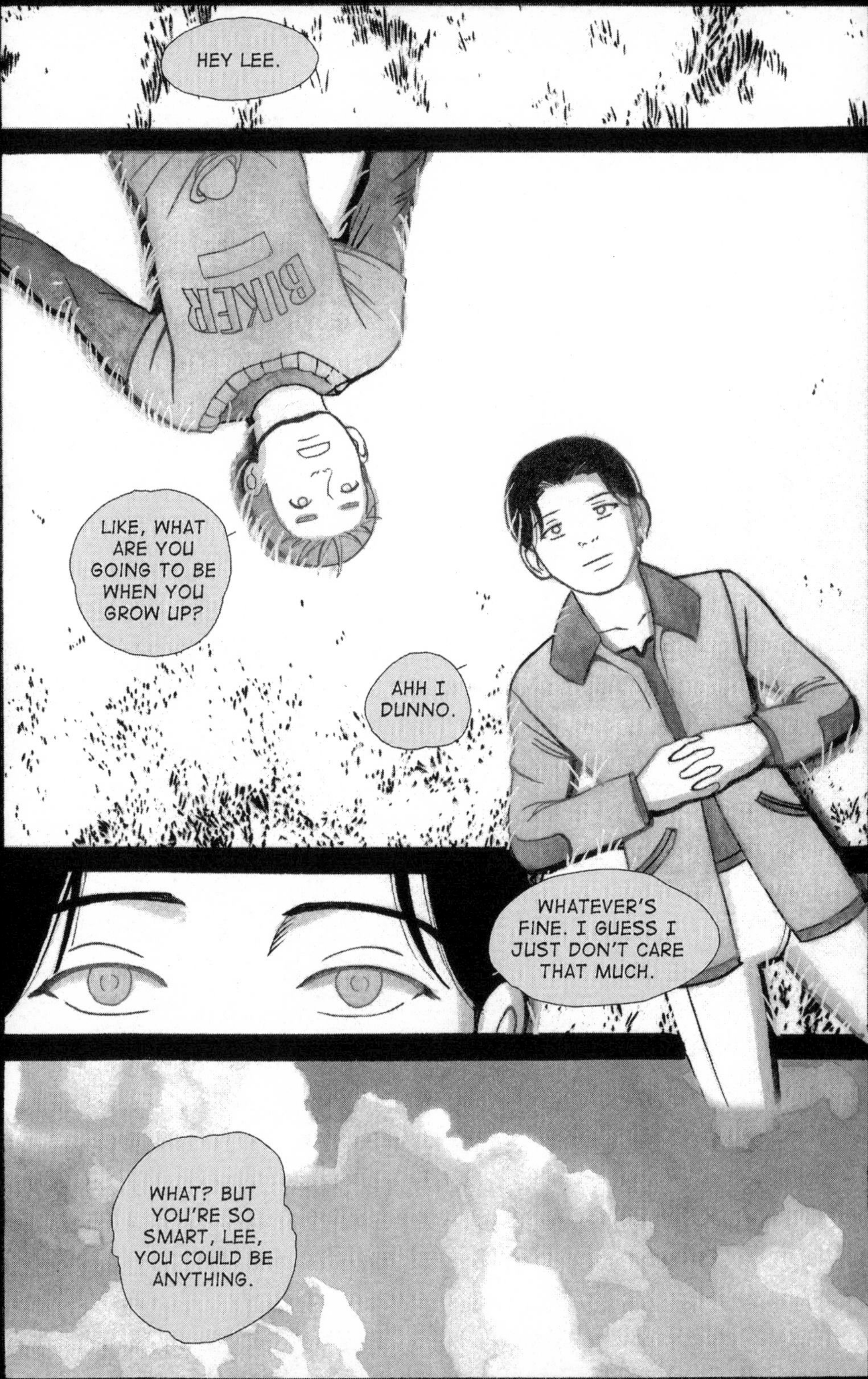
HEY LEE.
LIKE, WHAT ARE YOU GOING TO BE WHEN YOU GROW UP?
AHH I DUNNO.
WHATEVER'S FINE. I GUESS I JUST DON'T CARE THAT MUCH.
WHAT? BUT YOU'RE SO SMART, LEE, YOU COULD BE ANYTHING.

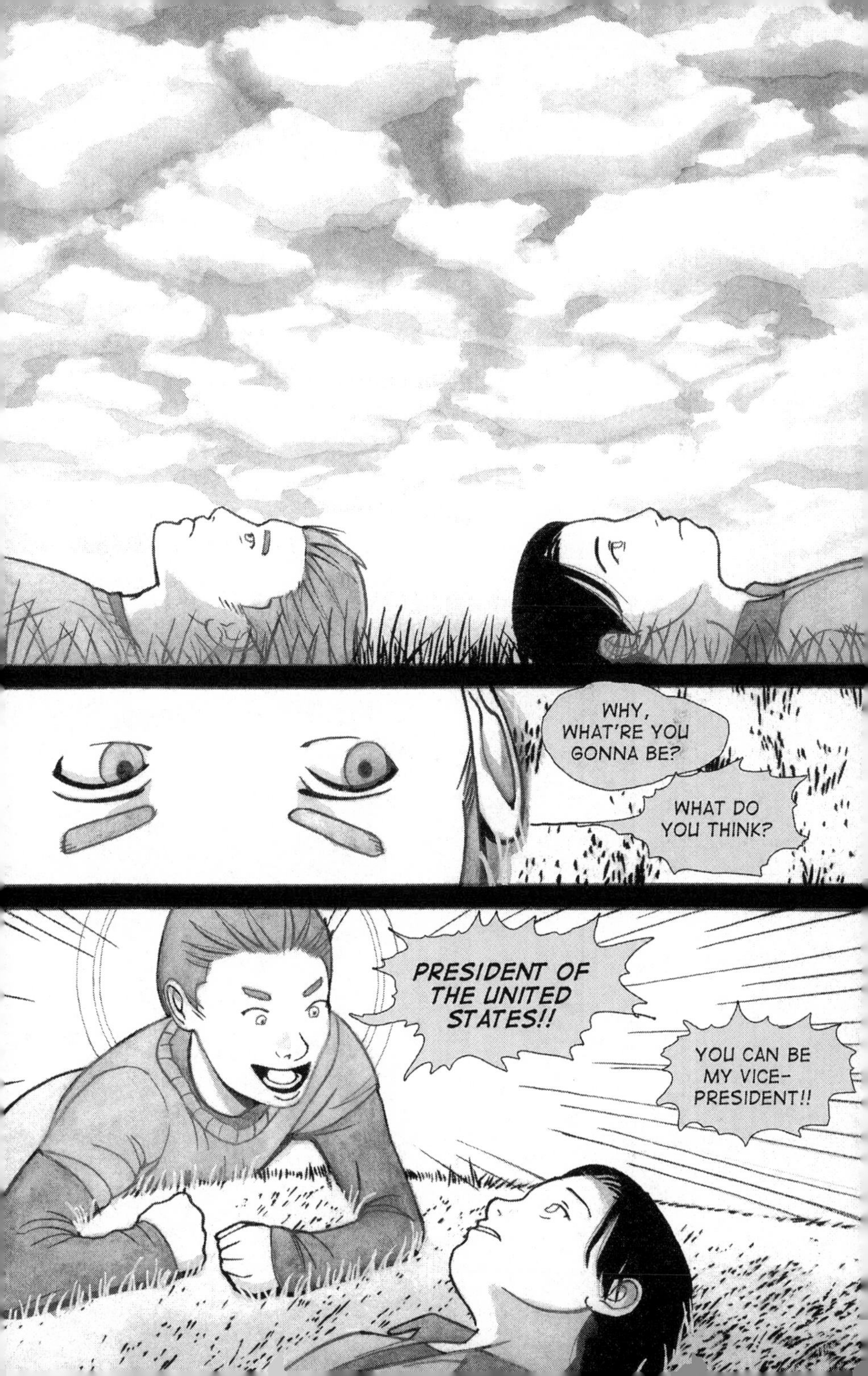
WHY, WHAT'RE YOU GONNA BE?
WHAT DO YOU THINK?
PRESIDENT OF THE UNITED STATES!!
YOU CAN BE MY VICE-PRESIDENT!!

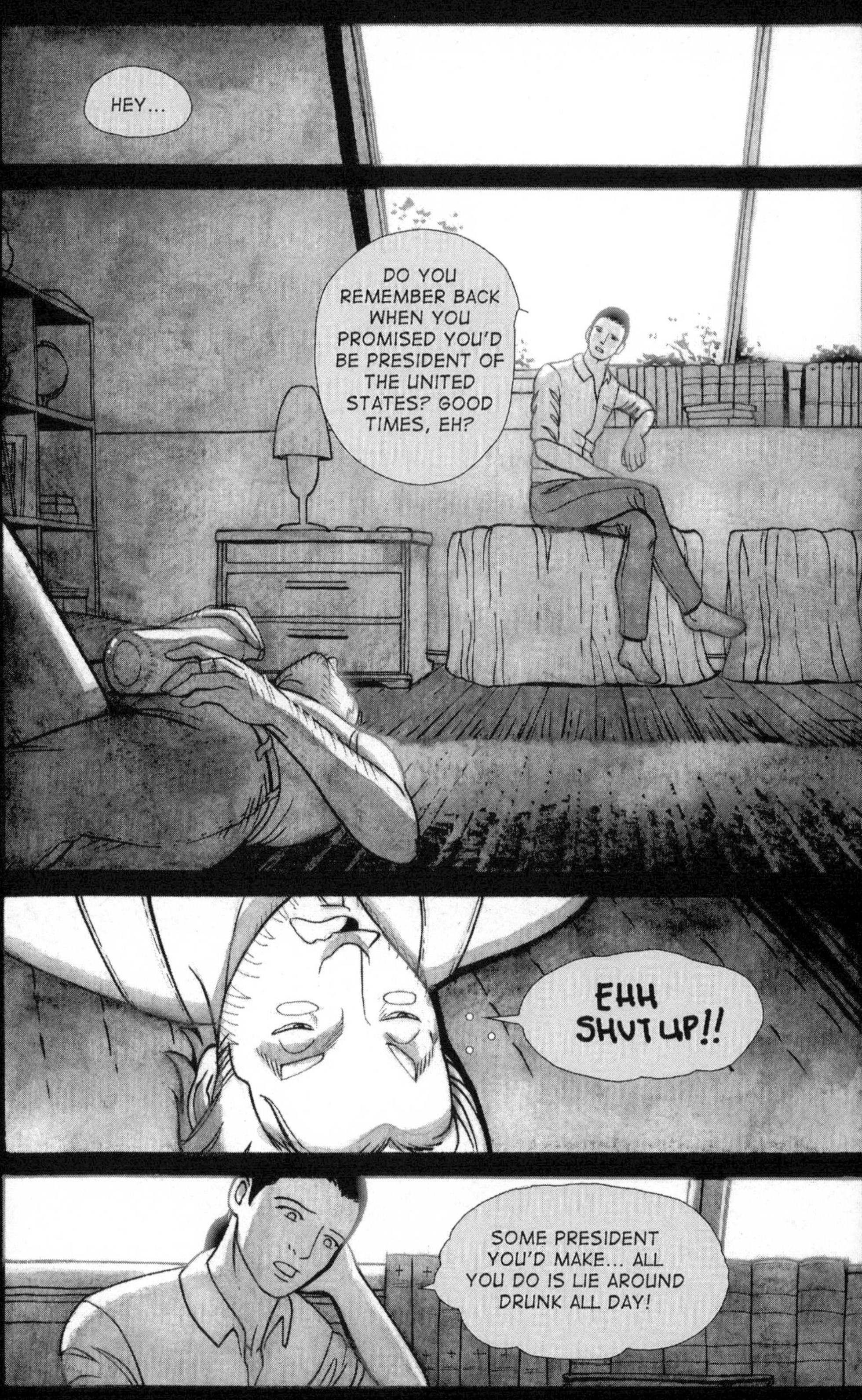
HEY...
DO YOU REMEMBER BACK WHEN YOU PROMISED YOU'D BE PRESIDENT OF THE UNITED STATES? GOOD TIMES, EH?
EHH SHUT UP!!
SOME PRESIDENT YOU'D MAKE... ALL YOU DO IS LIE AROUND DRUNK ALL DAY!

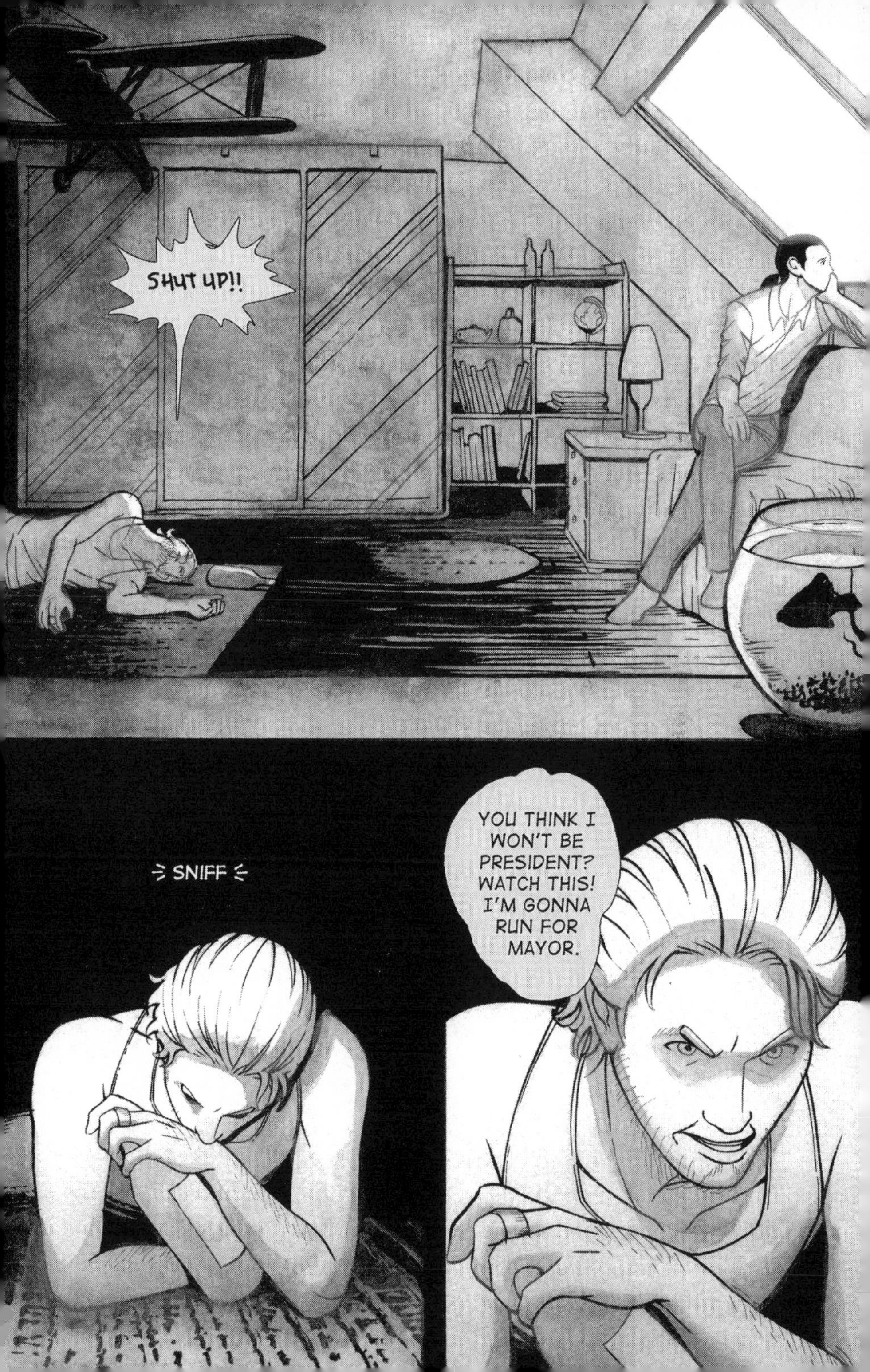
SHUT UP!!
SNIFF
YOU THINK I WON'T BE PRESIDENT? WATCH THIS! I'M GONNA RUN FOR MAYOR.

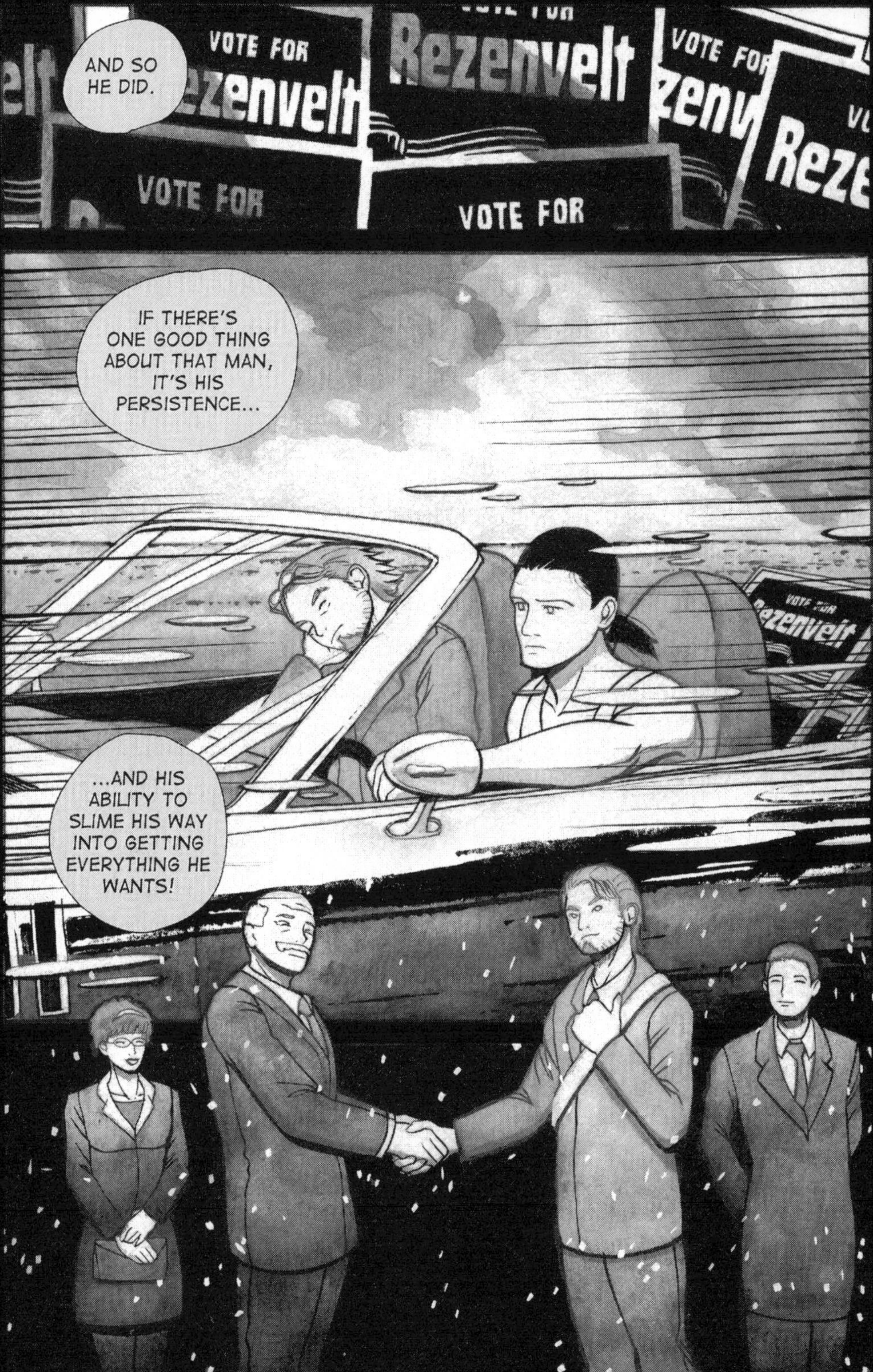
AND SO HE DID.
VOTE FOR Rezenvelt
IF THERE'S ONE GOOD THING ABOUT THAT MAN, IT'S HIS PERSISTENCE...
...AND HIS ABILITY TO SLIME HIS WAY INTO GETTING EVERYTHING HE WANTS!

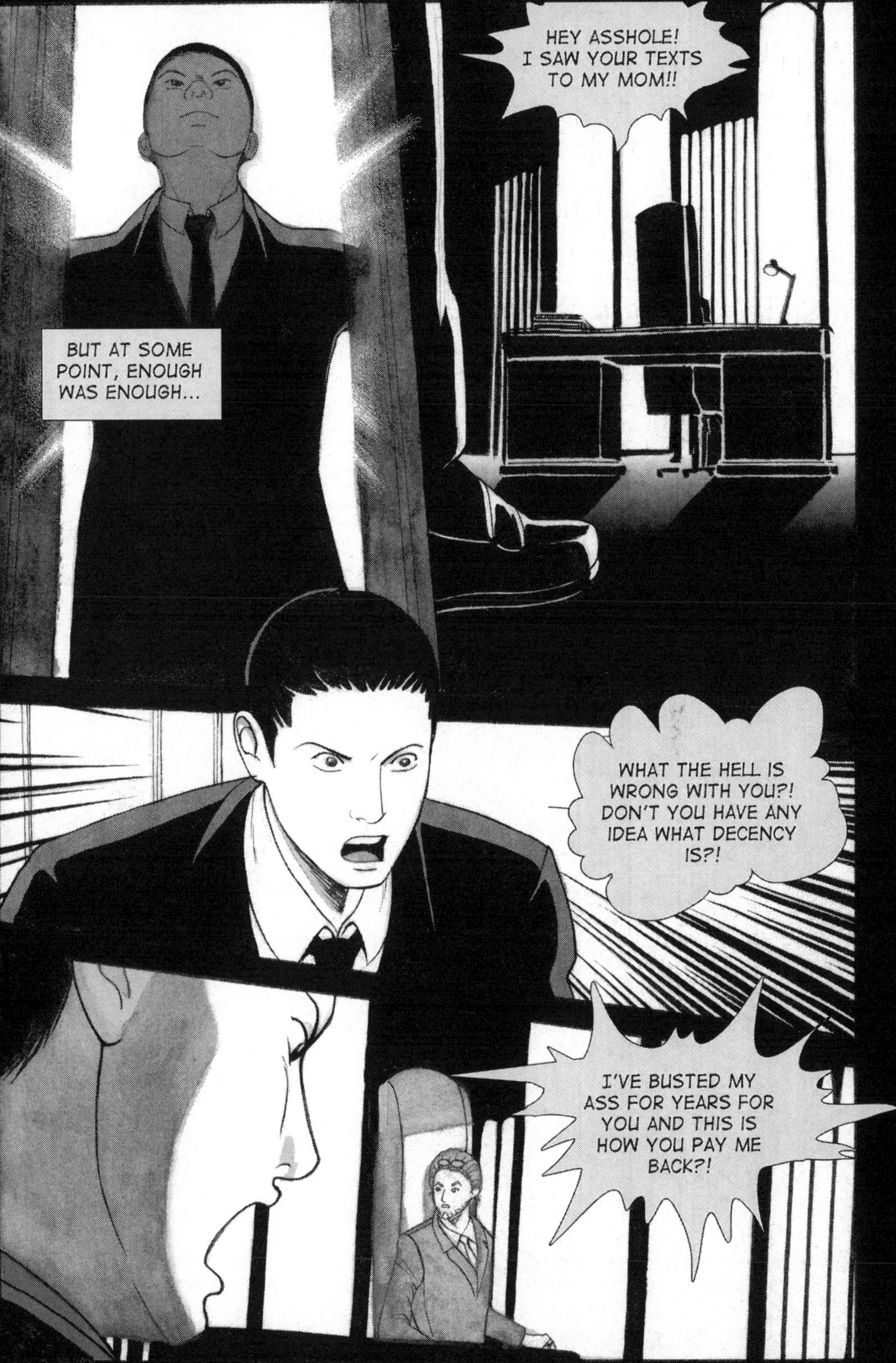
BUT AT SOME POINT, ENOUGH WAS ENOUGH...
HEY ASSHOLE! I SAW YOUR TEXTS TO MY MOM!!
WHAT THE HELL IS WRONG WITH YOU?! DON'T YOU HAVE ANY IDEA WHAT DECENCY IS?!
I'VE BUSTED MY ASS FOR YEARS FOR YOU AND THIS IS HOW YOU PAY ME BACK?!

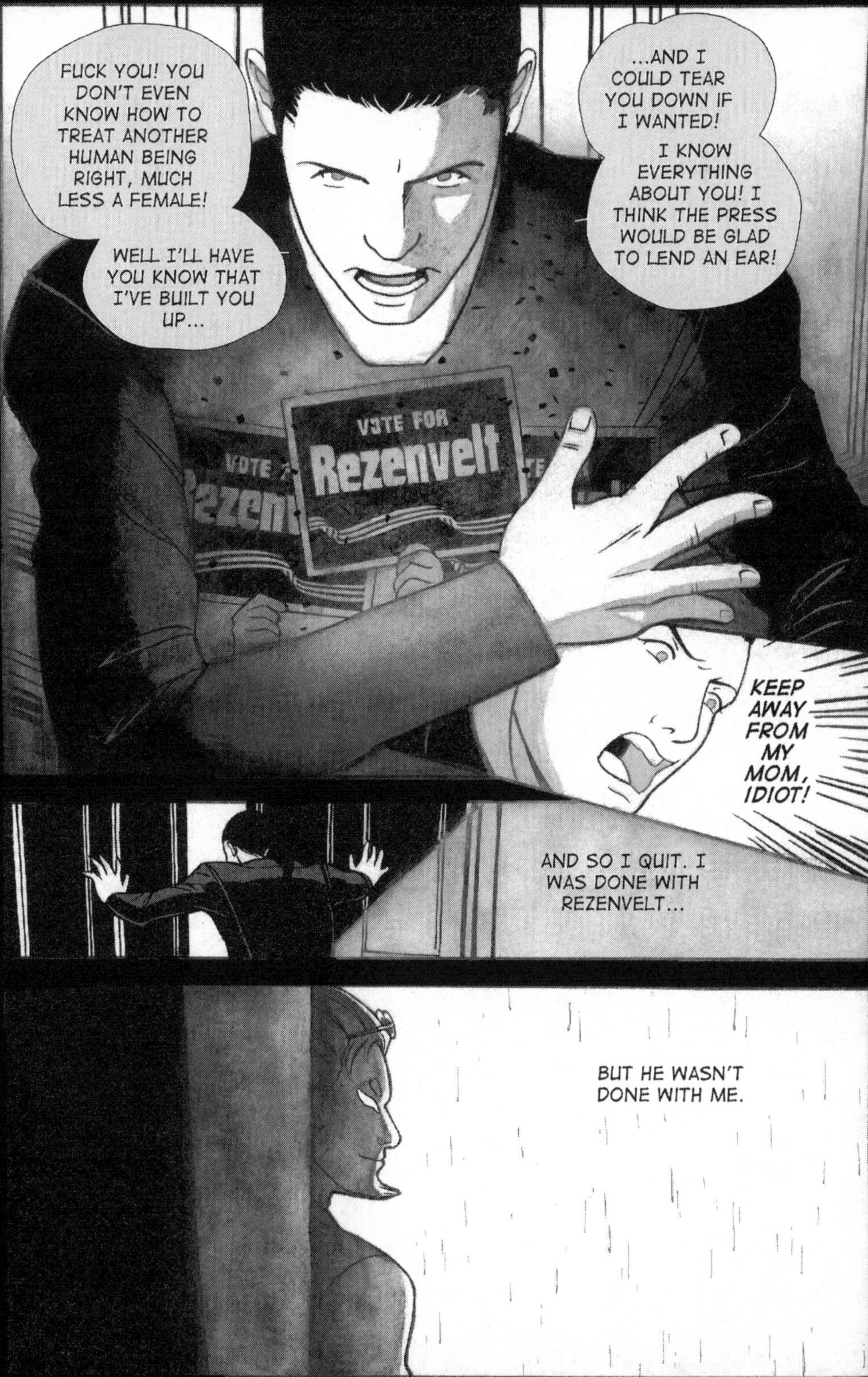
FUCK YOU! YOU DON'T EVEN KNOW HOW TO TREAT ANOTHER HUMAN BEING RIGHT, MUCH LESS A FEMALE!
WELL I'LL HAVE YOU KNOW THAT I'VE BUILT YOU UP...
...AND I COULD TEAR YOU DOWN IF I WANTED!
I KNOW EVERYTHING ABOUT YOU! I THINK THE PRESS WOULD BE GLAD TO LEND AN EAR!
VOTE FOR Rezenvelt
KEEP AWAY FROM MY MOM, IDIOT!
AND SO I QUIT. I WAS DONE WITH REZENVELT...
BUT HE WASN'T DONE WITH ME.

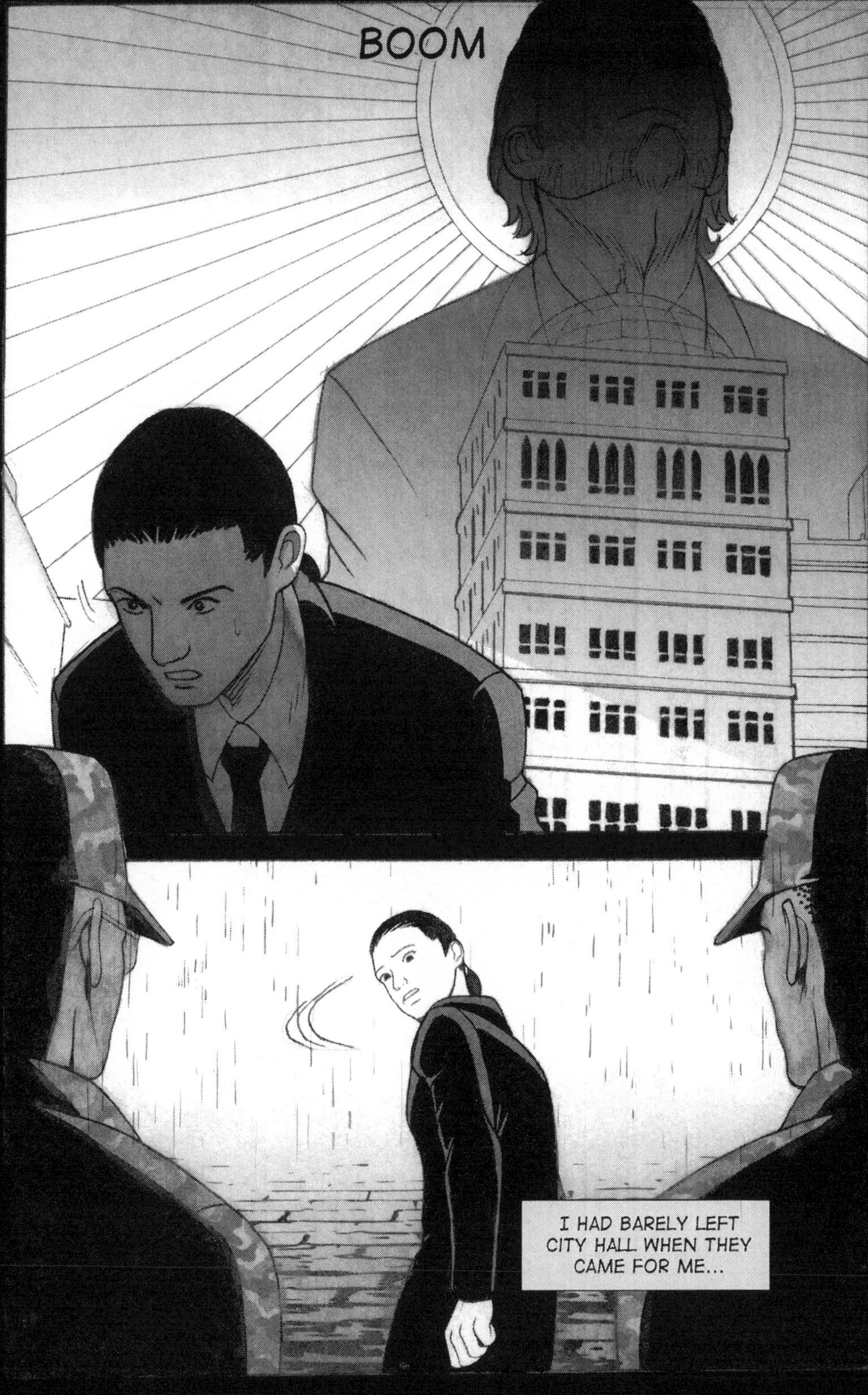
BOOM
I HAD BARELY LEFT CITY HALL WHEN THEY CAME FOR ME...

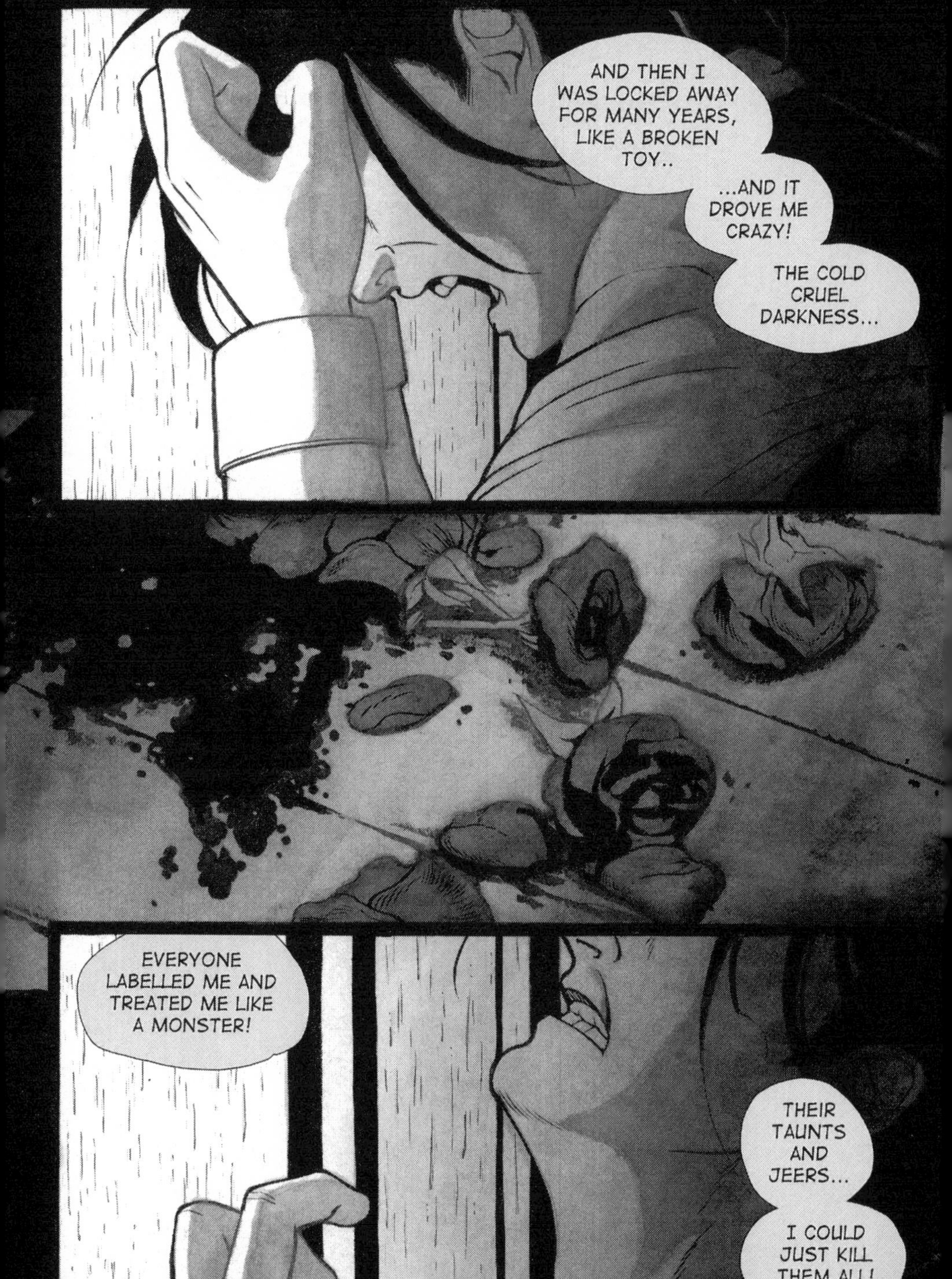
AND THEN I WAS LOCKED AWAY FOR MANY YEARS, LIKE A BROKEN TOY..
...AND IT DROVE ME CRAZY!
THE COLD CRUEL DARKNESS...
EVERYONE LABELLED ME AND TREATED ME LIKE A MONSTER!
THEIR TAUNTS AND JEERS...
I COULD JUST KILL THEM ALL!

ONE DAY, WE
ENDED UP VISITING
THAT CAVE.

THERE WAS A
SHEER DROP INTO
A BED OF SPIKES.

IT WAS TERRIFYING.

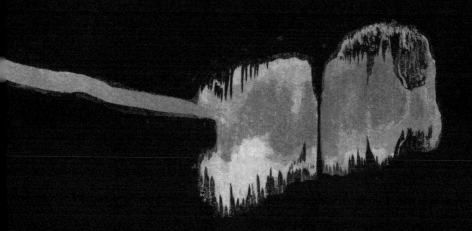

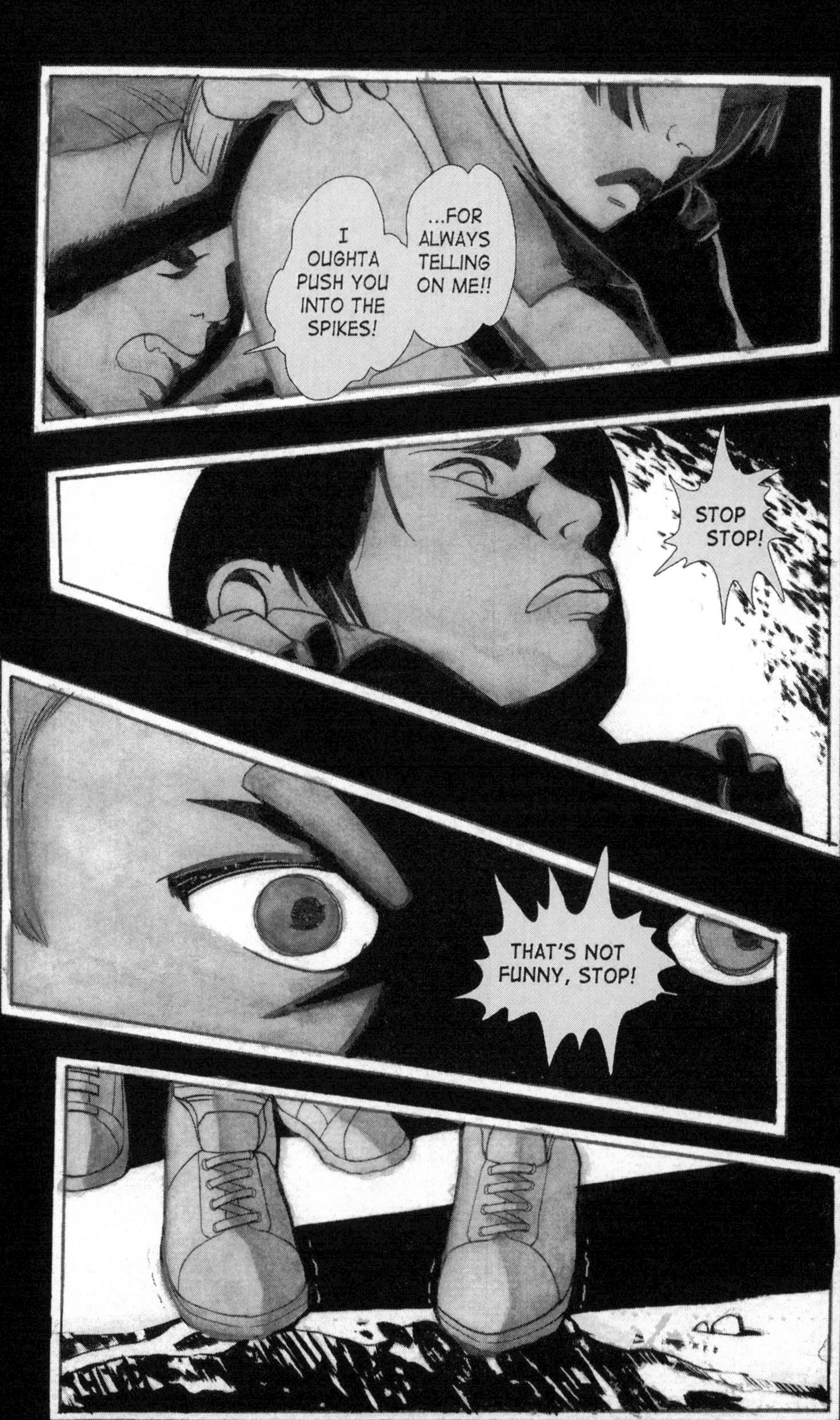

I OUGHTA PUSH YOU INTO THE SPIKES!
...FOR ALWAYS TELLING ON ME!!
STOP STOP!
THAT'S NOT FUNNY, STOP!

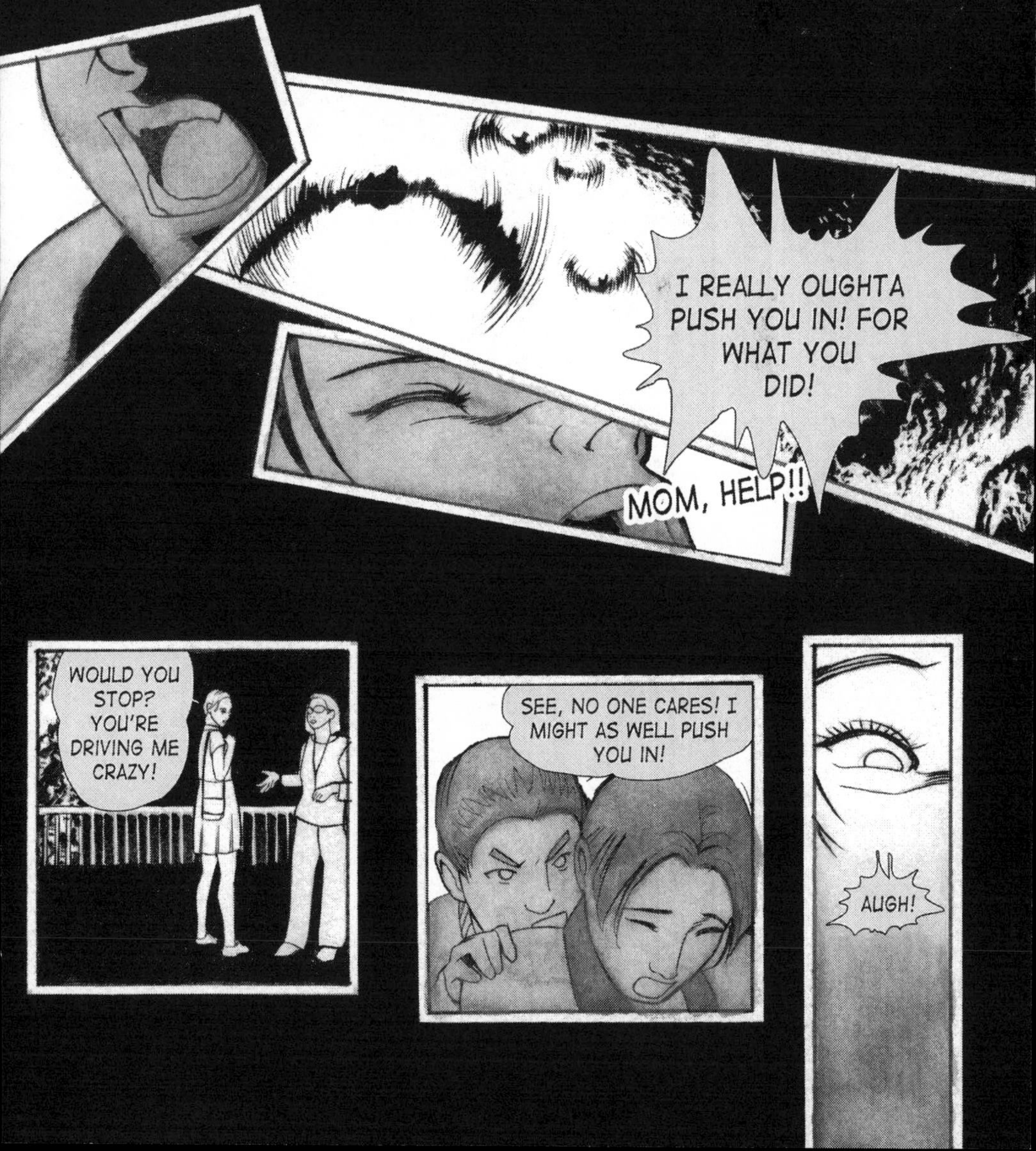
I REALLY OUGHTA PUSH YOU IN! FOR WHAT YOU DID!
MOM, HELP!!
WOULD YOU STOP? YOU'RE DRIVING ME CRAZY!
SEE, NO ONE CARES! I MIGHT AS WELL PUSH YOU IN!
AUGH!

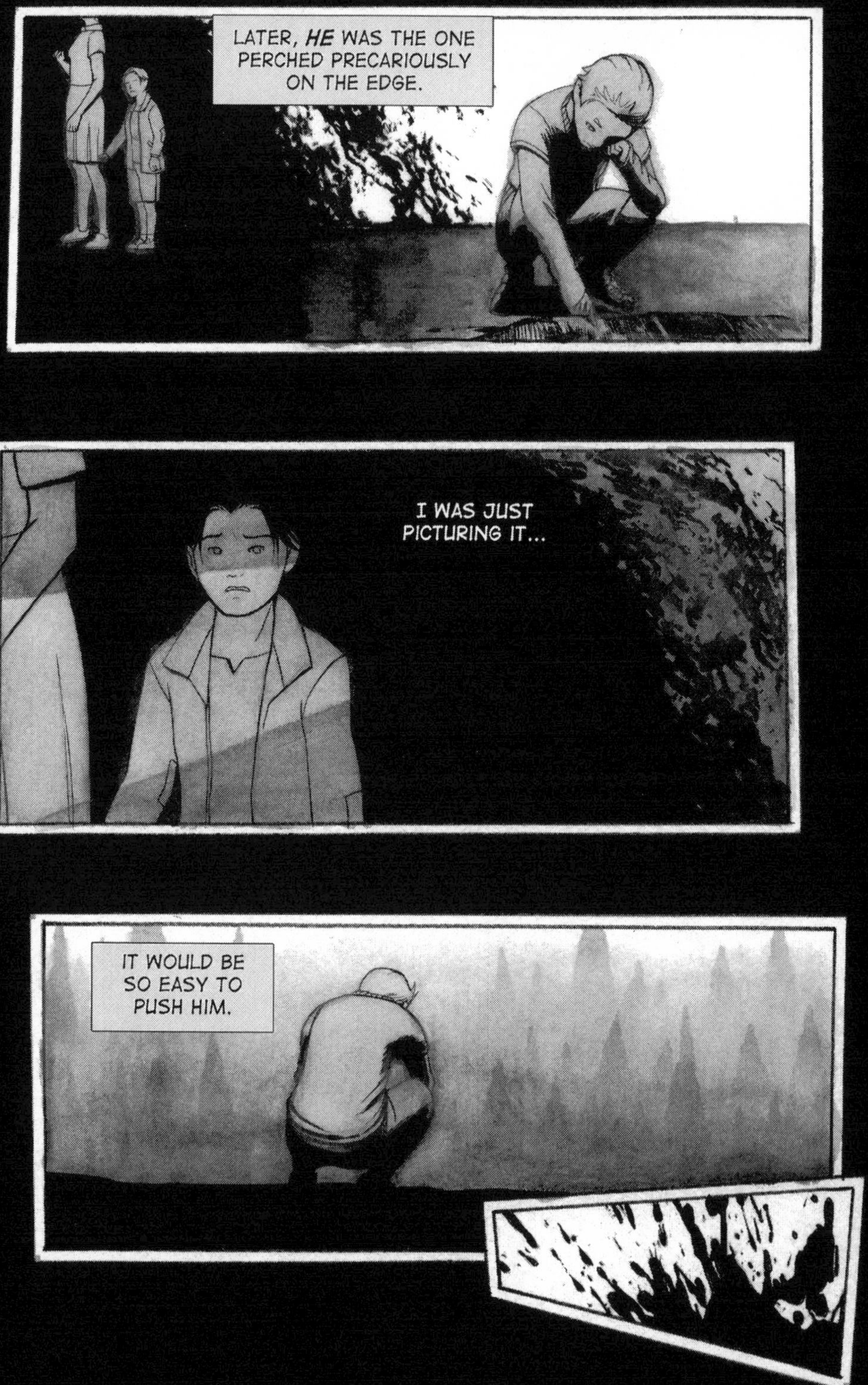
LATER, *HE* WAS THE ONE PERCHED PRECARIOUSLY ON THE EDGE.
I WAS JUST PICTURING IT...
IT WOULD BE SO EASY TO PUSH HIM.

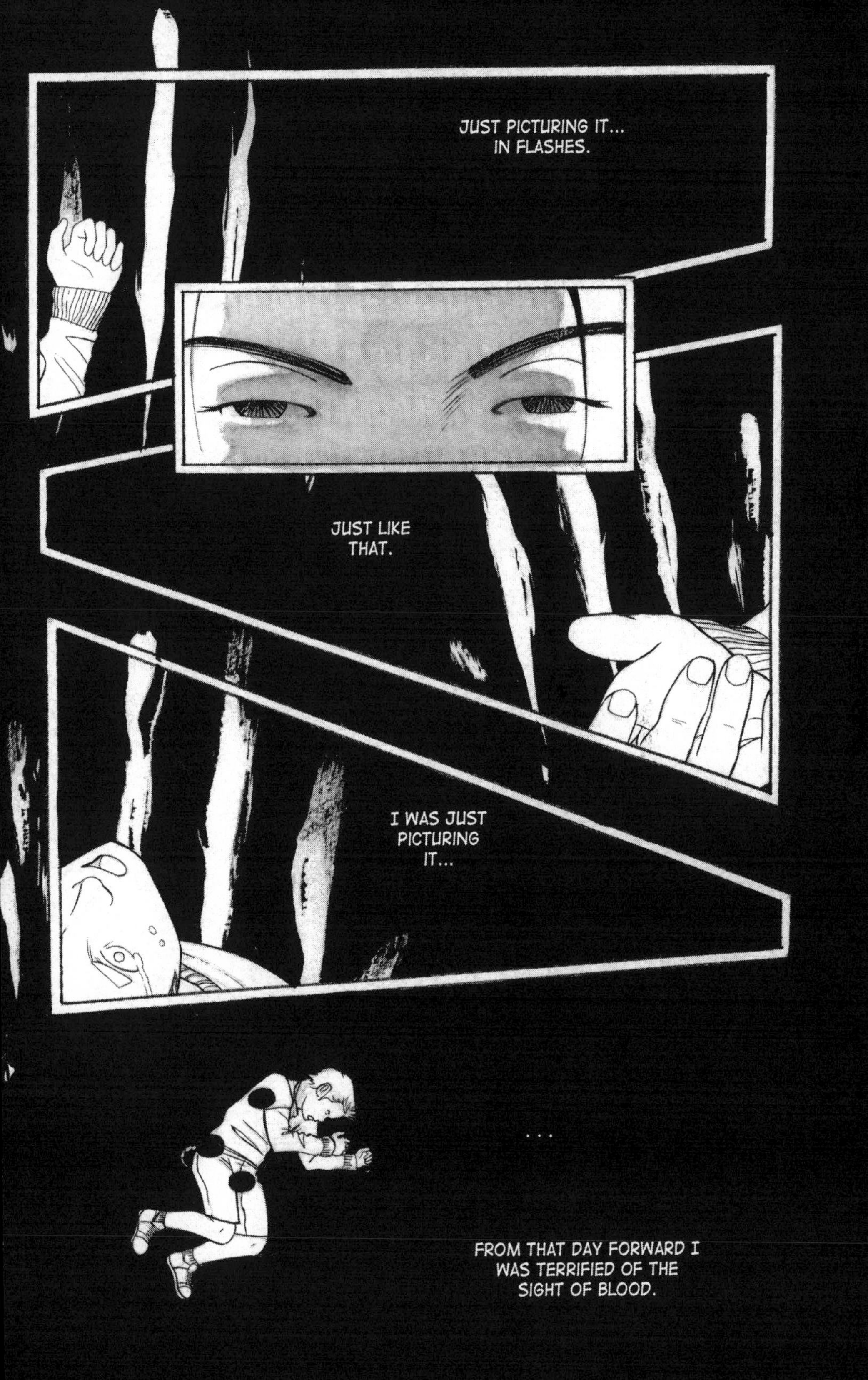
JUST PICTURING IT... IN FLASHES.
JUST LIKE THAT.
I WAS JUST PICTURING IT...
. . .
FROM THAT DAY FORWARD I WAS TERRIFIED OF THE SIGHT OF BLOOD.

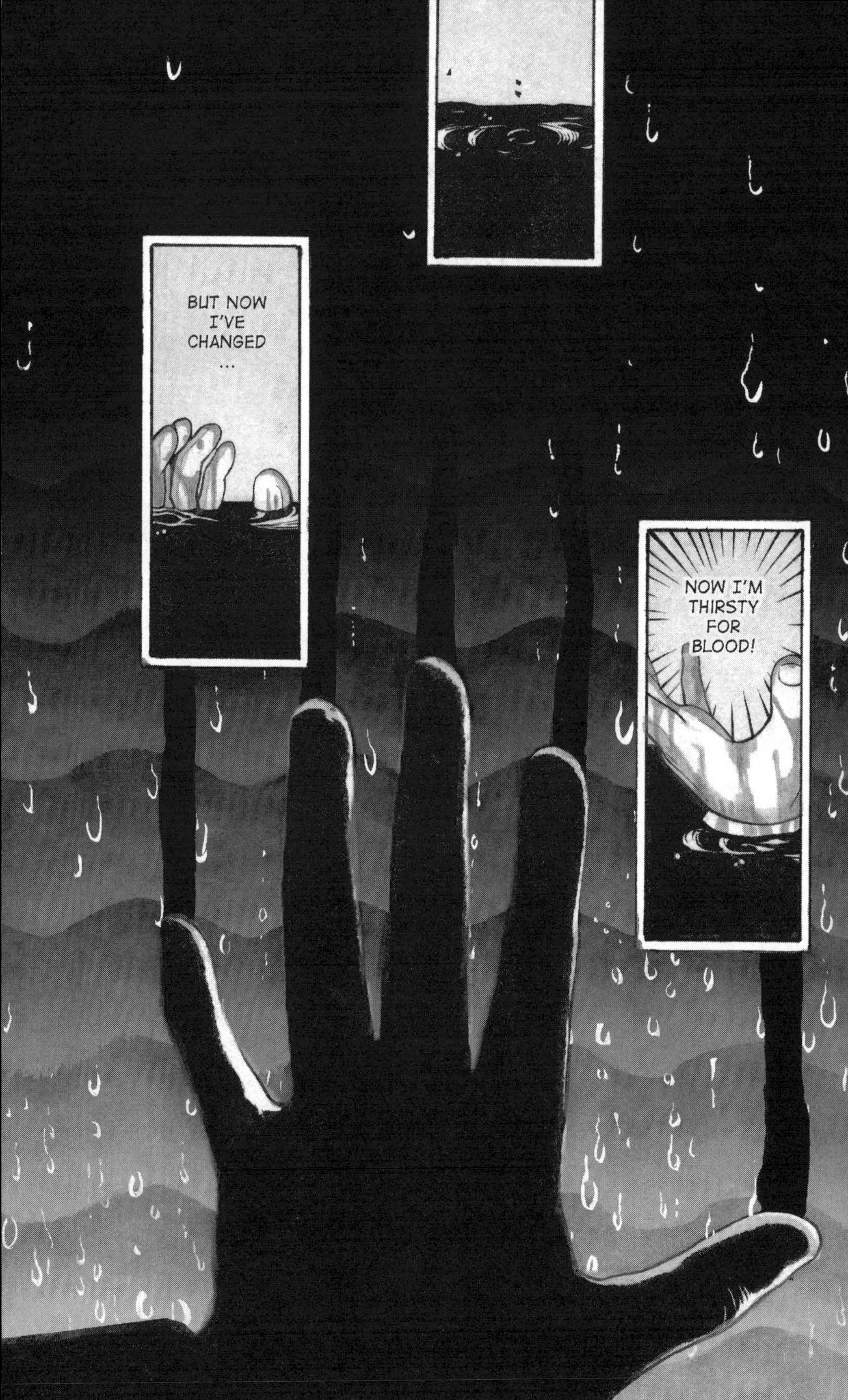
BUT NOW I'VE CHANGED ...
NOW I'M THIRSTY FOR BLOOD!

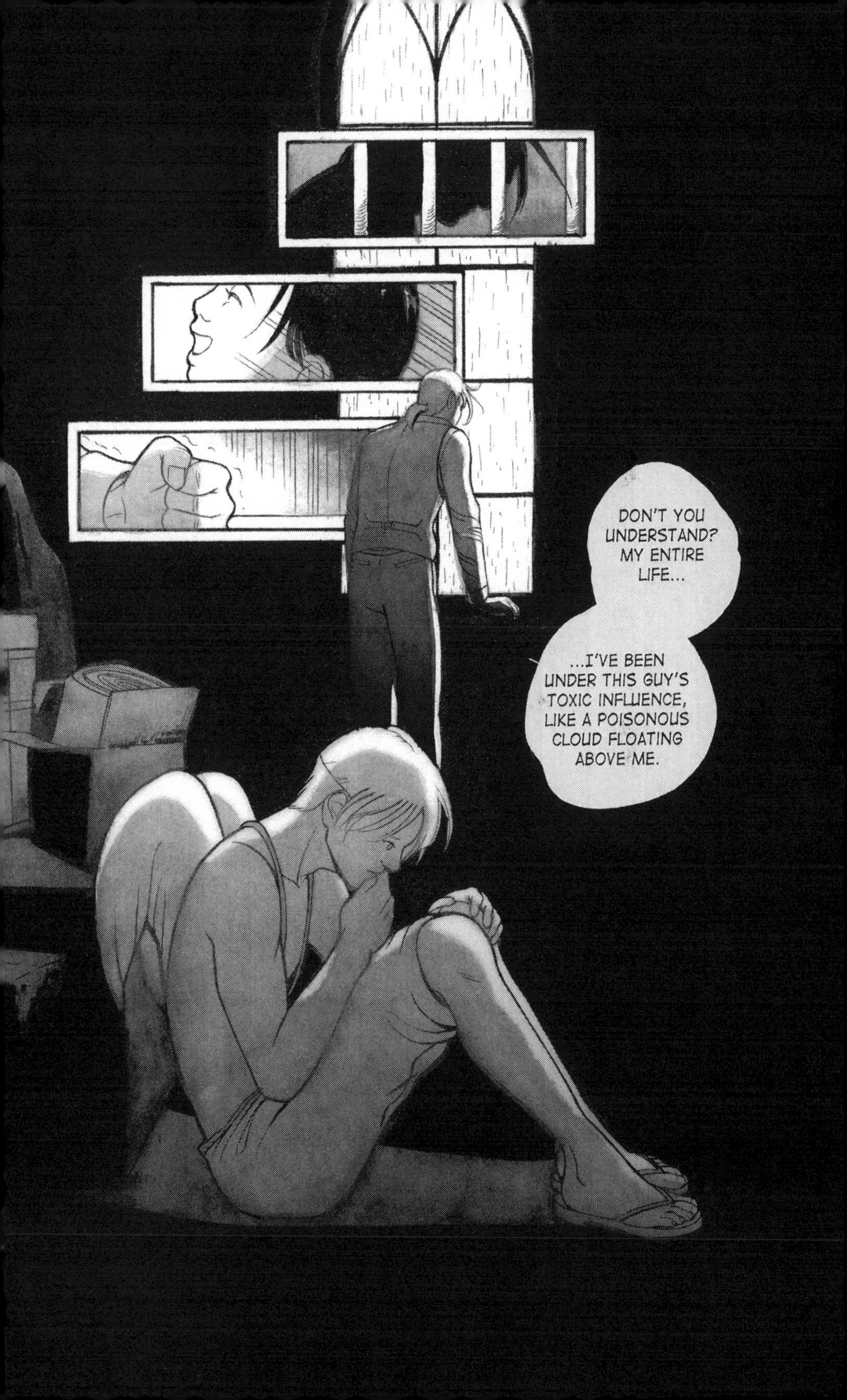
DON'T YOU UNDERSTAND? MY ENTIRE LIFE...
...I'VE BEEN UNDER THIS GUY'S TOXIC INFLUENCE, LIKE A POISONOUS CLOUD FLOATING ABOVE ME.

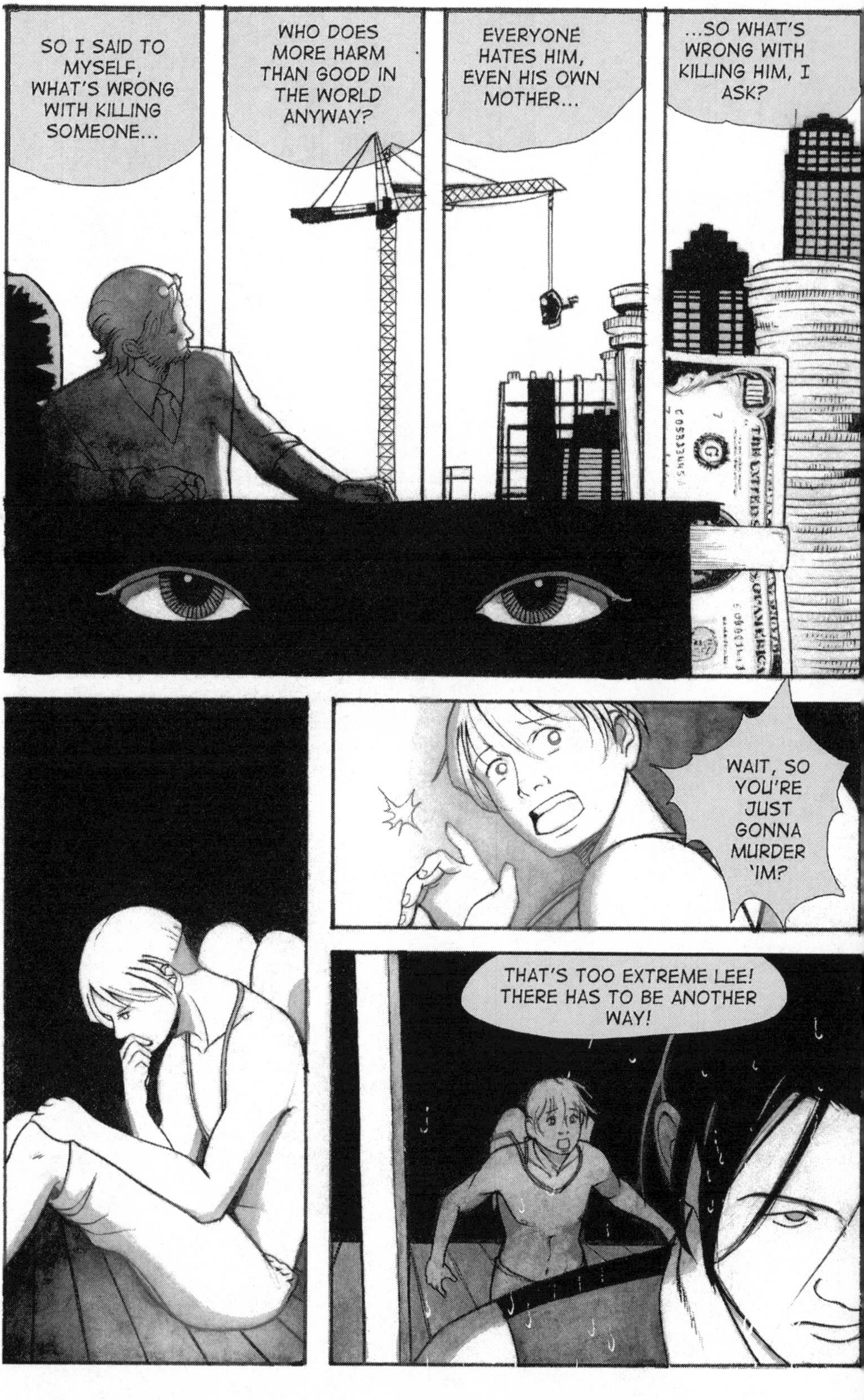
SO I SAID TO MYSELF, WHAT'S WRONG WITH KILLING SOMEONE...
WHO DOES MORE HARM THAN GOOD IN THE WORLD ANYWAY?
EVERYONE HATES HIM, EVEN HIS OWN MOTHER...
...SO WHAT'S WRONG WITH KILLING HIM, I ASK?
WAIT, SO YOU'RE JUST GONNA MURDER 'IM?
THAT'S TOO EXTREME LEE! THERE HAS TO BE ANOTHER WAY!

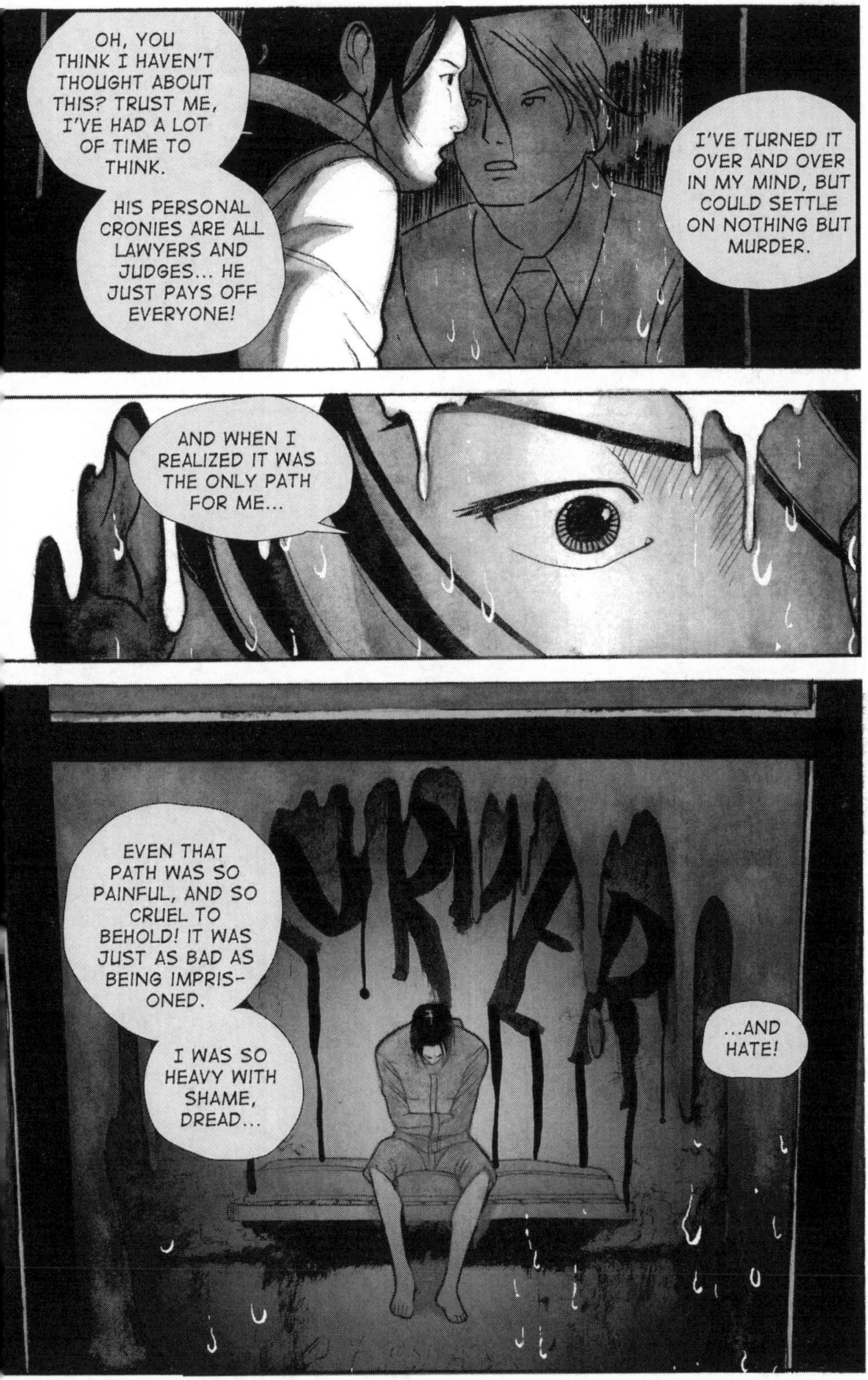
OH, YOU THINK I HAVEN'T THOUGHT ABOUT THIS? TRUST ME, I'VE HAD A LOT OF TIME TO THINK.
HIS PERSONAL CRONIES ARE ALL LAWYERS AND JUDGES... HE JUST PAYS OFF EVERYONE!
I'VE TURNED IT OVER AND OVER IN MY MIND, BUT COULD SETTLE ON NOTHING BUT MURDER.
AND WHEN I REALIZED IT WAS THE ONLY PATH FOR ME...
EVEN THAT PATH WAS SO PAINFUL, AND SO CRUEL TO BEHOLD! IT WAS JUST AS BAD AS BEING IMPRIS-ONED.
I WAS SO HEAVY WITH SHAME, DREAD...
...AND HATE!

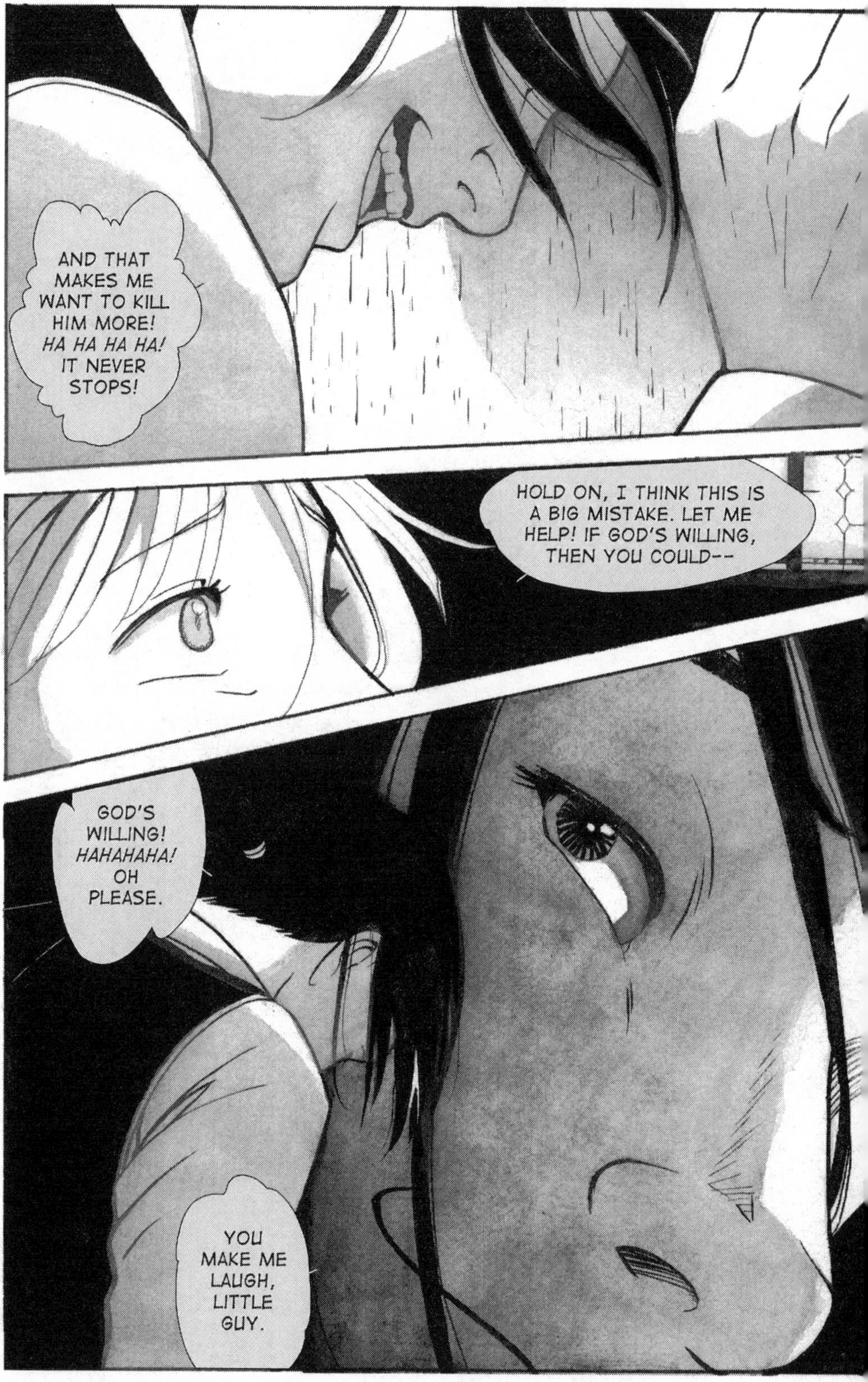
AND THAT MAKES ME WANT TO KILL HIM MORE! *HA HA HA HA!* IT NEVER STOPS!
HOLD ON, I THINK THIS IS A BIG MISTAKE. LET ME HELP! IF GOD'S WILLING, THEN YOU COULD--
GOD'S WILLING! *HAHAHAHA!* OH PLEASE.
YOU MAKE ME LAUGH, LITTLE GUY.

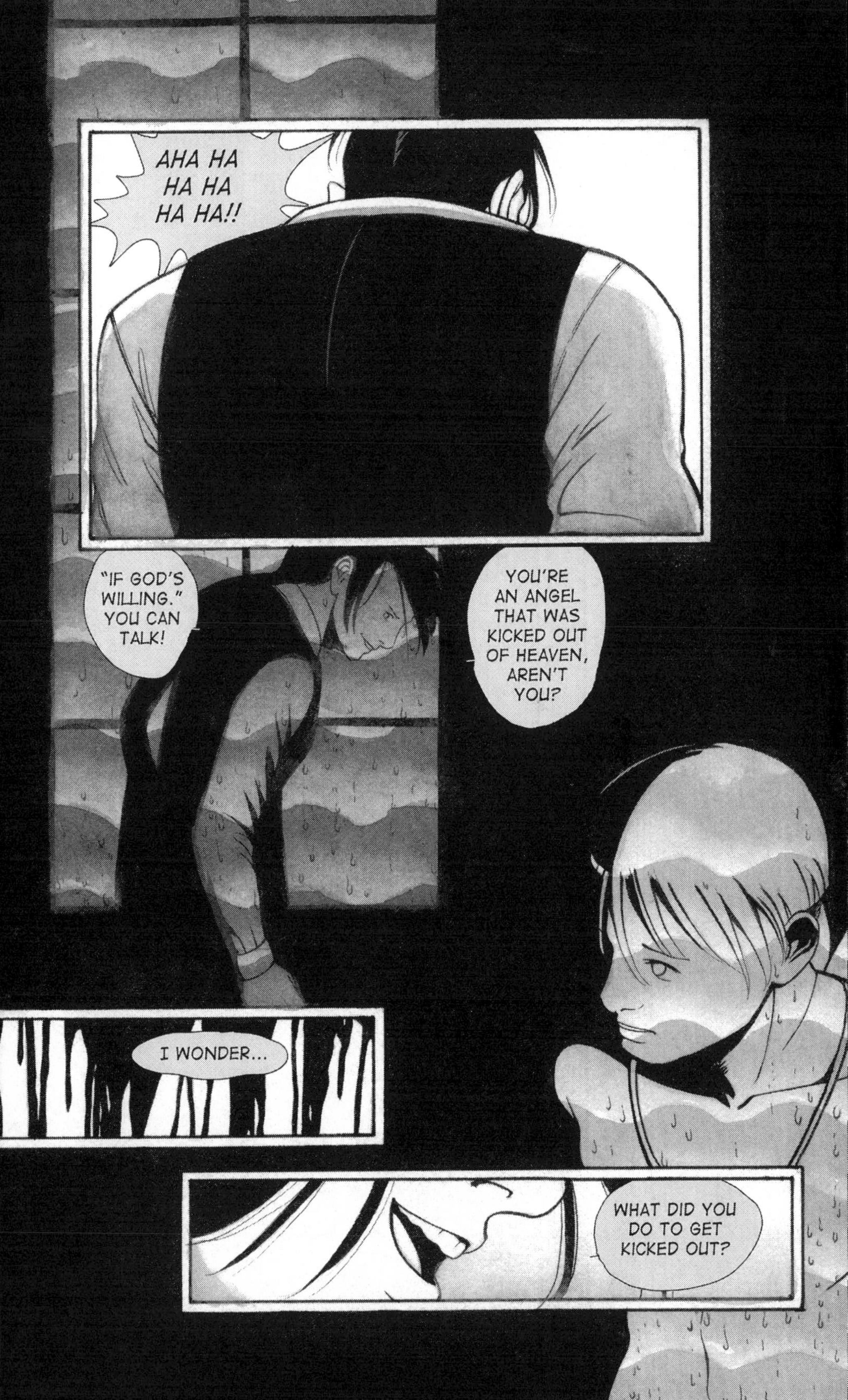
AHA HA HA HA HA HA!!
"IF GOD'S WILLING." YOU CAN TALK!
YOU'RE AN ANGEL THAT WAS KICKED OUT OF HEAVEN, AREN'T YOU?
I WONDER...
WHAT DID YOU DO TO GET KICKED OUT?

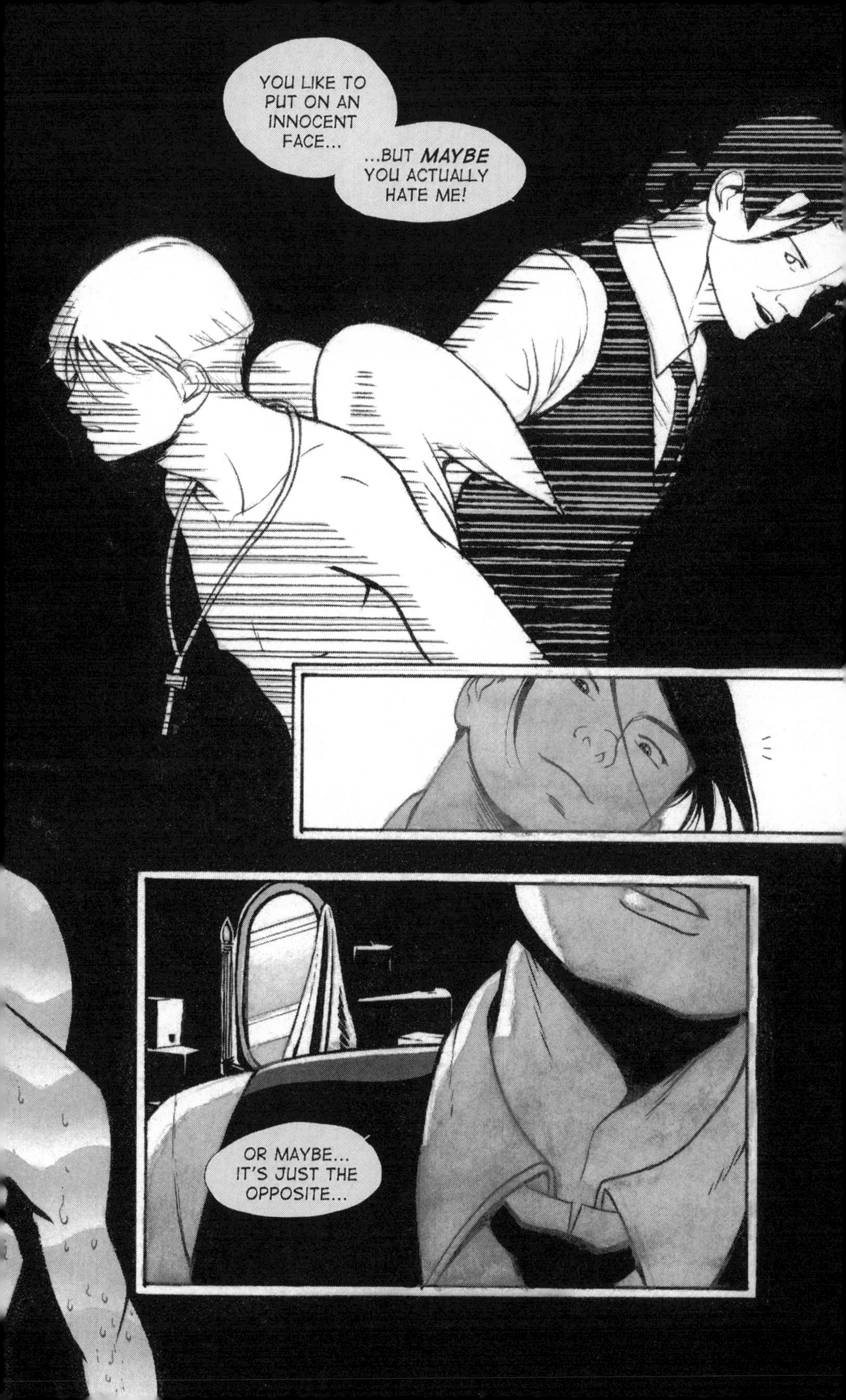
YOU LIKE TO PUT ON AN INNOCENT FACE...
...BUT *MAYBE* YOU ACTUALLY HATE ME!
OR MAYBE... IT'S JUST THE OPPOSITE...

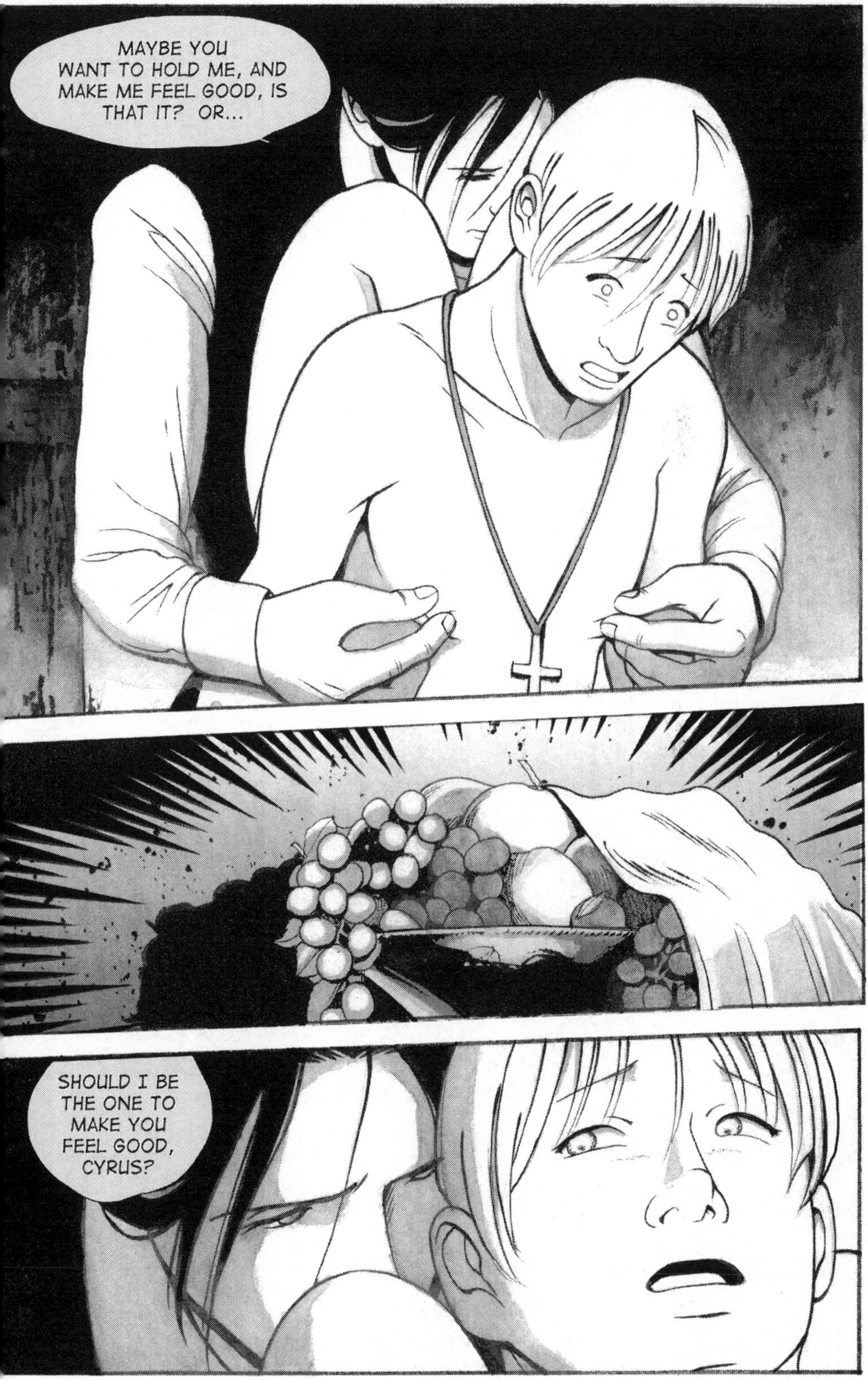
MAYBE YOU WANT TO HOLD ME, AND MAKE ME FEEL GOOD, IS THAT IT? OR...
SHOULD I BE THE ONE TO MAKE YOU FEEL GOOD, CYRUS?

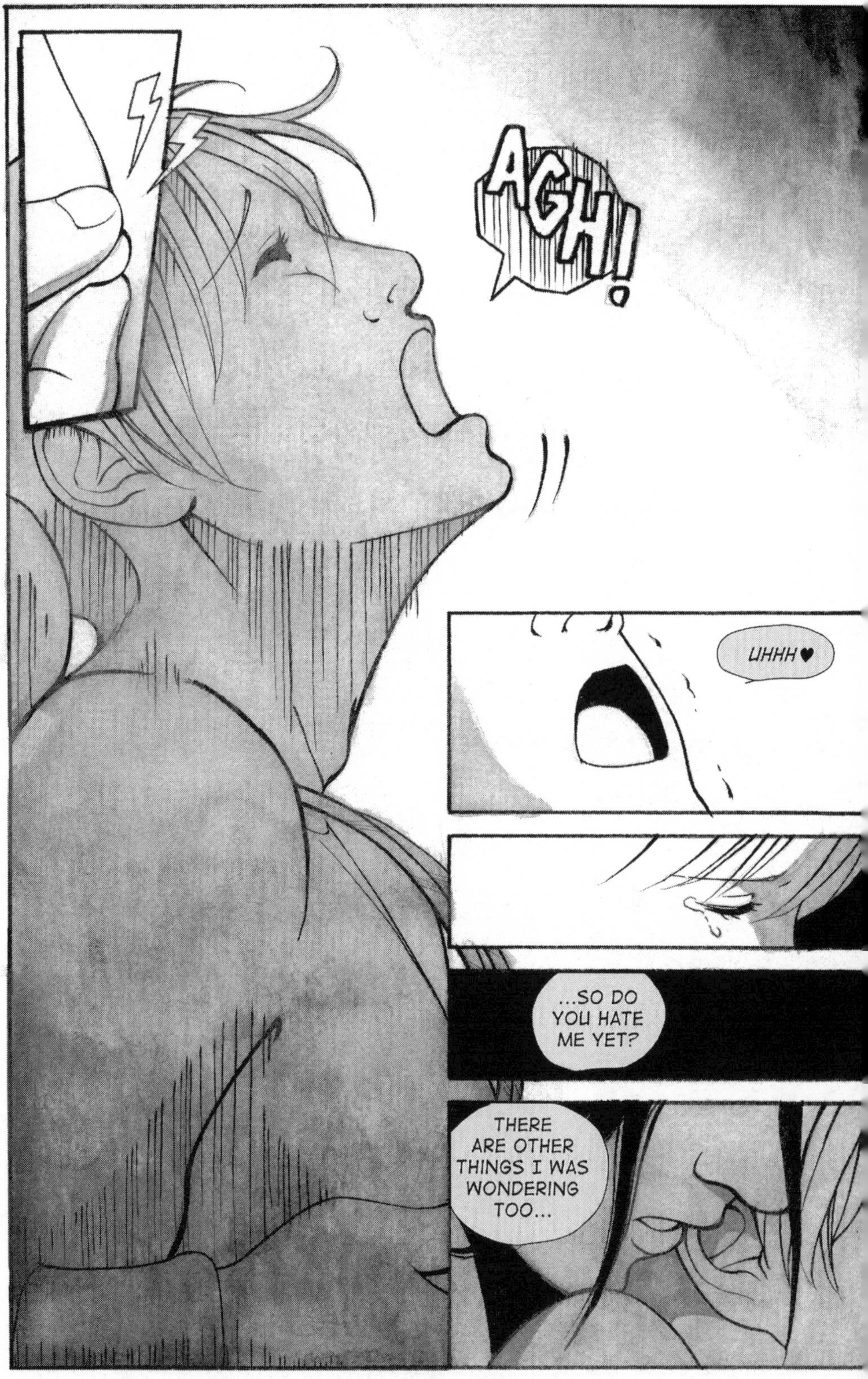
AGH!
UHHH♥
...SO DO YOU HATE ME YET?
THERE ARE OTHER THINGS I WAS WONDERING TOO...

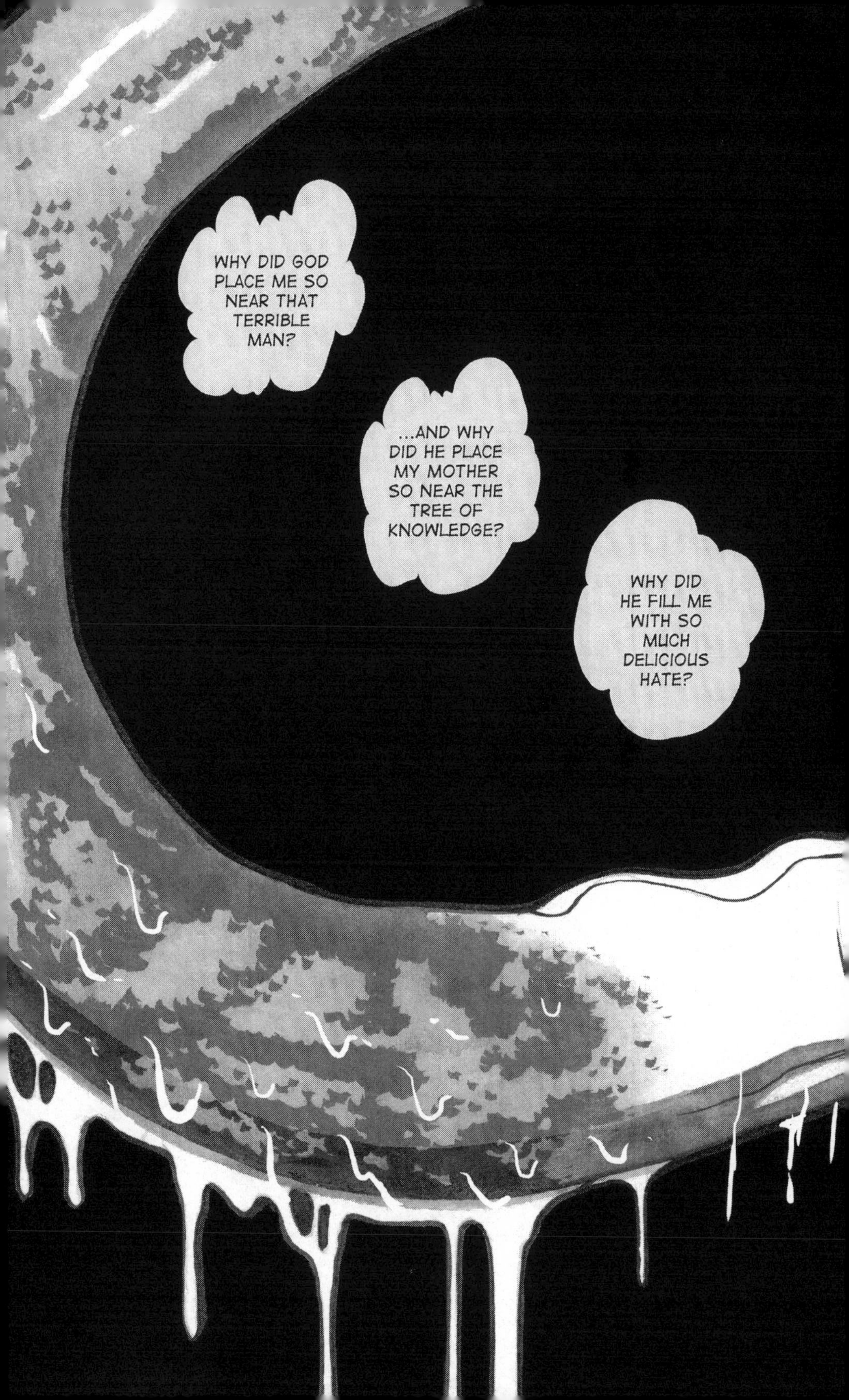
WHY DID GOD PLACE ME SO NEAR THAT TERRIBLE MAN?
...AND WHY DID HE PLACE MY MOTHER SO NEAR THE TREE OF KNOWLEDGE?
WHY DID HE FILL ME WITH SO MUCH DELICIOUS HATE?

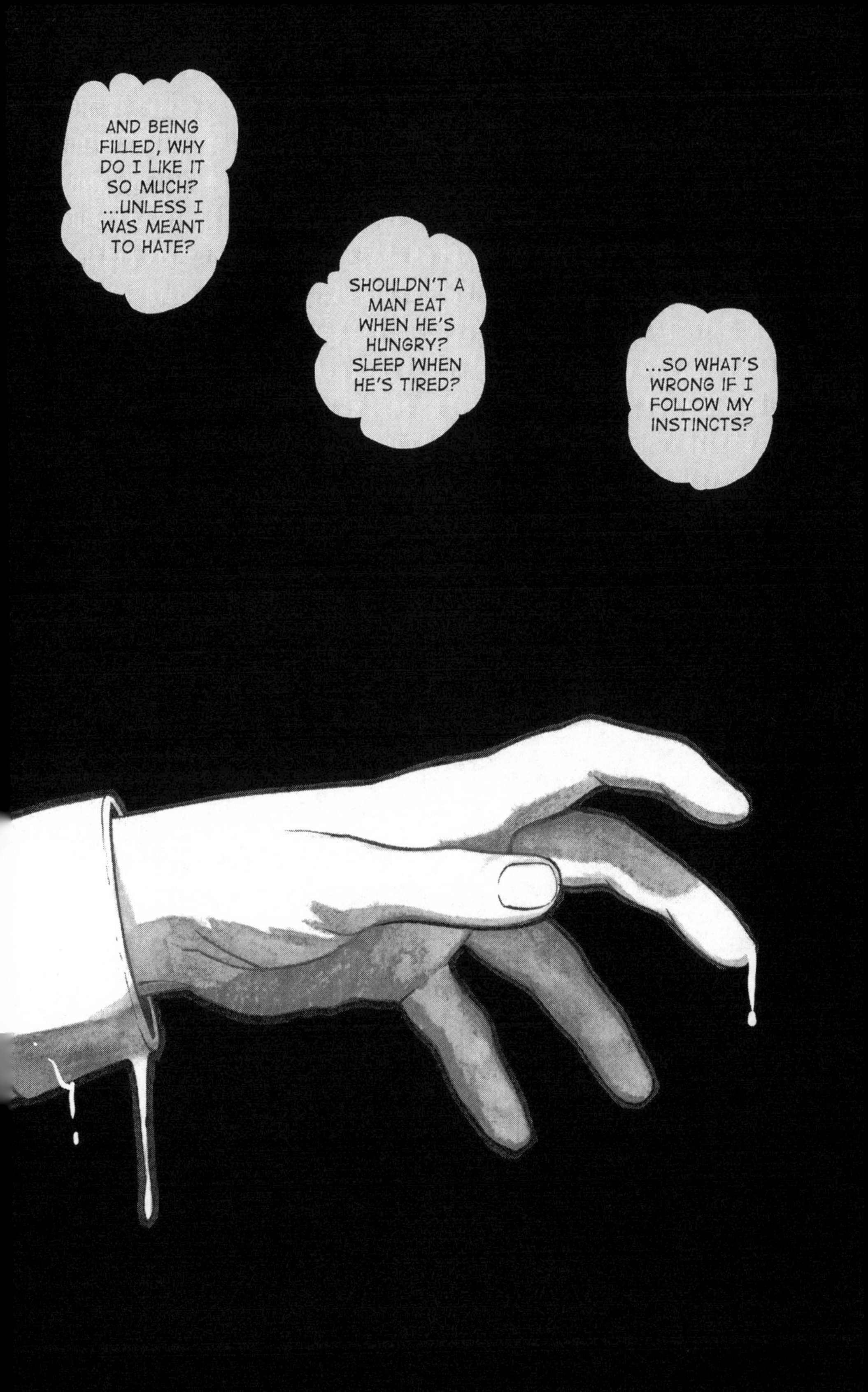
AND BEING FILLED, WHY DO I LIKE IT SO MUCH? ...UNLESS I WAS MEANT TO HATE?
SHOULDN'T A MAN EAT WHEN HE'S HUNGRY? SLEEP WHEN HE'S TIRED?
...SO WHAT'S WRONG IF I FOLLOW MY INSTINCTS?

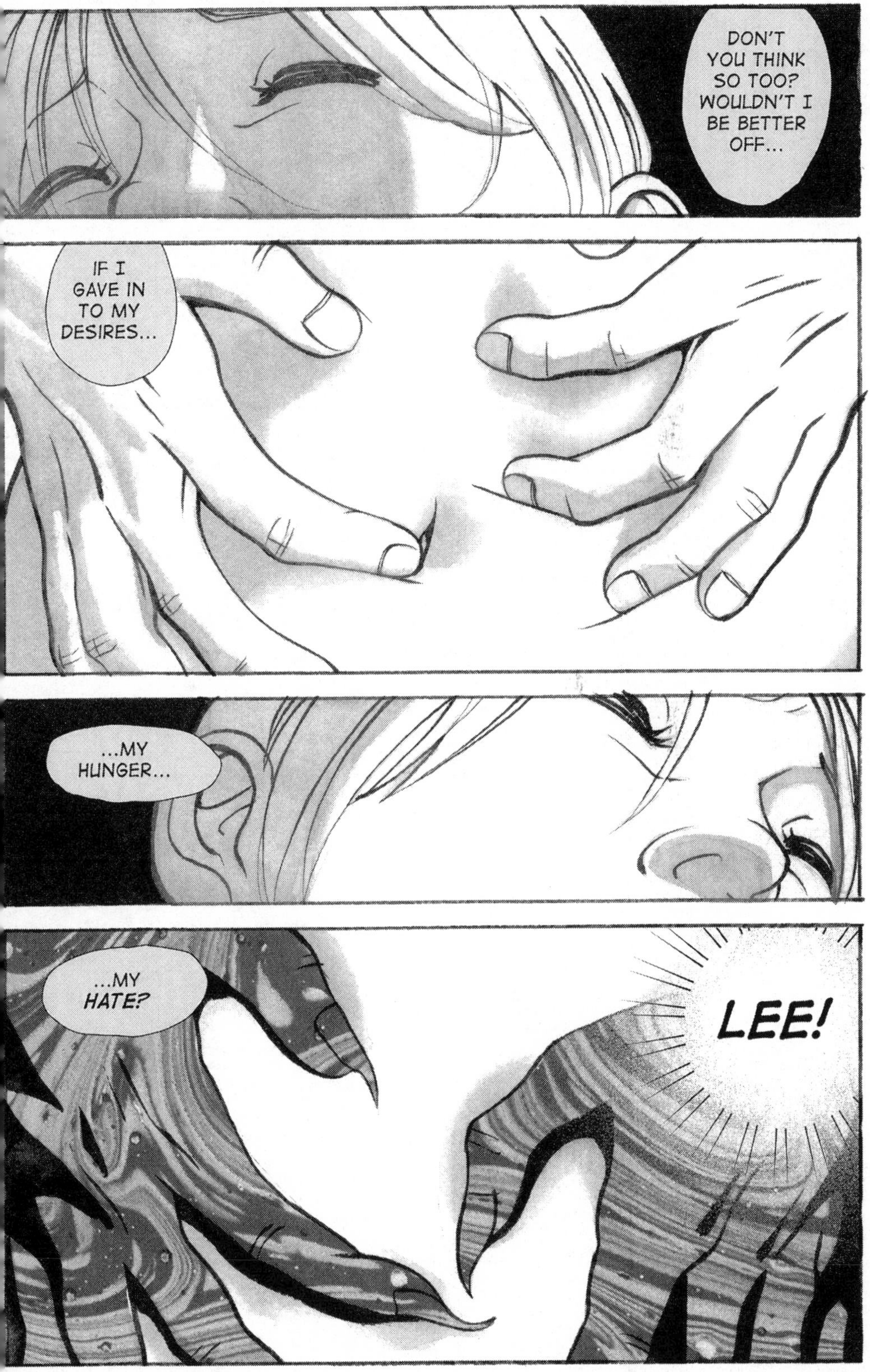
DON'T YOU THINK SO TOO? WOULDN'T I BE BETTER OFF...
IF I GAVE IN TO MY DESIRES...
...MY HUNGER...
...MY *HATE?*
LEE!

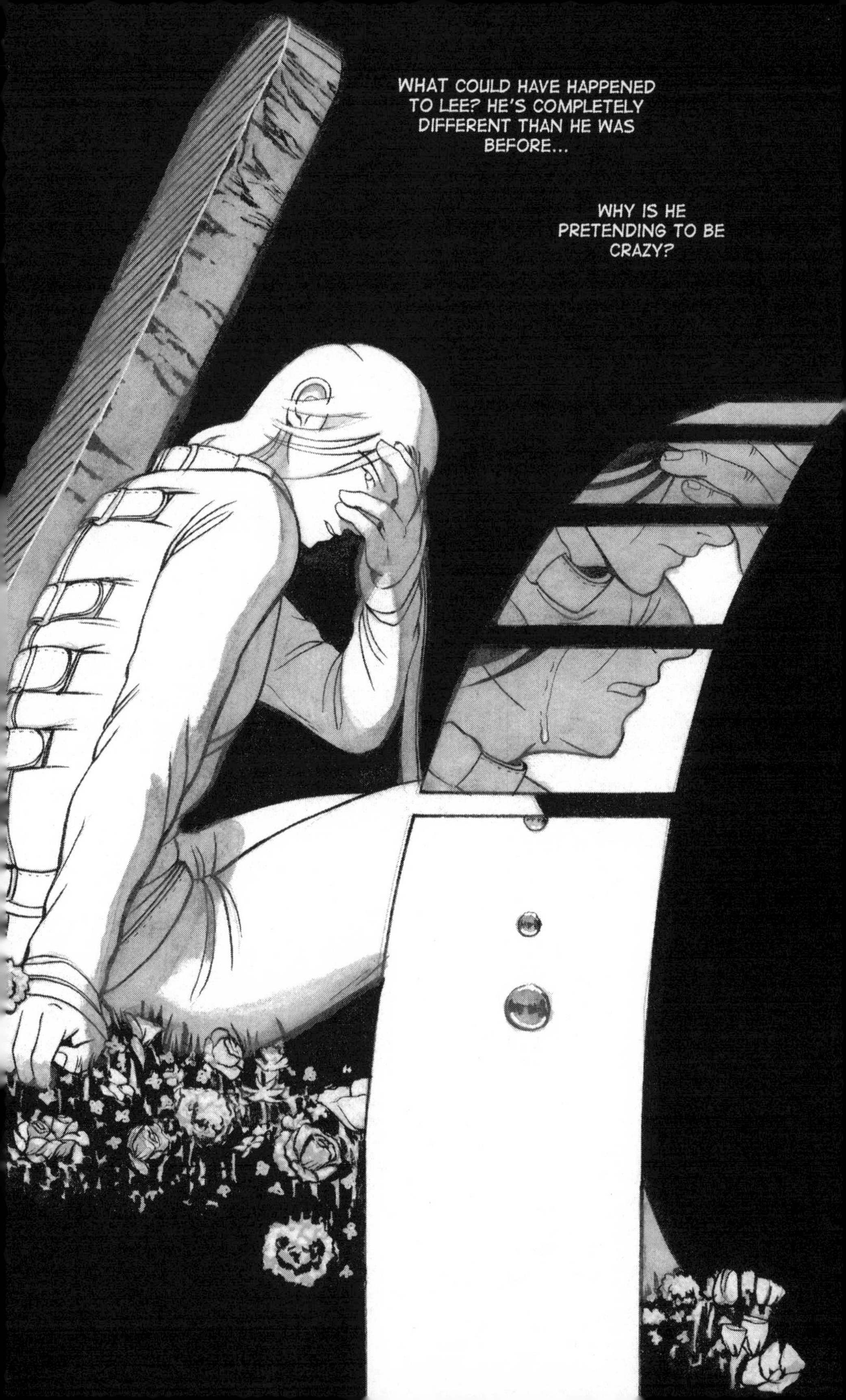
WHAT COULD HAVE HAPPENED TO LEE? HE'S COMPLETELY DIFFERENT THAN HE WAS BEFORE...
WHY IS HE PRETENDING TO BE CRAZY?

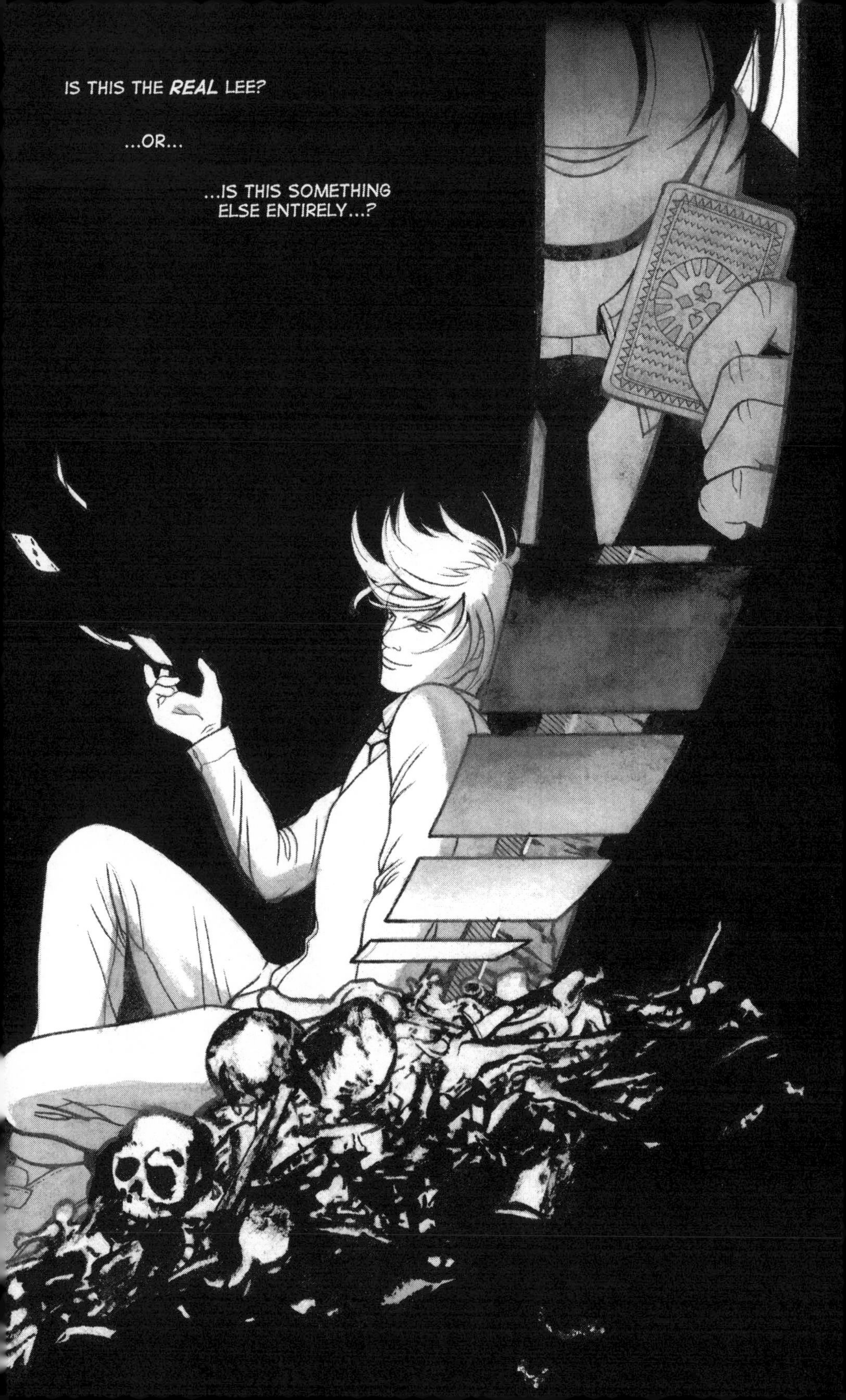
IS THIS THE *REAL* LEE?
...OR...
...IS THIS SOMETHING ELSE ENTIRELY...?

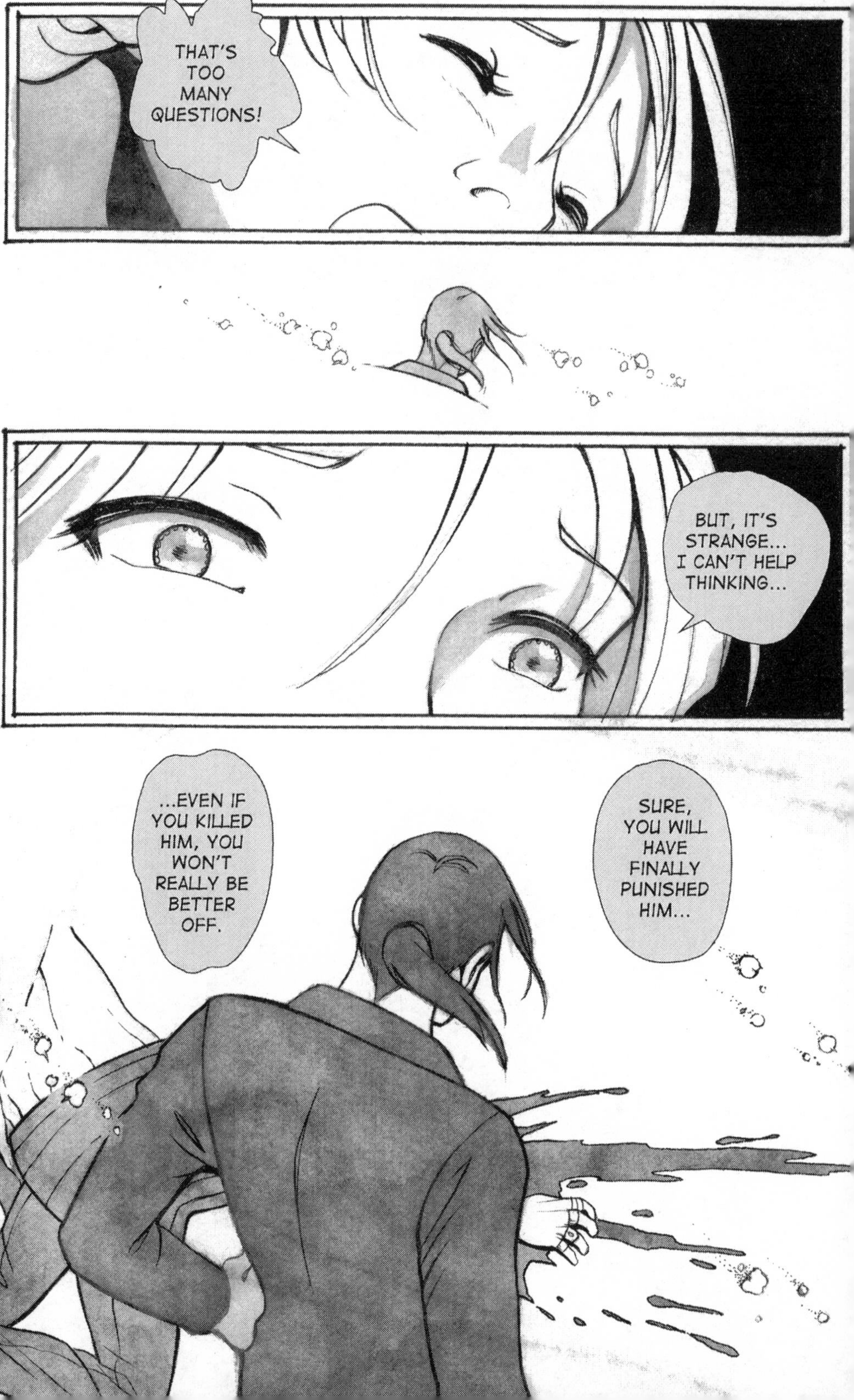
THAT'S TOO MANY QUESTIONS!
BUT, IT'S STRANGE... I CAN'T HELP THINKING...
SURE, YOU WILL HAVE FINALLY PUNISHED HIM...
...EVEN IF YOU KILLED HIM, YOU WON'T REALLY BE BETTER OFF.

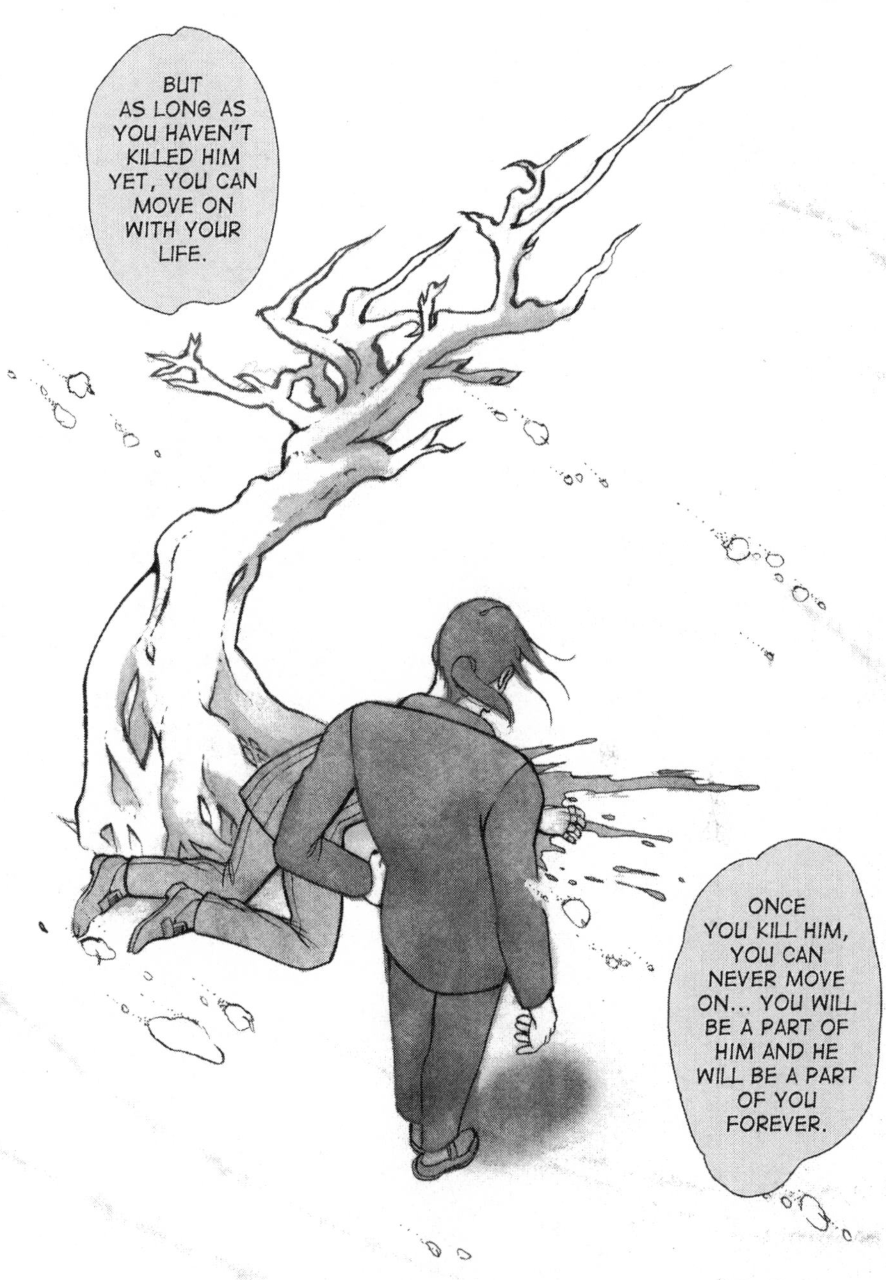
BUT AS LONG AS YOU HAVEN'T KILLED HIM YET, YOU CAN MOVE ON WITH YOUR LIFE.
ONCE YOU KILL HIM, YOU CAN NEVER MOVE ON... YOU WILL BE A PART OF HIM AND HE WILL BE A PART OF YOU FOREVER.

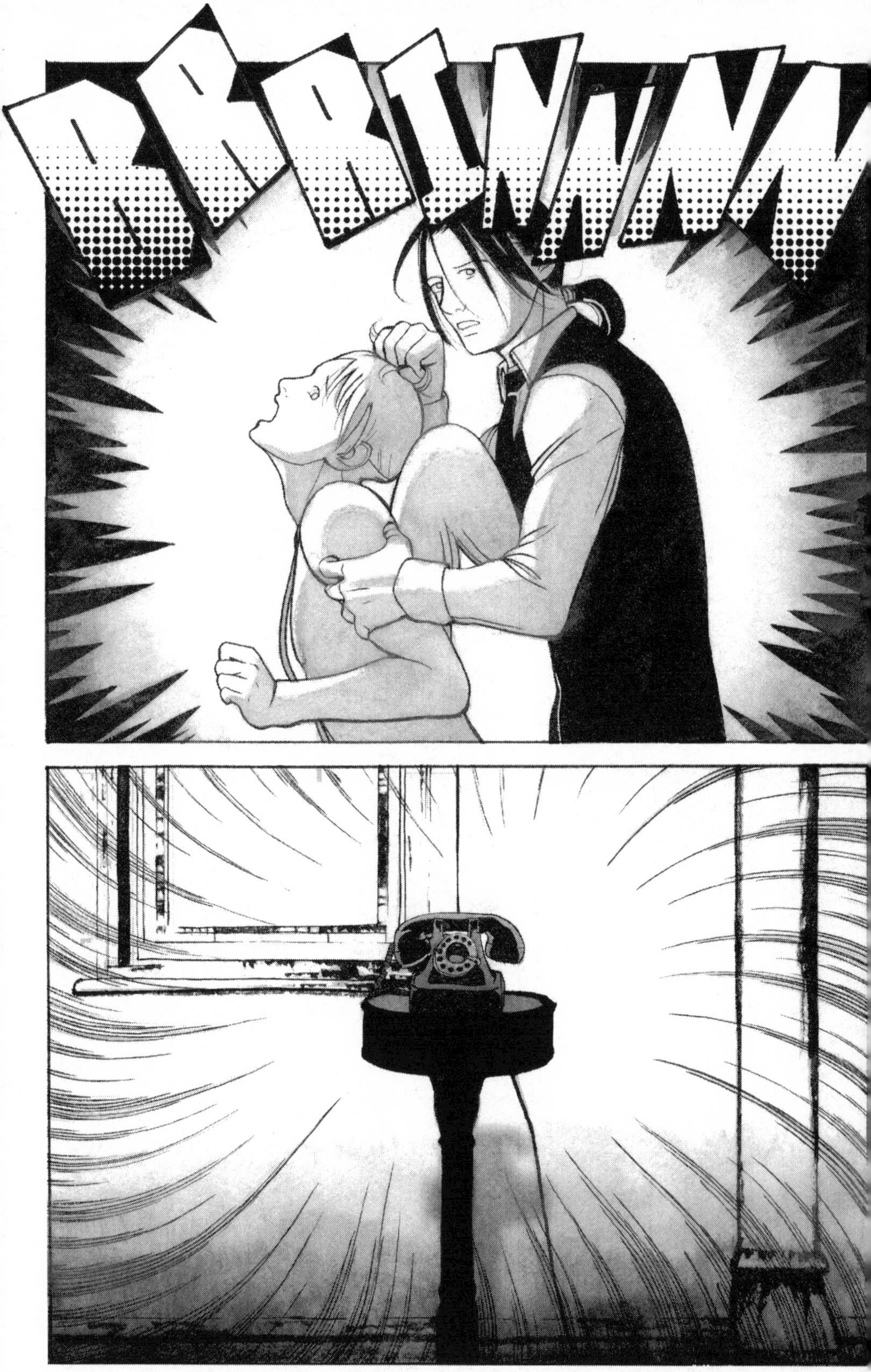
BRRINNN

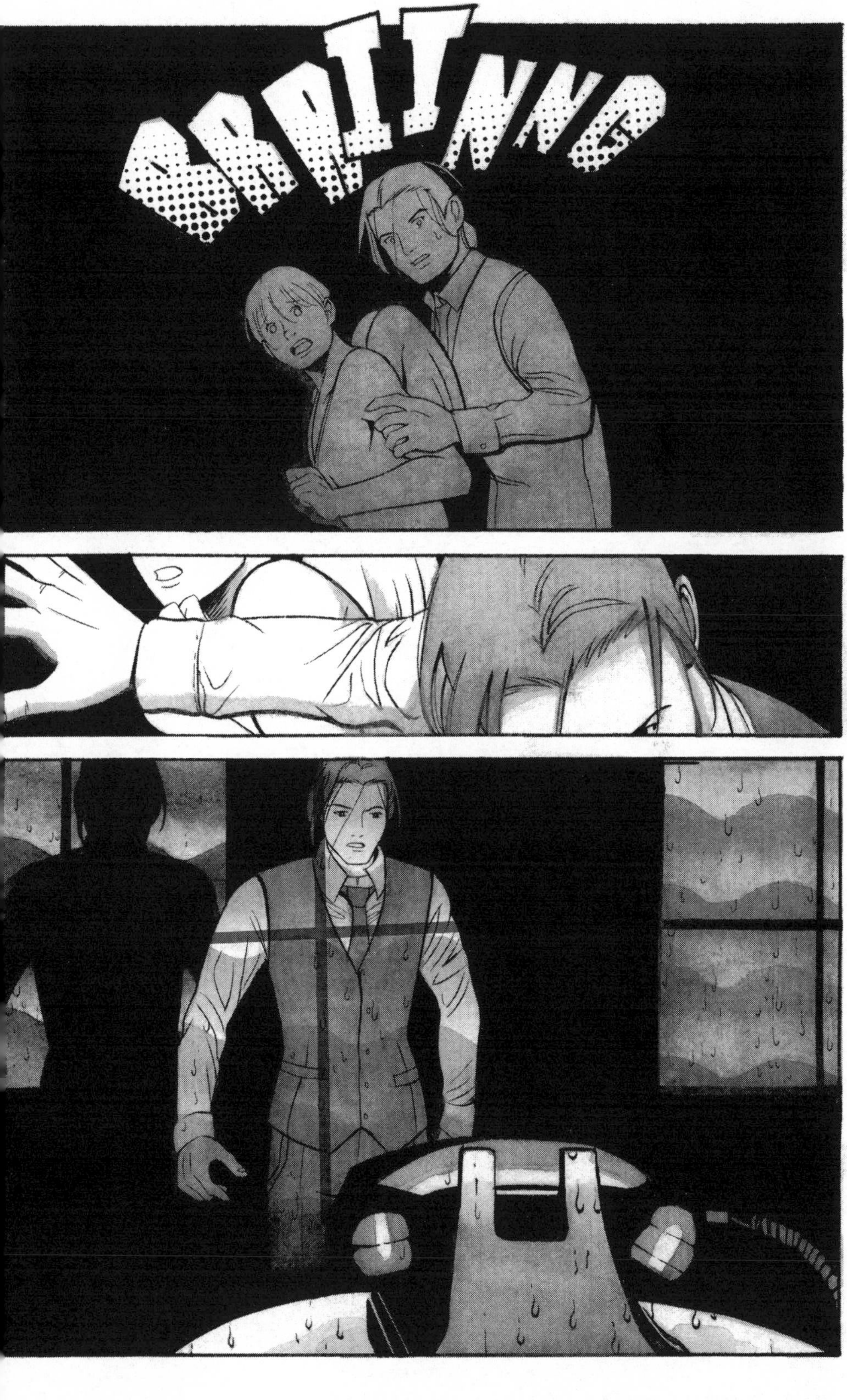
BRRIINNG

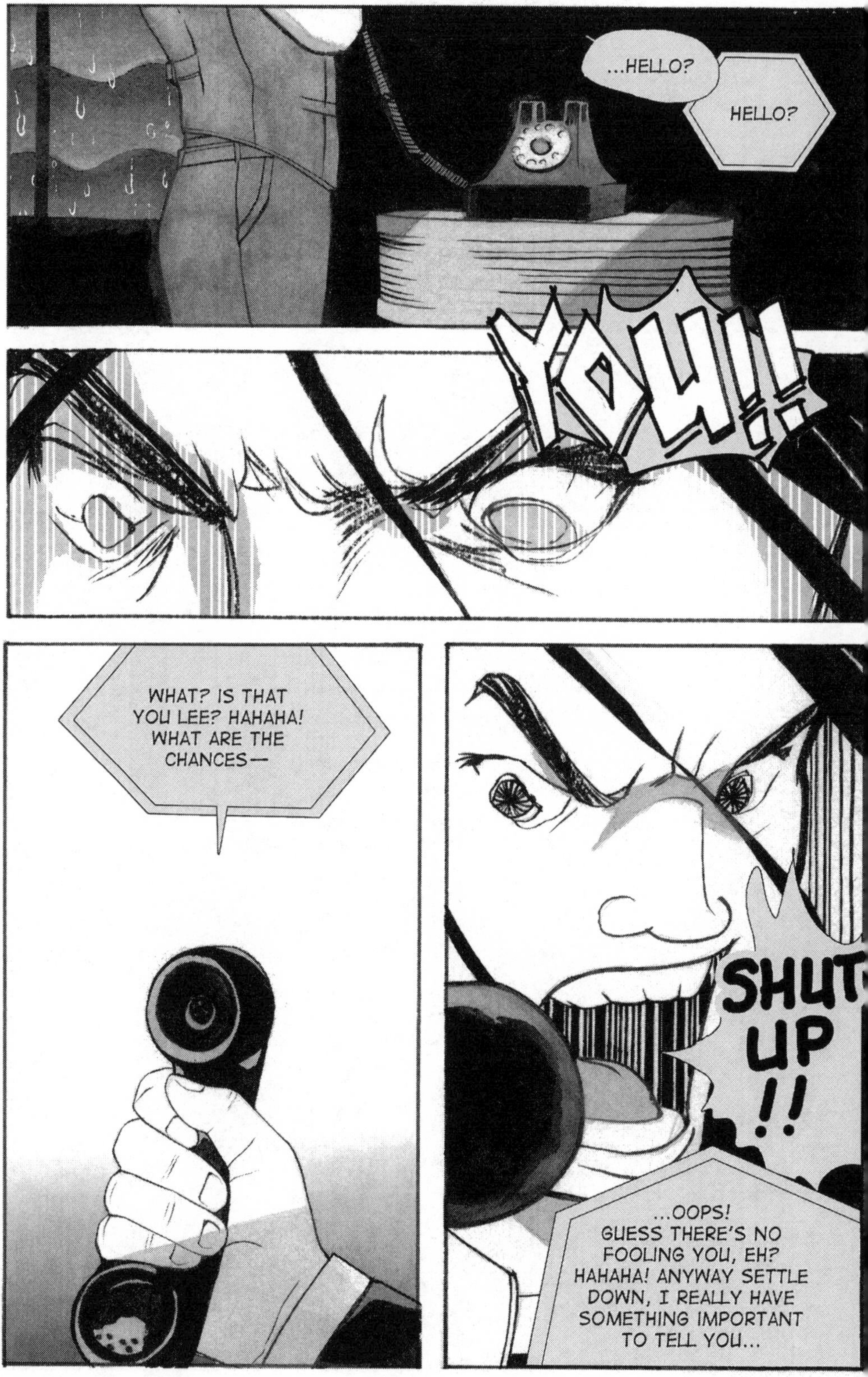
...HELLO?
HELLO?
YOU!!
WHAT? IS THAT YOU LEE? HAHAHA! WHAT ARE THE CHANCES—
SHUT UP!!
...OOPS! GUESS THERE'S NO FOOLING YOU, EH? HAHAHA! ANYWAY SETTLE DOWN, I REALLY HAVE SOMETHING IMPORTANT TO TELL YOU...

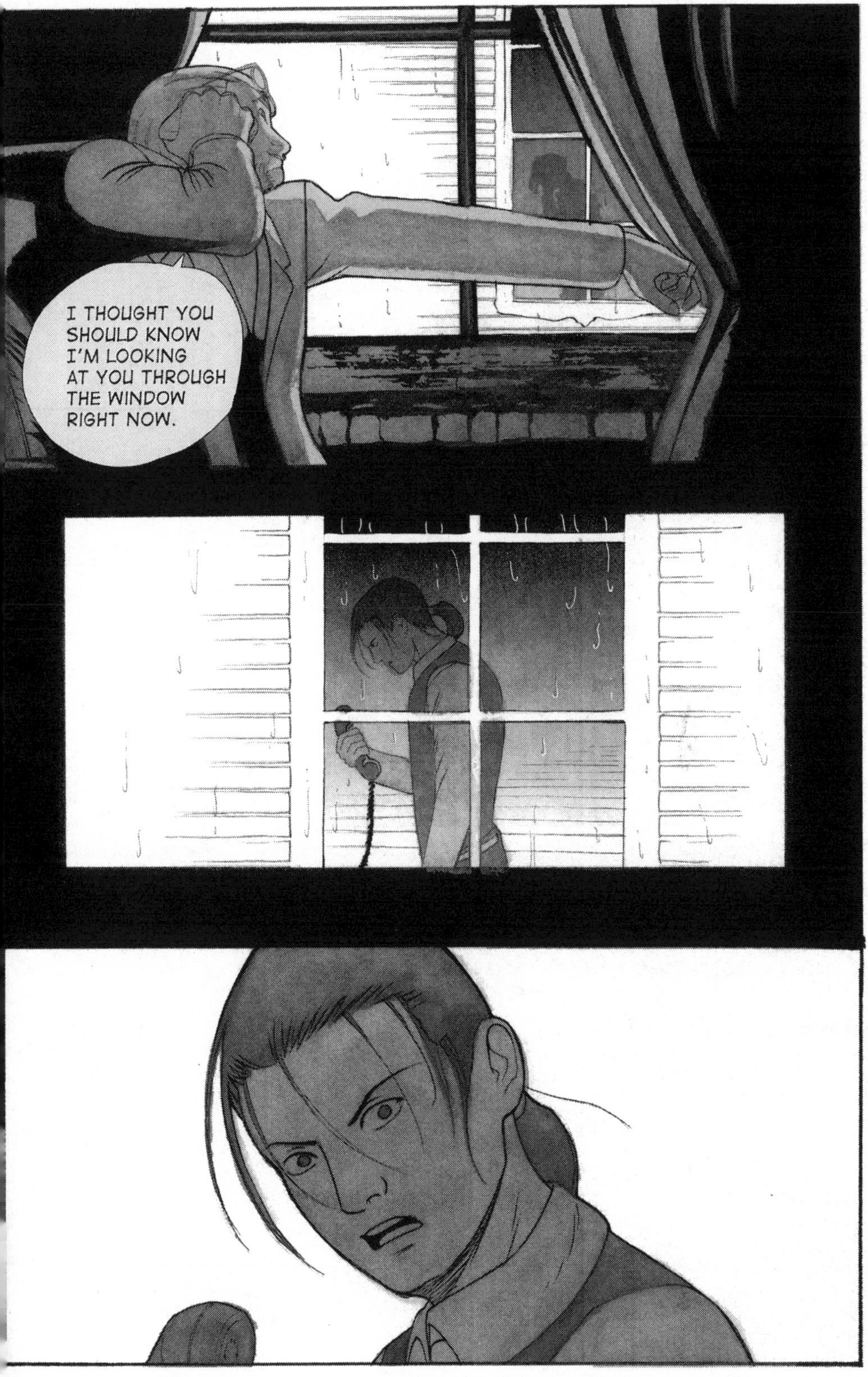
I THOUGHT YOU SHOULD KNOW I'M LOOKING AT YOU THROUGH THE WINDOW RIGHT NOW.

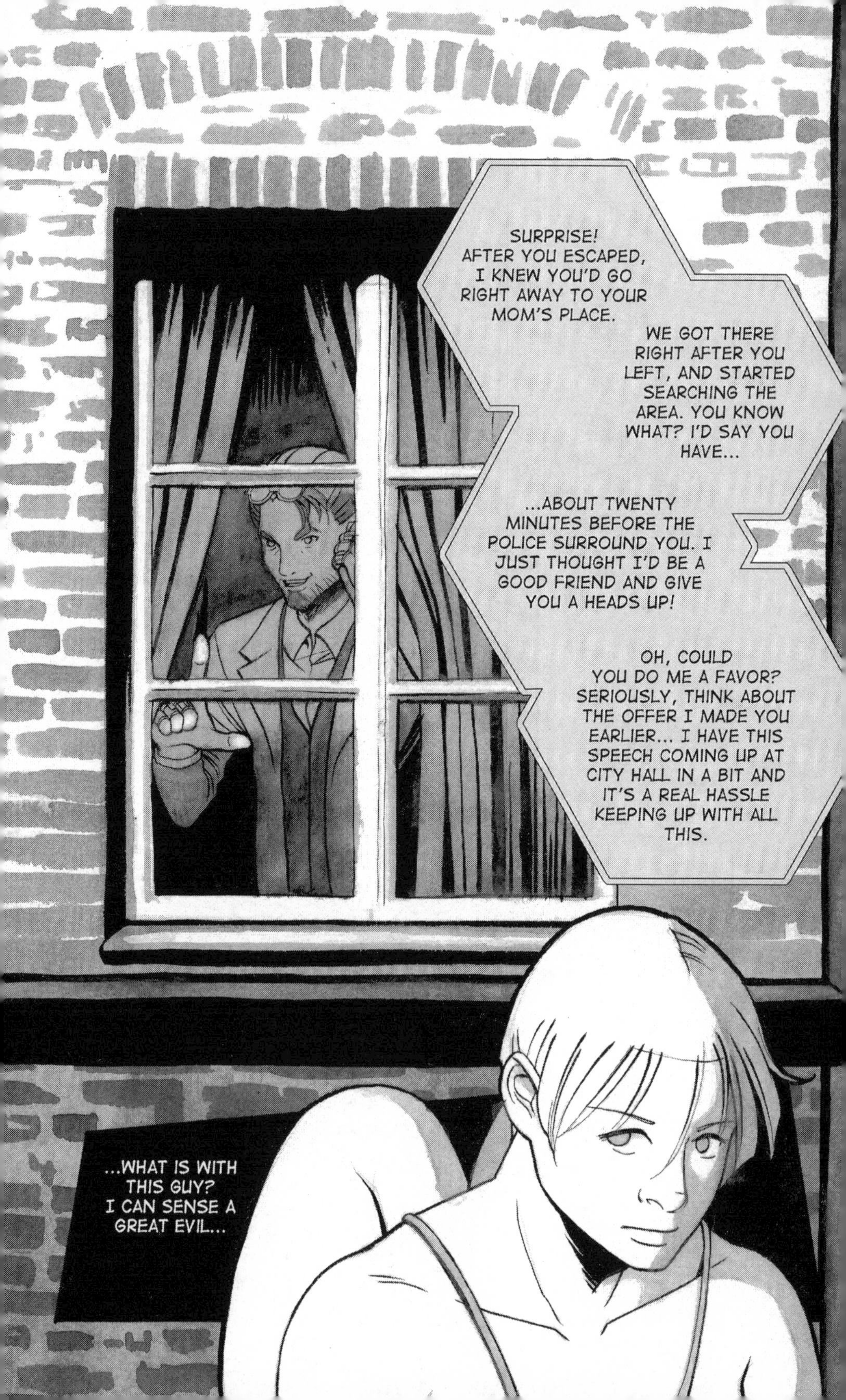
SURPRISE! AFTER YOU ESCAPED, I KNEW YOU'D GO RIGHT AWAY TO YOUR MOM'S PLACE.
WE GOT THERE RIGHT AFTER YOU LEFT, AND STARTED SEARCHING THE AREA. YOU KNOW WHAT? I'D SAY YOU HAVE...
...ABOUT TWENTY MINUTES BEFORE THE POLICE SURROUND YOU. I JUST THOUGHT I'D BE A GOOD FRIEND AND GIVE YOU A HEADS UP!
OH, COULD YOU DO ME A FAVOR? SERIOUSLY, THINK ABOUT THE OFFER I MADE YOU EARLIER... I HAVE THIS SPEECH COMING UP AT CITY HALL IN A BIT AND IT'S A REAL HASSLE KEEPING UP WITH ALL THIS.
...WHAT IS WITH THIS GUY? I CAN SENSE A GREAT EVIL...

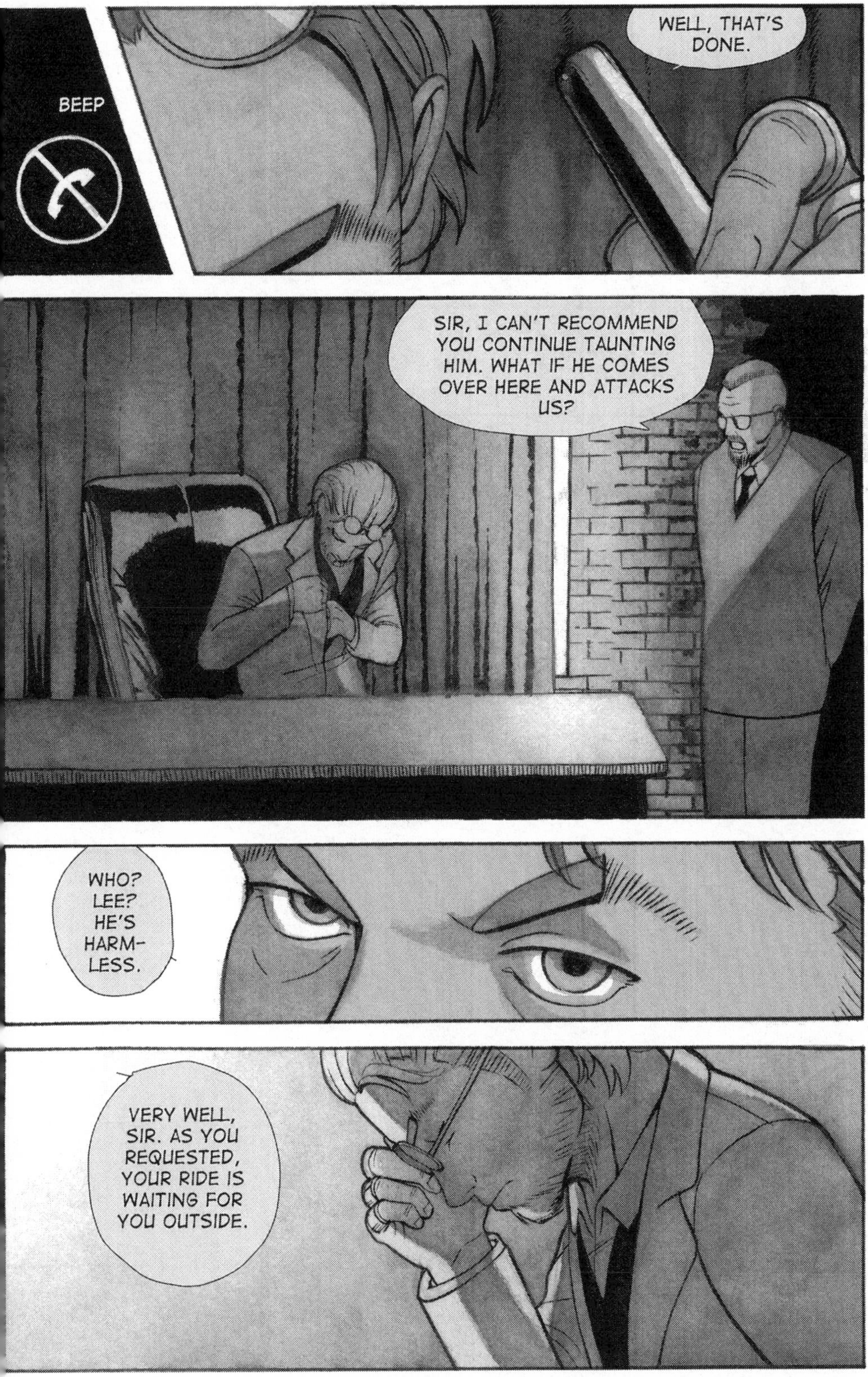
BEEP
WELL, THAT'S DONE.
SIR, I CAN'T RECOMMEND YOU CONTINUE TAUNTING HIM. WHAT IF HE COMES OVER HERE AND ATTACKS US?
WHO? LEE? HE'S HARM-LESS.
VERY WELL, SIR. AS YOU REQUESTED, YOUR RIDE IS WAITING FOR YOU OUTSIDE.

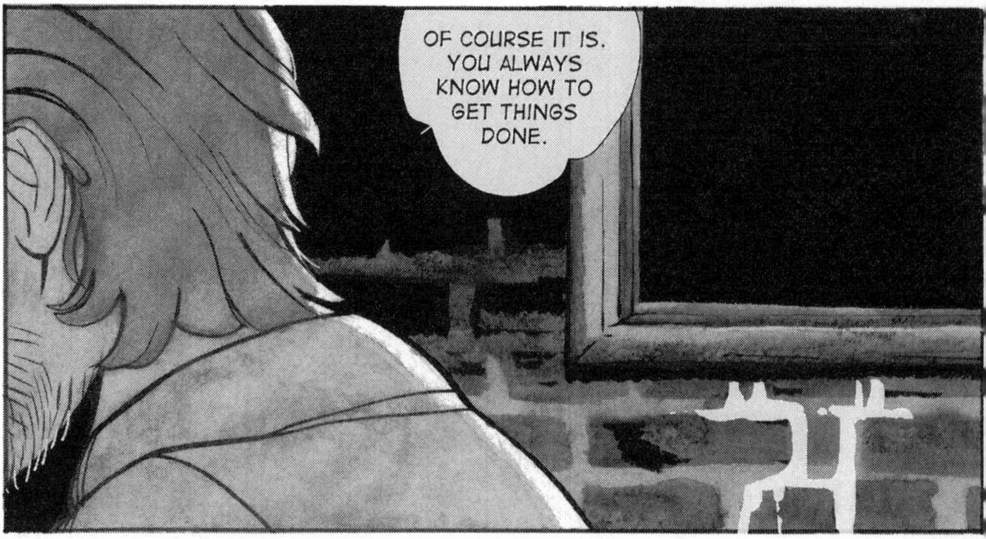
OF COURSE IT IS. YOU ALWAYS KNOW HOW TO GET THINGS DONE.

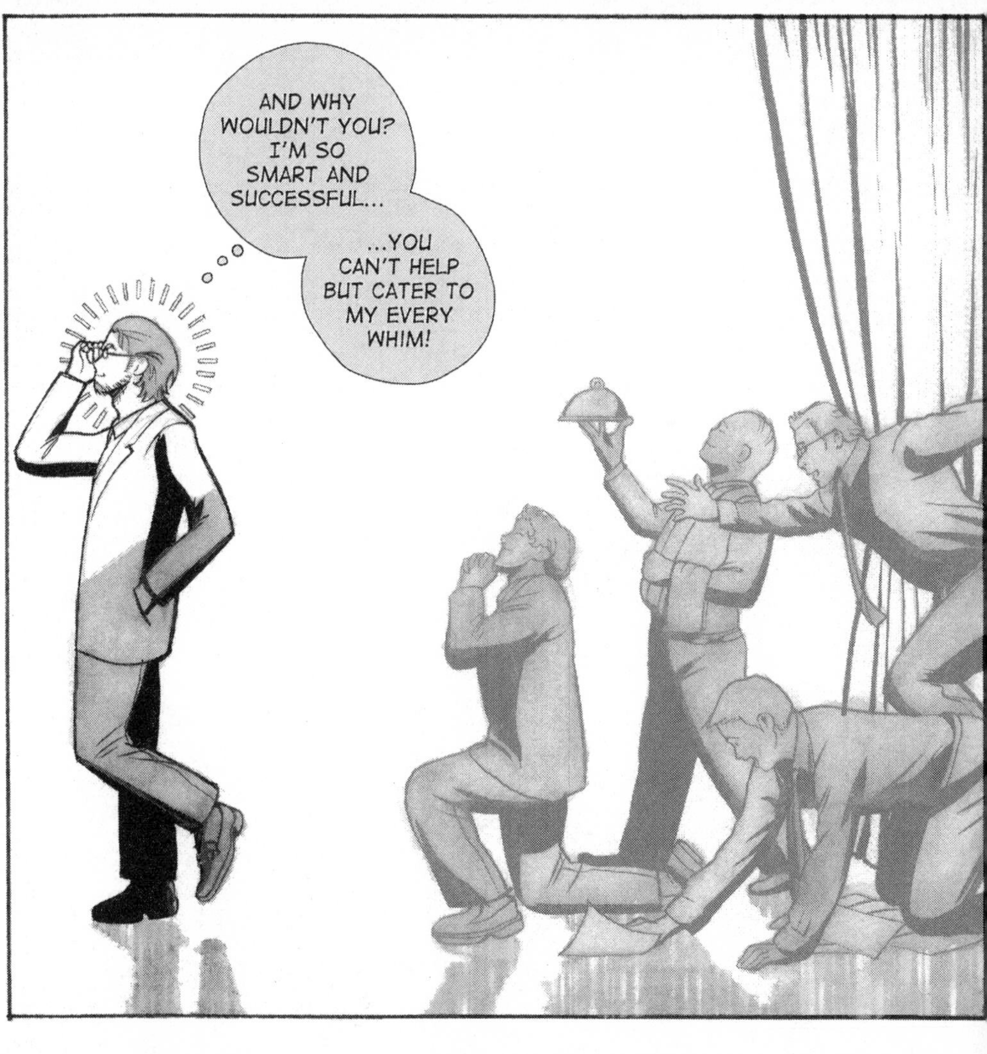
AND WHY WOULDN'T YOU? I'M SO SMART AND SUCCESSFUL...
...YOU CAN'T HELP BUT CATER TO MY EVERY WHIM!

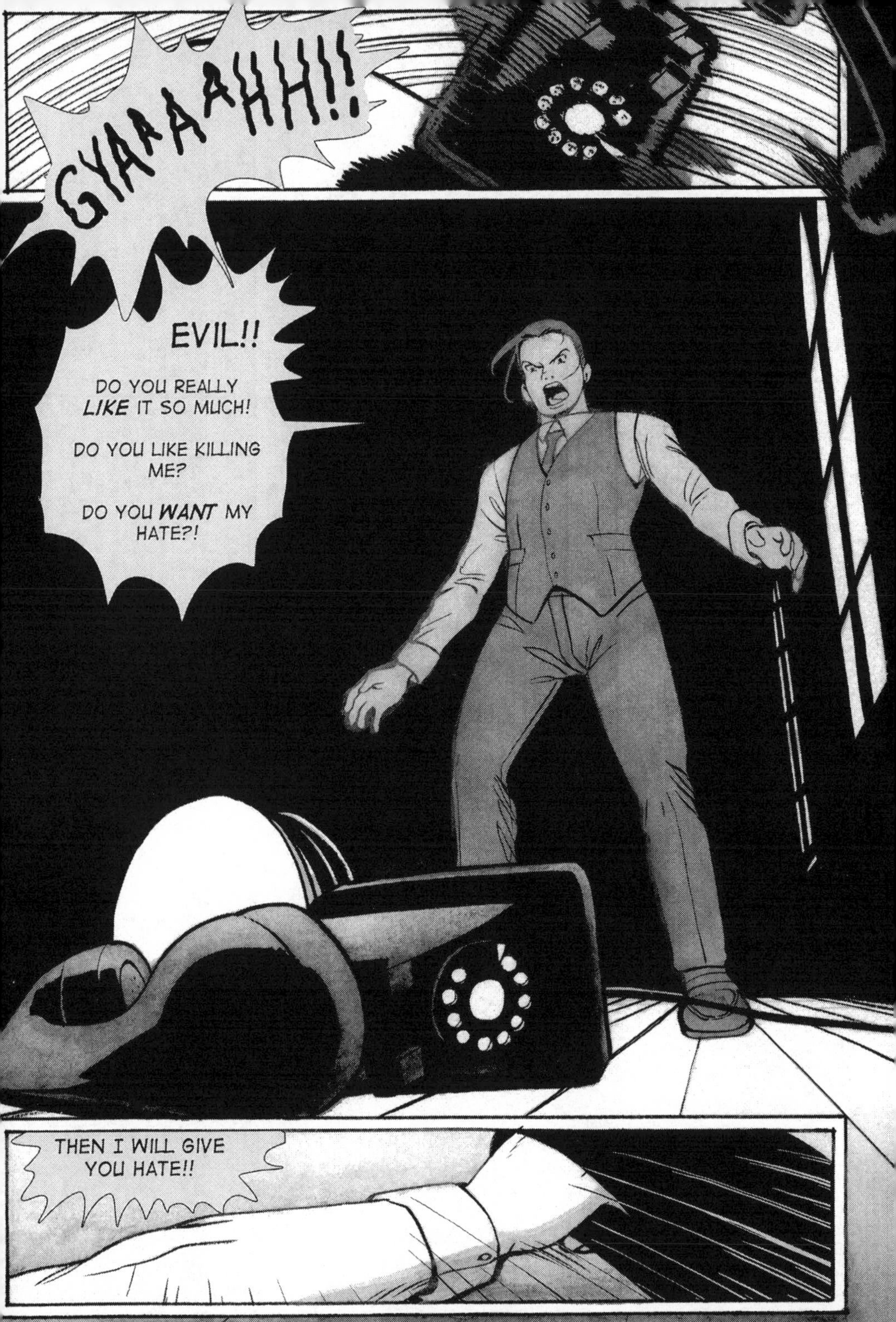
GYAAAHH!!
EVIL!!
DO YOU REALLY LIKE IT SO MUCH!
DO YOU LIKE KILLING ME?
DO YOU WANT MY HATE?!
THEN I WILL GIVE YOU HATE!!

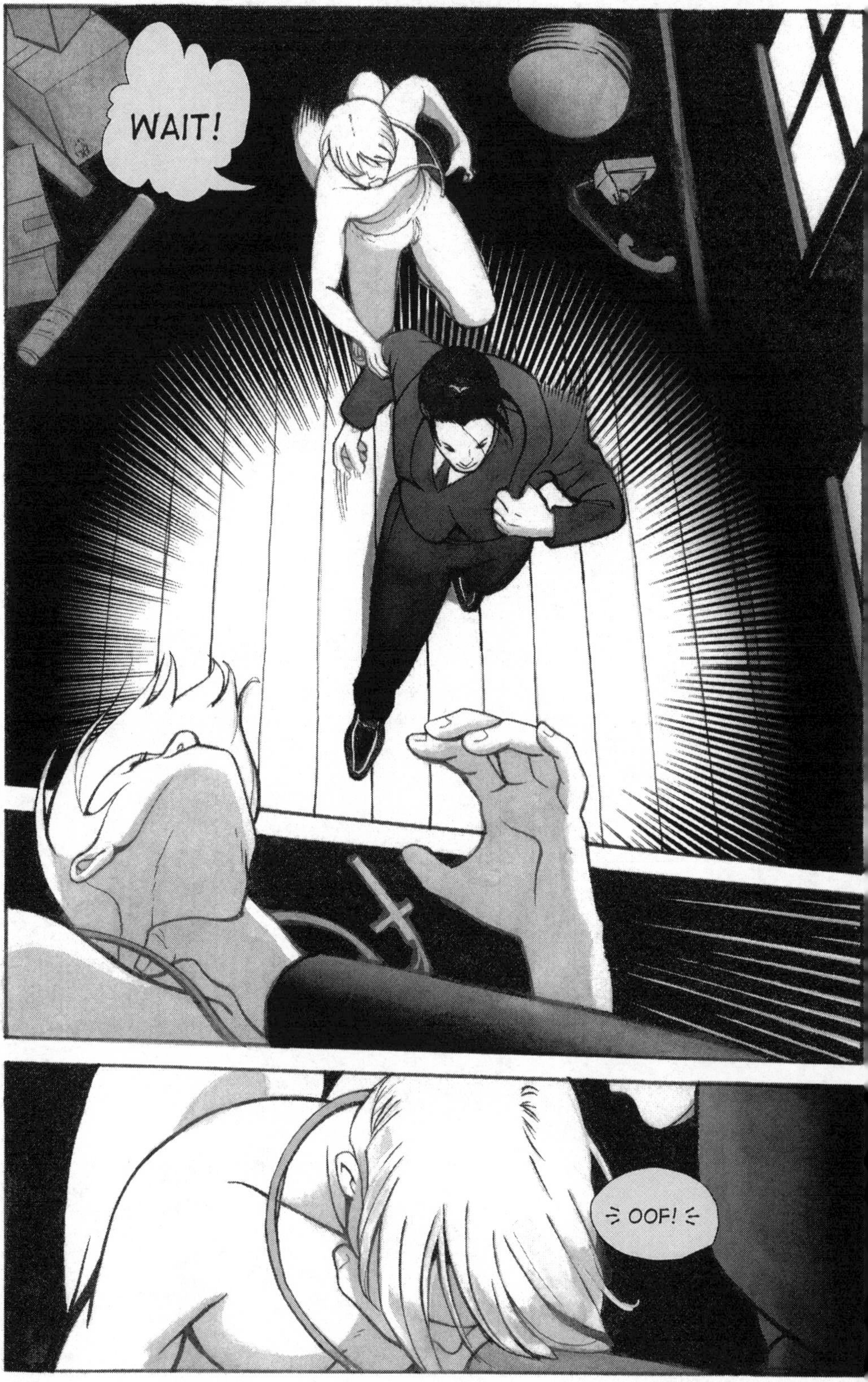
WAIT!
OOF!

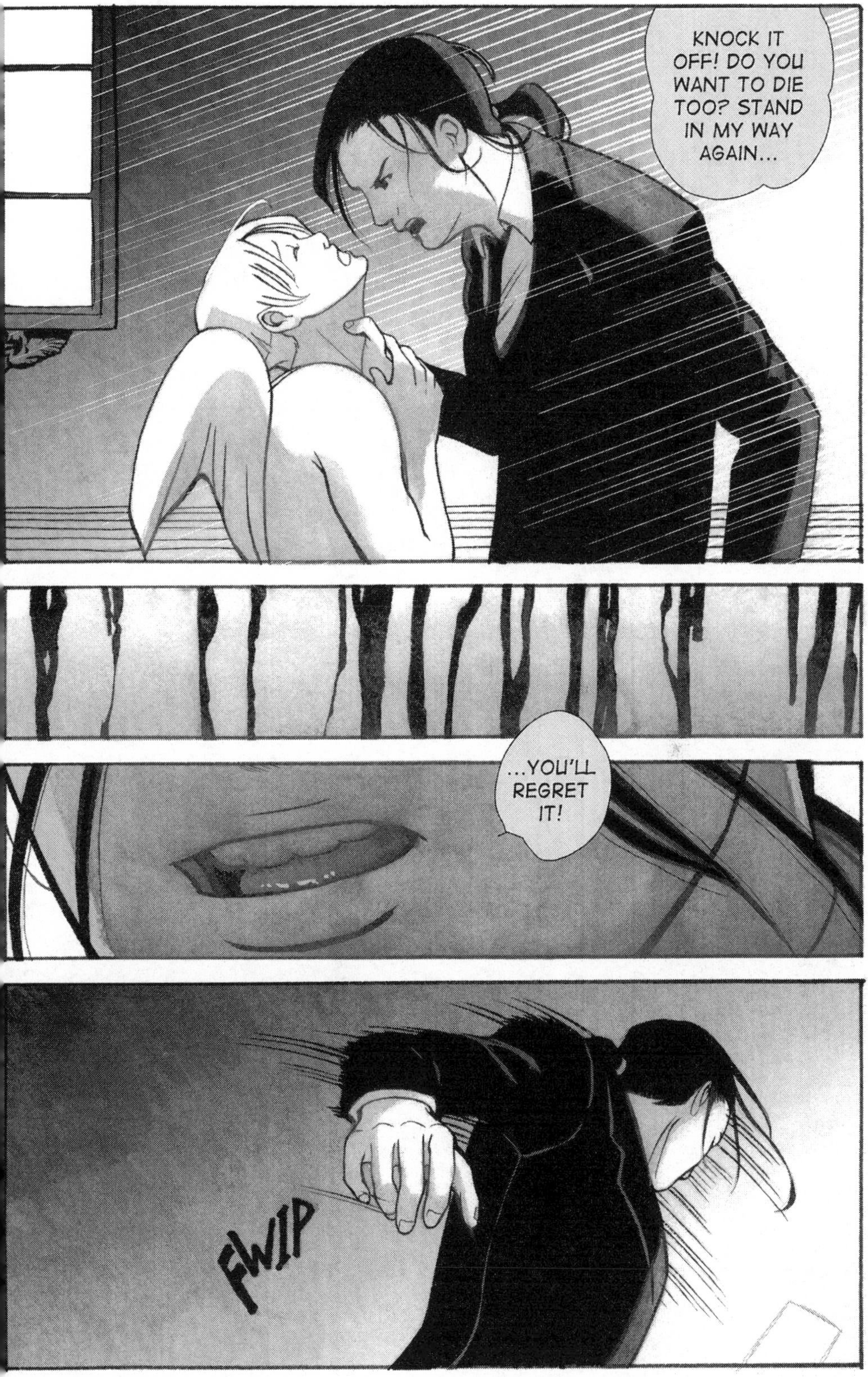
KNOCK IT OFF! DO YOU WANT TO DIE TOO? STAND IN MY WAY AGAIN...
...YOU'LL REGRET IT!
FWIP

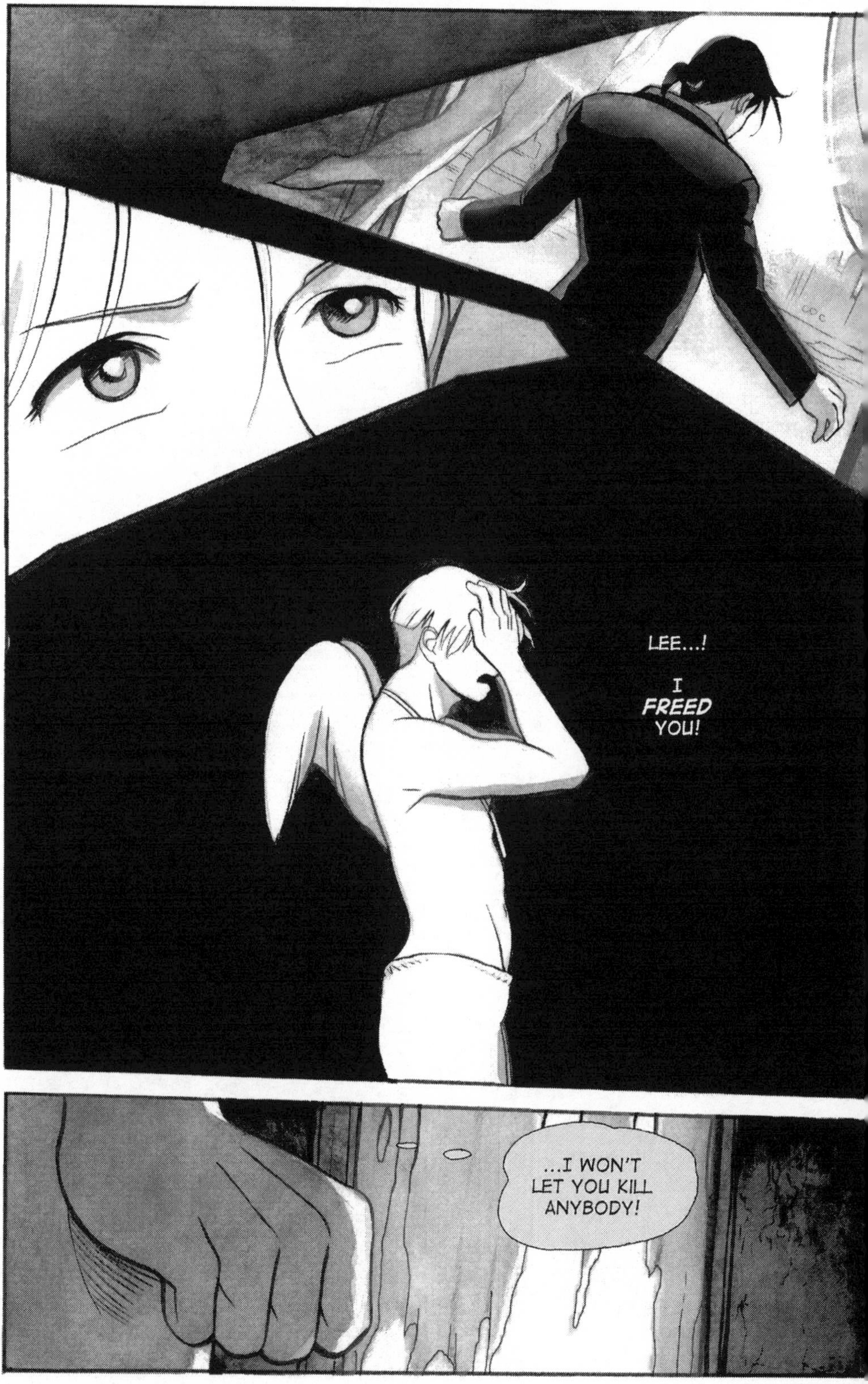
LEE...!
I *FREED* YOU!
...I WON'T LET YOU KILL ANYBODY!

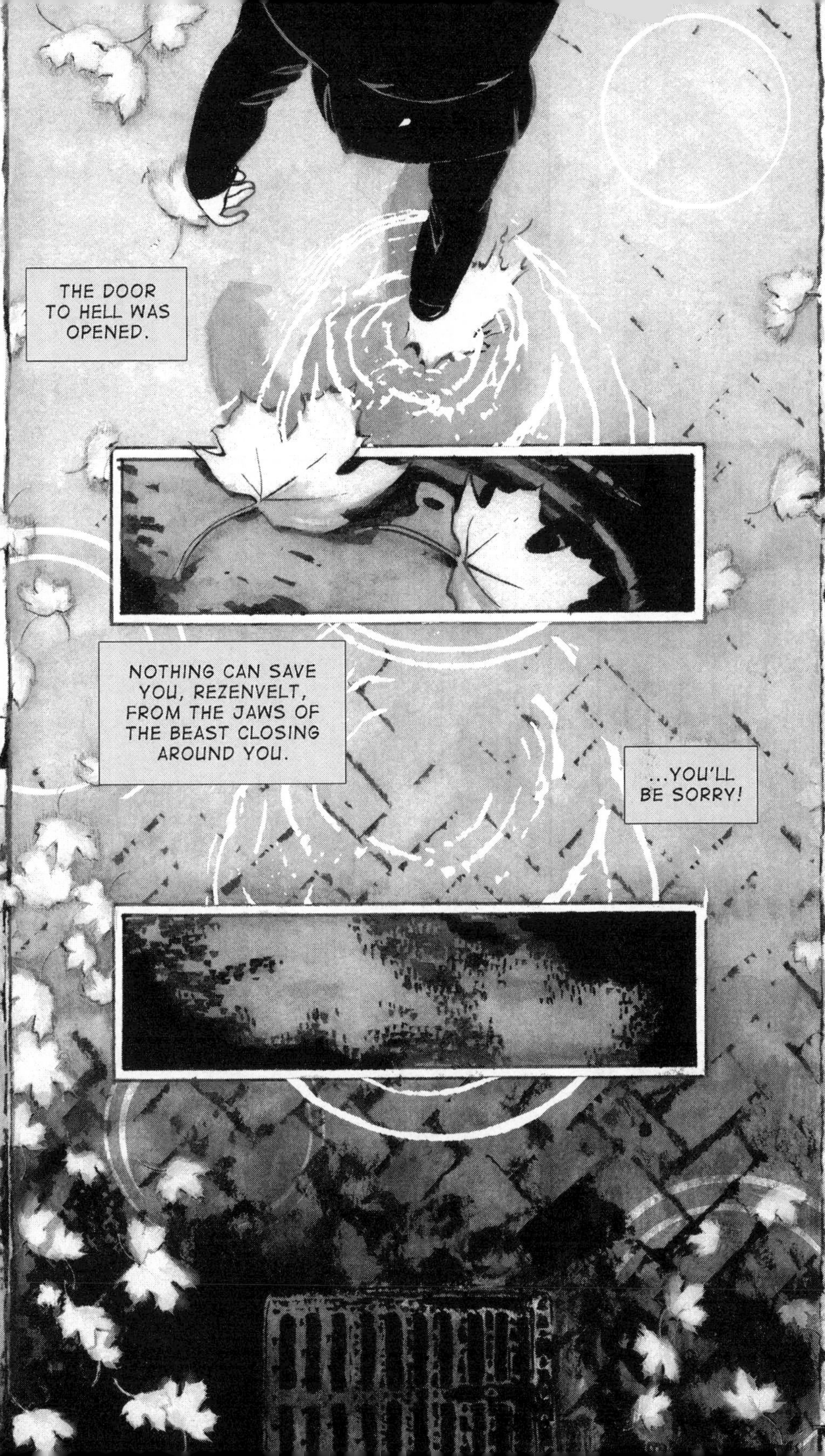
THE DOOR TO HELL WAS OPENED.
NOTHING CAN SAVE YOU, REZENVELT, FROM THE JAWS OF THE BEAST CLOSING AROUND YOU.
...YOU'LL BE SORRY!

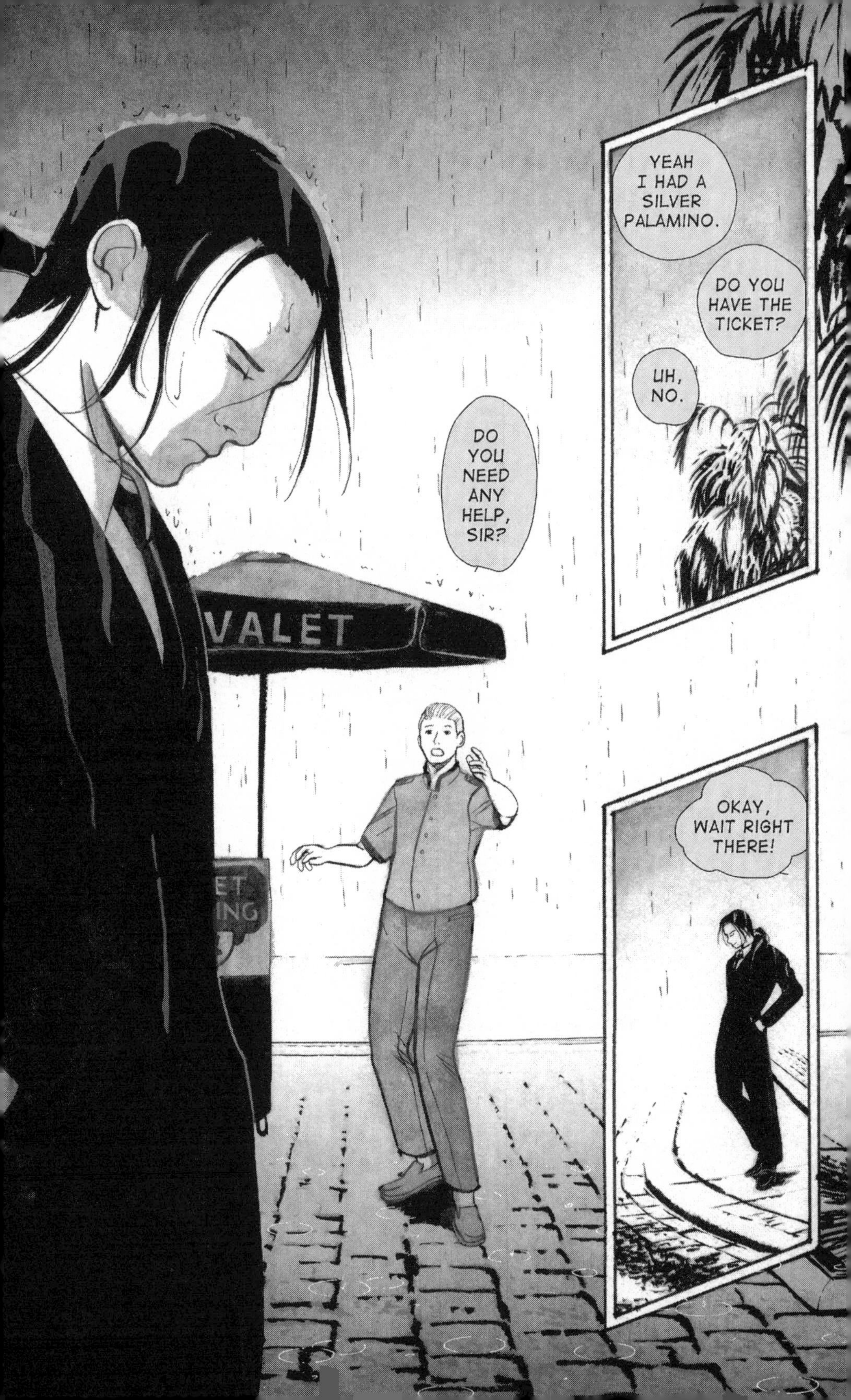
VALET
DO YOU NEED ANY HELP, SIR?
YEAH I HAD A SILVER PALAMINO.
DO YOU HAVE THE TICKET?
UH, NO.
OKAY, WAIT RIGHT THERE!

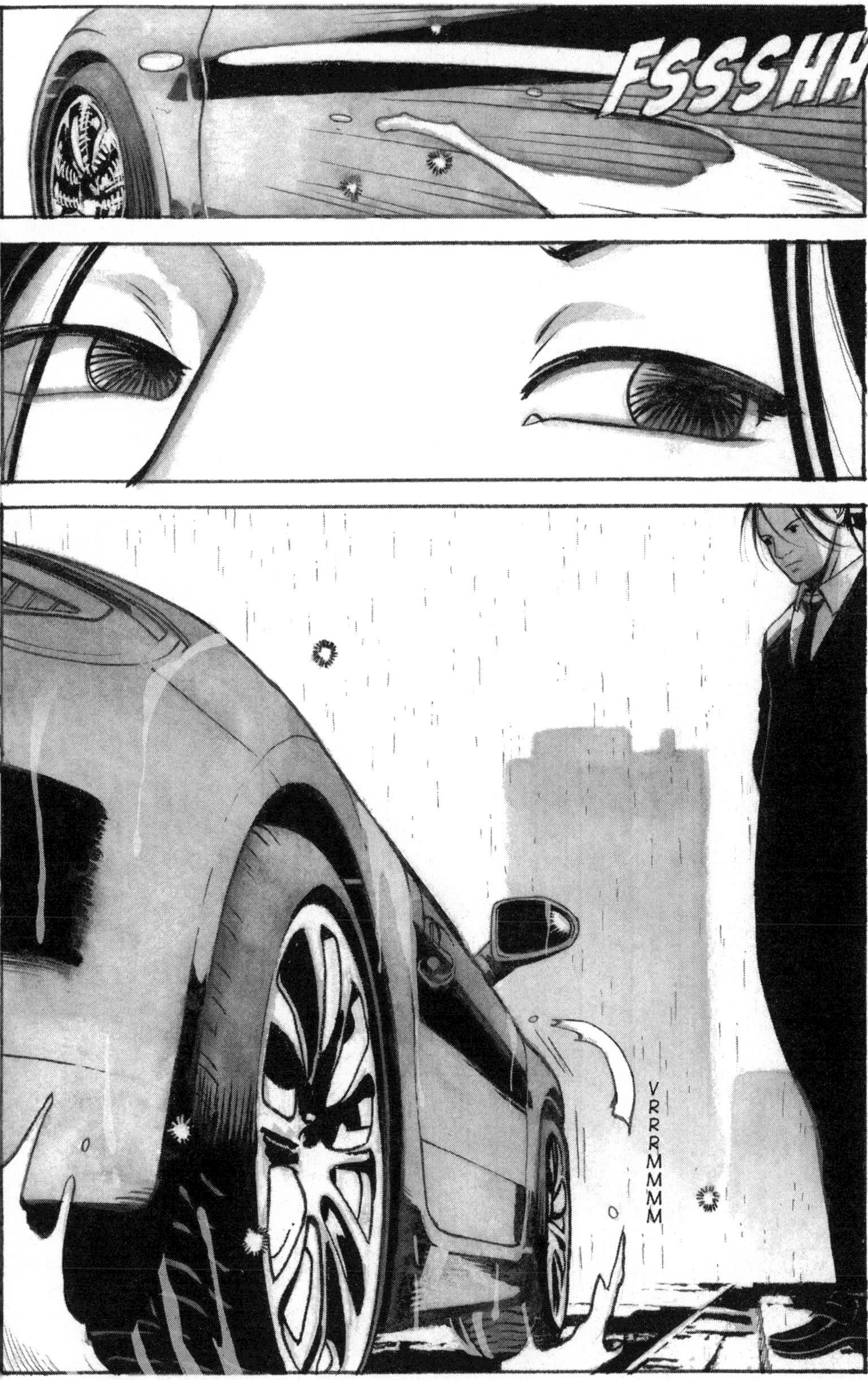
FSSSHH
VRRRMMMM

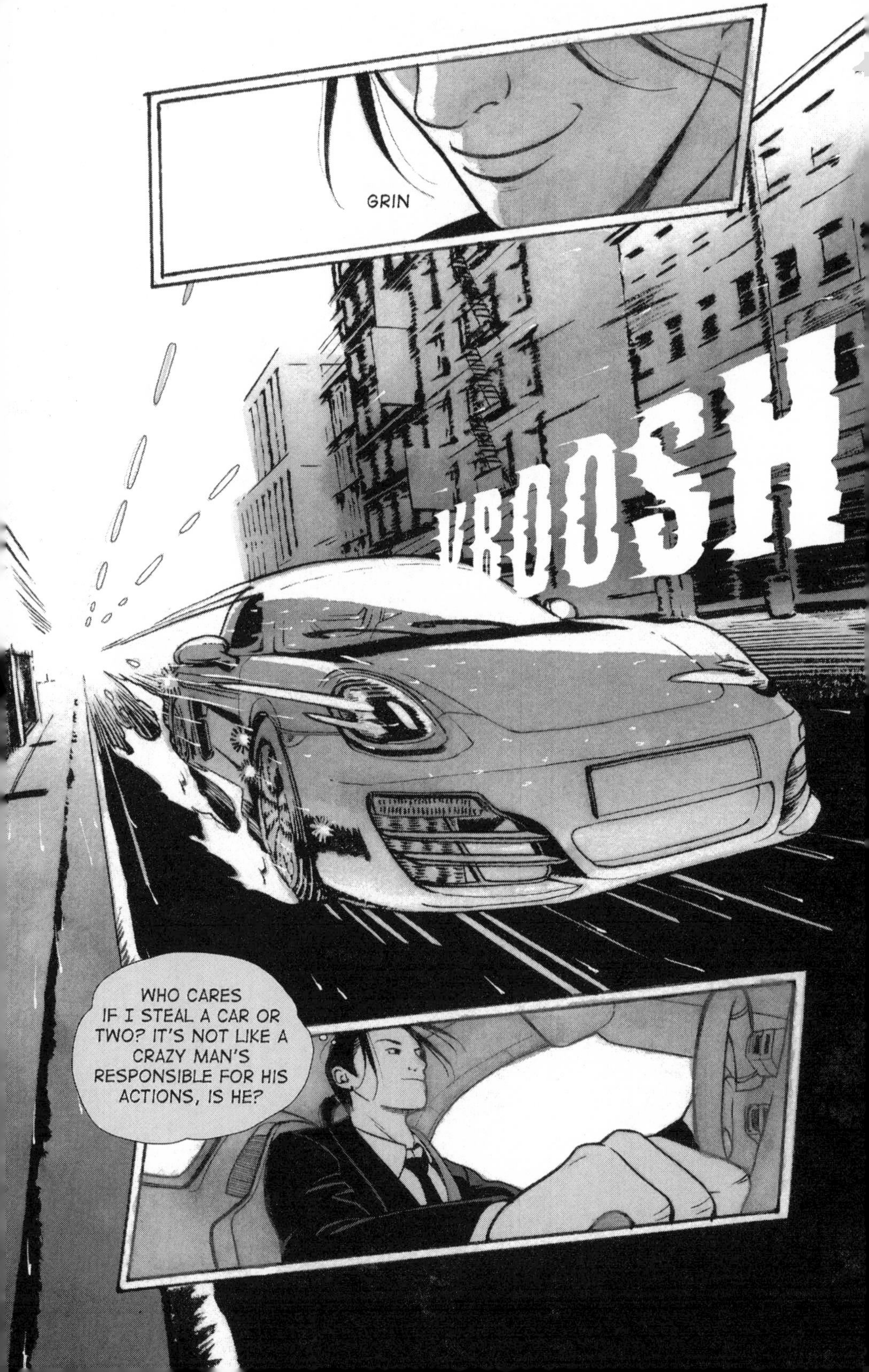
GRIN
VROOSH
WHO CARES IF I STEAL A CAR OR TWO? IT'S NOT LIKE A CRAZY MAN'S RESPONSIBLE FOR HIS ACTIONS, IS HE?

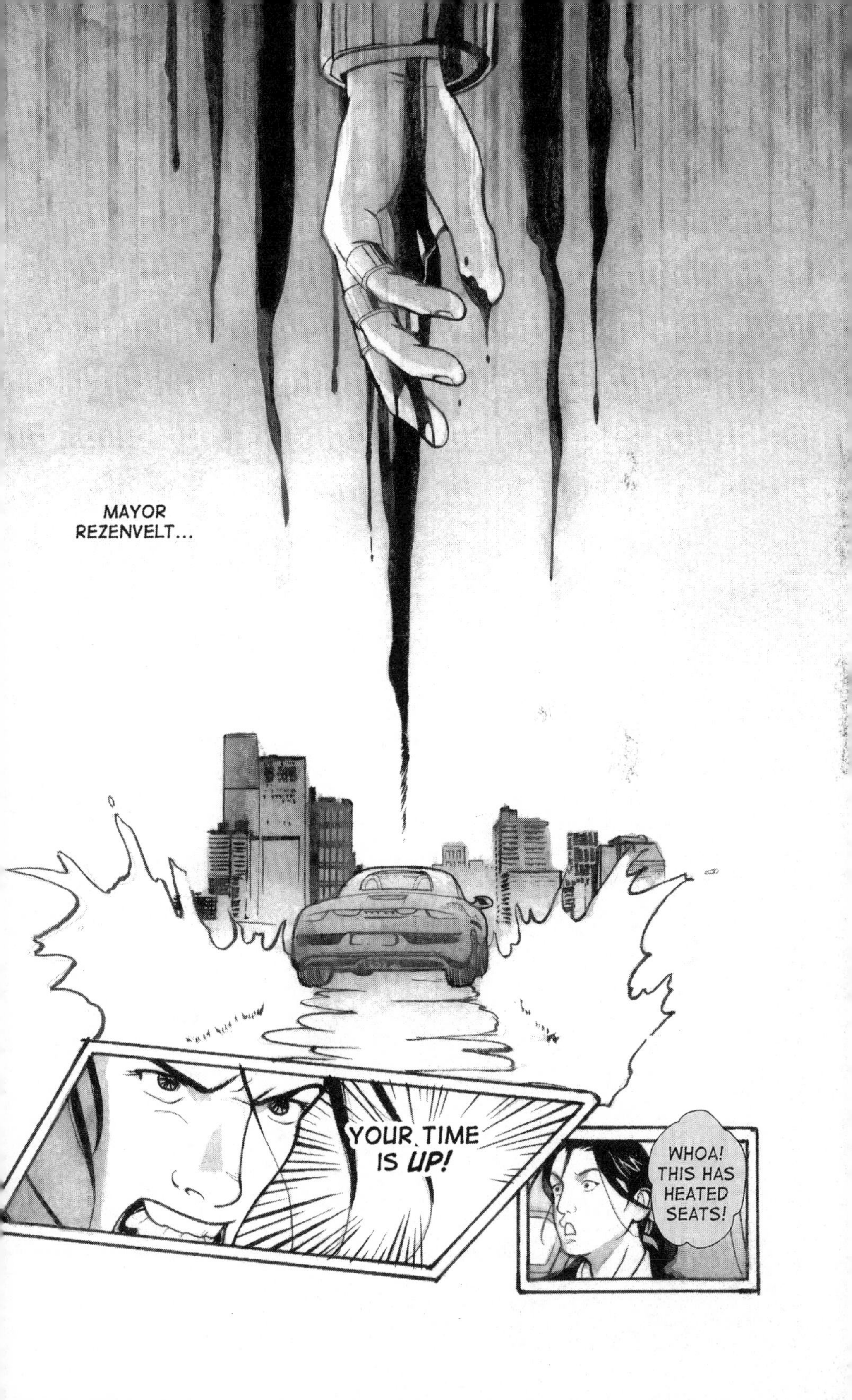
MAYOR REZENVELT...
YOUR TIME IS UP!
WHOA! THIS HAS HEATED SEATS!

BURNING...
BOILING...

I CAN'T GET THERE FAST ENOUGH...

...MY RAGE TRAVELS AHEAD OF ME!

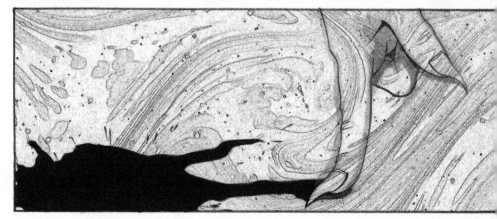

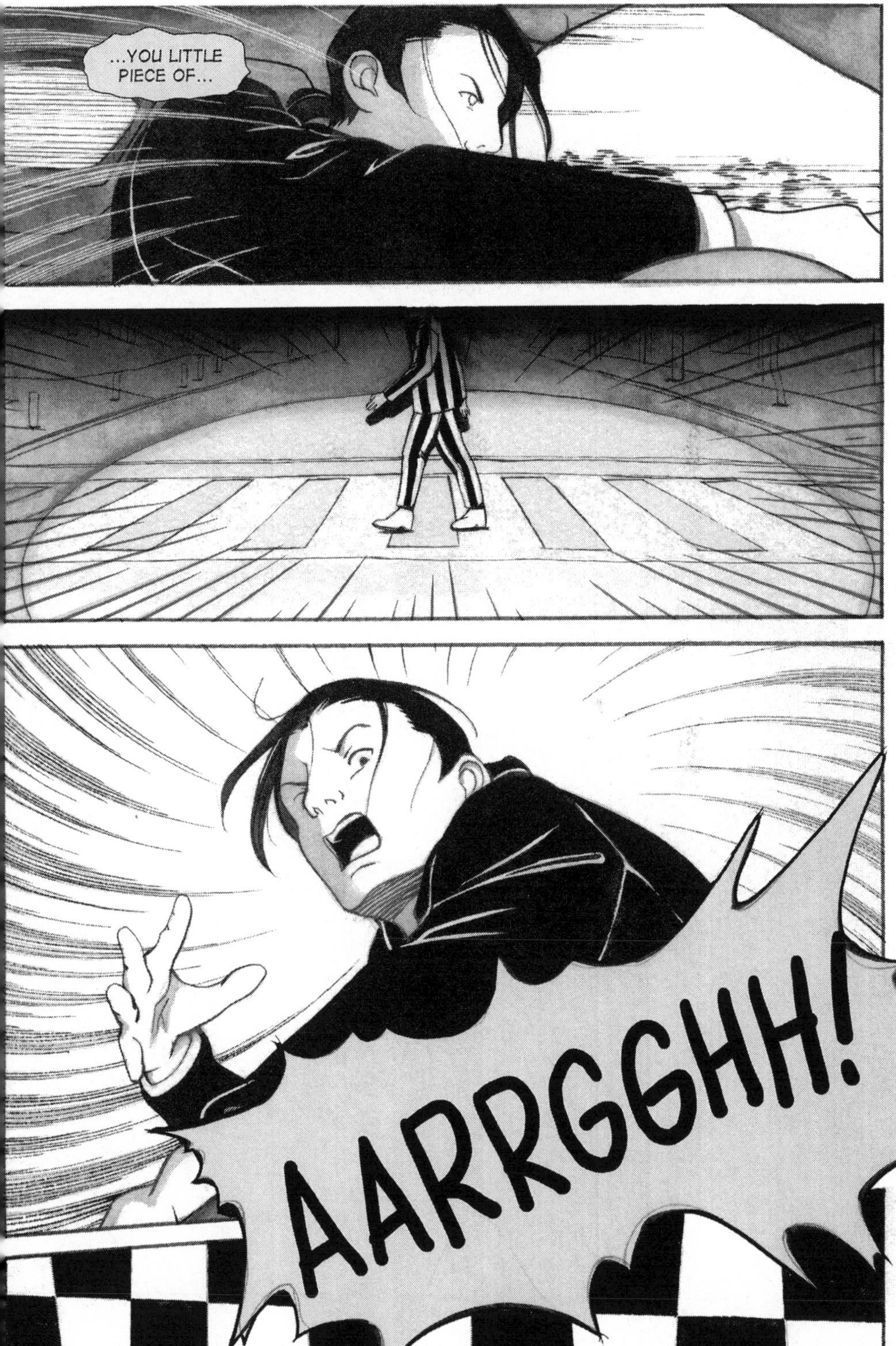
...YOU LITTLE PIECE OF...
AARRGGHH!

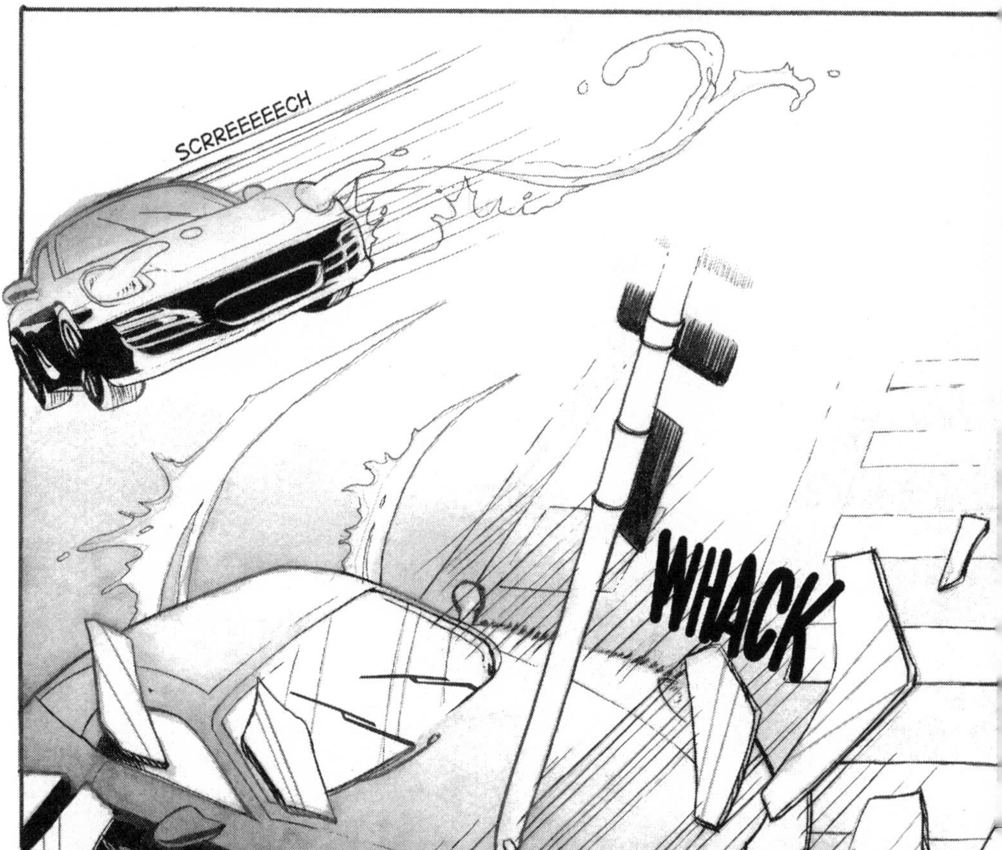
SCRREEEEECH
WHACK
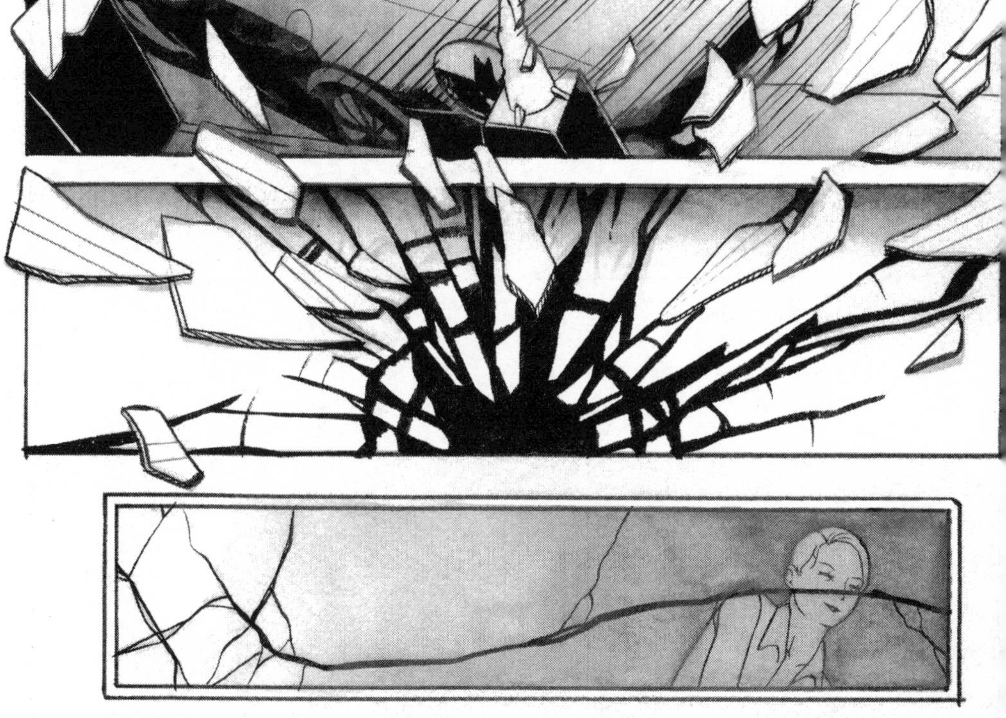

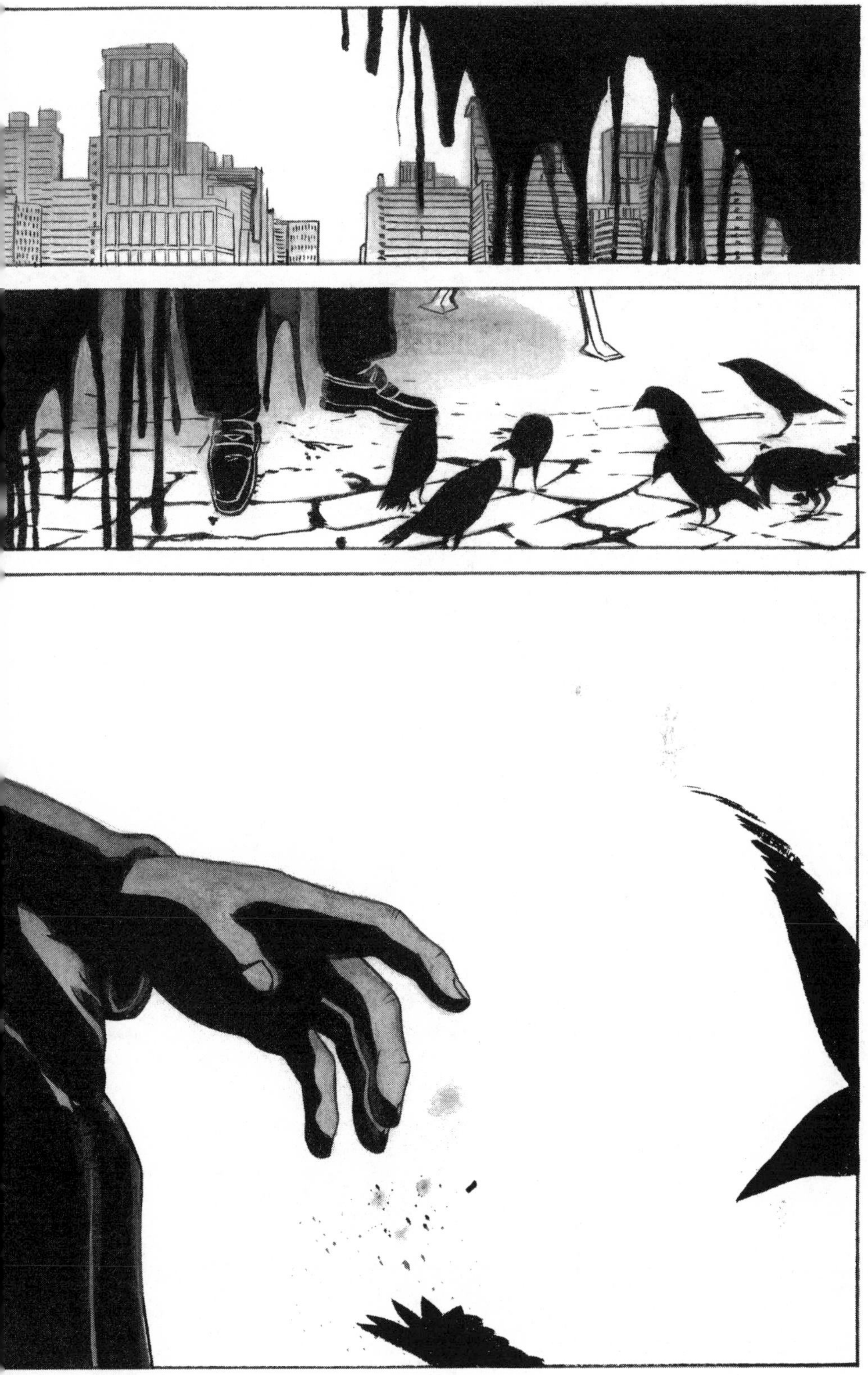

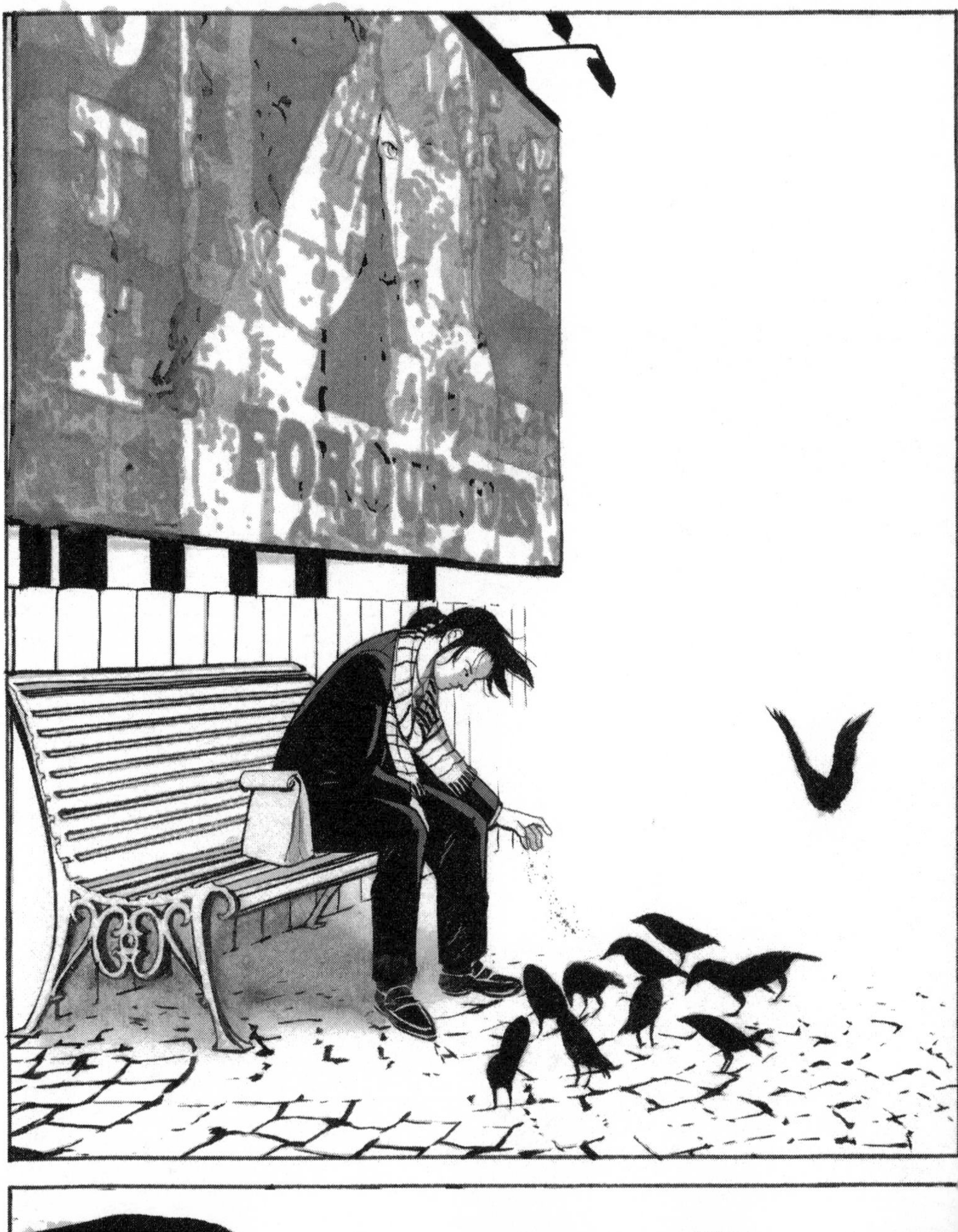
FOR OUR

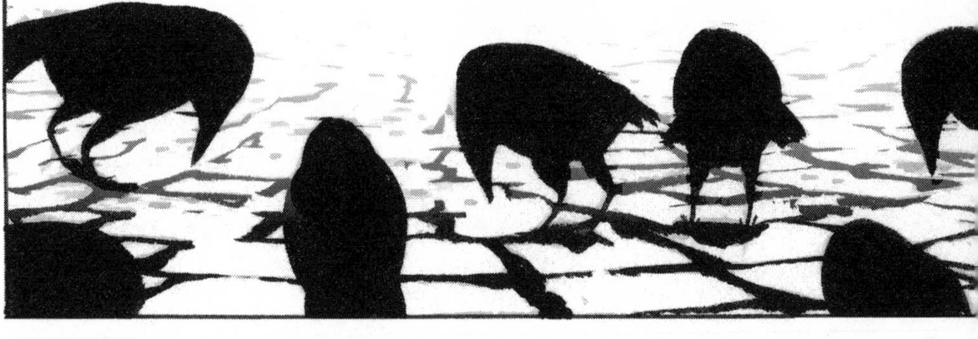

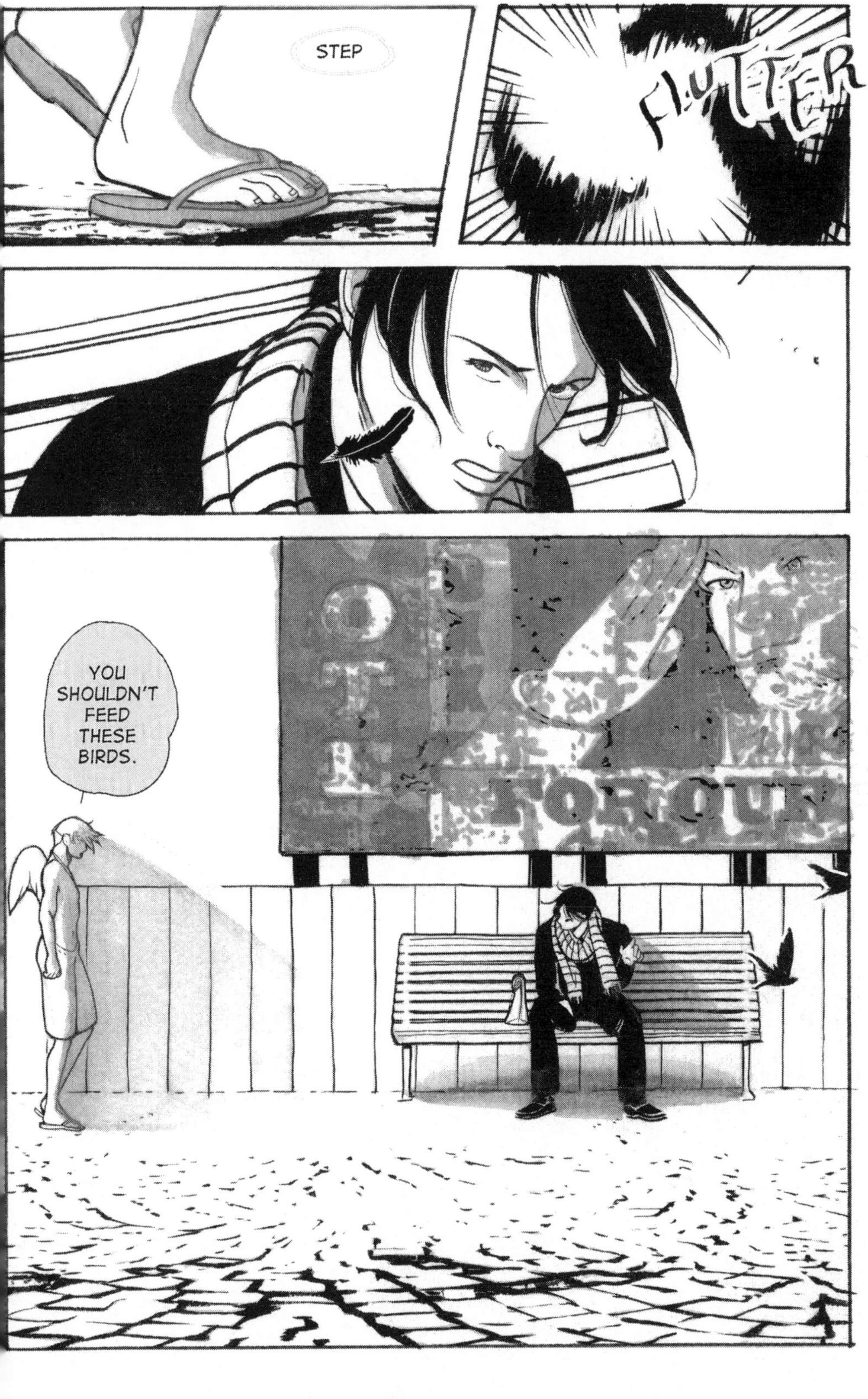
STEP
FLUTTER
YOU SHOULDN'T FEED THESE BIRDS.

OH, LEAVE ME ALONE!

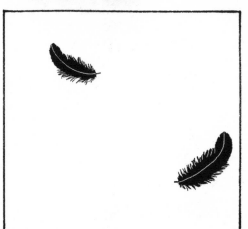

ARE YOU EVEN AWARE OF WHAT YOU ARE FEEDING THEM?

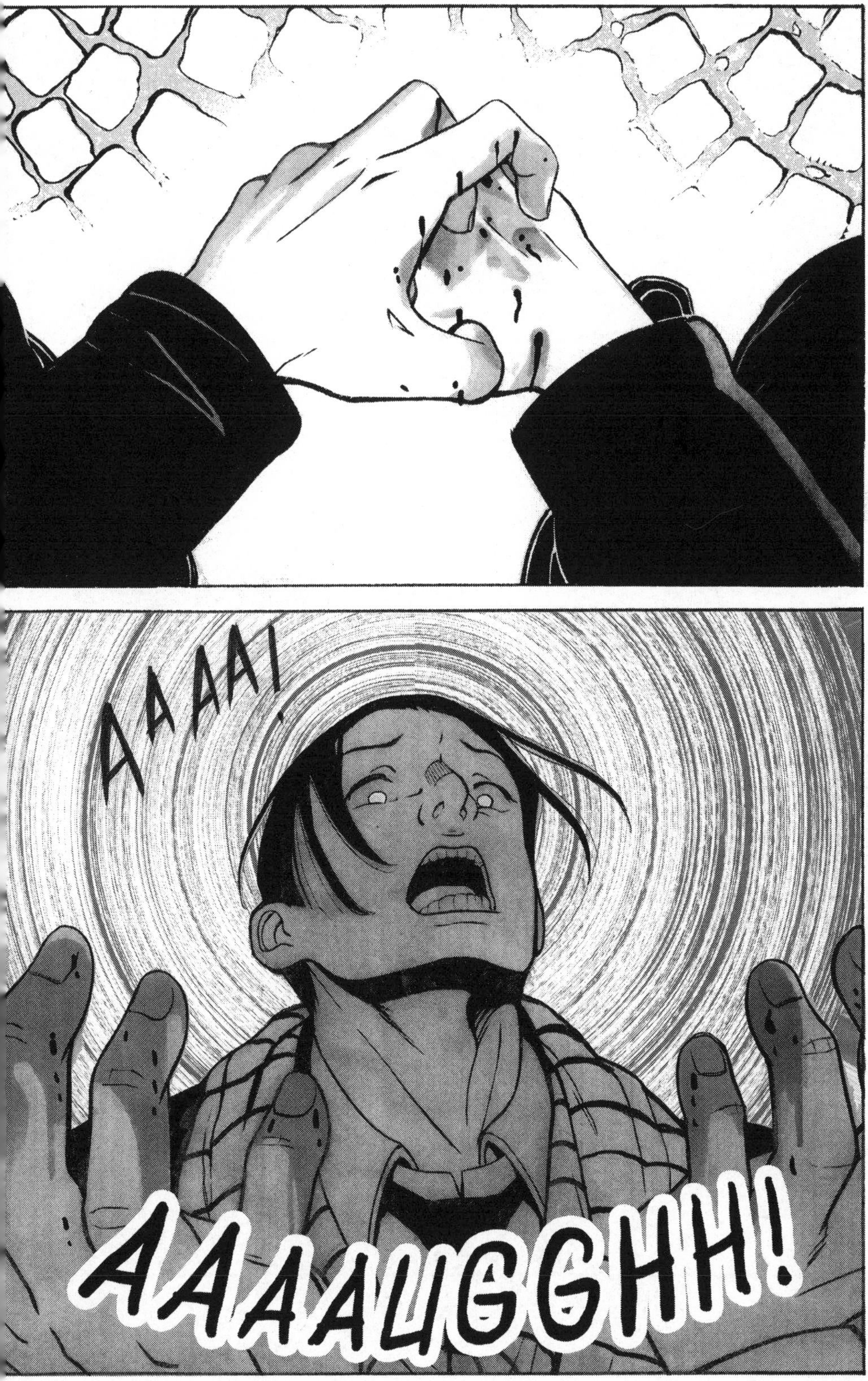
AAAA!
AAAAAUGGHH!

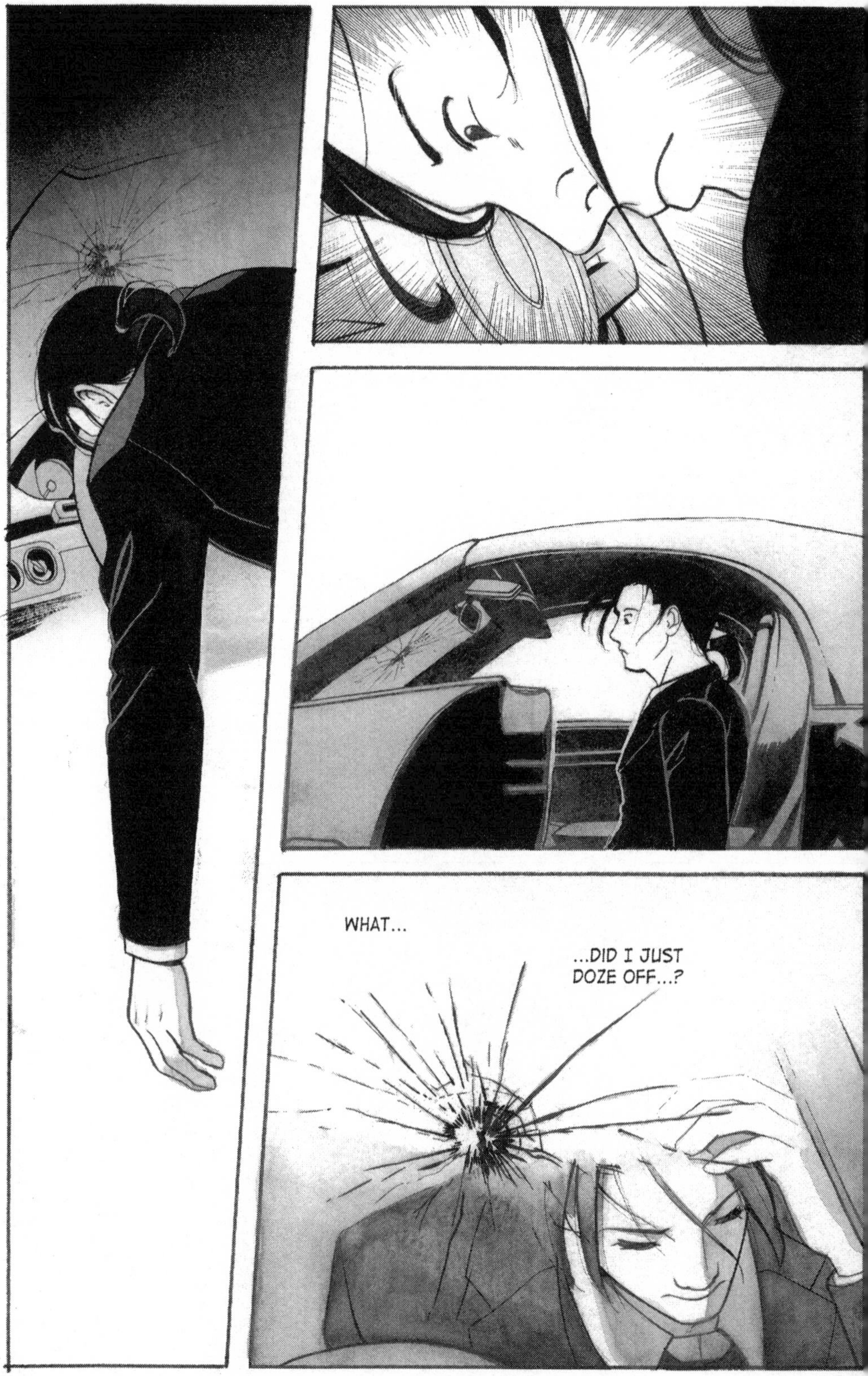
WHAT...
...DID I JUST DOZE OFF...?

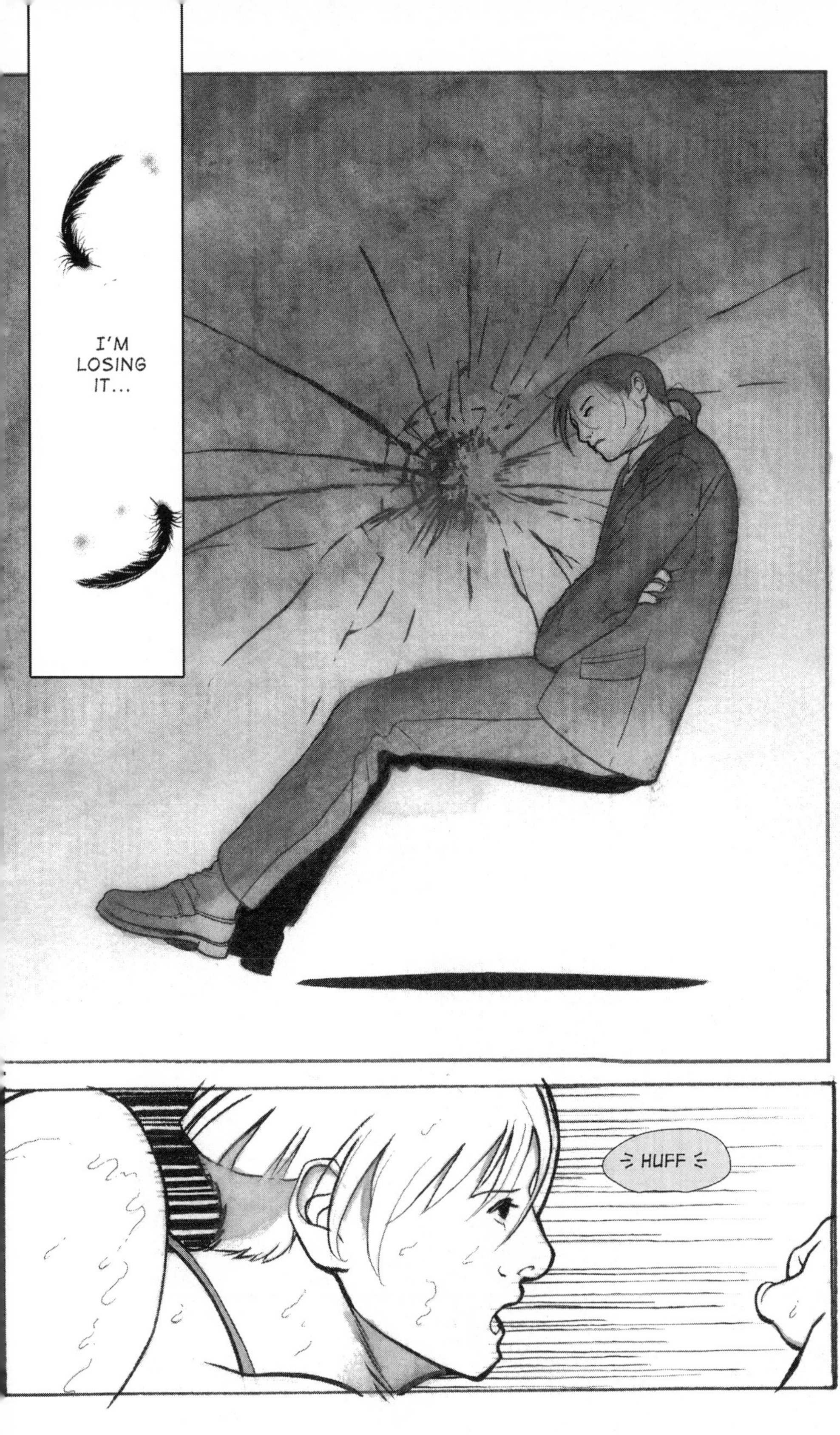
I'M LOSING IT...
HUFF

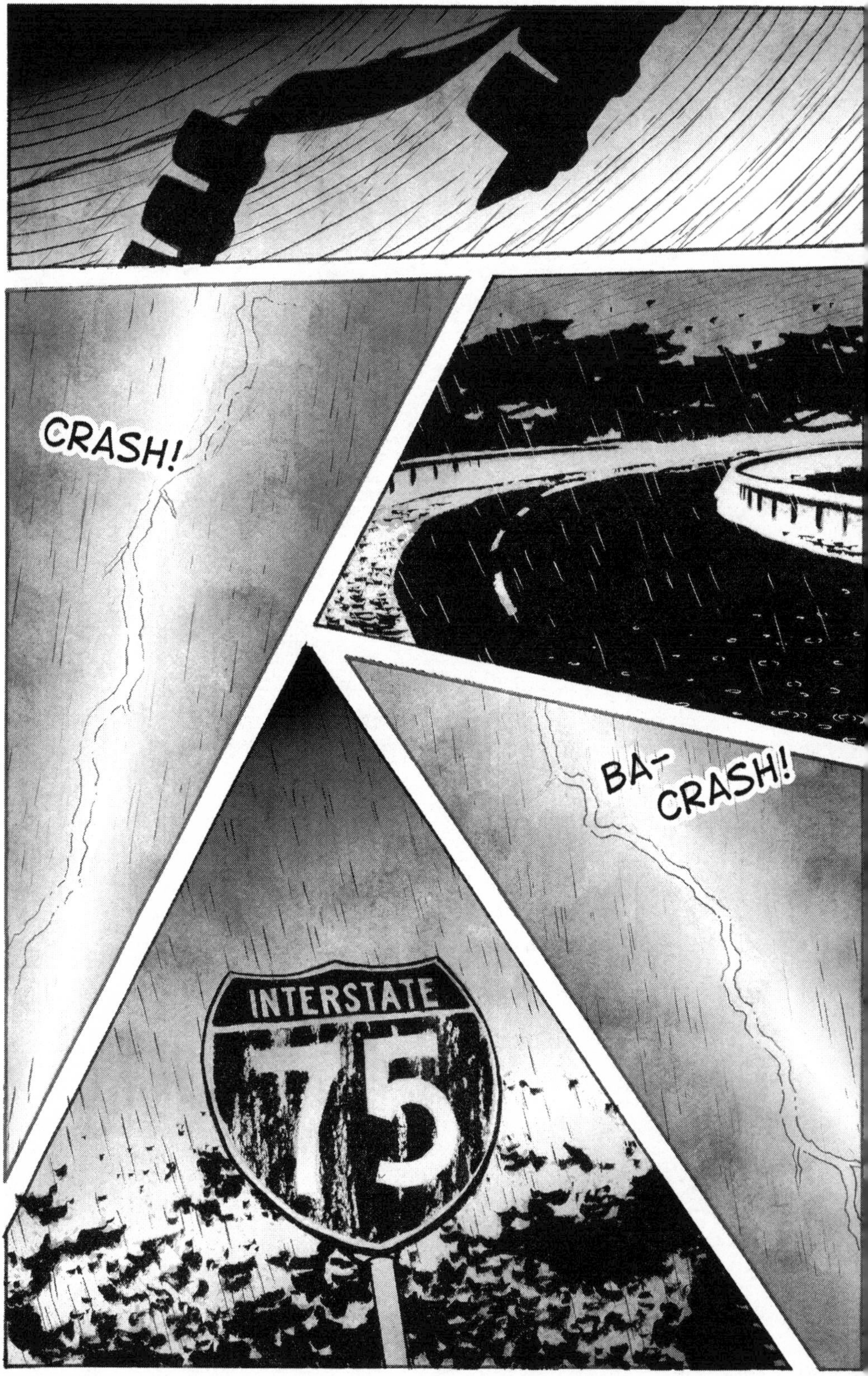
CRASH!
BA-CRASH!
INTERSTATE
75

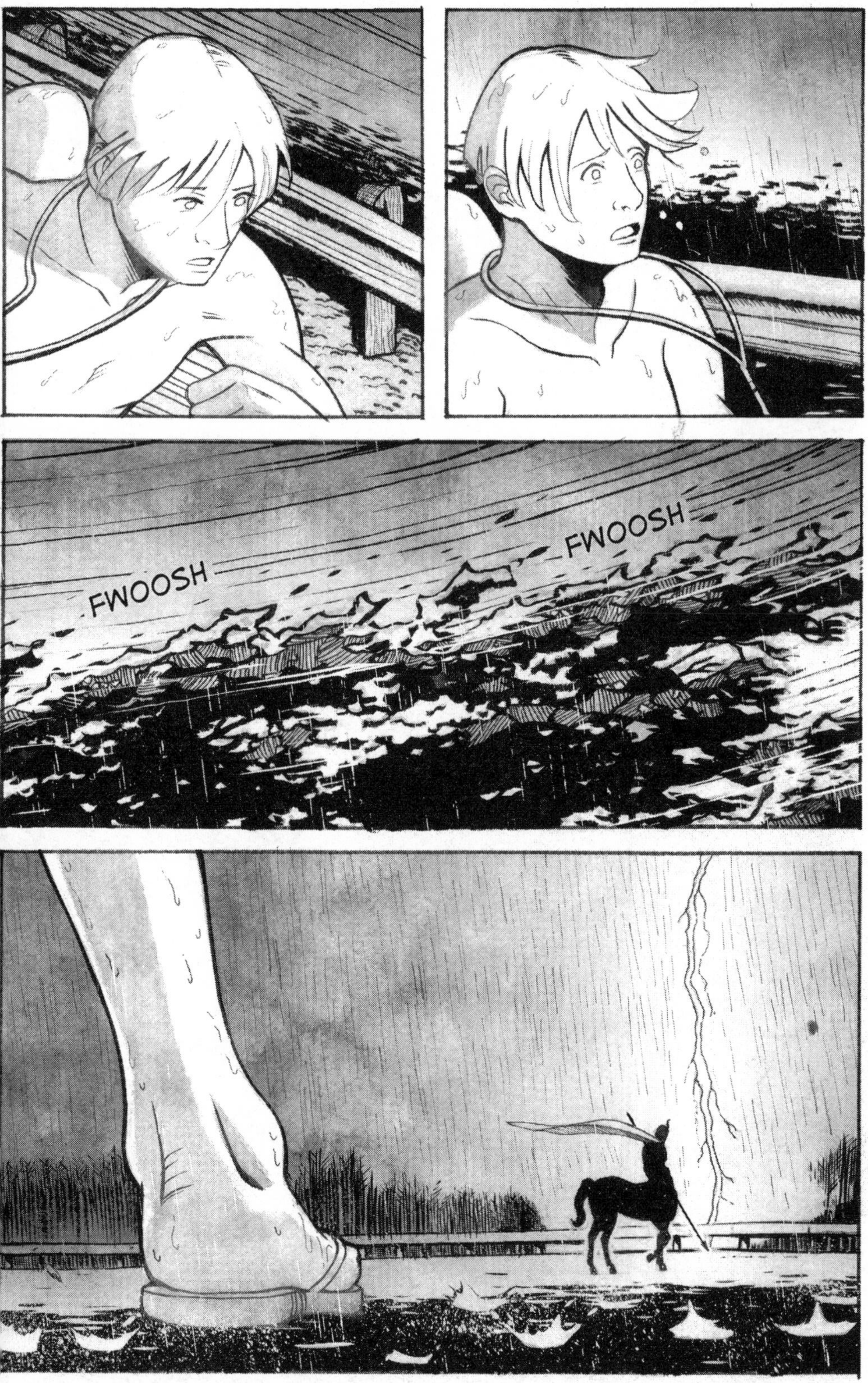
FWOOSH
FWOOSH

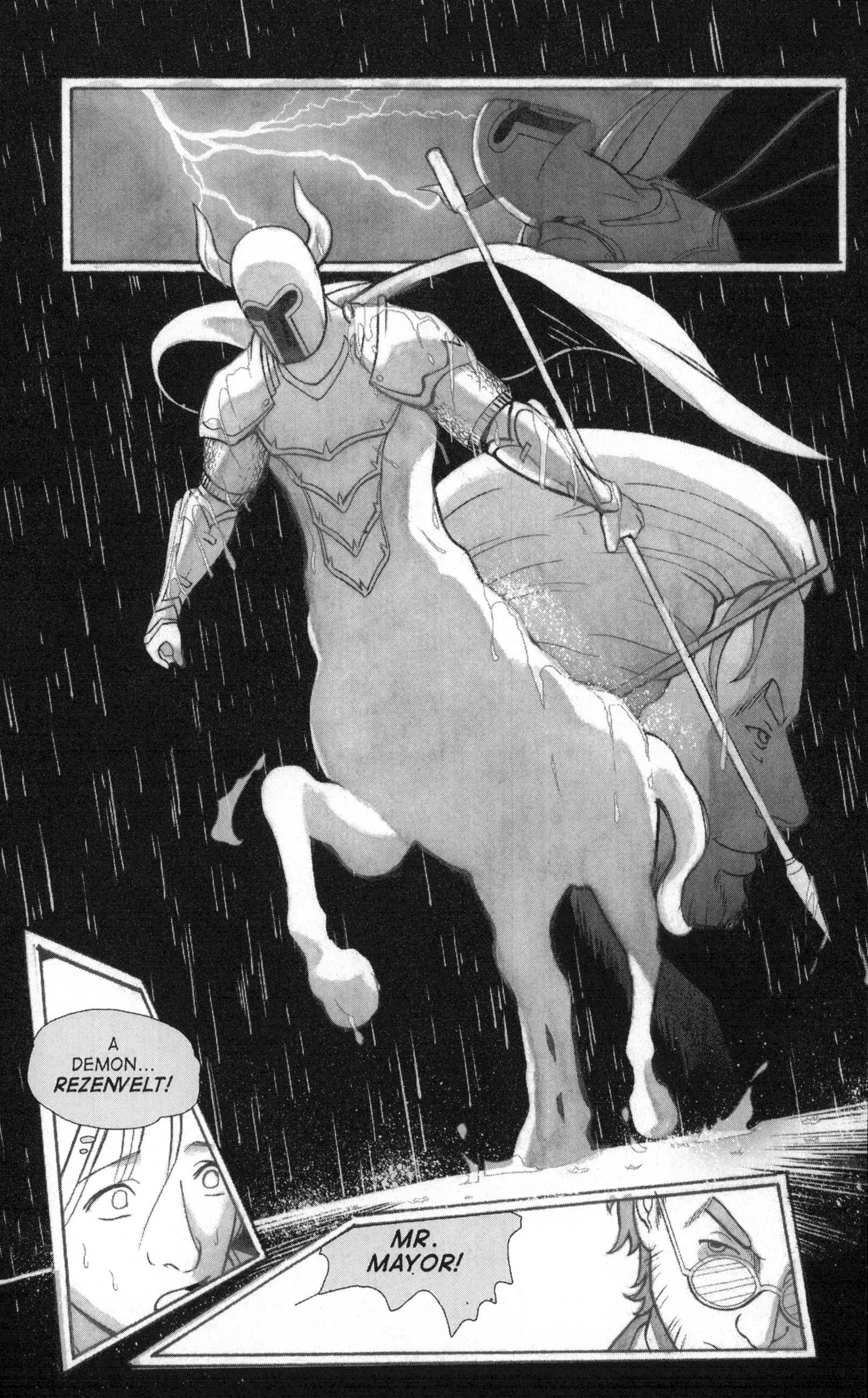
A
DEMON...
REZENVELT!
MR.
MAYOR!

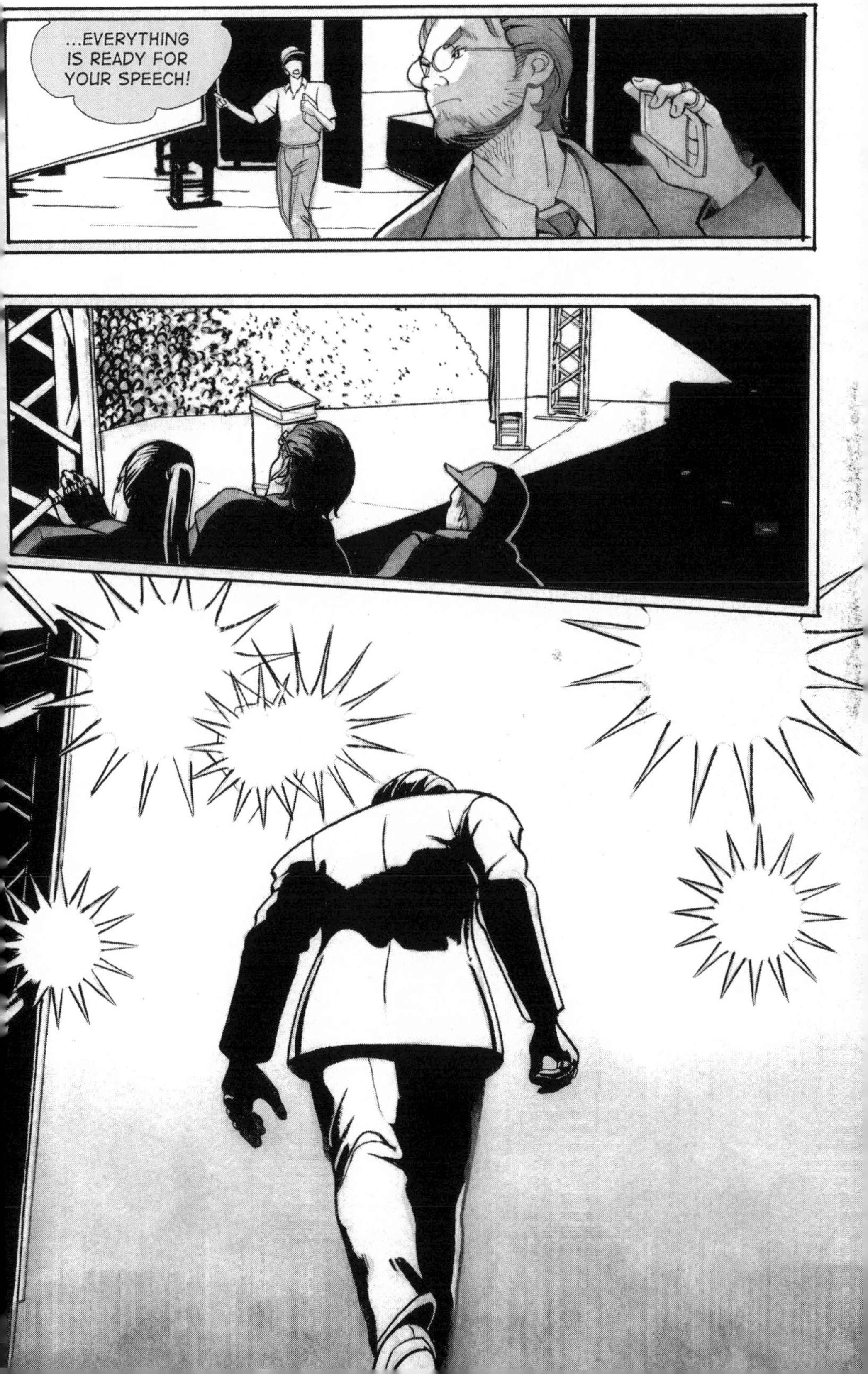
...EVERYTHING IS READY FOR YOUR SPEECH!

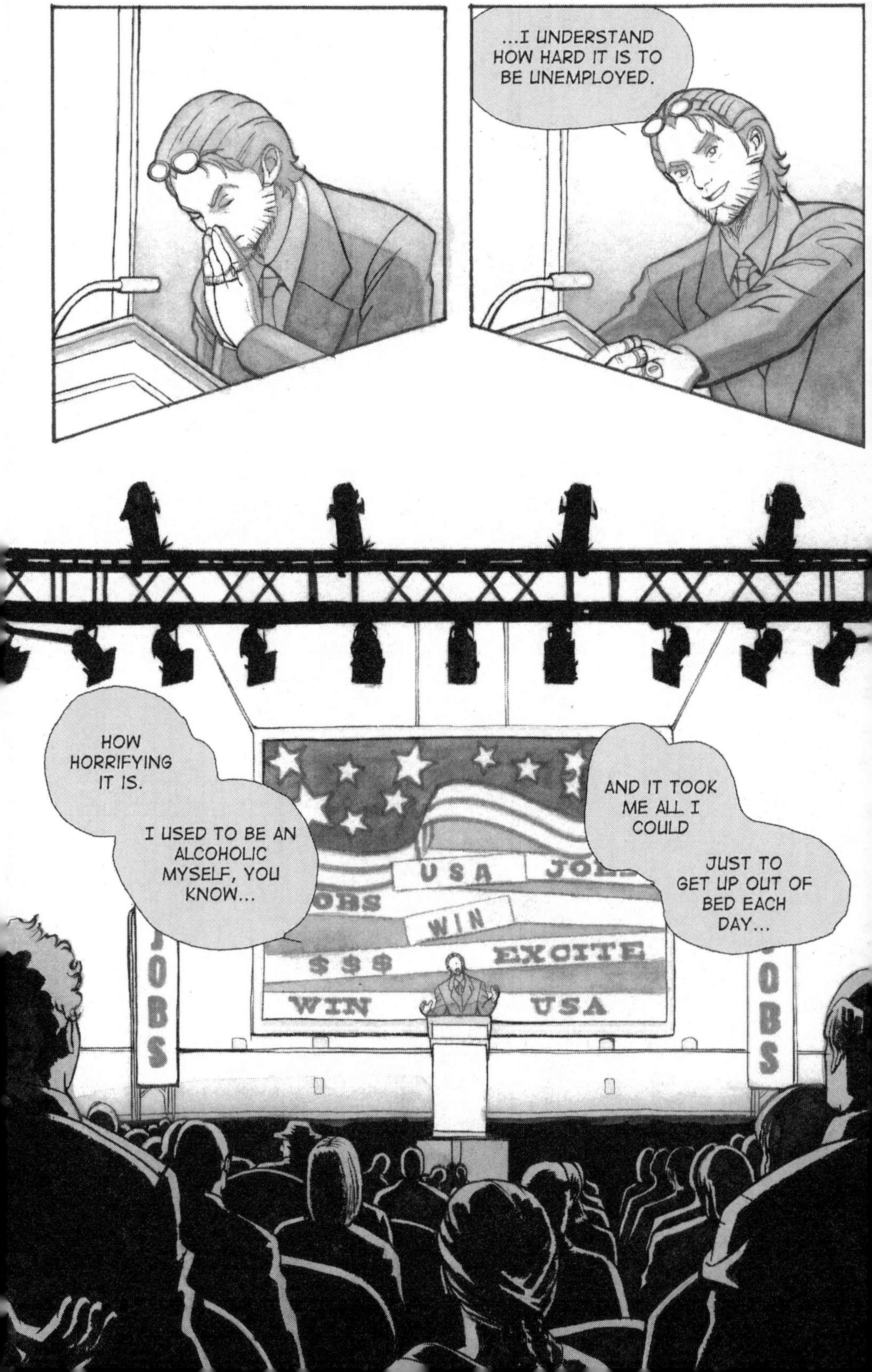
...I UNDERSTAND HOW HARD IT IS TO BE UNEMPLOYED.
HOW HORRIFYING IT IS.
I USED TO BE AN ALCOHOLIC MYSELF, YOU KNOW...
AND IT TOOK ME ALL I COULD
JUST TO GET UP OUT OF BED EACH DAY...
USA
JOBS
WIN
$$$
EXCITE
WIN
USA
JOBS
JOBS

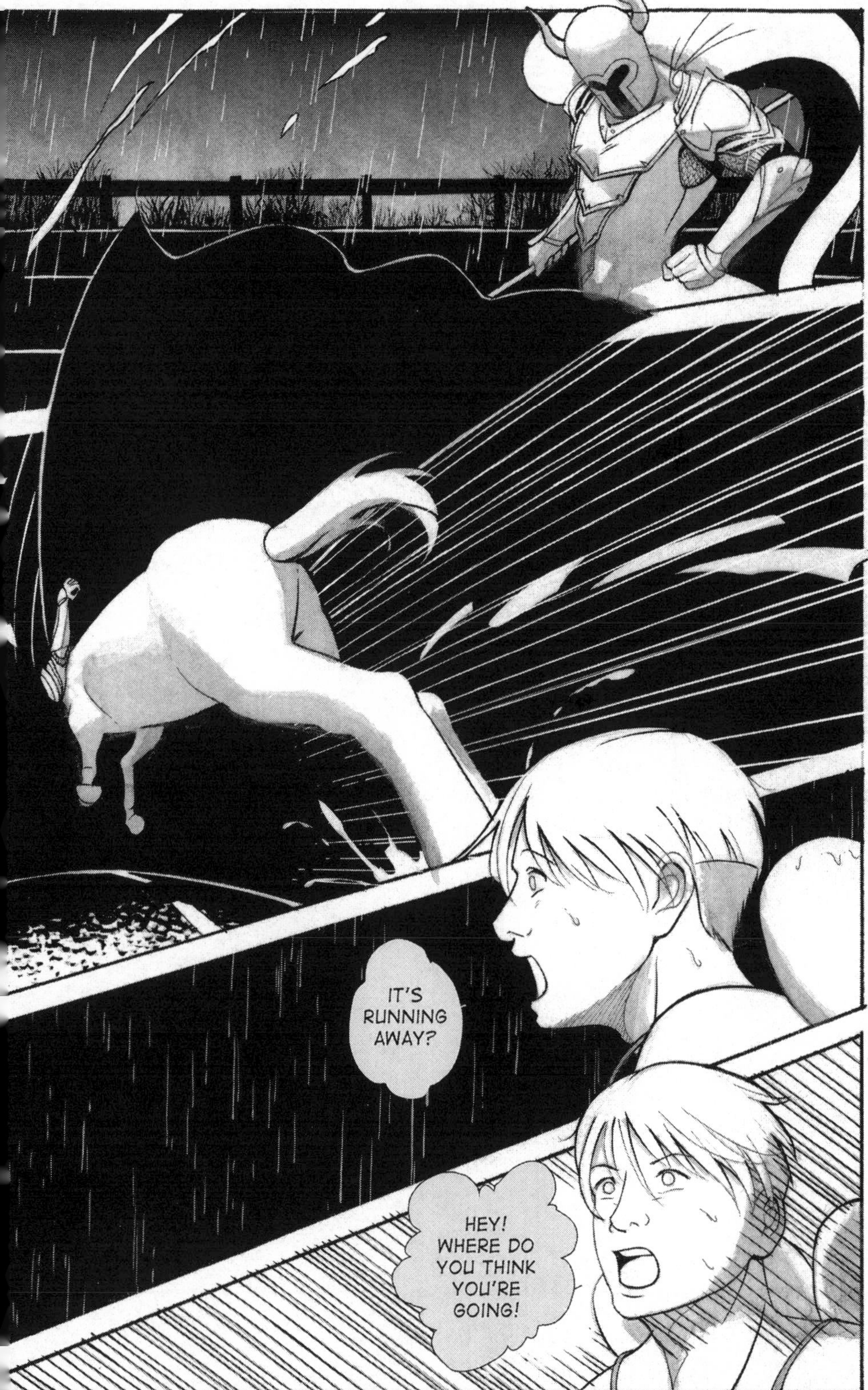
IT'S RUNNING AWAY?
HEY! WHERE DO YOU THINK YOU'RE GOING!

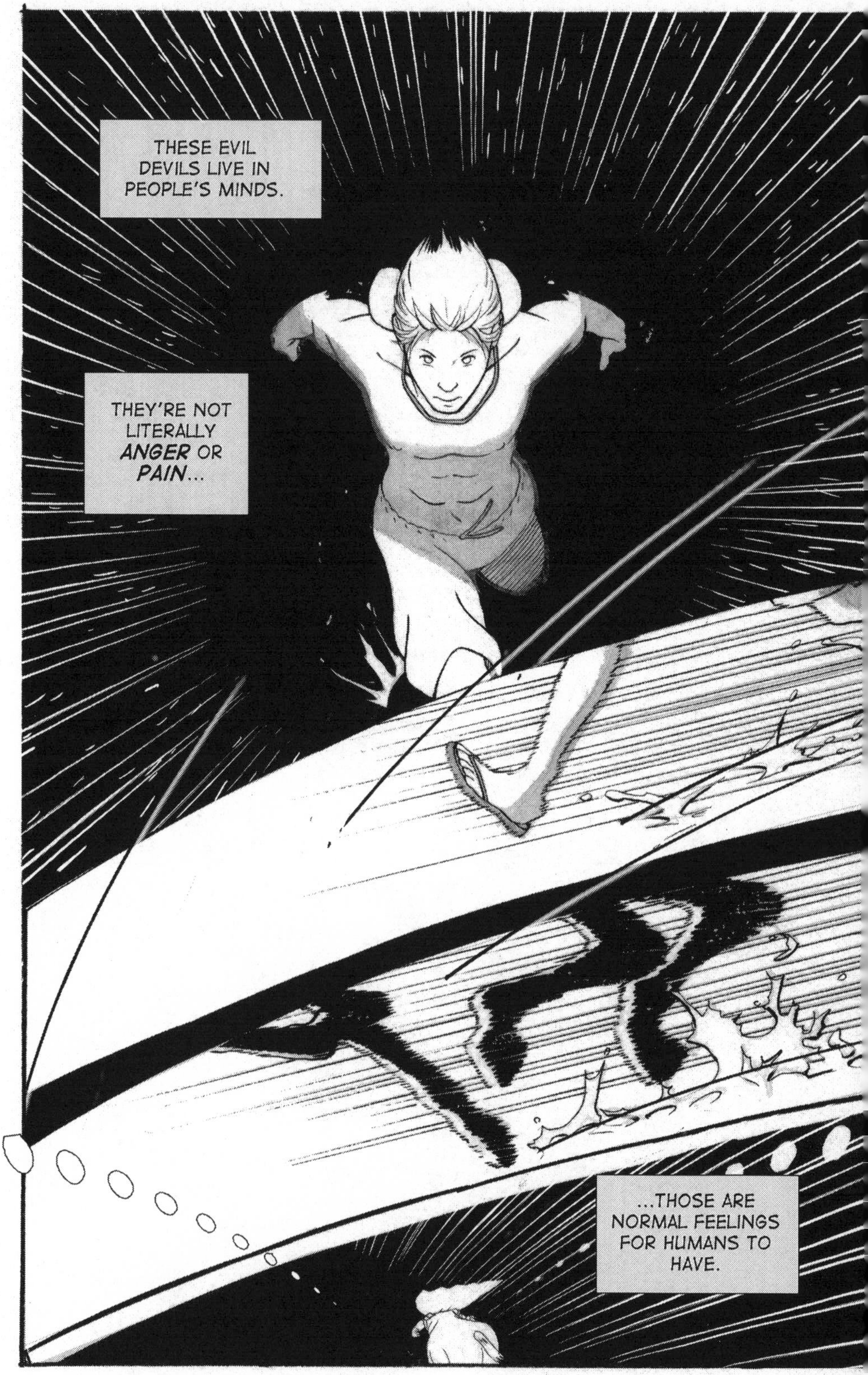
THESE EVIL DEVILS LIVE IN PEOPLE'S MINDS.
THEY'RE NOT LITERALLY *ANGER* OR *PAIN*...
...THOSE ARE NORMAL FEELINGS FOR HUMANS TO HAVE.

BUT SOMETIMES...

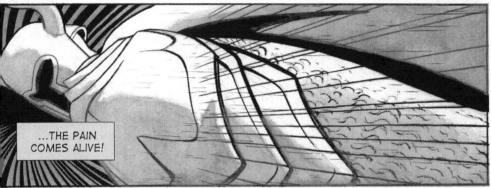

...THE PAIN COMES ALIVE!

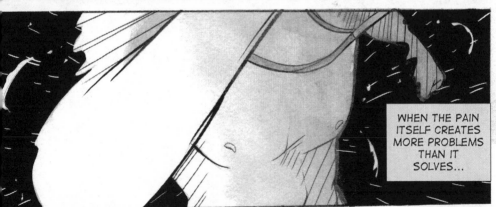

WHEN THE PAIN ITSELF CREATES MORE PROBLEMS THAN IT SOLVES...

...HURTING OTHERS, RUINING RELATIONSHIPS...

...IT LEADS TO EVEN MORE NEGATIVE FEELINGS, THUS COMPLETING THE VICIOUS CYCLE.

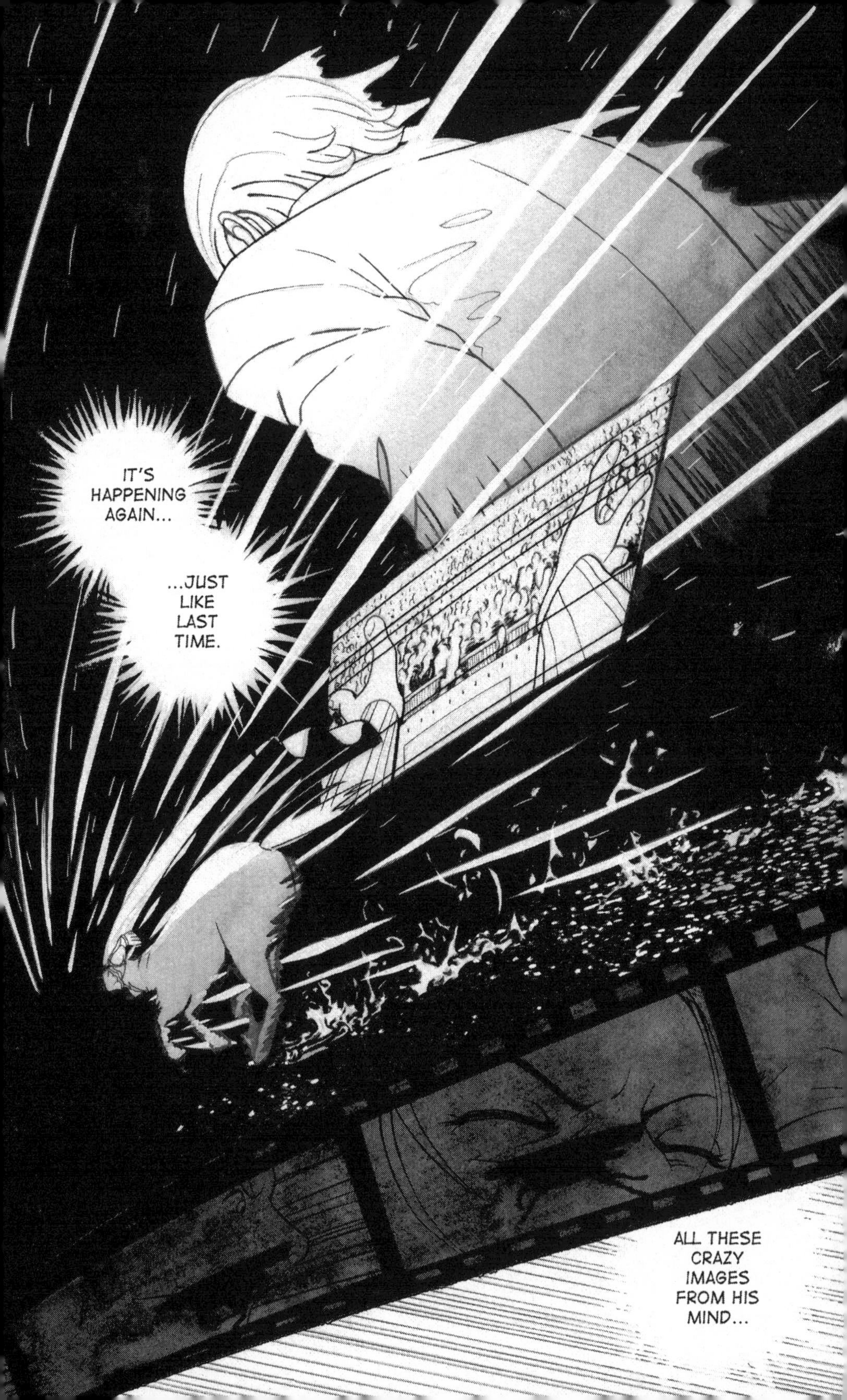

IT'S HAPPENING AGAIN...
...JUST LIKE LAST TIME.
ALL THESE CRAZY IMAGES FROM HIS MIND...

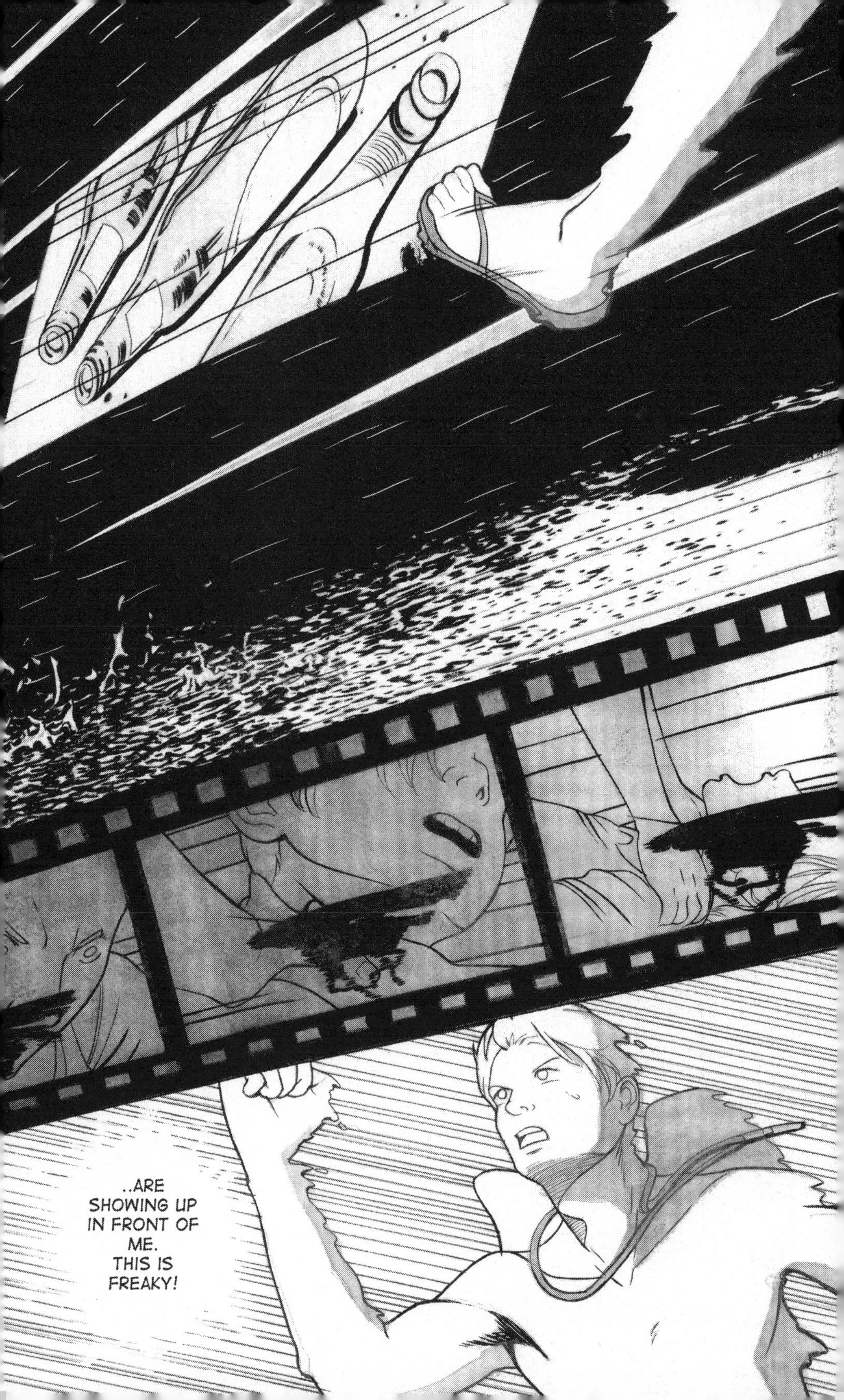
..ARE SHOWING UP IN FRONT OF ME. THIS IS FREAKY!

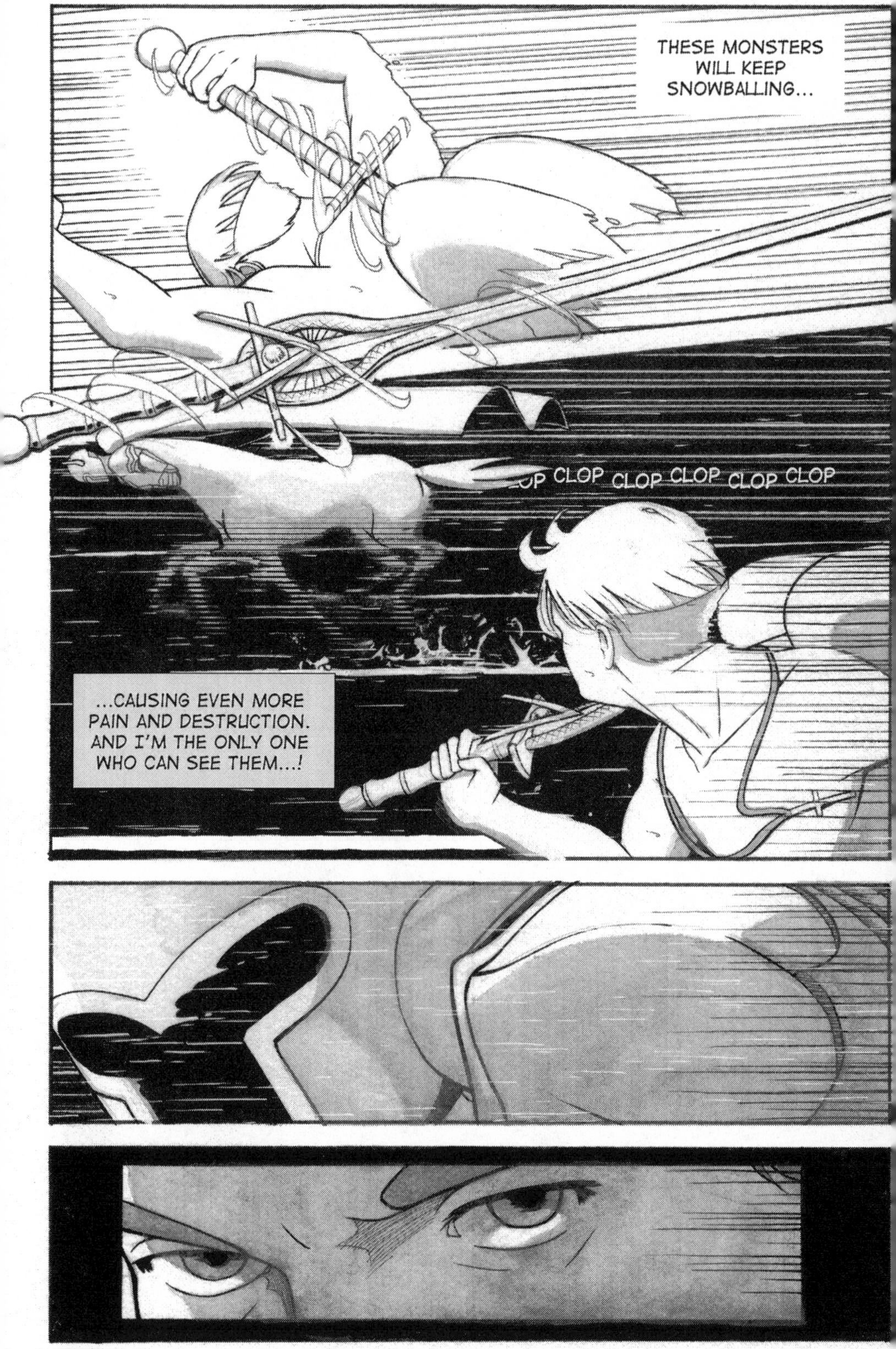
THESE MONSTERS WILL KEEP SNOWBALLING...
CLOP CLOP CLOP CLOP CLOP
...CAUSING EVEN MORE PAIN AND DESTRUCTION. AND I'M THE ONLY ONE WHO CAN SEE THEM...!

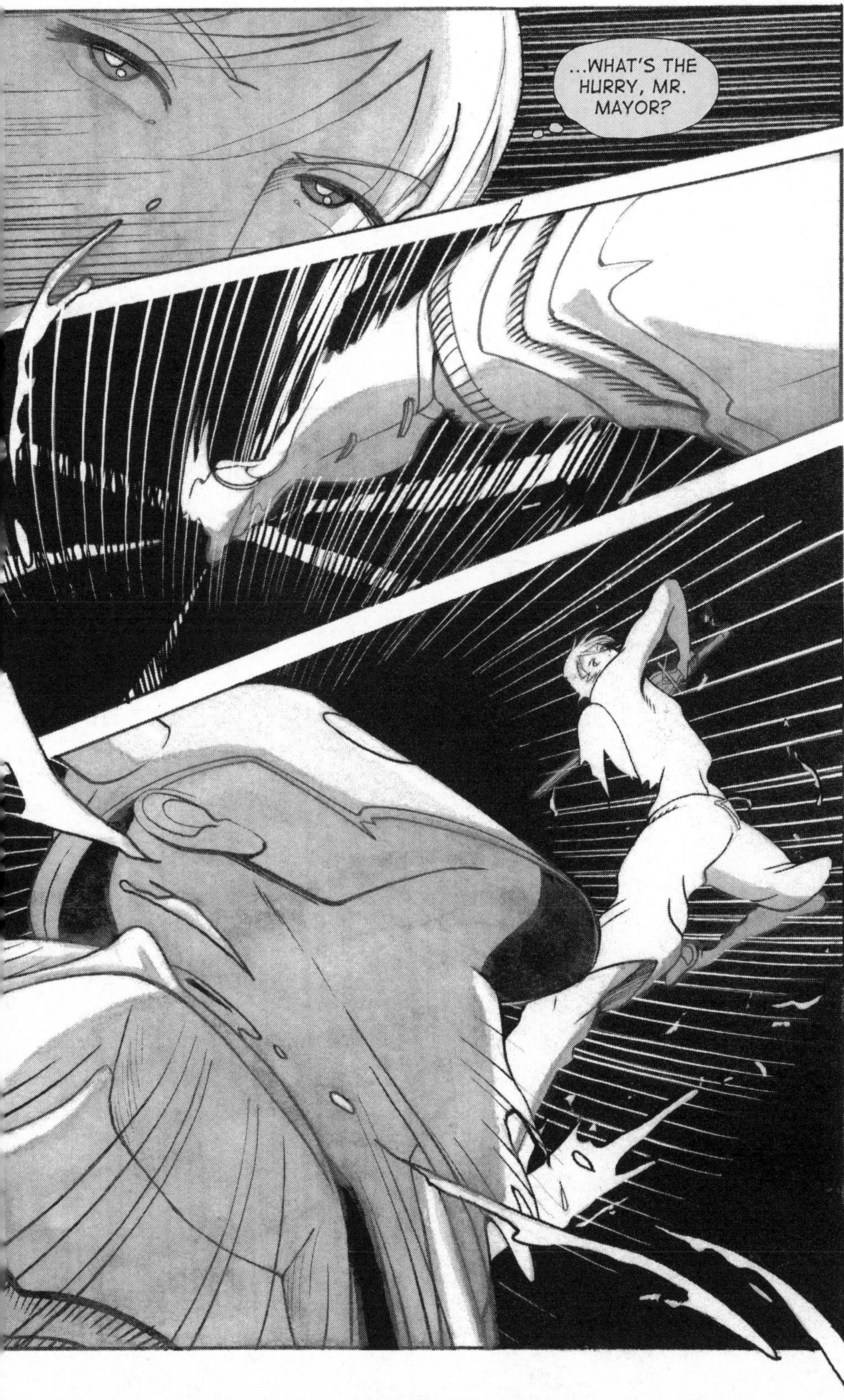
...WHAT'S THE HURRY, MR. MAYOR?

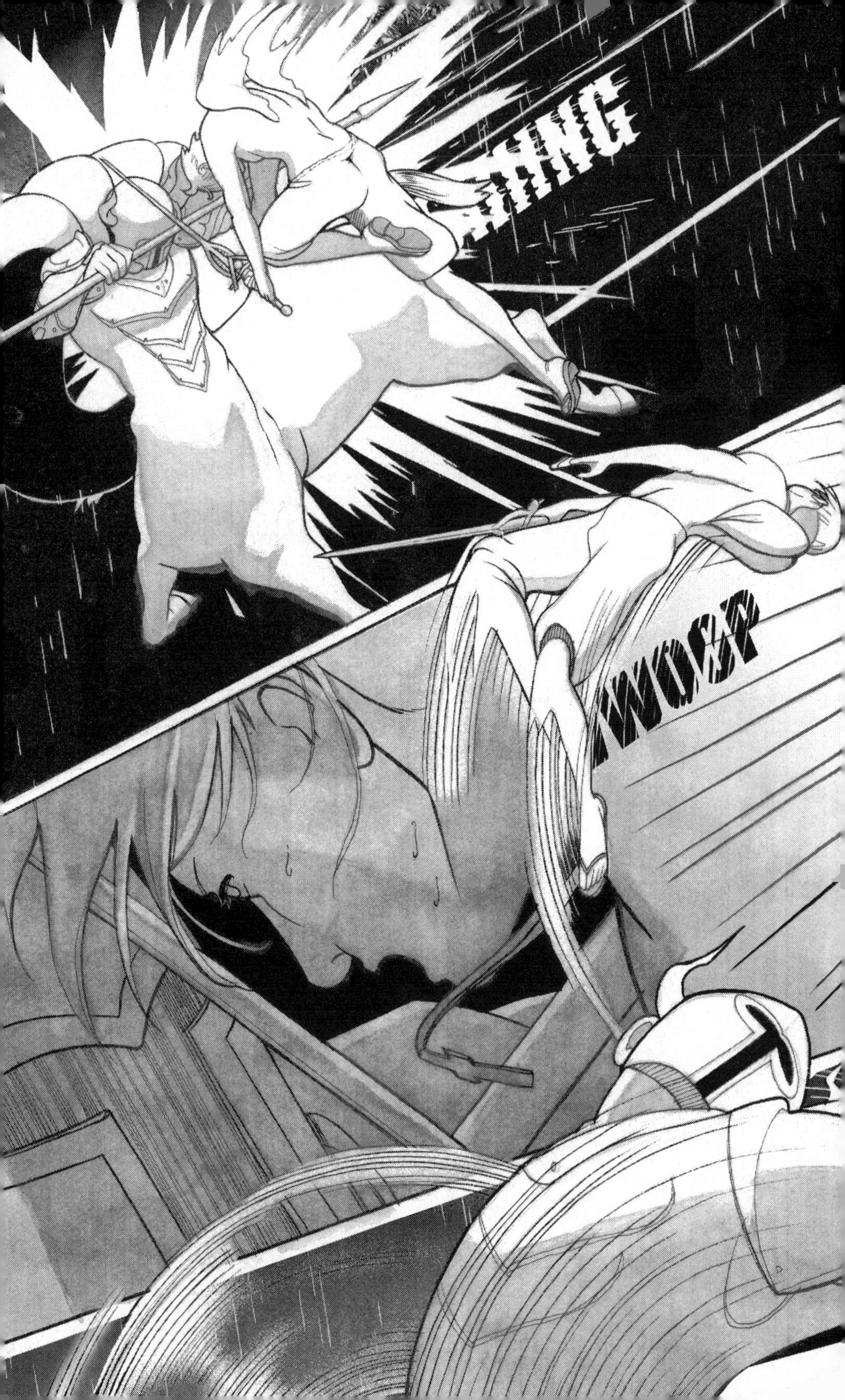
WOSP

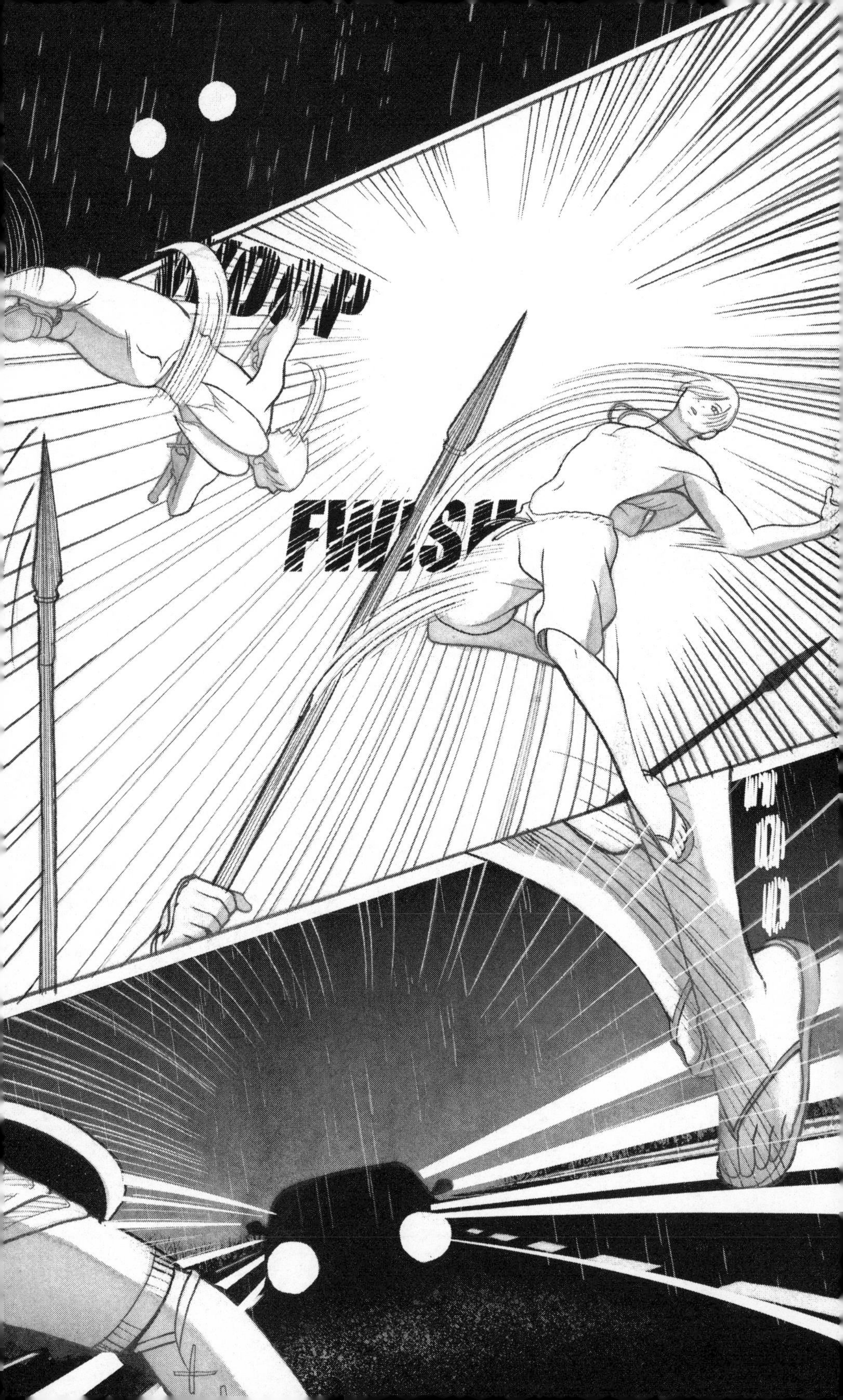
FWISH

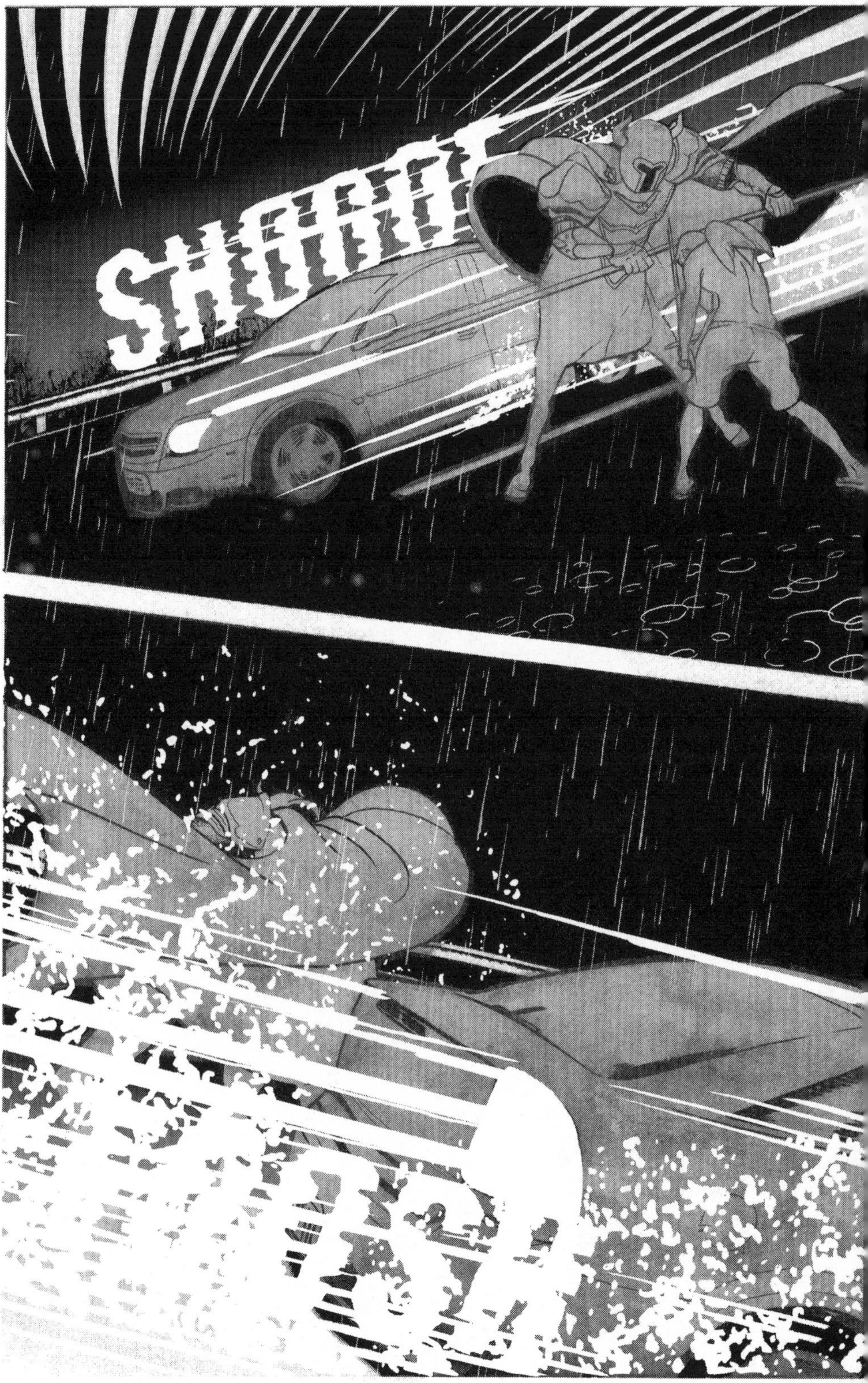

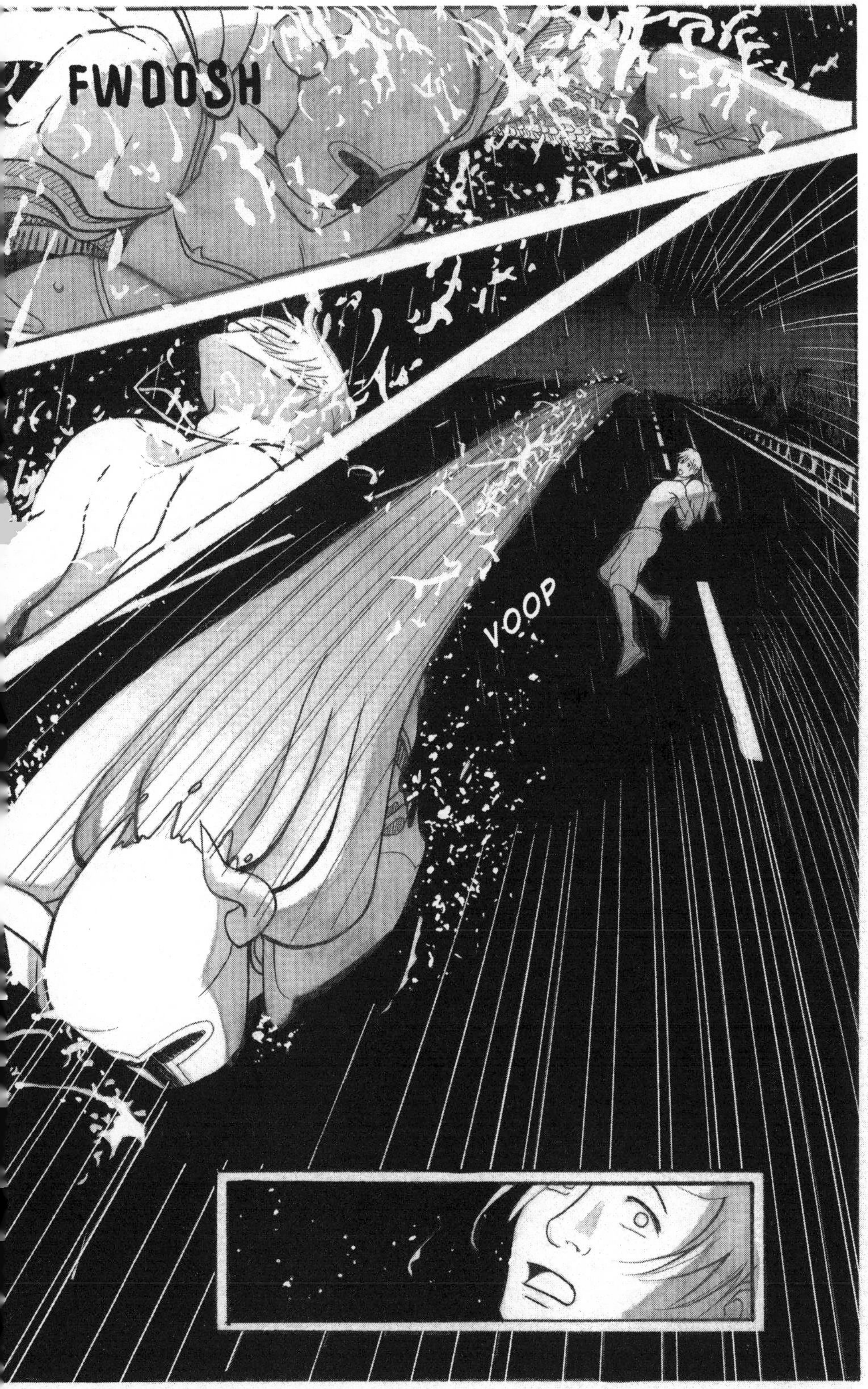
FWOOSH
VOOP

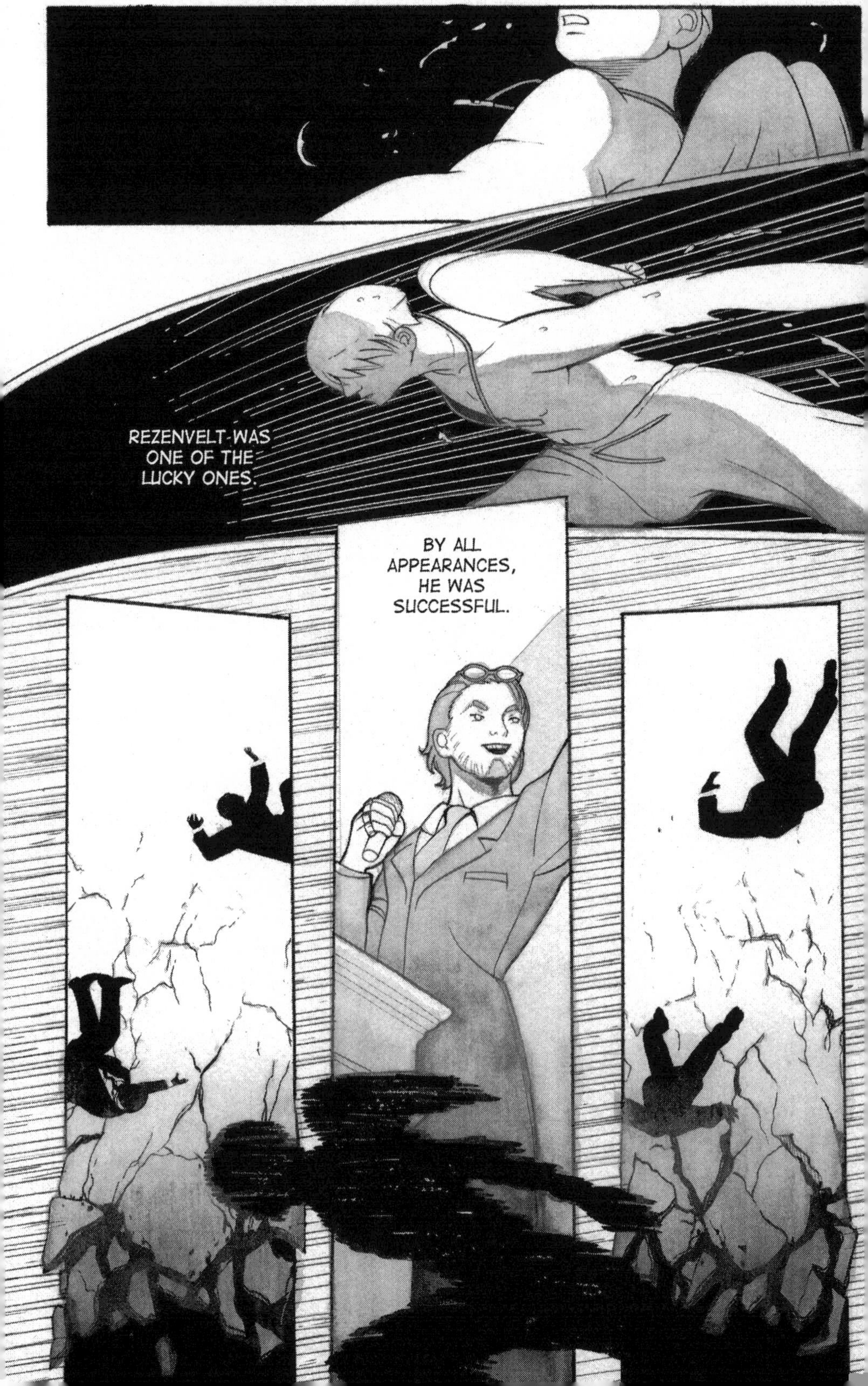
REZENVELT WAS ONE OF THE LUCKY ONES.
BY ALL APPEARANCES, HE WAS SUCCESSFUL.

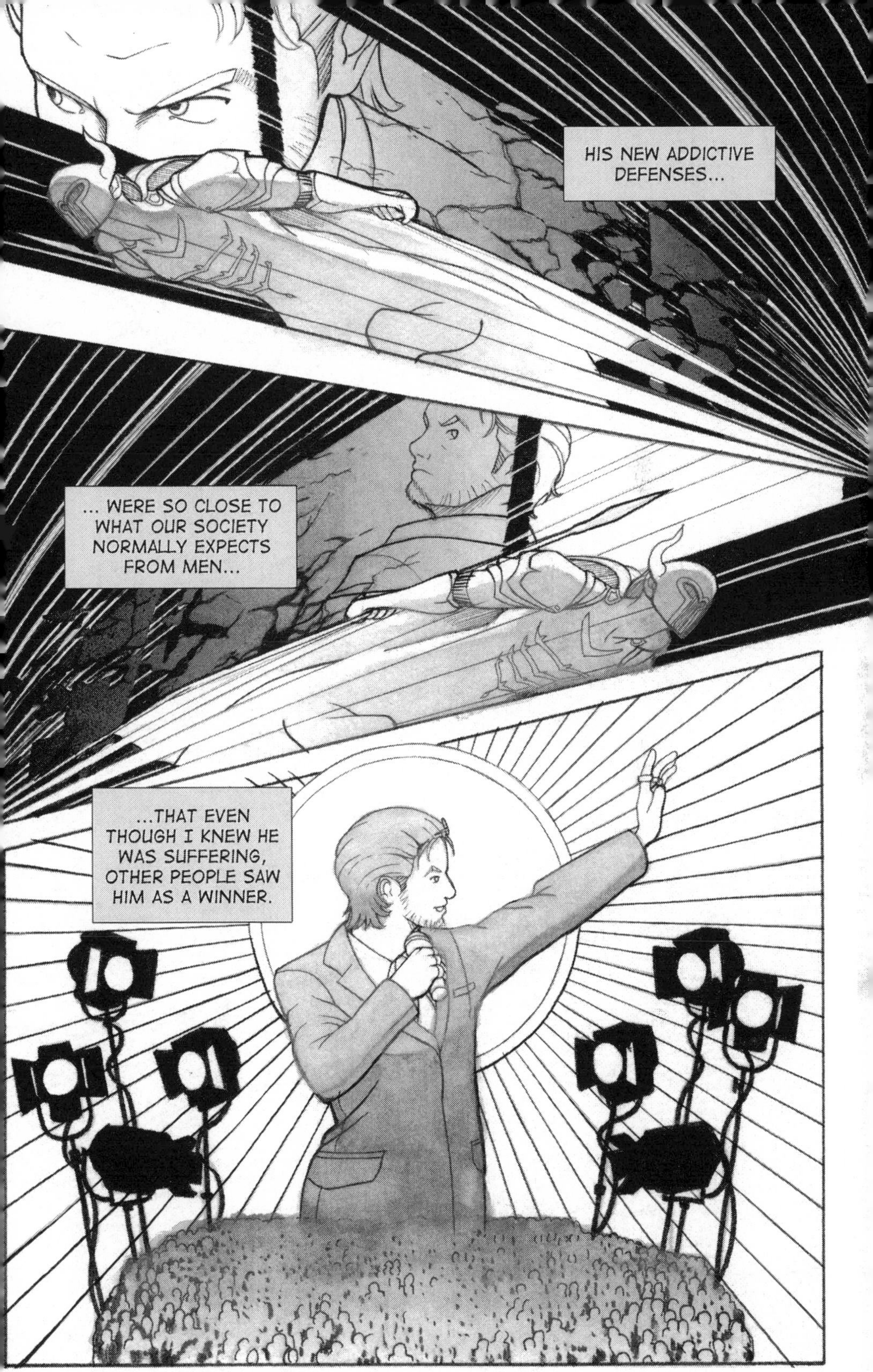
HIS NEW ADDICTIVE DEFENSES...
... WERE SO CLOSE TO WHAT OUR SOCIETY NORMALLY EXPECTS FROM MEN...
...THAT EVEN THOUGH I KNEW HE WAS SUFFERING, OTHER PEOPLE SAW HIM AS A WINNER.

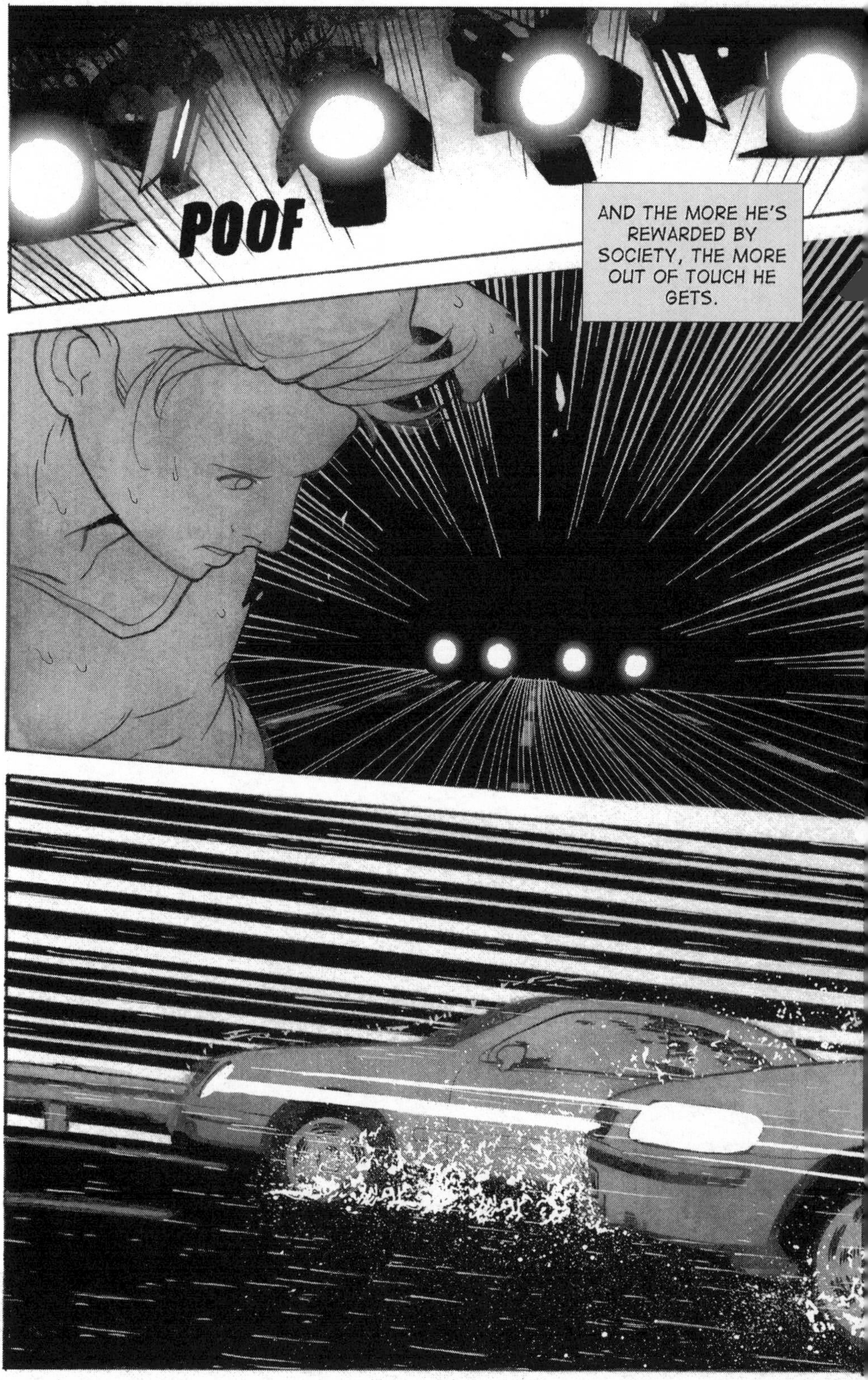
POOF
AND THE MORE HE'S REWARDED BY SOCIETY, THE MORE OUT OF TOUCH HE GETS.

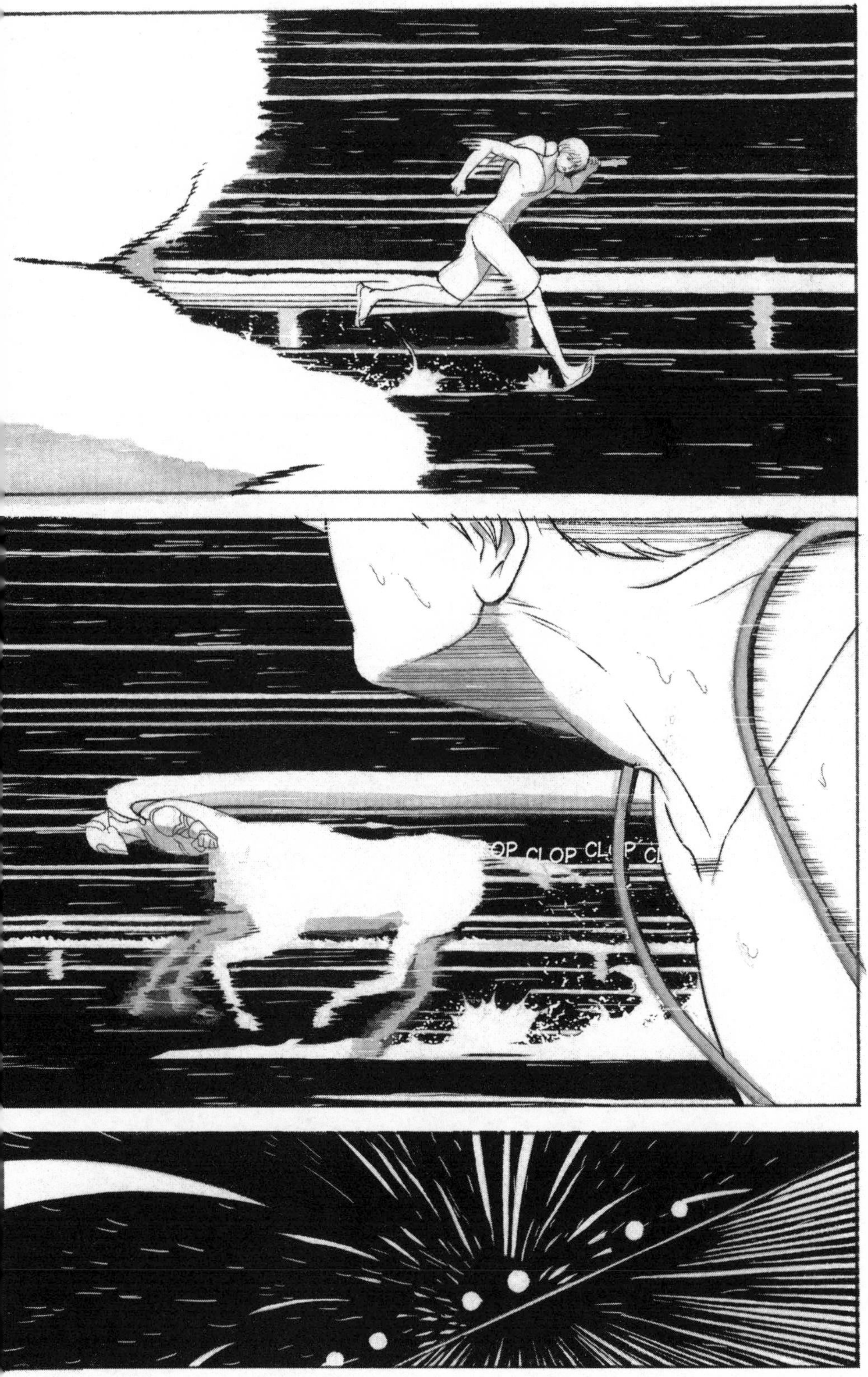
OP CLOP CLOP CL

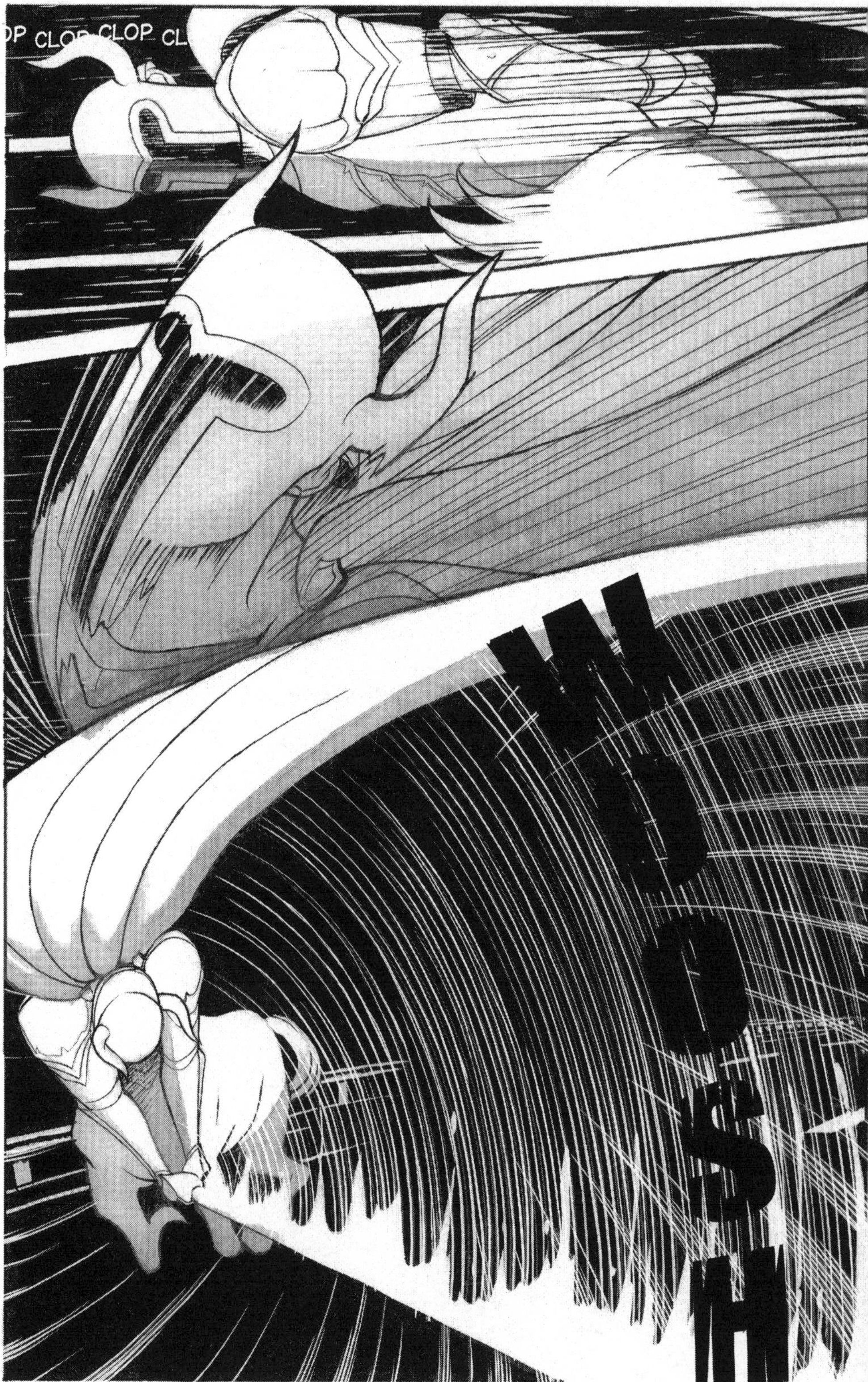

OP CLOP CLOP CL
WHOOSH

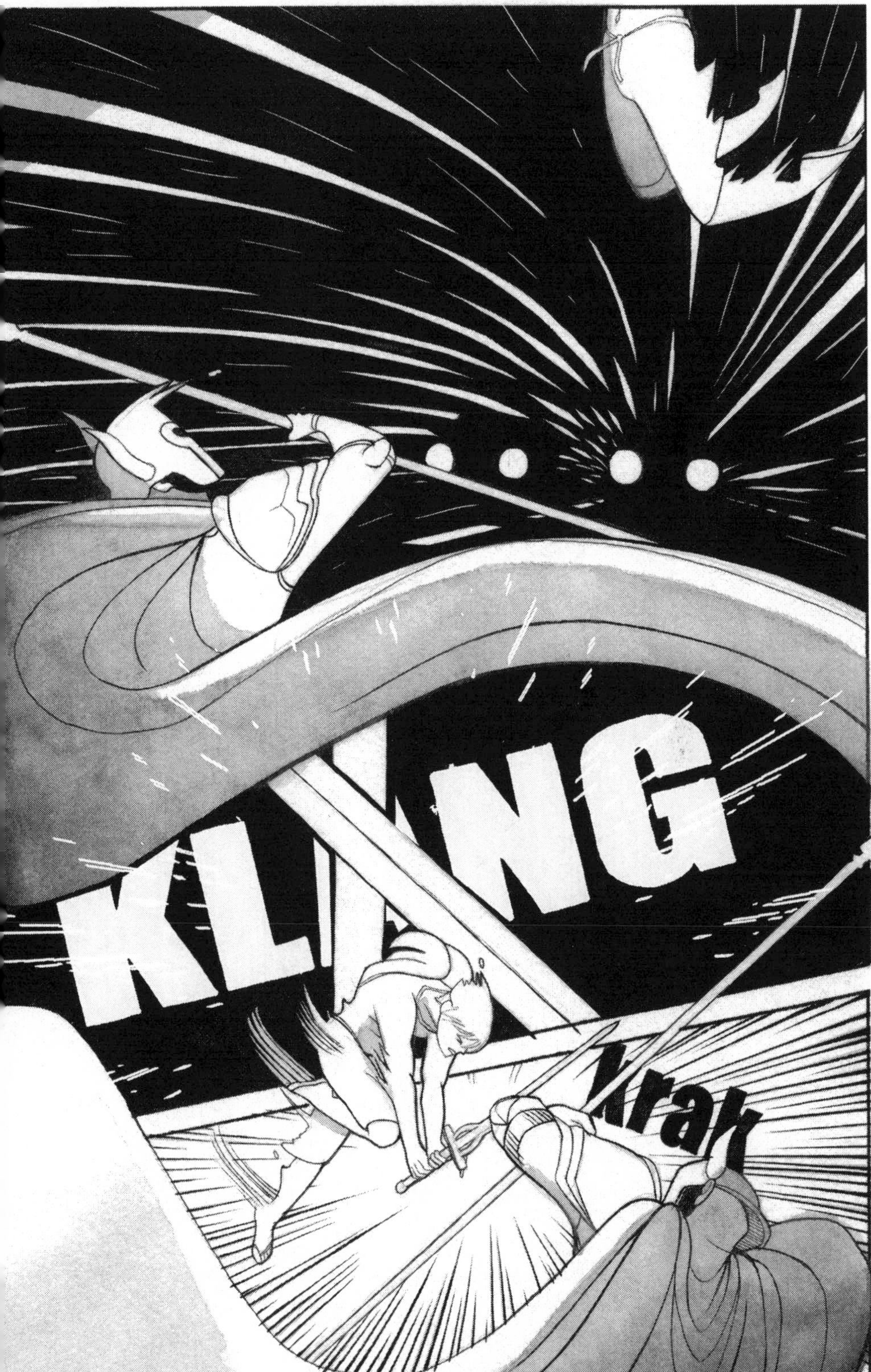
KLANG
KRAK

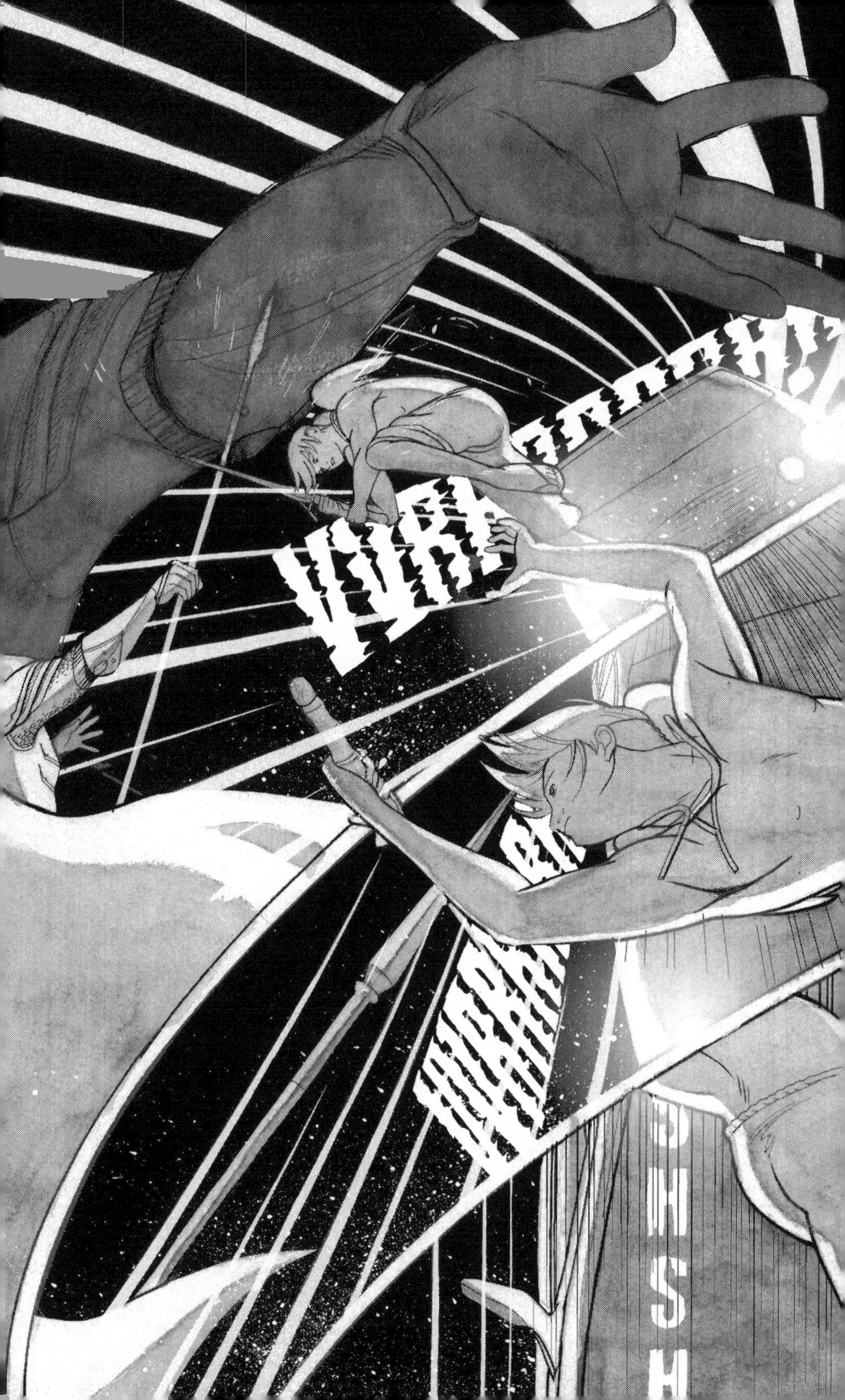

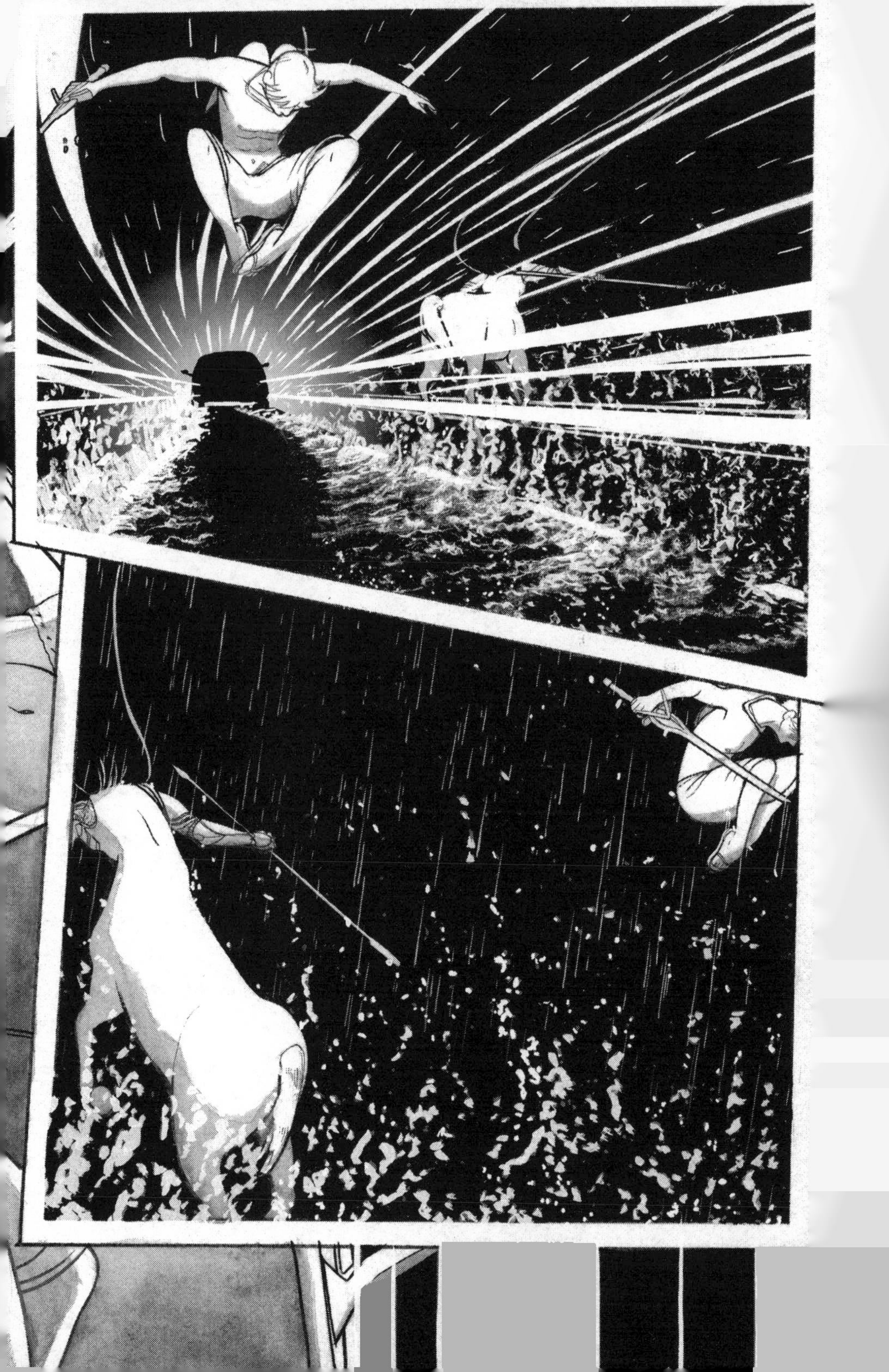

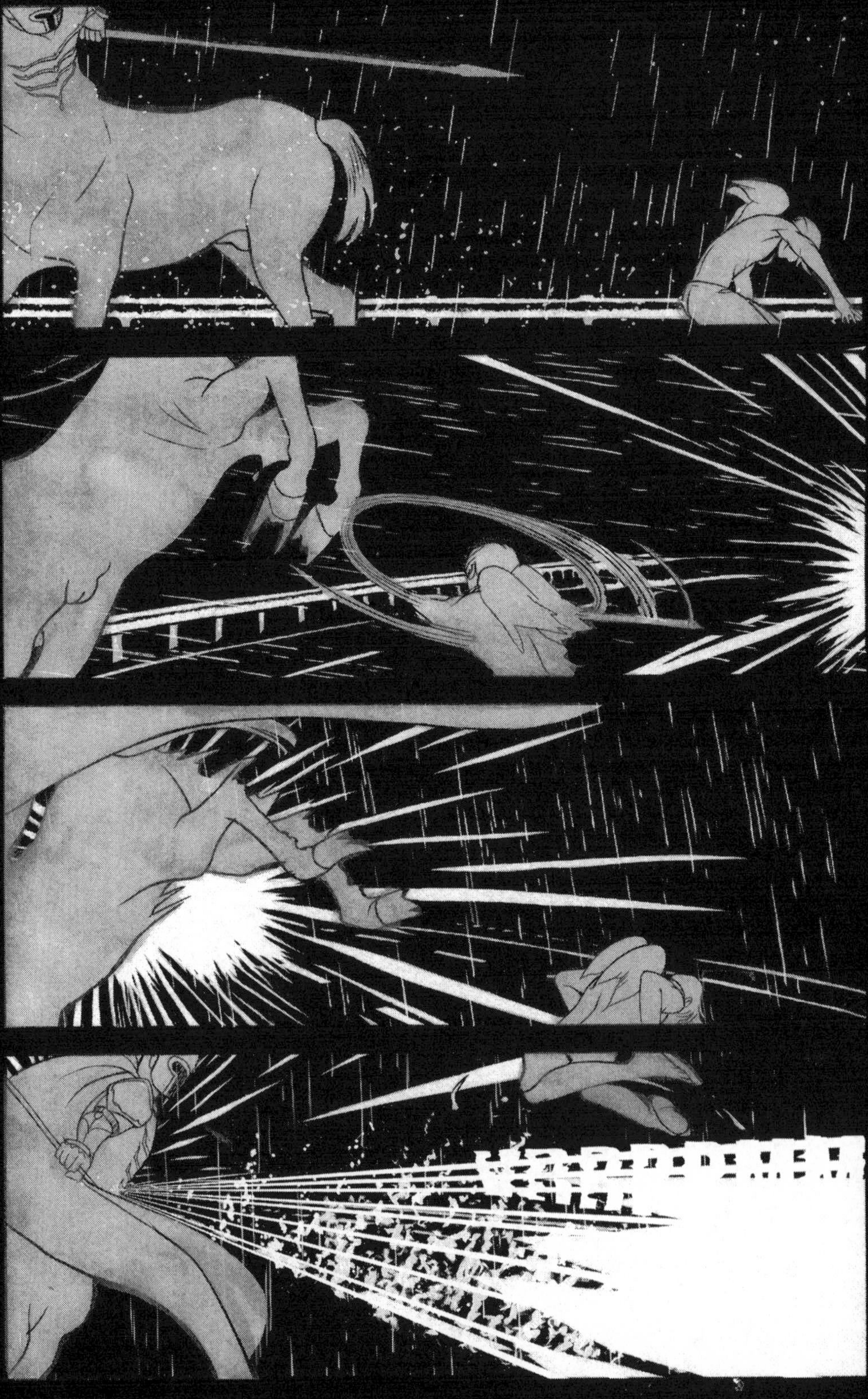

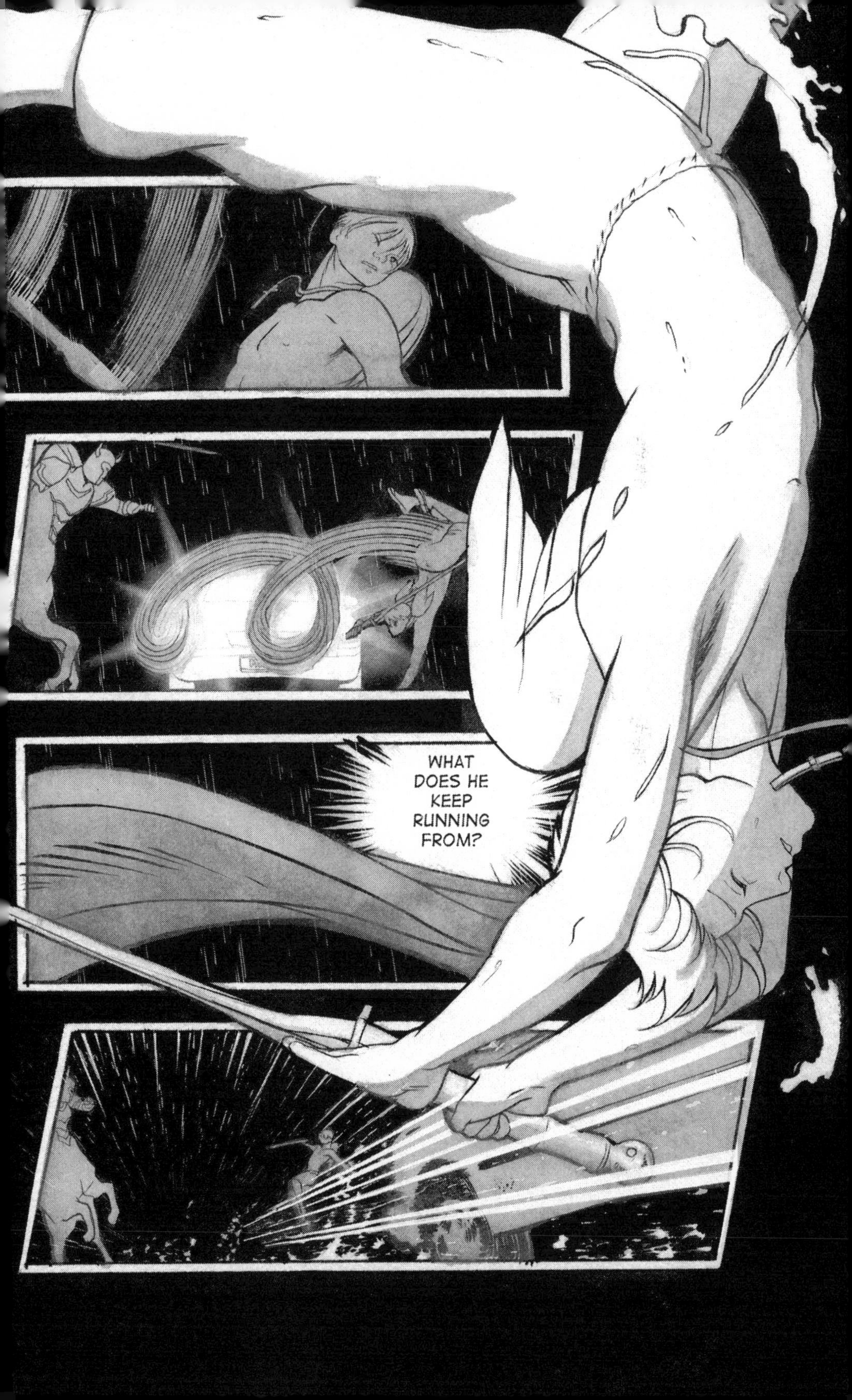
WHAT DOES HE KEEP RUNNING FROM?

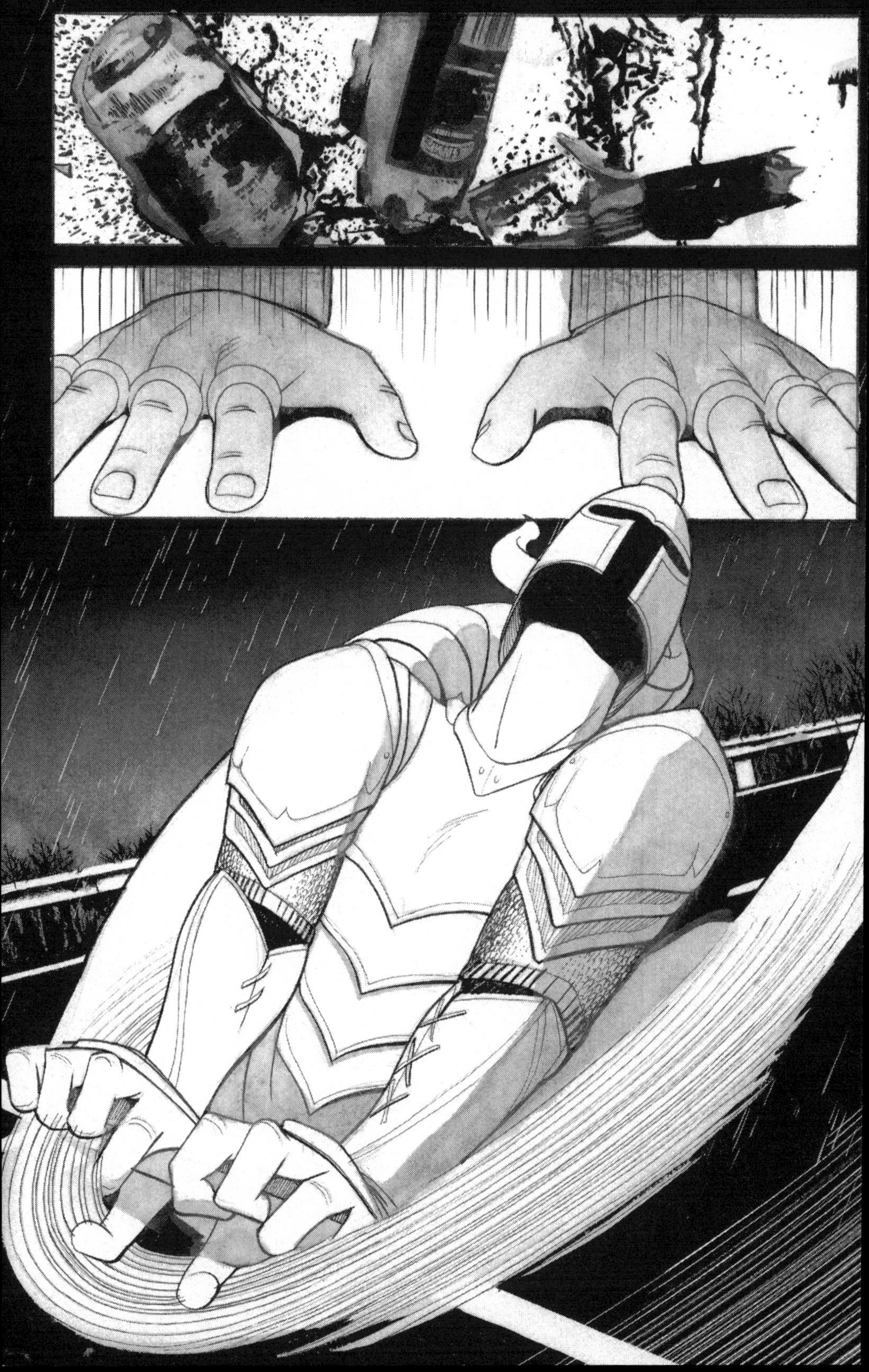

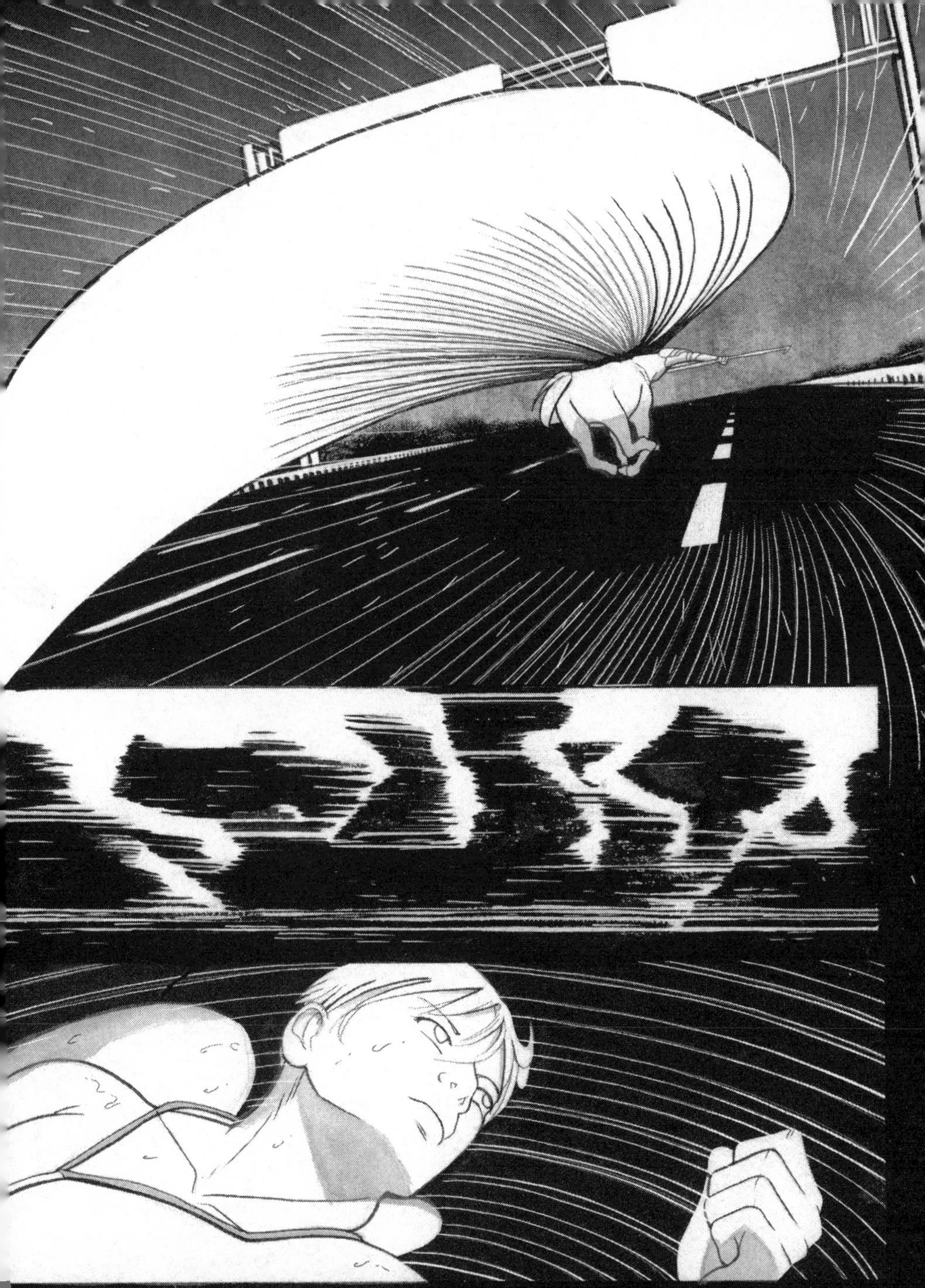

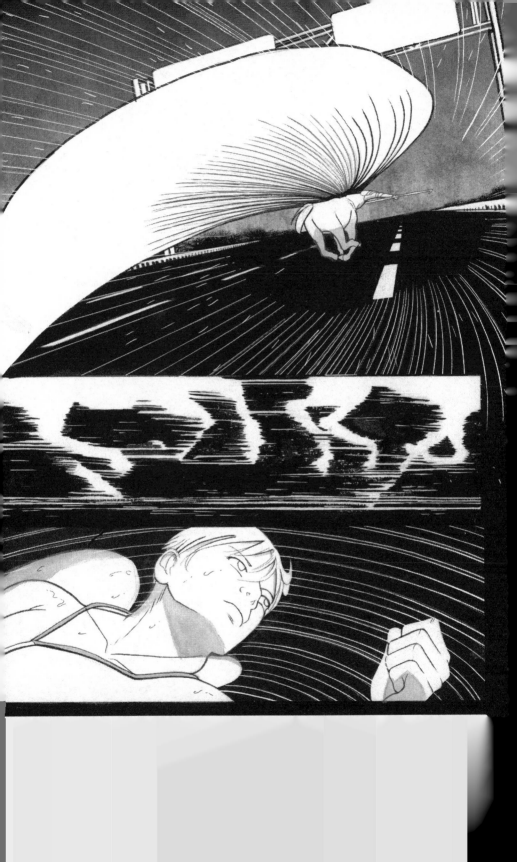

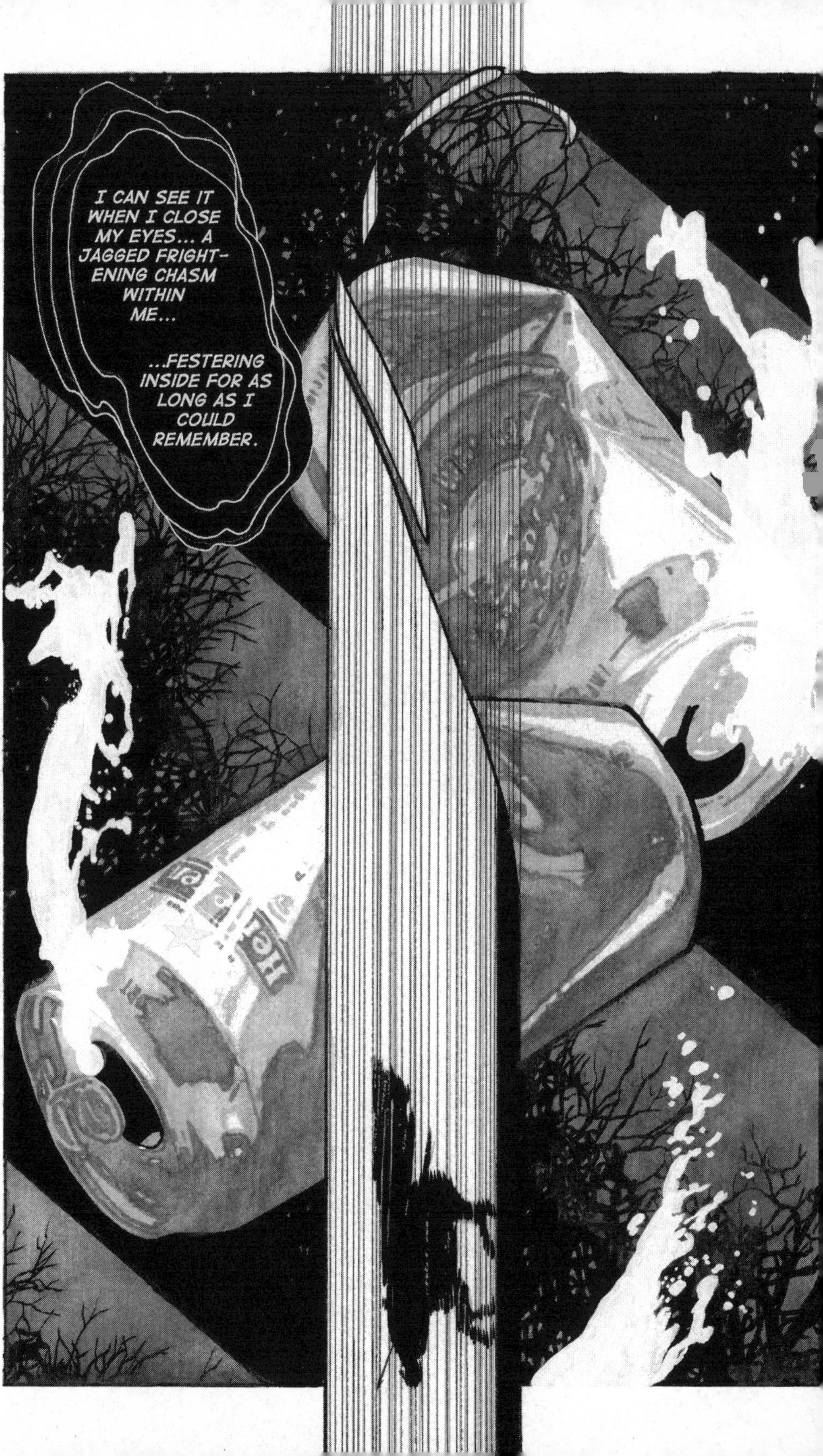
I CAN SEE IT WHEN I CLOSE MY EYES... A JAGGED FRIGHTENING CHASM WITHIN ME...
...FESTERING INSIDE FOR AS LONG AS I COULD REMEMBER.

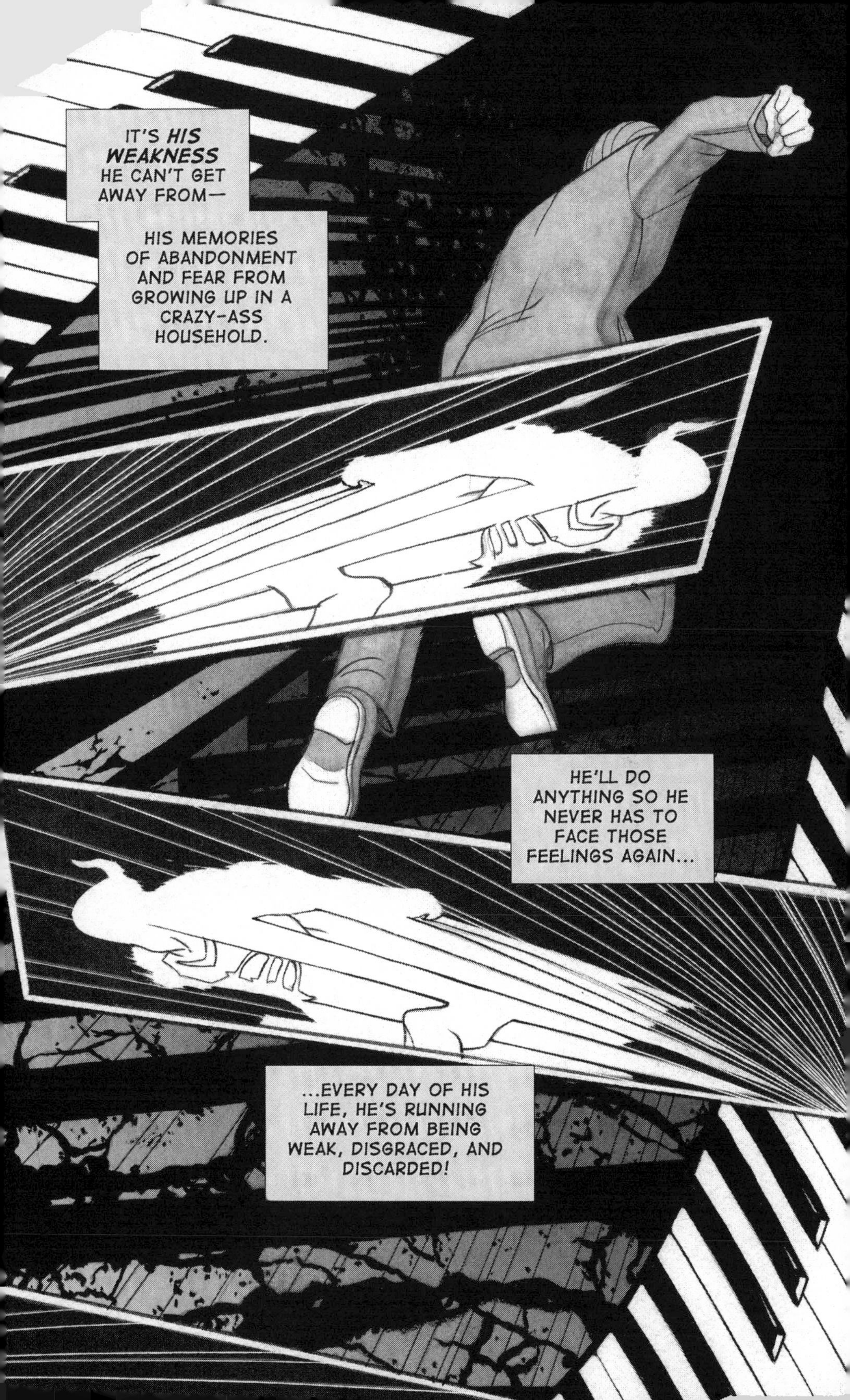
IT'S ***HIS WEAKNESS*** HE CAN'T GET AWAY FROM—
HIS MEMORIES OF ABANDONMENT AND FEAR FROM GROWING UP IN A CRAZY-ASS HOUSEHOLD.
HE'LL DO ANYTHING SO HE NEVER HAS TO FACE THOSE FEELINGS AGAIN...
...EVERY DAY OF HIS LIFE, HE'S RUNNING AWAY FROM BEING WEAK, DISGRACED, AND DISCARDED!

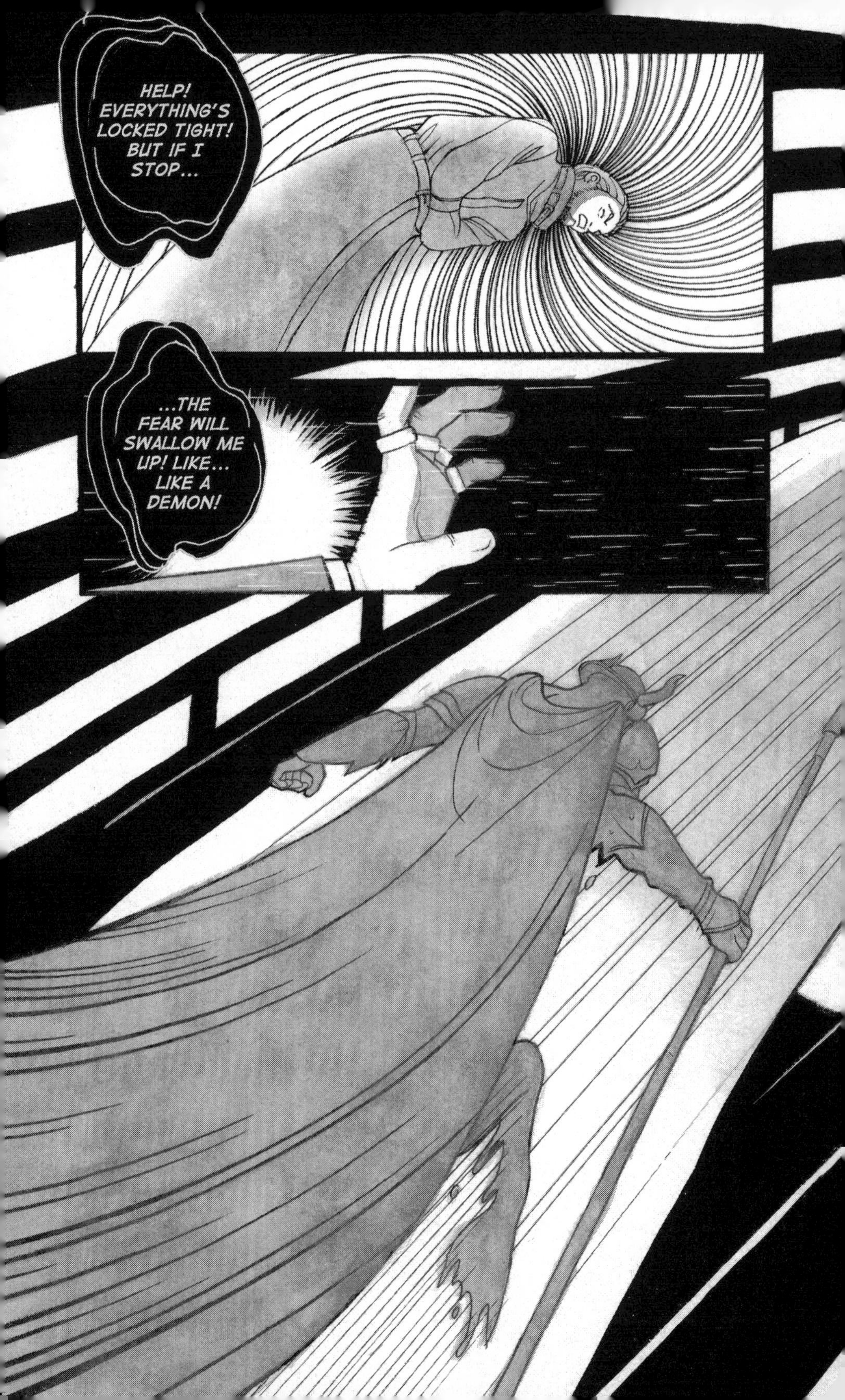
HELP! EVERYTHING'S LOCKED TIGHT! BUT IF I STOP...
...THE FEAR WILL SWALLOW ME UP! LIKE... LIKE A DEMON!

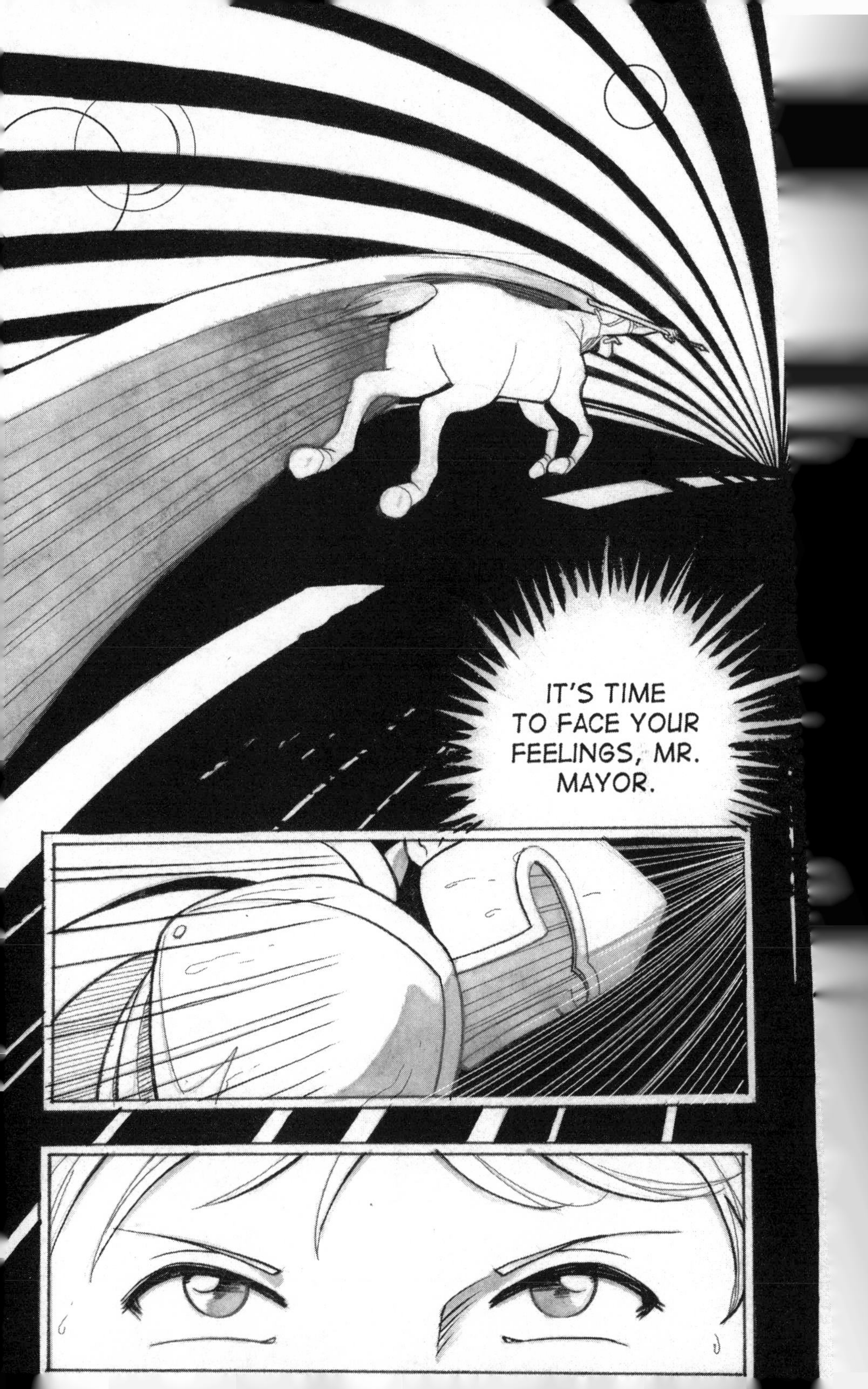
IT'S TIME TO FACE YOUR FEELINGS, MR. MAYOR.

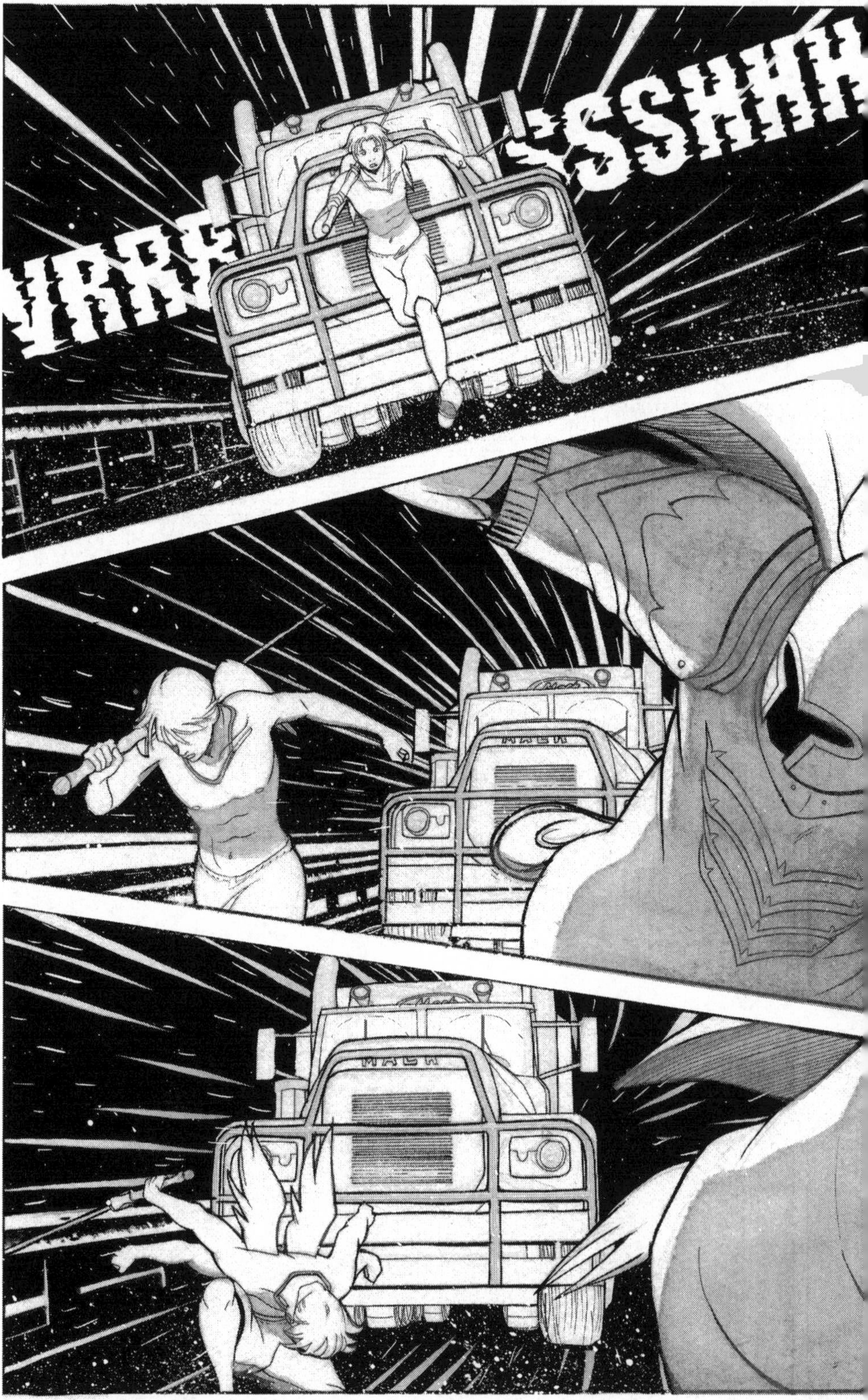

VRRR
SSHHH

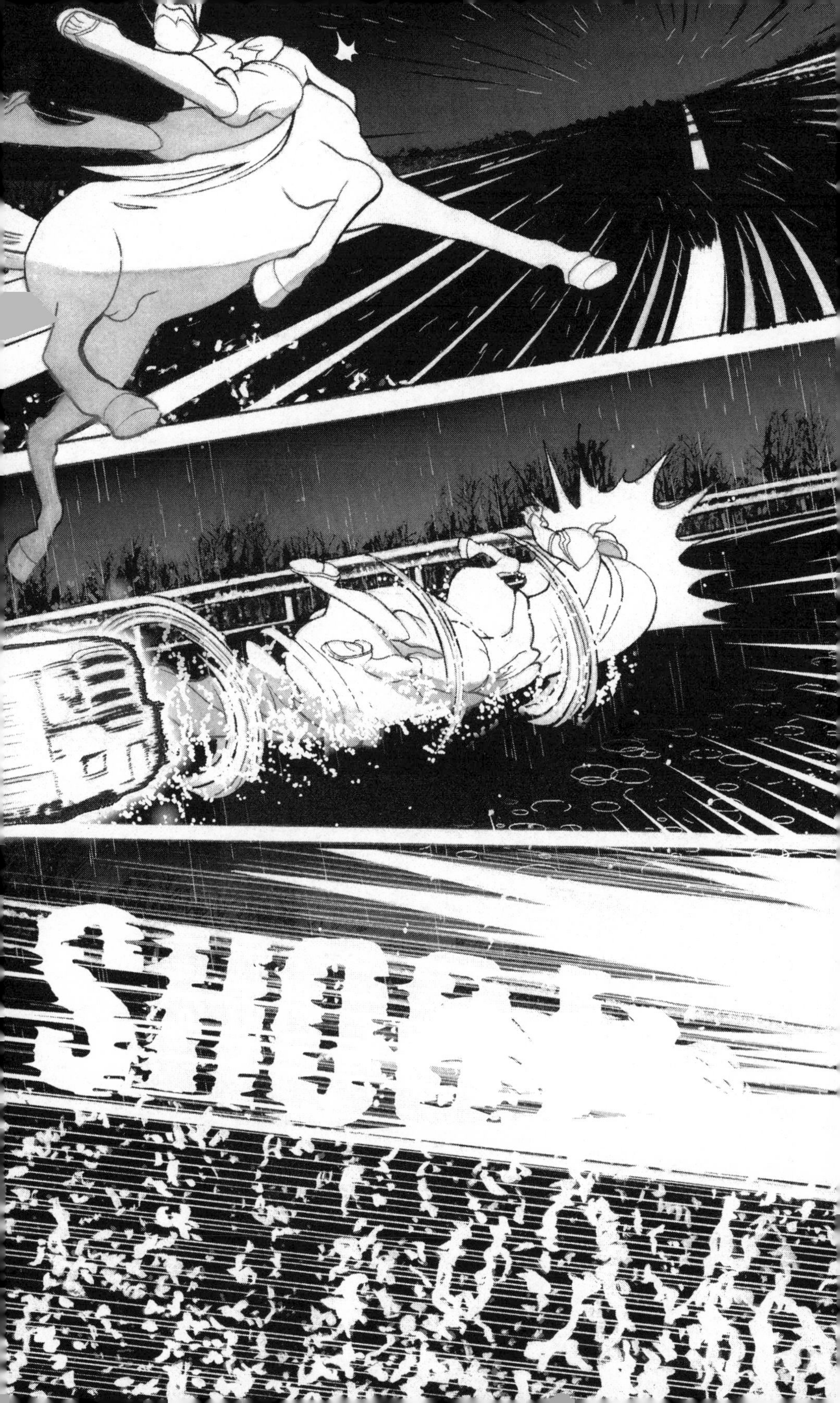
SHOO

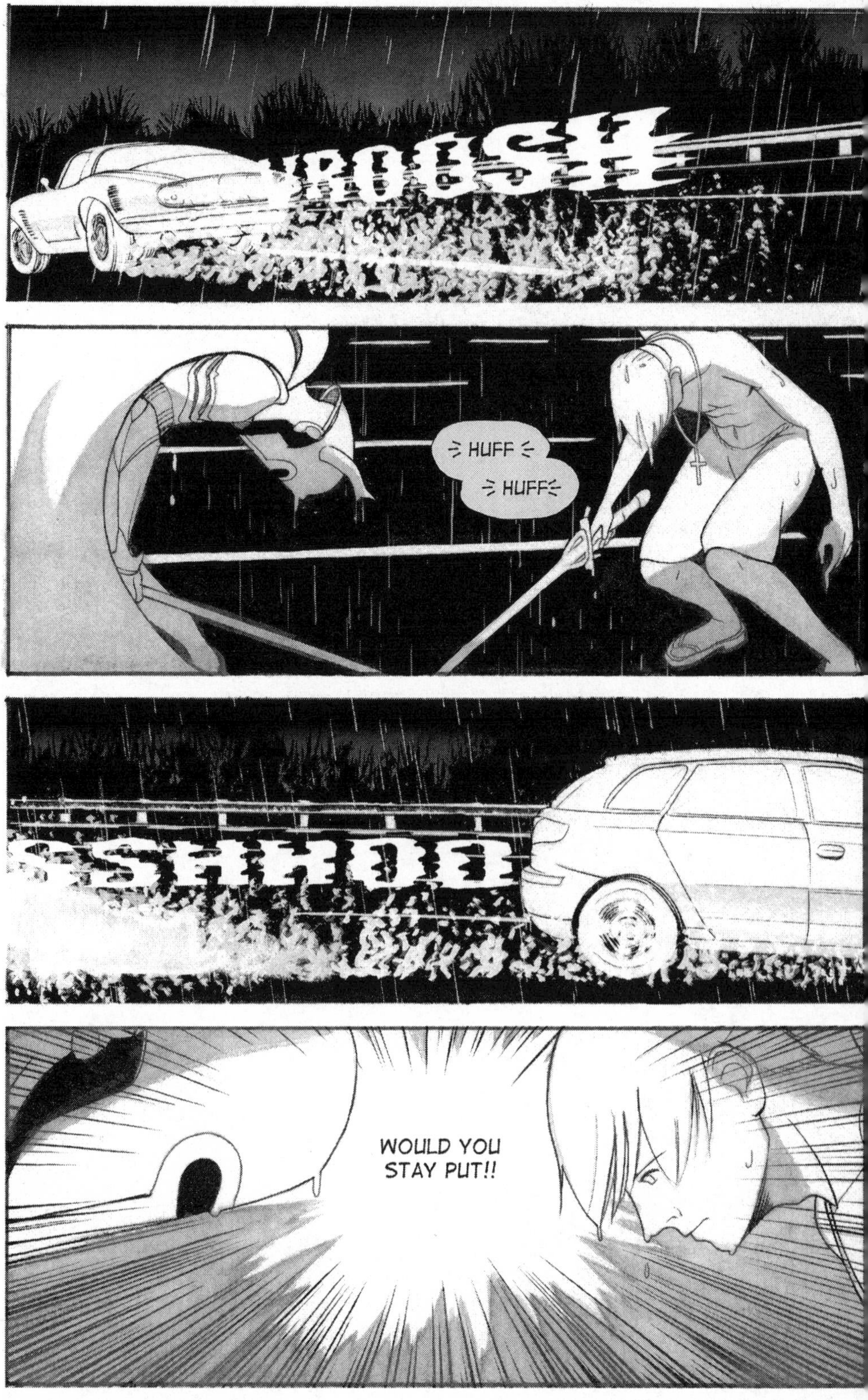

VROOSH
HUFF
HUFF
SHHOOO
WOULD YOU STAY PUT!!

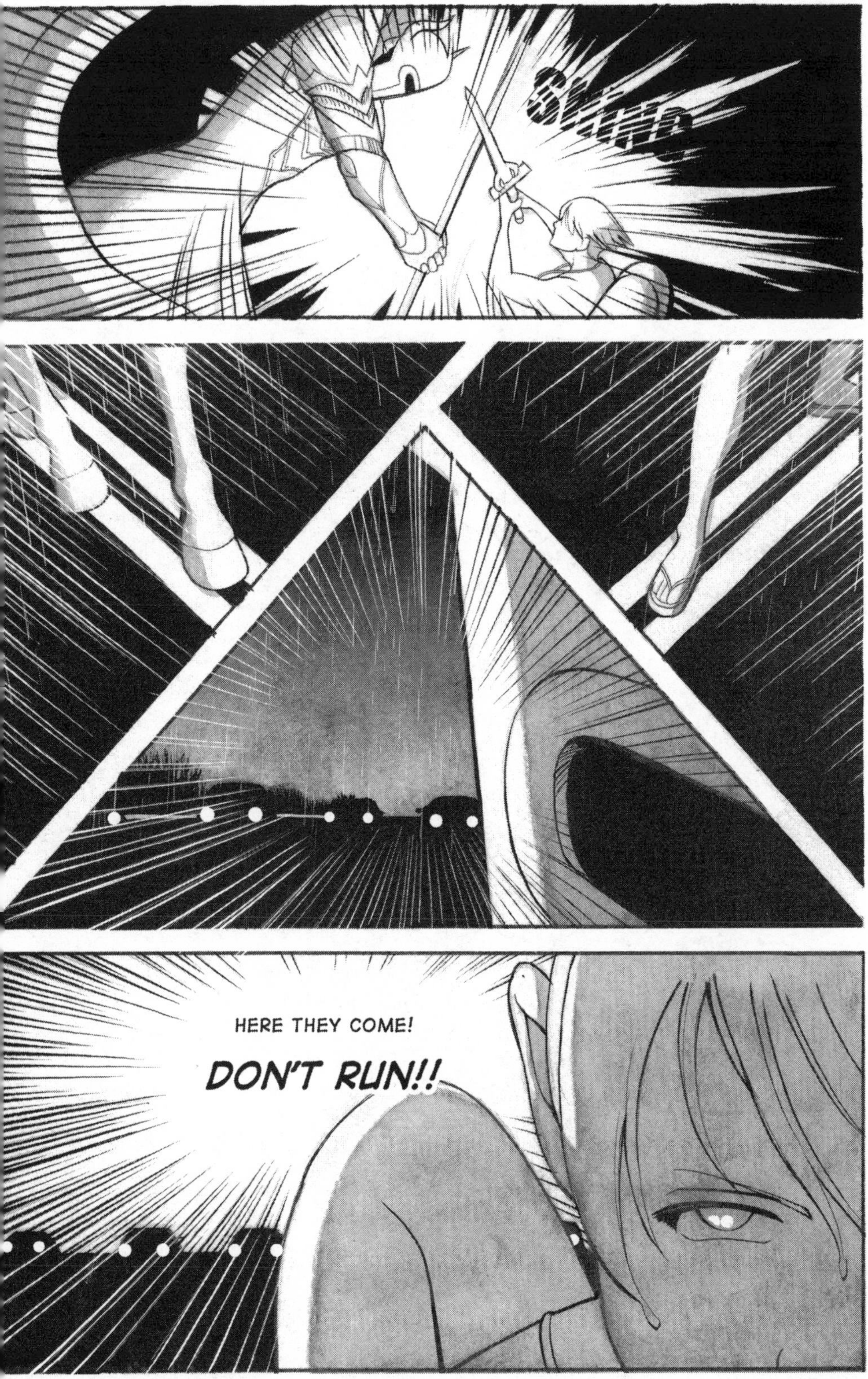
HERE THEY COME!
DON'T RUN!!

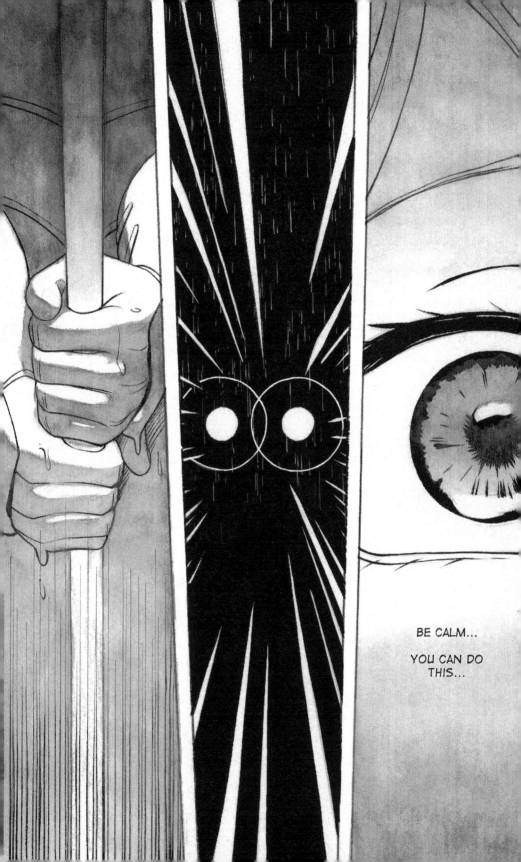

BE CALM...

YOU CAN DO
THIS...

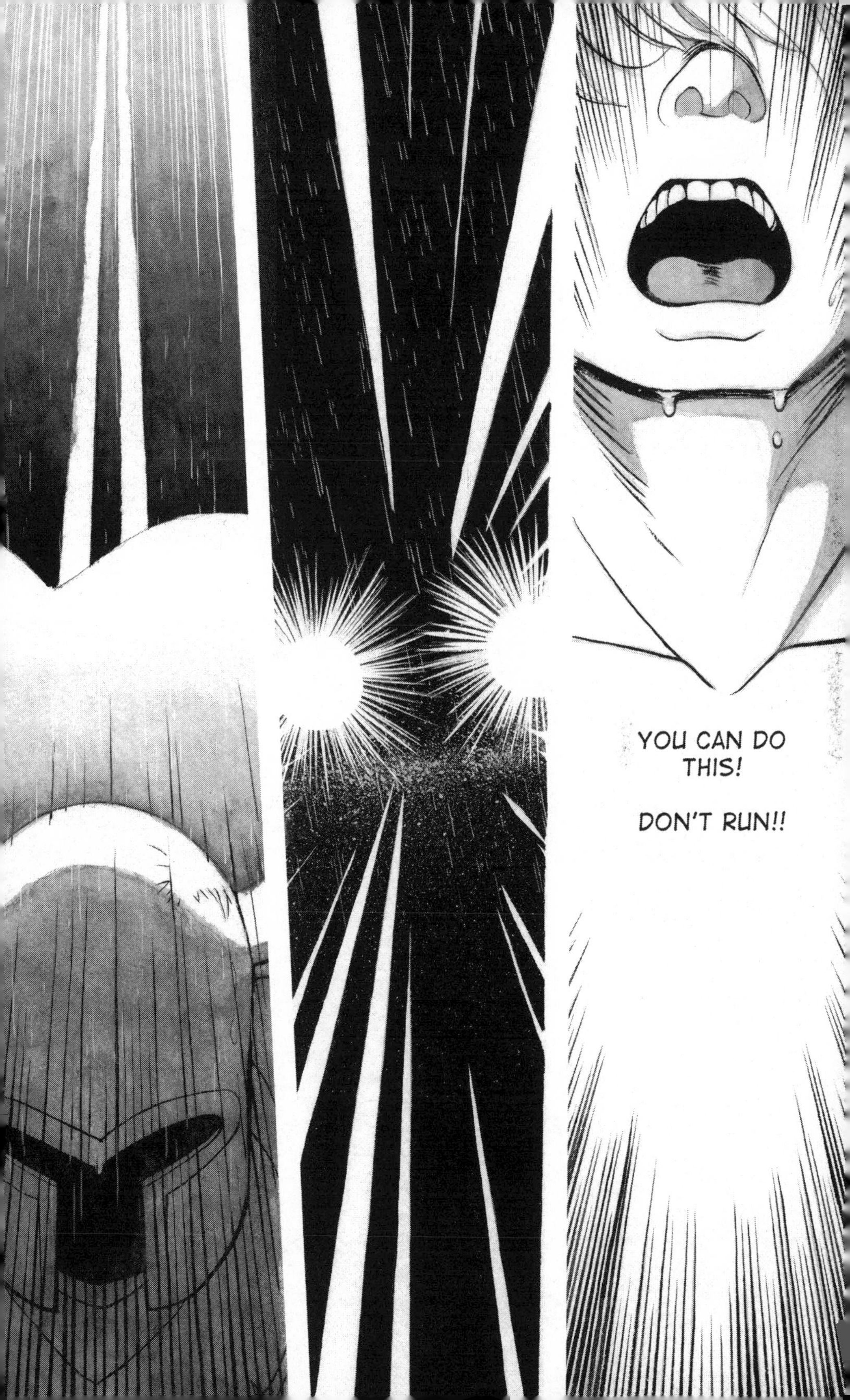
YOU CAN DO THIS!
DON'T RUN!!

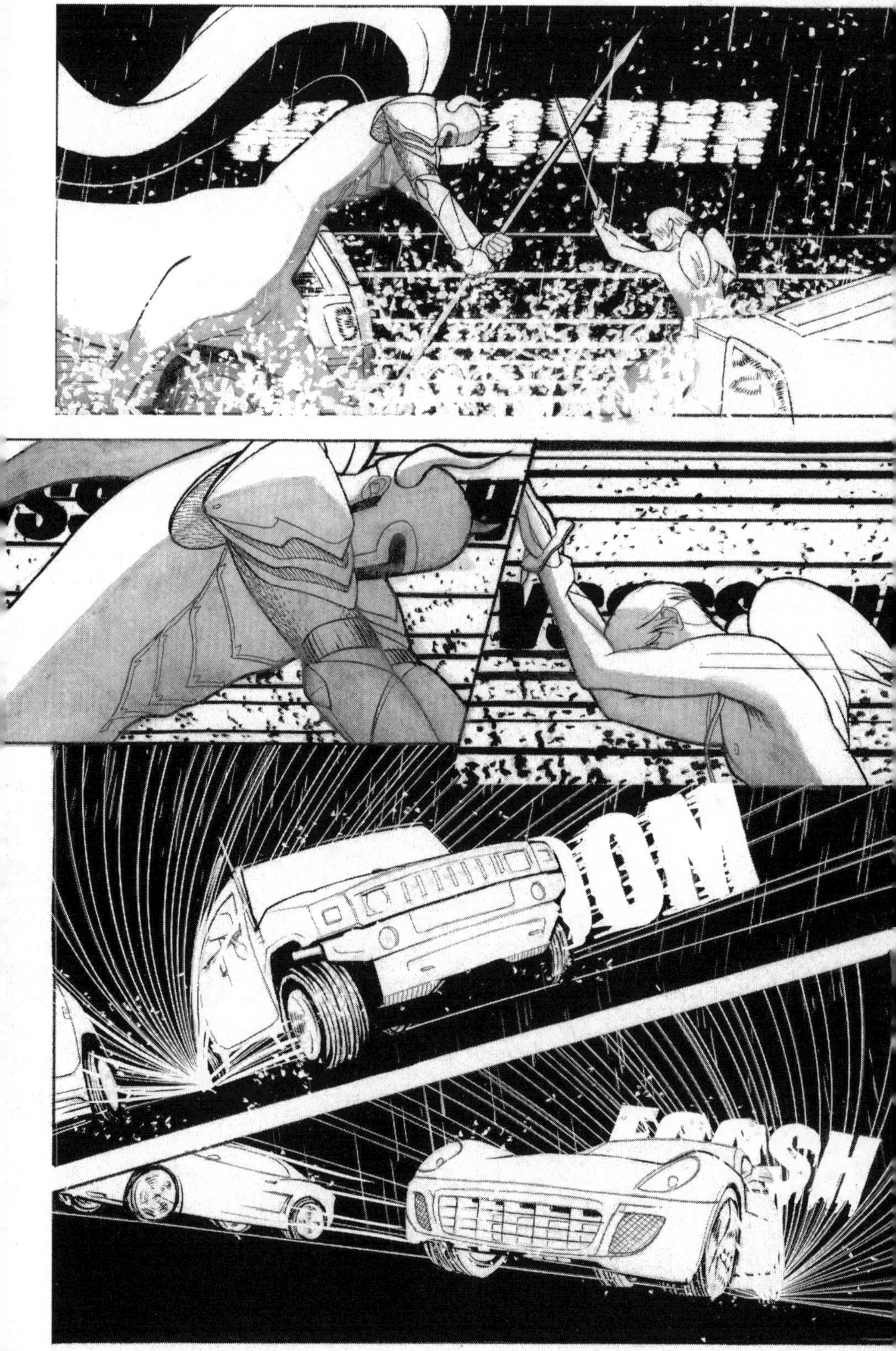
OM

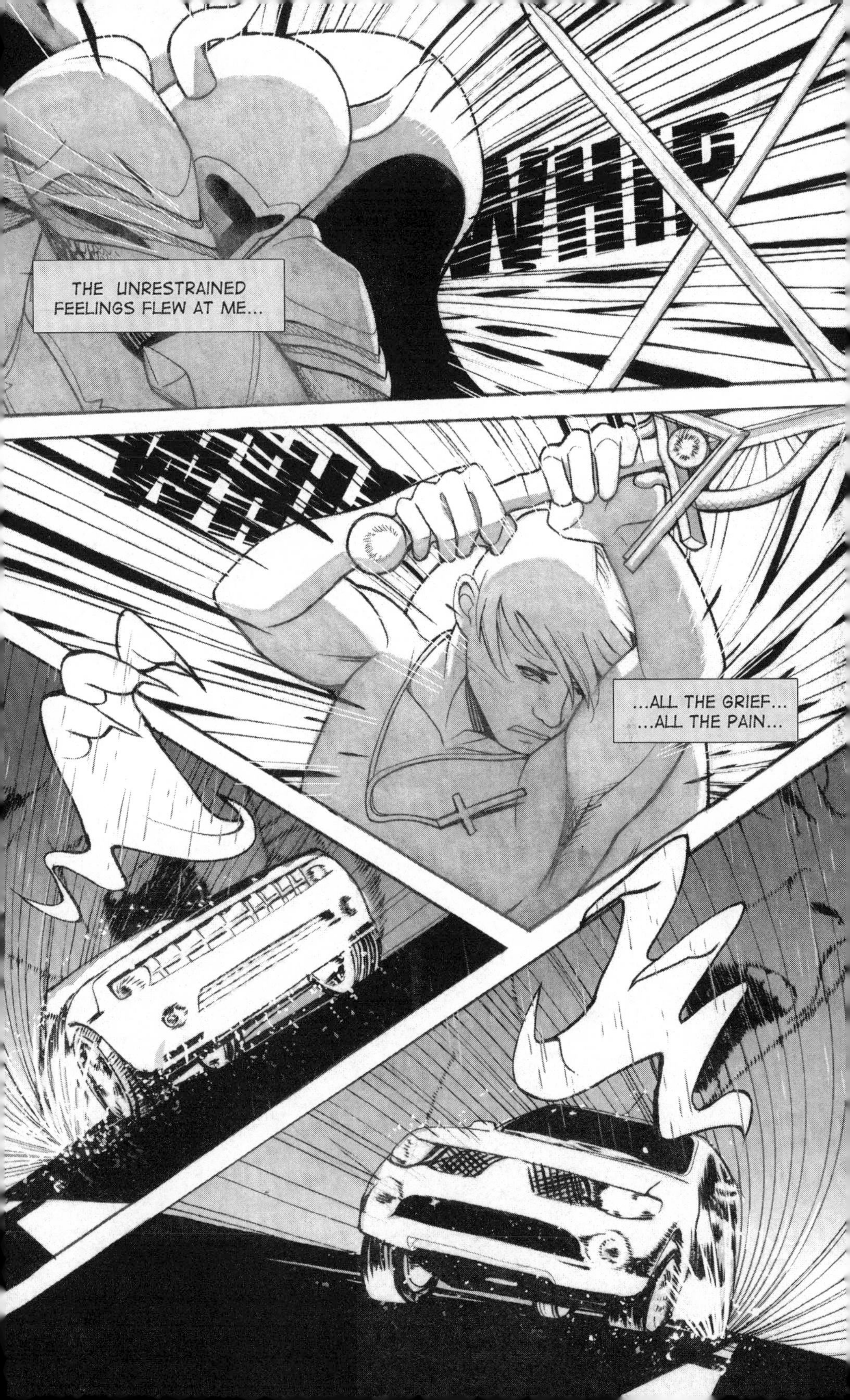
THE UNRESTRAINED FEELINGS FLEW AT ME...
...ALL THE GRIEF... ...ALL THE PAIN...

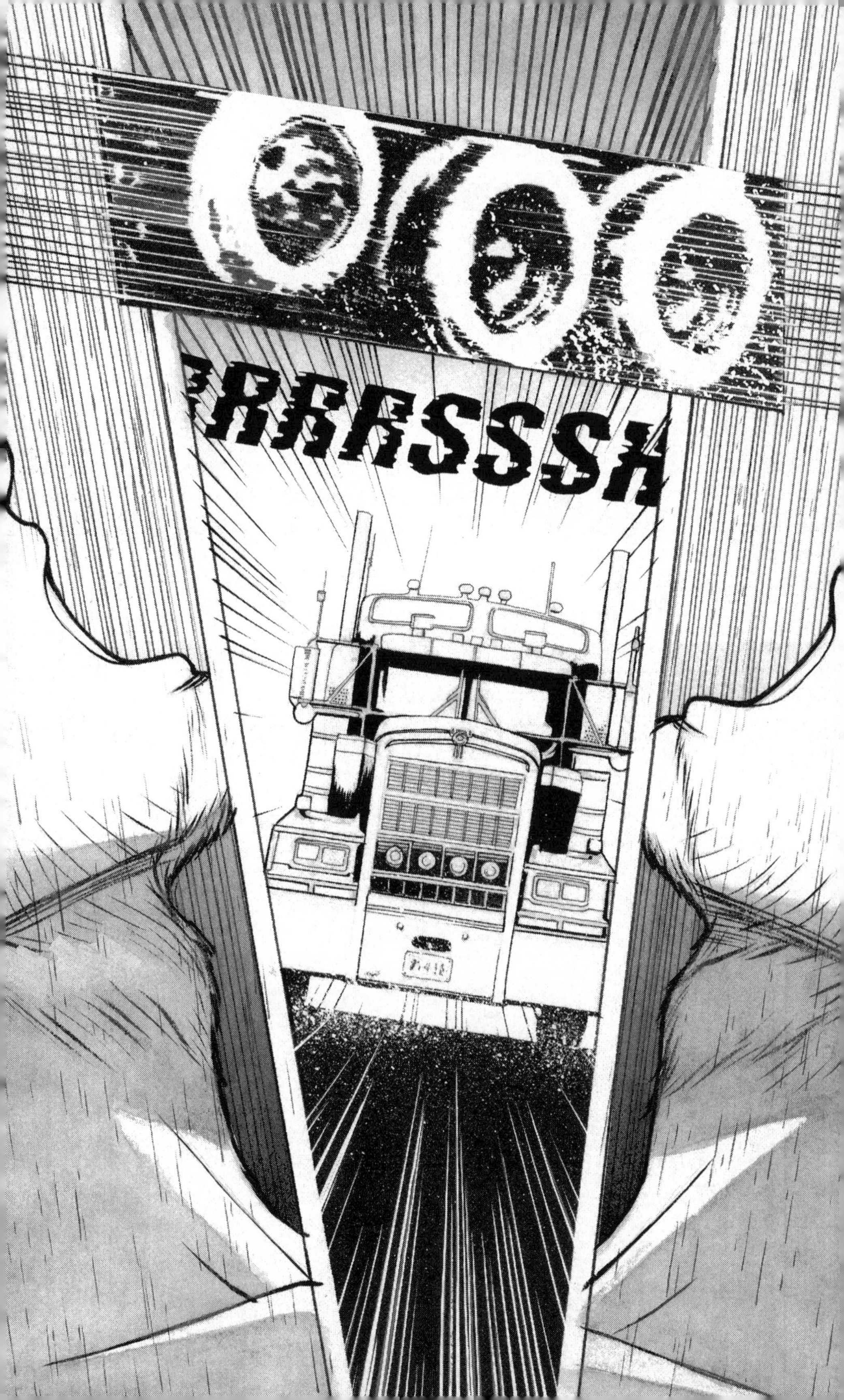
RRRSSSH

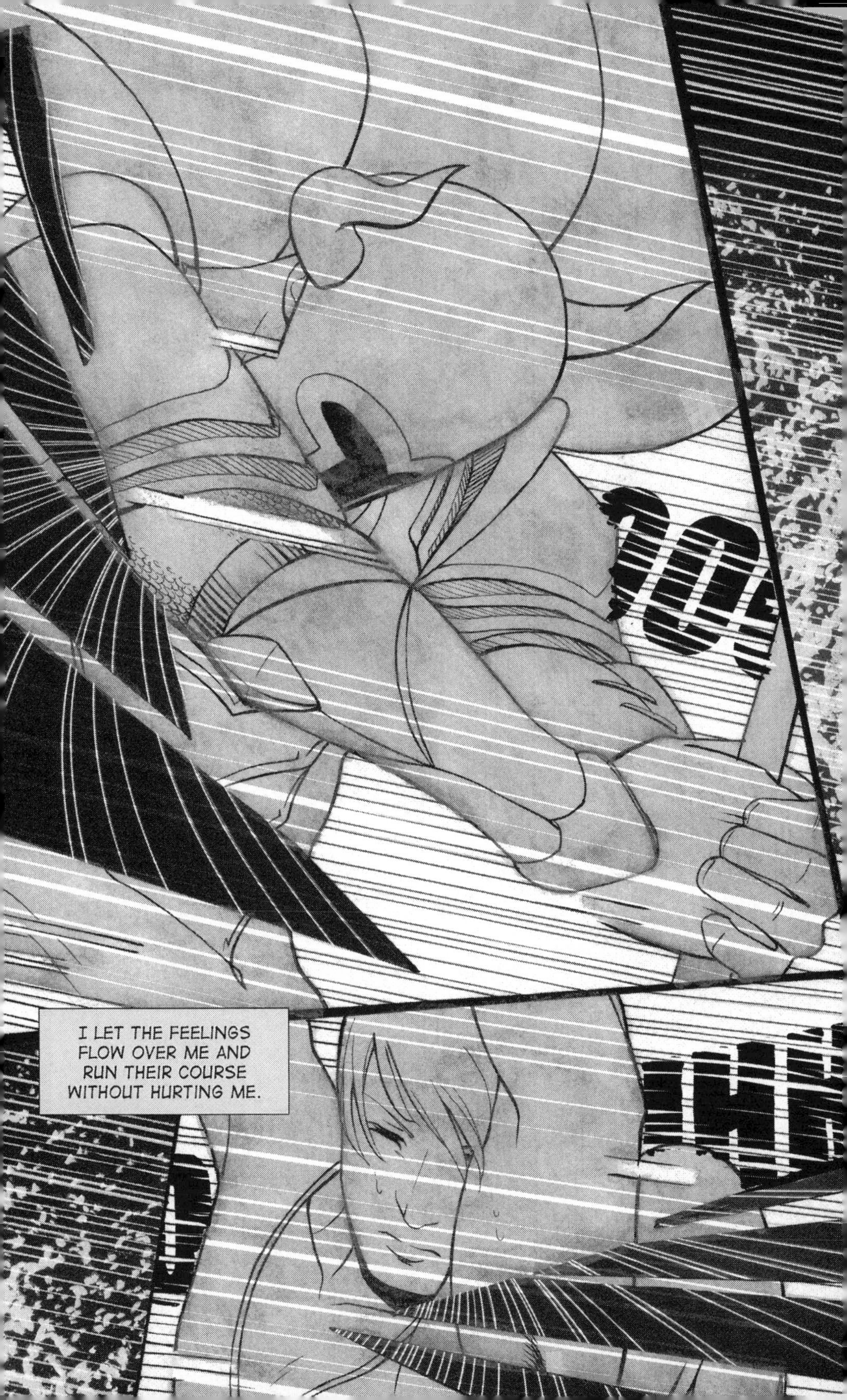
I LET THE FEELINGS FLOW OVER ME AND RUN THEIR COURSE WITHOUT HURTING ME.

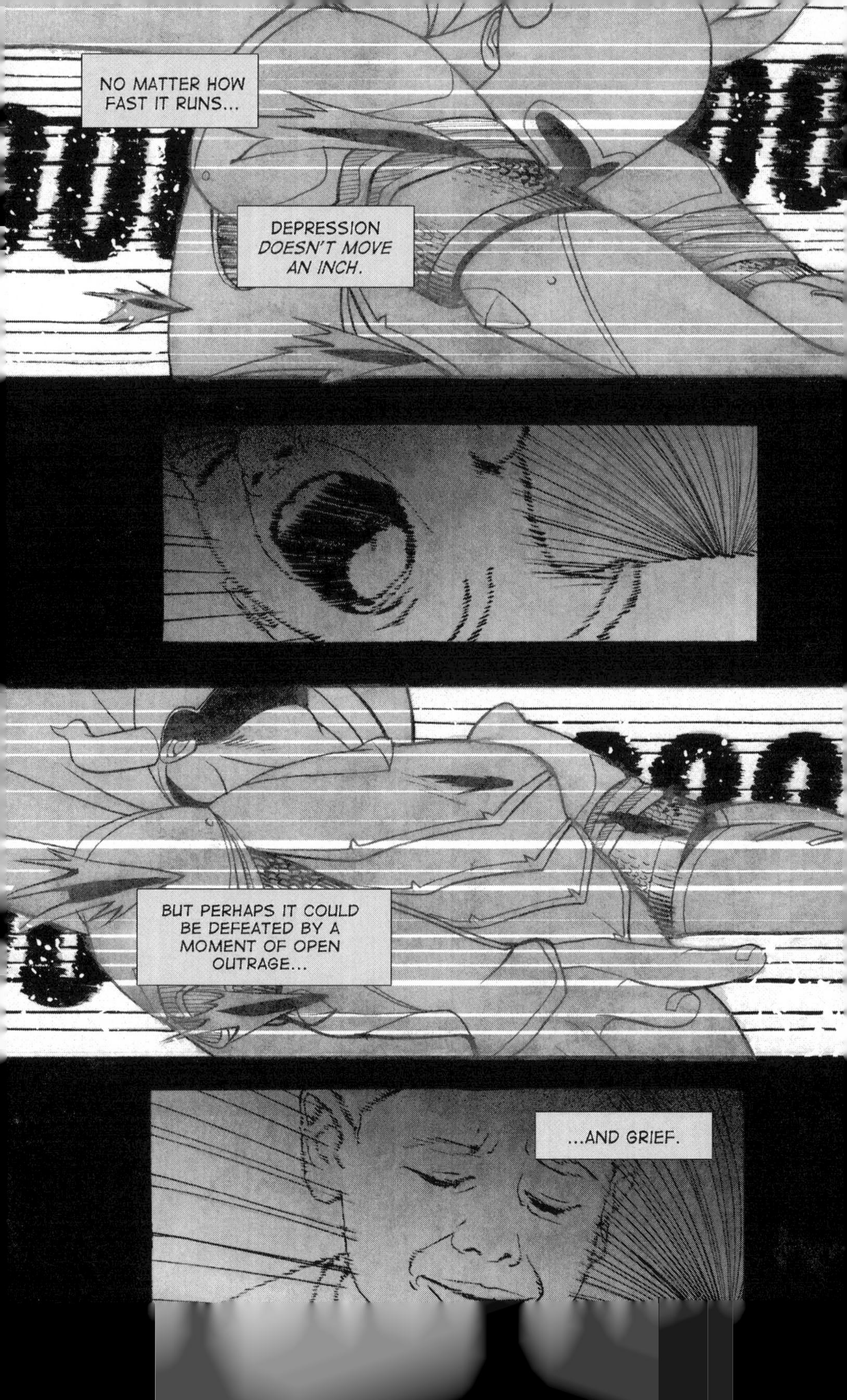
NO MATTER HOW FAST IT RUNS...
DEPRESSION *DOESN'T MOVE* AN INCH.
BUT PERHAPS IT COULD BE DEFEATED BY A MOMENT OF OPEN OUTRAGE...
...AND GRIEF.

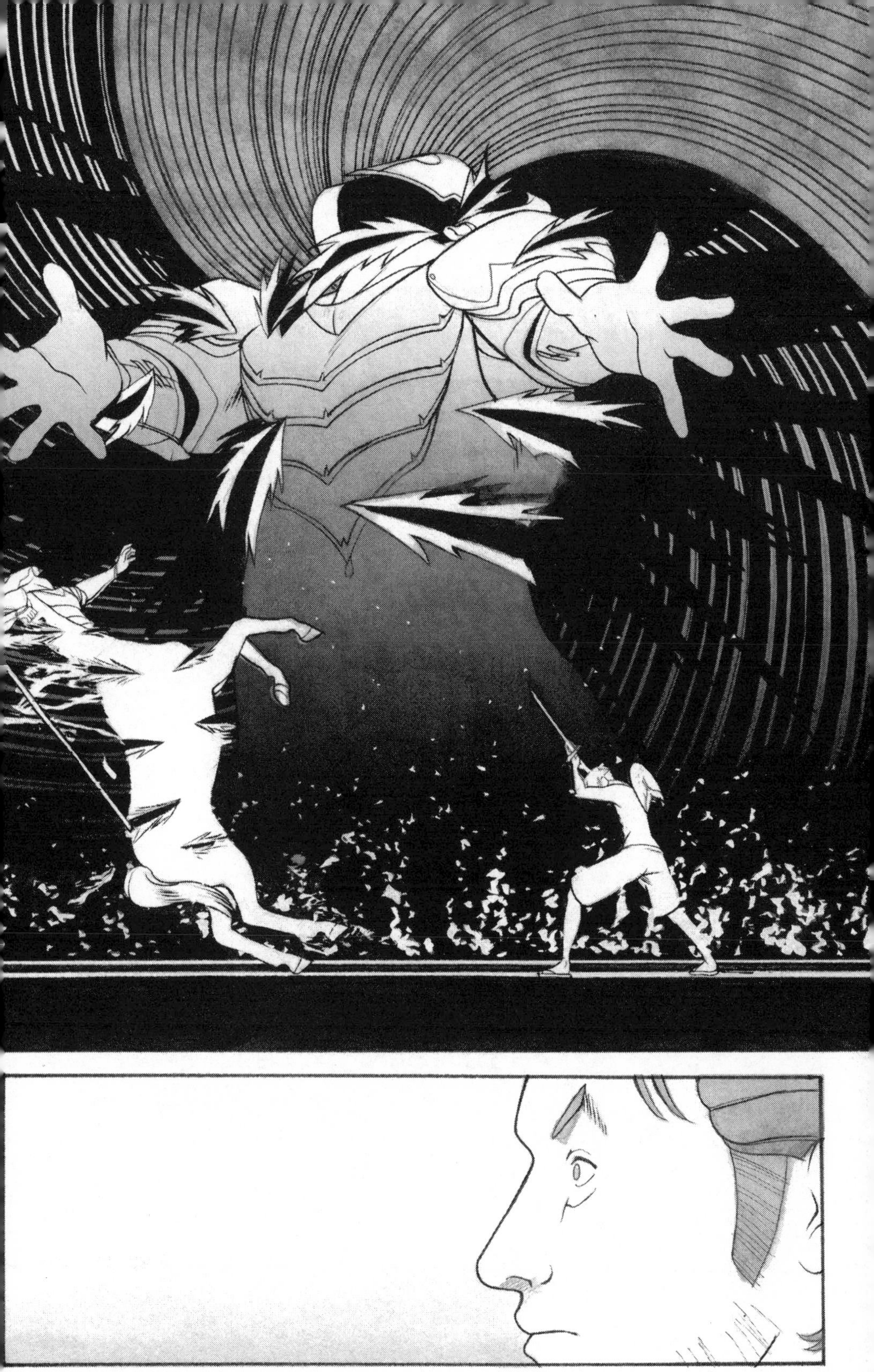

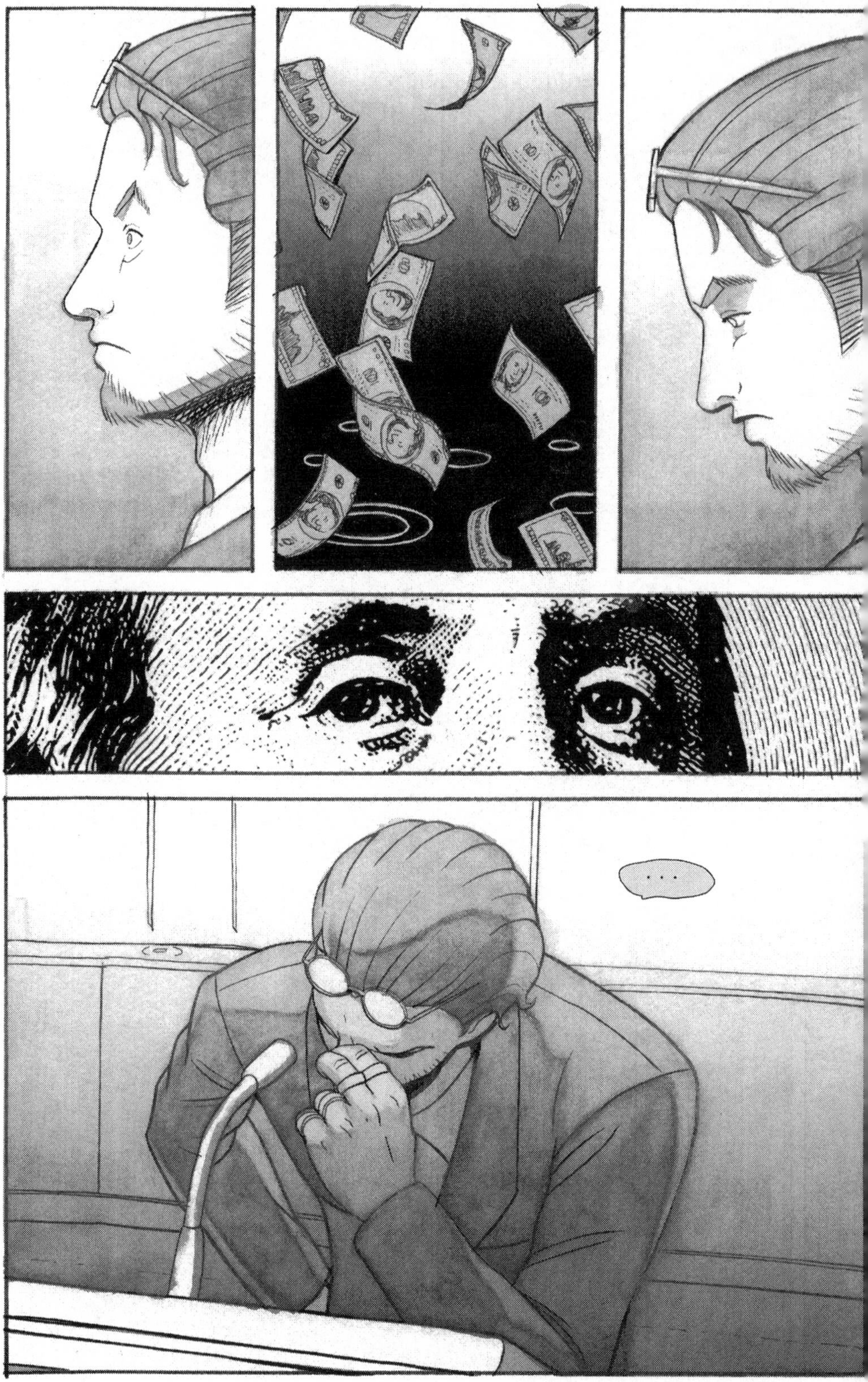
...

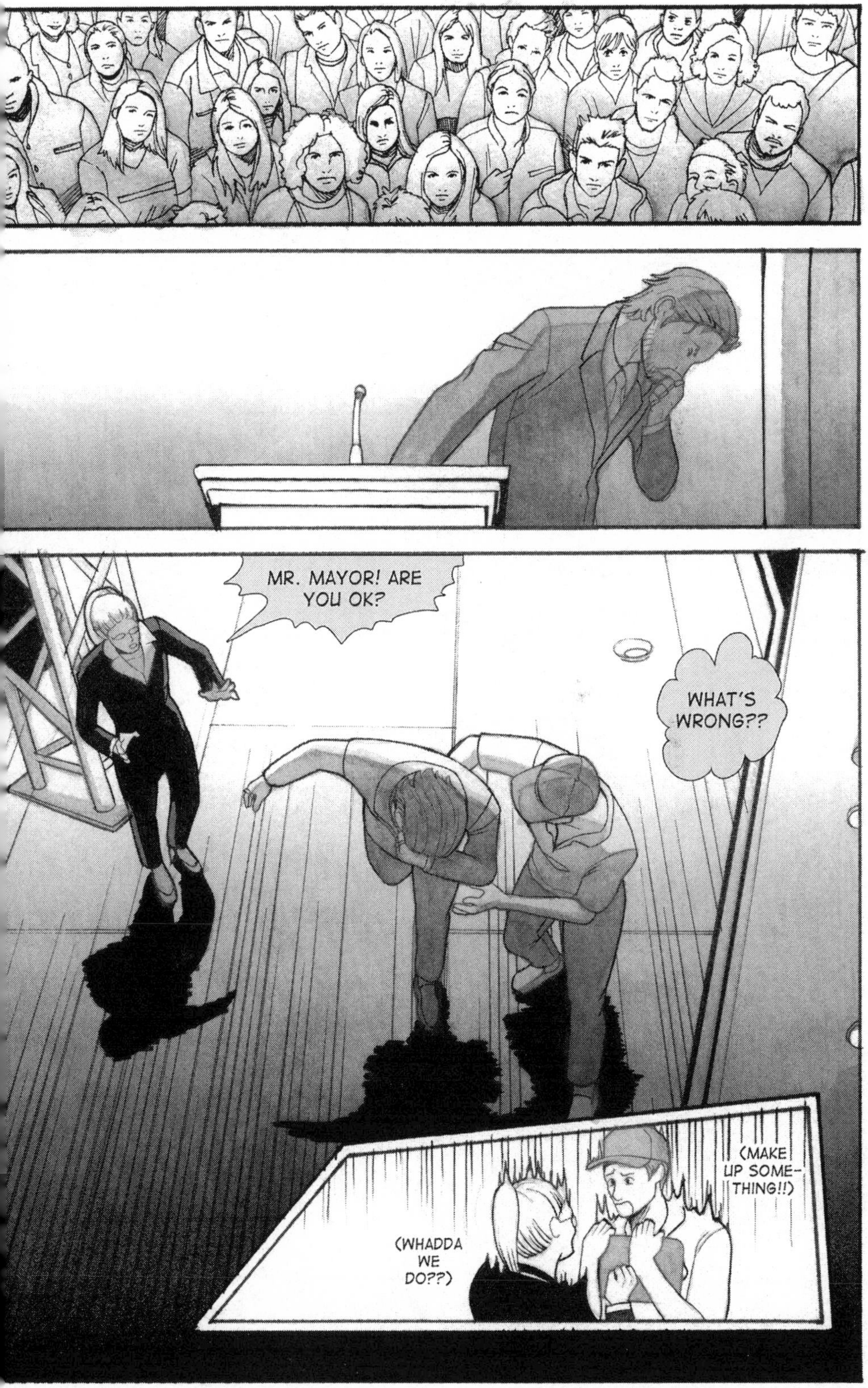
MR. MAYOR! ARE YOU OK?
WHAT'S WRONG??
(MAKE UP SOME-THING!!)
(WHADDA WE DO??)

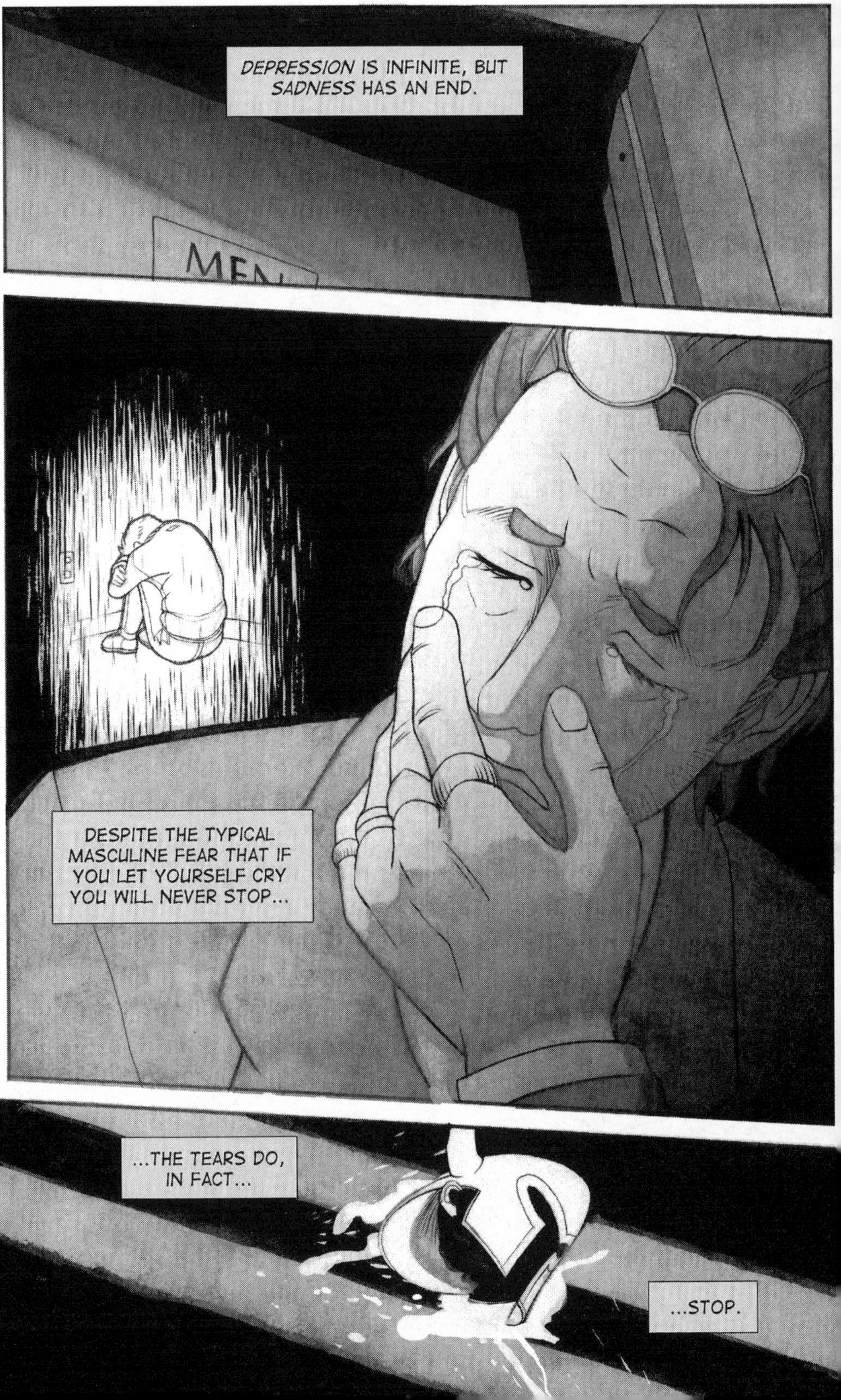
DEPRESSION IS INFINITE, BUT *SADNESS* HAS AN END.
MEN
DESPITE THE TYPICAL MASCULINE FEAR THAT IF YOU LET YOURSELF CRY YOU WILL NEVER STOP...
...THE TEARS DO, IN FACT...
...STOP.

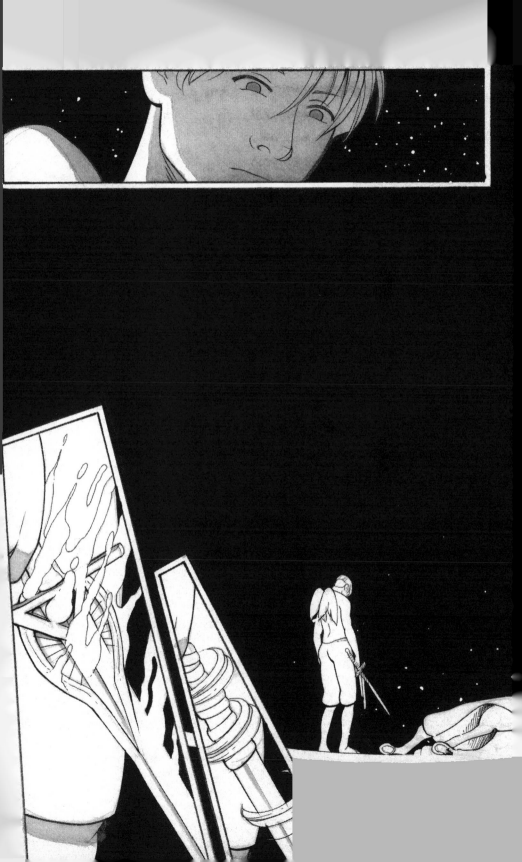

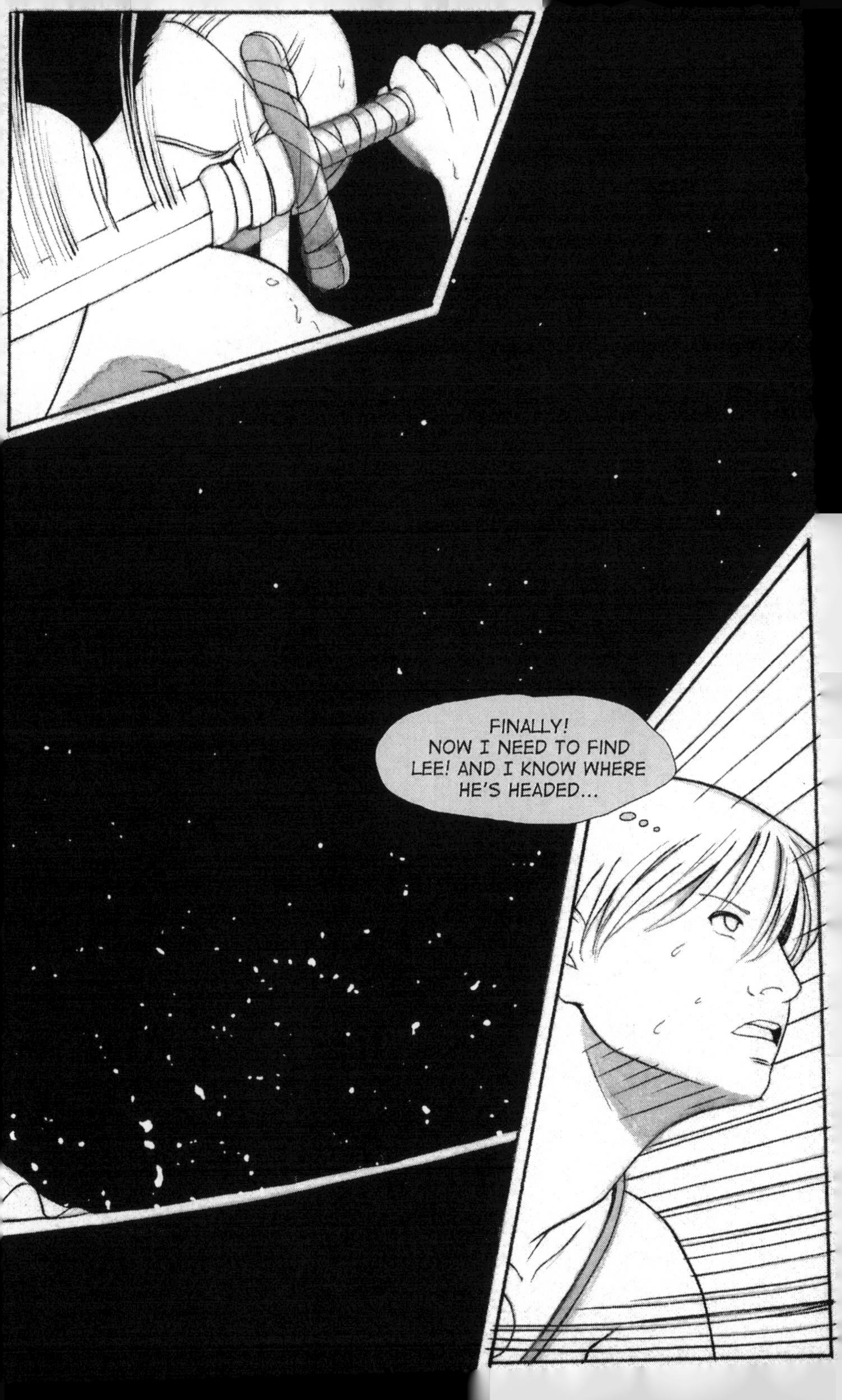
FINALLY!
NOW I NEED TO FIND
LEE! AND I KNOW WHERE
HE'S HEADED...

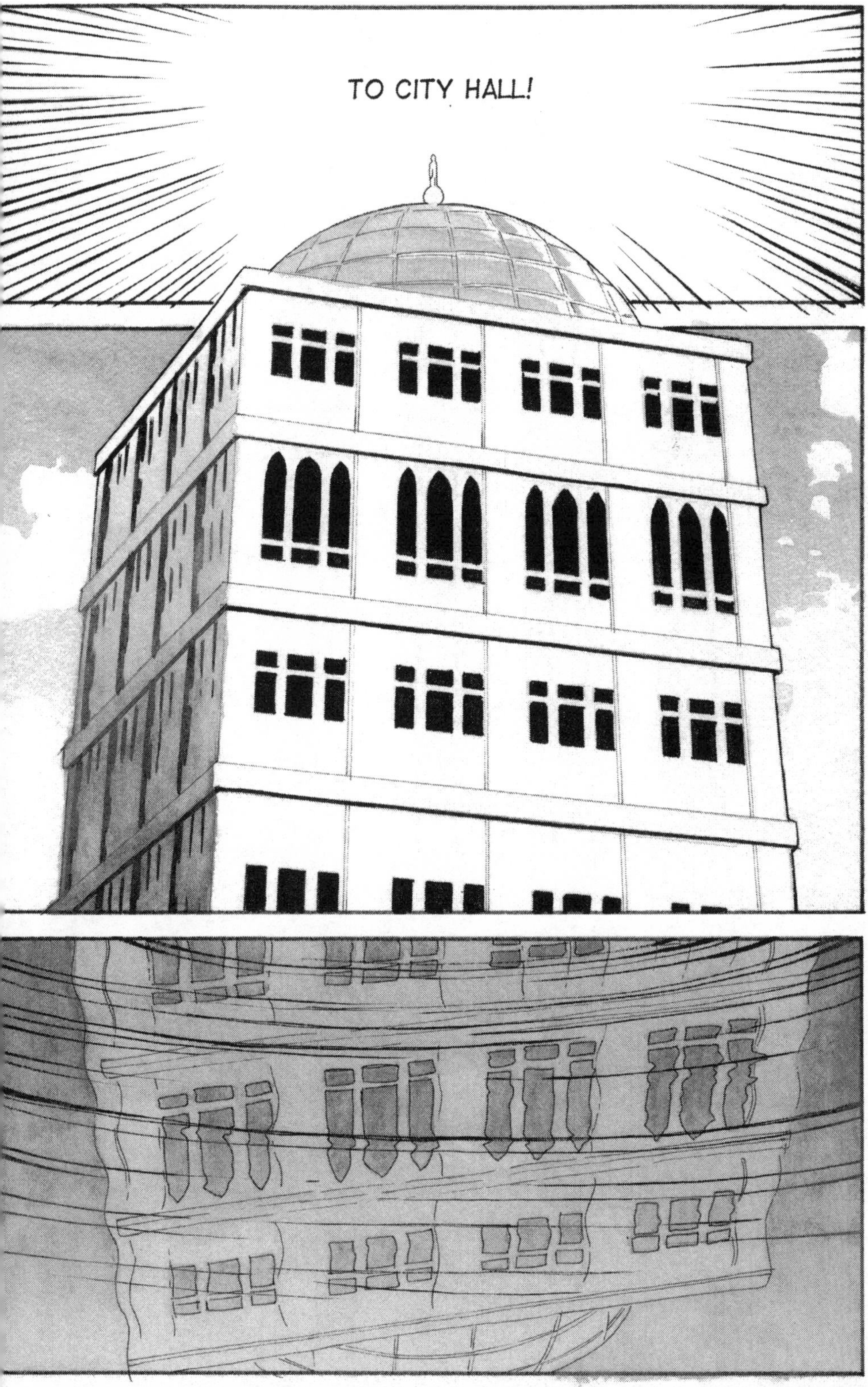
TO CITY HALL!

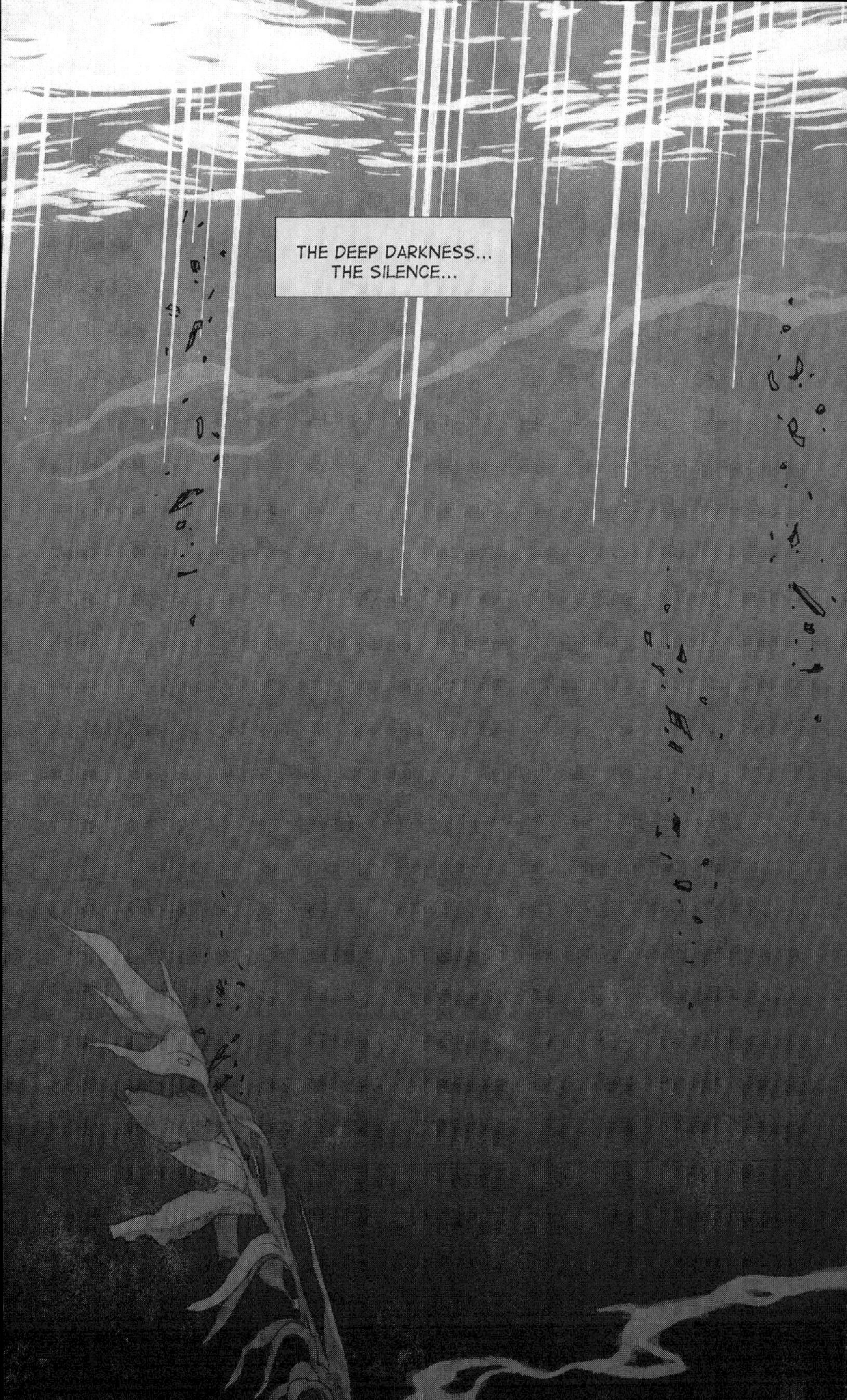
THE DEEP DARKNESS...
THE SILENCE...

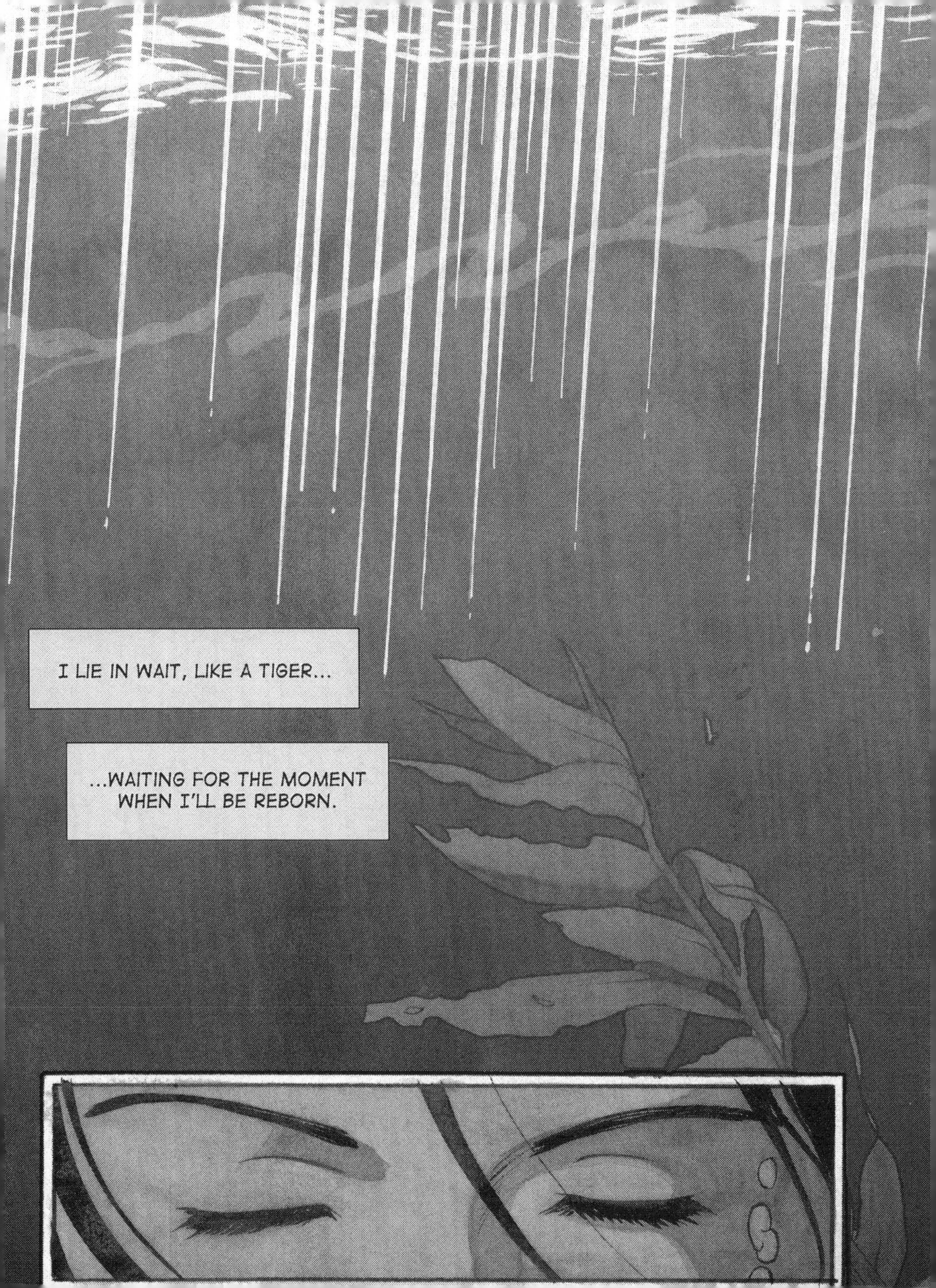
I LIE IN WAIT, LIKE A TIGER...
...WAITING FOR THE MOMENT WHEN I'LL BE REBORN.

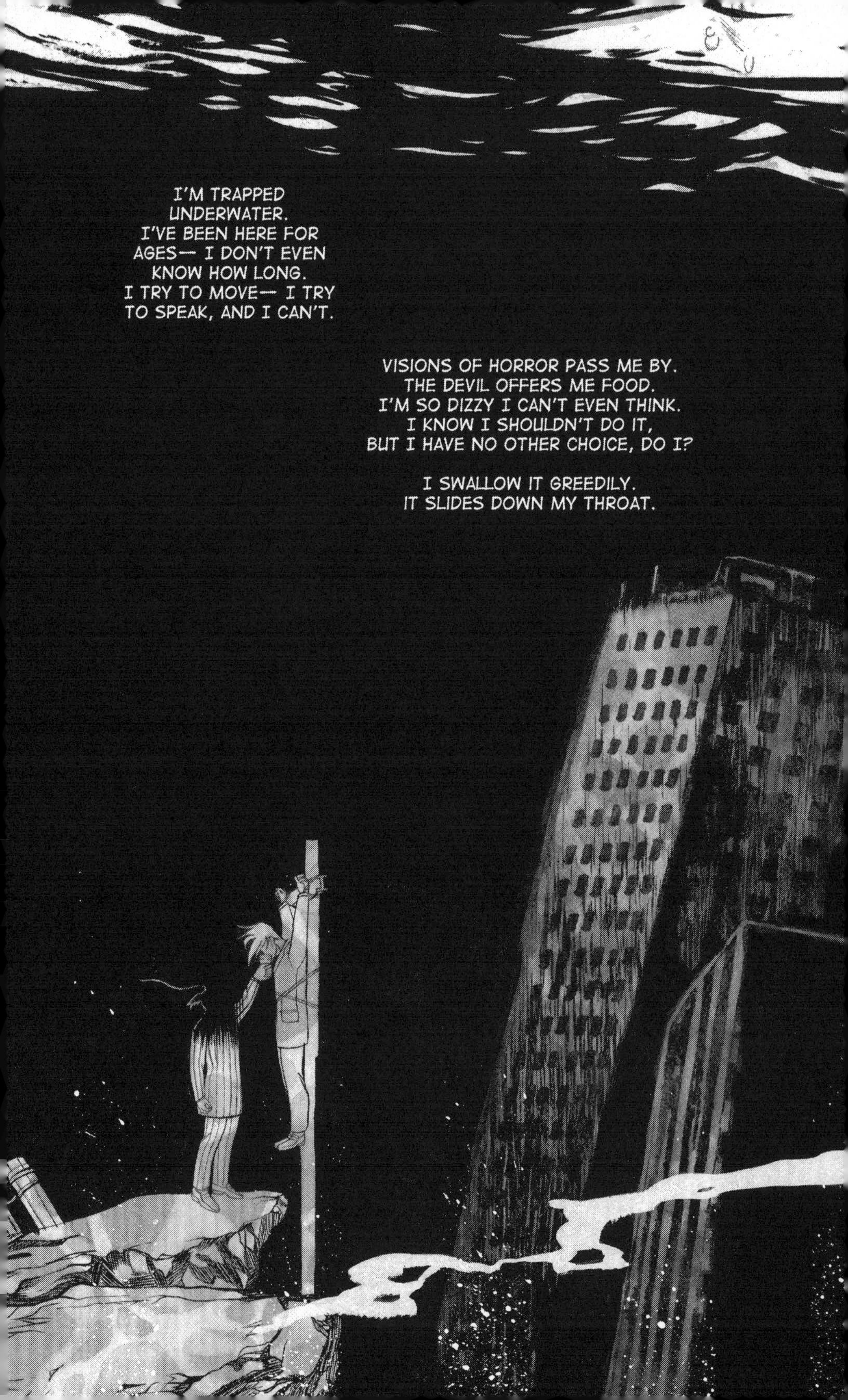
I'M TRAPPED UNDERWATER. I'VE BEEN HERE FOR AGES— I DON'T EVEN KNOW HOW LONG. I TRY TO MOVE— I TRY TO SPEAK, AND I CAN'T.
VISIONS OF HORROR PASS ME BY. THE DEVIL OFFERS ME FOOD. I'M SO DIZZY I CAN'T EVEN THINK. I KNOW I SHOULDN'T DO IT, BUT I HAVE NO OTHER CHOICE, DO I?
I SWALLOW IT GREEDILY. IT SLIDES DOWN MY THROAT.

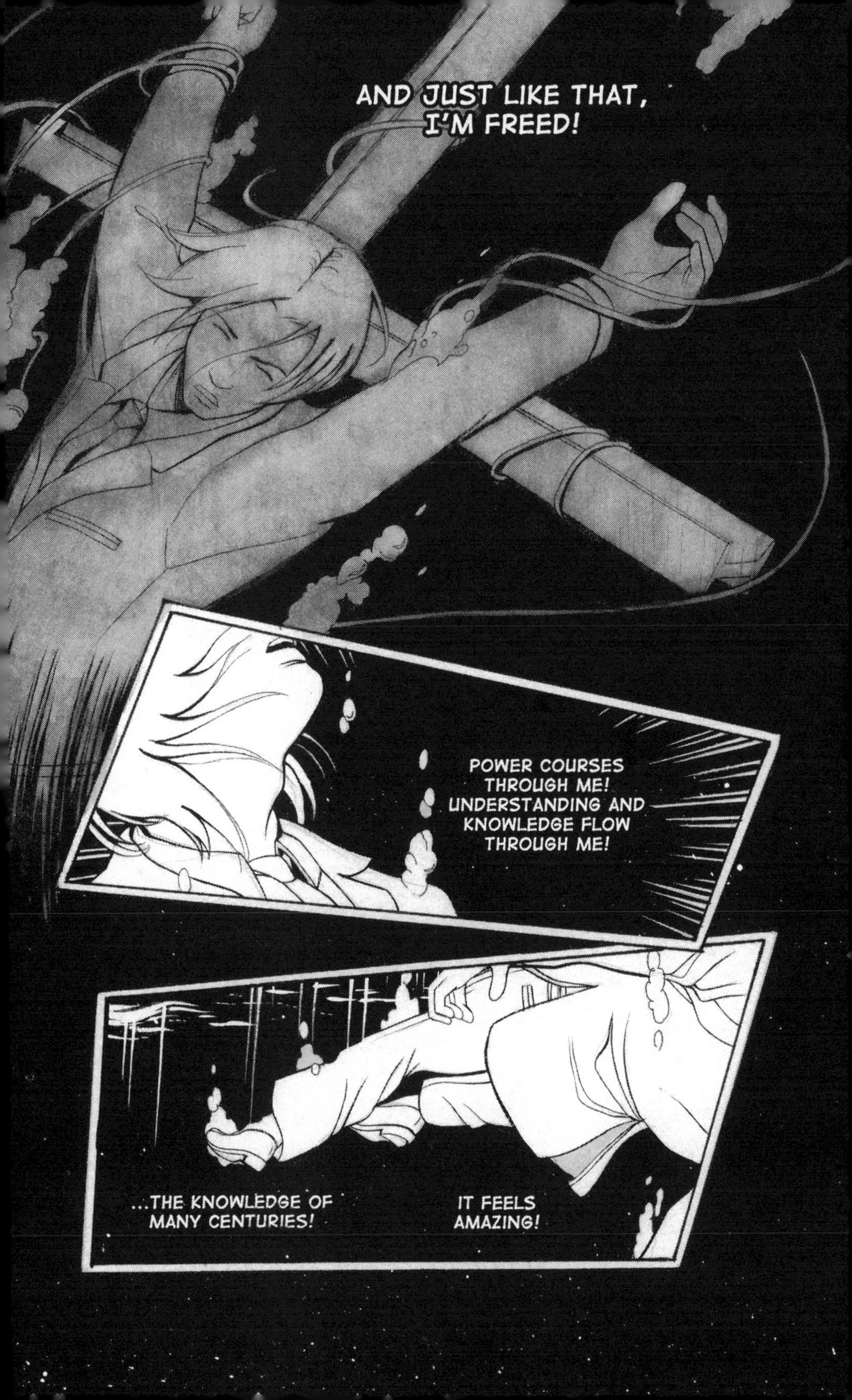
AND JUST LIKE THAT, I'M FREED!
POWER COURSES THROUGH ME! UNDERSTANDING AND KNOWLEDGE FLOW THROUGH ME!
...THE KNOWLEDGE OF MANY CENTURIES!
IT FEELS AMAZING!

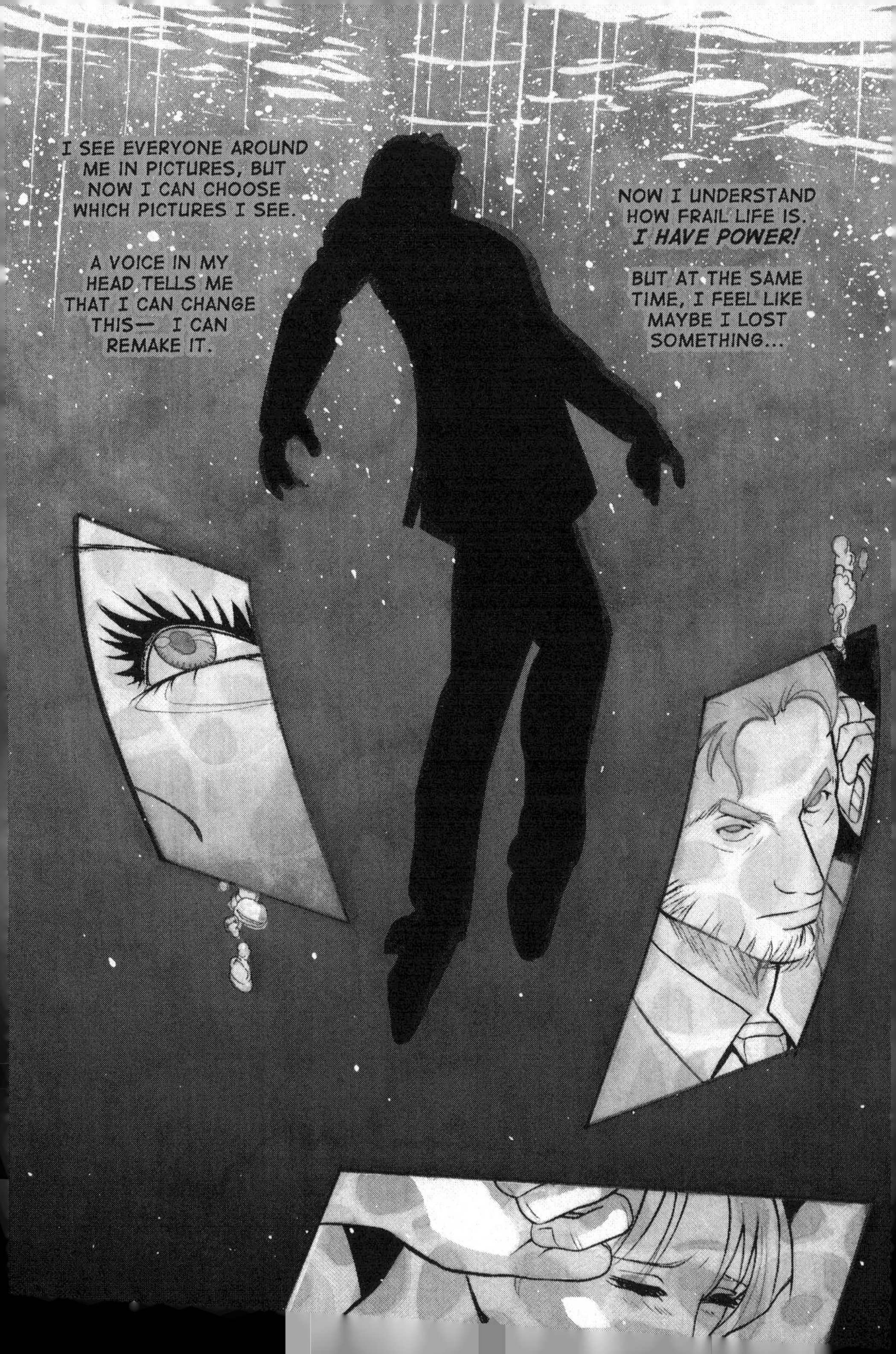
I SEE EVERYONE AROUND ME IN PICTURES, BUT NOW I CAN CHOOSE WHICH PICTURES I SEE.
A VOICE IN MY HEAD TELLS ME THAT I CAN CHANGE THIS— I CAN REMAKE IT.
NOW I UNDERSTAND HOW FRAIL LIFE IS. *I HAVE POWER!*
BUT AT THE SAME TIME, I FEEL LIKE MAYBE I LOST SOMETHING...

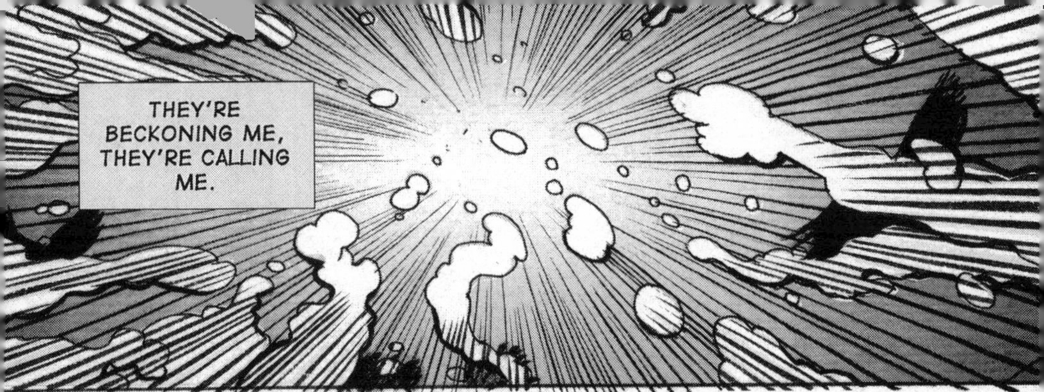
THEY'RE BECKONING ME, THEY'RE CALLING ME.

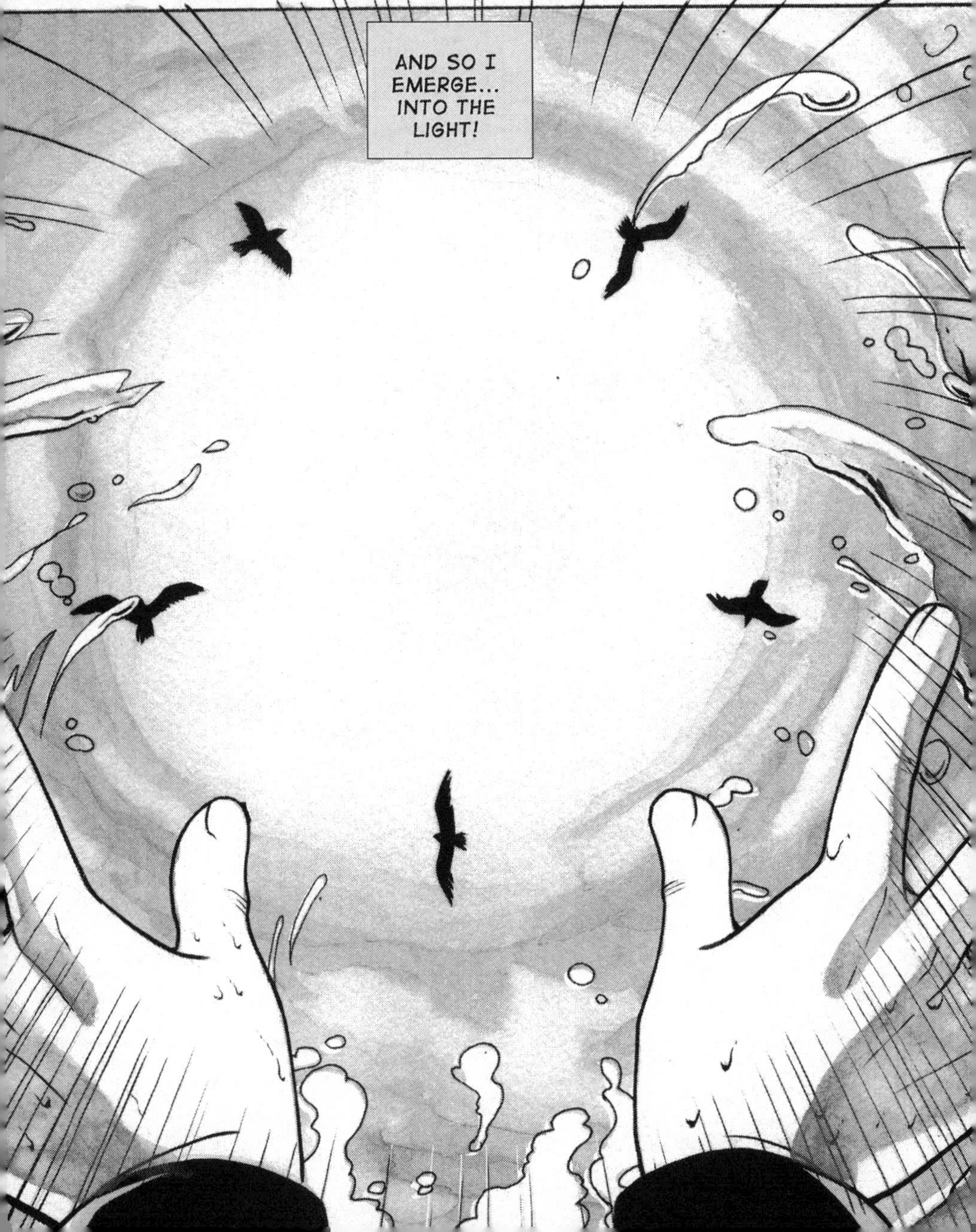
AND SO I EMERGE... INTO THE LIGHT!

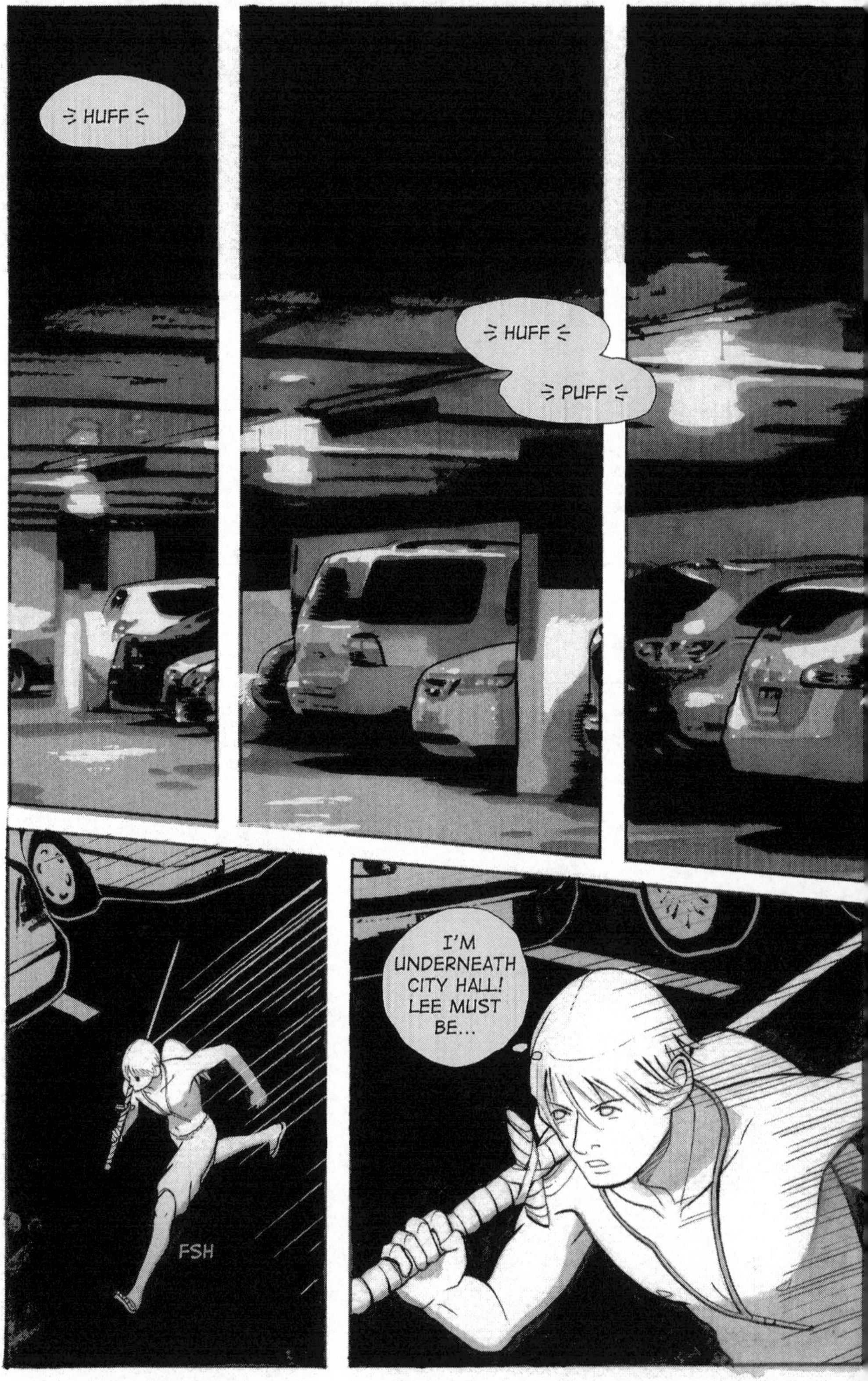
HUFF
HUFF
PUFF
FSH
I'M UNDERNEATH CITY HALL! LEE MUST BE...

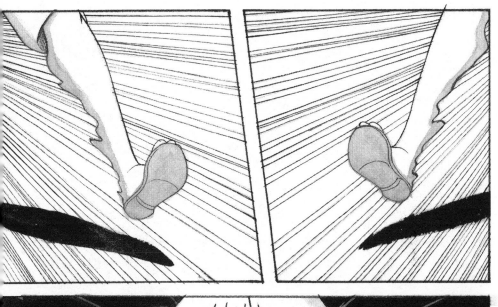

FOOSH

LEE!

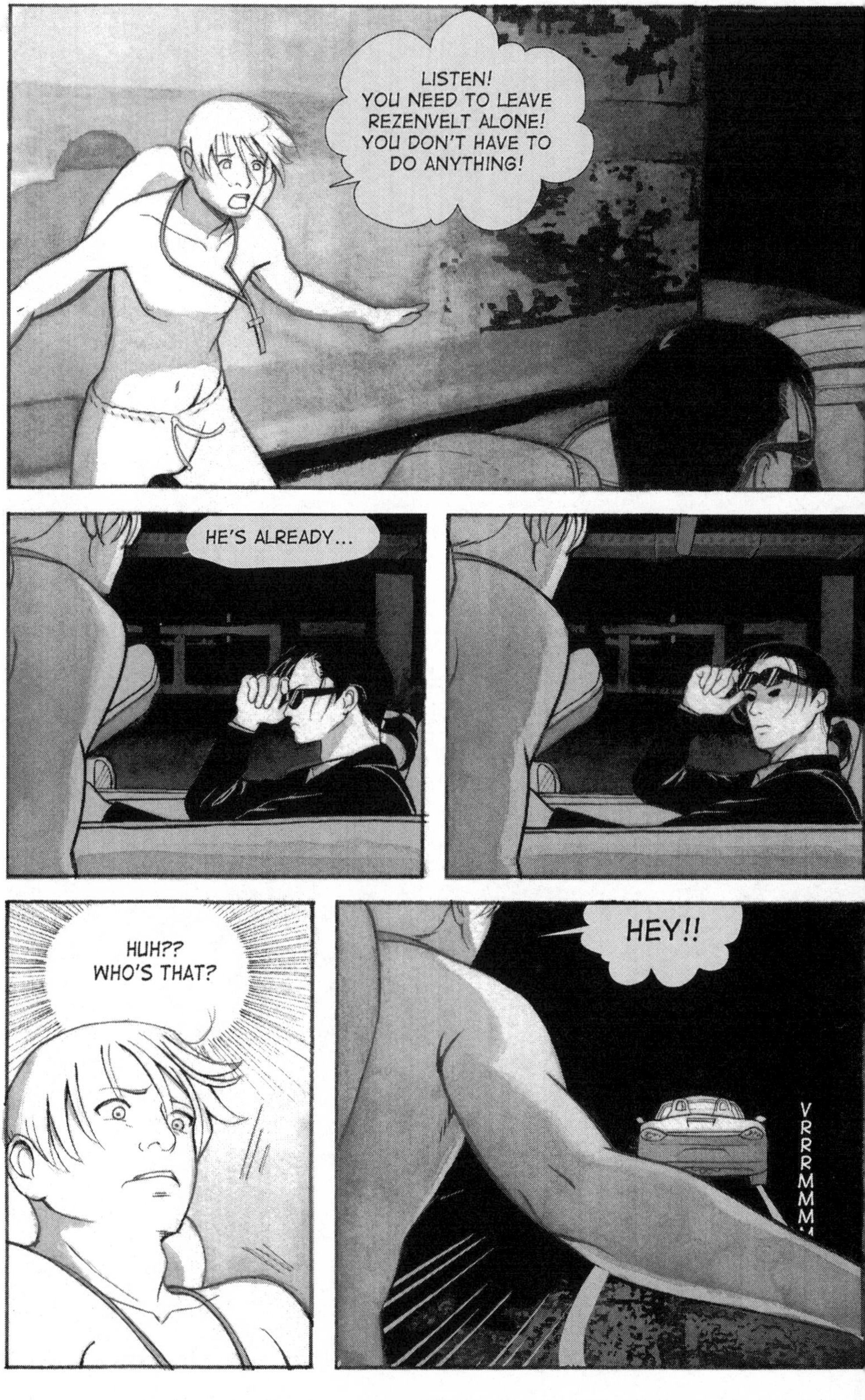
LISTEN!
YOU NEED TO LEAVE
REZENVELT ALONE!
YOU DON'T HAVE TO
DO ANYTHING!
HE'S ALREADY...
HUH??
WHO'S THAT?
HEY!!
VRRRMMM

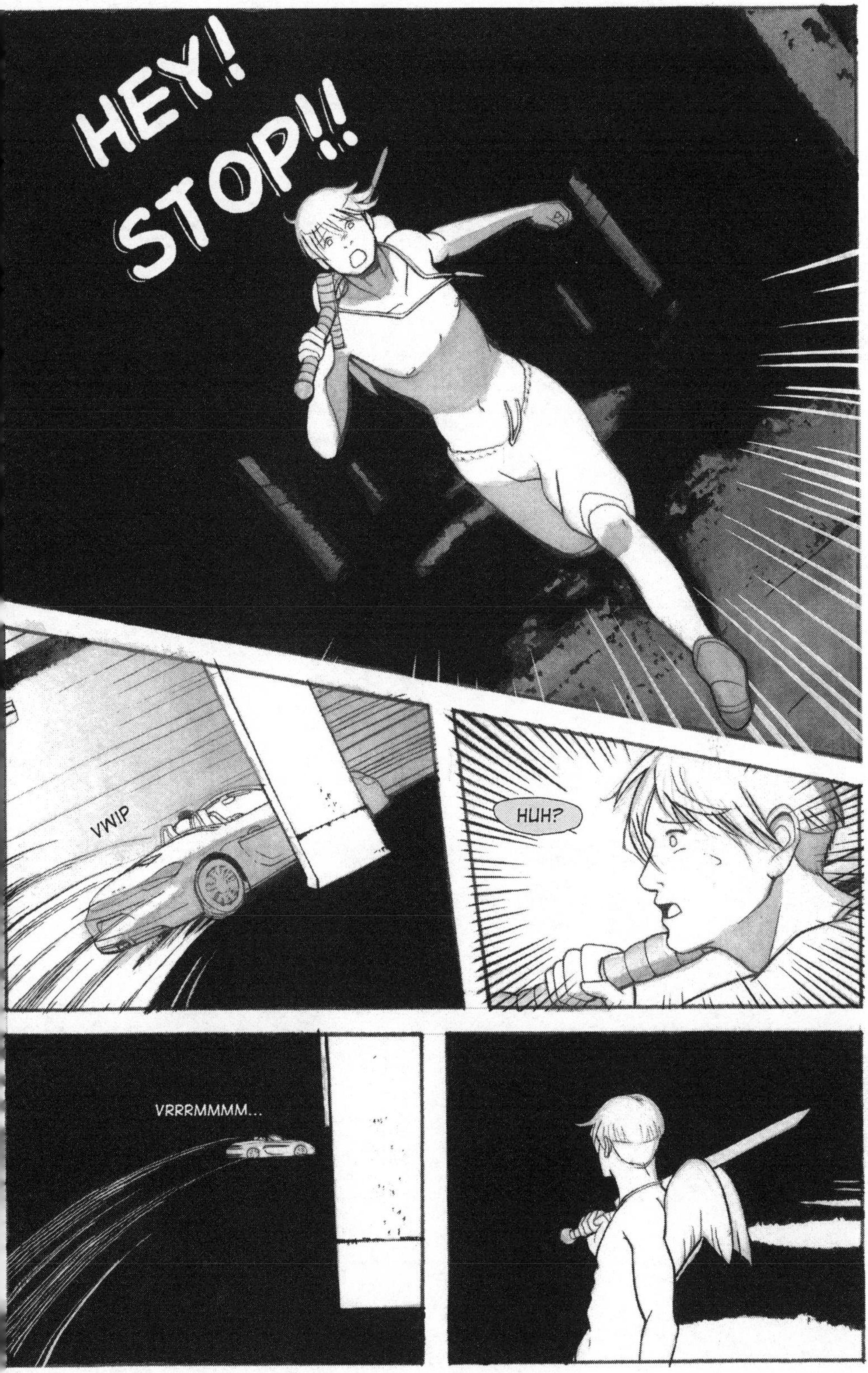
HEY! STOP!!
VWIP
HUH?
VRRRMMMM...

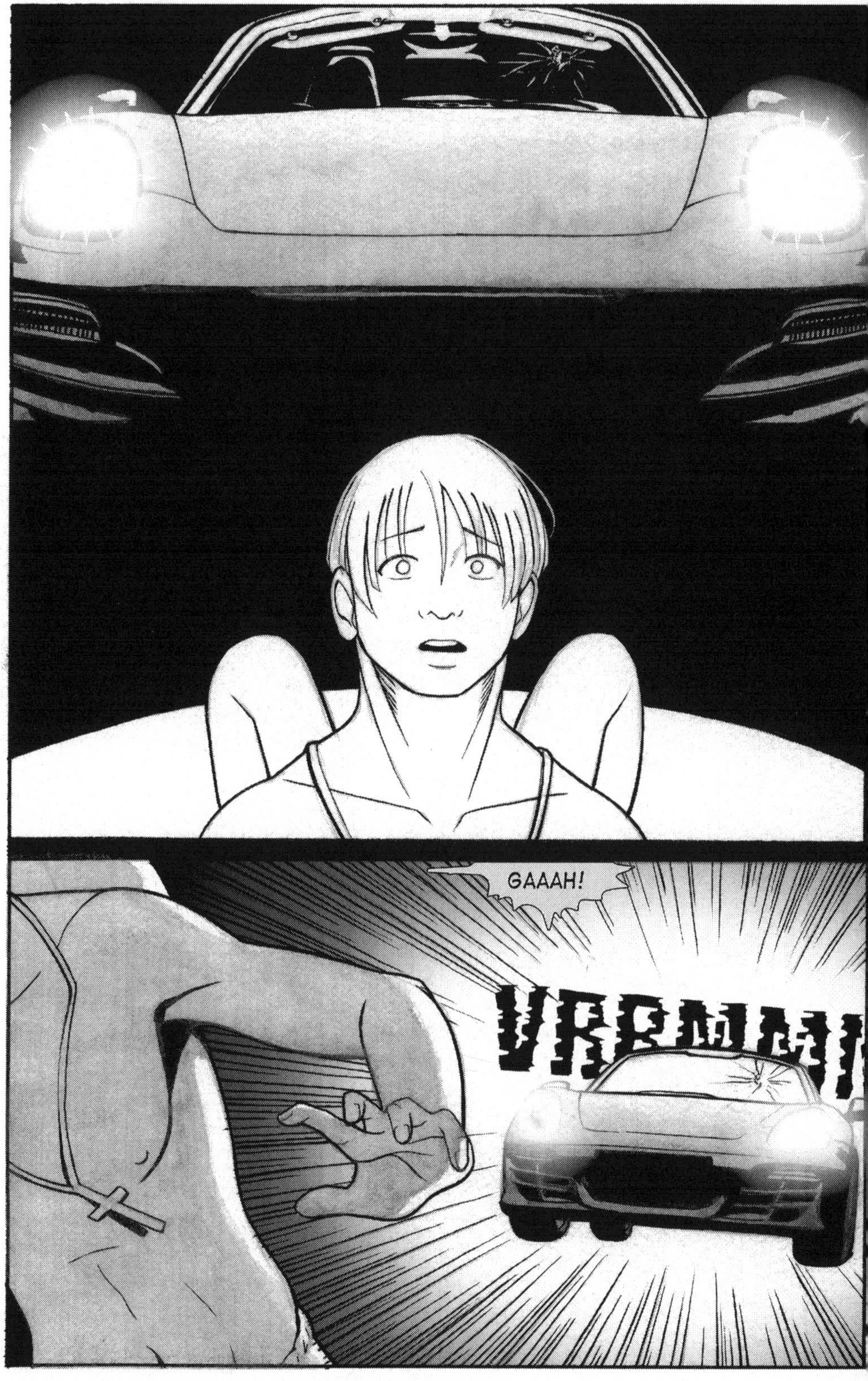
GAAAH!

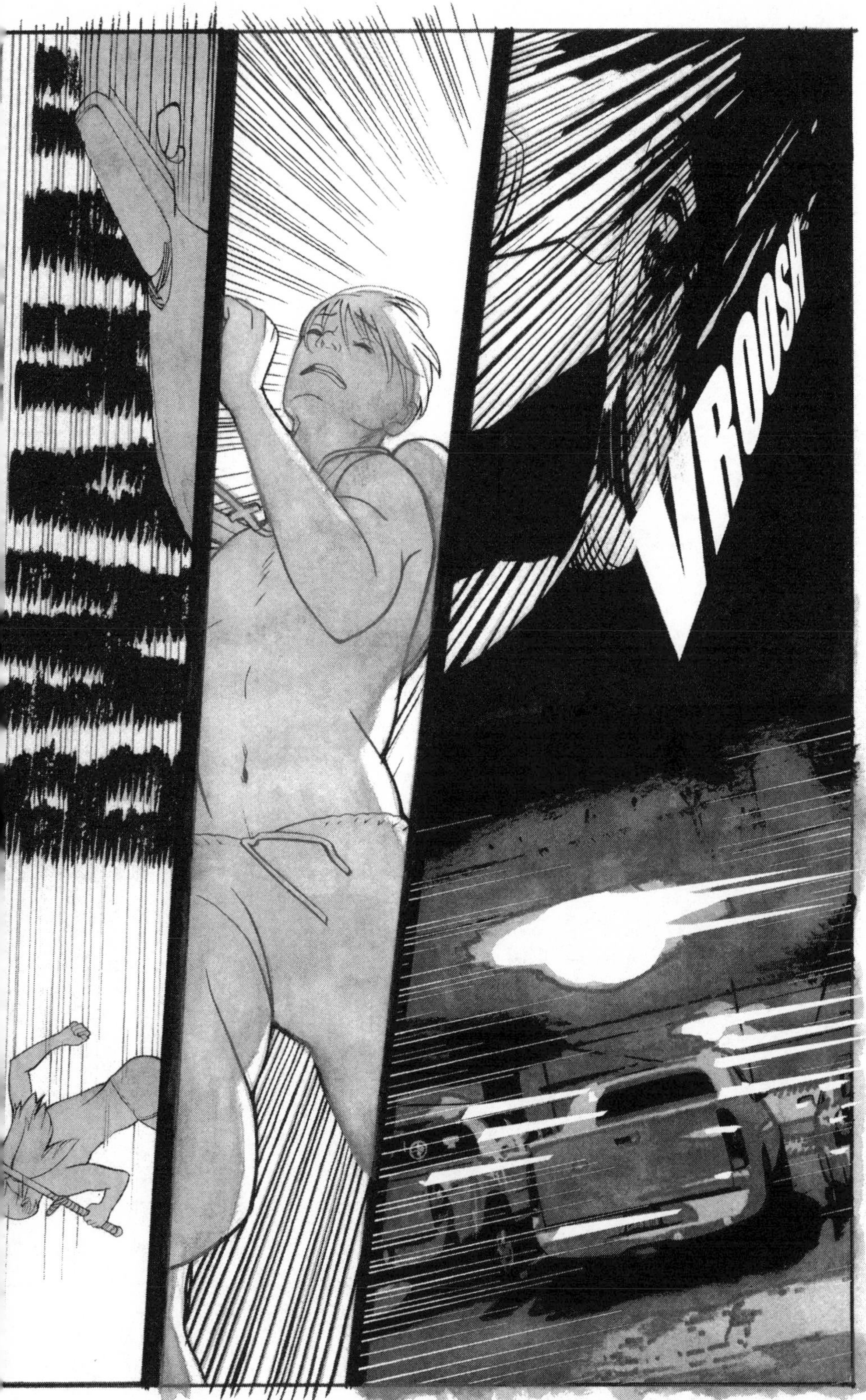
VROOSH

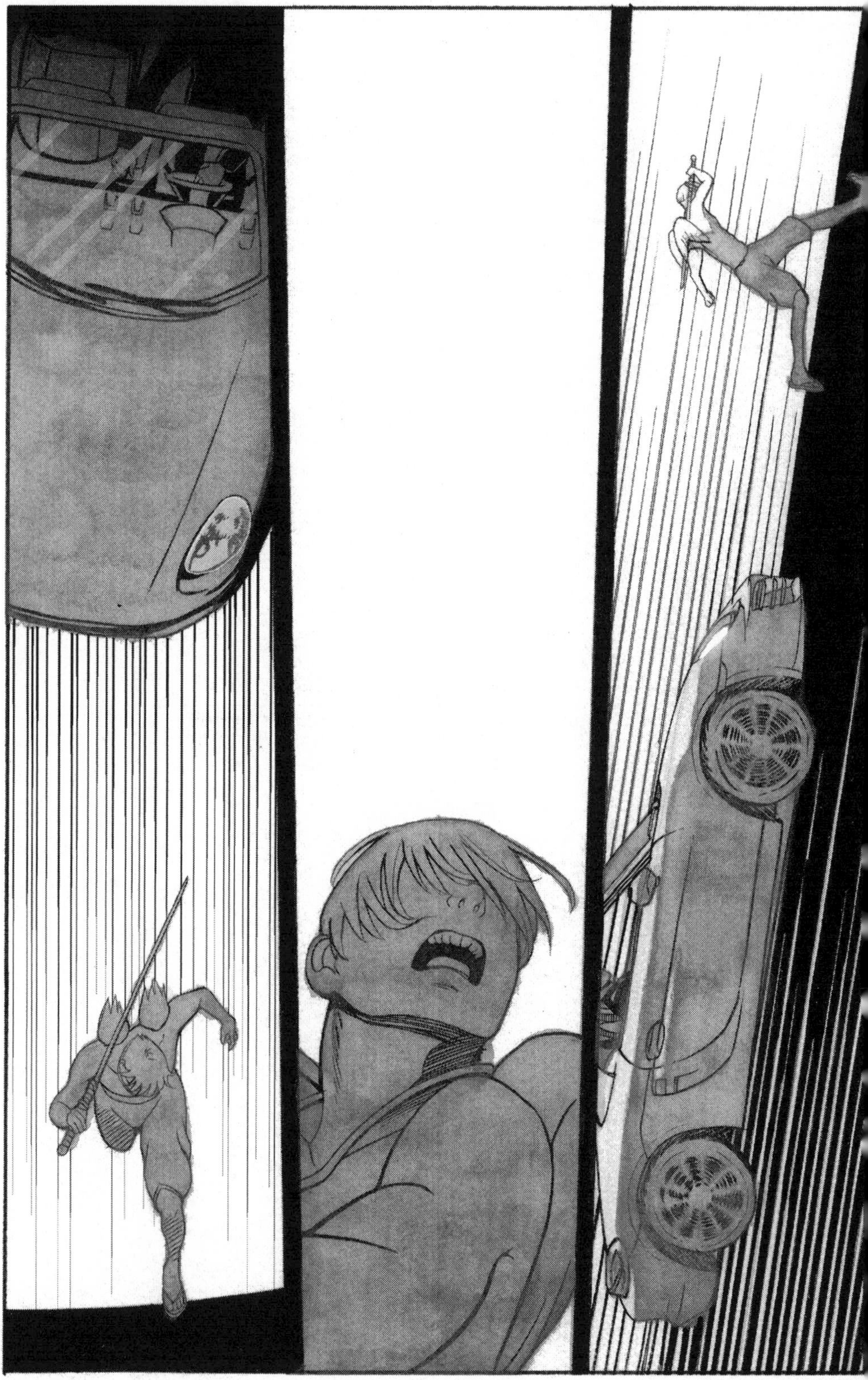

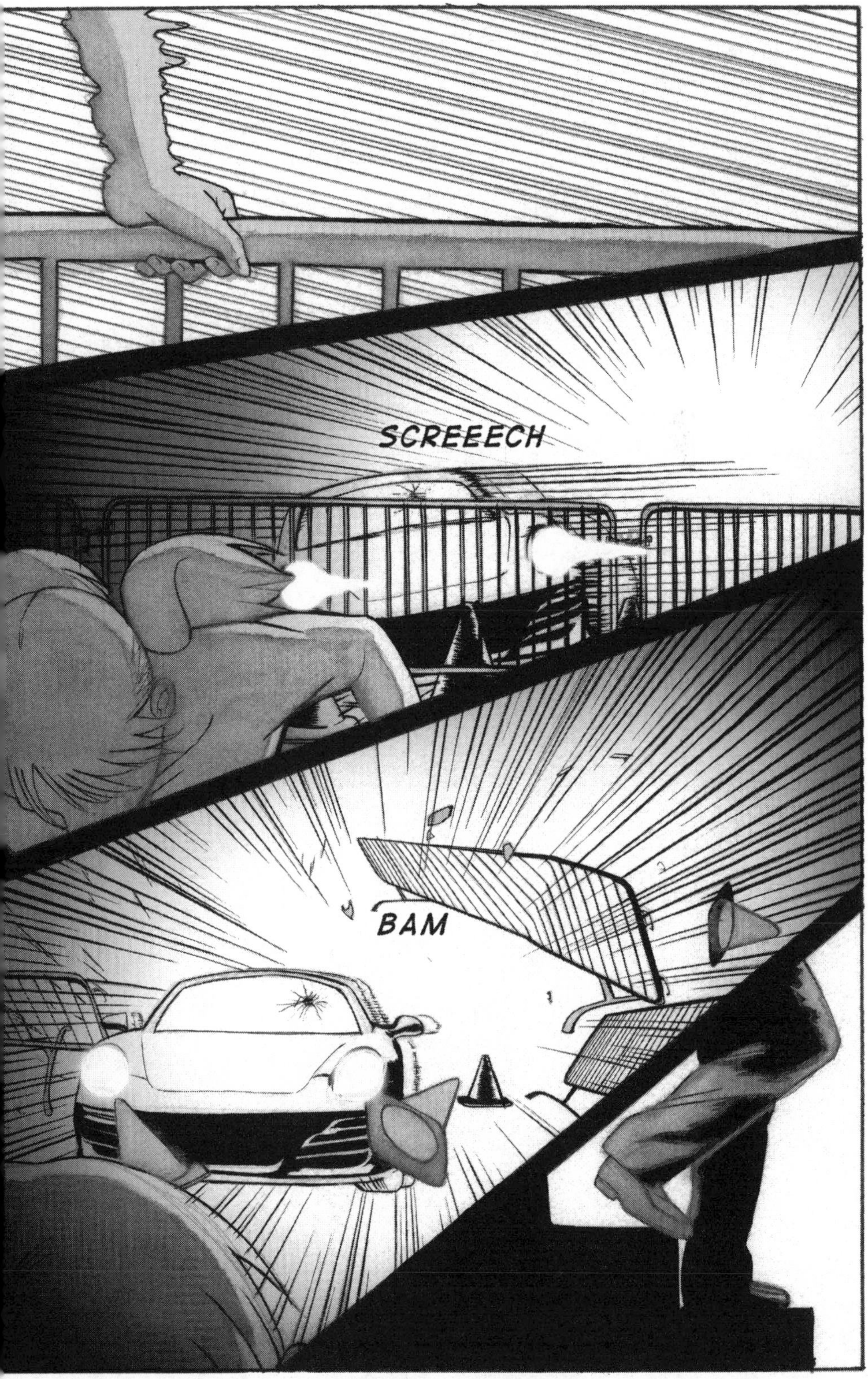
SCREEECH
BAM

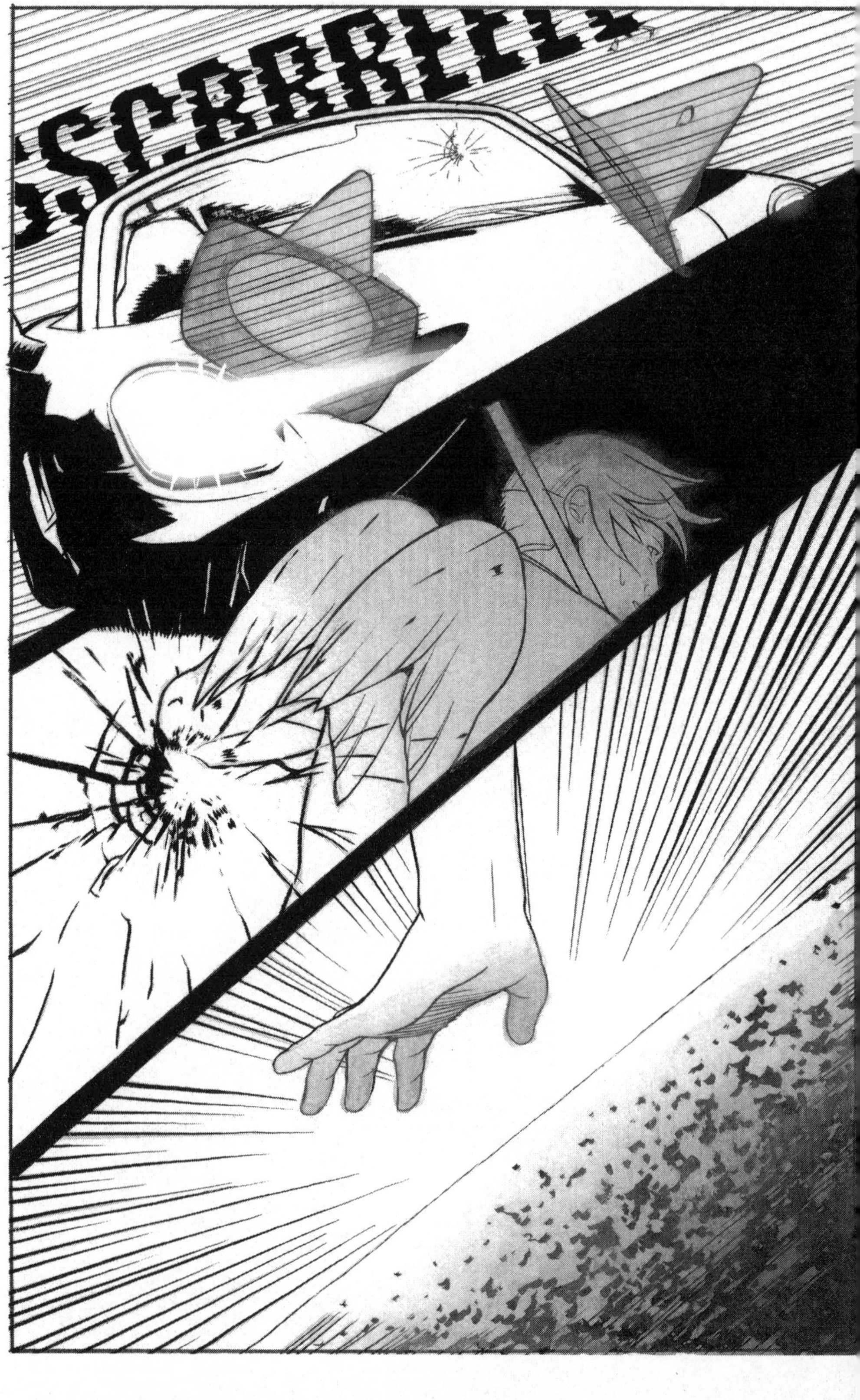
SCRRREEE

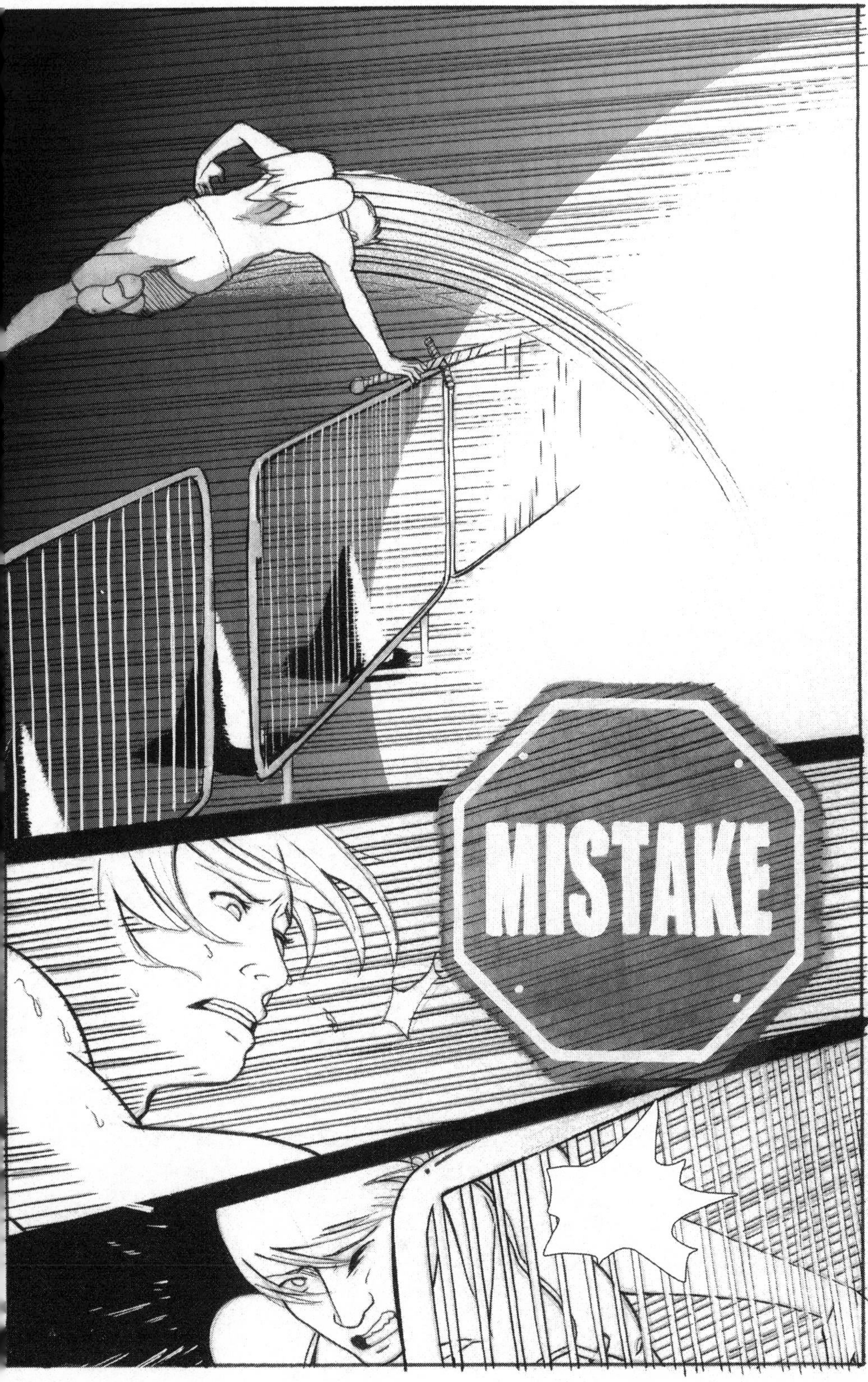
MISTAKE

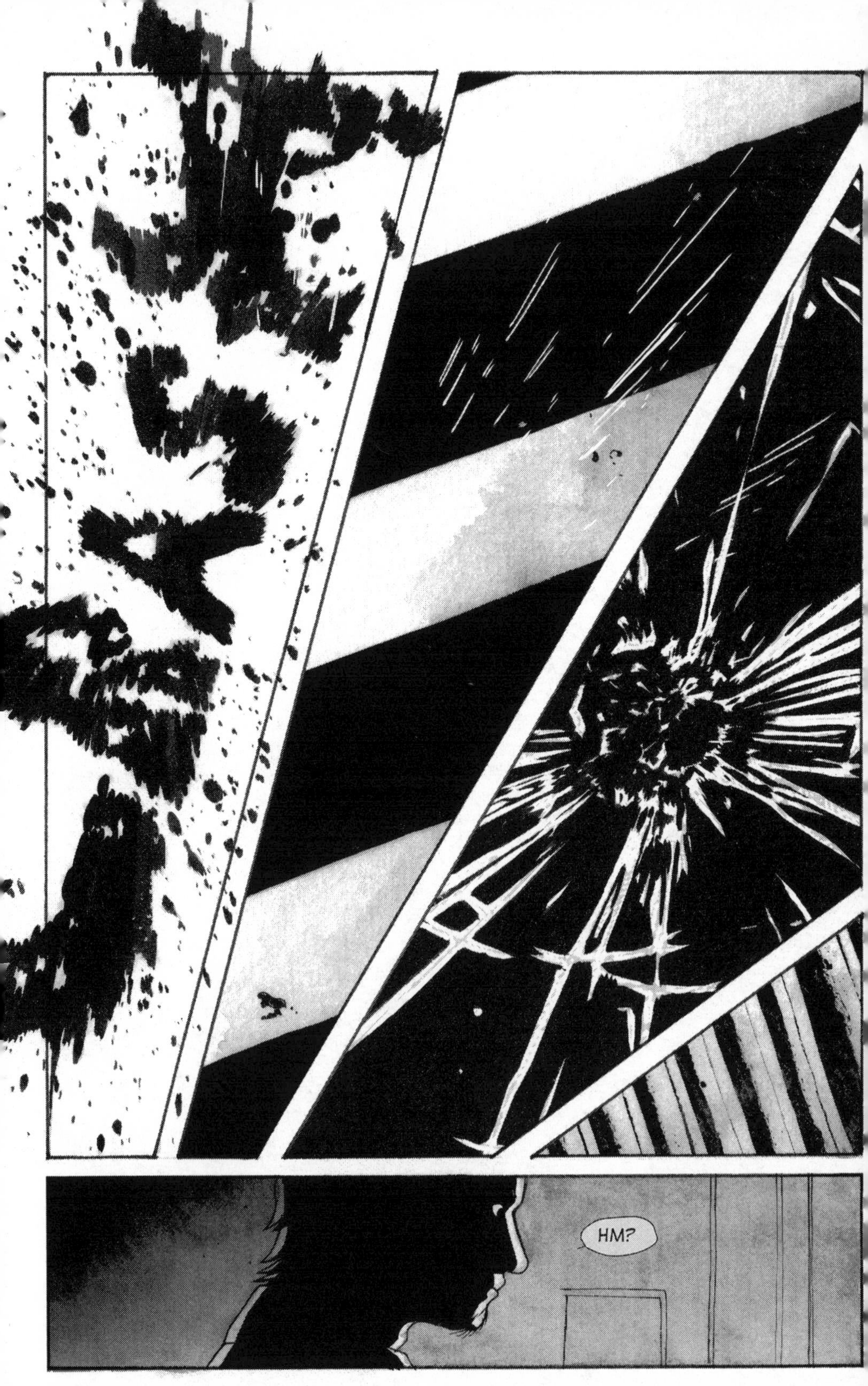
HM?

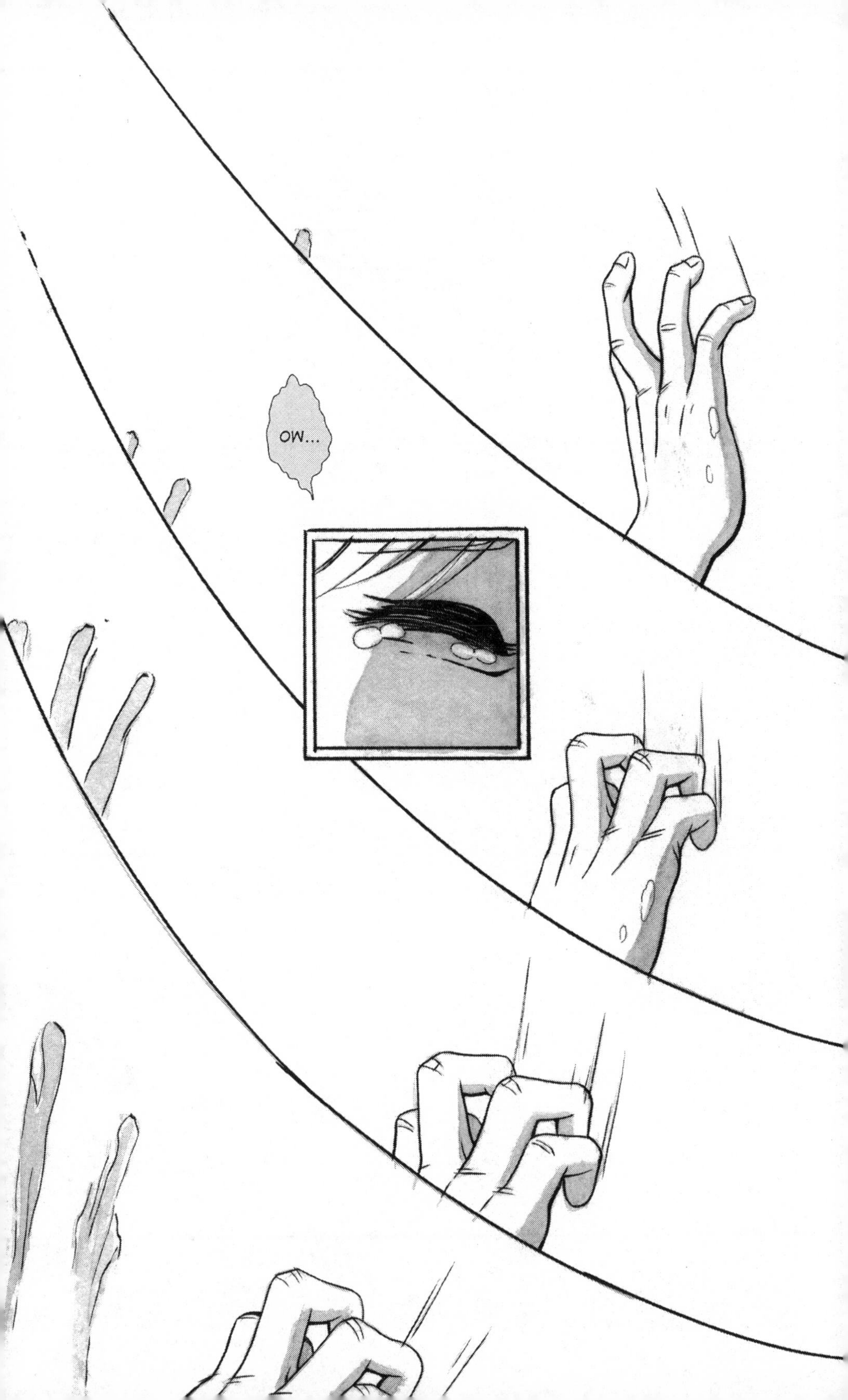
OW...

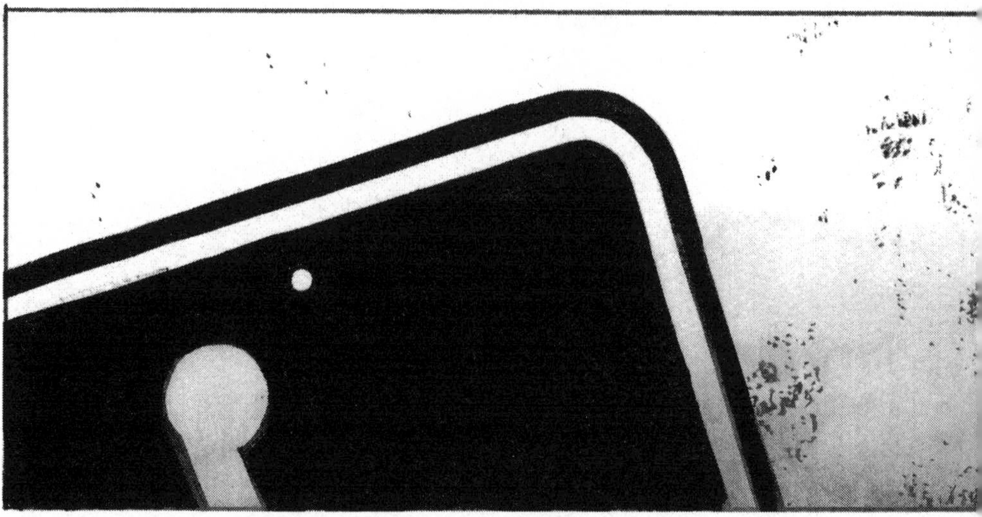

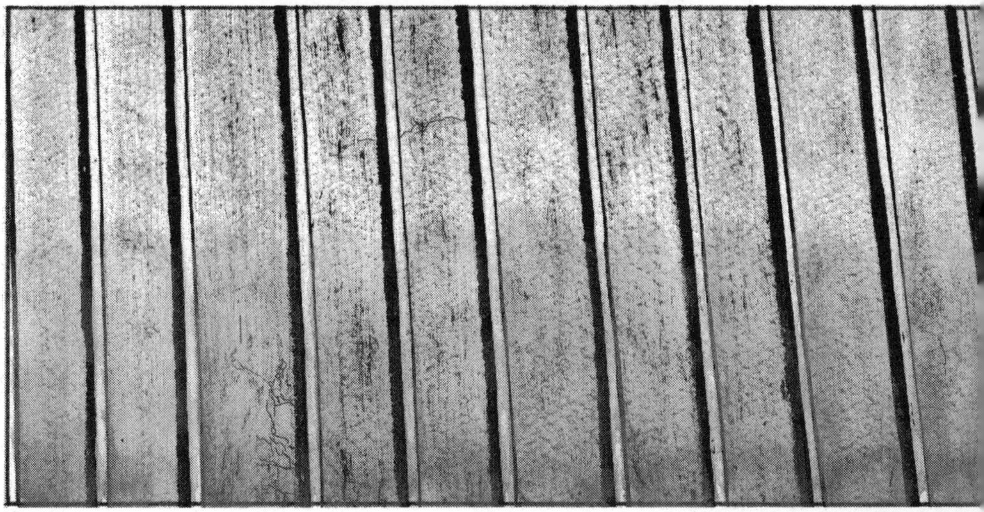

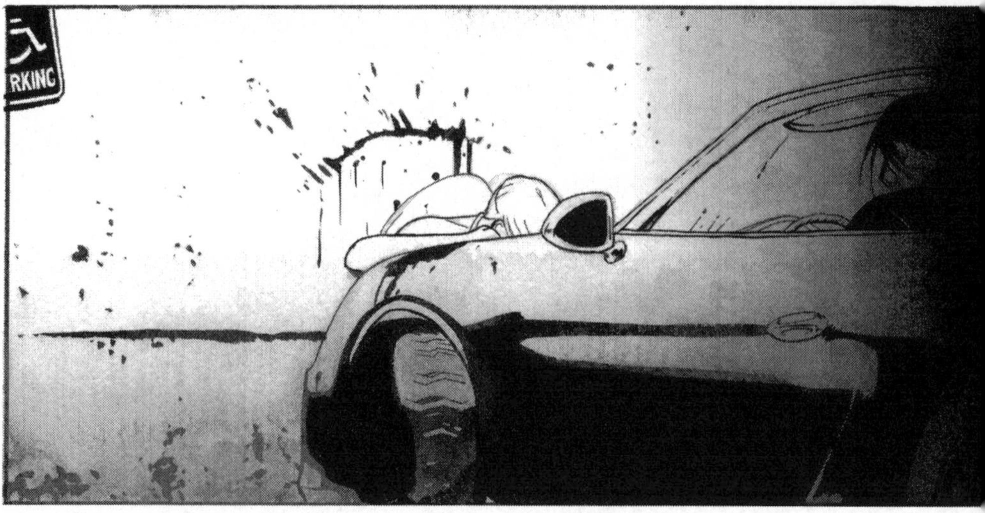
RKINC

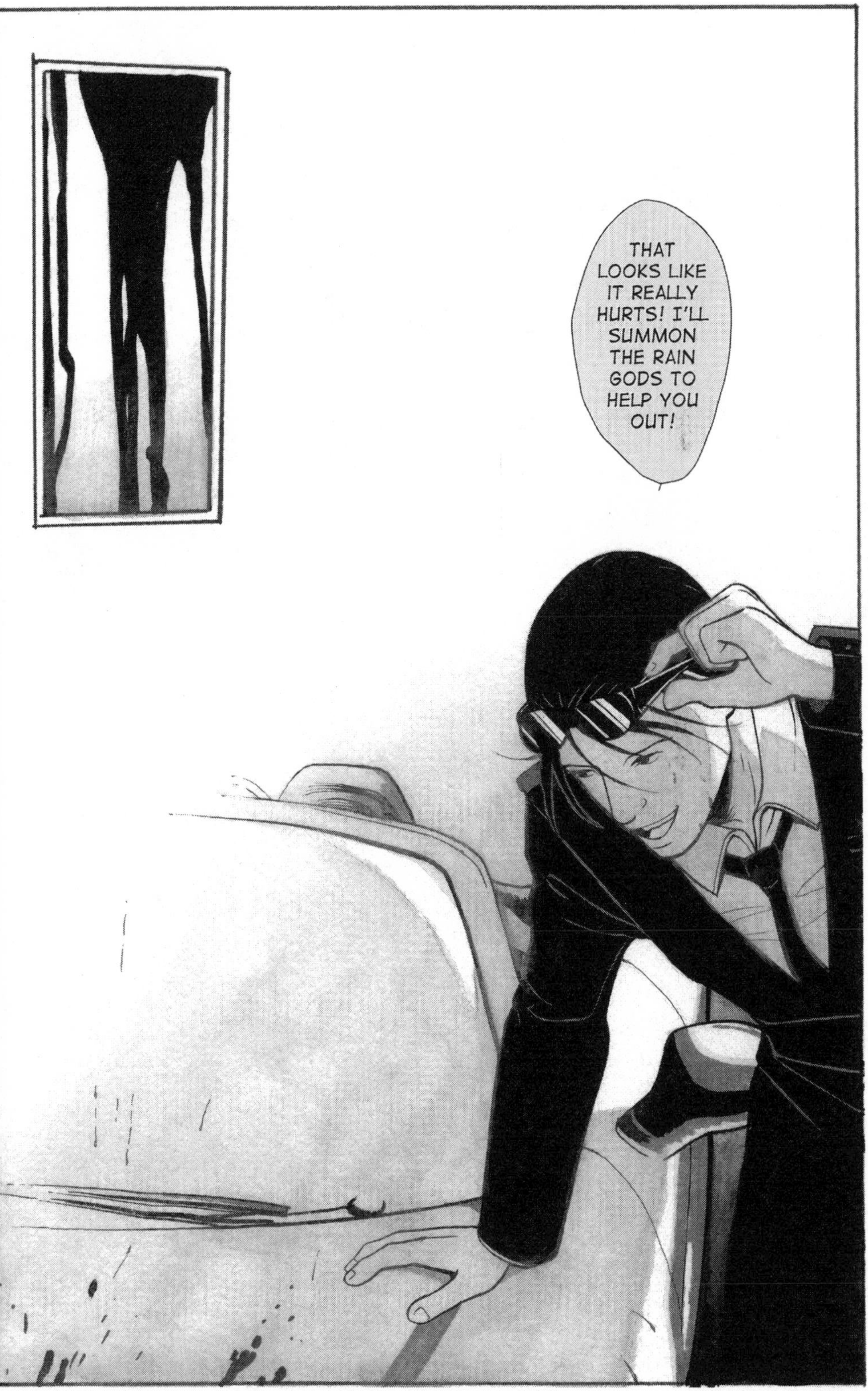
THAT LOOKS LIKE IT REALLY HURTS! I'LL SUMMON THE RAIN GODS TO HELP YOU OUT!

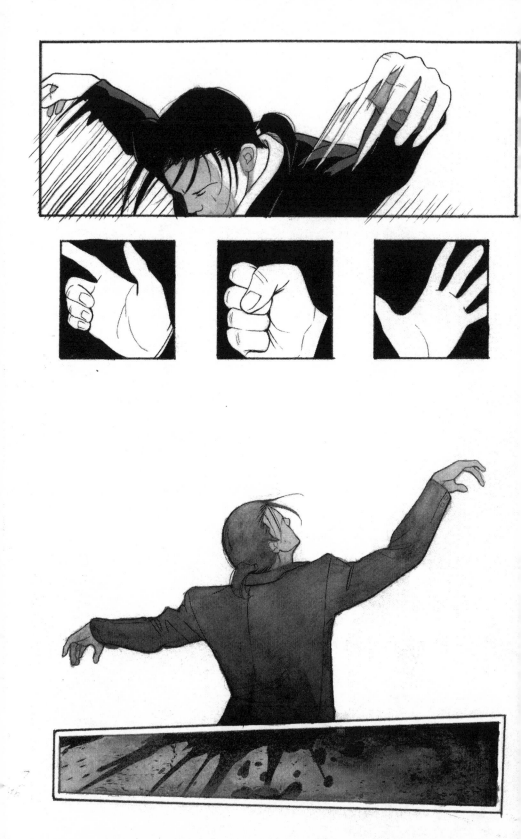

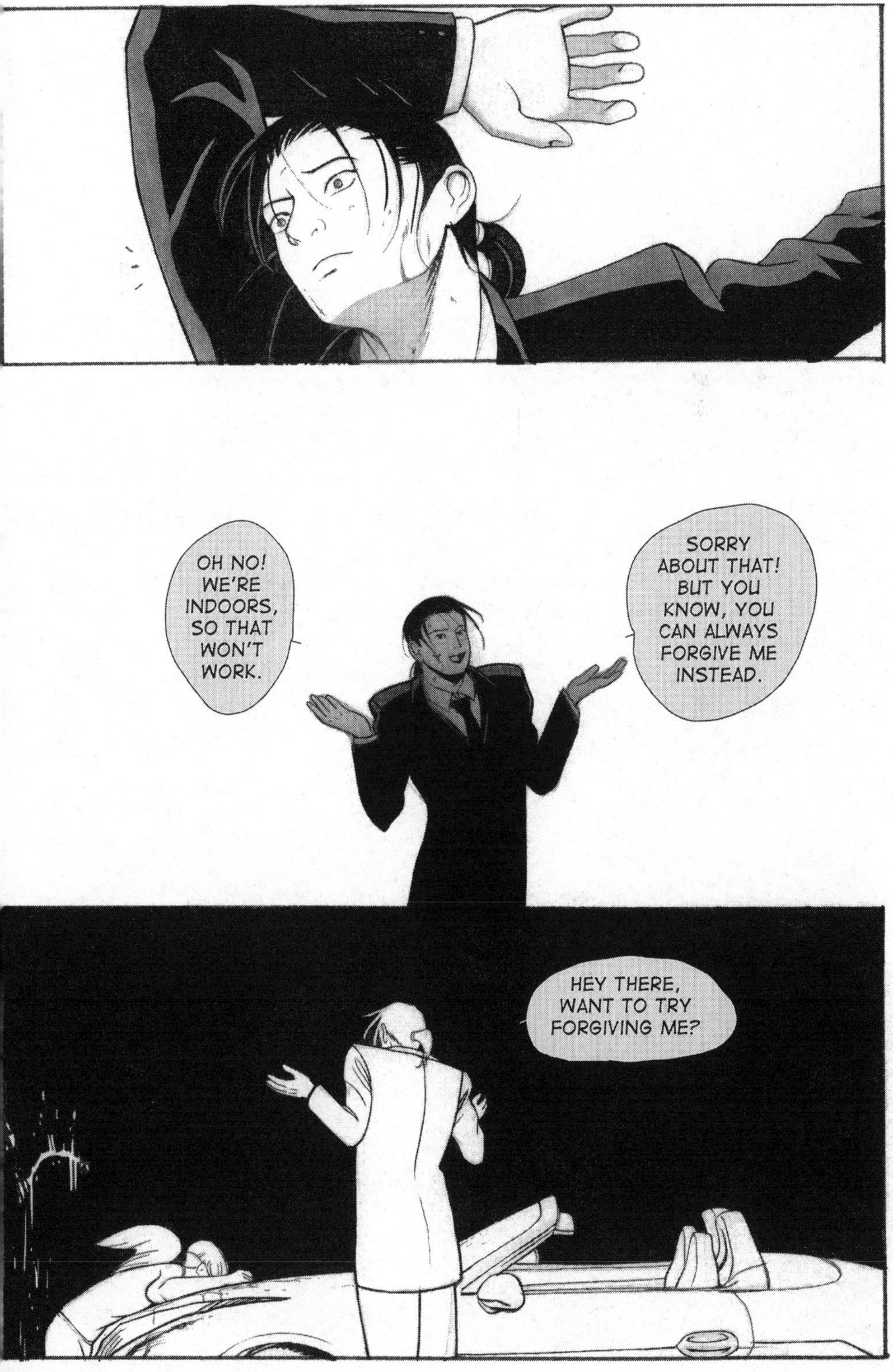
OH NO! WE'RE INDOORS, SO THAT WON'T WORK.
SORRY ABOUT THAT! BUT YOU KNOW, YOU CAN ALWAYS FORGIVE ME INSTEAD.
HEY THERE, WANT TO TRY FORGIVING ME?

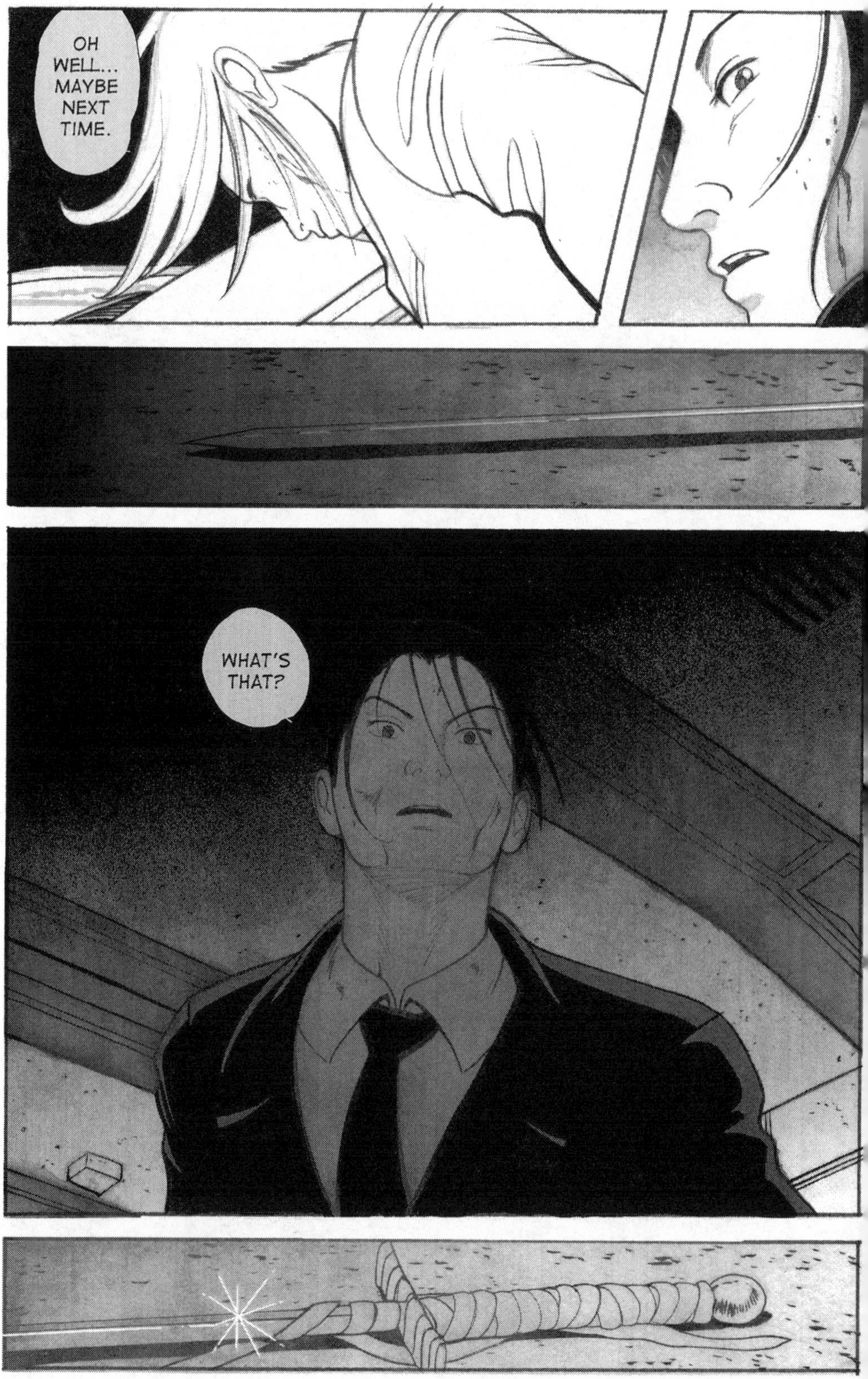
OH WELL... MAYBE NEXT TIME.
WHAT'S THAT?

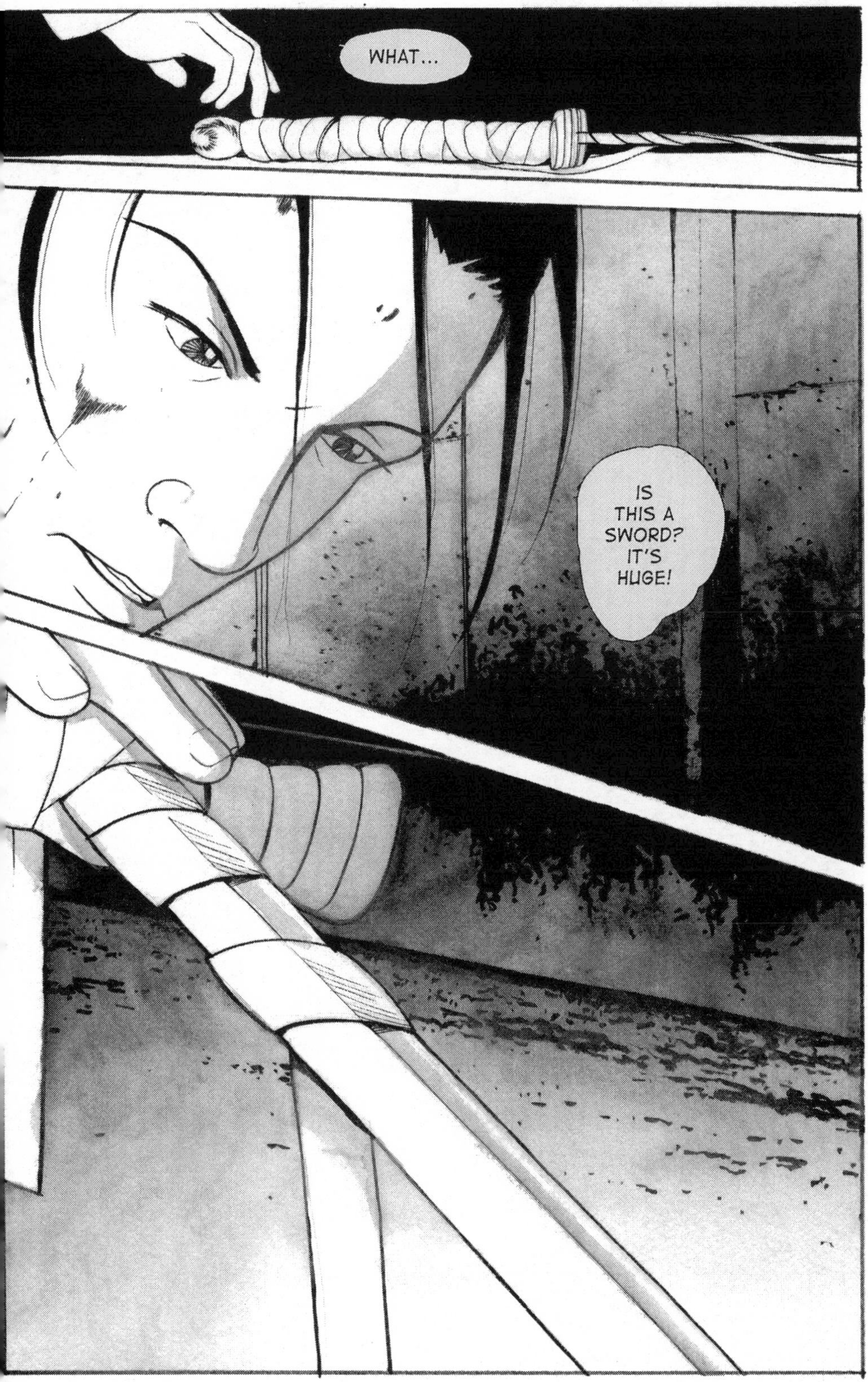
WHAT...
IS THIS A SWORD? IT'S HUGE!

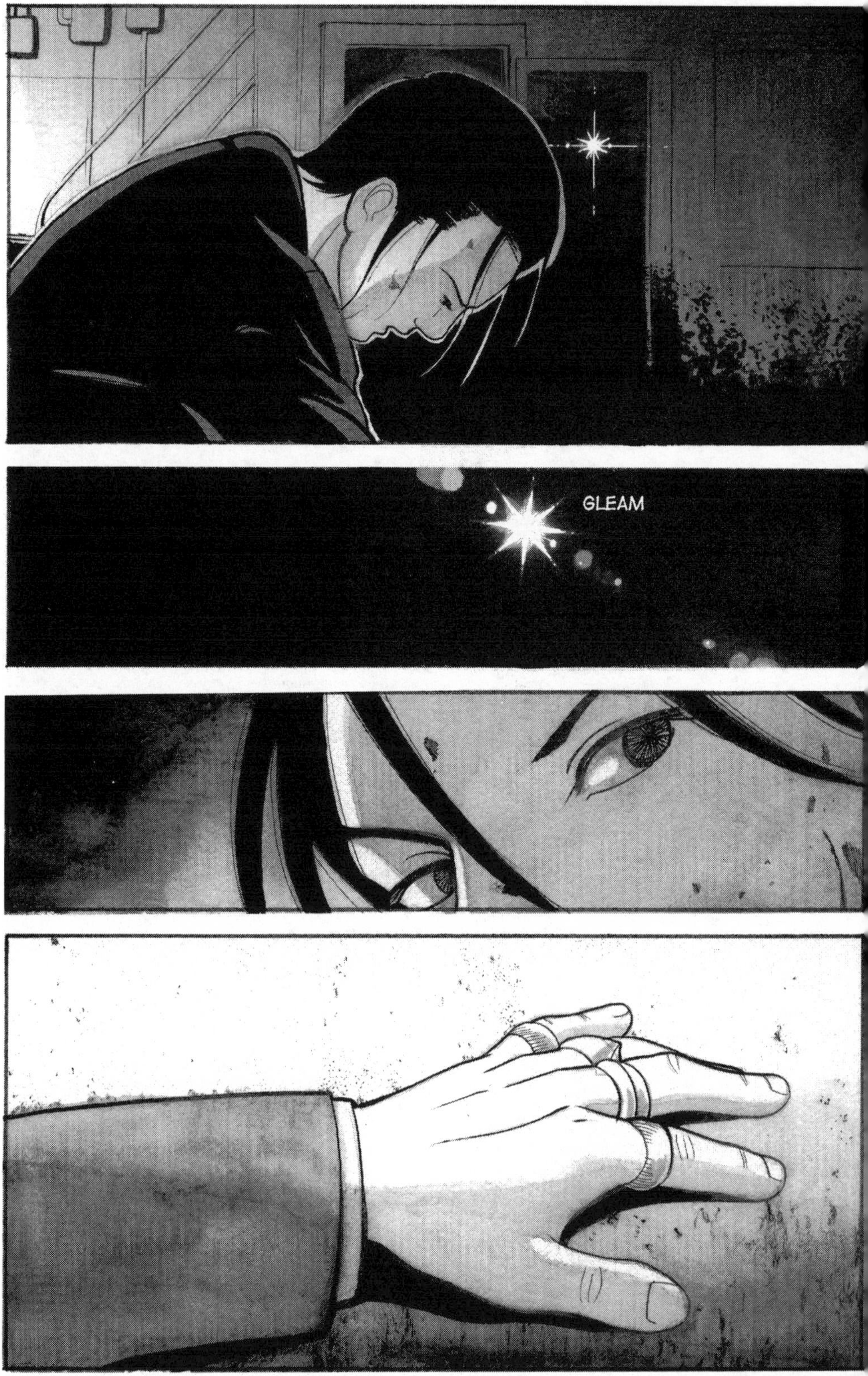
GLEAM

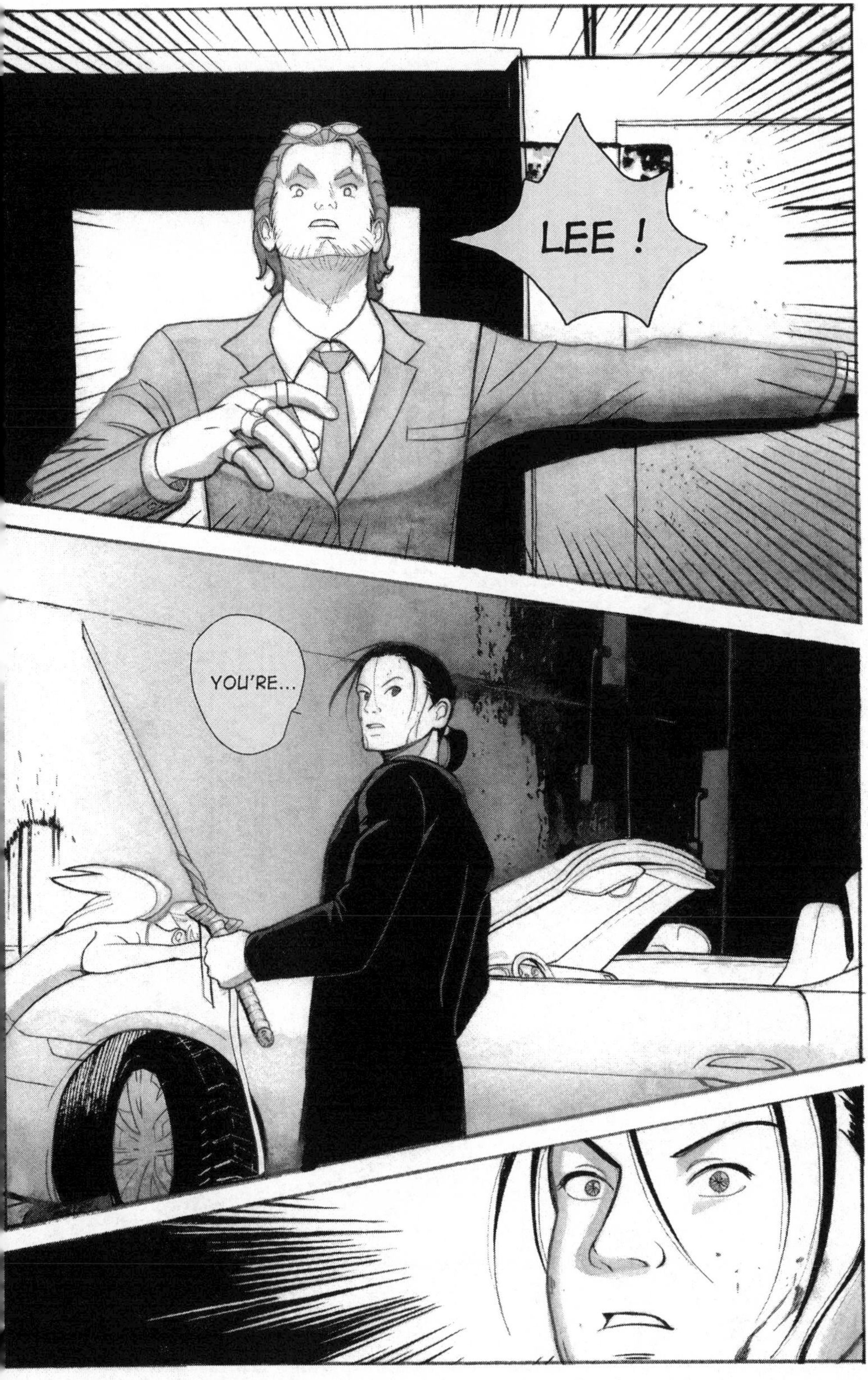
LEE !
YOU'RE...

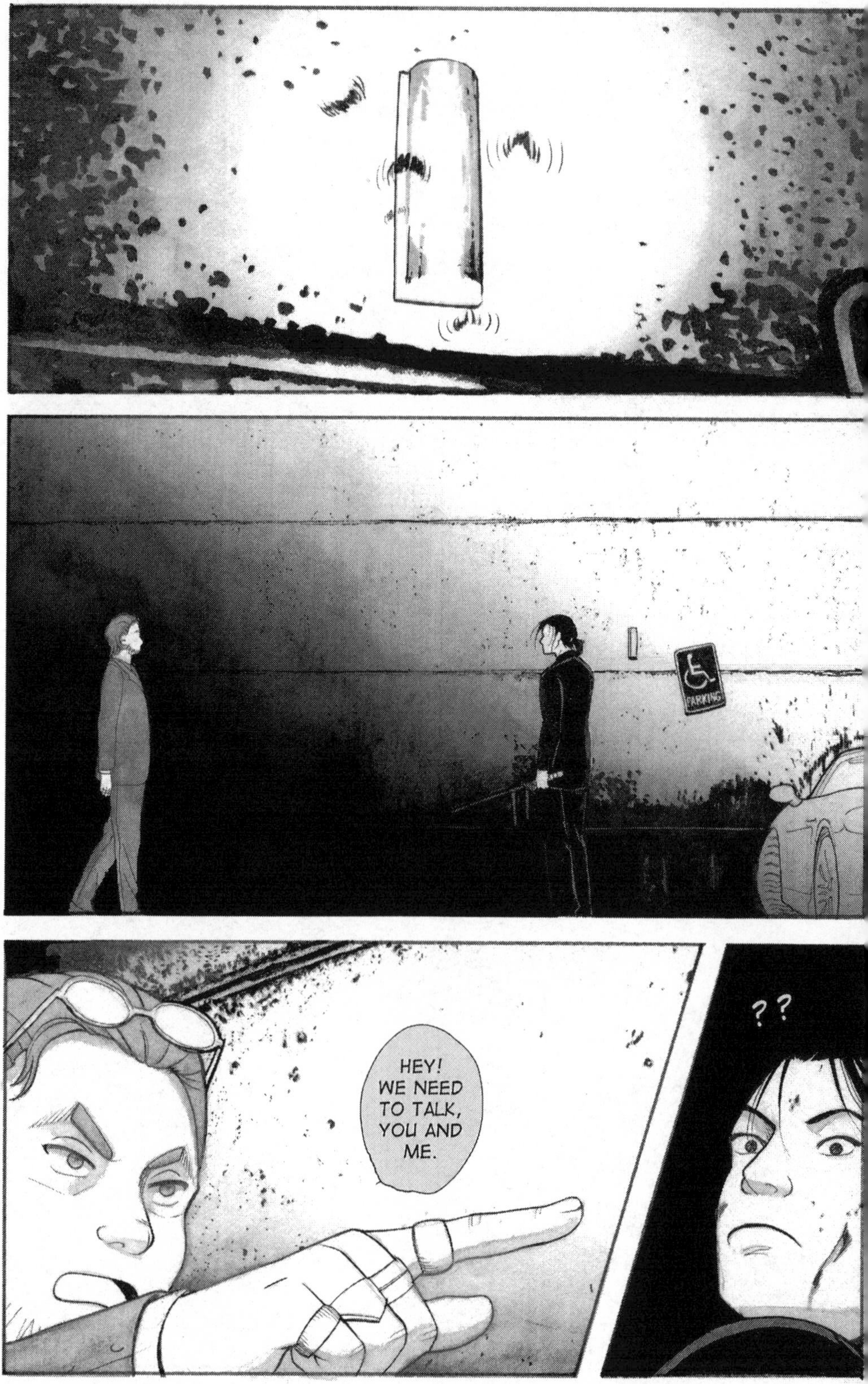
HEY! WE NEED TO TALK, YOU AND ME.
??

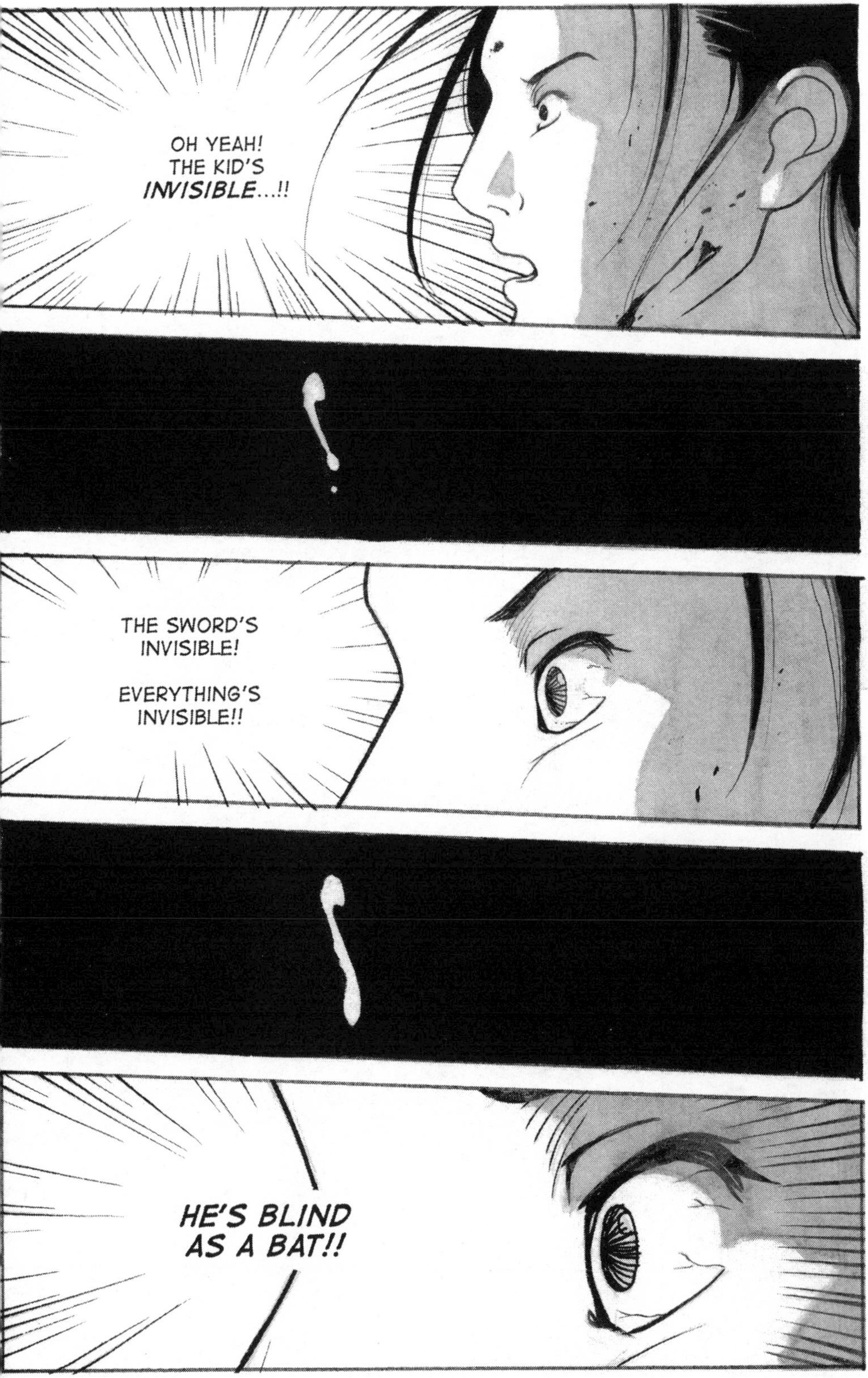
OH YEAH! THE KID'S *INVISIBLE*...!!
THE SWORD'S INVISIBLE!
EVERYTHING'S INVISIBLE!!
HE'S BLIND AS A BAT!!

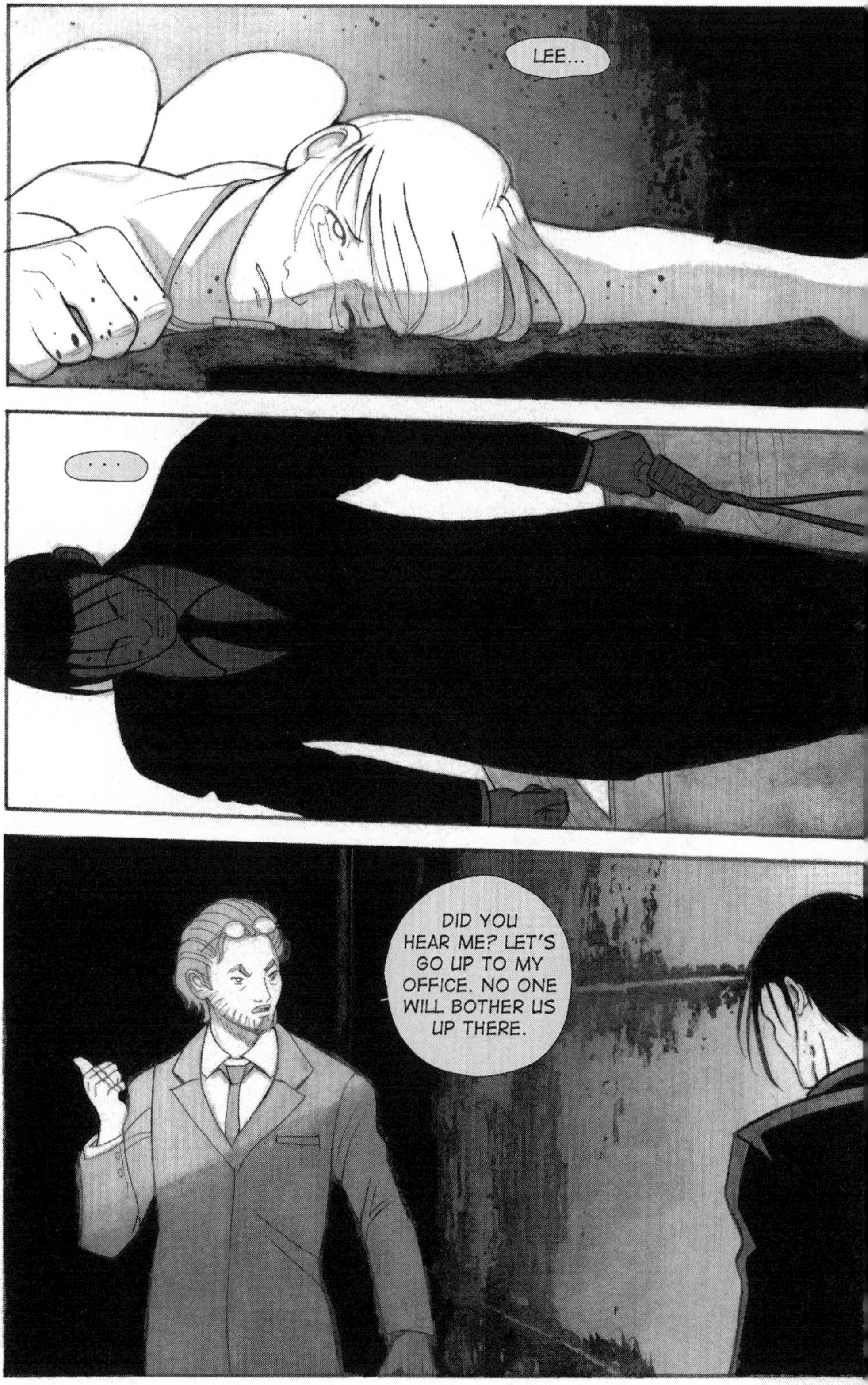
LEE...
. . .
DID YOU HEAR ME? LET'S GO UP TO MY OFFICE. NO ONE WILL BOTHER US UP THERE.

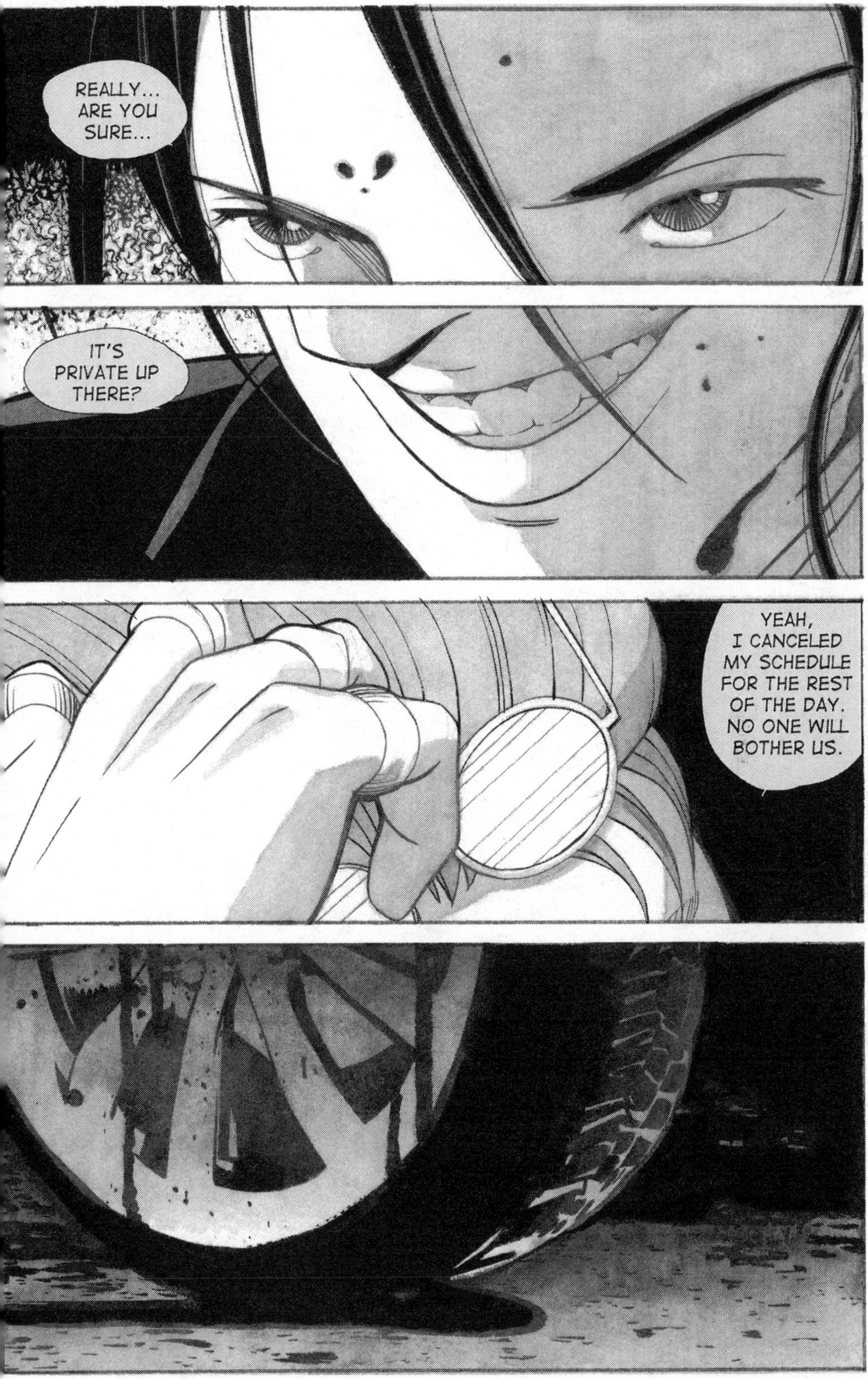
REALLY... ARE YOU SURE...
IT'S PRIVATE UP THERE?
YEAH, I CANCELED MY SCHEDULE FOR THE REST OF THE DAY. NO ONE WILL BOTHER US.

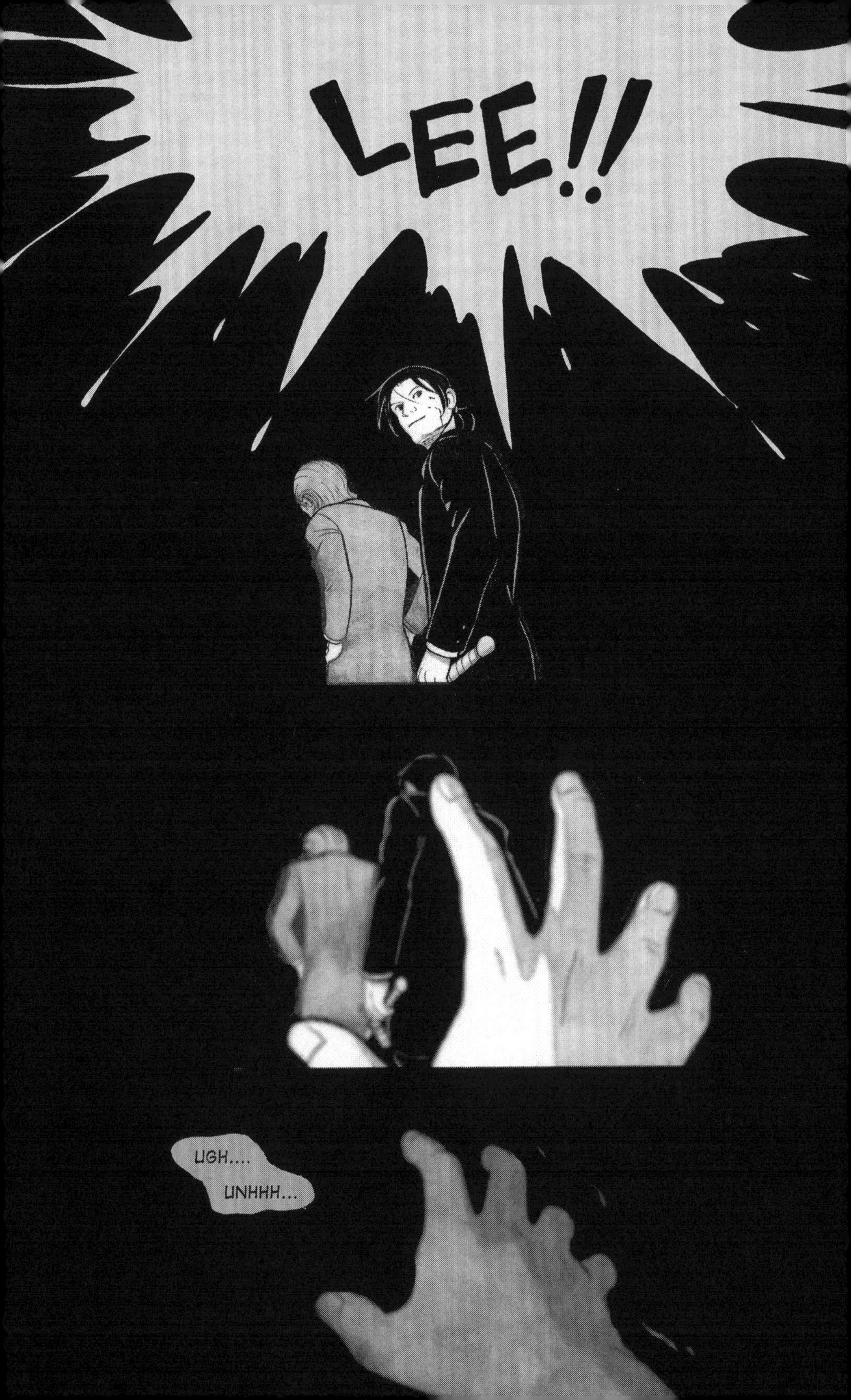
LEE!!
UGH....
UNHHH...

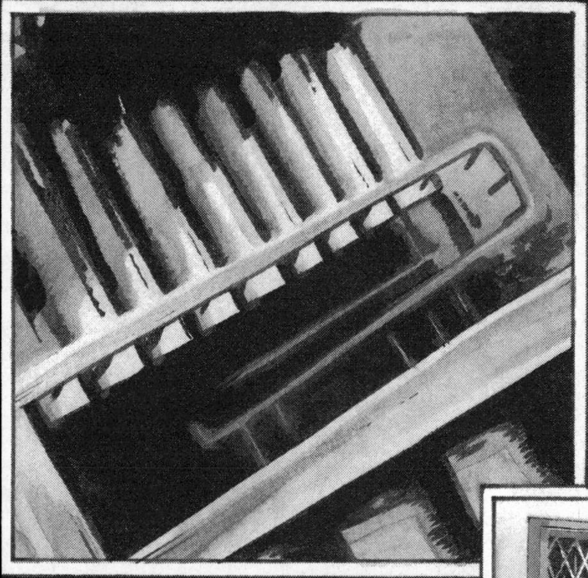

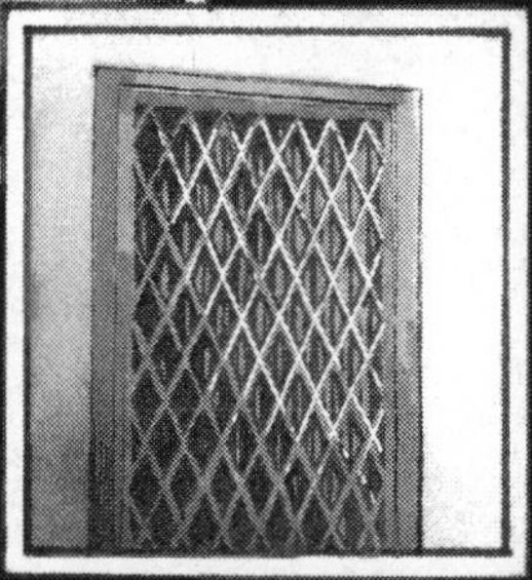

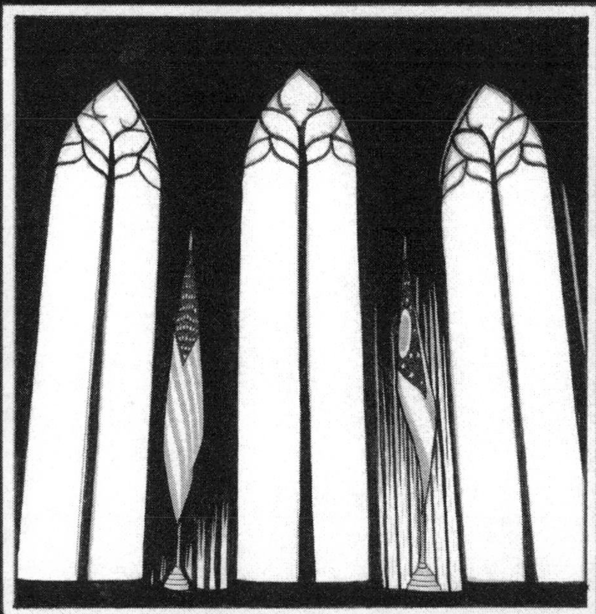

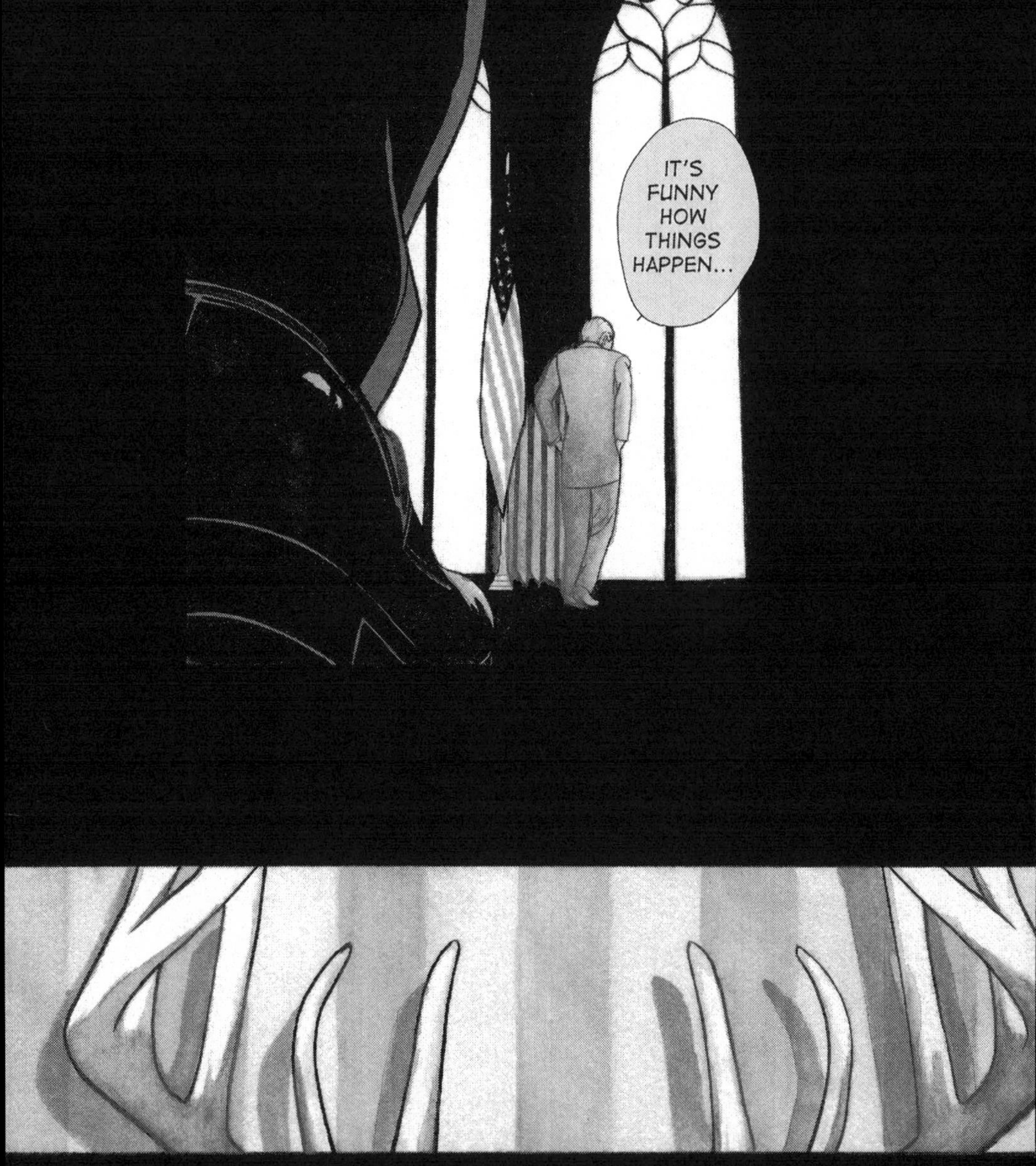
IT'S FUNNY HOW THINGS HAPPEN...

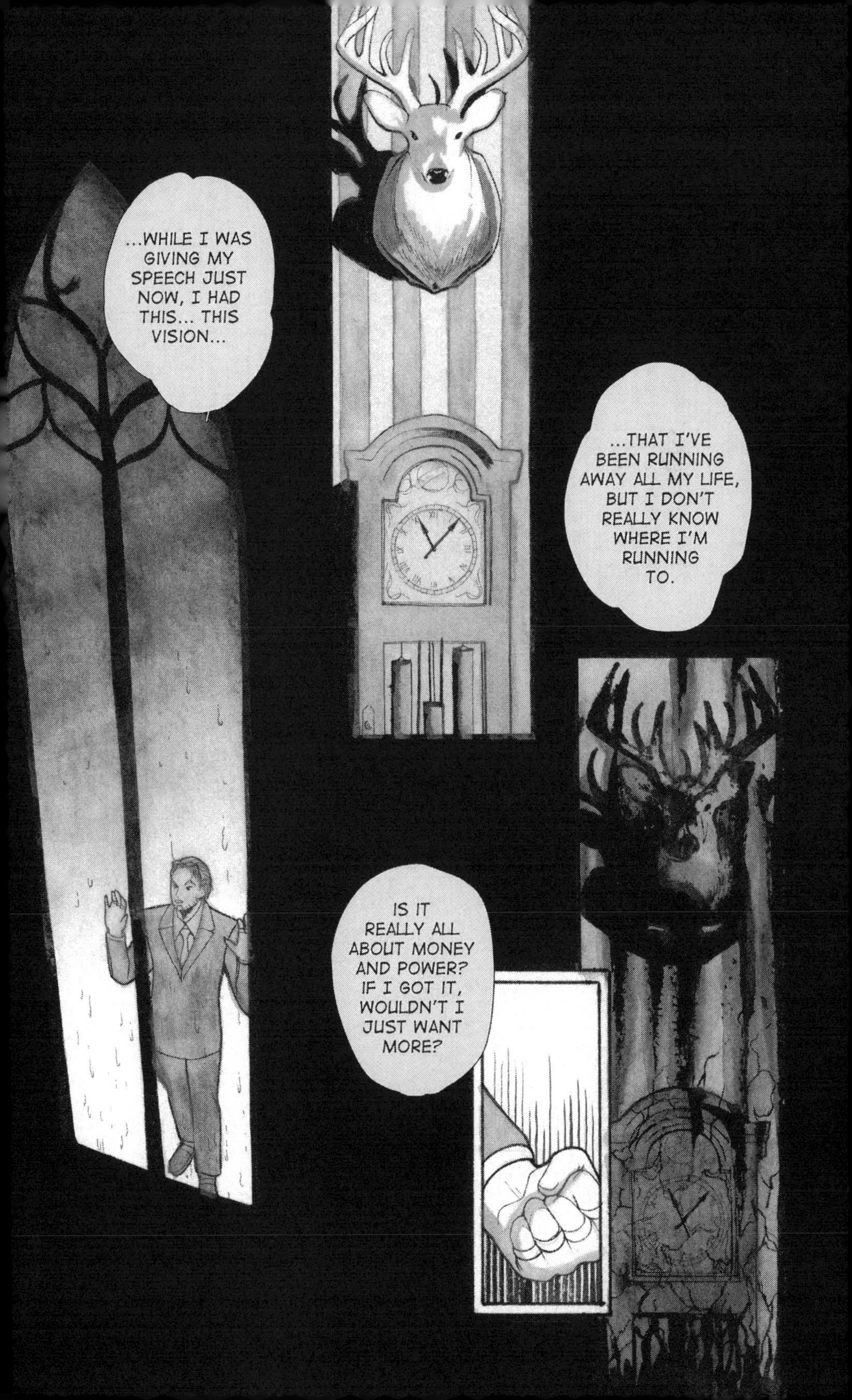
...WHILE I WAS GIVING MY SPEECH JUST NOW, I HAD THIS... THIS VISION...
...THAT I'VE BEEN RUNNING AWAY ALL MY LIFE, BUT I DON'T REALLY KNOW WHERE I'M RUNNING TO.
IS IT REALLY ALL ABOUT MONEY AND POWER? IF I GOT IT, WOULDN'T I JUST WANT MORE?

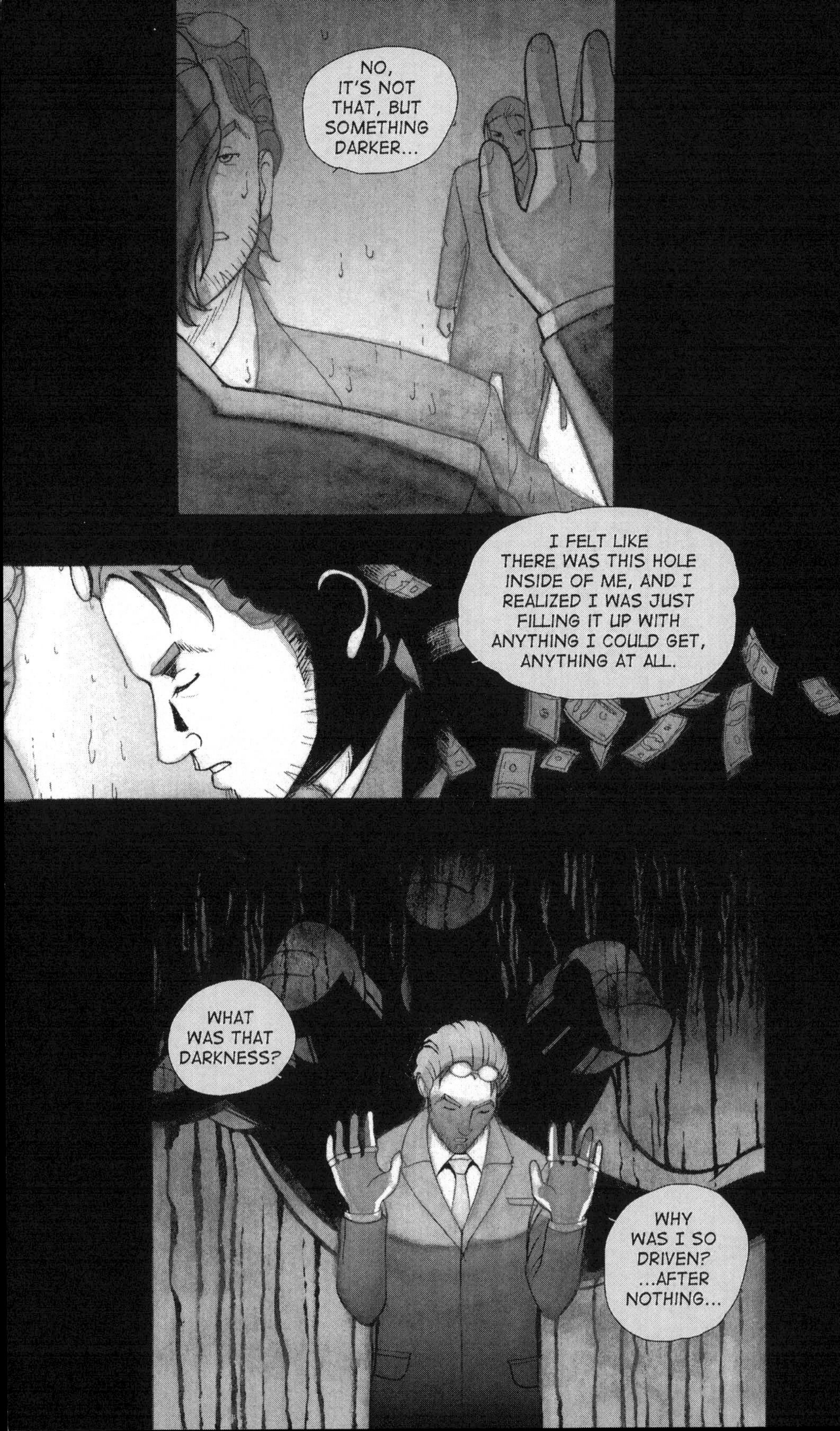
NO, IT'S NOT THAT, BUT SOMETHING DARKER...
I FELT LIKE THERE WAS THIS HOLE INSIDE OF ME, AND I REALIZED I WAS JUST FILLING IT UP WITH ANYTHING I COULD GET, ANYTHING AT ALL.
WHAT WAS THAT DARKNESS?
WHY WAS I SO DRIVEN? ...AFTER NOTHING...

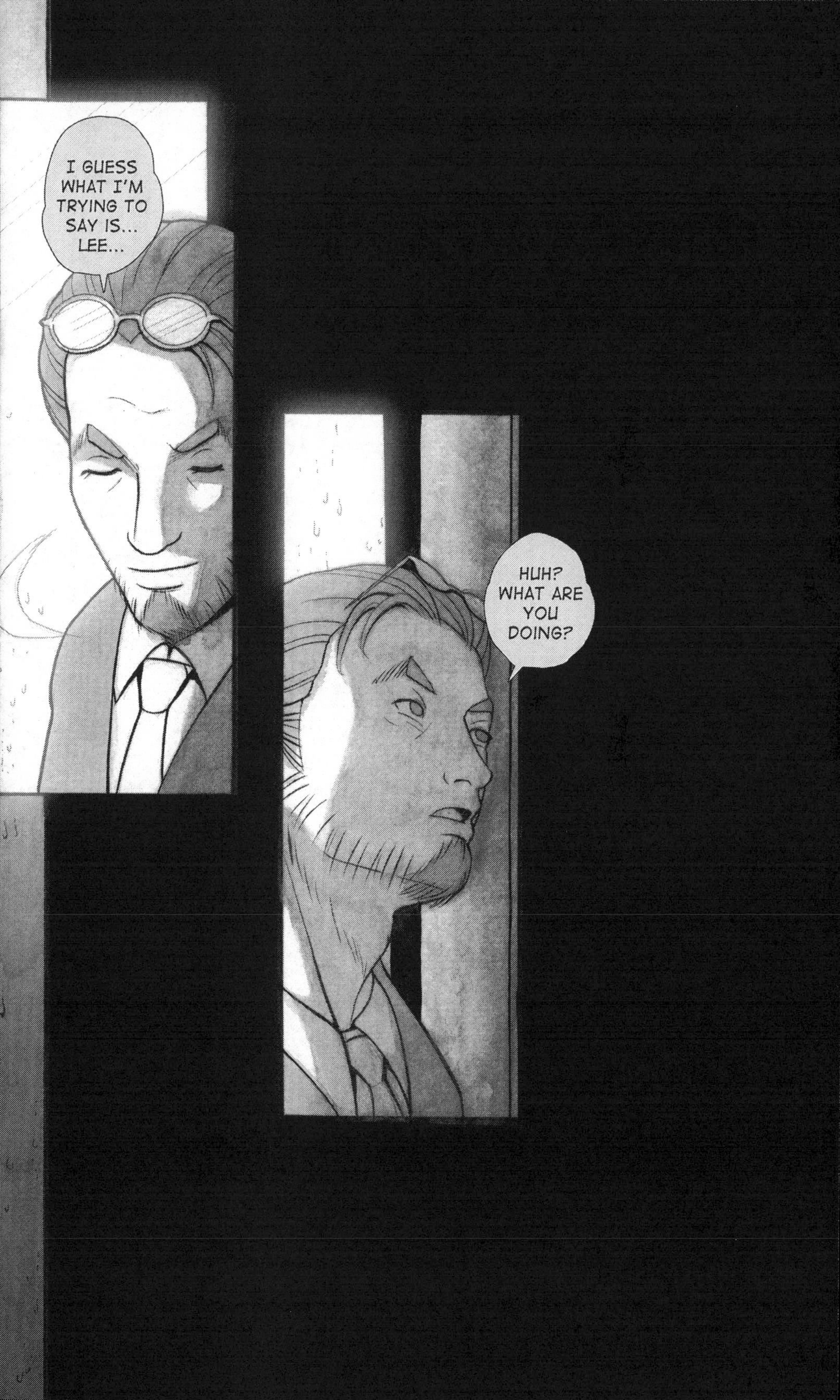
I GUESS WHAT I'M TRYING TO SAY IS... LEE...
HUH? WHAT ARE YOU DOING?

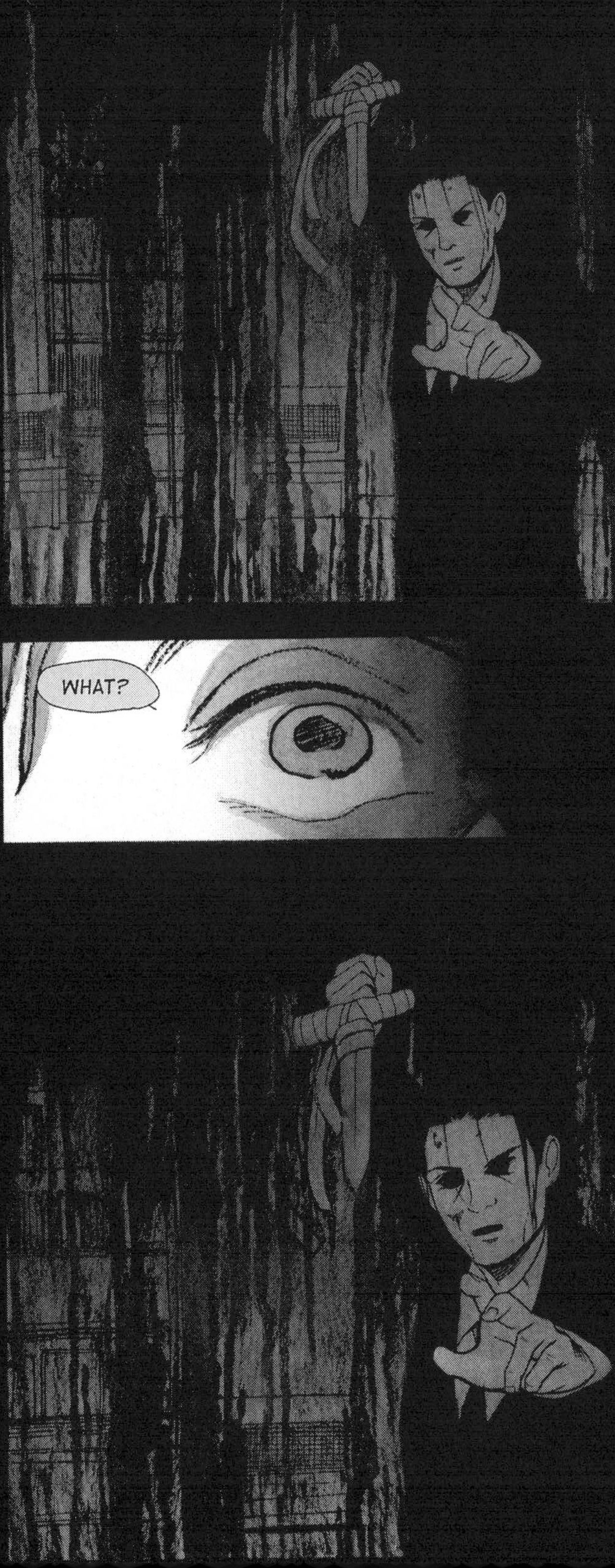
WHAT?

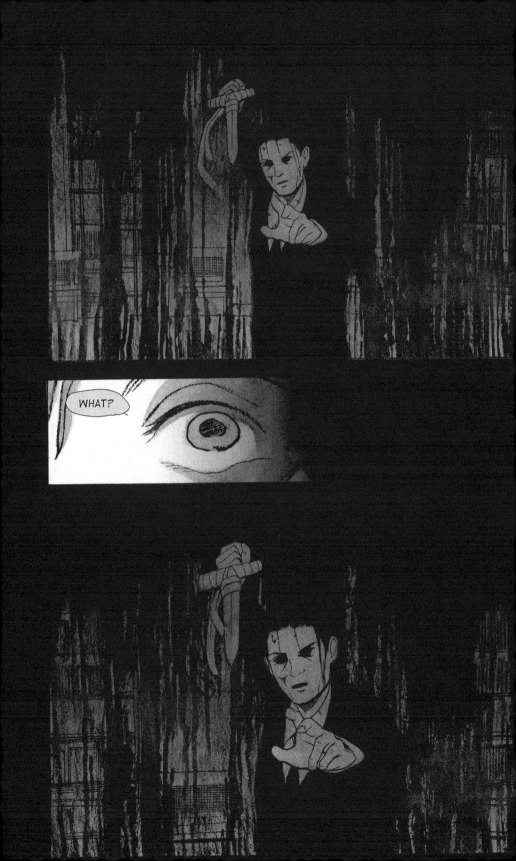

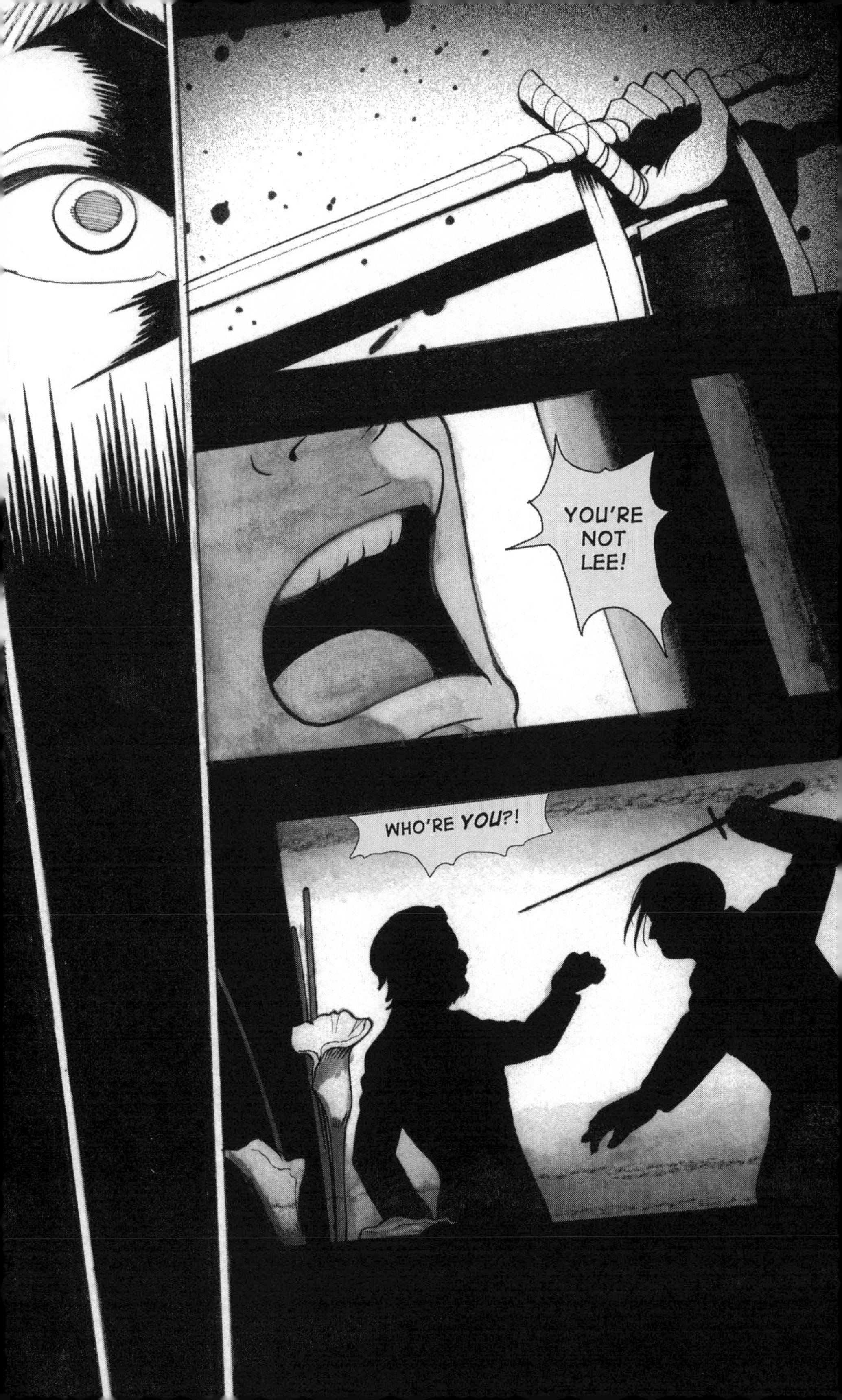
YOU'RE NOT LEE!
WHO'RE *YOU*?!

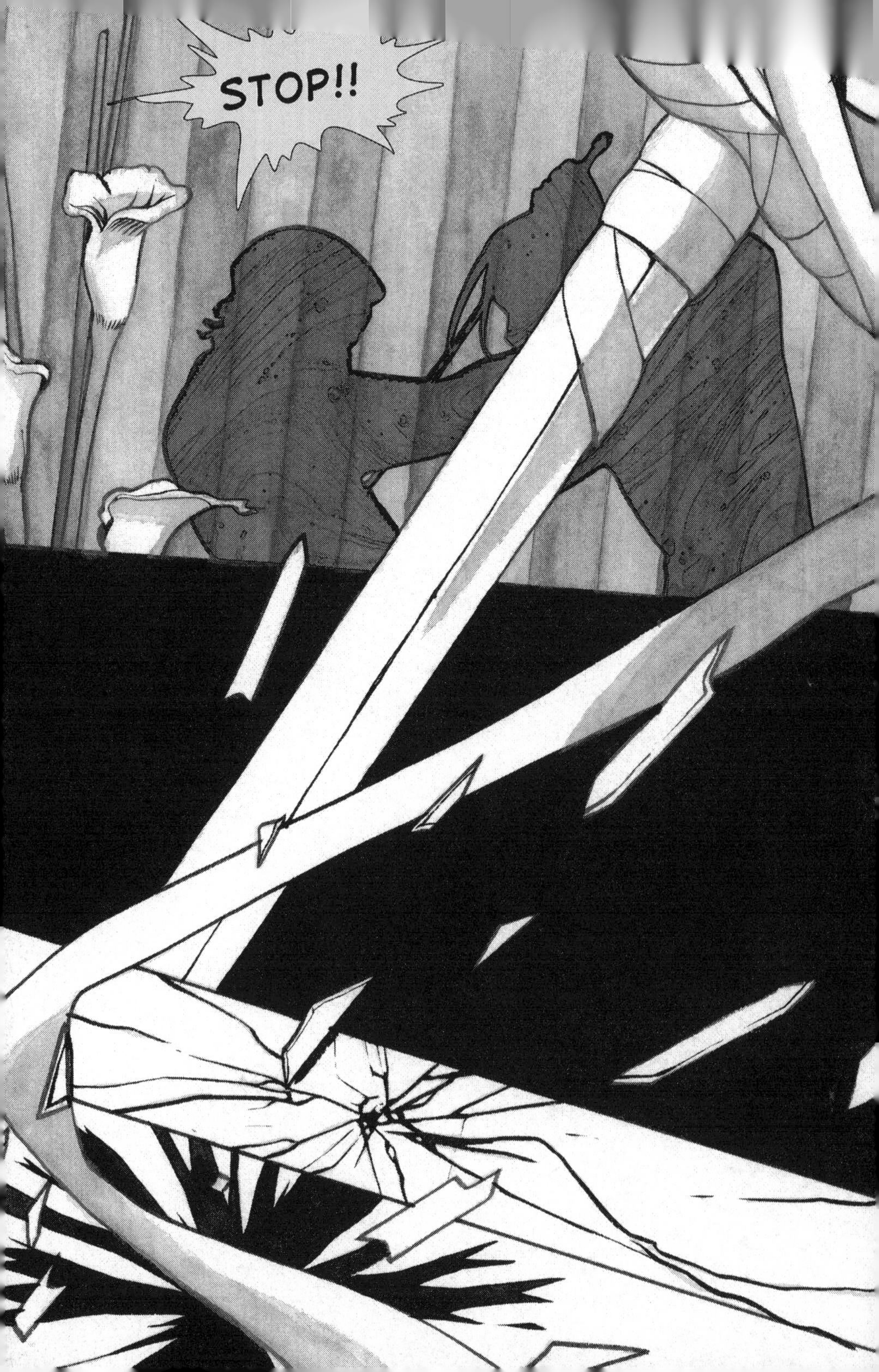
STOP!!

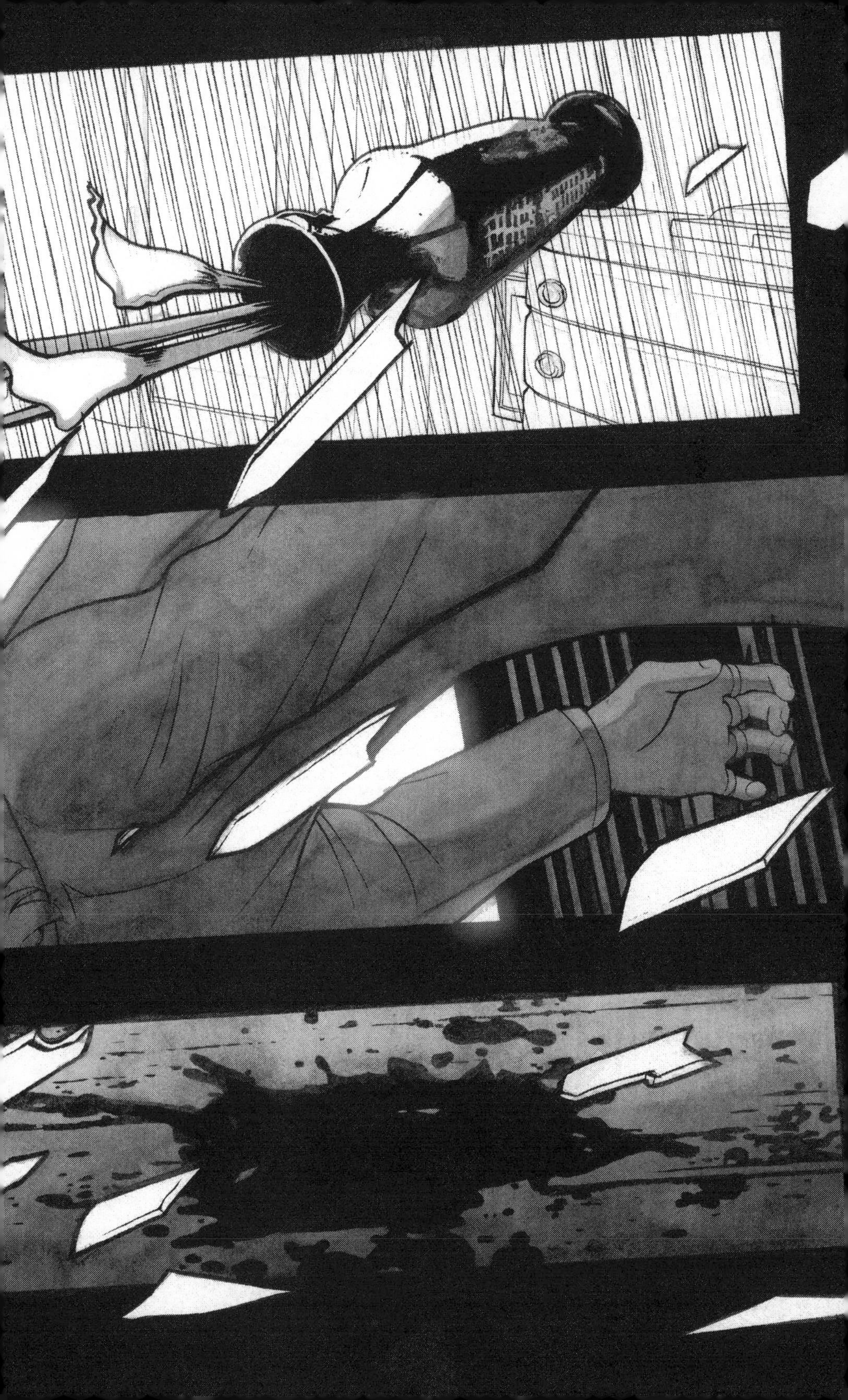

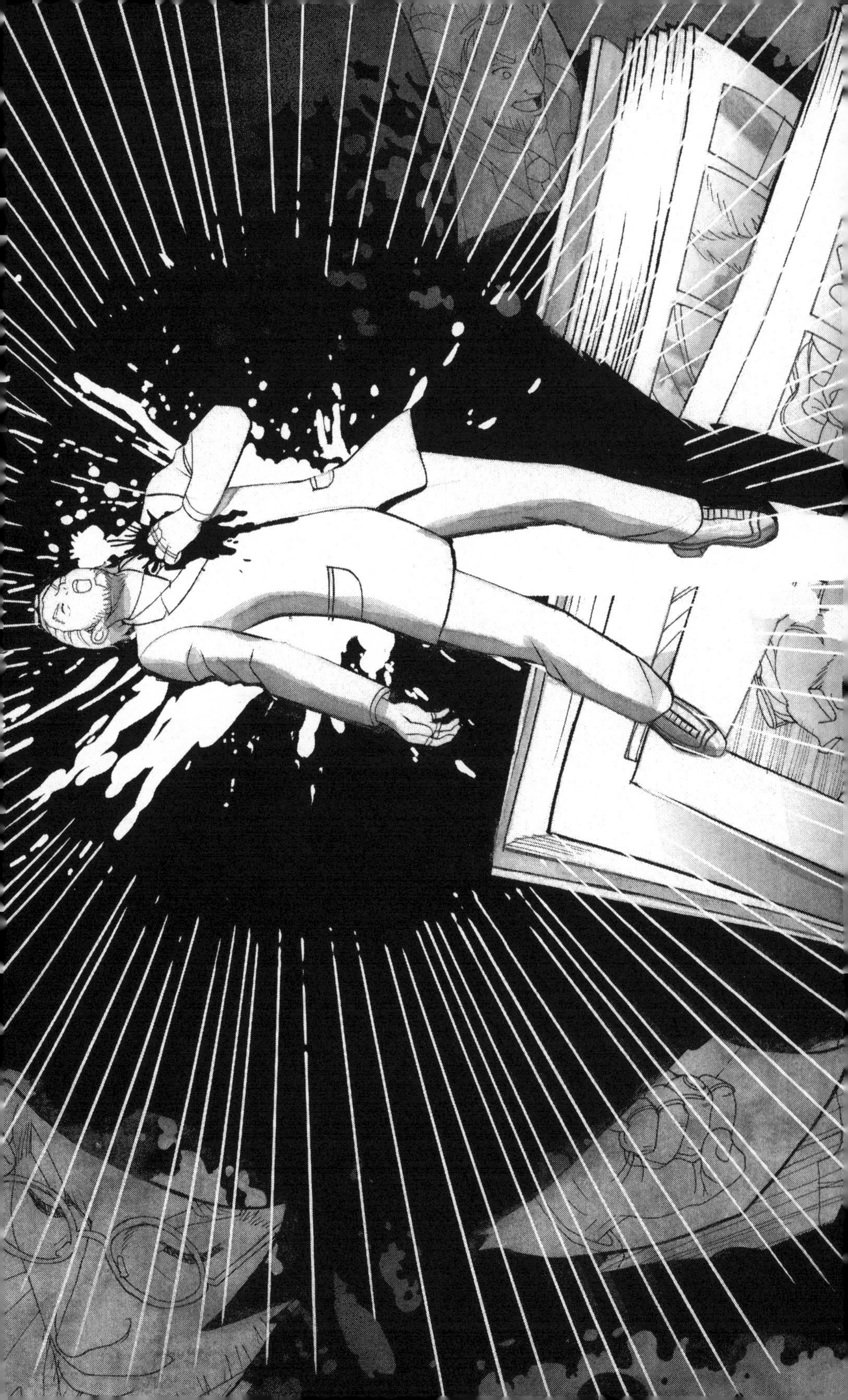

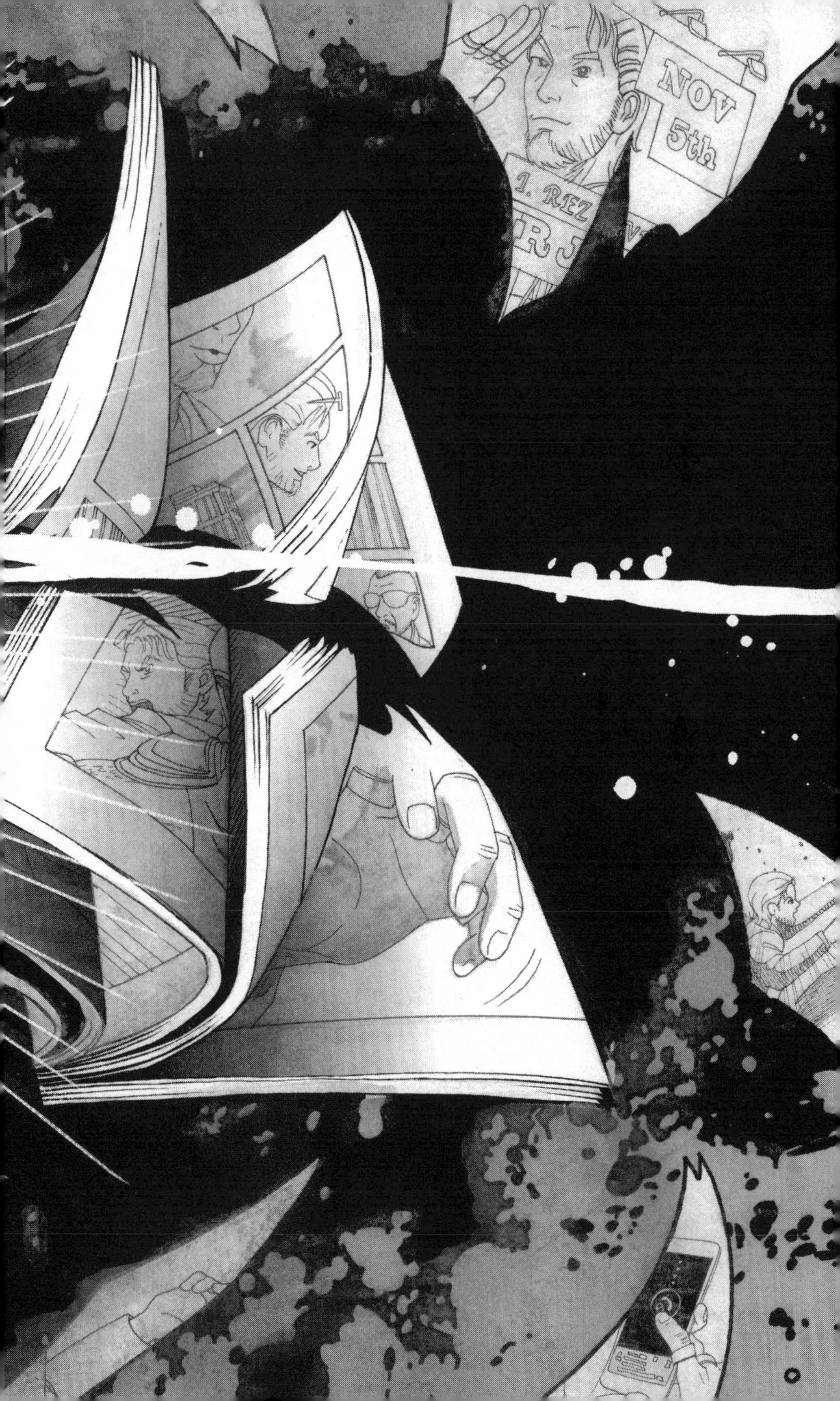
NOV
5th

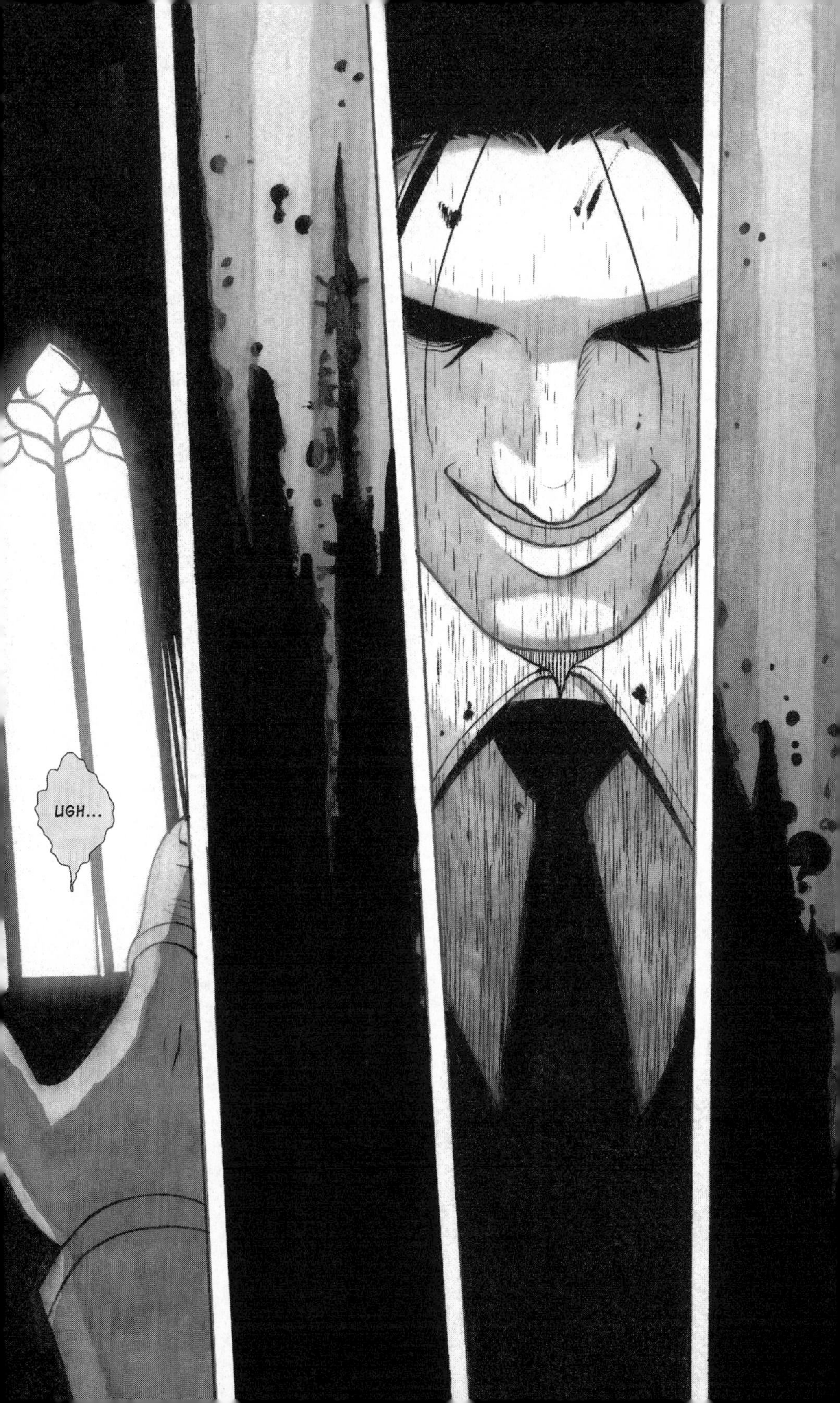
UGH...

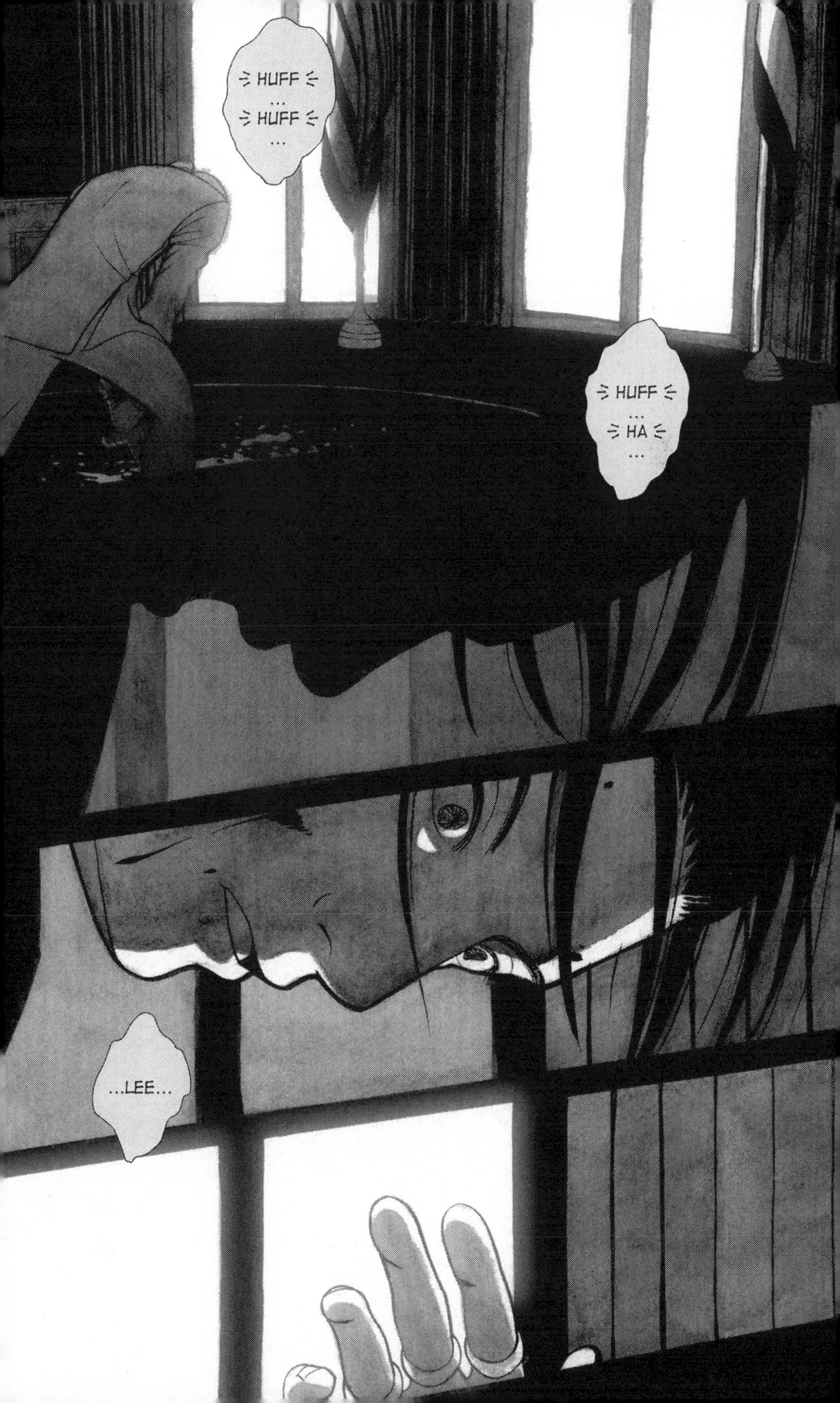
HUFF ... HUFF ...
HUFF ... HA ...
...LEE...

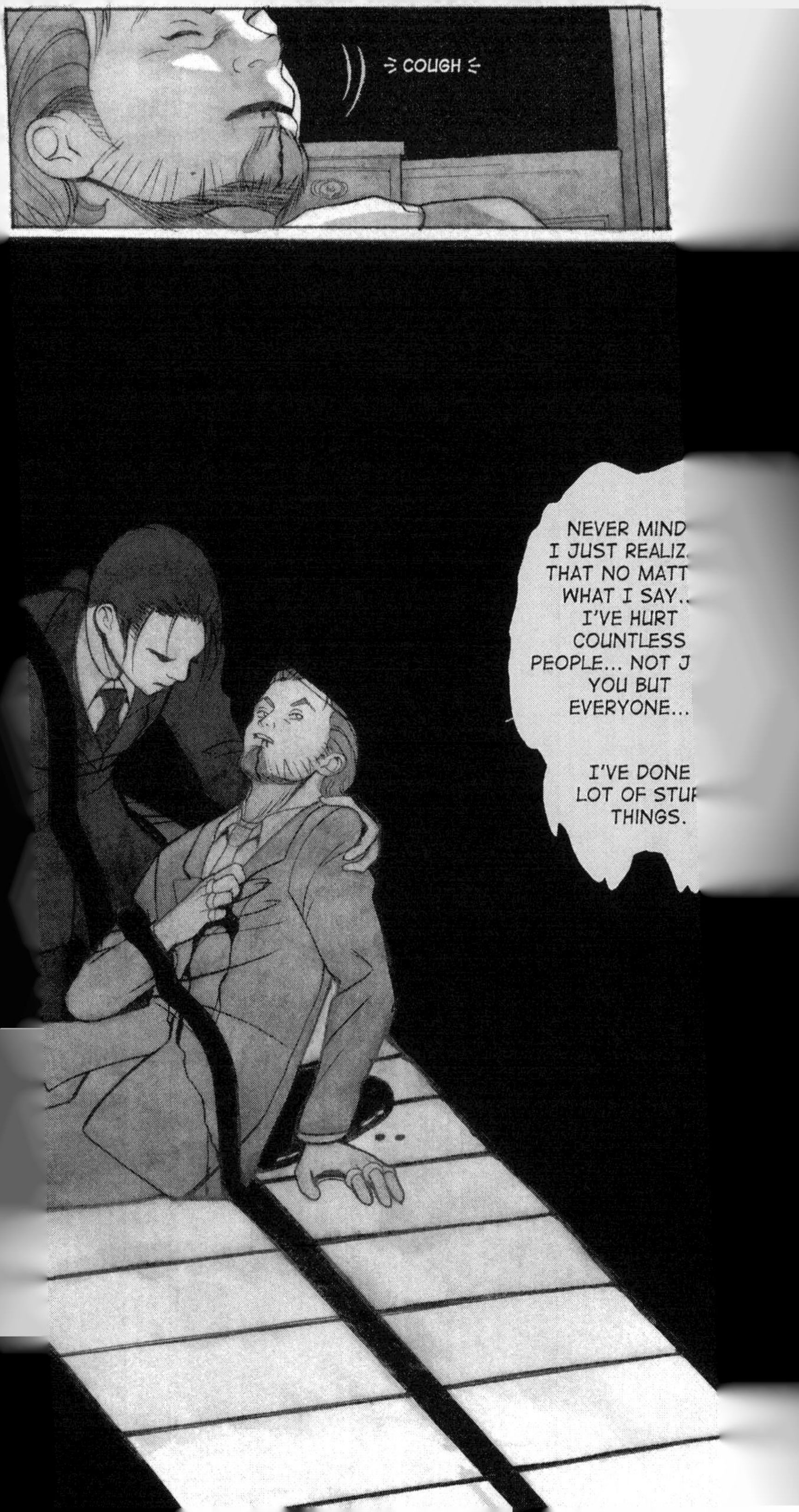
COUGH
NEVER MIND I JUST REALIZ THAT NO MATT WHAT I SAY.. I'VE HURT COUNTLESS PEOPLE... NOT J YOU BUT EVERYONE...
I'VE DONE LOT OF STU THINGS.

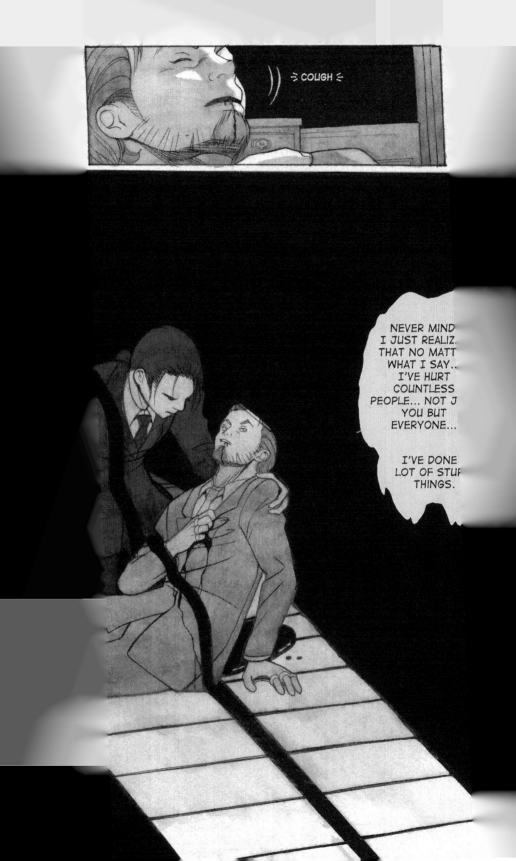

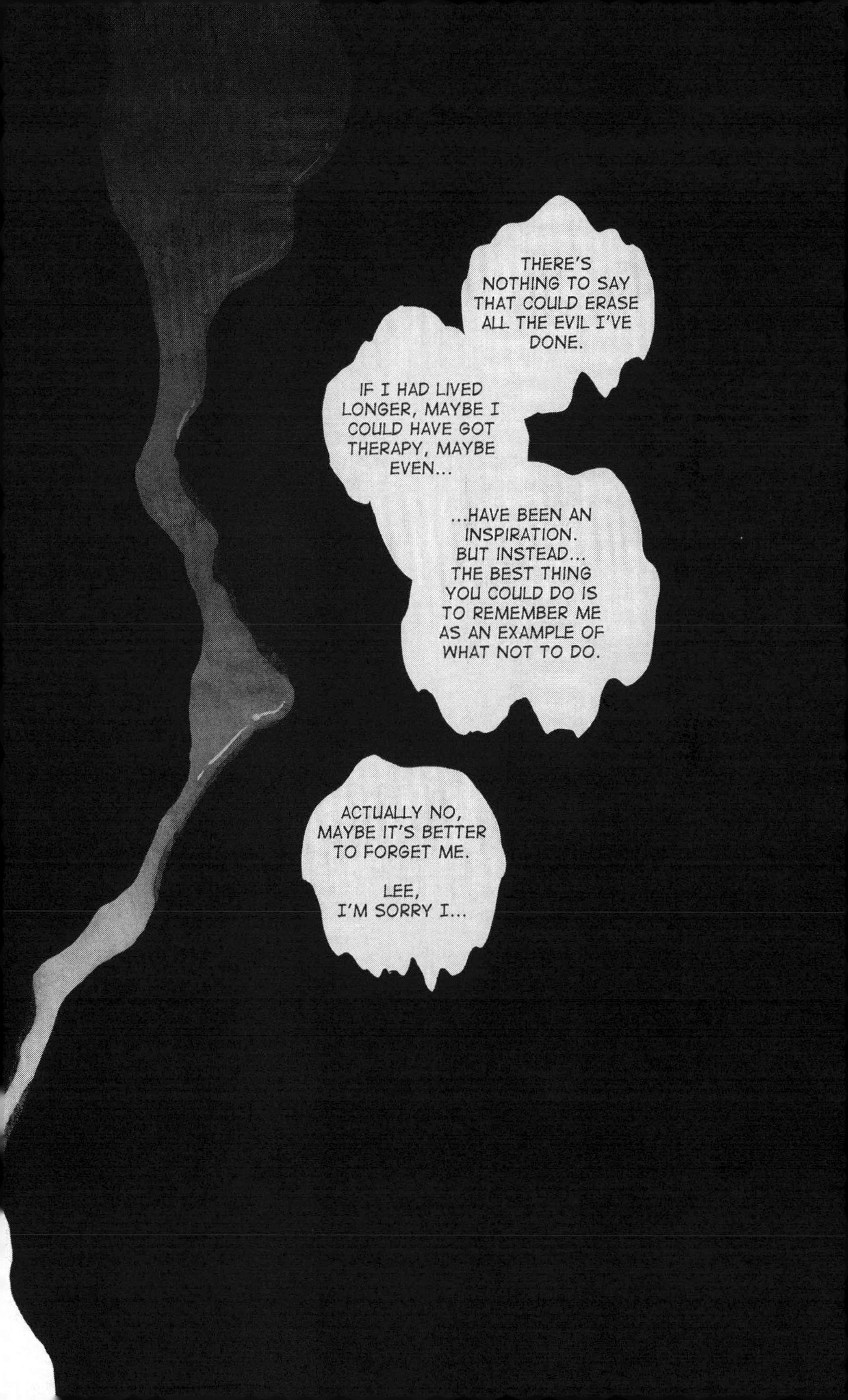
THERE'S NOTHING TO SAY THAT COULD ERASE ALL THE EVIL I'VE DONE.
IF I HAD LIVED LONGER, MAYBE I COULD HAVE GOT THERAPY, MAYBE EVEN...
...HAVE BEEN AN INSPIRATION. BUT INSTEAD... THE BEST THING YOU COULD DO IS TO REMEMBER ME AS AN EXAMPLE OF WHAT NOT TO DO.
ACTUALLY NO, MAYBE IT'S BETTER TO FORGET ME.
LEE, I'M SORRY I...

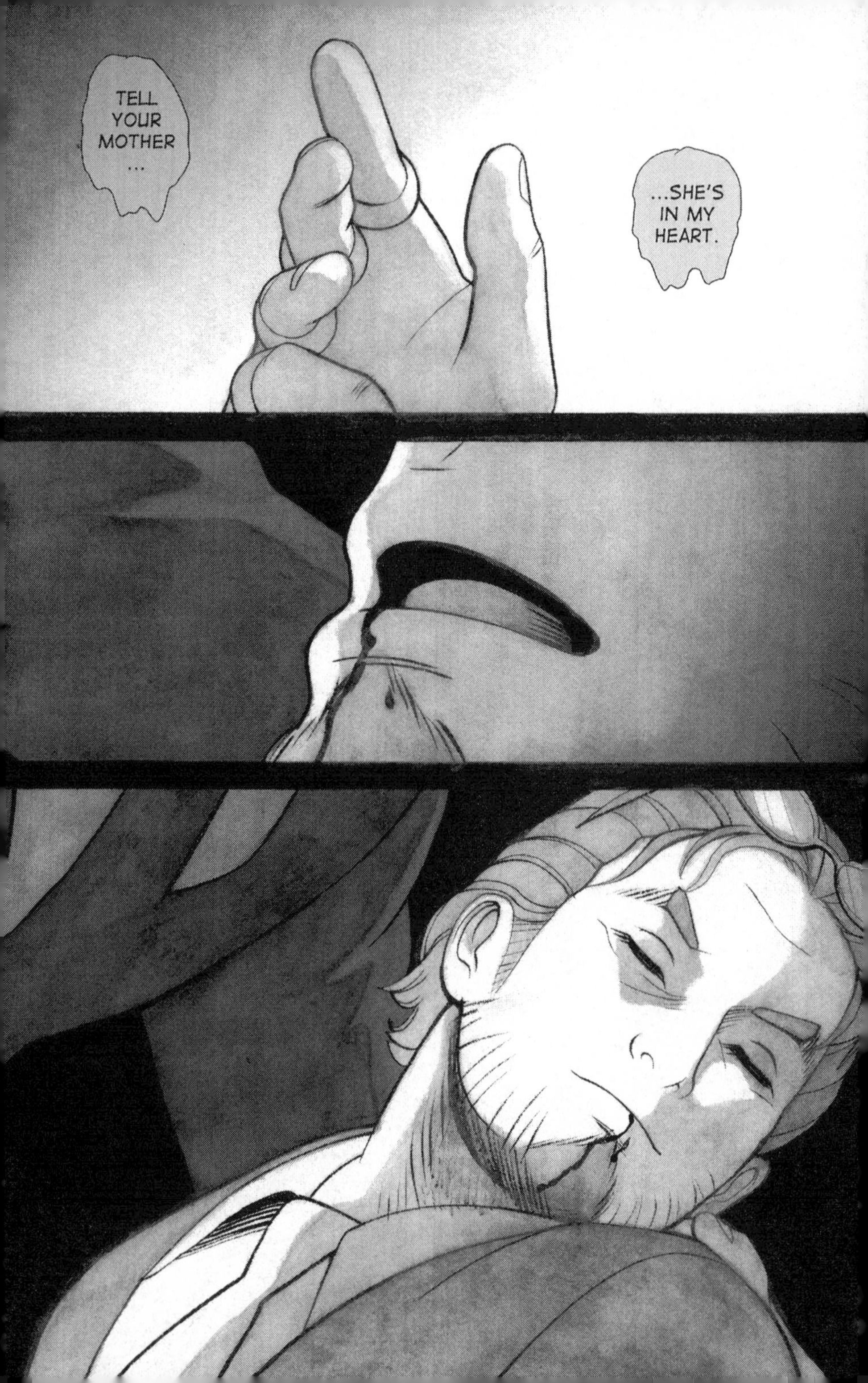
TELL YOUR MOTHER ...
...SHE'S IN MY HEART.

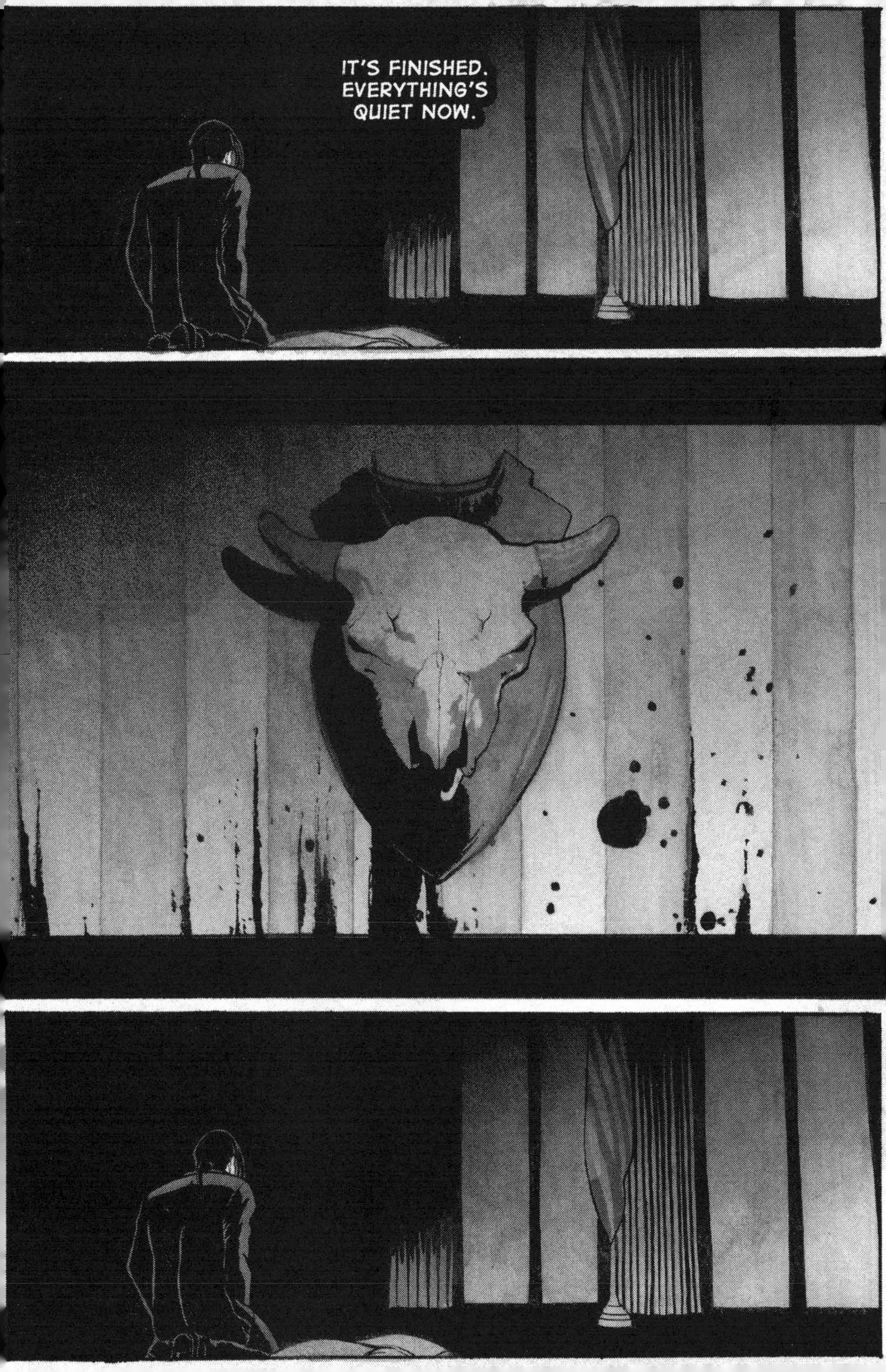
IT'S FINISHED. EVERYTHING'S QUIET NOW.

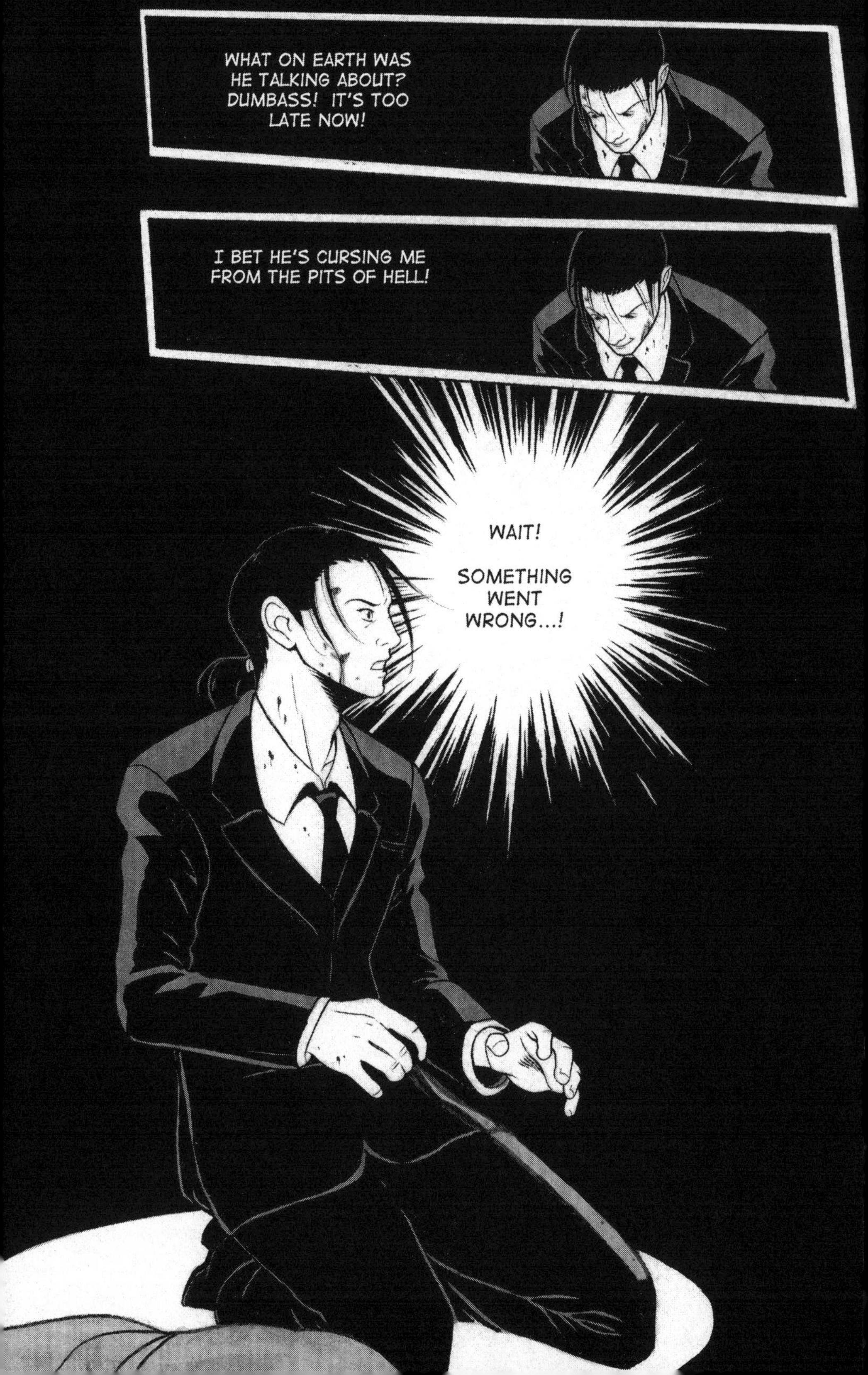
WHAT ON EARTH WAS HE TALKING ABOUT? DUMBASS! IT'S TOO LATE NOW!
I BET HE'S CURSING ME FROM THE PITS OF HELL!
WAIT!
SOMETHING WENT WRONG...!

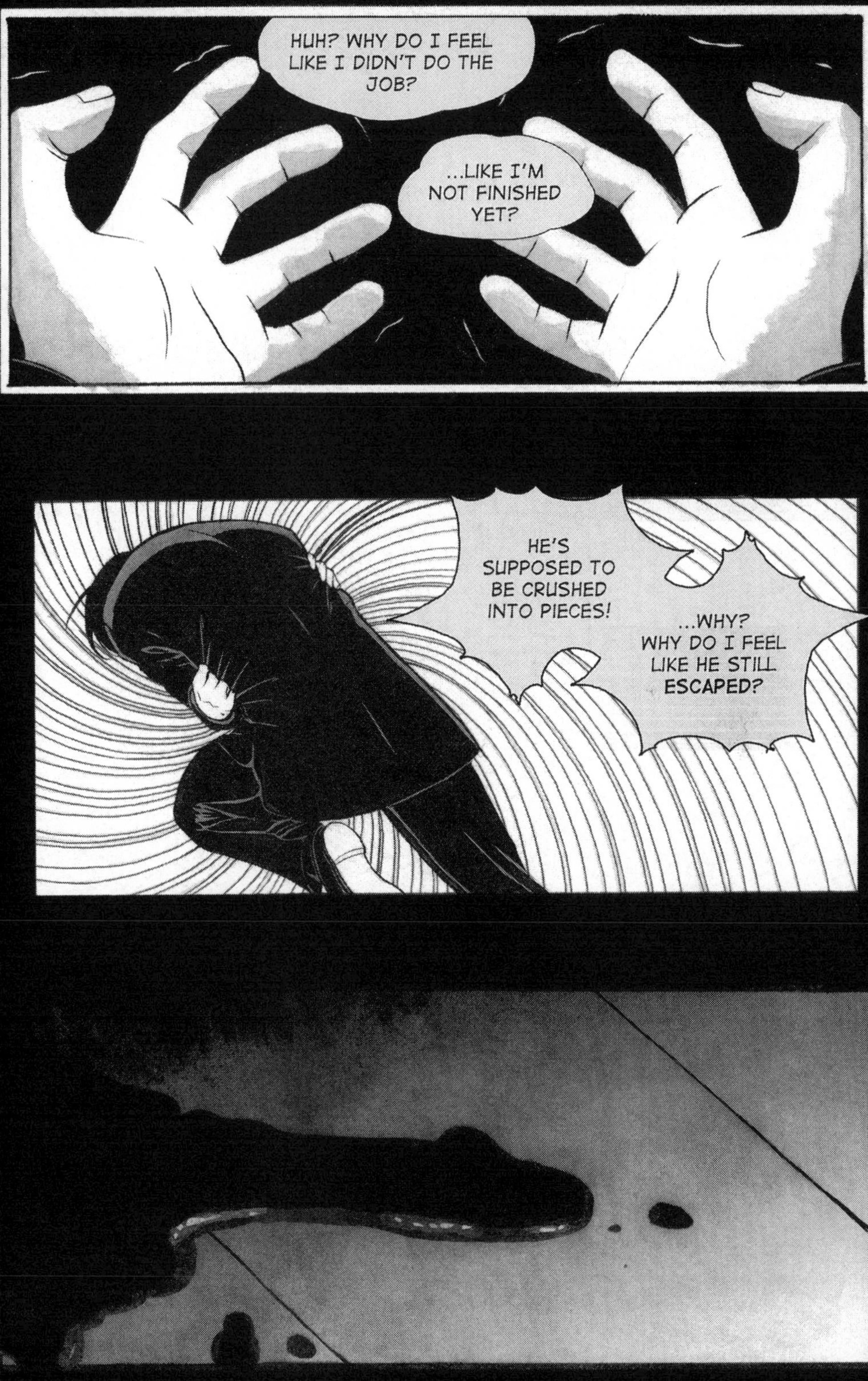
HUH? WHY DO I FEEL LIKE I DIDN'T DO THE JOB?
...LIKE I'M NOT FINISHED YET?
HE'S SUPPOSED TO BE CRUSHED INTO PIECES!
...WHY? WHY DO I FEEL LIKE HE STILL **ESCAPED?**

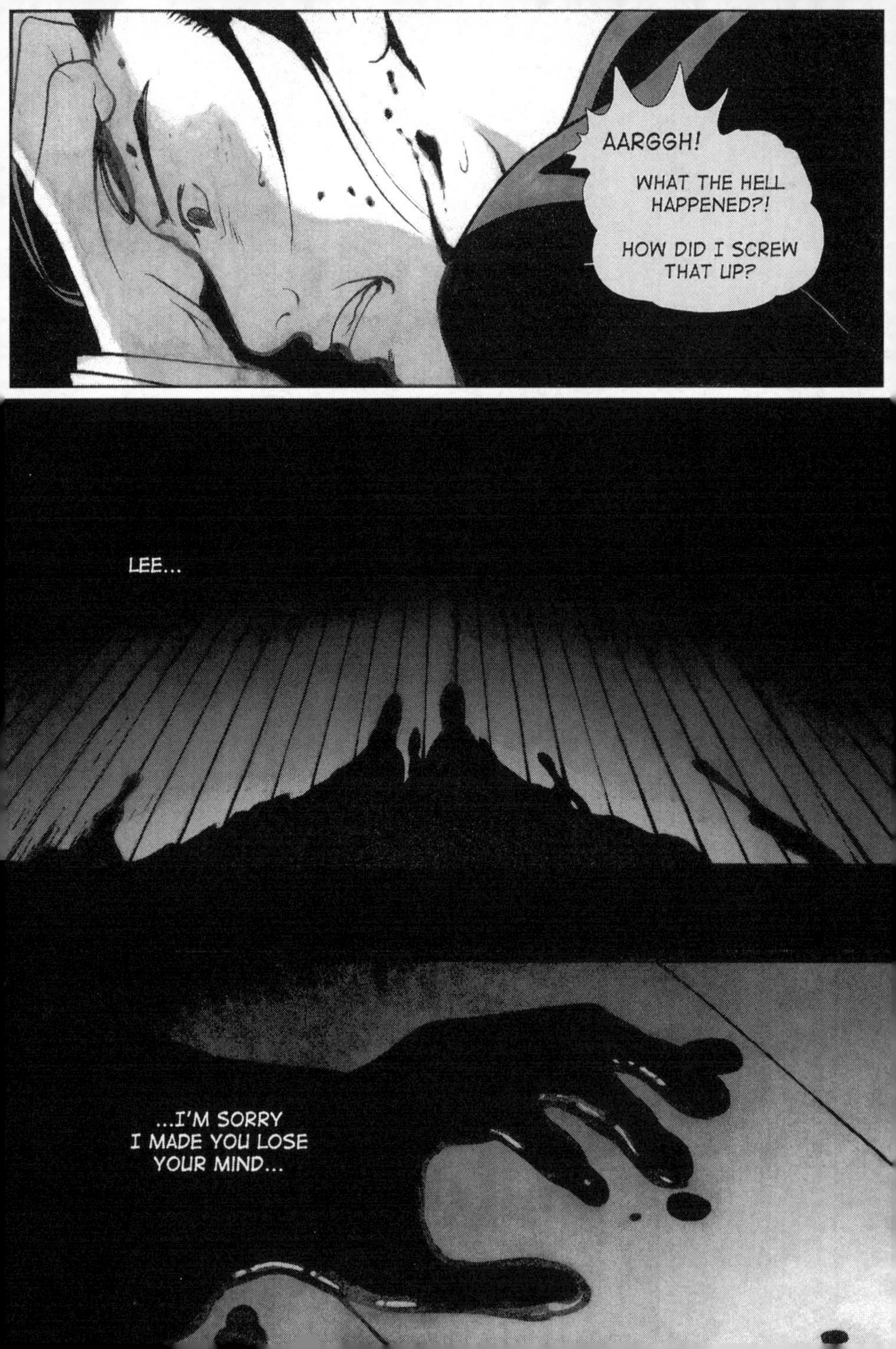
AARGGH!
WHAT THE HELL HAPPENED?!
HOW DID I SCREW THAT UP?
LEE...
...I'M SORRY I MADE YOU LOSE YOUR MIND...

HUH?!
. . .
LEE...
...I'M SORRY I MADE YOU LOSE YOUR MIND...
GAAH!

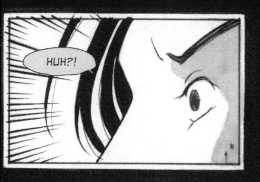

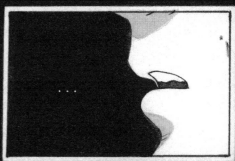

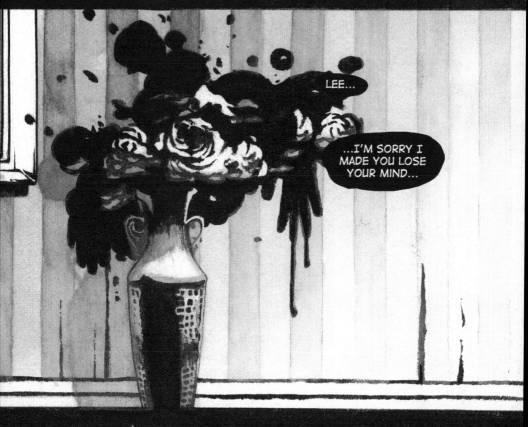

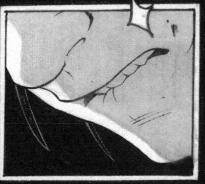

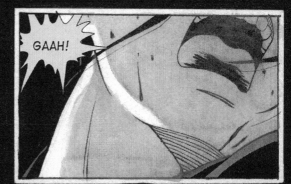

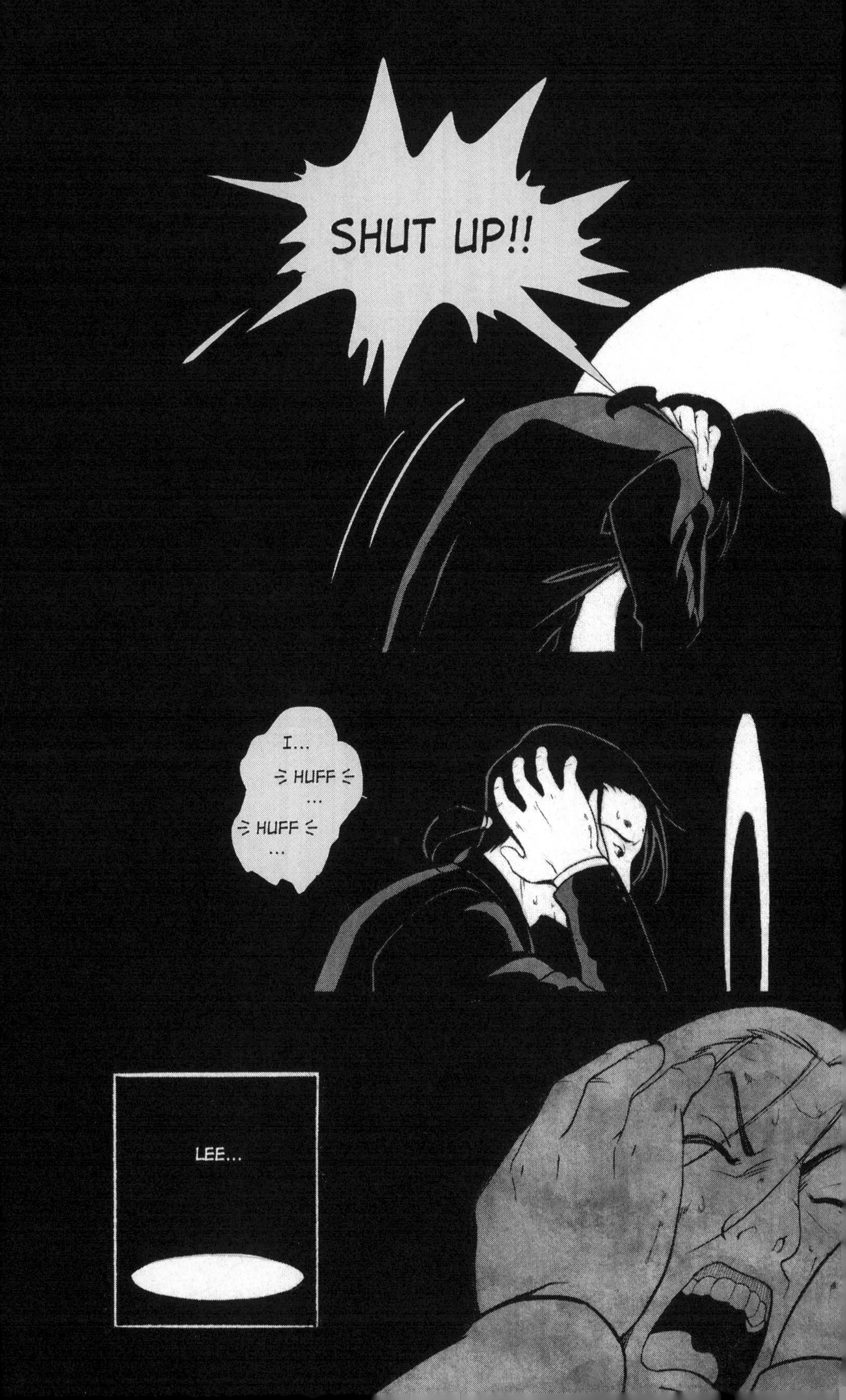
SHUT UP!!
I... HUFF ... HUFF ...
LEE...

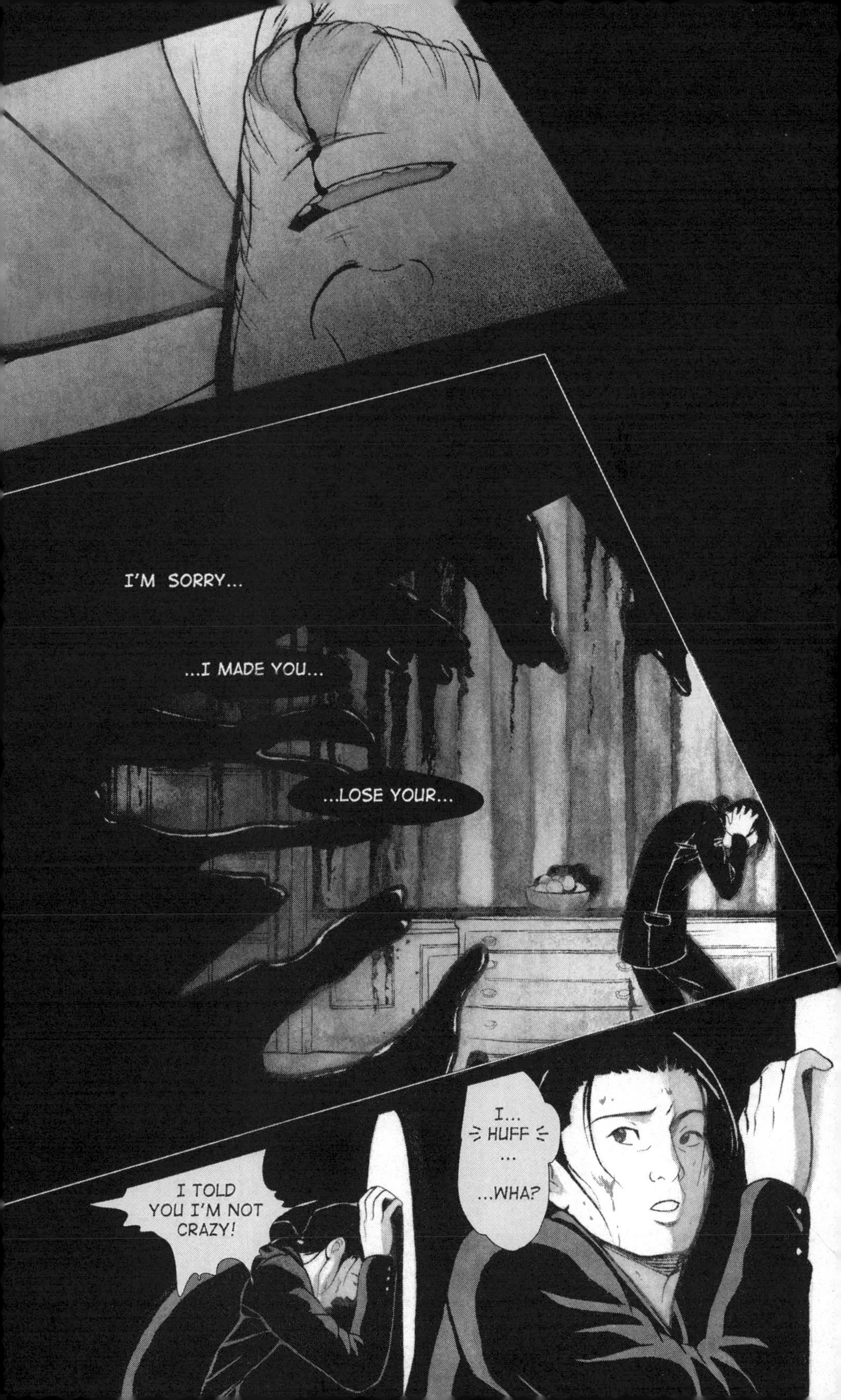

I'M SORRY...
...I MADE YOU...
...LOSE YOUR...
I... HUFF ... ...WHA?
I TOLD YOU I'M NOT CRAZY!

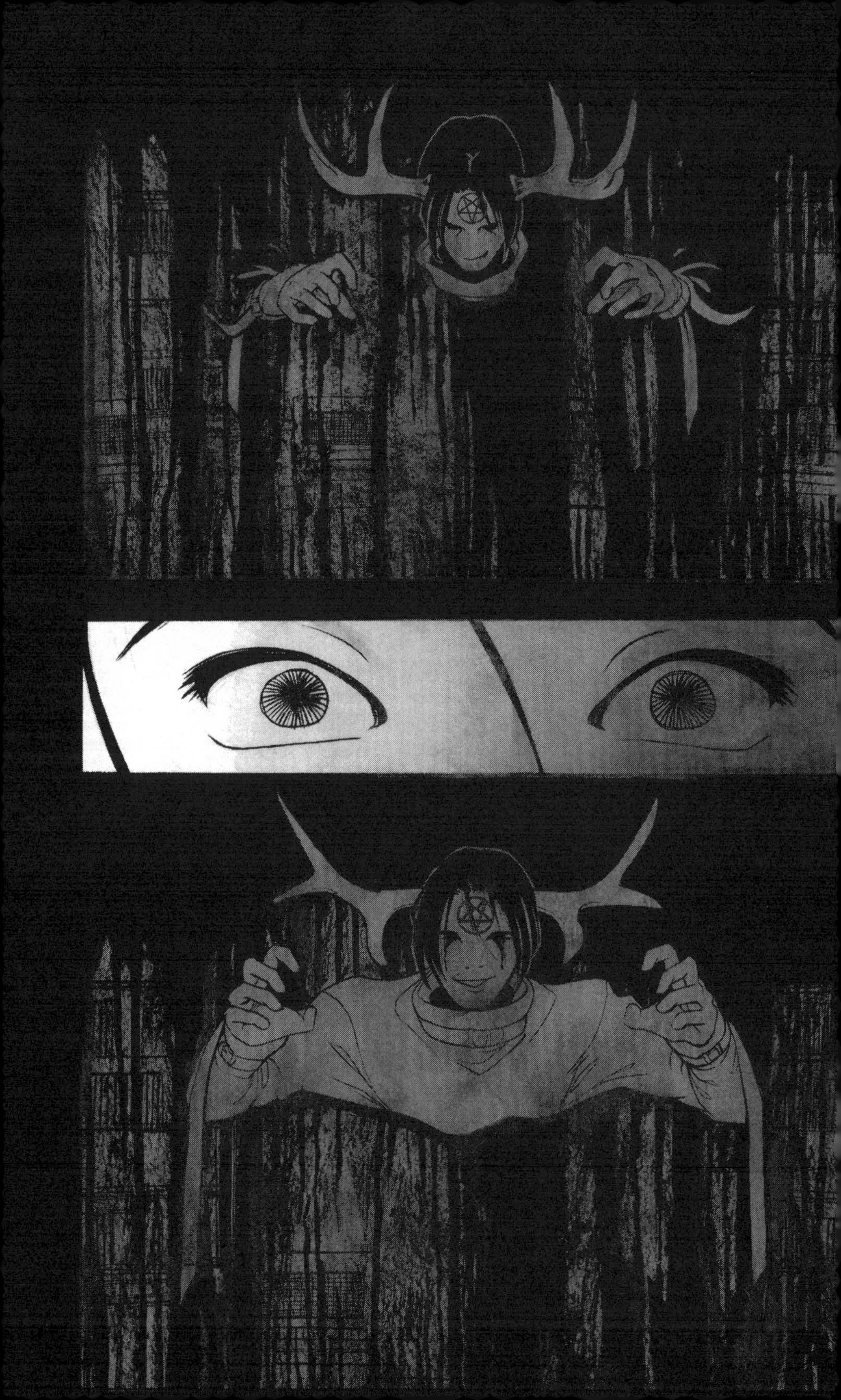

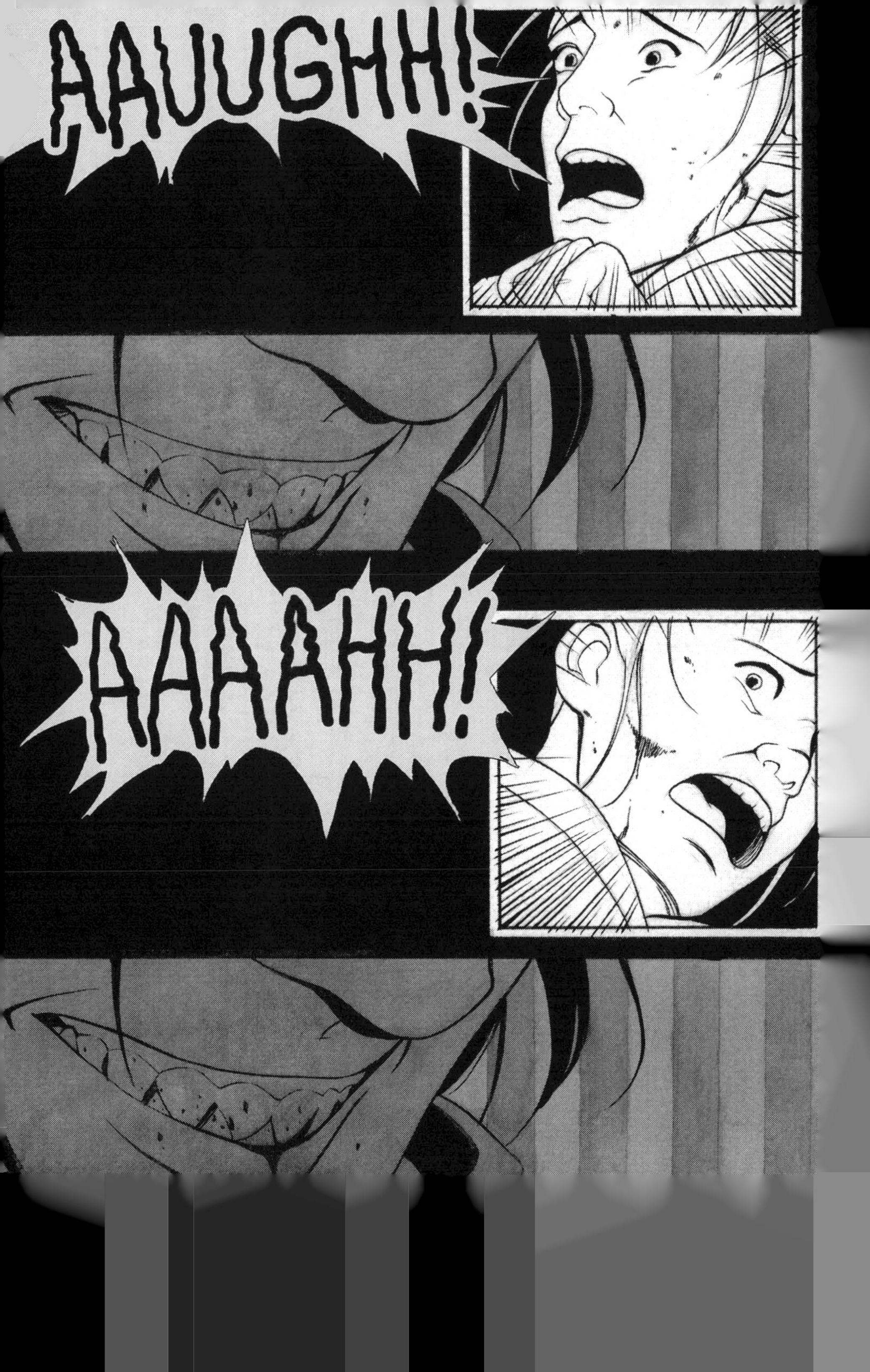
AAUUGHH!
AAAAHH!

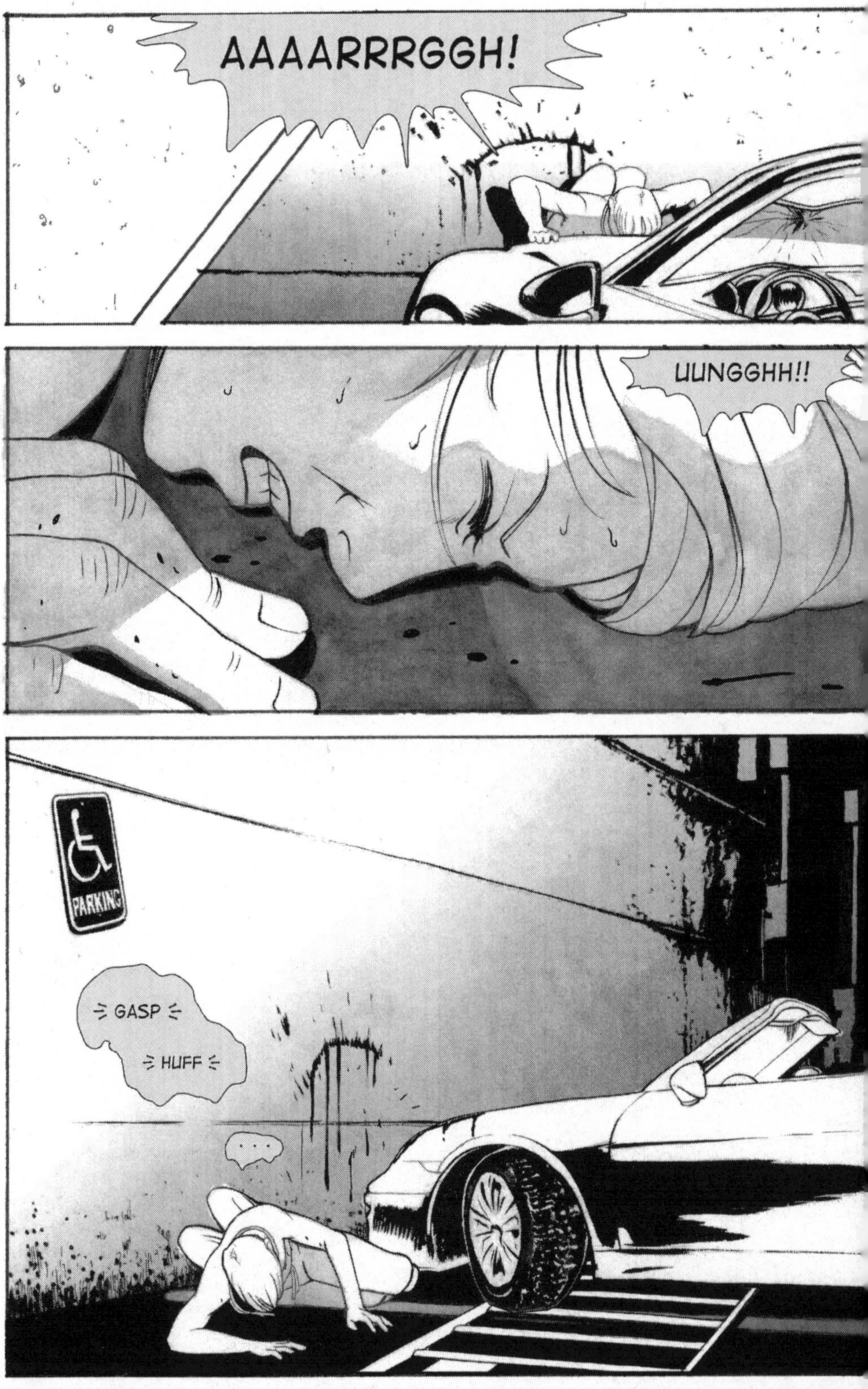
AAAARRRGGH!
UUNGGHH!!
PARKING
GASP
HUFF
. . .

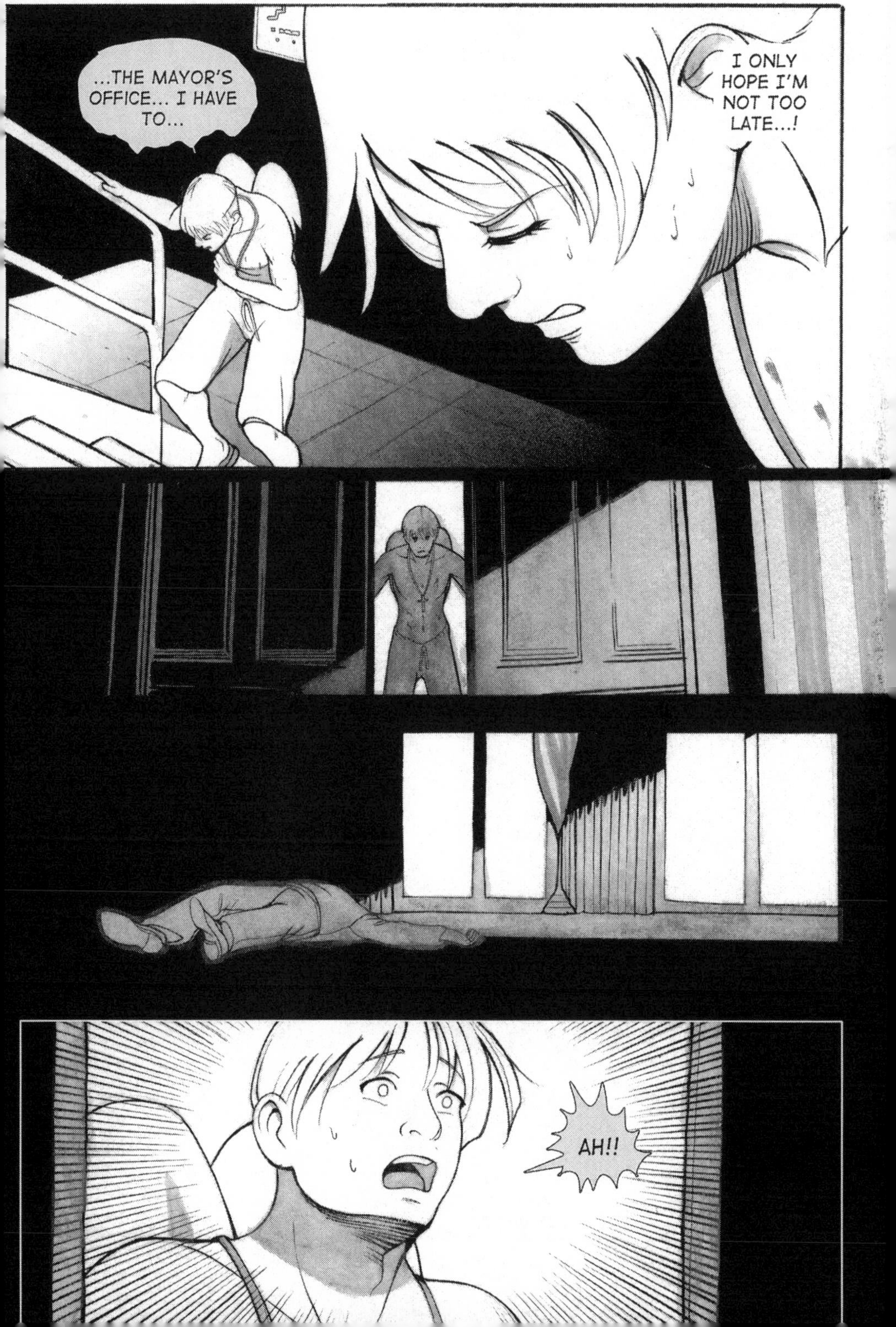
I ONLY HOPE I'M NOT TOO LATE...!
...THE MAYOR'S OFFICE... I HAVE TO...
AH!!

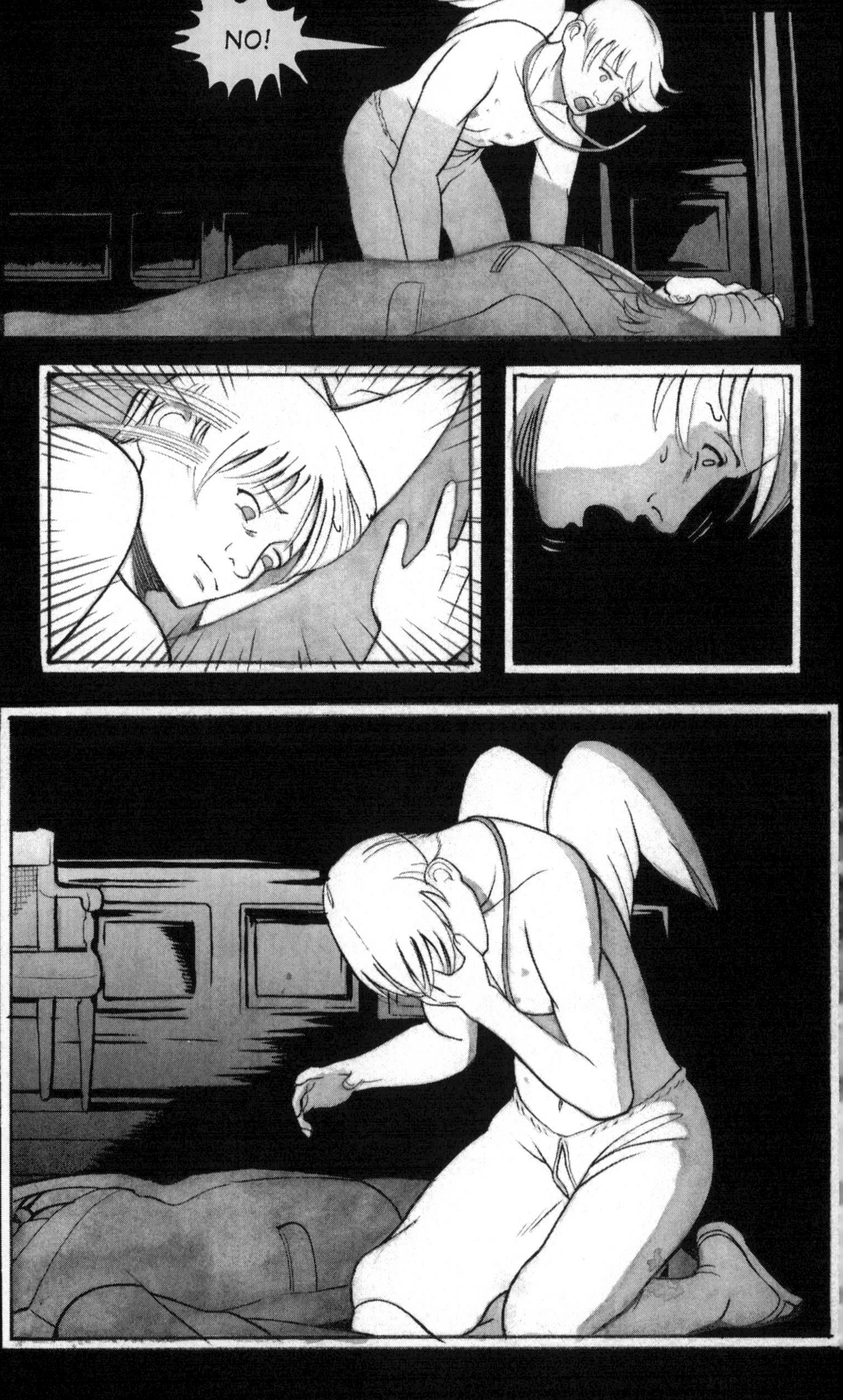
NO!

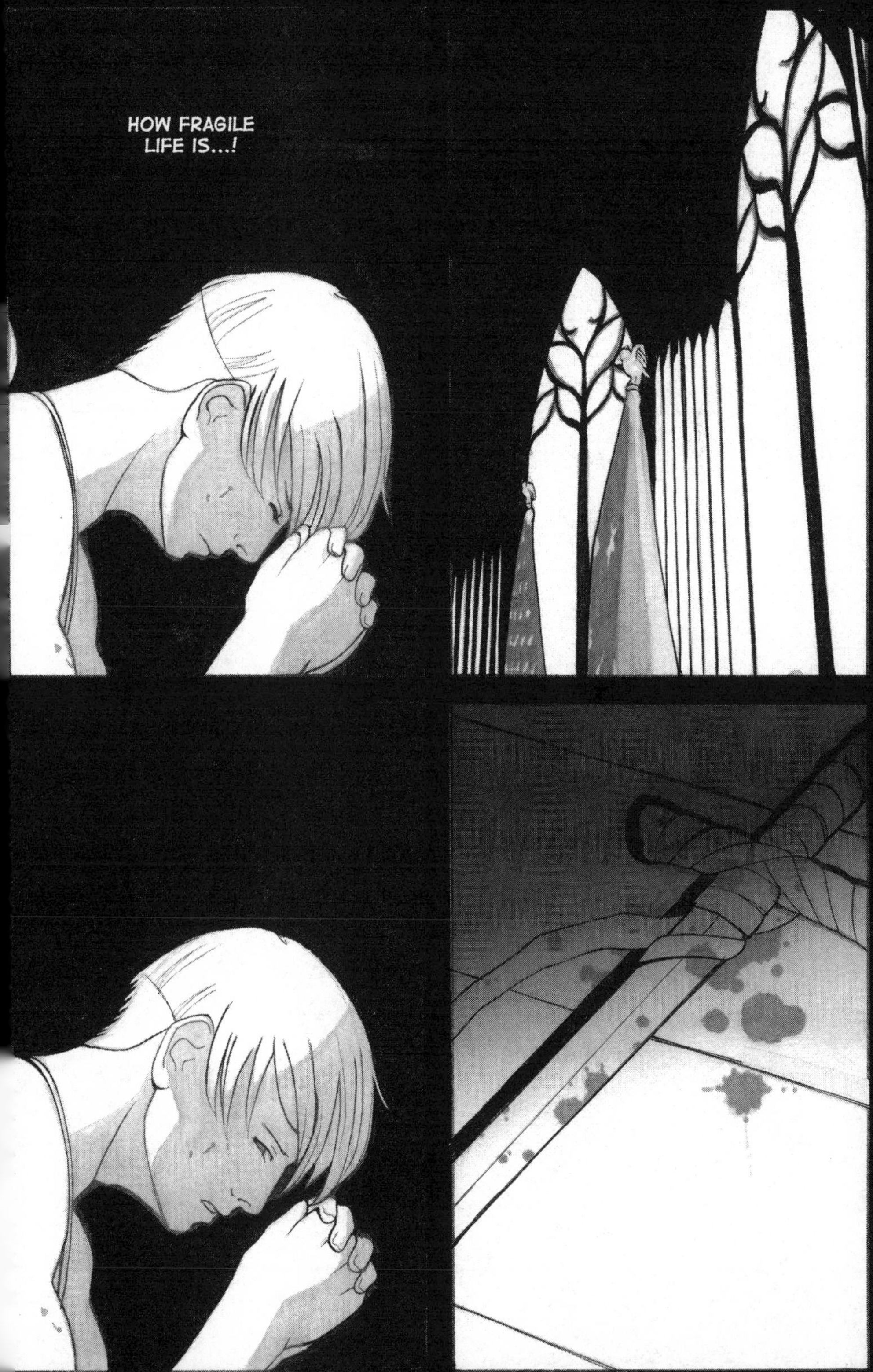
HOW FRAGILE LIFE IS...!

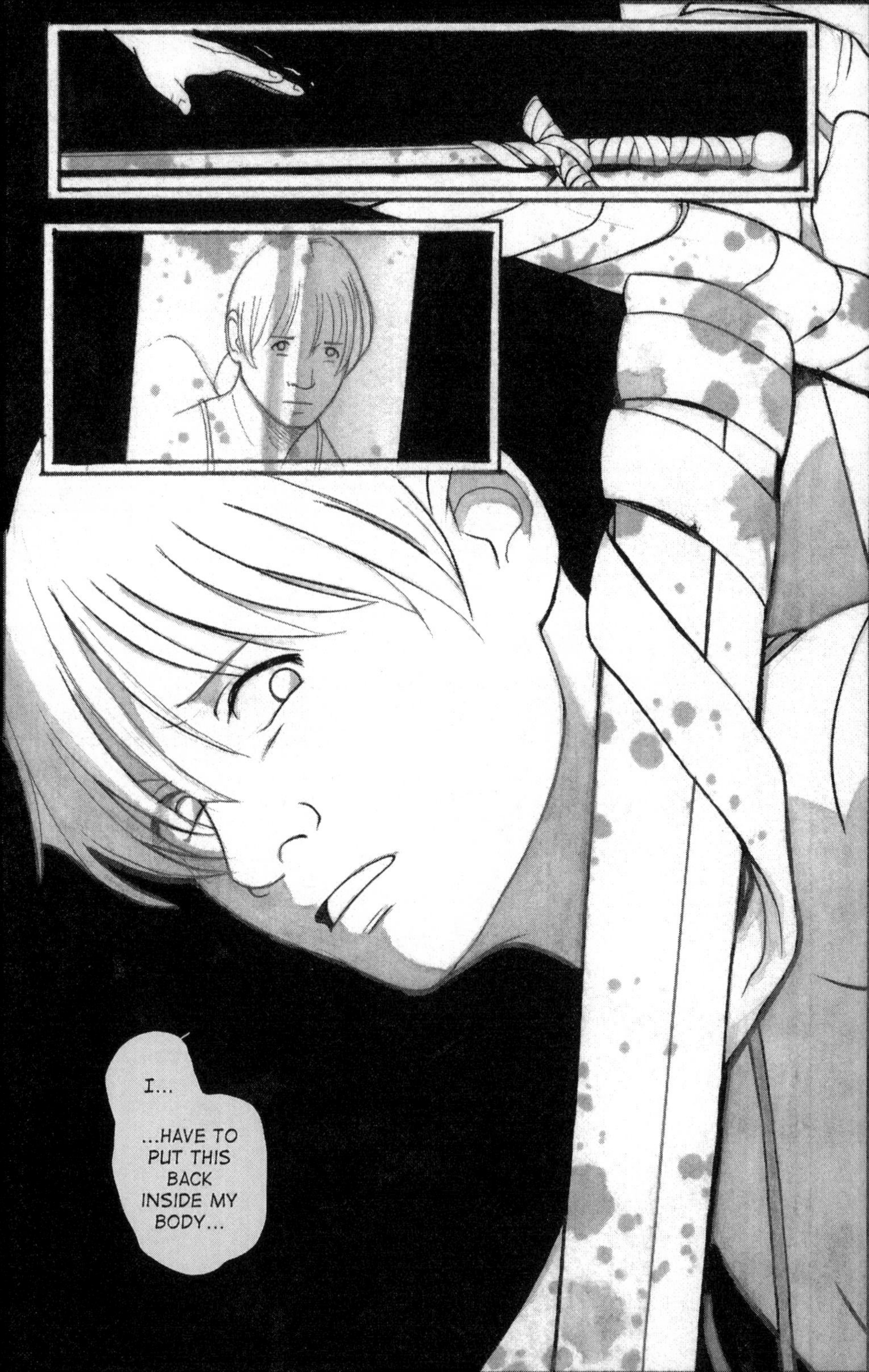
I...
...HAVE TO PUT THIS BACK INSIDE MY BODY...

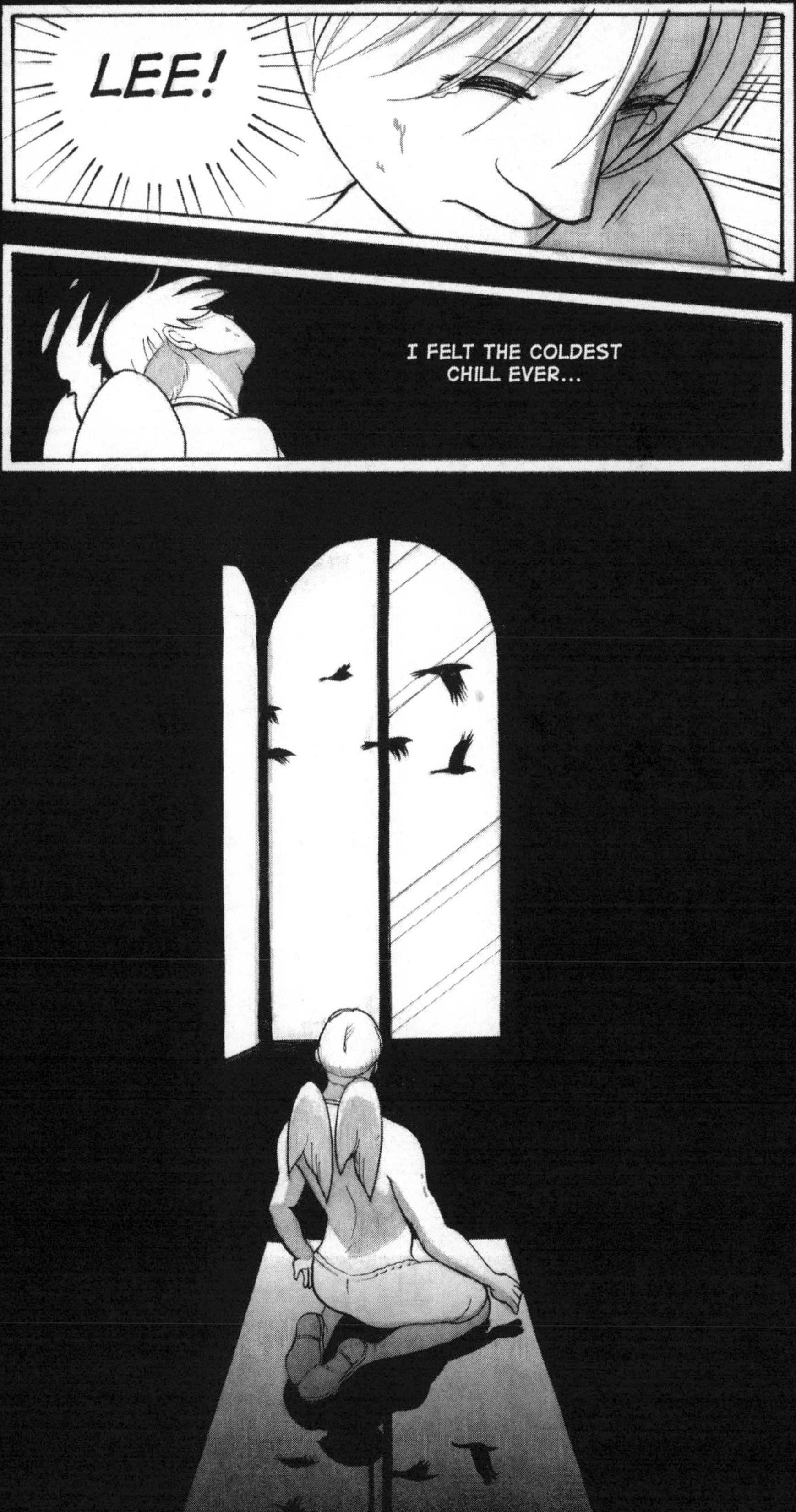
LEE!
I FELT THE COLDEST CHILL EVER...

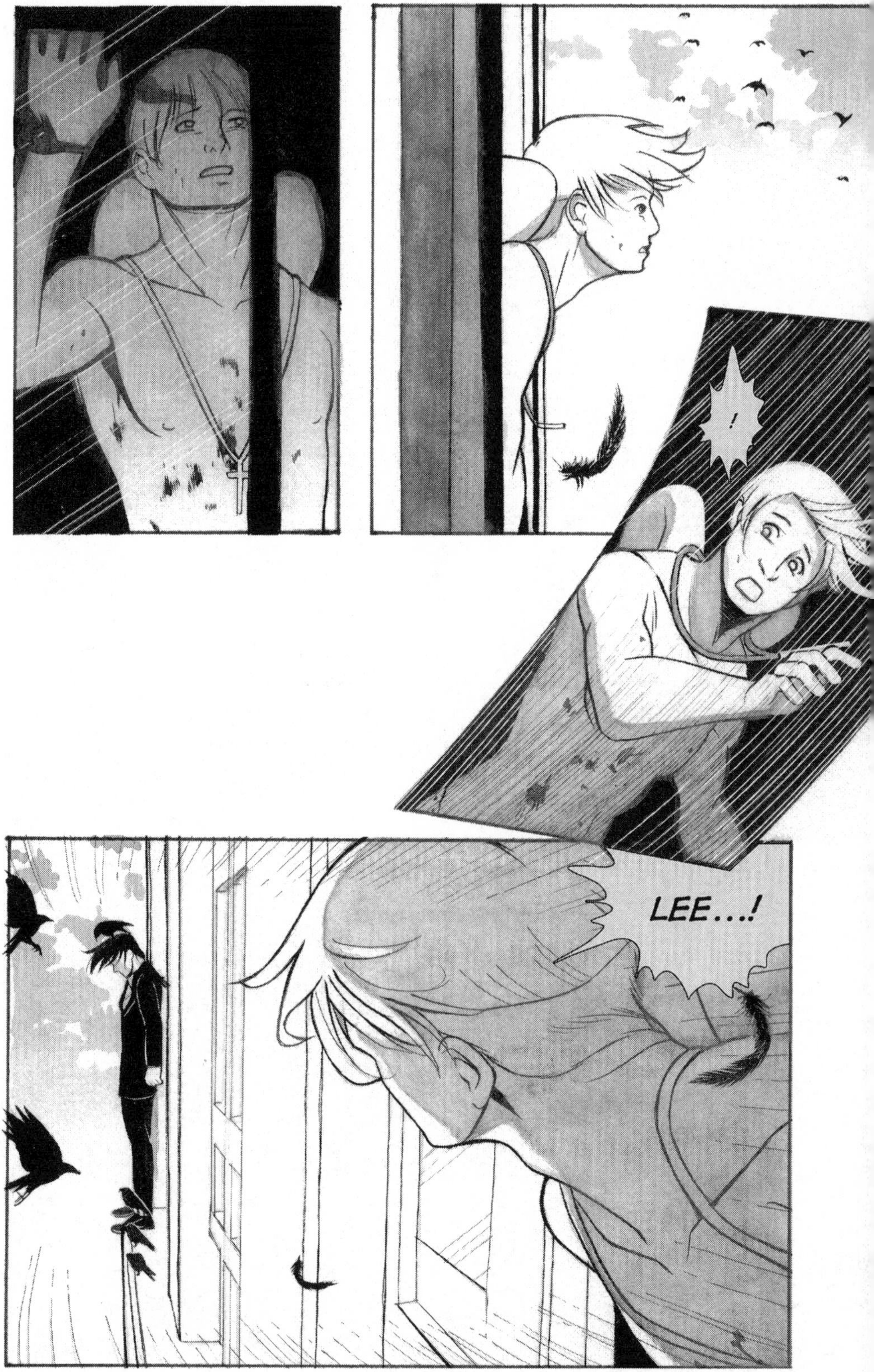
!
LEE...!

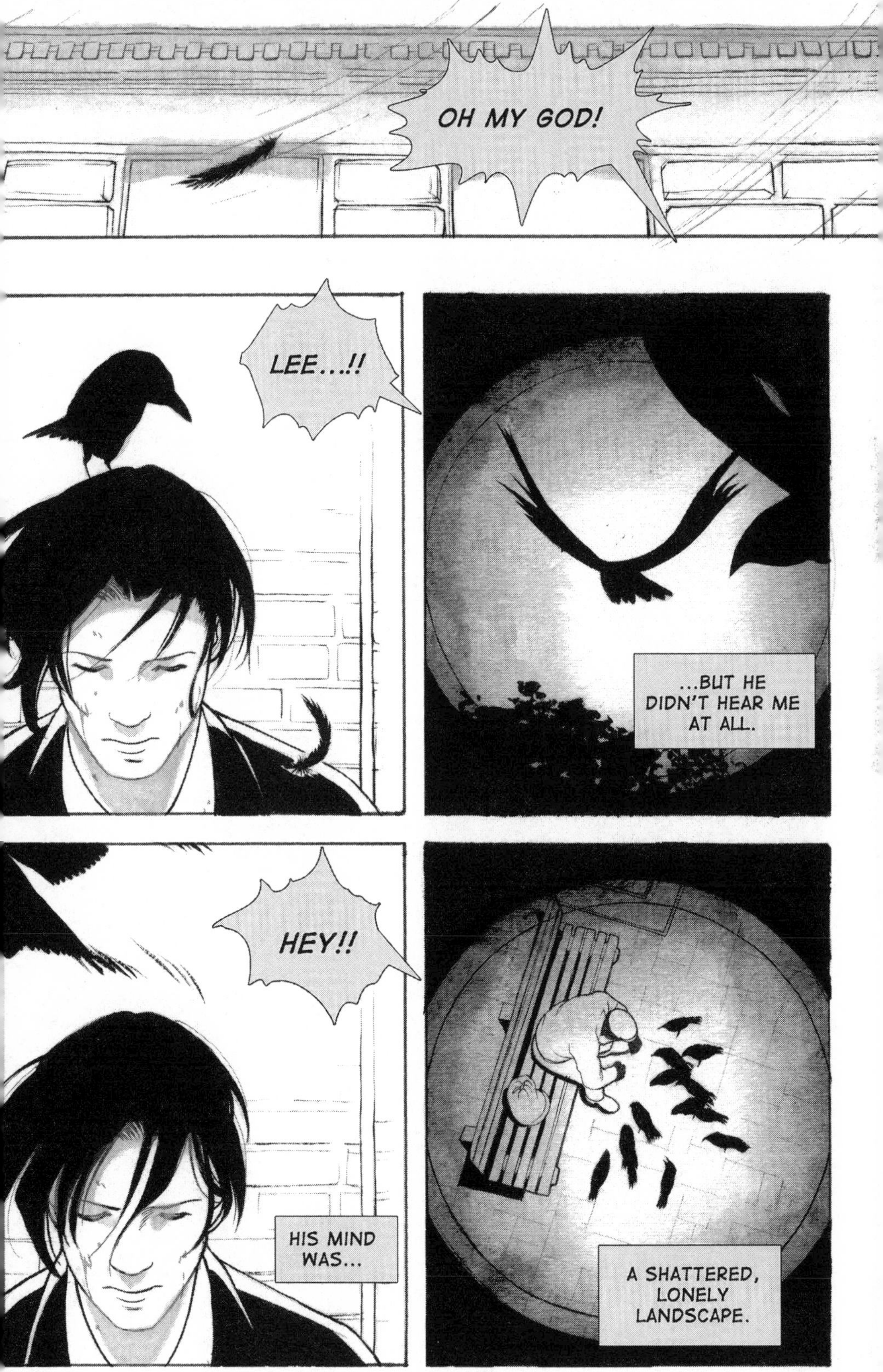
OH MY GOD!
LEE...!!
...BUT HE DIDN'T HEAR ME AT ALL.
HEY!!
HIS MIND WAS...
A SHATTERED, LONELY LANDSCAPE.

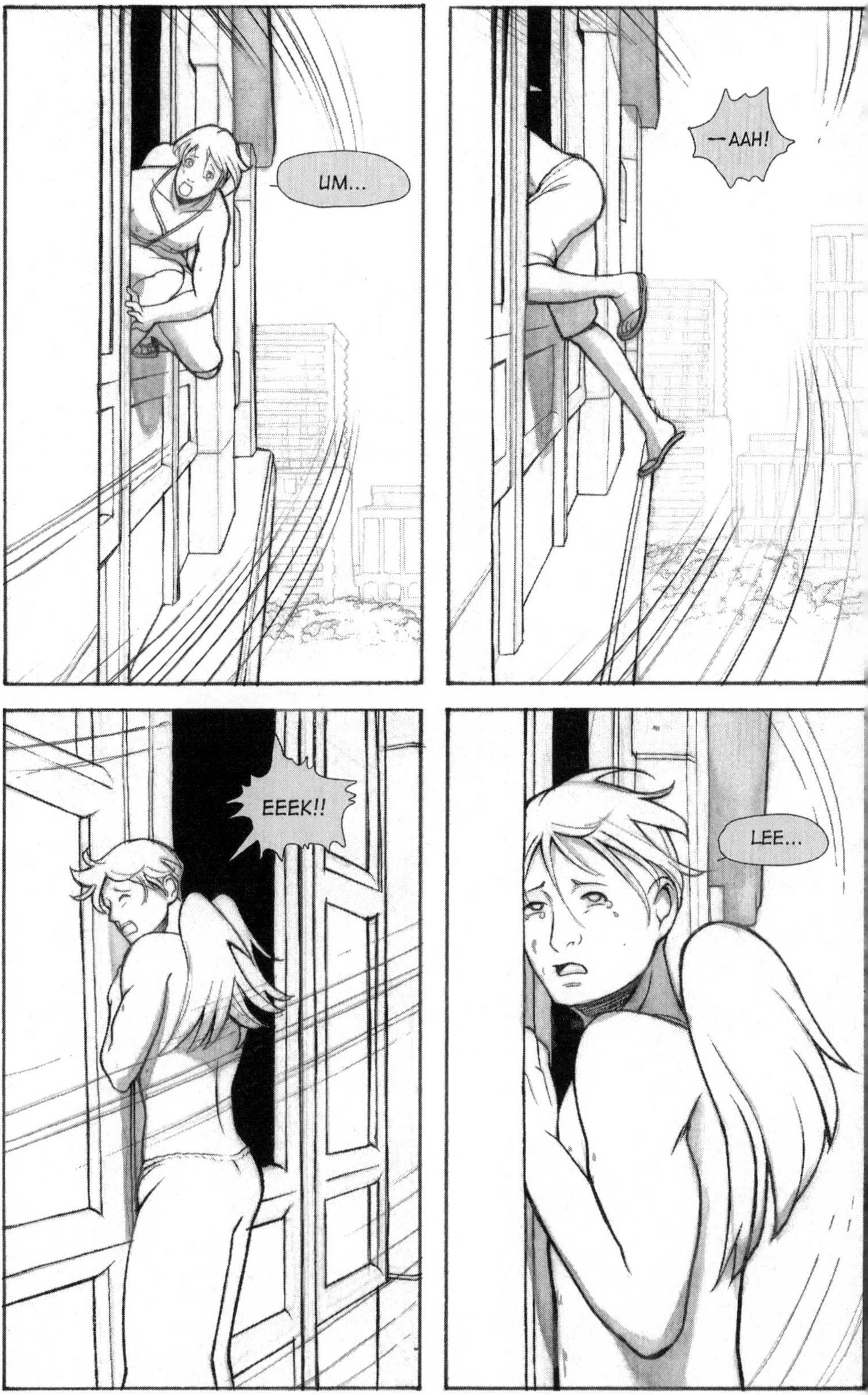
UM...
—AAH!
EEEK!!
LEE...

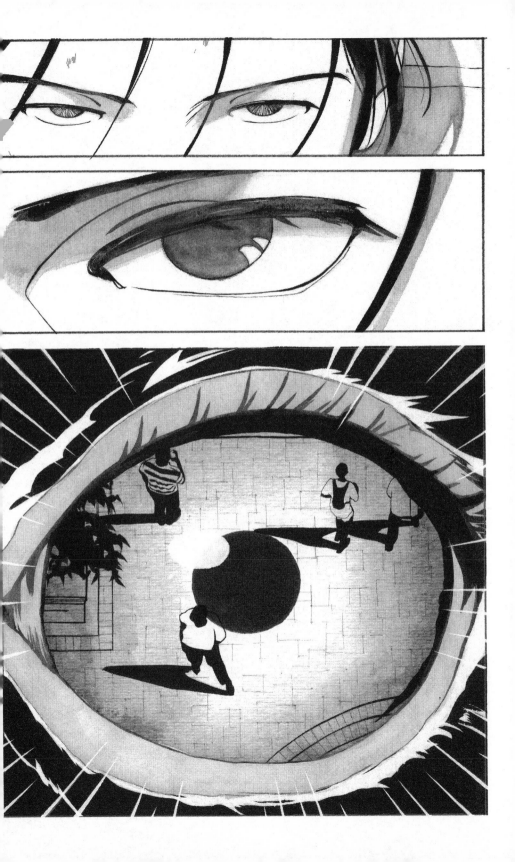

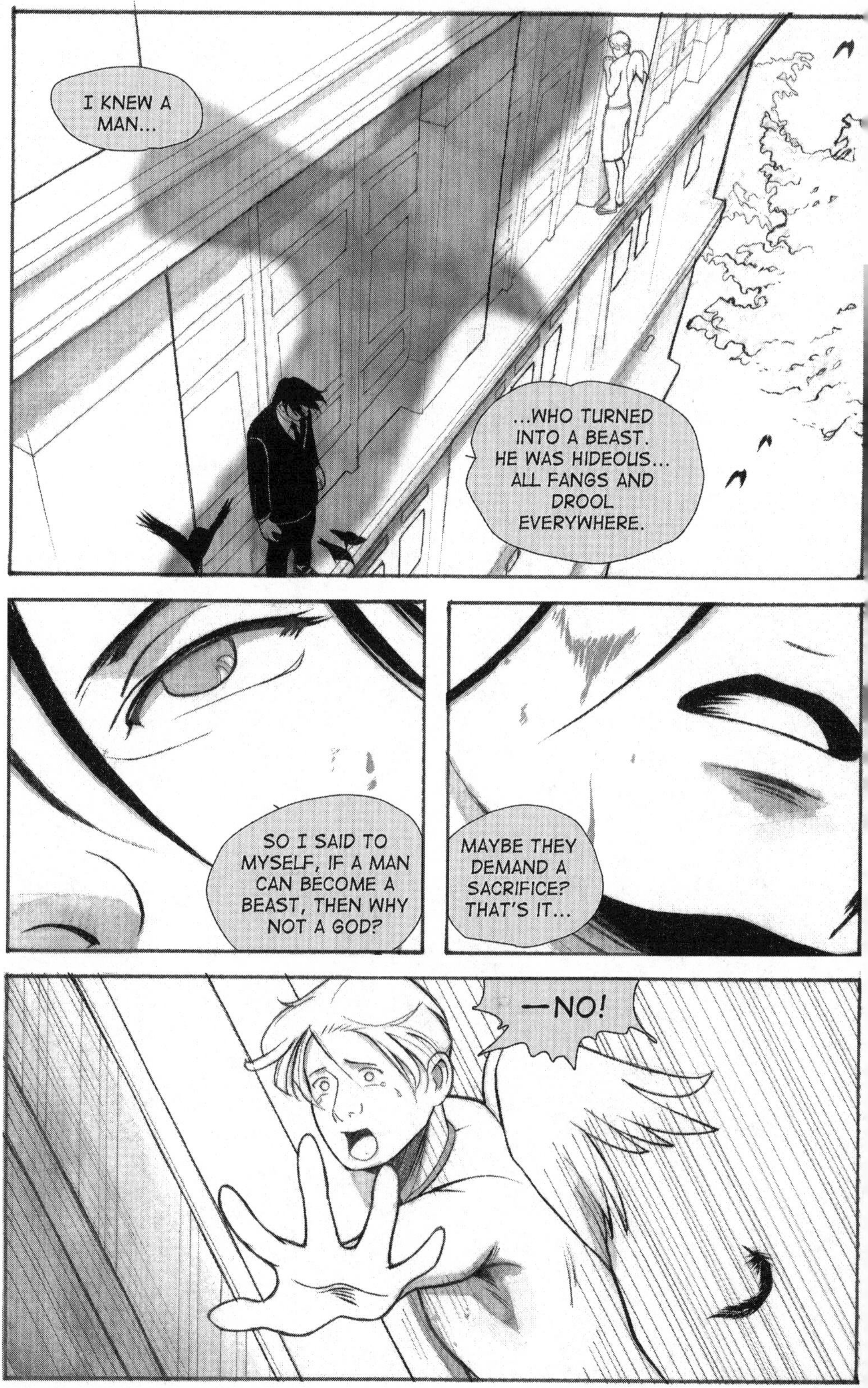
I KNEW A MAN...
...WHO TURNED INTO A BEAST. HE WAS HIDEOUS... ALL FANGS AND DROOL EVERYWHERE.
SO I SAID TO MYSELF, IF A MAN CAN BECOME A BEAST, THEN WHY NOT A GOD?
MAYBE THEY DEMAND A SACRIFICE? THAT'S IT...
—NO!

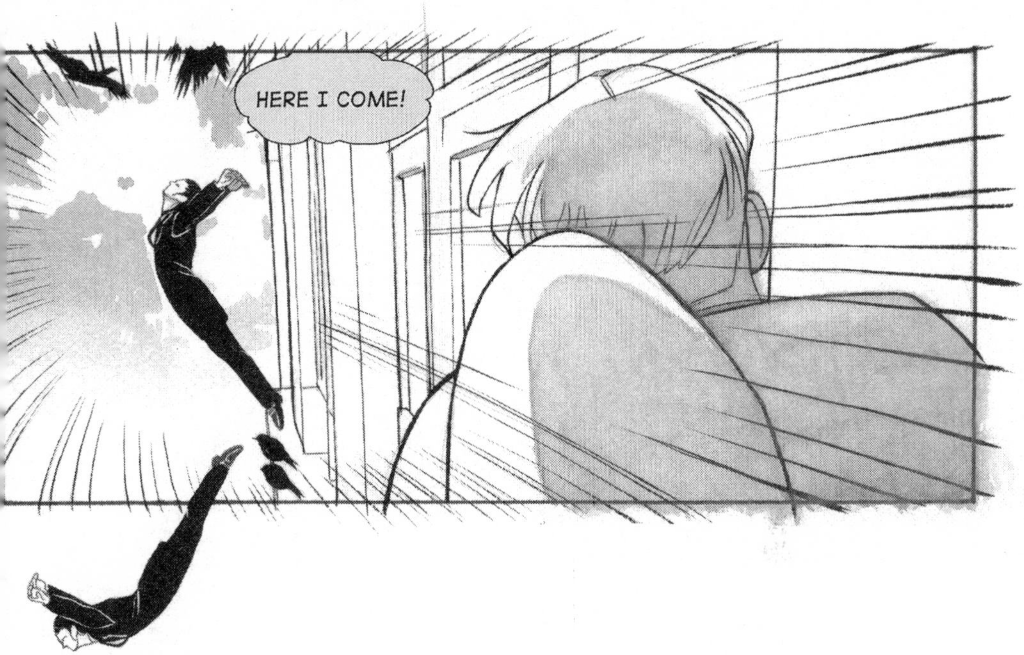
HERE I COME!

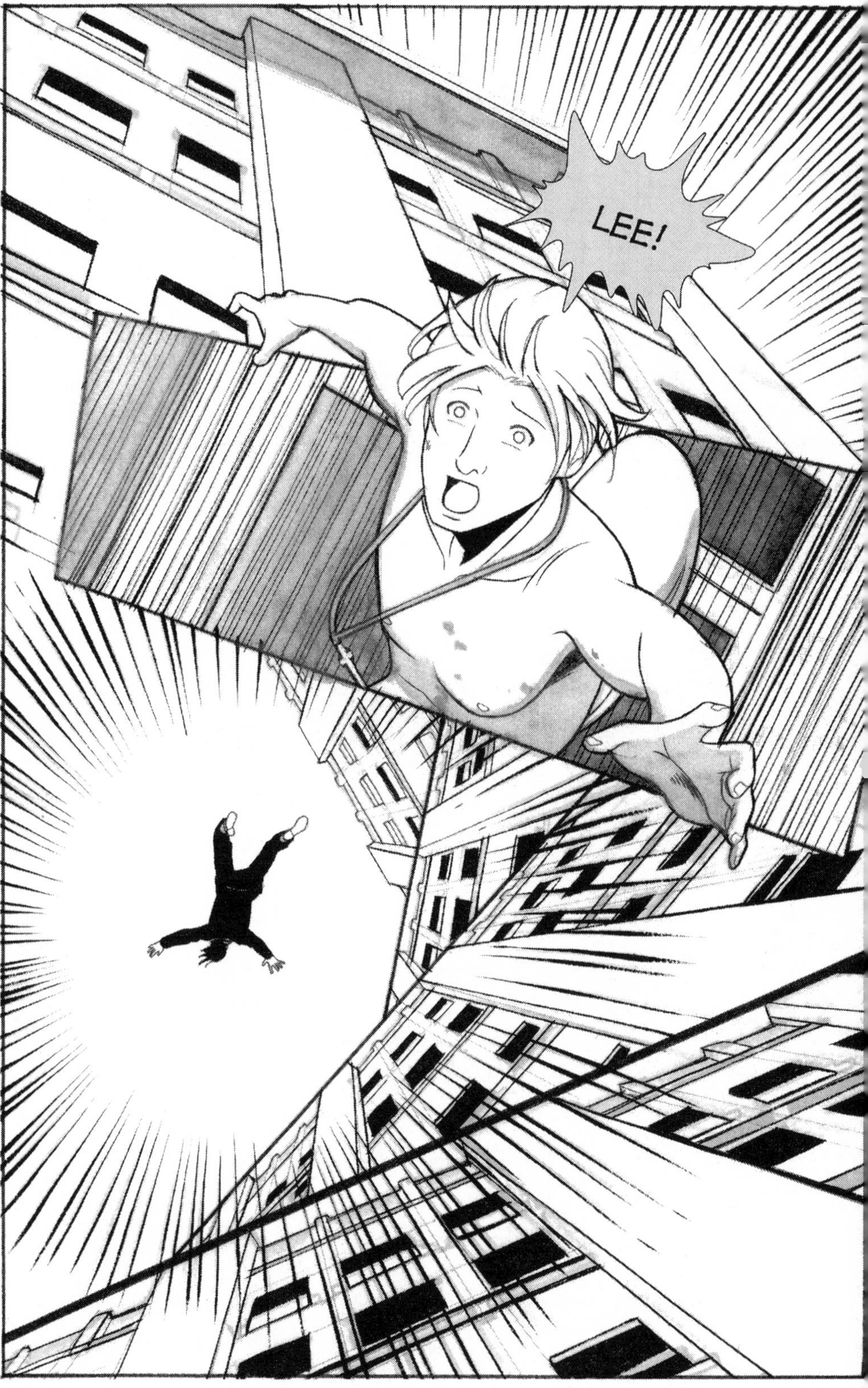
LEE!

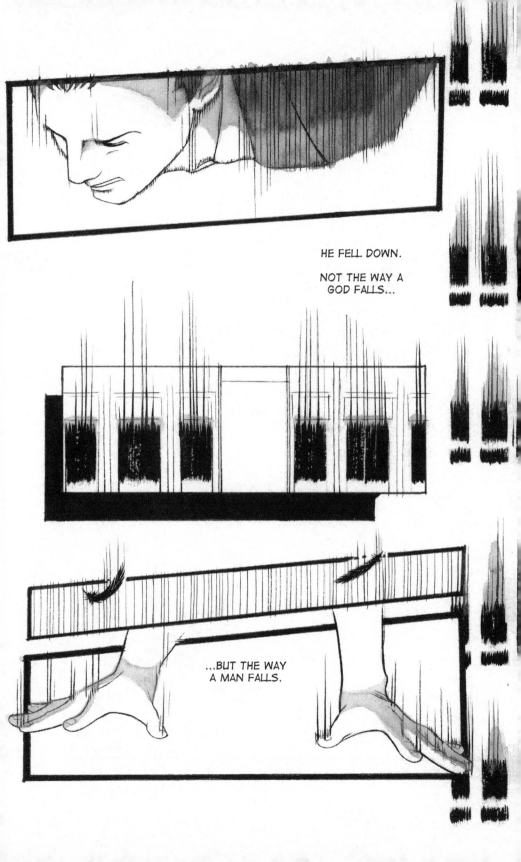

HE FELL DOWN.

NOT THE WAY A
GOD FALLS...

...BUT THE WAY
A MAN FALLS.

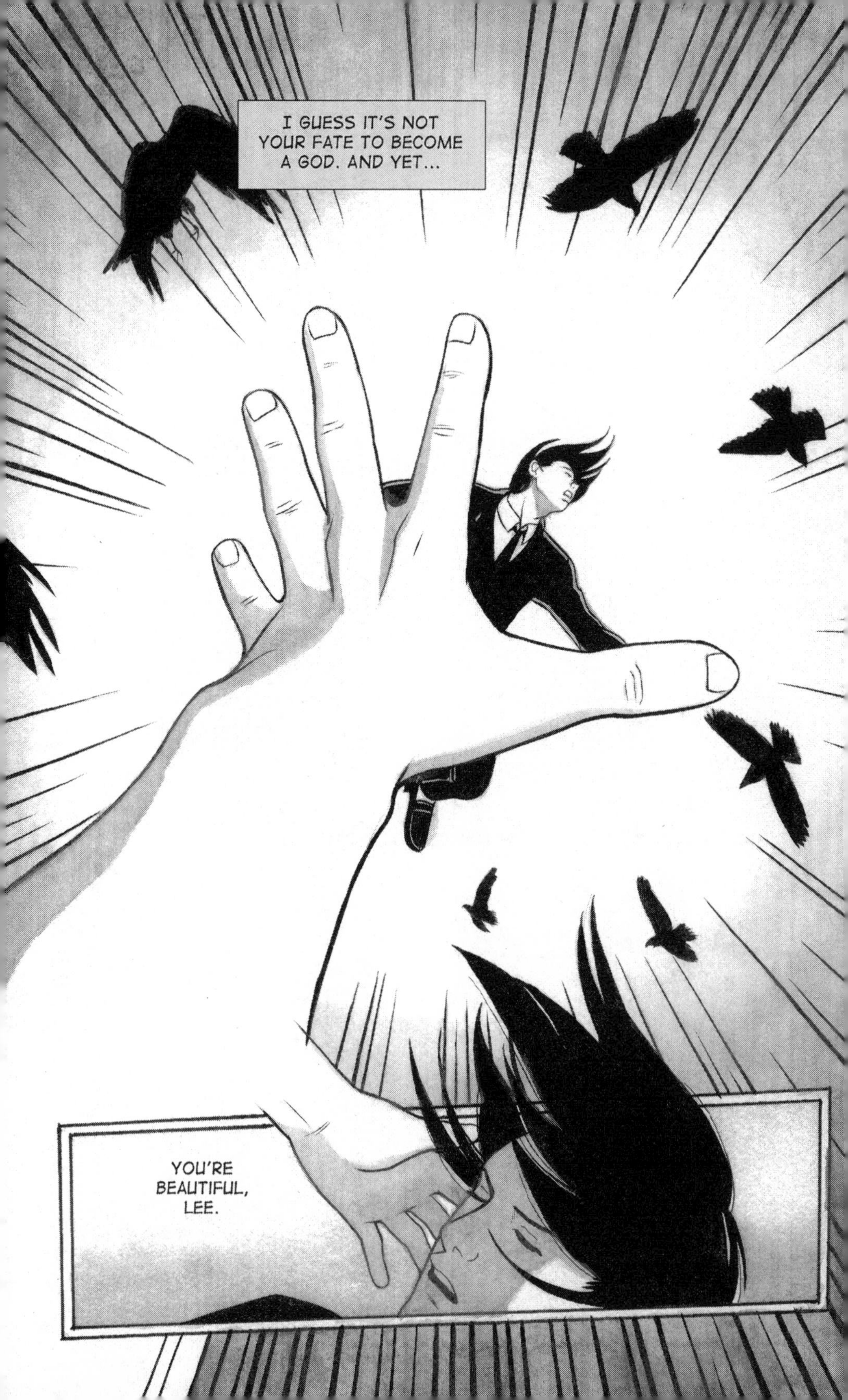
I GUESS IT'S NOT YOUR FATE TO BECOME A GOD. AND YET...
YOU'RE BEAUTIFUL, LEE.

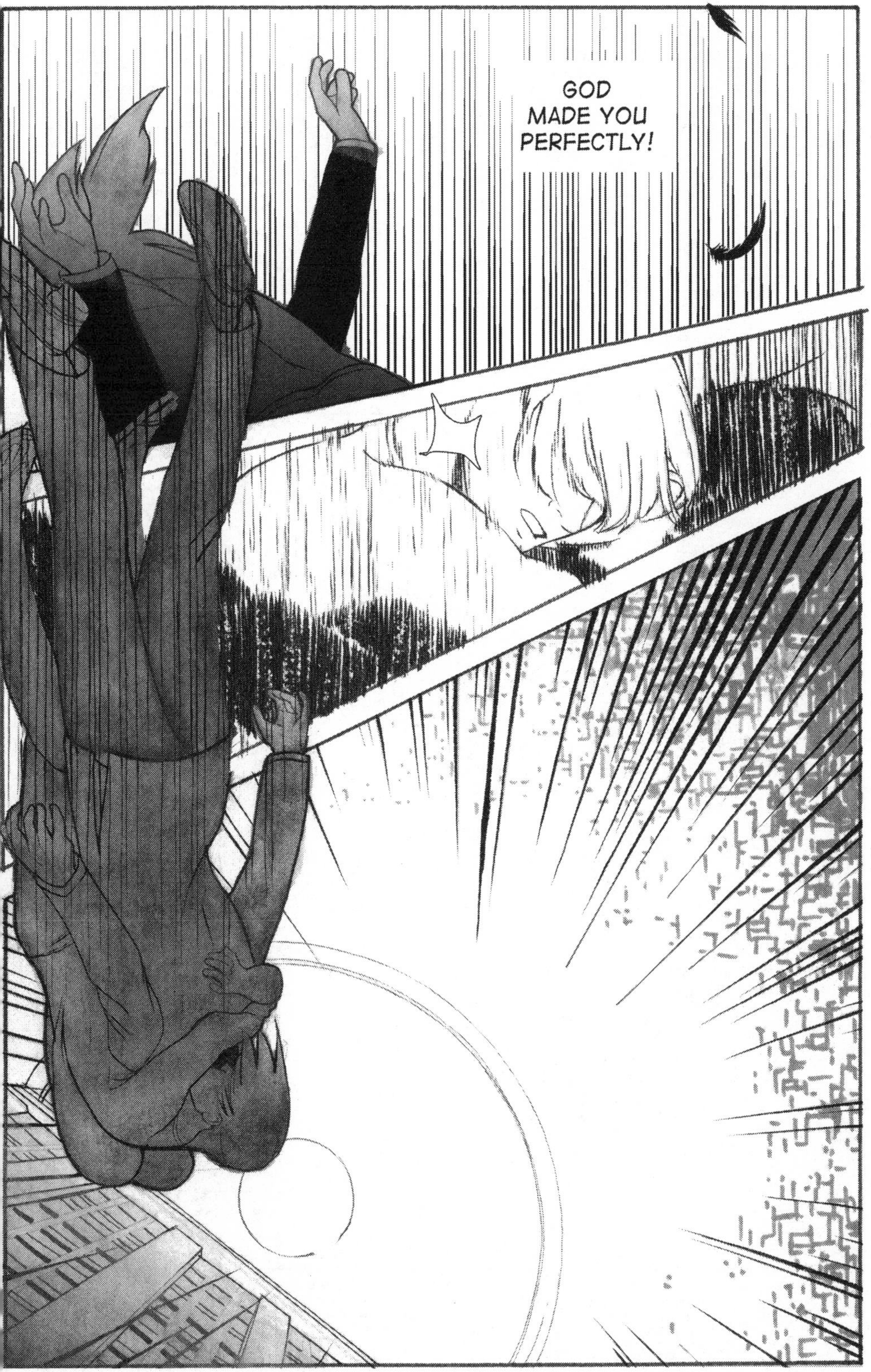
GOD
MADE YOU
PERFECTLY!

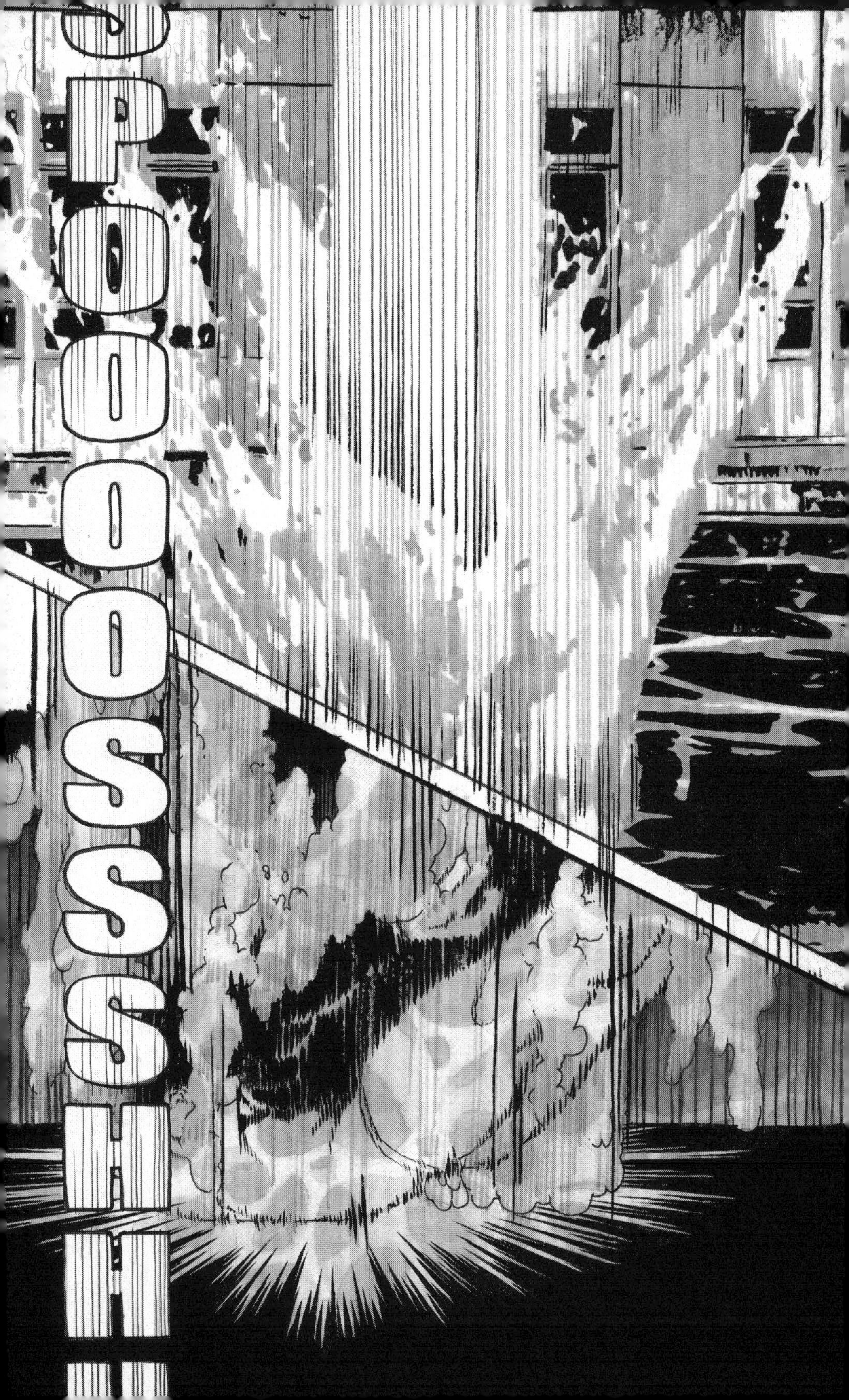
POOOOSSSHH

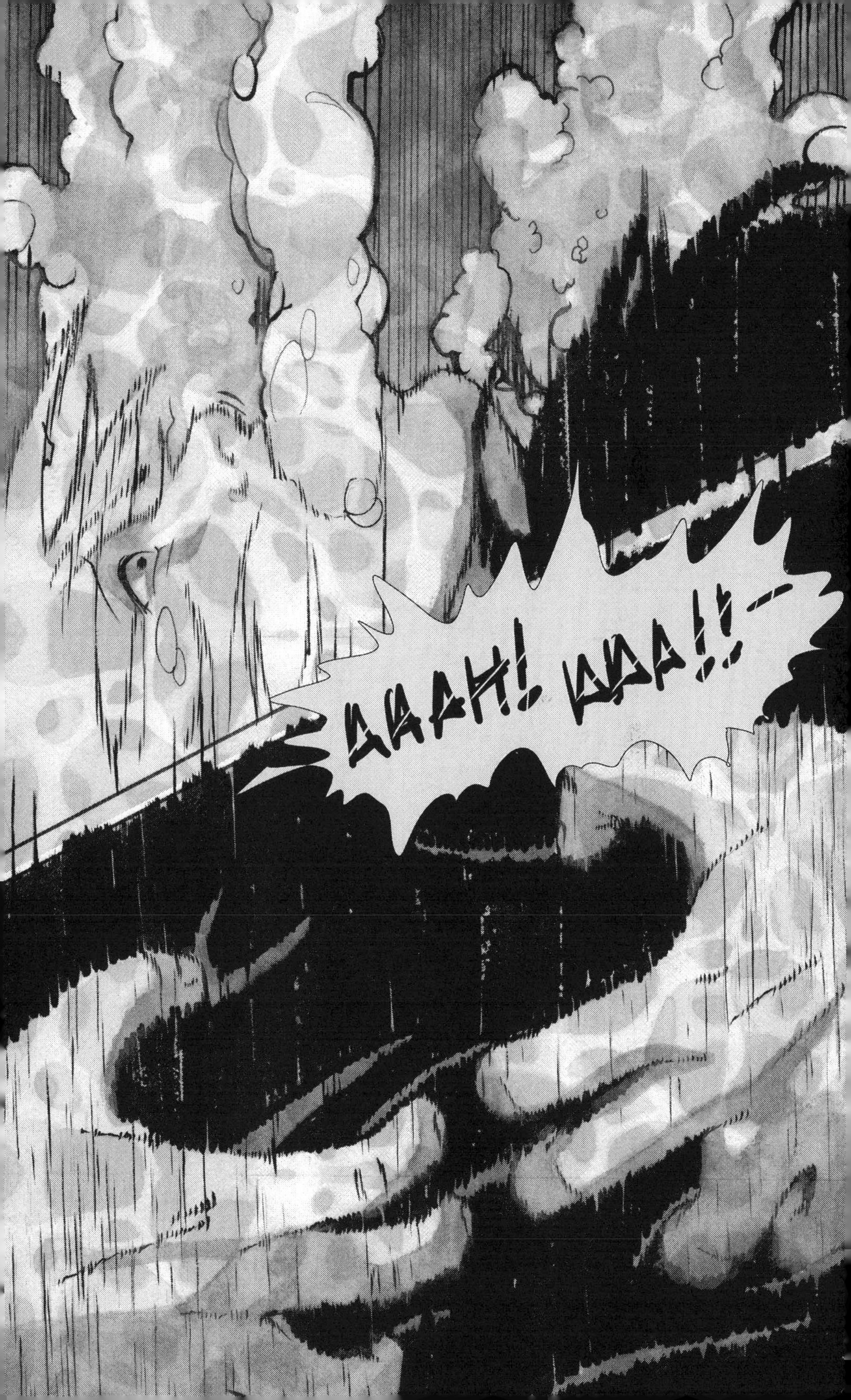
AAAH! AAA!!

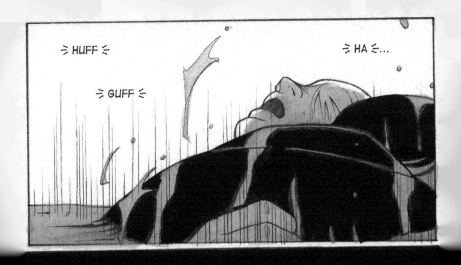

DID I MAKE IT?
THE WARM
WATER LAPS
MY SKIN.

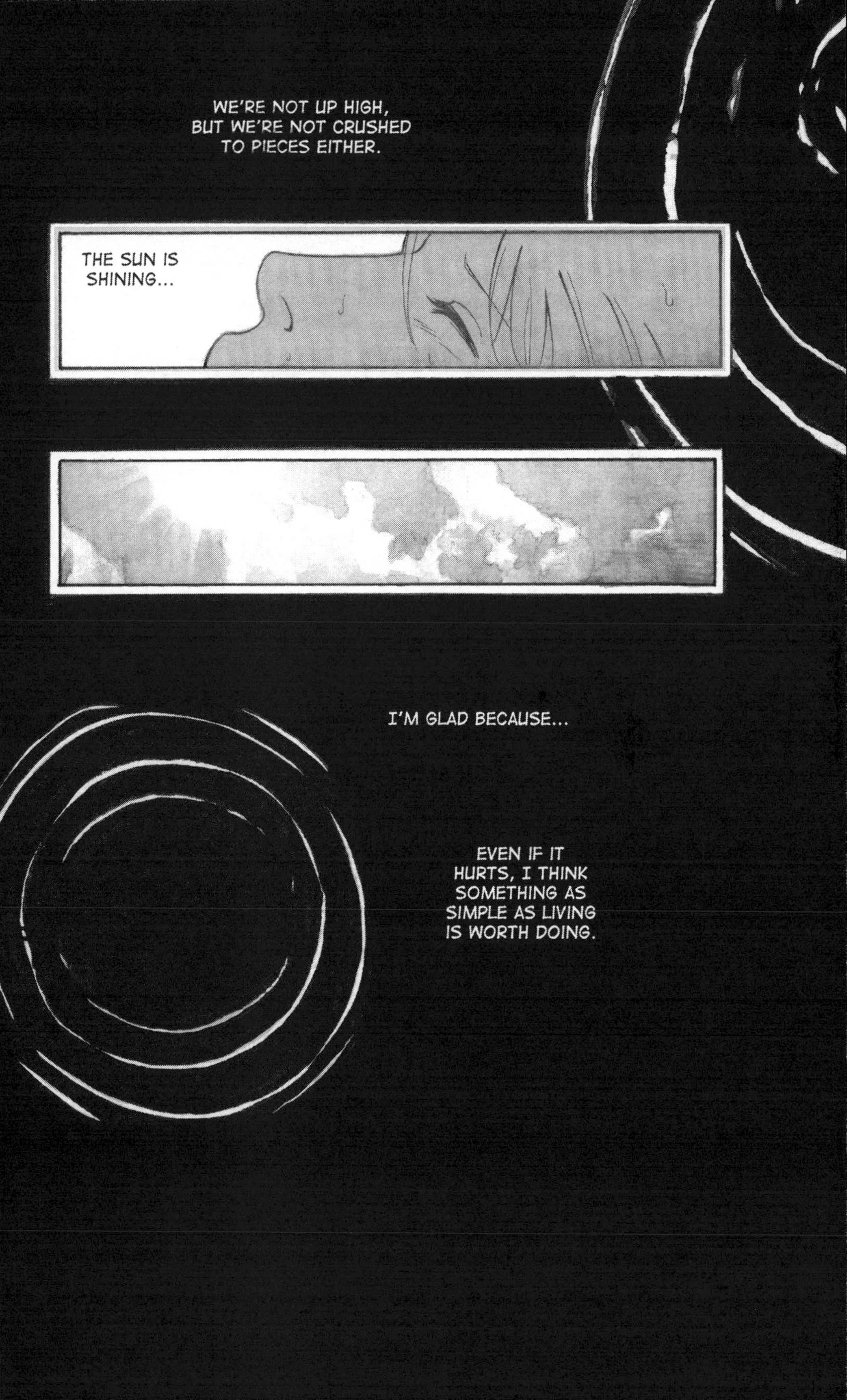
WE'RE NOT UP HIGH, BUT WE'RE NOT CRUSHED TO PIECES EITHER.
THE SUN IS SHINING...
I'M GLAD BECAUSE...
EVEN IF IT HURTS, I THINK SOMETHING AS SIMPLE AS LIVING IS WORTH DOING.

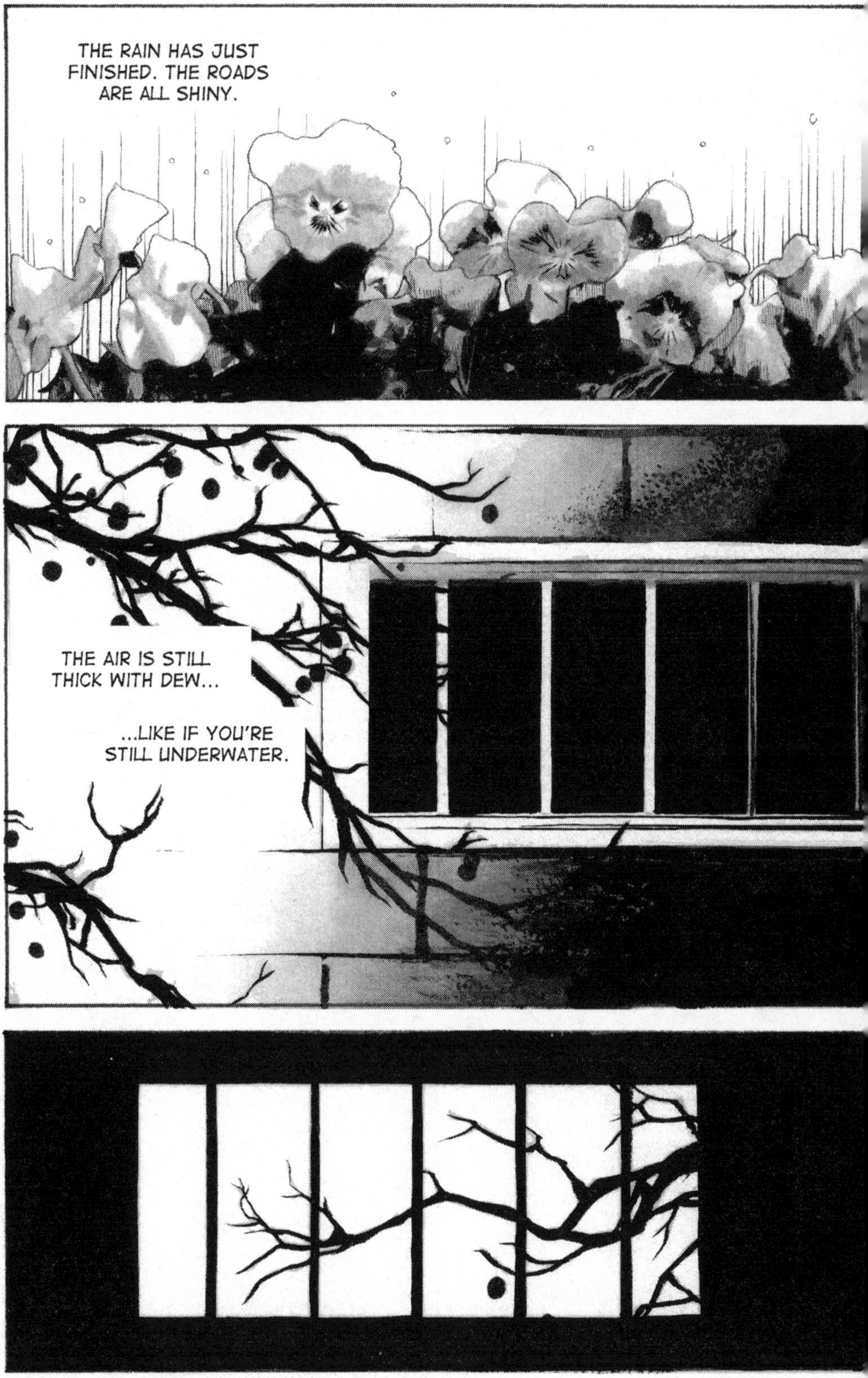
THE RAIN HAS JUST FINISHED. THE ROADS ARE ALL SHINY.
THE AIR IS STILL THICK WITH DEW...
...LIKE IF YOU'RE STILL UNDERWATER.

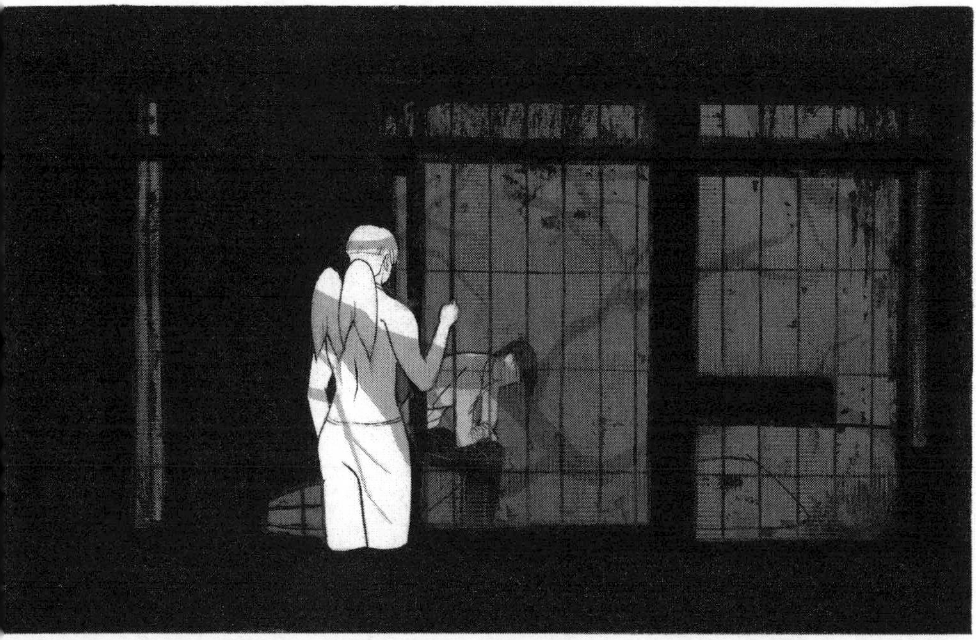
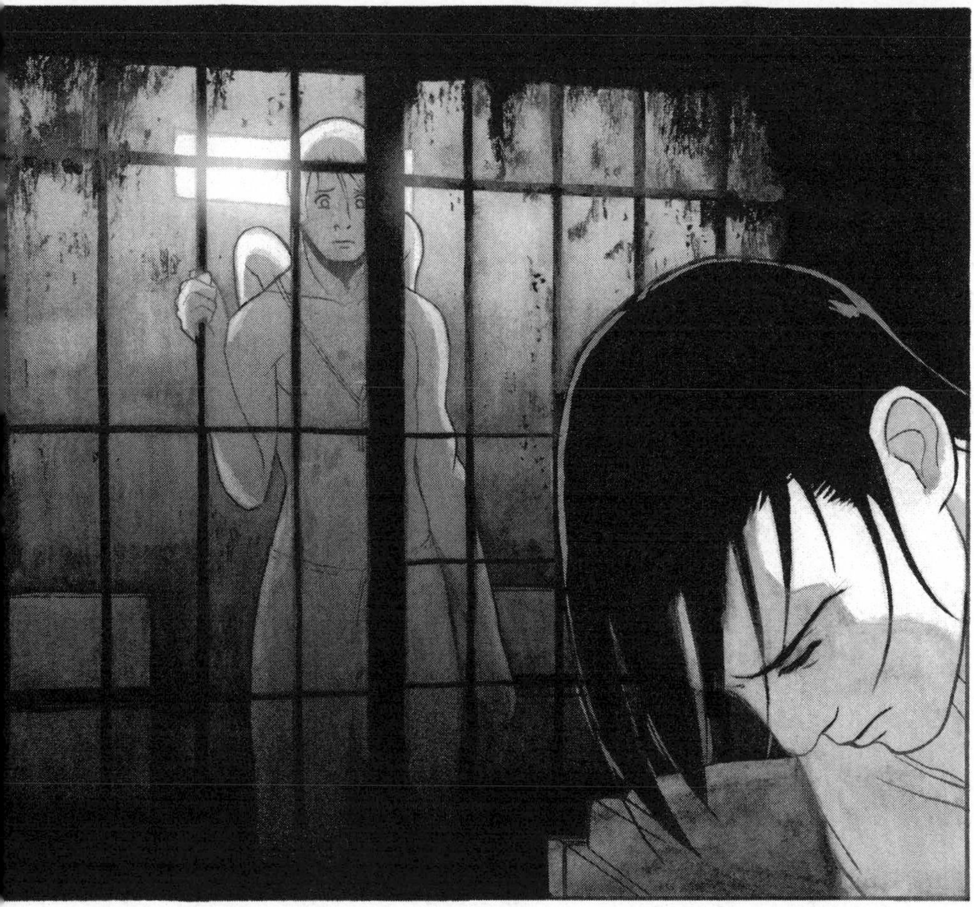

HE REFUSES TO
SAY ANYTHING TO
ME.

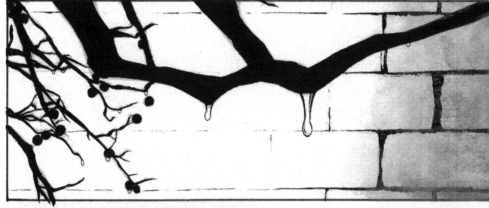

WHY?... WHY WON'T
YOU RESPOND?

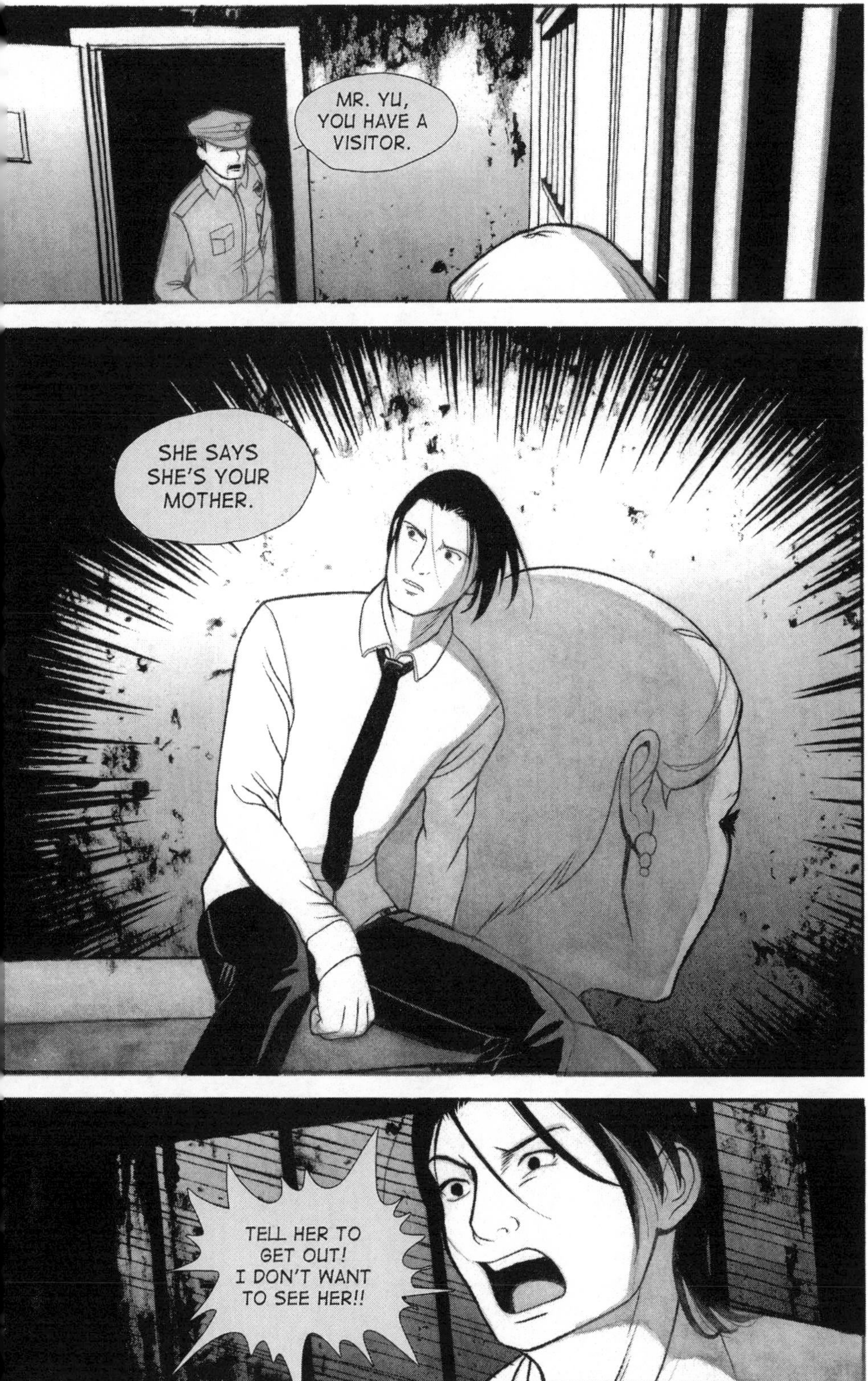
MR. YU, YOU HAVE A VISITOR.
SHE SAYS SHE'S YOUR MOTHER.
TELL HER TO GET OUT! I DON'T WANT TO SEE HER!!

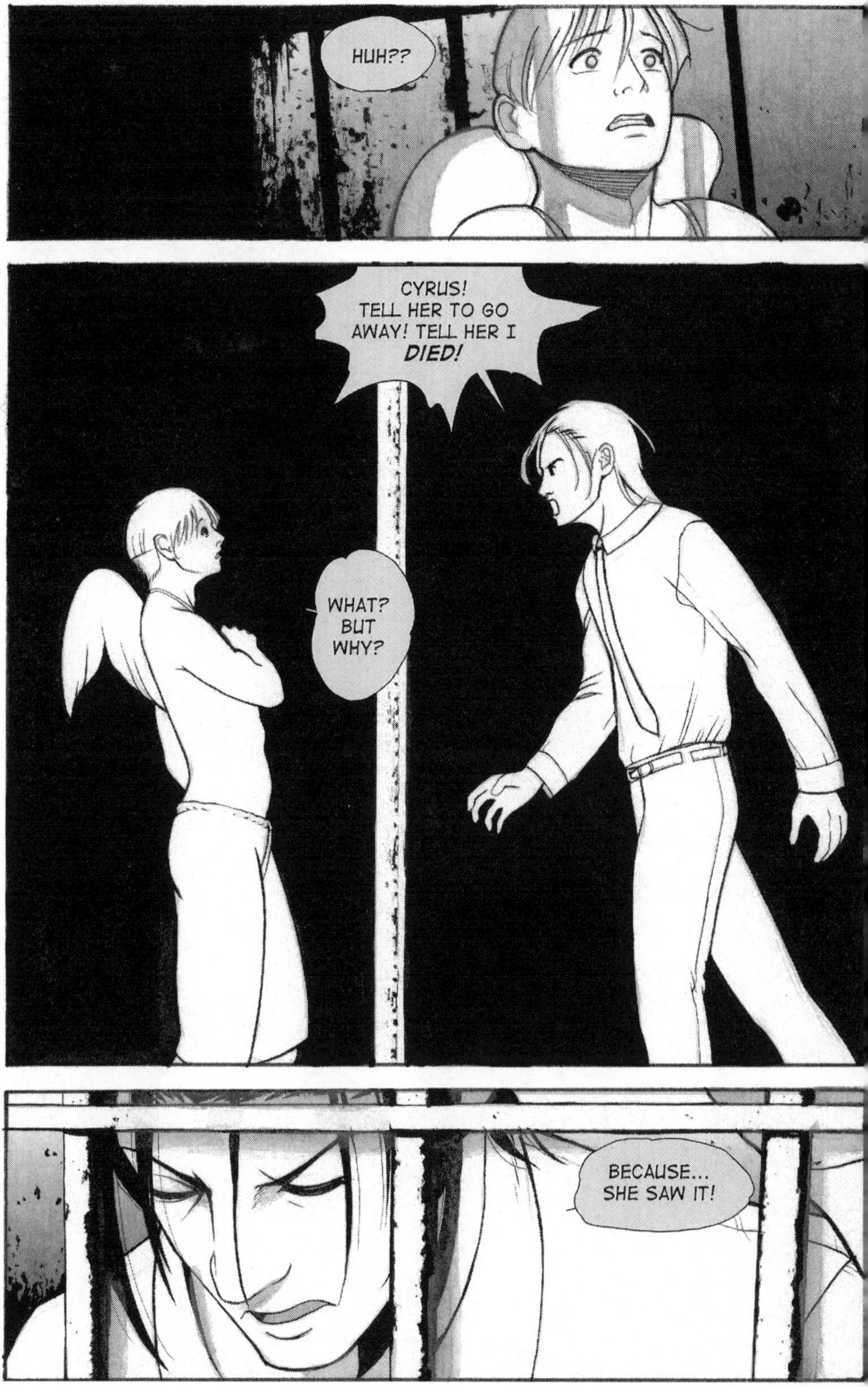
HUH??
CYRUS! TELL HER TO GO AWAY! TELL HER I *DIED!*
WHAT? BUT WHY?
BECAUSE... SHE SAW IT!

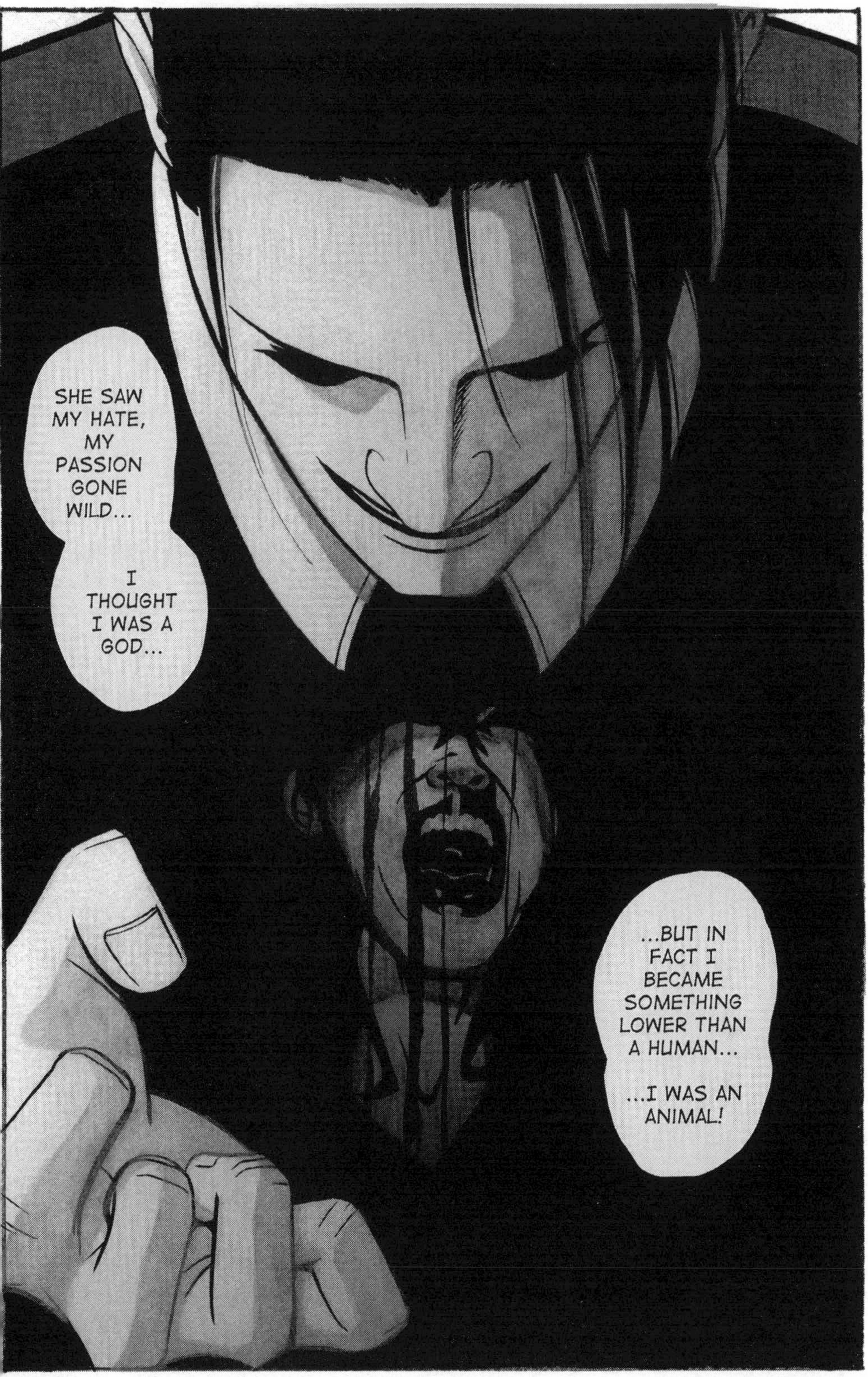
SHE SAW MY HATE, MY PASSION GONE WILD...
I THOUGHT I WAS A GOD...
...BUT IN FACT I BECAME SOMETHING LOWER THAN A HUMAN...
...I WAS AN ANIMAL!

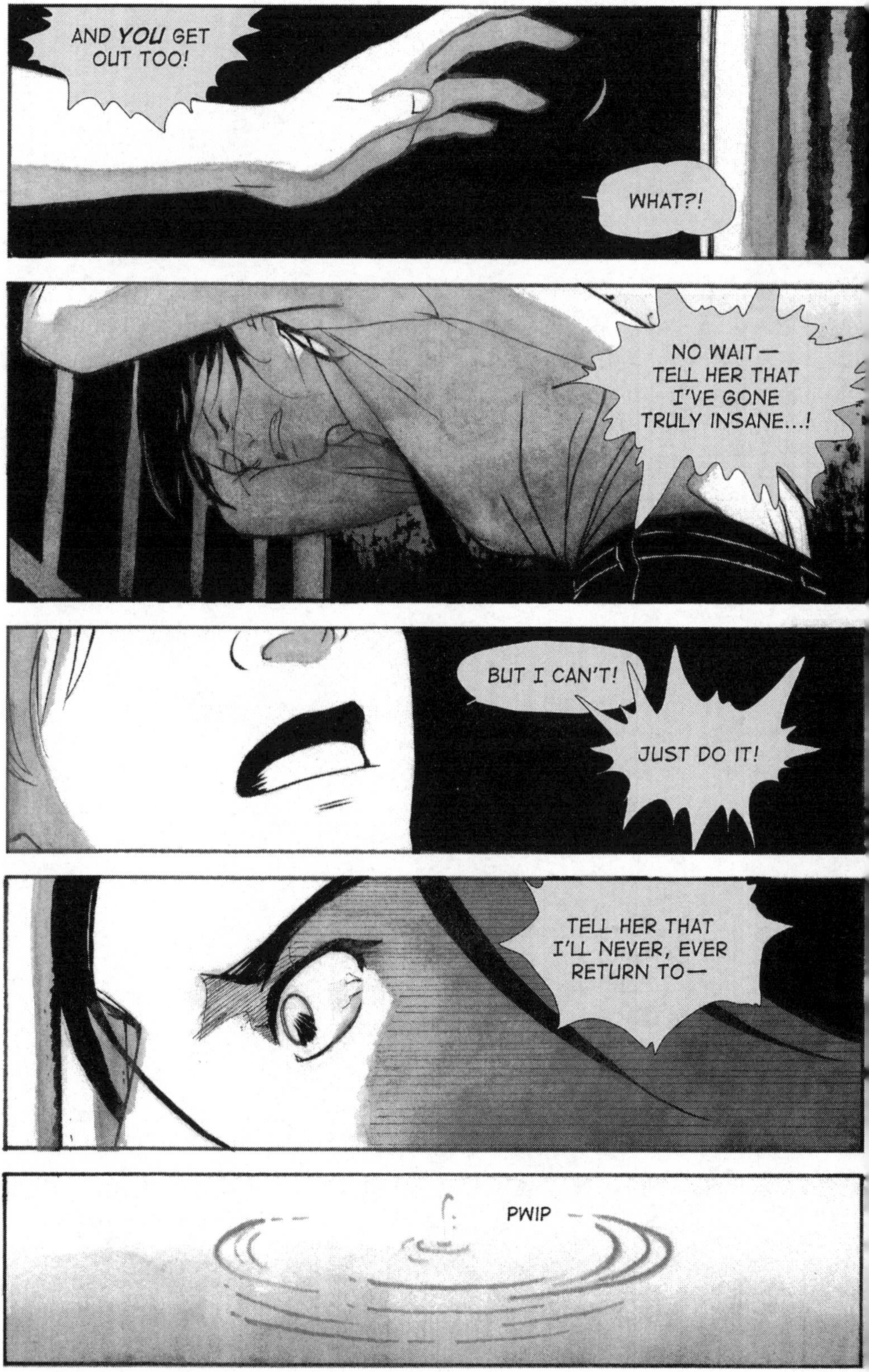
AND YOU GET OUT TOO!
WHAT?!
NO WAIT— TELL HER THAT I'VE GONE TRULY INSANE...!
BUT I CAN'T!
JUST DO IT!
TELL HER THAT I'LL NEVER, EVER RETURN TO—
PWIP

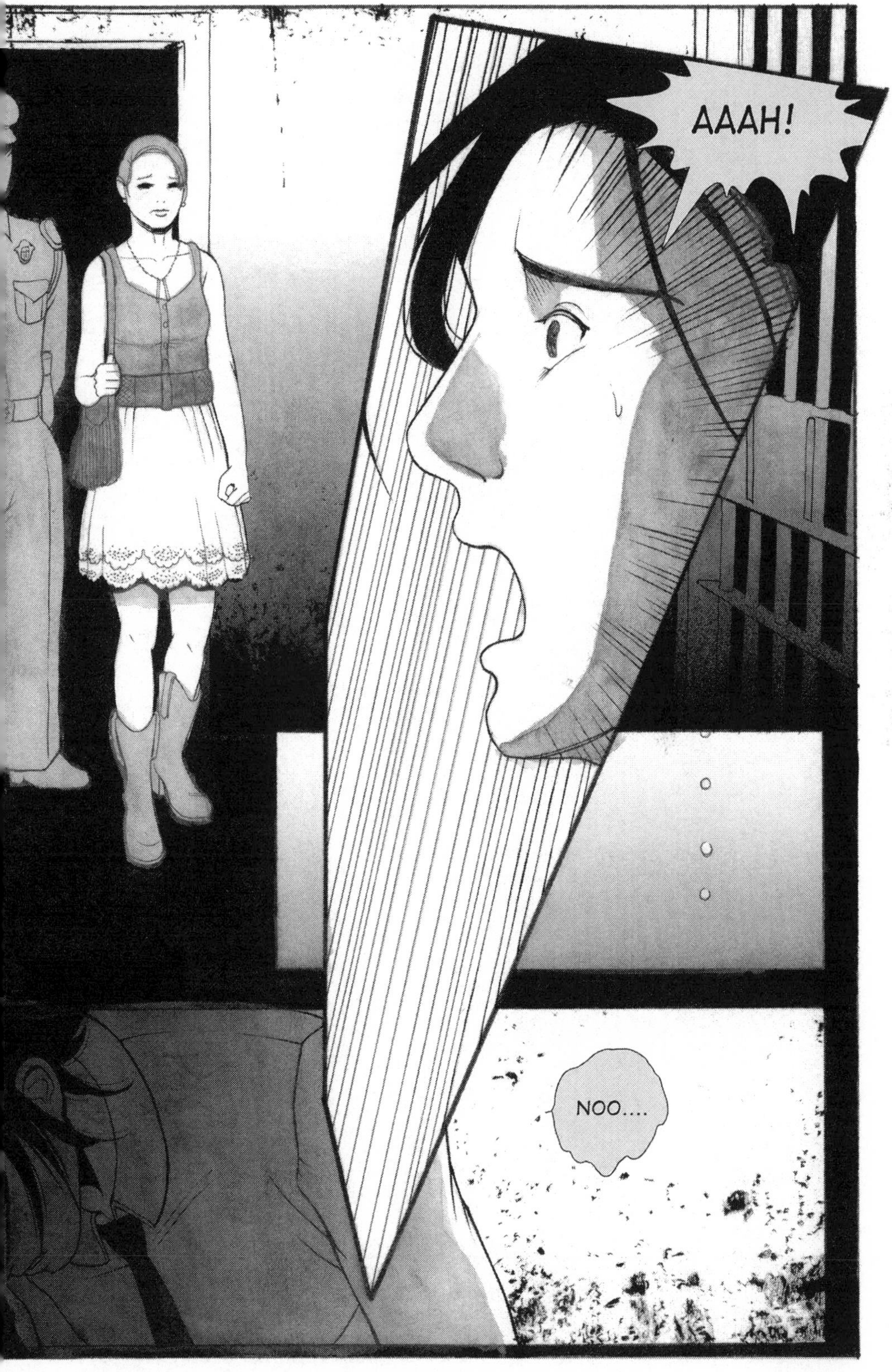
AAAH!
NOO....

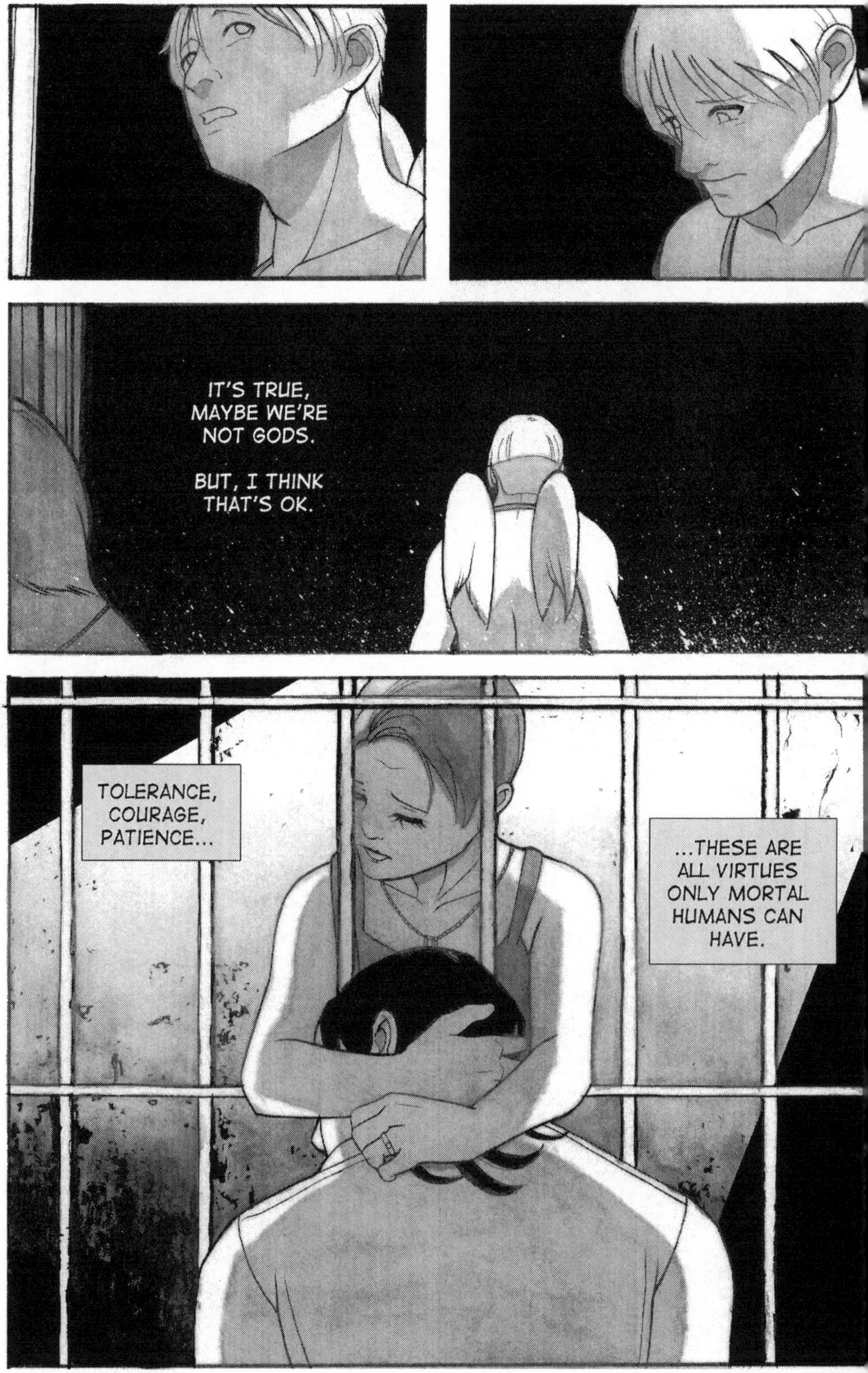
IT'S TRUE, MAYBE WE'RE NOT GODS.
BUT, I THINK THAT'S OK.
TOLERANCE, COURAGE, PATIENCE...
...THESE ARE ALL VIRTUES ONLY MORTAL HUMANS CAN HAVE.

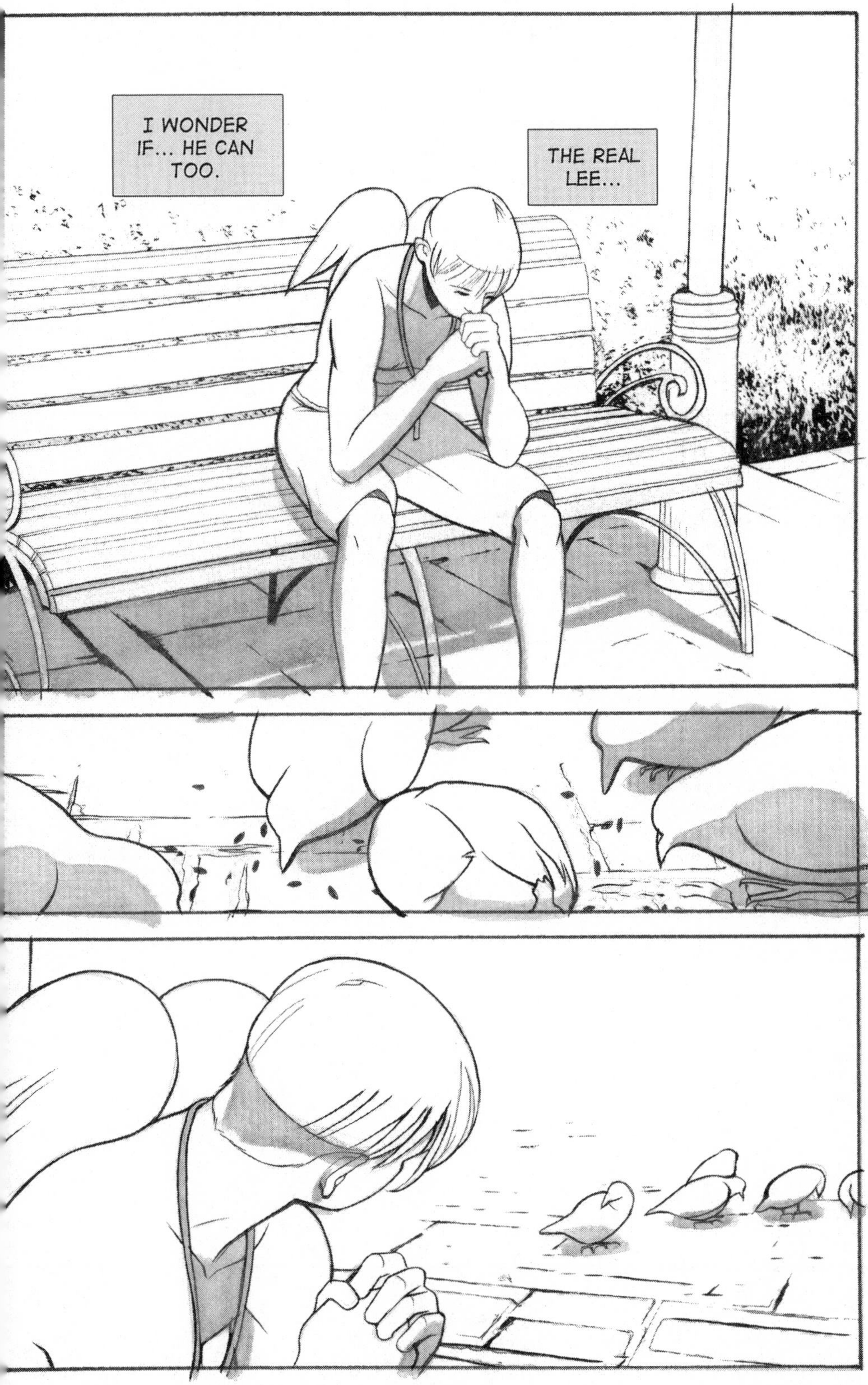
I WONDER IF... HE CAN TOO.
THE REAL LEE...

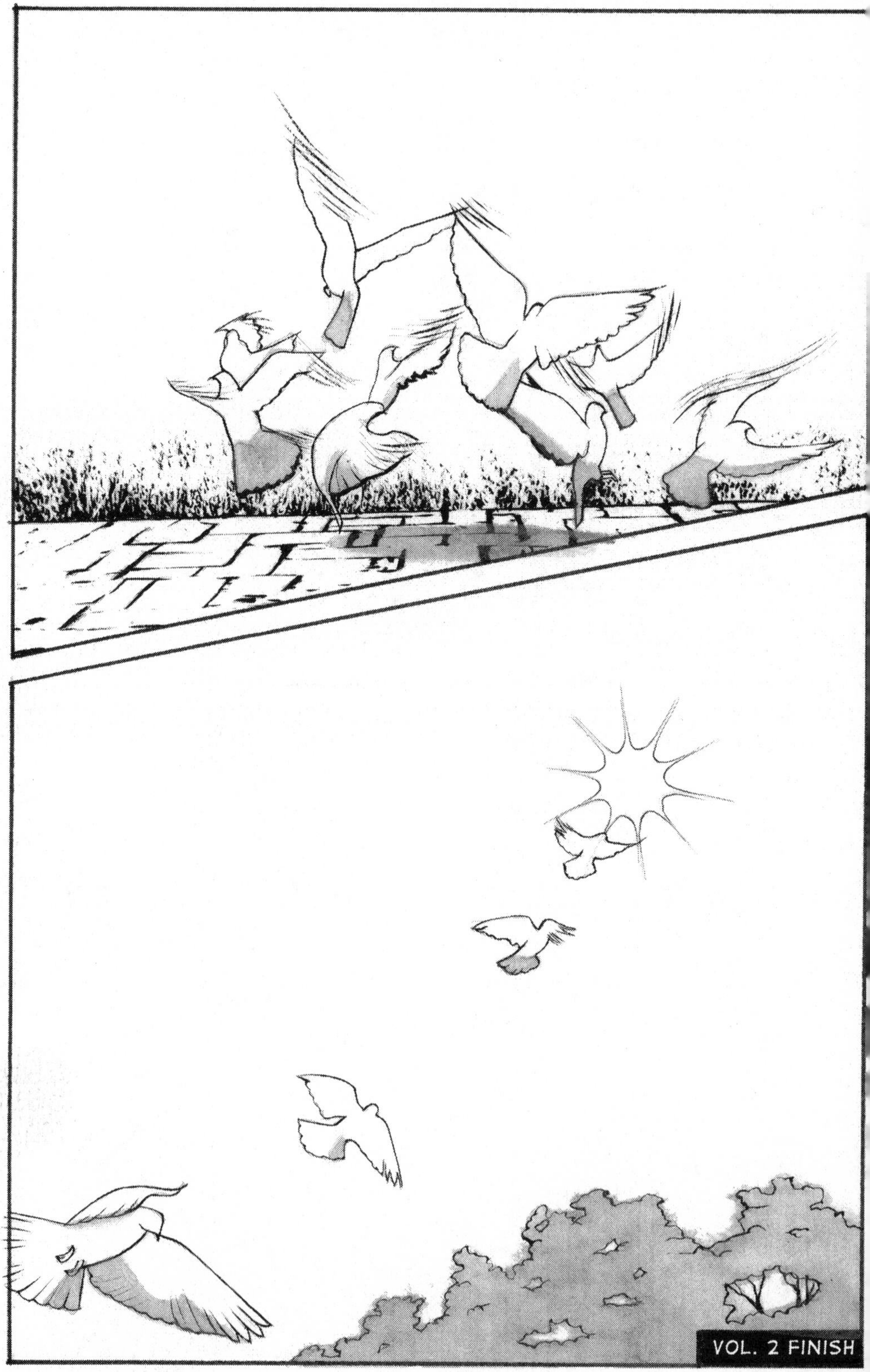
VOL. 2 FINISH

Thanks for reading Volume 2!

Guess what... you are holding in your hands 3 years of my life!! Hope you liked it! If you didn't, oh well it was fun to draw!

If you like my stuff, please post about it online + share with your friends. I am very bad at this!!! AND make sure you grab Angelboy Volume 3, in which you will will learn more about Cyrus' past! You'll love it! Don't miss it!!

—N.M.

Thank you to everyone who
left a review for Volume 1! I am very grateful.
Please leave a review for Volume 2 as well.

Go to www.angelboy.com
and subscribe to the newsletter.
I'll let you know when Volume 3 comes out!

49555641R00166

Made in the USA
San Bernardino, CA
28 May 2017